Bayesian Multilevel Models for Repeated Measures Data

This comprehensive book is an introduction to multilevel Bayesian models in R using brms and the Stan programming language. Featuring a series of fully worked analyses of repeated measures data, the focus is placed on active learning through the analyses of the progressively more complicated models presented throughout the book.

In this book, the authors offer an introduction to statistics entirely focused on repeated measures data beginning with very simple two-group comparisons and ending with multinomial regression models with many 'random effects'. Across 13 well-structured chapters, readers are provided with all the code necessary to run all the analyses and make all the plots in the book, as well as useful examples of how to interpret and write up their own analyses.

This book provides an accessible introduction for readers in any field, with any level of statistical background. Senior undergraduate students, graduate students, and experienced researchers looking to 'translate' their skills with more traditional models to a Bayesian framework will benefit greatly from the lessons in this text.

Santiago Barreda is a phonetician in the Linguistics Department at the University of California, Davis, USA, with a particular interest in speech perception.

Noah Silbert is a former Academic and is currently a practicing Stoic. His training and background are in phonetics, perceptual modeling, and statistics.

Bayesian Multilevel Models for Repeated Measures Data

A Conceptual and Practical Introduction in R

Santiago Barreda and Noah Silbert

LONDON AND NEW YORK

First published 2023
by Routledge
4 Park Square, Milton Park, Abingdon, Oxon OX14 4RN

and by Routledge
605 Third Avenue, New York, NY 10158

Routledge is an imprint of the Taylor & Francis Group, an informa business

© 2023 Santiago Barreda and Noah Silbert

The right of Santiago Barreda and Noah Silbert to be identified as authors of this work has been asserted in accordance with sections 77 and 78 of the Copyright, Designs and Patents Act 1988.

All rights reserved. No part of this book may be reprinted or reproduced or utilised in any form or by any electronic, mechanical, or other means, now known or hereafter invented, including photocopying and recording, or in any information storage or retrieval system, without permission in writing from the publishers.

Trademark notice: Product or corporate names may be trademarks or registered trademarks, and are used only for identification and explanation without intent to infringe.

British Library Cataloguing-in-Publication Data
A catalogue record for this book is available from the British Library

ISBN: 978-1-032-25962-8 (hbk)
ISBN: 978-1-032-25963-5 (pbk)
ISBN: 978-1-003-28587-8 (ebk)

DOI: 10.4324/9781003285878

Typeset in Times New Roman
by codeMantra

para mis chicas con pelo de nudo.

Contents

Preface	XV
Acknowledgments	xxiii

1 Introduction: Experiments and variables   1

1.1 Chapter pre-cap 1
1.2 Experiments and effects 1
    1.2.1 Experiments and inference 3
1.3 Our experiment 5
    1.3.1 Our experiment: Introduction 5
    1.3.2 Our experimental methods 7
    1.3.3 Our research questions 8
    1.3.4 Our experimental data 9
1.4 Variables 12
    1.4.1 Populations and samples 12
    1.4.2 Dependent and independent variables 13
    1.4.3 Categorical variables and 'factors' 14
    1.4.4 Quantitative variables 15
1.5 Inspecting our data 18
    1.5.1 Inspecting categorical variables 19
    1.5.2 Inspecting quantitative variables 20
1.6 Exercises 25
Reference 25

2 Probabilities, likelihood, and inference   26

2.1 Chapter pre-cap 26
2.2 Data and research questions 27
2.3 Empirical probabilities 28
    2.3.1 Conditional and marginal probabilities 30
    2.3.2 Joint probabilities 32
2.4 Probability distributions 34
2.5 The normal distribution 36
    2.5.1 The sample mean 37
    2.5.2 The sample variance (or standard deviation) 39

viii   *Contents*

2.5.3 The normal density 41

2.5.4 The standard normal distribution 41

2.6   *Models and inference 42*

2.7   *Probabilities of events and likelihoods of parameters 45*

2.7.1 Characteristics of likelihoods 48

2.7.2 A brief aside on logarithms 49

2.7.3 Characteristics of likelihoods, continued 50

2.8   *Answering our research questions 52*

2.9   *Exercises 54*

References 54

3   Fitting Bayesian regression models with *brms*   **55**

3.1   *Chapter pre-cap 55*

3.2   *What are regression models? 56*

3.3   *What's 'Bayesian' about these models? 58*

3.3.1 Prior probabilities 60

3.3.2 Posterior distributions 61

3.3.3 Posterior distributions and shrinkage 63

3.4   *Sampling from the posterior using* Stan *and* brms *63*

3.5   *Estimating a single mean with the* brms *package 64*

3.5.1 Data and research questions 64

3.5.2 Description of the model 65

3.5.3 Errors and residuals 66

3.5.4 The model formula 67

3.5.5 Fitting the model: Calling the brm function 68

3.5.6 Interpreting the model: The print statement 69

3.5.7 Seeing the samples 70

3.5.8 Getting the residuals 72

3.6   *Checking model convergence 73*

3.7   *Specifying prior probabilities 77*

3.8   *The log prior and log posterior densities 80*

3.9   *Answering our research questions 83*

3.10 *'Traditionalists' corner 83*

3.10.1 One-sample *t*-test vs. intercept-only Bayesian models 84

3.10.2 Intercept-only ordinary-least-squares regression vs. intercept-only Bayesian models 84

3.11 *Exercises 85*

4   Inspecting a 'single group' of observations using a Bayesian multilevel model   **87**

4.1   *Chapter pre-cap 87*

4.2   *Repeated measures data 87*

4.2.1 Multilevel models and 'levels' of variation 89

4.3   *Representing predictors with many levels 91*

4.4   *Strategies for estimating factors with many levels 93*

Contents   ix

4.4.1 Complete pooling 94
4.4.2 No pooling 95
4.4.3 (Adaptive) Partial pooling 96
4.4.4 Hyperpriors 97
4.5   *Estimating a multilevel model with* `brms` *98*
4.5.1 Data and research questions 99
4.5.2 Description of the model 100
4.5.3 Fitting the model 101
4.5.4 Interpreting the model 102
4.6   *'Random' effects 104*
4.6.1 Inspecting the random effects 105
4.7   *Simulating data using our model parameters 109*
4.8   *Adding a second random effect 112*
4.8.1 Updating the model description 113
4.8.2 Fitting and interpreting the model 114
4.9   *Investigating 'shrinkage' 115*
4.10 *Answering our research questions 117*
4.11 *'Traditionalists' corner 119*
4.11.1 Bayesian multilevel models vs. lmer 119
4.12 *Exercises 122*
References 122

5 Comparing two groups of observations: Factors and contrasts   123
5.1   *Chapter pre-cap 123*
5.2   *Comparing two groups 123*
5.3   *Distribution of repeated measures across factor levels 124*
5.4   *Data and research questions 126*
5.5   *Estimating the difference between two means with 'brms' 129*
5.5.1 Fitting the model 130
5.5.2 Interpreting the model 131
5.6   *Contrasts 132*
5.6.1 Treatment coding 133
5.6.2 Sum coding 133
5.6.3 Comparison of sum and treatment coding 135
5.7   *Sum coding and the decomposition of variation 135*
5.7.1 Description of the model 137
5.7.2 Fitting the model 138
5.7.3 Comparison of sum and treatment coding 139
5.8   *Inspecting and manipulating the posterior samples 140*
5.8.1 Using the hypothesis function 144
5.8.2 Working with the random effects 145
5.9   *Making our models more robust: The (non-standardized) t-distribution 149*
5.10 *Re-fitting with t-distributed errors 151*
5.10.1 Description of the model 154

x   *Contents*

5.10.2 Fitting and interpreting the model 155
5.11 Simulating the two-group model 157
5.12 Answering our research questions 159
5.13 'Traditionalists' corner 161
5.13.1 Bayesian multilevel models vs. lmer 161
5.14 Exercises 162

6   Variation in parameters ('random effects') and model comparison   164

6.1 Chapter pre-cap 164
6.2 Data and research questions 164
6.3 Variation in parameters across sources of data 165
6.3.1 Description of our model 168
6.3.2 Correlations between random parameters 171
6.3.3 Random effects and the multivariate normal distribution 174
6.3.4 Specifying priors for a multivariate normal distribution 176
6.3.5 Updating our model description 177
6.3.6 Fitting and interpreting the model 178
6.4 Model comparison 181
6.4.1 In-sample and out-of-sample prediction 182
6.4.2 Out-of-sample prediction: Adjusting predictive accuracy 185
6.4.3 Out-of-sample prediction: Cross-validation 190
6.4.4 Selecting a model 194
6.5 Answering our research questions 197
6.6 'Traditionalists' corner 198
6.6.1 Bayesian multilevel models vs. lmer 198
6.7 Exercises 199
References 200

7   Comparing many groups, interactions, and posterior predictive checks   201

7.1 Chapter pre-cap 201
7.2 Comparing four (or any number of) groups 201
7.2.1 Data and research questions 202
7.2.2 Description of our model 204
7.2.3 Fitting and interpreting the model 207
7.3 Investigating multiple factors simultaneously 209
7.3.1 Data and research questions 211
7.3.2 Description of the model 212
7.3.3 Fitting and interpreting the model 214
7.4 Posterior prediction: Using our models to predict new data 216
7.5 Interactions and interaction plots 220
7.6 Investigating interactions with a model 222
7.6.1 Data and research questions 223
7.6.2 Model formulas 223
7.6.3 Description of our model 225

Contents xi

7.6.4 Fitting and interpreting the model 226
7.6.5 Caulculating group means in the presence of interactions 229
7.6.6 Calculating simple effects in the presence of interactions 230
7.6.7 Assessing model fit: Bayesian R^2 232
7.7 Answering our research questions 235
7.8 Factors with more than two levels 239
7.9 'Traditionalists' corner 241
  7.9.1 Bayesian multilevel models vs. lmer 241
7.10 Exercises 242
References 242

8 Varying variances, more about priors, and prior predictive checks   **243**
8.1 Chapter pre-cap 243
8.2 Data and Research questions 243
8.3 More about priors 244
  8.3.1 Prior predictive checks 245
  8.3.2 More specific priors 248
8.4 Heteroskedasticity and distributional models 250
8.5 A 'simple' model: Error varies according to a single fixed effect 251
  8.5.1 Description of our model 251
  8.5.2 Prior predictive checks 254
  8.5.3 Fitting and interpreting the model 255
8.6 A 'complex' model: Error varies according to fixed and random effects 257
  8.6.1 Description of our model 257
  8.6.2 Fitting and interpreting the model 260
8.7 Answering our research questions 262
8.8 Building identifiable and supportable models 265
  8.8.1 Collinearity 266
  8.8.2 Predictable values of categorical predictors 268
  8.8.3 Saturated, and 'nearly saturated', models 271
8.9 Exercises 272
References 272

9 Quantitative predictors and their interactions with factors   **273**
9.1 Chapter pre-cap 273
9.2 Data and research questions 273
9.3 Modeling variation along lines 274
  9.3.1 Description of the model 277
  9.3.2 Centering quantitative predictors 278
  9.3.3 Fitting and interpreting the model 280
9.4 Models with group-dependent intercepts, but shared slopes 282
  9.4.1 Description of the model 282
  9.4.2 Fitting and interpreting the model 283

xii   *Contents*

      9.4.3 Interpreting group effects in the presence of shared (non-zero) slopes 286

  9.5   *Models with group-dependent slopes and intercepts 288*

      9.5.1 Description of the model 288

      9.5.2 Fitting and interpreting the model 290

      9.5.3 Interpreting group effects in the presence of varying slopes 292

  9.6   *Answering our research questions: Interim discussion 292*

  9.7   *Data and research questions: Updated 292*

  9.8   *Models with intercepts and slopes for each level of a grouping factor (i.e. 'random slopes') 293*

      9.8.1 Description of the model 294

      9.8.2 Fitting and interpreting the model 296

  9.9   *Models with multiple predictors for each level of a grouping factor 299*

      9.9.1 Description of the model 300

      9.9.2 Fitting and interpreting the model 301

      9.9.3 Model selection 303

  9.10 *Answering our research questions: Updated 305*

      9.10.1 A word on causality 307

  9.11 *Exercises 308*

  References 308

10 Logistic regression and signal detection theory models   309

  10.1 *Chapter pre-cap 309*

  10.2 *Dichotomous variables and data 309*

  10.3 *Generalizing our linear models 313*

  10.4 *Logistic regression 315*

      10.4.1 Logits 315

      10.4.2 The inverse logit link function 316

      10.4.3 Building intuitions about logits and the inverse logit function 319

  10.5 *Logistic regression with one quantitative predictor 320*

      10.5.1 Data and research questions 321

      10.5.2 Description of the model 321

      10.5.3 Fitting the model 324

      10.5.4 Interpreting the model 325

      10.5.5 Using logistic models to understand classification 329

      10.5.6 Answering our research question 334

  10.6 *Measuring sensitivity and bias 334*

      10.6.1 Data and research questions 338

      10.6.2 Description of the model 340

      10.6.3 Fitting and interpreting the model 342

      10.6.4 Answering our research questions 343

  10.7 *Exercises 345*

  References 345

Contents xiii

11 Multiple quantitative predictors, dealing with large models, and Bayesian ANOVA   346

11.1 Chapter pre-cap 347

11.2 Models with multiple quantitative predictors 347

11.3 Interactions between quantitative predictors 349

   11.3.1 Centering quantitative predictors when including interactions 351

   11.3.2 Data and research questions 353

   11.3.3 Description of the model 354

   11.3.4 Fitting the model 356

   11.3.5 Advantages of Bayesian multilevel models for large models 357

11.4 Bayesian Analysis of Variance 360

   11.4.1 Getting the standard deviations from our models 'manually' 363

   11.4.2 Using the BANOVA function 366

   11.4.3 Fitting and comparing the reduced model 367

11.5 A logistic regression model with multiple quantitative predictors 369

   11.5.1 Data and research questions 370

   11.5.2 Description of the model 371

   11.5.3 Fitting the model and applying a Bayesian ANOVA 372

   11.5.4 Categorization in two dimensions 372

   11.5.5 Model selection and misspecification 375

11.6 Exercises 381

References 381

12 Multinomial and ordinal regression   383

12.1 Chapter pre-cap 383

12.2 Multinomial logistic regression 383

   12.2.1 Multinomial logits and the softmax function 385

   12.2.2 Comparison to logistic regression 387

   12.2.3 Data and research questions 390

   12.2.4 Description of our model 391

   12.2.5 Fitting the model 394

   12.2.6 Interpreting the model 396

   12.2.7 Multinomial models and territorial maps 399

   12.2.8 Refitting the model without speaker random effects 404

   12.2.9 Answering our research questions 407

12.3 Ordinal (logistic) regression 407

   12.3.1 Cumulative distribution functions 412

   12.3.2 Data and research questions 415

   12.3.3 Description of the model 416

   12.3.4 Fitting and interpreting the model 418

   12.3.5 Listener-specific discrimination terms 422

   12.3.6 Answering our research questions 424

12.4 Exercises 426

References 426

xiv *Contents*

13 Writing up experiments: An investigation of the perception of apparent speaker characteristics from speech acoustics 427

  13.1 Introduction 428
    13.1.1 Fundamental frequency and voice pitch 428
    13.1.2 Variation in fundamental frequency between speakers 429
    13.1.3 Voice resonance and vocal-tract length 430
    13.1.4 Estimating vocal-tract length from speech 431
    13.1.5 Variation in vocal-tract length between speakers 431
    13.1.6 Perception of age, gender, and size 432
    13.1.7 Category-dependent behavior 435
    13.1.8 The current experiment 437

  13.2 Methods 437
    13.2.1 Participants 438
    13.2.2 Stimuli 438
    13.2.3 Procedure 439
    13.2.4 Data screening 439
    13.2.5 Loading the data and packages 440
    13.2.6 Statistical Analysis: Apparent height 441
    13.2.7 Statistical Analysis: Apparent gender 442

  13.3 Results: Apparent height judgments 443

  13.4 Discussion: Apparent height 445
    13.4.1 Age-dependent use of VTL cues on apparent height 446
    13.4.2 The effect of apparent gender on apparent height 447

  13.5 Conclusion: Apparent height judgments 447

  13.6 Results: Apparent gender judgments 448

  13.7 Discussion: Apparent gender judgments 450
    13.7.1 Effect of apparent age on the perception of femaleness 450
    13.7.2 Between-listener variation in gender perception 451
    13.7.3 Beyond gross acoustic cues in gender perception 452

  13.8 Conclusion: Apparent gender 453

  13.9 Next steps 453
    13.9.1 Research design, variable selection, etc. 453
    13.9.2 Non-linear models 454
    13.9.3 Other data distributions 454
    13.9.4 Multivariate analyses 455

  References 456

Index 457

Preface

This book presents an introduction to the statistical analysis of repeated measures data using Bayesian multilevel regression models. Our approach is to fit these models using the brms package and the *Stan* programming language in R. This book introduces mathematical and modeling concepts in plain English, and focuses on understanding the visual/geometric consequences of different regression model structures rather than on rigorous mathematical explanations of these.

Statistical modeling is as much a coding challenge as it is a mathematical challenge. As any programmer with some experience knows, copying existing scripts and modifying them slightly is an excellent way to learn to code, and often a new skill can be learned shortly after an understandable example can be found. To that end, rather than use a different toy data set for every new topic introduced, this book presents a set of fully worked analyses involving increasingly complicated models fit to the same experimental data.

We were both trained as linguists, and the experiment we analyze in this book is an experiment investigating a 'linguistic' research question (kind of). However, the sorts of models described in this book are useful for researchers in psychology, cognitive science, and many related (and unrelated) disciplines. In general, the information in this book will be useful to anyone that has similar sorts of data that they want to analyze regardless of the specifics of their research areas, and it should be straightforward to extend the concepts outlined in this book to models that predict different sorts of data.

Bayesian multilevel models and repeated measures data

A more complete explanation of the following is presented in Chapters 2–4, however, we can say something about this here. A Bayesian model is one which bases reasoning on *posterior probabilities* rather than *likelihoods*. A multilevel model is one in which you simultaneously model variation in your data, and in your parameters. The 'multi(ple) levels' are a metaphor: There is variation in the data (conceptually 'below'), and in the parameters of the probability distributions generating this data (conceptually 'above'). A Bayesian multilevel model puts these concepts together and uses posterior probabilities to make inferences about variation in data and in parameters.

Repeated measures data is data where multiple observations come from the same 'source' (discussed in more detail in Section 4.2). Basically, any time you have data with more than one observation from any given source, you have repeated measures data. Repeated measures data is very common in linguistics and the norm in

xvi *Preface*

many areas of research. For example, you might ask participants in an experiment to hit a button as soon as they hear a buzz, and repeat this for 100 trials per participant. Repeated measures data can naturally lead to independent data-level variation (the lower level) and parameter-level variation (the upper level). For example, reaction times to hit a button vary within-participants (the data/lower level), but average reaction times will also likely vary between participants (the upper/parameter level) in a systematic manner. Using multilevel models to analyze repeated measures data lets you independently model these two levels of variation. Using a *Bayesian* multilevel model allows you to build flexible models that provide you with all sorts of useful information.

One obstacle to the proper analysis of repeated measures data is that this requires models that are relatively 'complicated' and therefore usually not taught at the beginner level. In order to learn how to model repeated measures data, a student is often first expected to learn 'traditional' statistical approaches and designs. After this foundation is laid, the student can then move to the sorts of models they can *actually* use for their work, mainly multilevel models that can handle repeated measures data. This approach has several drawbacks: It takes a long time, spends substantial energy on statistical approaches that most will rarely if ever use in their work, and front-loads difficult and abstract concepts before students can start working with data they really understand. As a result, students may become discouraged, become convinced that they're 'not good at math', and may not realize how much they already intuitively understand about statistics.

This book starts with multilevel models and doesn't look back. It presents a realistic and complicated data set, and focuses from (nearly) the start (Chapter 4) on realistic models that could actually be used in modern, publishable research.

What's missing from this book

There was a time when every other Spider-Man movie started with Peter Parker being bitten by a spider and getting his powers, costume, etc. Filmmakers didn't trust that viewers know how Spider-Man got his powers, or that they could easily get this information somewhere, and so chose to spend precious movie minutes retelling what is perhaps the least interesting Spider-Man story. The problem is, the longer you spend on Peter Parker getting bit, the less time you can spend on Spider-Man swinging between buildings at high velocity. In the same way, many statistics books tell the statistics 'origin story' over and over, to the detriment of getting to the sorts of really interesting models people actually need. In other cases, when complicated models are discussed they are presented in a style and language only appropriate for an advanced reader, or with simple examples using toy data.

This book tries to find the 'Goldilocks zone' between too much and too little information: We assume you know who Spider-Man is or can easily find his origin story. This book omits a basic introduction to R in addition to a detailed explanation of how the code used in the book works. It also omits a lot of explanation that is required to 'really' understand topics, for example, correlation, which we introduce but only spend a few pages on. However, there are hundreds or thousands of excellent introductions to R, and even more places to find good information about basic statistical concepts like correlations. Rather than spend precious book pages on really getting

Preface xvii

into every topic that comes up, this book aims to spend as much time as possible flying between buildings at high velocity, or the statistical equivalent.

As a result, this book is narrowly focused on a specific subject: Introduction to Bayesian multilevel models for repeated measures data. It's not a general introduction to statistics nor to Bayesian models, or any number of other things. This narrow(ish) focus is both a strength and a weakness. We feel that it is a strength because it allows this book to cover material and provide examples of the sorts of models that are frequently needed in many disciplines, but also rarely discussed in statistics textbooks (often missing entirely or featuring in 1–2 chapters tucked away at the back). It's a weakness because it means the book is to some extent 'incomplete' in terms of providing a full introduction to the field of (Bayesian) statistics, as noted above. As a result, the ideal reader will know a little about statistics or have some resources on introductory statistics on hand (e.g. books, Wikipedia) to look up things they might not know or understand. Similarly, the book does not spend much time explaining how the things we do in R work, though examples of everything are given, and the code is commented and made as transparent as we could.

At the other end of the spectrum, this book is also missing many 'more complicated' but useful topics. For example, the book is entirely focused on linear modeling and does not discuss non-linear modeling. We also do not discuss missing data, multivariate dependent variables, or transformations of the dependent variables, among other topics. However, all of these things, and more, are easily doable using *Stan* and `brms`.

Statistics as procedural knowledge

Although statistical knowledge might seem like declarative knowledge, in many ways it is much more similar to procedural knowledge. You would never read a chapter from a French textbook once and expect to have memorized all the vocabulary and irregular forms. Similarly, you would never practice a piano piece a single time and assume that you are just 'bad at the piano' because you can't play it flawlessly. And yet a student may read a chapter from this book once and feel disappointed that they do not already understand the concepts.

We suggest thinking of acquiring statistical knowledge like learning a language, or musical instrument. It is normal, and in fact should be expected, that the reader will need to read some parts of the text multiple times, and *practice*, before being able to really *understand* all of the concepts presented here. We do not think getting good at statistics is about 'brain power' (whatever that is), as much as it is about a desire to learn, a genuine interest in the topic, and perseverance. In this way, learning statistics is very much like learning a language or an instrument. Buying a piano doesn't make you good at the piano, only practice does. Reading a grammar of Spanish or even moving to Spain will not teach you Spanish, only getting out there and talking to people will. To get good at statistics, you need to practice using statistics.

To that end, this book provides examples of analyses and data that can be re-analyzed in many similar yet different ways. As a result, readers have an opportunity to fit several parallel models, interpret them, make sure they understand them, and so on. In doing so, and in returning to challenging content periodically to 'practice', we hope that readers will be able to support their understanding of the content in the book.

xviii *Preface*

Practice vs brain power

John von Neumann was perhaps the greatest mathematical mind the world has ever seen. A glance at his contributions to mathematics on his Wikipedia page reveals an astonishing breadth and depth of mathematical abilities. Some quotes from his contemporaries about von Neumann (from his Wikipedia page):

- "I have sometimes wondered whether a brain like von Neumann's does not indicate a species superior to that of man." – Hans Bethe
- "Johnny was the only student I was ever afraid of. If in the course of a lecture I stated an unsolved problem, the chances were he'd come to me at the end of the lecture with the complete solution scribbled on a slip of paper." – George Pólya

And yet when a graduate student complained about not *understanding* some mathematical abstraction, von Neumann is said to have replied:

- "Young man, in mathematics you don't *understand* things. You just get *used to them*." – John von Neumann

This was von Neumann's experience, it has certainly been our experience, and it will likely be yours. Some things will make no sense the first, second, third, …, maybe even the tenth time you see them. And then one day they will. It won't be clear when or why they changed from confusing to sensible, but all of the sudden a combination of repetition, practice, and *time* will make the difference. It is likely that no amount of thinking and raw brain power alone will help you *understand* statistics right away on a first pass.

That being said, many of the things we talk about in this book will come up in every chapter, so if things don't all make sense right away that's fine since you will have plenty of chances to *get used to them*. Things will make more sense bit by bit as we learn how to use more and more complicated models. After reading a few chapters, you should come back and read earlier chapters again (and again). You may notice that a lot of things are discussed in an earlier chapter that you did not notice the first time you read it.

How to use this book

The chapters of this book, from Chapter 3 on, are organized in terms of regression model components, e.g., intercepts, slopes, interactions, and 'random' effects. We will discuss how these relate to experimental designs, statistical concepts, and the geometry of figures based on the data and model coefficients. In each chapter, we will learn how to use these components to 'build' progressively more complicated models to answer more complicated research questions. An analogy may be drawn to learning to be a carpenter. A chair is usually not carved out of a single block of wood, but rather assembled out of several discrete components (i.e., the flat seat, the cylindrical legs, supports for stability, etc.). As a result, learning to build a chair requires that the carpenter first learn to make the individual components and then learn to put them together in a specific way.

The example analyses in each chapter are presented with the general structure of a lab report or academic write-up. This is done as a pedagogical tool to help readers 'copy' the work they see in each chapter and modify this to suit their needs. The general structure for the presentation of new model components: (1) Introduce a type of research question (e.g., are the means of these groups the same?). Explain how this relates to model design concepts and give an example of real-world data associated with this sort of design. (2) Present the structure of a model that can be used to analyze the data, and to answer this sort of research question. Fit the model. (3) Interpret the model output and coefficients. Explain what all the information presented in the model output means, and explain how coefficients relate to our research question. (4) Beyond coefficient values, discuss what the model 'means' and attempt to provide an answer to our research questions based on the model. These chapter components correspond approximately to the (1) introduction, (2) methods, (3) results, and (4) discussion/conclusion sections found in a typical research paper.

Since we think learning statistics requires practice and repetition, this book is intended to allow readers to follow along with the analyses in the book, and to modify these to fit and interpret their own models. A possible sequence might be: (1) Repeat the exact analyses in a chapter, (2) Modify the model in the chapter slightly and interpret it, and (3) Fit new data using a model structure like that included in each chapter. Of course, step two above can be extended indefinitely for most chapters because in each case we present only a very small set of the very large number of possible models that could be fit to the data in each chapter.

Supplemental resources

The code needed to follow along with all the analyses presented in the book is provided in each chapter. There is also a book website that presents an online version of the book, and the code necessary to make all the plots in the book. Finally, the book's GitHub page (https://github.com/santiagobarreda/bmmrmd) contains. `Rmd` files containing all the code chunks, and the code to make the figures in the book. The book GitHub page also contains all the models referred to in the book, which can be downloaded using the `bmmb::get_models` function.

Our target audience

Although we think no statistical background is needed to use this book, readers with some statistical background will be in a better position to take full advantage. This book does assume a basic familiarity with R. However, the book provides fully worked examples of all analyses (including the scripts to generate all figures) so that readers only need to know enough R to follow along. We identify a few (non-exhaustive) types of people who might get good use out of this book: The self-starter, the convert, and the instructor.

The self-starter

The self-starter is a person interested in multilevel models, who has little to no background in statistics, and perhaps little to no knowledge of R. However, the self-starter enjoys learning on their own and is motivated to use Wikipedia, Stack Overflow, Google, and so on in order to supplement the information in this book. In particular, self starters may benefit by 'going along for the ride' to some extent and focusing on

xx *Preface*

practicing and working through examples without expecting to *understand* everything the first time.

The convert

Converts are readers who are already proficient with more 'traditional' analysis methods and may want to 'translate' their skills over to a Bayesian framework. As much as possible, this book adopts the jargon of more 'traditional' methods, and we also provide explicit comparisons with other sorts of models at the end of several chapters. If this sort of reader is reasonably familiar with R, and in particular if they are familiar with the `lme4` package, the content and examples in this book should be very accessible.

The instructor

Linguistics, and many disciplines with similar sorts of data, are in the early stages of a paradigm shift toward Bayesian statistical methods. Although we don't include many of the smaller exercises found in the typical statistics textbook, the book was written for use as a (semi) introductory book for a senior undergraduate or graduate statistics class. In addition, the data and scripts provided allow for a broad range of in-class activities and out-of-class assignments to be easily created based on the topics covered in each chapter. The exercises suggested at the end of each chapter involve the analysis and interpretation of models similar in structure to what is presented in each chapter. The result of this is that the exercises we suggest resemble the actual analyses that students will need to carry out when they eventually analyze their own data.

For example, students can be asked to replicate an analysis from a chapter but to make some modifications, analyzing a different dependent variable or re-parameterizing the model in some way. Because of the open-ended nature of the data exploration and the incredible customizability of Bayesian multilevel models, assignments using the same data set and analysis scripts can easily vary from very simple to quite sophisticated. In addition, since usable models are presented from the fourth chapter on, students can use the course to analyze their own repeated measures data, building and interpreting progressively more complicated models as the course progresses.

What you need installed to use this book

In order to use this book, you need to install R, which you can get for free online. If your R installation is more than one year old you may want to consider updating R right now and will also want to update R periodically. That's because some of the packages we will use in this book sometimes don't play nice with 'older' (relatively speaking) versions of R. If you're trying to do something and R crashes for no apparent reason, it may be time to update R and all your packages. You will also need to install (minimally) the `brms`, `devtools`, and `bmmb` packages. You can get the first two by running `install.packages('packageName')`. You can get the `bmmb` package from the package GitHub by running:

```
devtools::install_github("santiagobarreda/bmmb")
```

After installing `devtools` of course. We also recommend installing RStudio, an integrated development environment (IDE) for R. This is basically just software that makes it more convenient to use R, and it honestly *does* make it very convenient. Installing RStudio is only recommended, but we recommend it like we recommend indoor plumbing: After trying it we think you won't want to live without it.

Why go Bayesian?

We do not use Bayesian statistics because of an affinity for Bayesian arguments regarding the philosophy of knowledge gathering, although we do think these topics are very interesting. Instead, we use Bayesian statistics and suggest you should also use them, because it lets you do things that are difficult to do with other approaches, gives you information that other approaches don't, and gives you flexibility and resilience that may be difficult to find elsewhere. Even though we think Bayesian modeling has its advantages, we are not like the proverbial man with the hammer, we do not think that every problem requires a Bayesian solution. Instead, you may find that the models in this book are best for some situations, and other sorts of models are best for other situations.

That being said, the flexibility provided by Bayesian modeling is an enormous advantage, and it is difficult to find through other approaches. Returning to the woodworking analogy, learning to 'build' Bayesian models from their components lets you build exactly the 'furniture' (model) you want. In contrast, working with some traditional models feels more like going to Ikea, you can pick from a set of predetermined models, but are often constrained in terms of how these pre-built pieces can be modified.

Why brms?

The `brms` package is a useful way for us to use the *Stan* programming language, the real star of the show. We could write our own models for all of the analyses presented in this book and fit them directly in *Stan*. However, `brms` will do this for us more quickly, more easily, and with fewer mistakes. It also writes highly efficient models that fit quickly in *Stan*. In addition, the helper functions in the package make working with the posterior samples very simple and work well with a wide range of other packages related to *Stan*. However, despite the fact that this book uses `brms` exclusively for model building and fitting, we don't really think of this book as being *about* `brms`. The information presented in this book applies to modeling more generally and is also useful for people that write their own models directly in *Stan*. The main difference is these readers would need to do a lot of things 'by hand' or find other solutions to many of the things the `brms` package makes very simple to do.

It takes a village (of books)

As noted above, this book omits some basic information that can be found in many places online. It also does not get into some more complicated topics or in-depth explanations of some aspects of statistical modeling more generally. We recommend the following books to provide information that readers may want, but that is not present in this book.

xxii *Preface*

Before this book

These books introduce more 'classic' (non-Bayesian) models and traditional statistical approaches. Such models are usually not multilevel models and often cannot handle repeated measures data.

Myers, J. L., Well, A. D., & Lorch, R. F. (2013). *Research design and statistical analysis*. London: Routledge.
Winter, B. (2019). *Statistics for linguists: An introduction using R*. London: Routledge.

During this book

These books provide a lot of additional information about Bayesian statistics and modeling in general and discuss many things not covered in this book. However, they spend very little time on repeated measures data.

Kruschke, J. (2014). *Doing Bayesian data analysis: A tutorial with R, JAGS, and Stan*. Frankfurt: Elsevier Science.
Gelman, A., Hill, J., & Vehtari, A. (2020). *Regression and other stories*. Cambridge: Cambridge University Press.
Gelman, A., & Hill, J. (2006). *Data analysis using regression and multilevel/hierarchical models*. Cambridge: Cambridge University Press.

After this book

If you finish this book and think most of it made sense, you may find these books useful.

McElreath, R. (2020). *Statistical rethinking: A Bayesian course with examples in R and Stan*. Chapman and Hall/CRC.
Gelman, A., Carlin, J. B., Stern, H. S., Dunson, D. B., Vehtari, A., & Rubin, D. B. (2013). *Bayesian data analysis*, Third Edition. London: Taylor & Francis.

Acknowledgments

We would like to thank Sunny Zhou, Scott Perry, Michelle Cohn, and Mike Stuart, for their helpful comments and suggestions. I (Santiago) would like to thank Terry Nearey for introducing Noah and I, and for always insisting that things be done properly. I would also like to thank my parents for too many things to list, my daughters for keeping me company while I worked on the book, and my wife for all her encouragement and support; the book couldn't exist without her.

1 Introduction

Experiments and variables

Each chapter of this book will involve the analysis of data from a single perceptual experiment carried out by a group of 15 listeners. In this chapter, we will discuss the data for our experiment, introduce concepts related to variables and probabilities, and provide a very basic introduction to R along the way. As noted in the preface, a working knowledge of R is assumed and a familiarity with basic statistics is probably helpful, though not strictly necessary. The preface also provides suggested readings for those wanting to do some background reading on R or statistical inference and provides information about the software you need installed to follow along with the examples in the book.

1.1 Chapter pre-cap

In this chapter, we discuss the use of experiments for scientific inference, in addition to some inherent problems associated with inferences based on limited amounts of observations. After this, we describe the perceptual experiment that will be analyzed in this book, including a discussion of its structure, aims, procedures, and resulting data. Following the introduction of the experiment, we discuss variables and the way that we use these in experiments to make inferences. After that, we introduce some R data types, and the relationship between these and different kinds of variables is presented. Finally, we present some ways to visualize different sorts of variables and the relationships between them.

1.2 Experiments and effects

An **experiment** is a procedure or process that can help answer some research questions. Obviously, when defined so broadly, almost anything can be an experiment. In fact, when a child touches a hot stove to see what 'red' feels like, they are conducting an experiment which provides essential information about their world. In an academic context, experiments are expected to be **scientific**. However, there is no definition of *scientific* that is not socially and historically contingent. What is considered 'scientific' is determined by what scientists in a specific time and place consider to be scientific, and this can change and has changed, substantially over time.

At the moment, in most contexts, a research project is 'scientific' when it generally conforms to the **scientific method**. Of course, just as with **science** and scientific, there is no *single* scientific method, and no single 'true' definition that can be referred to. Instead, the scientific method consists generally of a process in which researchers: (1) Ask

DOI: 10.4324/9781003285878-1

2 Introduction: Experiments and variables

questions based on gaps in their knowledge about the world, (2) Collect data using codified procedures developed to avoid certain pitfalls and maximize the chance that the collected data can answer their questions, (3) Evaluate their questions in light of their data, and (4) Reach conclusions where possible, and synthesize their conclusions with their previous knowledge about the world.

Modern 'scientific' work usually involves the collection of empirical measurements, the quantification of patterns in these measurements, and the qualitative description of the quantitative patterns in the measurements. As a result, much modern scientific work yields large quantities of numeric values, observed under different conditions, which the researcher must then (statistically) analyze in order to understand. For example, imagine an experiment about whether caffeine makes people read faster. Subjects are asked to drink either a cup of coffee or a cup of decaf. After a 30-minute wait, they are asked to read a passage aloud and the duration of the reading is measured. Basically, we are measuring two different values, "the amount of time it takes people to read a passage of text after drinking decaf" and "the amount of time it takes people to read a passage of text after drinking regular coffee".

The experiment outlined above allows us to ask: is "the amount of time it takes people to read a passage of text after drinking decaf" *the same* as "the amount of time it takes people to read a passage of text after drinking regular coffee"? Another way to look at this is that we are interested in the **effect** of caffeine on reading times. By 'effect' we mean the degree to which caffeine is associated with changes in the characteristics of our observation (reading times) in some way. For example, if the average reading times were the same in both groups, we would conclude that "caffeine has no *effect* on reading times". In contrast, if reading times were 800 milliseconds shorter in the caffeine group, we might conclude "caffeine has the effect of reducing reading times by 800 milliseconds".

The relationship between statistical effects and causality is tricky. In some cases, like with caffeine and reading times, it seems reasonable that the caffeine is actually *causing* faster reading times since caffeine is associated with increased energy. However, we want to be sure to not imply that effects are *necessarily* causal. For example, decaf might also speed up reading times (relative to cold water) due to a placebo effect. This would suggest that some of the increase in reading times with regular coffee is due to people's *expectations* regarding its effect, in addition to the actual effect of caffeine. So, increased reading times after drinking regular coffee allows us to establish an *association* between these observations but does not in any way *prove* that one is causing the other. So, our use of the term *effect* should be interpreted as meaning 'association' rather than 'cause'.

Our experiment on reading times is specifically constructed to investigate the effect of caffeine on reading times. If the speakers in our experiment were randomly assigned to conditions, there is no particular reason to expect that their reading times would be different *in the absence* of caffeine. So, if we find that people read faster in the caffeine group, we may establish an association between caffeine and an increase in speaking rate. Combined with our knowledge of the physiological effect of caffeine on human listeners, we may conclude that this association suggests that caffeine consumption causes a difference in reading times. However, it's important to keep in mind that it is our world knowledge that allows us to make a causal inference and not the statistical association on its own. If we found a statistical association between wearing a green

Introduction: Experiments and variables 3

t-shirt and reading times, we should be more hesitant to make claims about a causal relationship.

This same logic applies in situations where we do not randomly assign subjects to groups, as long as we are careful in creating equivalent groups. Consider the same experiment about speaking rate carried out with groups based on speaker gender rather than drinking coffee. In this case, the question would be "is the amount of time it takes men to read this passage of text the same amount of time that it takes women to read this passage of text". If the speakers are generally similar in important characteristics (e.g. dialect, cultural background, and education levels) *apart* from gender, then any group differences may be attributable to the effect of gender on speaking rate (although establishing causal relationships is a difficult thing, as noted above, and involves more than simply randomization).

What we are describing in the above paragraphs are **controlled experiments**, experiments where the researcher takes an active role in ensuring the 'fairness' of the experiment. The notions of control and fairness are somewhat hazy and are perhaps more gradient than discrete (i.e. 'controlled' vs. 'uncontrolled'). However, some situations clearly do not lead to 'fair' outcomes. For example, what if the caffeine group of readers were all first-language English speakers, and the decaf group had a substantial number of second-language speakers with little experience reading in English. The caffeine group may very well read faster simply because they are more polished readers, independent of any effects of caffeine. Whenever possible, researchers avoid situations like this by exerting *control* over their experiments, both in the structure of their experiments and in the recruiting and assignment of their participants to experimental conditions.

Due to random between-speaker variation (among other things), there is no chance whatsoever that average reading times across both groups will be exactly identical, even if caffeine has no effect on reading times at all. In addition, if you re-ran the experiment with the same people and sentences, there is no chance that both group means would be the same across experiments. Basically, any two given group means are always expected to differ due to chance alone. And yet, there is the possibility that caffeinated reading times are *systematically* different – i.e. different in a way that the random variation of groups across replications is not. So, how can we ever establish that our measures are *actually* different and don't just *appear* to be different because of randomness? It is precisely this problem that has motivated scientists to use statistical analyses to help answer their research questions.

1.2.1 Experiments and inference

This book is about statistical inference. We will talk about the 'statistics' part in more detail in the next chapter, but we can talk about the 'inference' part now. **Inference** is a form of reasoning that allows you to go from a set of observations or premises to a conclusion about some facts. For example, you may arrive at a newly discovered island and see white cats wandering around. If you are there for a while and continue to observe only white cats, you may conclude "all the cats on this island are white". If you do this you have made what is called an **inductive** inference: You have gone from a set of observations (the cats you saw) to a general conclusion about all the cats on the island.

4 *Introduction: Experiments and variables*

Often, experiments are not just about observing and measuring certain effects, but also about drawing inferences regarding those effects. For example, in the reading time experiment described above, the researchers are not specifically interested in the reading times of the people in the experiments (i.e. the cats they saw) but rather in the reading times of people more generally (i.e. all the cats on the island).

Since inductive inference seeks to go from limited observation to general rules or principles, it has a central weakness. For example, your inference that only white cats exist on the island is on solid ground until you see a cat that is not white. Can you be sure this won't happen? You can't, because you don't know what you don't know and you can't be sure that what hasn't happened yet will never happen. This is called **the problem of induction** and it is a fundamental weakness of inductive reasoning.

Another problem faced when using experiments to gather knowledge is the fallacy of affirming the consequent, also known as the fallacy of the converse. Affirming the consequent arises when a researcher works backward from their "then" statement to their "if" statement. For example consider the statement: "If caffeine speeds up reading, then reading times will be faster for the caffeine group". Even if it's true that the reading times are faster for the caffeine group, it is not necessarily true that it is caused by the caffeine.

The problem is that the caffeine group reading faster is a *necessary* but not *sufficient* condition for the conclusion that 'caffeine speeds up reading'. Affirming the consequent does not mean that if/then statements are not useful, but simply that they cannot be used to prove the truth of the premises in a logically necessary manner. For example, consider the statement: "If am the king of England, this coin flip will be heads". This silly example shows that the truth of the second part of the statement does not prove the first.

We actually *do* think it would be reasonable to conclude that caffeine is causing the increase in reading times based on the experiment outlined above, given enough participants. However, it's useful to be aware of the fundamental limitations of trying to understand general patterns given limited sets of observations. It's also useful to think about how we can reason in a way that might minimize the odds of inferential mistakes, especially by including our general knowledge of the world (and the specific topic) in our reasoning. For example, rather than observing white cats and leaving it at that, we can ask: Why are the cats white? Do evolutionary pressures cause them to be white? How do their genetics ensure that all members of the species will be white? Is there any chance non-white cats could enter the population? Considering the answers to questions like this, in combination with our observations, can make inferences like "all cats on this island are white" more reliable.

The examples above involved the effect of caffeine on reading times. We are interested in generalizing to the human population based on what is a tiny sample of humans, relatively speaking. If we make the claim "caffeine speeds up reading times", are we extending that to all humans, or at least to all English speakers? Past, present, and future? That is a bold claim based on a small number of data points, or it would be in the total absence of any world knowledge and prior expectations. Of course, we know that caffeine is a stimulant and seems reasonably likely to make people read faster. The finding fits within our larger worldview and, as a result, we may accept it as likely to be 'true'. In contrast, suppose that the two groups had instead drank plain water, one 'regular' and one dyed with blue food coloring. In this situation, we may be skeptical of a large effect for food coloring. This is because there is no reason to suppose that there is an effect. Since this finding does not conform to any prior knowledge about the world, it is the sort of inference that may turn out to be less reliable, in the long run.

1.3 Our experiment

As noted above, each chapter in this book will feature the analysis of data from the same perceptual experiment. In this section, we provide an overview of the experiment, its design, the general research questions it can address, and an overview of the resulting data. A more thorough explanation of the issues at hand and the design of the experiment can be found in Chapter 13.

1.3.1 Our experiment: Introduction

Any two speakers will likely 'sound' different from each other even when they are saying the 'same' word. These between-speaker differences can, in some cases, be systematically associated with speaker characteristics such as age, height, and gender. So, tall speakers tend to sound one way, while shorter speakers tend to sound another way. As a result, although it may sound odd to talk about how tall someone *sounds*, listeners are able to use the acoustic information in a speaker's voice to *guess* the speaker's age, gender, size, and so on. This information is referred to as the speaker's **indexical characteristics**: Social and physical information regarding the speaker that is understood from the way someone speaks.

We can ask two different questions with respect to assessments of indexical characteristics from speech: (1) Are they accurate, and (2) How do listeners arrive at their guesses? Generally speaking, listeners are often not very accurate in their judgments of indexical characteristics, however, they are consistent in the errors that they tend to make. For example, if one voice is incorrectly assumed to belong to a particular sort of speaker, it will often be the case that this mistake is a regular occurrence.

The 'guessing' of speaker characteristics is dominated by two acoustic cues: Voice pitch and voice resonance. Voice **pitch** can be thought of as the 'note' someone produces with their speech. When you sing you produce different notes by producing different pitches. The pitch of a sound is related to the vibration rate of the thing that produced the sound because repetitive vibration produces a repetitive sound wave that humans perceive as a pitch. Human voice pitch is regulated by changing the vibration rate of the vocal folds in your larynx. You can feel this vibration if you hum a song and press your fingers against the middle of the front of your neck. Pitch is an **auditory sensation**, a *feeling* you have in relation to a periodic acoustic event, a sound. When you hear two sounds, if you can order them based on which sound is 'lower/higher' than the other, then they differ in pitch. Since this quality cannot be directly measured, scientists measure the **fundamental frequency** (f0) of the sound to quantify its pitch. The f0 of a sound is measured in **Hertz** (Hz), which measures the number of times a sound wave repeats itself in a second.

Smaller things tend to vibrate at higher rates than larger things. This holds for vocal folds as well; shorter vocal folds tend to vibrate at higher rates than longer vocal folds, thereby producing speech with a higher pitch. As a result, larger speakers tend to produce speech with a lower pitch than smaller speakers. Since the vocal folds grow as one grows into adulthood, voice pitch is a good indicator of age between young childhood and adulthood, but is less useful to distinguish adults of different ages. Basically, pitch may help you distinguish a 5-year-old from an 18-year-old, but not an 18-year-old from a 30-year-old.

In addition to general age-related changes, the vocal folds tend to increase in size during puberty for most males so that post-pubescent males tend to produce speech with a lower pitch than the rest of the human population. As a result of these relations, a voice with a lower voice pitch is more likely to be produced by someone who is *older*, *taller*, and more likely to be *male* than a voice with a higher pitch. The relationships between age, height, gender, and f0 are presented in Figure 1.1. The height information used throughout this book is available in the `height_data` data included in the `bmmb` package and is from Fryar et al. (2012).

Resonance can be thought of as the 'size' of a sound. For example, a violin and a cello can be playing the same note (with the same pitch), but the cello will 'sound' bigger. This is because lower frequencies resonate in its larger structure. In the same way, speakers with longer **vocal tracts** (the space from the vocal folds to the lips) tend to 'sound' bigger by producing speech with lower frequencies overall. We don't really have good words to describe what resonance 'sounds' like, but a small resonance (short vocal tract) sounds 'heliumy'. When a person breathes helium and speaks, their pitch does not go up, but their *resonance* frequencies increase. Acoustically and perceptually, this mimics the effects of having a very short vocal tract (for more information on this, see Chapter 13).

Long vocal tracts sound like slow-motion speech (think of someone saying "nooooooooooooooooooo….." when something bad is happening in slow motion in a movie), and this is because slowing down the playback of a recording simulates a lowering of resonance frequencies in speech (along with the pitch). In fact, size simulation by resonance manipulation is how the recordings for 'Alvin and the chipmunks' were originally created. A low-pitched male singer was recorded singing abnormally slow, and the recording was sped up in order to simulate speech with a very high resonance (and an associated very short vocal tract). If you wonder what an increased resonance sounds like, there is a gas called 'sulfur hexafluoride' that mimics this effect (because

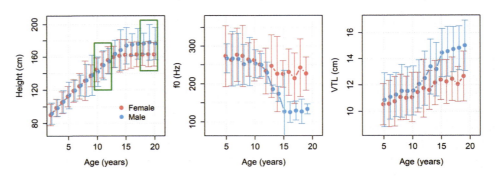

Figure 1.1 (left) Average height of males and females in the United States of America, organized by age (Fryar et al. 2012). (middle) Average f0 produced by male and female speakers from five years of age until adulthood (Lee et al. 1999). (right) Average acoustic vocal tract length (VTL) of male and female speakers from five years of age until adulthood (Lee et al. 1999). The average adult male VTL was set to 15 cm. Error bars indicate two standard deviations.

it is very dense). Examples of people increasing their voice resonance by inhaling this gas can be found on YouTube.

There are many ways to measure the resonance of a voice. In our data, we will use speech acoustics to directly estimate the length of the vocal tract that produced it, in centimeters (in the manner described in Chapter 13). So, our measure of voice resonance will not be acoustic at all but will instead measure the physical correlate of the vocal tract expected to have produced the speech sound.

In general, a lower voice resonance suggests a longer vocal tract length in centimeters. There is a strong positive relationship between vocal tract length and body length (i.e. height) across the entire human population. This means that if a person is taller than another, their vocal tract is expected to be longer and their voice resonance is expected to be lower. Since height increases from birth into adulthood, this means that voice resonance can be used to predict both height and age. In addition, adult males tend to be somewhat taller than adult females in most populations, with an average difference of about 15 cm in the United States. As a result, voice resonance can be used to infer the gender of adult speakers, and possibly that of children as well. These relationships are shown in Figure 1.1.

In summary, voice pitch and voice resonance are independent ways that someone can acoustically 'sound' bigger/smaller, older/younger, and male/female. The experiment to be described below is a **perceptual experiment** involving **behavioral measures**, meaning we observed people's *behavior* in reaction to the stimuli. In this experiment, human listeners listened to auditory stimuli (words) and were asked to answer questions regarding what they heard. The experiment was designed to investigate the way that speech acoustics are used by listeners to determine the age, gender, and height of speakers, and the way that these decisions affect each other.

1.3.2 Our experimental methods

Our listeners were 15 speakers of American English. Listeners were presented with the word "heed" produced by 139 different speakers of Michigan English. These speech samples were recorded by Hillenbrand et al. (1995) and are available on the GitHub page associated with this book. So, this experiment featured 139 unique **stimulus** sounds that the listeners in the experiment were asked to respond to. The stimuli used were produced by 48 adult females, 45 adult males, 19 girls (10–12 years of age), and 27 boys (10–12 years of age). These speakers showed substantial variation in their voice pitch and resonance as measured by their f0 and estimated vocal tract length (as will be discussed in Section 1.5).

In addition to the natural acoustic variation that exists between speakers, voice resonance was also manipulated experimentally. All stimuli were manipulated by shifting the spectral envelope down by 8%, simulating an increase in speaker size of approximately 8% (all other things being equal). The downward shift of the spectral envelope results in a perceptually lower resonance which should 'sound bigger' to listeners. This acoustic manipulation is similar to the one carried out to make voices such as those of 'Alvin and the Chipmunks' sound small, but in reverse (and the pitch was not affected).

Each listener responded to all 278 stimuli (139 speakers × 2 resonance levels), for a total of 4,170 observations across all listeners (15 listeners × 278 stimuli). Stimuli were presented one at a time, randomized along all stimulus dimensions. This means that tokens were thrown in one big pile and selected at random in a way that the properties

8 Introduction: Experiments and variables

of an upcoming stimulus were never predictable based on the previous one. For each trial, listeners were presented with a single word at random and were asked to:

a   Indicate whether they thought the speaker was a "boy 10–12 years old", a "girl 10–12 years old", a "man 18+ years old", or a "woman 18+ years old". This is the **apparent speaker category**.

b   Estimate the height of the speaker in feet and inches (converted to centimeters for this book). This is the **apparent speaker height**.

Our intention is to analyze the apparent speaker category and height judgments provided by listeners in order to address specific research questions (discussed in the following section). To do this, we will use acoustic descriptions of the different speakers' voices, focusing on the fundamental frequency of their speech, and the vocal tract length implied by their speech (estimated as described in Chapter 13). In addition, we will investigate how listeners' judgments about the speaker's age, gender, and height can affect *each other* and the use of speech acoustics.

1.3.3 Our research questions

This experiment is meant to investigate how listeners use speech acoustics to estimate the height of unknown talkers. The results will also let us investigate the relationship between the perception of talker size and the perception of talker category. Specific research questions will be discussed in each chapter, however, a general overview will be provided here. The expectations to be outlined below are based on the empirical relationships between these measurements and characteristics outlined above, shown in Figure 1.1, and on previous research (discussed in Chapter 13).

The assumption is that listeners are familiar with the relationships between apparent speaker characteristics and speech acoustics, and 'somehow' use the information in speech to guess speaker characteristics. For example, if we know that a speaker with an f0 of 100 Hz is usually an adult male and is usually about 176 cm tall, we might expect listeners will identify speech stimuli with an f0 near 100 Hz as produced by an adult male speaker who is about 176 cm tall.

Listeners were asked to provide two responses, speaker height and speaker group. The four-speaker groups can be split according to two characteristics: The age of the group and the gender of the group (boy = male child, girl = female child, man = male adult, woman = female adult). So, we can consider that listeners reported the height, age, and gender of the speaker, for each sound they listened to.

Lower frequencies, whether f0 or resonances are expected to be associated with taller and older speakers. For post-pubescent speakers, low frequencies, particularly in f0, can also be an indicator of maleness. In general, we expect that the perception of maleness will be associated with the perception of taller speakers, in particular for older speakers. The perception of adultness should be associated with taller speakers for either gender, however, the difference in height between boys and men tends to be larger than that between girls and women.

Finally, it's also possible that the acoustic information in voices is used differently based on the apparent category of the speaker. For example, maybe listeners use f0 one way when they think the speaker is an adult and another way when they think the speaker is a child. In addition, it's possible that different listeners use acoustic

Introduction: Experiments and variables 9

information in idiosyncratic ways that are systematic within-listener, but which differ arbitrarily from each other between listeners.

1.3.4 Our experimental data

The data associated with this experiment is available in the bmmb package (discussed in the preface), and can be accessed using the code below:

```
# load package
library ("bmmb")

# load data
data (exp_data_all)
```

The code above loads our data and places it into our workspace in an object called exp_data_all. Below we use the head function to see the first six lines of the data for the experiment. Our data is in **long format**, so each row is a different individual observation and each column is a different piece of information regarding that observation. Each individual trial (a single row) represents an individual listener's response to a single stimulus word played to them. So, we know that this data frame has 4,170 rows to represent the 4,170 observations in our data.

```
# see first 6 rows
head (exp_data_all)
##   L C height R S C_v  vtl  f0 dur G A G_v A_v
## 1 1 g  165.6 a 1   b 12.2 277 237 f c   m   c
## 2 1 w  173.2 b 1   b 12.2 277 237 f a   m   c
## 3 1 w  165.6 a 2   b 12.4 287 317 f a   m   c
## 4 1 g  147.8 b 2   b 12.4 287 317 f c   m   c
## 5 1 g  165.6 a 3   b 11.6 219 277 f c   m   c
## 6 1 g  158.8 b 3   b 11.6 219 277 f c   m   c
```

If this were data that you collected and wanted to analyze, you would likely have it somewhere on your hard drive in a CSV file, or some equivalent data file. If you were to open this data in Excel (or a similar software), you would see your data arranged in rows and columns. Below we write our data out as a CSV file so that we can have a look at it outside of R.

```
write.csv (exp_data_all, "exp_data_all.csv", row.names = FALSE)
```

We can get more information about our data using the str function, which tells us that our data is stored in a data frame. A **data frame** is a collection of vectors that can be of different types, but which must be of the same length. A **vector** is a collection of elements of the same kind. Below, we see that the str function tells us about the vectors comprised by our data frame.

```
str (exp_data_all)
## 'data.frame':   4170 obs. of  13 variables:
```

10 *Introduction: Experiments and variables*

```
##   $ L      : int  1 1 1 1 1 1 1 1 1 1 ...
##   $ C      : chr  "g" "w" "w" "g" ...
##   $ height : num  166 173 166 148 166 ...
##   $ R      : Factor w/ 2 levels "a","b": 1 2 1 2 1 2 1 2 1 2 ...
##   $ S      : int  1 1 2 2 3 3 4 4 5 5 ...
##   $ C_v    : Factor w/ 4 levels "b","g","m","w": 1 1 1 1 1 1 1 1 1 1 ...
##   $ vtl    : num  12.2 12.2 12.4 12.4 11.6 11.6 11.9 11.9 12.1 12.1 ...
##   $ f0     : int  277 277 287 287 219 219 260 260 244 244 ...
##   $ dur    : int  237 237 317 317 277 277 318 318 242 242 ...
##   $ G      : chr  "f" "f" "f" "f" ...
##   $ A      : chr  "c" "a" "a" "c" ...
##   $ G_v    : Factor w/ 2 levels "f","m": 2 2 2 2 2 2 2 2 2 2 ...
##   $ A_v    : Factor w/ 2 levels "a","c": 2 2 2 2 2 2 2 2 2 2 ...
```

We see four kinds of vectors in our data: `int` indicating that the vector contains integers, `num` indicating that the vector contains floating-point numbers (i.e. numbers that can have decimal points), `chr` indicating that the vector contains elements made up of characters (i.e. letters or words), or numbers being treated as if they were letters (i.e. as symbols with no numeric value), and `Factor` which indicates that the vector contains categorical predictors (discussed below). The information represented in each column of our data frame is:

- `L`: An integer from 1 to 15 indicating which *listener* responded to the trial.
- `C`: A letter representing the apparent speaker category (`b` = boy, `g` = girl, `m` = man, `w` = woman) reported by the listener for each trial.
- `height`: A floating-point number representing the *height* (in centimeters) reported for the speaker on each trial.
- `R`: A letter representing the *resonance* scaling for the stimulus on each trial. The coding is `a` (actual) for the unmodified resonance and `b` (big) for the modified resonance (intended to sound bigger).
- `S`: An integer from 1 to 139 indicating which *speaker* produced the trial stimulus.
- `C_v`: A letter representing the *veridical* (actual) speaker category (`b` = boy, `g` = girl, `m` = man, `w` = woman) for each trial.
- `vtl`: An estimate of the speaker's *vocal tract length* in centimeters.
- `f0`: The vowel *fundamental frequency* (f0) measured in Hertz.
- `dur`: The *duration* of the vowel sound, in milliseconds.
- `G`: The *apparent gender* of the speaker indicated by the listener, `f` (female) or `m` (male).
- `A`: The *apparent age* of the speaker indicated by the listener, `a` (adult) or `c` (child).
- `G_v`: The *veridical gender* of the speaker indicated by the listener, `f` (female) or `m` (male).
- `A_v`: The *veridical age* of the speaker indicated by the listener, `a` (adult) or `c` (child).

Since more than one person who read earlier versions of this book complained about the short variable names, we want to explain why we used names like `A` and not `apparent_age`, and `L` instead of `Listener`. When we get to more complicated models, `A:G:f0:L` is a manageable amount of characters for a variable name, while

Introduction: Experiments and variables 11

`apparent_age:apparent_gender:f0:Listener` is not. The latter may be nicer in the short term but becomes impossible to deal with in a compact manner in plots and on the page. The only way to feature compact descriptions and printouts for the more complicated models in the second half of this book was to go with the short variable names from the start. By using the short names, we can have consistent naming in the text, in the formal mathematical descriptions of our models, and in the information printed in the R console. Since the same data is used in every chapter and the same handful of variables are used in every chapter, we hope that this decision will not be too vexing for the reader.

We can access the individual vectors that make up our data frame in many ways. One way is to add a `$` after the name of our data frame, and then write the name of the vector after. This is shown below for our vector of heights.

```
exp_data_all$height
```

Running the command above will write out the entire vector on your screen, which includes all 4,170 observations of height responses that make up our data. Using the `head` function will show you the first six elements of an object, and you can get specific elements of the vector using brackets as shown below.

```
# show the first six
head(exp_data_all$height)
## [1] 165.6 173.2 165.6 147.8 165.6 158.8

# show the first element
exp_data_all$height[1]
## [1] 165.6

# show elements 2 to 6
exp_data_all$height[2:6]
## [1] 173.2 165.6 147.8 165.6 158.8
```

Below, we use two sets of brackets to retrieve the height vector using its position in the data frame (first example) or its name (second example).

```
head(exp_data_all[[3]])
## [1] 165.6 173.2 165.6 147.8 165.6 158.8

head(exp_data_all[["height"]])
## [1] 165.6 173.2 165.6 147.8 165.6 158.8
```

We can also retrieve the height vector by using a single set of parentheses as shown below. This method relies on treating the data frame as a matrix whose elements are arranged on a grid. Each element of the grid can then be accessed by providing x and y grid coordinates in single brackets as in `[x,y]`. Below we retrieve the entire third column by specifying a column number (or name) but leaving the row number unspecified.

12 *Introduction: Experiments and variables*

```
head(exp_data_all[,3])
## [1] 165.6 173.2 165.6 147.8 165.6 158.8

head(exp_data_all[,"height"])
## [1] 165.6 173.2 165.6 147.8 165.6 158.8
```

We use the same method to recover the entire first row of the data frame, and then the second element of the first row (or, from another perspective, the first element of the second column).

```
exp_data_all[1,]
##   L C height R S C_v  vtl  f0 dur G A G_v A_v
## 1 1 g  165.6 a 1   b 12.2 277 237 f c   m   c

exp_data_all[1,2]
## [1] "g"
```

1.4 Variables

Each of the columns in the `exp_data_all` data frame can be thought of as a different variable. **Variables** are placeholders for some value, whether we know it or not. For example, you can say "my weight is x pounds" or "this data represents a response provided by experimental subject x". In our data, our variables take on different values from trial to trial, and the values of these variables tell us about the different outcomes and conditions associated with the trial. In this section, we're going to discuss different aspects of variables, especially as they pertain to the analysis of experimental data.

1.4.1 Populations and samples

Anything that varies from observation to observation in an unpredictable manner can be thought of as a **random variable**. For example, your exact weight varies from day to day around your 'average' weight. In principle, you could probably explain exactly why your weight varies if you were so inclined. However, in practice, you are probably not exactly sure *why* your weight is a bit higher one day and a bit lower the next. So, your weight is a random variable not necessarily because it is *impossible* to know why it varies, but simply because you don't currently have the means to predict its exact value for any given observation.

In order to answer questions about reasonable values for variables of interest, scientists often collect measurements of that variable. These measurements can help us understand the most probable values of this variable, and the expected range of the variable, even if its value for any given observation is unpredictable. For example, although you may not know your exact weight on any given day, if you weigh yourself with some regularity you may have enough observations to have a pretty good idea of what your weight might be tomorrow. In addition, your expectation may be so strong that a large deviation from it would be more likely to result in your buying a new scale than believing the measurement.

Introduction: Experiments and variables 13

A **sample** is a finite set of observations – measurements of a variable – that you actually have. The **population** is the entire, possibly infinite, set of possible outcomes associated with the random variable. For example, the population of "f0 produced by adult women in the United States" contains all possible values of f0 produced by the entire set of women from the United States. Our sample is the specific set of observations we have from the speakers we observed.

Usually, a scientist will collect a sample to make inferences about the population. In other words, we are interested in the general behavior of the variable itself, not just in the small number of instances that we observed. For example, Hillenbrand et al. collected their data to make inferences about speakers of American (or Michigan) English in general, and not because they were particularly interested in the speakers in their sample. Similarly, we are not specifically interested in the opinions of the 15 listeners in our data, but in what their behavior might tell us about the population of human listeners in general.

1.4.2 Dependent and independent variables

We can make a very basic distinction between variables that we want to explain or understand, and variables that we *use* to explain and understand. The variables we want to explain are our **dependent variables**, and they are usually the variables we measure or observe in an experiment. The variables that we use to explain and understand our measurements are our **independent variables** (sometimes called explanatory variables).

Dependent variables can often be **random**, which means their values are not knowable **a priori** (before observation). For example, you may have some expectations about what your weight might be before you get on a scale, but in general, you can't know exactly what it will say with certainty before collecting the observation. Although the exact values of our dependent variables can vary somewhat unpredictably from trial to trial, in the context of an experiment, there is the general expectation that these values will *depend* in some way on the other variables in the experiment. For example, in this book we will analyze experimental data. In this experiment, we modified the resonance frequencies of stimuli so that some are expected to 'sound' bigger than others. As a result, we expect an association between values of apparent height and the R (Resonance) variable in our data. In other words, the value of apparent height *depends* on the value of R.

Variables that help predict the response (dependent) variable are sometimes referred to as independent variables because their values are not considered to depend on those of the other predictors. More specifically, we can say the values of our independent variables are not assumed to depend on the values of the other variables within the context of our experiment, or in a manner that directly relates to the relevant research questions.

Our experiment has two response variables: the apparent height (`height`) reported for each trial, and the apparent speaker category (`C`) reported for each trial. Our experiment also involves several variables that could be used to understand our responses (i.e. every other variable in the data). Whether a variable is dependent or independent depends on the research question and on the structure of the model more than on some inherent property of variables and data. For example, the data in `exp_data_all` could be used to understand variation in voice pitch (`f0`) across speaker groups. In

14 *Introduction: Experiments and variables*

this case, `f0` would be the dependent variable and the veridical speaker category (`C_v`) would be the independent variable. Another researcher may choose to model how perceived height varies as a function of f0 and speaker group. In this case, `height` would be the dependent variable, and `f0` and `C_v` would be the independent variables.

1.4.3 Categorical variables and 'factors'

Categorical variables, also sometimes called **nominal**, are variables that take on some set of non-numeric, usually character values. Often, categorical variables are the labels that we apply to objects or groups of objects. For example, gender is a categorical variable with possible values of 'male' and 'female', among others. In our experiment data, `C`, `S`, `L`, `R`, `C_v`, `A`, `G`, `A_v`, and `G_v` are categorical variables. Categorical predictors are often called **factors**. Factors can take on a limited number of values, called **levels**. For example, if your factor is 'word category' your factor levels may be 'verb' and 'noun'. If your factor is 'first language', your levels may be 'Mandarin', 'English', 'Italian', and 'Hindi'.

A `factor` is a data type in R. A vector of factors is very similar to a vector of words, but it has some additional properties that are useful. For example, consider our `C_v` predictor, which tells us which category each speaker falls into. When `C_v` is treated as a vector of factors, rather than a character vector, our nominal labels will have associated numerical values. Many R functions turn nominal (non-numeric) predictors into factors and doing this yourself gives you control over how this will be handled.

```
# see the first 6 observations
head (exp_data_all$C_v)
## [1] b b b b b b
## Levels: b g m w

# it has levels
levels(exp_data_all$C_v)
## [1] "b" "g" "m" "w"

# each level has numerical values
table (exp_data_all$C_v, as.numeric (exp_data_all$C_v))
##
##         1     2     3     4
##   b   810     0     0     0
##   g     0   570     0     0
##   m     0     0  1350     0
##   w     0     0     0  1440
```

By default, factor levels are ordered alphabetically. You can control this behavior by re-ordering the factor levels as below:

```
# re order
exp_data_all$C_v_f = factor (exp_data_all$C_v, levels = c('w','m','g','b'))

# the new order is evident
levels (exp_data_all$C_v_f)
## [1] "w" "m" "g" "b"
```

```
# note that 'm' is now the second category
xtabs ( ~ exp_data_all$C_v + exp_data_all$C_v_f)
##                    exp_data_all$C_v_f
## exp_data_all$C_v     w      m      g      b
##               b      0      0      0    810
##               g      0      0    570      0
##               m      0   1350      0      0
##               w   1440      0      0      0
```

Although our factors seem to have an 'order' this is only because items can only be discussed and presented one at a time, and so there must be some order in our nominal variables at some level of organization. For example, when presenting effects and plotting figures, you literally do have to decide to show one effect first and another second. However, the ordering of factors is **exchangeable** meaning it does not in any way affect our analysis. For example, the listeners and speakers in our experiment received unique numbers. However, listener 1 is not the listener who 'most' has the quality of 'listener', and speaker 8 is not twice the 'speaker' (or anything else) that speaker 4 is. In other words, although we must commit to some order in our factors to organize our data, this ordering is arbitrary and not meaningful.

There is a special kind of categorical variable, called an **ordinal** variable, where the ordering of the categories *is* meaningful. These variables are halfway between numbers and labels: They faithfully represent the order (**rank**) of categories but not the magnitude of the difference between values. For example, consider the first-, second-, and third-place runners in a race. These are *ordinal* labels. You know who finished before/after who but don't know anything about how much of a difference there was between the runners. As a result, these variables seem to have some of the properties of numbers, while not being totally like 'real' numbers. We will discuss the prediction of ordinal dependent variables in more detail in Chapter 12.

1.4.4 Quantitative variables

Unlike nominal variables, quantitative variables let us represent the relative ordering of different observations *and* the relative differences between them. Some examples of quantitative variables are time, frequency, and weight. In our experiment data, height is a quantitative dependent variable, and f0, vtl, and dur are quantitative independent variables.

A distinction is made between **continuous** and **discrete** quantitative variables. Continuous variables have infinitely small spaces between adjacent elements (like real numbers), at least in principle. On the other hand, discrete variables have gaps between the possible values of the variable, like integers. For example, things like time are naturally continuous, while things like counts are naturally discrete.

When we use a quantitative variable as our dependent variable, there is usually the expectation that it is continuous rather than discrete. However, in practice all measures stored on computers are discrete and many continuous values (e.g. reaction times) can be measured with maximal precision, resulting in discrete values. For example, a chronometer that measures reaction times to the millisecond contains only 1,000 possible values between zero and one second. Similarly, human height is difficult to measure up to much less than a centimeter of precision, making height measurements effectively discrete. Below are some more

16 *Introduction: Experiments and variables*

questions that will help you decide if you should treat a variable as quantitative, even if it is discrete:

- Is the variable on a ratio or interval scale? This is a prerequisite for a quantitative value to be used as a dependent variable. An interval scale means that differences between values are meaningful, and a ratio scale additionally means that 0 is meaningful.
- Is the underlying value continuous? Many variables are discrete in practice due to limitations in measurement. However, if the underlying value is continuous (e.g. height, time), then this can motivate treating the measurement as a quantitative dependent variable since fractional values 'make sense'. For example, even if you measure time only down to the nearest millisecond, a value of 0.5 milliseconds is possible and interpretable. In contrast, a value of 0.5 people is not.
- Are there a large number (>50) of possible values the measured variable can take? For example, a die can only take on 6 quantitative values, which is not enough.
- Are most/all of the observed values far from their bounds? Human height does not really get much smaller than about 50 cm and longer than about 220 cm, so it is technically bounded. However, in most cases, our observations are expected to not be away from these boundaries.

If you answered yes to all or most of these questions, it is probably ok to treat your discrete variable as if it were quantitative, though this determination really needs to be made on a case-by-case basis.

1.4.5 *Logical variables*

Before finishing with variables, we need to talk about one type that does not appear in our data, but that will come up often. These are referred to as **Boolean** variables in many other situations; however, they are referred to as **logical** variables in R. Logical variables can only take one of two values: TRUE and FALSE. Below we use two equal signs to test for the equality of two values, and != to check for inequality. Notice that we can check for the equality of numbers or characters.

```
2 == 1
## [1] FALSE

"hello" == "hello"
## [1] TRUE

"hello" != "hello"
## [1] FALSE
```

We can also check for inequalities between numbers:

```
2 > 1
## [1] TRUE
```

```
2 >= 1
## [1] TRUE

2 < 1
## [1] FALSE

2 >= 1
## [1] TRUE
```

One useful fact is that the logical values of TRUE and FALSE have numeric values of 1 and 0, as seen below. In each case, TRUE is equal to 1 so the expression evaluates to 2.

```
TRUE + 1
## [1] 2

(2 == 2) + 1
## [1] 2
```

When logical operators are applied to vectors, the operation is evaluated for each element of the vector, as below, and a vector of logical values is returned. When combined with the numeric values of logical variables, this means that we can easily calculate the number of times a certain condition was met in the vector.

```
# are the values less than or equal to 3?
c(1,2,3,4,5,6,7,8,9,10) <= 3
##  [1]  TRUE  TRUE  TRUE FALSE FALSE FALSE FALSE FALSE FALSE FALSE
```

Below, we find whether each element of the vector is greater then or equal to three. This results in a vector of logical values equivalent to a vector of ones and zeros. When we find the sum of the vector of logical values, we find the number of times in which the condition was met. Below, we see that three of the elements in this vector satisfy our condition.

```
logical_vector = c(1,2,3,4,5,6,7,8,9,10) <= 3

as.numeric (logical_vector)
##  [1] 1 1 1 0 0 0 0 0 0 0

sum (logical_vector)
## [1] 3

sum (c(1,2,3,4,5,6,7,8,9,10) <= 3)
## [1] 3
```

There is one other very important use for vectors of logical values, and this is to extract subsets of your data that meet certain conditions. Below we create a vector of logical values that indicate whether the f0 for a trial is below 175 Hz or not. We can see

18   *Introduction: Experiments and variables*

that this vector has 4,170 elements, one for every row in our data, and that 1,290 trials satisfied our condition. This is nothing more than a bigger version of the same process we just carried out above with our `logical_vector`.

```
# TRUE if f0 < 175
f0_idx = exp_data_all$f0 < 175

str (f0_idx)
##  logi [1:4170] FALSE FALSE FALSE FALSE FALSE FALSE ...

sum (f0_idx)
## [1] 1290
```

Recall that we can access individual rows of our data frames, that is the individual observations of our data, by placing this information before a comma inside brackets following the name of the data frame (as seen below). When we use a logical vector in this way, the effect is to include every row that equals `TRUE` and to omit every row that equals `FALSE` in the vector. Below we use our `f0_idx` vector to create a new data frame called `low_f0` containing only productions with f0 below 175 Hz.

```
# get only rows where f0 < 175, i.e. where f0_idx is TRUE
low_f0 = exp_data_all[f0_idx,]

nrow(low_f0)
## [1] 1290

max(low_f0$f0)
## [1] 172
```

We can use the `!` operator, which basically means 'not', to flip each `TRUE` to `FALSE` (and vice versa). When `f0_idx` is flipped to select a subset of a data frame, the result is to select those rows where speaker f0 is greater than or equal to 175 Hz.

```
# get only rows where f0 >= 175, i.e. where f0_idx is FALSE
high_f0 = exp_data_all[!f0_idx,]

nrow(high_f0)
## [1] 2880

min(high_f0$f0)
## [1] 175
```

1.5 Inspecting our data

After running an experiment but before your statistical analysis, you should inspect the patterns in your data. This gives you an opportunity to make sure the data has the characteristics you expect, and that there weren't any errors during the collection of your data or with the design of your experiment.

Introduction: Experiments and variables 19

1.5.1 Inspecting categorical variables

One of the most useful functions for understanding the distribution of categorical variables is the `table` function. This function makes a **cross-tabulation** (or **contingency table**) of the variables passed to the function. If a single factor is passed, the function returns the number of times each level of the factor is found in the data. Since each of our listeners listened to 278 stimuli, we expect that each level of the factor L (representing listeners) will appear 278 times in our data, confirmed below.

```
table (exp_data_all$L)
##
##   1   2   3   4   5   6   7   8   9  10  11  12  13  14  15
## 278 278 278 278 278 278 278 278 278 278 278 278 278 278 278
```

We can use this approach to confirm basic expectations about our data and to rule out problems with the design of the experiment. This is always a good idea since mistakes happen, and sometimes only get noticed when attempting to process the data. For example, if any of the levels above appeared more than or fewer than 278 times, we would have a problem.

We can also provide two (or more) factors at a time and the `table` function will return counts for every combination of factor levels. The table below reflects the fact that each listener heard 54 boys, 38 girls, 90 men, and 96 women, for a total of 278 responses per listener. When you provide multiple factors to `table`, it will vary the first factor along the rows of the table and the second factor along the columns of the table. If a third factor is provided, it makes a different table for factors one and two, for each level of factor three. More and more factors can be provided to the function, but these tables become harder and harder to work with.

```
# table of listener and veridical speaker category
table (exp_data_all$C_v, exp_data_all$L)
##
##      1  2  3  4  5  6  7  8  9 10 11 12 13 14 15
##   b 54 54 54 54 54 54 54 54 54 54 54 54 54 54 54
##   g 38 38 38 38 38 38 38 38 38 38 38 38 38 38 38
##   m 90 90 90 90 90 90 90 90 90 90 90 90 90 90 90
##   w 96 96 96 96 96 96 96 96 96 96 96 96 96 96 96
```

Below we see that unlike our veridical categories, the distribution of *apparent* speaker categories varies across listeners. This is because the equal distribution of speakers for each listener is an aspect of the experimental design. However, the manner in which listeners interpreted each voice, whether they thought it sounded like a boy or girl, for example, may vary across individual listeners.

```
# table of listener and apparent speaker category
table (exp_data_all$C, exp_data_all$L)
##
##      1   2   3   4   5   6   7   8   9  10  11  12  13  14  15
##   b 42  89  59  90  59  59  67  58  51  12  68  40  98  95  63
```

20   *Introduction: Experiments and variables*

```
##    g   58   45   24   50   44   34   32   29   44   60   24   34   16   23   43
##    m   83   89   90   84   90   92   88   90   89   93   86   95   88   88   89
##    w   95   55  105   54   85   93   91  101   94  113  100  109   76   72   83
```

We can visualize relationships between categorical variables using a mosaic plot. In Figure 1.2, we see mosaic plots representing the two tables shown immediately above. Mosaic plots use rectangles of different sizes to reflect the relative frequencies of different combinations of categorical variables. In the left mosaic plot, we see that the size of the rectangle for each category is identical across listeners. This tells us these variables do not affect each other: Changing the listener does not affect the distribution of veridical speaker category in any way. In contrast, the distribution of apparent speaker category *is* affected by the listener and this is shown in the right plot where columns differ randomly from each other.

Below we make a three-dimensional table and inspect the table and each dimension. Notice that to index the table along the third dimension, we need to add two commas inside the brackets.

```
tmp_tab = table (exp_data_all$C, exp_data_all$L, exp_data_all$R)
tmp_tab
tmp_tab[,,1]
tmp_tab[,,2]
```

When we plot the relationship between apparent speaker class, listener, and resonance (i.e. actual vs. big), we see a three-way relationship between the variables (Figure 1.3). First, we see that the chances of observing different speaker categorizations depend on the listener. Second, we see that the chances of observing each category depend on resonance. And third, we see that the effect of resonance potentially affects each listener in a somewhat different way. The first chapters of this book will focus on understanding patterns in continuous variables. However, we will discuss the prediction and modeling of categorical dependent variables beginning in Chapter 10.

1.5.2 Inspecting quantitative variables

Using R, we can easily find useful information about any quantitative variable. Below, we calculate the sample mean, the number of observations, the sample

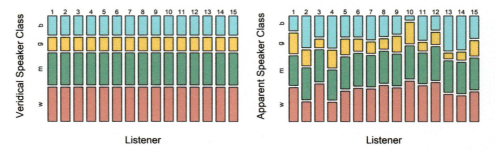

Figure 1.2 Comparisons of mosaic plots showing variables that do not (left), and do (right), affect each other.

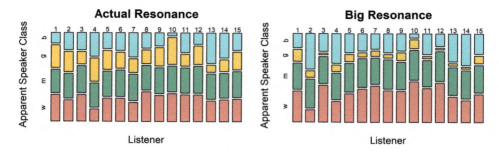

Figure 1.3 Mosaic plots highlighting a three-way relationship: The two-way listener by apparent speaker class relationship varies as a function of the third variable, resonance (indicated along the top of each plot).

standard deviation, and some important quantiles for our speaker height judgments. The **quantiles** of a set of observations are values such that a given percentage of observations fall above and below the value. Quantiles are found by finding cutoff values that are greater than x% of the sampled values. For example, the 50% quantile, also called the **median**, is the value such that 50% of the distribution is below it, and the 25% quantile (the *first quartile*) is the value such that 25% of the distribution is below it.

```
# calculate the mean
mean (exp_data_all$height)
## [1] 162.8

# find the number of observations
length (exp_data_all$height)
## [1] 4170

# find quantiles
quantile (exp_data_all$height)
##     0%    25%    50%    75%   100%
## 106.7  154.9  164.8  173.5  198.1
```

We can use this information to make some basic, and potentially useful, statements about our data. The mean and median are 162.8 and 164.8 cm, respectively, and height values range from 106.7 to 198.1 cm. However, there are not many observations at the extremes, and 50% of values are between 154.9 and 173.5 cm. We know this because these are the values of the first and third **quartiles**, the 25% quantiles that divide our distribution into four equal parts. Since 75−25=50, we know that 50% of the distribution of observations must fall inside of these boundaries.

We can look at the distribution of apparent height judgments in several ways, as seen in Figure 1.4. In the top row, each point indicates an individual production. Points are jittered (randomly shifted) along the *y*-axis to make them easier to distinguish so that dense and sparse locations can be compared.

22 Introduction: Experiments and variables

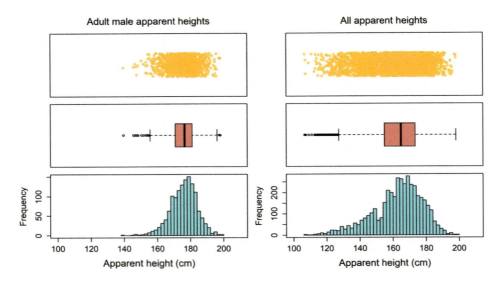

Figure 1.4 Each column presents the same data in three different ways: (top) As individual jittered points, (middle) as a boxplot, and (bottom) as a histogram.

In the middle row, we see a **box plot** of the same data. The edges of the box correspond to the 25% and 75% quantiles of the distribution, and the line in the middle of it corresponds to the median. So, the box spans the **interquartile range** of your observations and 50% of observations are contained in the box. The boxplot **whiskers** extend from the edge of the boxplots. By default, these extend out 1.5 times the interquartile range. These whiskers are simply intended to give you an estimate of the amount of 'typical' variation in your sample. Beyond the whiskers, we see individual **outliers**, points considered to be substantially different from the rest of the sample. We can see that the boxplot does a good job of summarizing the information in the top plots, and provides information related to both average apparent height values and to the expected variability in these values.

The bottom row presents what is known as a **histogram** of the same data. The histogram divides the x-axis into a set of discrete sections ('bins') and gives you the count (or frequency) of observations in each bin. Bins with lots of observations are relatively taller (more *dense*) than bins with fewer observations in them. As a result, histograms can be used to summarize where observations tend to be. For example, we can see that the bins under the interquartile range have the most observations, and that values further from the median value become increasingly less frequent. In addition, histograms can provide us with information that boxplots can't. For example, in the right column, we see that our distribution of height judgments actually has a little gap at around 150 cm. This information does not really come across in the boxplot representation of the same data.

Scatter plots are plots that represent two quantitative variables at a time using a set of points on a coordinate space. Each point represents a single observation, the x-axis location represents the value of one variable, and the y-axis location represents the value of the other variable. Scatter plots are useful to understand relationships

Introduction: Experiments and variables 23

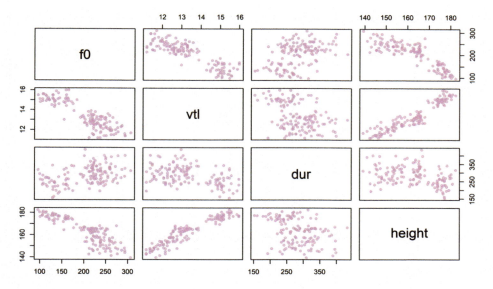

Figure 1.5 A pairs plot of the continuous variables in our data, showing different sorts of relationships between f0 (fundamental frequency in Hertz), VTL (vocal tract length in centimeters), dur (duration in milliseconds), and height (apparent speaker height in centimeters).

between quantitative predictors. Below we consider the relationships between our quantitative predictors using a pairs plot (`pairs`). A pairs plot creates scatter plots for all pairs of quantitative variables provided, resulting in n^2 plots for *n* variables. Each plot in (Figure 1.5) contains a single point for each different stimulus used in this experiment (height values represent averages across all listeners).

In the plot above, we can see several apparent relationships between our quantitative variables. For example, pitch (`f0`) and vocal tract length (`vtl`) are *negatively* related. This means that as the value of `f0` increases (left to right), the value of `vtl` decreases (top to bottom). In other words, if the f0-vtl relationship were a hill it would have a negative, decreasing, slope. In contrast, we see that `height` and `vtl` enter into a positive relationship: As you increase `vtl`, `height` also increases. Finally, we see that duration (`dur`) and `height` do not seem to have much of a relationship. Unlike the other two scatterplots which looked a bit like ramps or lines, the scatter plot of `dur` and `height` resembles a Rorschach test inkblot. This suggests either that these two variables are not strongly related, or that the nature of the relationship is more complicated than what can be understood using these simple plots.

1.5.3 Exploring continuous and categorical variables together

We can also consider the relationships between our quantitative and categorical variables. We can use the boxplot function as below:

```
boxplot (y ~ factor)
```

24 *Introduction: Experiments and variables*

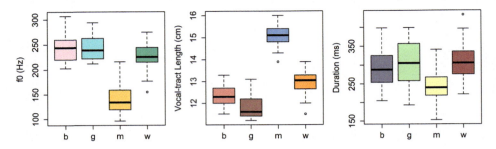

Figure 1.6 Boxplots showing the distribution of different quantitative variables in our data according to the veridical speaker categories of boy (b), girl (g), man (m), and woman (w).

To make a set of boxplots for the variable y. The function call above will create a plot with a separate box for each level of the factor in the function call. In Figure 1.6, we see different quantitative variables organized according to veridical speaker category. For example, the left plot shows the distribution of observations of f0 for boys, girls, men, and women, respectively. In this case, the differences between the boxplots for each level of the factor tell us about the values of f0 usually observed for speakers in that category.

Another way to think of the relationships between our categorical and quantitative variables is using scatter plots with different points, as in Figure 1.7. In the scatter plots below, each point indicates a single speaker from our experiment, and the position of each point is determined by the f0, vocal tract, and average apparent height for the speaker. However, rather than using meaningless symbols, each point is labeled using a letter which indicates the veridical category that the speaker falls into. Using plots like the one below helps us understand the relationship between our acoustic predictors and our speaker categories. For example, it's clear that adult males are fairly distinct acoustically compared to the other speaker categories. In addition, it seems that boys, girls, and women are easier to separate along the vocal tract length dimension than the f0 dimension.

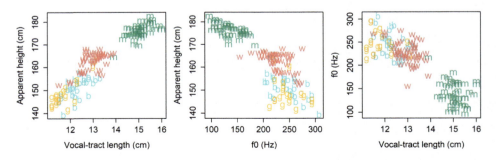

Figure 1.7 Speakers plotted according to their fundamental frequency (f0), vocal tract length, and average apparent height. Letters indicate if speaker is a boy (b), girl (g), man (m), or woman (w).

1.6 Exercises

The analyses in the main body of the text all involve only the unmodified 'actual' resonance level. Responses for the stimuli with the simulated 'big' resonance will be reserved for exercises throughout. You can get the 'big' resonance data in the `exp_ex` data frame, or all the data in the `exp_data_all` data frame. For now, it would be useful to compare the results in `exp_data` and `exp_ex` using the techniques covered in this chapter. The data is quite similar but not exactly the same, so familiarizing yourself with the apparent height variable in `exp_ex`, and any differences between `exp_data` and `exp_ex`, will help your analyses later on.

Reference

Fryar, C. D., Gu, Q., & Ogden, C. L. (2012). Anthropometric reference data for children and adults: United States, 2007–2010. *Vital and Health Statistics*. Series 11, Data from the National Health Survey, 252, 1–48.

2 Probabilities, likelihood, and inference

In the previous chapter, we introduced some data and talked about variables and experiments. In this chapter, we're going to talk about probabilities and explain how they can be used to make inferences about our data and research questions. Before beginning this chapter we should note that it's normal if some, or many, of the topics to be discussed don't make sense the first time you read this chapter. Things will make more sense once you start to actually build models and it becomes less hypothetical and more practical.

In addition, as noted in the preface, it's a mistake to think that you can read a chapter in a statistics textbook once and move on having fully absorbed the content. If many of the topics in this chapter are new to you, you should probably: (1) Read this chapter, (2) wait a few days and read it again, and then (3) wait a few more days (or weeks) and read it again. It may also be useful to return to this chapter even once you are working through the following chapters. In our experience, you may find that you *see* information for the first time that was there all along, but that finally makes sense given your increased experience with the subject.

Finally, we want to note that what we present below is a teeny tiny slice of statistical inference based on the assumption of normally distributed data (or actually, errors). In Chapter 5, we will introduce another error distribution (t), and in Chapter 10, we will model binary dependent variables using logistic regression. In each case, those models require us to change aspects of the details outlined below. However, the same general principles still apply with respect to the relationships between data, likelihoods, and the estimation of credible parameter values.

2.1 Chapter pre-cap

In this chapter, we introduce important statistical concepts such as probability, probability distributions, and likelihoods. The discussion in this chapter centers around the Gaussian/Normal distribution, and making inferences related to the population mean parameter. First, we introduce conditional, marginal, and joint probabilities, and the importance of assuming the independence of observations. Then, we present probability densities and the normal distribution, and discuss the parameters of this distribution in detail. Following this, we introduce likelihood functions, and discuss logarithms and the use of log-likelihoods. Finally, we outline the use of likelihood functions and statistical models to make inferences about credible values of parameters.

DOI: 10.4324/9781003285878-2

2.2 Data and research questions

We're going to think about a hypothetical value "the average apparent height of adult males". To put it another way, we might wonder "how tall do men 'sound'?". The apparent heights of men cannot be known *a priori*. In other words, you don't know how tall a random man will 'sound' until you actually observe the judgment. For this reason, "the average apparent height of men" can be modeled as a random variable. We're going to think about how we can use our experimental data to try to answer the following two questions:

(Q1) How tall does the average adult male 'sound'?
(Q2) Can we set limits on credible average apparent heights based on the data we collected?

These two questions can be thought of as relating to the central location and the spread of the data, respectively. Answering the first question tells you what values your variable tends to take on, while answering the second question tells you how much variation you can expect around the most typical values. Scientific research is often focused on questions such as (Q1) regarding the central location, the average value, of some variable. For example, someone might ask "how tall do adult male speakers sound?" and you can say, for example, "I have some data that suggests 174 cm is a reasonable estimate". However, reliable inference requires answering question (Q2) as well, and determining what range of values are plausible for a certain variable.

Think of the (actual) average height of the people in a large city. You can go out and sample 100 people and find the mean (average) of your sample, arriving at a single estimate of the population mean. Now imagine that 50 people went out in the same city and each sampled 100 random people. There is no chance that every one of those 50 people would find identical means across all of their samples. Instead, there will be a distribution of sample means, in the same way, there is a distribution of the original data used to calculate the means. Another way to look at this is that there is some degree of **uncertainty** involved when answering any research question. As a result of uncertainty, it can be difficult to rule out alternative possible answers to our research questions. For example, if 174 cm is a good estimate, what about 173.99 cm? What about 173 cm? 172 cm? Where do estimates of average height stop being 'good'? Without being able to say what is *not* a good estimate, it's not quite as useful to be able to say what *is*.

A related issue arises with respect to the interpretation of the magnitude of effects. Imagine that you read about a miracle diet that was guaranteed to make you lose one gram of weight a day. You know that is not very impressive. How? Because you understand that a difference of one gram is not large relative to the variation that exists in the weight of a human body on a daily basis. You could gain the weight back (and more) by drinking a teaspoon of water. Without knowing how much human weight tends to vary between and within people, it's impossible to know whether a reduction of one gram constitutes a meaningful change in the mass of a human. In contrast, a diet that causes one gram of weight loss in the average mouse may actually be of interest to mice owners, as this may be a large value relative to natural variation in the weight of a mouse.

28 *Probabilities, likelihood, and inference*

So, we see that imposing limits on credible ranges for our average values can be as important as finding the average values themselves. Further, in order to properly contextualize values and effects, we need to have some idea about the underlying variation in the measurements. Clearly, we need some principled way to 'guess' reasonable ranges based on our sample of observations, in addition to just talking about average values. In this chapter, we will discuss how statistics provides us with a framework to answer (Q1) and (Q2) above using only our sample of values and a (statistical) model.

In order to discuss the apparent heights of adult males, we need to extract the subset of speakers judged to be adult males from our data. Below we load the book package (bmmb) and select the relevant rows from our experimental data. Recall that our experiment contained an acoustic manipulation such that speech resonances were changed to make speakers sound bigger (see Section 1.3.2). In the main text, we're going to focus only on the unmodified productions, the 'natural' speech produced by the men in our sample. To do this, we are going to use the data in exp_data, which contains only the trials involving unmodified productions.

```
# Load book package
library (bmmb)

# Load experimental data
data (exp_data)

# Take only rows produced by men (`m`)
men = exp_data[exp_data$C_v == 'm',]
mens_height = men$height
```

We can have a look at some of the quantiles (see Section 1.4.4) to get an idea of what range of values this variable tends to have. We see that the minimum and maximum values are 139.7 and 192.3 cm, that 174.5 cm is the median, and that half of the observed height judgments for adult males fell between 169.2 and 179.1 cm.

```
quantile (mens_height)
##     0%    25%    50%    75%   100%
## 139.7 169.2 174.5 179.1 192.3
```

Obviously, inspecting the distribution of our observed height judgments only gives us direct information about the judgments we actually observed. To make inferences about the probable characteristics of the height judgments we have *not* observed, or to talk about height judgments for adult males more generally, we rely on methods of statistical inference, as will be described below.

2.3 Empirical probabilities

The **sample space** of a variable is the set of all possible outcomes/values that a variable can take. Classic examples are a coin flip, which can take on the values 'heads' or 'tails', or the roll of a standard six-sided die, which can take on the values one through six. In other cases, the sample space may have an infinite or practically infinite number of members. For example, since time is continuous, there are an infinite number of durations an event may have, given adequate precision in measuring time. If we think of the human population, or the population of fish in the sea, these are theoretically finite but practically infinite. It would be extremely difficult to fully sample either of these populations and impossible to do so before they changed substantially (e.g. before some members have died and others have been born).

The **probability** of an event/outcome is the number of times an outcome occurs relative to the number of all possible outcomes that can occur (i.e. all of the outcomes in the sample space). For example, there are six possible outcomes when you roll a die. As a result, the probability of any one outcome is 1/6 (0.17), and the probability of observing an even number is 3/6 (0.5). Actually, this is an extremely brief, and vastly oversimplified, presentation of probability, a topic that could occupy one's entire career. There are actually many ways to conceive of probability mathematically and philosophically. For more detailed, rigorous expositions, see Ross (2019) for a good introductory text, Parzen (1960) for a more classical, and advanced, approach, and Jaynes (2003) for a distinctly Bayesian treatment of the subject.

By convention, the probability of each event is assigned a value between 0 and 1, and the total probability of all of the possible outcomes in the sample space is equal to one. As a result of this, you know that a probability of 0.5 means something is expected to occur half the time (i.e. on 50% of trials), and a probability of 0.25 indicates that something should happen 25% of the time, about one in every four trials.

Empirical probabilities are the probabilities of different outcomes in a sample of data. For example, we can flip a coin 100 times and observe 65 heads. This means that the empirical probability of observing heads in our data is 0.65 (65% of trials). Empirical probabilities can also be referred to as relative frequencies or proportions. Later, we're going to talk about *theoretical* probabilities based on mathematical models.

Suppose we want to know the probability of observing an apparent height judgment over 180 cm in our sample. To calculate the empirical probability of this occurring in our data we need to find (1) the number of times it occurred, and (2) the total number of observations for the variable. We can do this easily using the logical operators and variables discussed in Chapter 1. Below, we find the total number of outcomes that satisfy our restrictions (being over 180 cm) and divide this by the total number of observations being considered.

```r
# the evaluation in the parenthesis will return 1 if true, 0 if false
# number of observations the fall above the threshold
sum (mens_height > 180)
## [1] 136

# divided by total number of events
sum (mens_height > 180) / length (mens_height)
## [1] 0.2015

# a shortcut to calculate probability, mean = sum/length
mean (mens_height > 180)
## [1] 0.2015
```

30 *Probabilities, likelihood, and inference*

The top value is the frequency of the occurrence. This is not so useful because this number can mean very different things given different sample sizes (e.g. 136/675, 136/675,000). The middle and bottom values have been divided by the total number of observations. As a result, these now represent an estimate of the probability of occurrence in a way that is independent of the total number of observations.

2.3.1 Conditional and marginal probabilities

Figure 2.1 presents boxplots of the overall distribution of height judgments in our data (left), and of the distribution of these provided by each listener individually. We can see that height judgments range from about 140 to 200 cm, with most responses falling between 170 and 180 cm. Notice that our overall boxplot does not give us any information about the ranges used by different listeners, nor even the fact that the data was contributed by different listeners. This overall distribution of height responses is the **marginal distribution** of height judgments. The marginal distribution of a variable is the overall distribution, *across* all values of all other variables. The marginal boxplot on the left compresses all of the listener-specific boxplots on the right into one single box. It's common to denote marginal probabilities using notation like this . $P(\text{variable})$, meaning we might refer to the marginal probability of height responses like this $P(\text{height})$.

A look at Figure 2.1 reveals that the probability of observing a height response of over 180 cm can depend substantially on the listener that provided it (e.g. compare listener 7 vs listener 12). Recall that height is a quantitative variable and listener is a categorical predictor (a factor) with 15 levels, one for each listener (see Section 1.4.3). We can talk about how height judgments vary across the levels of our listener factor (i.e. for different listeners) by considering the **conditional probability** of height *given* the listener. A conditional probability is the probability of an outcome given that some other outcome has occurred. For example, rather than ask "what is the probability of observing an apparent height over 180 cm?", we can ask "what is the probability of observing an apparent height over 180 cm *given* that we are observing data from listener 12?". Conditional probabilities basically reduce the sample space by including only the subset of events that satisfy the given condition.

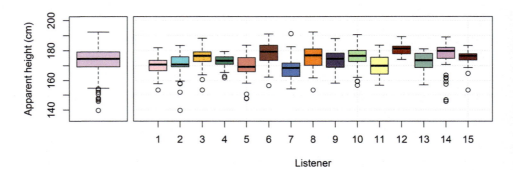

Figure 2.1 (left) Boxplot showing all height judgments for adult male speakers in our experiment. (right) Individual boxplots for each listener's responses.

Conditional probabilities are often denoted like this $P(\text{outcome variable} \mid \text{conditioning variable})$, which in this case would look like $P(\text{height} \mid L)$. For example, the first box in the right plot of Figure 2.1 is the distribution of $P(\text{height} \mid L = 1)$, and the second box is the distribution of $P(\text{height} \mid L = 2)$. Below we divide our vector of height judgments (`mens_height`) into those contributed by listener 7 and listener 12. We then find the probability of observing a height judgment over 180 cm conditional on the listener and see that these can differ quite a bit from each other.

```
# create subsets based on listener
L07 = mens_height[men$L==7]
L12 = mens_height[men$L==12]

# find the conditional probability of height>180 for each listener
mean (L07 > 180)
## [1] 0.04444

mean (L12 > 180)
## [1] 0.6444
```

In the boxplots in Figure 2.1, we see that apparent height distributions vary substantially as a function of the value of `L`, our listener variable. Contrast this with the boxplots seen in Figure 2.2, which shows the distribution of stimulus durations conditional on listener. Since every individual recording had a fixed duration and all listeners heard the same sounds, we know that the distribution of stimulus durations is identical across all levels of the listener variable. As a result, we can see that all of the conditional distributions of duration given listener look just like each other, and just like the marginal probability. This tells us that duration and listener are *statistically independent*.

When two variables are **statistically independent**, the distribution of one variable is not affected by the values of the other. As a result, the conditional distribution of one variable given the other will be the same as its marginal distribution, as seen in Figure 2.1. This can be stated for the general case as $P(\text{variable} \mid \text{conditioning variable}) = P(\text{variable})$. In our example in Figure 2.1, $P(\text{height} \mid L = 7)$ is *not* equal to $P(\text{height} \mid L = 12)$, and neither

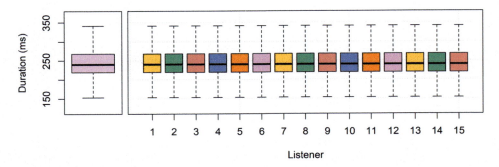

Figure 2.2 (left) Boxplot showing the duration of stimuli for adult male speakers in our experiment. (right) Individual boxplots for the stimuli presented to each listener.

32   *Probabilities, likelihood, and inference*

of these is equal to the marginal distribution. As a result, we conclude that the apparent height and listener variables in our data are not independent. Instead, they are **statistically dependent**, meaning that these variables *are* related to each other in some way and that knowing the value of one may tell you something about probable values of the other.

2.3.2 Joint probabilities

Joint probabilities reflect the probability of two or more things occurring together. We can refer to the joint probability of A and B using the notation $P(A \cap B)$ or $P(A \& B)$. Here are some important things to know about joint probabilities:

1   The formula for calculating the joint probability of two outcomes A and B is given by $P(A \cap B) = P(A \mid B) \cdot P(B)$. This means that the probability of A and B is equal to the conditional probability of A given B, multiplied by the marginal probability of B. In plain English, this means that the joint probability of A and B being true is equal to the probability that A is true assuming B is true, times the probability that B is true.
2   Recall from Section 2.3.1 that when A and B are independent $P(A \mid B) = P(A)$. In other words, when A and B are independent, the conditional probability that A is true given that B is true equals the marginal (unconditional) probability that A is true. As a result of this, when A and B are independent, $P(A \mid B) \cdot P(B) = P(A) \cdot P(B)$. Thus, when A and B are independent, their joint probability can be found by simply multiplying their individual marginal probabilities.
3   The probability of A and B is equal to the probability of B and A. As a result of this $P(A \cap B) = P(B \cap A)$, and as a result of that $P(A \mid B) \cdot P(B) = P(B \mid A) \cdot P(A)$. This relation is very important and will become useful later.

We can demonstrate the above properties using the empirical probabilities in our data. Consider the joint probability of observing a response in our data that was contributed by listener seven (`L='12'`), and also being longer than 250 ms in duration. We can find this by joining two logical variables using the `&` (and) symbol as shown below.

```
# TRUE if the listener is 12
L12 = (men$L=='12')

# TRUE if the duration is greater than 250 ms
dur_250 = men$dur > 250

# The probability of A and B
mean (L12 & dur_250)
## [1] 0.02815

mean (men$L=='12' & men$dur > 250)
## [1] 0.02815
```

So, we see that the probability of observing this event is 0.028, indicating that we expect this in about 3% of trials. Below, we see that this same joint probability can be calculated based on $P(A \cap B) = P(A \mid B) \cdot P(B)$.

```
# Marginal probability of observing listener 12 (i.e. P(L=12))
p_L12 = mean (men$L=='12')

# Subset containing only listener 12
L12 = men[men$L == '12',]

# Probability of dur>250 given listener 12 (i.e. P(dur>250 | L=12))
p_dur_250_given_L12 = mean (L12$dur > 250)

# Joint probability = P(dur>250 | L=12) * P(L=12)
p_dur_250_given_L12 * p_L12
## [1] 0.02815
```

Because of the experimental design, we know that every listener heard the same vowel durations (see Section 1.3 for a review of the experimental design). This means that duration is independent of the listener: Knowing who the listener is in no way changes the fact that every listener heard the same number of trials with durations longer than 250 ms. As a result of this independence, we could also have calculated the joint probability of the above events by simply multiplying their marginal probabilities, as seen below.

```
# Joint probability = P(dur>250) * P(L=12)
mean (dur_250) * mean (p_L12)
## [1] 0.02815
```

This shortcut will not work for variables that are not independent. For example, let's consider the probability of observing a height judgment of greater than 180 cm provided by listener 12. Below we calculate this the *wrong* way by multiplying the marginal probabilities, substantially underestimating the probability of the event. The problem is that this method of calculation does not take into account that listener 12 was among the most likely listeners to report heights greater than 180 cm.

```
# TRUE if the listener is 12
L12 = (men$L=='12')

# TRUE if the height is over 180
over_180 = men$height > 180

# Empirical joint probability of the observation
mean(men$L=='12' & men$height > 180)
## [1] 0.04296

# Wrong: multiplying marginal probabilities
mean(L12) * mean(over_180)
## [1] 0.01343
```

34 *Probabilities, likelihood, and inference*

Below we calculate the joint probability correctly by using the conditional probability.

```
# Marginal probability of observing listener 12
p_L12 = mean (men$L=='12')

# Subset containing only listener 12 (i.e. given listener 12)
L12 = men[men$L == '12',]

# Conditional probability of a height > 180 given listener 12
p_over_180_given_L12 = mean (L12$height > 180)

# Correct joint probability
p_over_180_given_L12 * p_L12
## [1] 0.04296
```

This highlights a very important point: The calculation of joint probabilities is much (much) simpler when you can assume that your observations are independent. For example, consider the comparison of the joint probability of four events, one for independent events, and another for dependent events:

Independent events :
$$P(A \& B \& C \& D) = P(A) \cdot P(B) \cdot P(C) \cdot P(D)$$
Dependent events :
$$P(A \& B \& C \& D) = P(A \mid B, C, D) \cdot P(B \mid C, D) \cdot P(C \mid D) \cdot P(D)$$

This means that to calculate the joint probability of dependent events, we may need to calculate many conditional probabilities. Although this may not matter when calculating the joint probability of a handful of observations, calculating the joint probability of hundreds or thousands of correlated variables can become difficult if not impossible in practice.

2.4 Probability distributions

A probability distribution is a function that assigns probabilities to the different possible outcomes in a sample space. We will illustrate and discuss exactly what this means with reference to histograms. In the left plot of Figure 2.3, we see a histogram of counts. This histogram shows the number of times different ranges of height values were observed. The height values are indicated on the x-axis, and the heights of the bars reflect the number of times that different ranges of heights were observed. As a result, the bars of the histogram tell you about the values of the variable that are more or less frequent. This sort of representation makes it difficult to compare distributions across samples of different sizes. For example, if the number of observations were tripled (and if the relative frequency of each height observation was preserved), the heights of the bars in the histogram would also triple.

Probabilities, likelihood, and inference 35

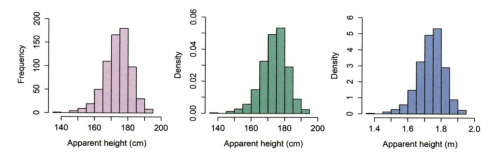

Figure 2.3 (left) A histogram of adult male height judgments showing counts in each bin. (middle) The same data from the left plot, this time showing the density of the distribution. (right) The same data from the middle plot, this time with heights expressed in meters.

Histograms can also be used to show the **probability densities** associated with different values, i.e. the amount of probability 'mass' per unit of the variable of interest. In the middle of Figure 2.3, we see a histogram that shows the **density** of the distribution of height judgments, i.e. the thickness of the distribution at different locations along the number line. The values of the density, and the heights of the bars of the density histogram, are constrained by the fact that the area under the curve must equal one since these reflect probabilities. In the case of our histograms, this means that the total area of all the bars (rectangles) is constrained to equal one. As a result of this, when variables have wide ranges densities tend to be very small (as in the middle panel in Figure 2.3).

In the right plot of Figure 2.3, we present heights in meters rather than centimeters. This has the effect of substantially increasing the values of the density (100-fold) but does not otherwise affect the shape of the distribution. The relationship between variable ranges and density values means that densities can't really be interpreted in an absolute sense – they always reflect the amount of probability per unit. So, if you change the unit, you change the interpretation of the corresponding density. For example, a density value of 0.06 means very different things in the middle and right histograms in Figure 2.3. As a result, density values should be interpreted relative to other density values only along the same x-axis (i.e. given the same variable). A higher density in one location tells us that values in that vicinity are more probable than values in locations with lower densities, and differences in densities reflect differences in the relative probabilities of different values.

Probability distributions sometimes have shapes that can be represented using mathematical functions. These functions typically have a limited number of **parameters** that determine their exact shape. Think of parameters as the properties of a system that can be 'set' separately from each other. For example, a radio has three parameters: Tuner frequency, band (AM/FM), and volume. A toaster may have only one, a single knob determining the degree of toasting required. The more parameters something has, the more complicated it is (e.g. an airplane may have thousands).

Consider the code below, which defines a slope and intercept and draws a line based on these parameters. You can change the values of the intercept and the slope and draw many kinds of lines. However, there's no way to change the characteristics of a

36 *Probabilities, likelihood, and inference*

line other than by changing its slope and intercept: A line is entirely defined by these parameters.

```
intercept = 3
slope = 1
x = seq (-10,10,.1)
y = intercept + x*slope

plot (x,y, type='l',lwd=3,col=4)
```

Sometimes the same sorts of probability density shapes pop up over and over, and these shapes are often well-defined mathematically. **Parametric probability distributions** are those density shapes that can be represented using curves that vary in terms of a limited number of parameters. Just like with lines, the characteristics of a parametric probability distribution are entirely defined by the values of its parameters.

2.5 The normal distribution

The distribution of many random variables (at least approximately) follows what's known as the **normal** or **Gaussian** distribution. This means that if you take a sample of a random variable and arrange observations into bins, the resulting histogram will tend to have the familiar bell-shaped curve (seen in the histograms in Figure 2.3). Normal distributions have two parameters, meaning they differ from each other in only two ways: A mean (μ) and a variance (σ^2). The normal distribution has the following important characteristics:

1   The distribution is symmetrical – i.e. observations above and below the mean are equally likely.
2   The probability of observing a given value decreases as you get further from the mean (i.e. *average*) value.
3   It's easy to work with, very well understood, and (approximately) normally distributed data arises in many domains.

The mean (μ) of a normal distribution determines the location of the distribution along the number line. When the mean of a normal distribution changes, the whole shape of the distribution 'slides' along the number line. The mean is the 50% halfway point of the 'mass' of the distribution (i.e. with a normal distribution, the mean is identical to the median). If the distribution were a physical object, its mean would be its center of gravity and you would balance the distribution on your fingertip at this point. The mean of a normal distribution is also the **expected value** of that variable. For discrete variables, the *expected value* ($\mathbb{E}$) is the sum of all possible values of y multiplied by the probability of observing each value, $P(y)$, as in (2.1).

$$\mathbb{E}(y_{[i]}) = \sum_{i=1}^{\infty} y_{[i]} P(y_{[i]}) \tag{2.1}$$

For example, for the roll of a single die the possible outcomes are the integers from 1 to 6 and each has a 1/6 chance of occurring. To calculate the expected value, we multiply each outcome by 1/6 and sum the resulting values (1/6, 2/6, 3/6, 4/6, 5/6, 6/6), resulting

Probabilities, likelihood, and inference   37

in 3.5. So, the expected value of a roll of a single die is 3.5. This is why the game of craps involves rolling two dice and centers on whether a player rolls a 7: This is the most probable outcome. Continuous variables have an analogous formula defining the expected value with an integral and a **probability density function** ($f(y)$), as seen below. A probability density function is just a function that assigns some value, e.g. $f(y) = x$, for the different values of a variable (e.g. y).

$$\mathbb{E}(y) = \int_{-\infty}^{\infty} yf(y)\,dy \qquad (2.2)$$

The $y_{[i]}P\left(y_{[i]}\right)$ part in the discrete equation above is analogous to the $yf(y)$ in the continuous equation. In each case, the first element (y) represents a possible value and the second element ($P(y)$, or $f(y)$) multiplies this by a value reflecting the probability that this value is observed. In the discrete case we use probabilities ($P(y)$) and add our terms up (with Σ). For the continuous case we use the density ($f(y)$) and integrate (i.e. find the area under the curve) across a given interval (with $\int dy$).

The variance (σ^2), or standard deviation ($\sigma = \sqrt{\sigma^2}$), of a normal distribution determines its *spread* along the x-axis. When the standard deviation changes, the distribution is stretched wide or made very narrow, but stays in the same place. Since every distribution has an area under the curve equal to one (i.e. they all have the same 'volume'), distributions with smaller variances must necessarily be more dense.

In principle, a given probability distribution can be thought of as having a set of 'true', fixed parameters. For example, we might imagine that the average apparent height of adult male speakers is exactly 175.91254… cm. This is questionable at least in part because, as noted earlier, many real-life populations are practically infinite and constantly changing. In any case, even if 'true', fixed parameters exist, in most situations we can't be certain of what the true parameters of a distribution are. Instead, we must be satisfied with estimating the values of parameters based on our samples.

Estimates of our population parameters based on our sample are called **statistics**. **Statistical inference** consists of using statistics (based on our sample) to make inferences about the characteristics of the overall population (i.e. the 'true' parameters). In the case of the normal distribution we're interested in two statistics: the sample mean and the sample standard deviation.

2.5.1 The sample mean

The sample mean is our 'best' guess for the population mean, i.e. the expected value of the distribution. We'll be more specific about what 'best' means later, but for now, we can just say that if you don't know the population mean parameter for a given normal distribution, and all you have is a sample of observations, the sample mean will provide you the best available estimate. The formula for the sample mean is given in equation (2.3). Initially, reading these mathematical formulas may seem daunting. However, learning to read these is just a skill that is developed with practice. In addition, you will begin to see the same 'chunks' or structures come up in formulas over and over, and reading these becomes much easier once you start to recognize the meaning of these repetitive structures intuitively.

$$\hat{\mu}_y = \sum_{i=1}^{n} y_{[i]}/n \qquad (2.3)$$

38 *Probabilities, likelihood, and inference*

The sample mean is an estimator of the expected value. In (2.3), the division by n reflects the fact that we treat each of our n observations as equally likely, estimating each probability as $1/n$. If we were to replace $\frac{1}{n}$ with $P(y)$ above, equation (2.3) starts to look a lot more like (2.1).

Equation (2.3) says that the sample mean of y ($\hat{\mu}_y$) is equal to the sum of all of the elements of the vector y, divided by n, where n is equal to the length of the y vector (i.e. the number of observations). We use the little hat symbol ($\hat{\mu}$) to indicate that this is an estimate of the mean, and to distinguish it from the population mean, which we cannot observed directly and goes hatless (μ). The summation (Σ) symbol represents the repetitive adding of whatever is to the right of the symbol to some total. The summation begins at the number below the Σ and performs one operation for every integer value of i between the starting point and the end point (indicated below and above the Σ). The counter variable, in this case i, is also often used to index values of a vector (or other structure) that is being summed.

This behavior is similar to a `for` loop in R. Below we define the variable `n` (equal to the length of the vector) and initialize a variable to receive the summation (`mean_height`). The `for` loop then proceeds to increment a count variable (`i`) from one to n along the integers. For each iteration, it adds the value of the vector, divided by n, to the summation variable `mean_height`. As we can see below, this results in a value identical to that returned by the `mean` function in R.

```r
# initialize values
n = length (mens_height)
mean_height = 0

# summation equivalent to equation 2.3
for (i in 1:n) mean_height = mean_height + mens_height[i]/n

# replicates values of the mean function
mean (mens_height)
## [1] 173.8
mean_height
## [1] 173.8
```

Here are some useful things to know about sample means, in no particular order:

1 The mean of a set of observations is affected by addition and multiplication. Adding a to each member of a set of observations increases its mean by $a>$, and multiplying observations by b results in a change in the mean by the same factor.
2 The mean of the sum of two sets of variables (of the same length) x and y is equal to $\mu_x + \mu_y$. In other words, the average of the sum is just the sum of the averages.
3 The sum of the sample's deviations from the sample mean equals zero (seen in (2.4)). This means that the sum of the distances between positive and negative differences from the sample mean exactly balance out. To some extent this makes sense since the mean is the 'center of gravity' of a distribution. It's worth noting that this does not apply to deviations from the *population* mean since the population mean is not estimated from the characteristics of a sample. So, there is no

Probabilities, likelihood, and inference 39

guarantee that some set of observations will 'balance out' around the population mean.

$$0 = \sum_{i=1}^{n} y_{[i]} - \hat{\mu}_y \tag{2.4}$$

2.5.2 The sample variance (or standard deviation)

The formula to calculate the sample variance is seen in (2.5). Note that it is quite similar to the structure of (2.3) and clearly involves the averaging of a value. In fact, if we were to replace $\left(y_{[i]} - \mu_y\right)^2$ with $y_{[i]}$, the two equations would be identical. The value being averaged consists of a difference $(y_{[i]} - \mu_y)$ followed by a squaring operation. So, we see that what's being averaged is squared deviations from the sample mean. This is what the variance is: The expected value of squared deviations around the mean of the variable.

$$\hat{\sigma}_y^2 = \sum_{i=1}^{n} \left(y_{[i]} - \hat{\mu}_y\right)^2 / n \tag{2.5}$$

Below we see that we can use a `for` loop to recreate equation (2.5). However, we don't manage to exactly recreate the output of the `var` (variance) function included in R.

```
# initialize values
n = length (mens_height)
variance_height = 0
mean_height = mean (mens_height)

# equivalent to equation 2.5 above
for (i in 1:n) variance_height =
  variance_height + (mens_height[i]-mean_height)^2/n

# this time the values don't match
var (mens_height)
## [1] 60.27
variance_height
## [1] 60.18
```

This is because R does not use (2.5) to estimate variances but rather (2.6).

$$\hat{\sigma}_y^2 = \sum_{i=1}^{n} \left(y_{[i]} - \hat{\mu}_y\right)^2 / (n-1) \tag{2.6}$$

Above we said that the sample mean is our 'best' estimate of the population mean given a sample. A more formal way to state this is that the sample mean is the value which minimizes the sample variance. In other words, if we choose *any* value of μ_y to calculate the sample variance other than the sample mean, the variance will *necessarily* be larger. However, we know that our sample mean is just an *estimate* of the population

40 *Probabilities, likelihood, and inference*

mean and will never be exactly equal to it. As a result of this, the true variance must be greater than the sample variance when calculated using the sample mean. We can put it like this: $\sum_{i=1}^{n}\left(y_{[i]}-\hat{\mu}_y\right)^2 \le \sum_{i=1}^{n}\left(y_{[i]}-\mu_y\right)^2$, the sum of squares around the sample mean will always be less than or equal to the sum of squares around the population mean. For reasons that we won't get into (but which aren't too complicated), this expected difference may be offset by dividing the squared deviations by $(n-1)$ rather than n as in (2.6). We can update our R code to reflect this change, and see that this now matches the calculation of the variance carried out by R.

```r
# initialize variable
variance_height = 0

# equivalent to 2.6 above
for (i in 1:n)
    variance_height = variance_height + (mens_height[i]-mean_height)^2/(n-1)

# this time the values do match
var (mens_height)
## [1] 60.27
variance_height
## [1] 60.27
```

The sample standard deviation (σ) is simply the square root of the sample variance, as in (2.7).

$$\hat{\sigma}_y = \sqrt{\hat{\sigma}_y^2} = \sqrt{\sum_{i=1}^{n}\left(y_{[i]}-\mu_y\right)^2 / (n-1)} \qquad (2.7)$$

Here are some useful things to know about variances, in no particular order:

1   Variances are always positive, and can only be zero for variables that do not actually take on different values (i.e. constants).
2   The variance of a set of observations is not affected by addition. So, adding or subtracting some arbitrary value from a data set will not affect the variance of that data.
3   Multiplication *does* affect the variances of a set of values. Multiplying numbers by x results in a change of the variances equal to x^2. So, if we took our heights and multiplied them by 10 to express them in millimeters, we would expect the value of σ_{height}^2 to increase by a value of $10^2 = 100$. Since standard deviations are the square roots of variances, this implies that multiplying data by x results in an increase in the standard deviation of the data by a factor of x.
4   The variance of the sum of variables depends on whether they are independent or not. When variables are independent, the sum of their variances is simply equal to $\sigma_x^2 + \sigma_y^2$ for variables x and y. However, when variables are not independent, the variance can be much greater or smaller than this based on the nature of the relationship between the variables. As a result, just as with the calculation of joint probabilities, we need to take into account whether variables are independent or not when we consider the variance of their sum.

Probabilities, likelihood, and inference 41

2.5.3 The normal density

The parameters of a probability distribution are used to draw its shape, which can be used to make inferences about likely values. Think back to high school math and the function defining the shape of a parabola $y = a(x - h)^2 + k$. This function draws a shape based on the settings of its parameters a, h and k. The a parameter determines the width of the parabola (and whether it points up or down), while the vertex of the parabola will have x and y axis coordinates of h and k respectively. In the same way, the formula defining the density of the normal distribution draws a shape given the settings of its μ and σ parameters.

The formula for the probability density function of the normal distribution is seen in (2.8). The function returns a density value for the probability distribution based on the value of x, and the values of its parameters. The equation in (2.8) features **exponentiation** $(\exp(x))$, that is, raising the base $e = 2.718...$ (Euler's number) to some power as in e^x. In (2.8), the value being exponentiated is $-\dfrac{1}{2\sigma^2}(x - \mu)^2$.

$$f(x) = \frac{1}{\sigma\sqrt{2\pi}} \cdot \exp\left(-\frac{1}{2\sigma^2}(x - \mu)^2\right) \tag{2.8}$$

It's much more common to denote exponentiation like e^x rather than $\exp(x)$. However, for now we will use the latter notation for two reasons. First, it makes the exponent bigger and more isolated, which can both make equations easier to read. Second, this makes it look just like the R function `exp(x)`, which makes it easier to remember what it is and what it does.

2.5.4 The standard normal distribution

The **standard normal distribution** is a normal distribution with a mean of zero and a standard deviation of one. Variables drawn from a standard normal distribution are often represented by the symbol z (sometimes called a **z score**). Any normally distributed variable can be turned into a standard normal variable by an operation known as **standardization**, which consists of **centering** and then **scaling** the variable as in (2.9). To center a variable we subtract the mean from the value of each observation, making the new mean equal to zero. By dividing our observations by the standard deviation, we scale these values so that the new standard deviation is equal to one (since anything divided by itself is equal to one).

$$z = (x - \mu) / \sigma \tag{2.9}$$

Figure 2.4 presents our height data again, but this time compares the data to its centered and standardized versions.

Equation (2.10) re-arranges the terms in (2.9) to isolate x on the left-hand side. From (2.10) we can see that any normally distributed variable can be thought of as a standard normal that has been multiplied by a standard deviation and then had a mean added to this product.

$$x = z \cdot \sigma + \mu \tag{2.10}$$

Normally distributed data is often discussed in terms of 'standard deviations from the mean'. This is because stating things in terms of standard deviations from the

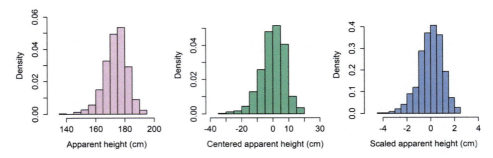

Figure 2.4 (left) A histogram of apparent height judgments for adult male speakers. (middle) The same data from the left plot, this time the data has been centered around the mean so that the new mean is zero. (right) The same data from the middle plot, this time the data has been scaled according to the standard deviation so that the standard deviation is now one (and the mean is still zero).

mean effectively standardizes a variable, making all variables seem standard normal. For example, if someone says "my test score was two standard deviations above the mean" what do you know about their score? You don't know what the mean is, nor what the standard deviation is. All you know is that their score is two distance units (standard deviations) above the mean, so their test score can be thought of as a standard normal variable like z. This is despite the obvious fact that the true average test score was not zero and the true average standard deviation was not one. This is an extremely useful property because it means that we can discuss the probability of any given event from any given normal distribution in consistent terms. For example, we can say that an observation four standard deviations from the mean is very unusual in *any* normal distribution. This means that if you have an observation equal to 140, the mean is 174, and the standard deviation is 8, you know that this observation is very improbable. That is because it is 4.25 (34/8) standard deviations from the mean of 174.

2.6 Models and inference

Models are simplified representations that help us understand things. For example, we may want to understand the movement of balls on a billiards table, perhaps to create a video game about playing pool. To do this we may assume the balls are spherical and that their mass is evenly distributed about their volume, among other things. Neither of these things is exactly true but assuming this helps us keep our model simple and manageable. It also helps us build our model in terms of things, like regular spheres, whose properties and behaviors are well understood and easy to work with.

To build an *exact* model for our billiards game we would need to include friction from the felt on the table, the effect of wind resistance, the gravitational effect of the moon, and a large number of other factors. As a result, a perfect or exact model is not really possible for most things (and maybe for anything?). And yet, the simulation of realistic behavior of billiard balls is easy and can be done with great accuracy, suggesting that a simplified model can still be useful to understand the behavior of the more-complicated phenomenon it is meant to represent.

Probabilities, likelihood, and inference 43

In general, it's impossible to know what the 'true' data distribution is, so *perfect* inference is not possible. As a result, scientists often use theoretical probability distributions to make inferences about real-life populations and observations. If our measurements more or less follow the 'shape' predicted by the theoretical normal distribution, we may be able to use the characteristics of an appropriate normal distribution to make inferences about our variables. Using a normal distribution to make inferences about your data is like using a mathematical model for spheres to understand the behavior of billiard balls. The billiard balls are *spherical enough* to allow us to make useful predictions based on the simplified model.

It's useful to keep in mind that reality will never exactly conform to our model. This can result in unpredictable errors in our conclusions. In general, the things you don't know you don't know are the things that will cause the most problems. If you had known that your model was wrong, you would have fixed it! Further, using models to make inferences about the general properties of data assumes that the things you have not seen are more or less just like those you have. Under those conditions then the conclusions you draw may be reliable. It's important to keep this limitation in mind because you never know for sure that what you have not seen will conform to your model, and as a result, the fit between a model and some set of observations can never definitively *prove* the truth of the relations encoded in the model (this is related to the problem of induction, discussed in Section 1.2.1).

Parametric distributions can be used to establish **theoretical probabilities**, that is expectations about which events are and are not likely based on the general shape expected for the distribution. Basically, if we expect our distribution of values to have the shape of the normal distribution, we can use the shape of the normal distribution to make inferences about our distribution of values. When we used *empirical probabilities* above, our probabilities were estimated only with respect to the data we observed. However, when we refer to *theoretical* probability distributions we can also think about the behavior of values we did not observe or the behavior of the distribution in general.

In order to calculate theoretical probabilities you first need to commit to a model of the data. You may be thinking, what model? It may seem too simple to be a model, but by assuming that our data can be understood as coming from a normal distribution with some given μ and σ, we've already created a simple model for our data. This is analogous to committing to a spherical shape for the model of our billiard balls: Saying that you expect your data to be normally distributed commits you to a certain distribution 'shape' and to more and less probable parameter values for your variable.

In Figure 2.5, we compare the histogram of apparent height judgments to the density of a normal distribution with a mean equal to the sample mean (μ = 173.8 cm) and a standard deviation equal to the sample standard deviation (σ = 7.8 cm) of our `mens_height` vector. The density was drawn using the `dnorm` function, which draws a curve representing the shape of a theoretical normal distribution with a given mean and standard deviation. Clearly, there is a good alignment between our random sample of real-world data and the theoretical normal density. This suggests that we could potentially use the shape of the *theoretical* normal distribution to talk about the characteristics of our observed random sample of data. Although the distribution of our sample is unlikely to be perfectly normal, it is *normal enough* to make the comparison worthwhile.

The average female over 20 in the United States is 162.1 cm, according to the information in `height_data`. A vertical line has been placed at this value in Figure 2.5. We

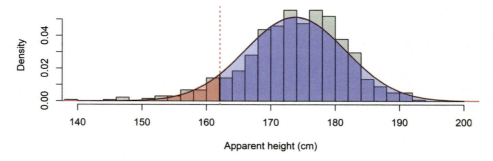

Figure 2.5 The histogram shows the empirical distribution of height judgments for adult male speakers in our data. The shaded area shows the theoretical density of the equivalent normal distribution. The red area corresponds to the theoretical probability of observing a height under 162 cm, based on the shape of the normal density.

might wonder, what is the probability of observing a height judgment for an adult male that is shorter than this average adult female height? Asking this question is equivalent to asking: What is the area under the curve of the density above, to the *left* of the vertical line? Since the *total* area of the density is always equal to one, the area of the red portion below corresponds to a percentage/probability of observing values less than 162.1 cm. One way to answer this question is to calculate the empirical probability of observing an apparent height of less than 162.1 cm for male speakers in our data. Another way to do this is by calculating the *theoretical probability* by finding the proportion of values expected to be less than 162.1 cm in the normal distribution that has approximately the same 'shape' as our data distribution (i.e. the one seen in Figure 2.5).

Below, we use the function `pnorm` to find the proportion of values that are expected to be less than 162.1 cm. This function takes in a value, a mean, and a standard deviation. It then tells you the proportion of the distribution that is to the *left* of (i.e. less than) a given value. Below, we use parameters estimated from our sample to run the `pnorm` function, as these are our best guesses of the population parameters. The output of this function is equal to the area of the red section in the density in Figure 2.5. As we can see, the theoretical and empirical probabilities are very similar to one another. If we subtract this area from one, we get the area under the curve to the *right* of the vertical line, the blue section of the density above.

```
# empirical probability of height < 162.1
mean (mens_height < 162.1)
## [1] 0.07704

# Red area of distribution, x < 162.1
pnorm (162.1, mean (mens_height), sd(mens_height))
## [1] 0.0661

# Blue area of distribution, x > 162.1
1 - pnorm (162.1, mean (mens_height), sd(mens_height))
## [1] 0.9339
```

Probabilities, likelihood, and inference   45

Imagine you had 1 pound of clay and you were asked to make a shape *exactly* like the normal density above. This shape should be perfectly flat and should have a constant depth (like a coin). If you had this shape made of clay and used a knife to remove the part to the left of 162.1 cm (the red subsection) and weighed it, it should weigh 6.6% of a pound (0.066 pounds). The 'area under the curve' of this clay sculpture would just correspond to the amount of clay in a certain area, and in this case, we know that only 6.6% of the clay should be in that section of the shape. The area under the curve, the probability, is just the amount of the *stuff* in the density that falls below/above a certain point, or between two points. The `pnorm` function allows you to slice and 'weigh' the sections of the distribution to tell you how much of it is in any given interval.

This is what our theoretical probabilities tell us: *If* height judgments come from a normal distribution, *and* that distribution has a mean and standard deviation that is close to the sample estimates, *then* we expect (in the long run) that 6.6% of height judgments will be lower than 162.1 cm. What we are expressing here is effectively a conditional probability, we're saying *if* the parameters have certain values, *and* the probability distribution has a certain shape, *then* we expect certain height judgments to be more or less probable. Of course, if you change any part of that, either the values of the parameters or the probability distribution, then your estimated theoretical probabilities are likely to change. This is an important thing to keep in mind because it means that inference based on theoretical probabilities can change when our assumptions change, and many of these assumptions cannot be 'proven' true or false.

2.7 Probabilities of events and likelihoods of parameters

We're going to switch from talking about *probabilities* to talking about *likelihoods*. When we talk about a probability, we are talking about the probability of observing some particular data/event/outcome, given some parameter(s). A **likelihood** inverts this, and places the focus on different *parameter* values, given some observed data. For example, you could say "how probable is it that a random man will sound shorter than 162.1 cm in height if the mean is 174 cm?". When stated this way, we are discussing the probability of observing *data* (apparent height < 162.1) from some fixed distribution. So, probability puts the *data* in question and takes the distribution for granted.

In contrast, you could ask "how likely is it that the average man sounds 162.1 cm tall, given some observations?". Now, we are discussing the likelihood of a particular mean *parameter* ($\mu = 162.1$) given some fixed data. So, likelihood puts the *parameters* in question and takes the data for granted. The likelihood of a parameter represents the joint probability (density) of observing all the data you observed, given specific parameter values. In other words, the likelihood relates to the probability of your first observation, *and* your second observation, *and* your third observation, and so on, for all observations, given the parameter value(s) of interest.

The **likelihood function** is a curve showing the relative likelihoods of different parameter values, given a fixed set of observations/data. The likelihood function tells you what parameter values are *credible* given your data. If a value is very unlikely, that means that it is not supported by your data. In other words, unlikely parameter estimates represent conclusions that your data is rejecting as not viable, and hence they are not credible. Here's a simple example of how you use likelihoods informally in your everyday life. Suppose your friend tells you they can hit about 90% of their three-point shots in basketball. You know this friend is prone to making spectacular claims, so you ask to watch them shoot.

46 Probabilities, likelihood, and inference

They heave up 100 shots, sinking 20/100, not too bad for an amateur, but not 90%. Do you believe that your friend sinks 90% of their shots overall? If you decide not to, it may be because their claim is extremely *unlikely*: A distribution which generates 90% successful shots is extremely unlikely to generate only 20 successes in 100 shots. In other words, given the data you have, a 'real' ability to score 90% of shots does not seem credible.

Every parameter for every probability distribution has a likelihood function, given some data. Here, we're only going to discuss the likelihood of the normal mean parameter, μ, in detail. The likelihood of the sample mean reflects the joint probability of observing all of your data, given different values of the mean, for a given standard deviation. An example of how this is calculated is given in Figure 2.6. The left plot shows the likelihood function for μ based on a random sample of ten height judgments from our data (indicated by the blue points at the bottom of the plot). We can see that the most *likely* values of μ are centered on the bulk of the observations, and that values become less likely as we deviate from them. The vertical dotted lines indicate three possible mean values that will be highlighted in this discussion.

The likelihood of a parameter value (e.g. $\mu = 174$ cm in the right plot of Figure 2.6) is equal to the product of the density of each observation in the sample, given the value of the parameter. This sounds like a mouthful but is actually deceptively simple. For example, to calculate the likelihood that $\mu = 174$, we:

1. Assume that the data is generated by a normal distribution with $\mu = 174$ and σ equal to your sample standard deviation (7.8 cm).
2. Find the height of the curve of the probability density over each point (indicated by the vertical lines in the right plot in Figure 2.6). This reflects the relative probability of each observation given your parameter value.
3. The joint probability of all of the observations (the likelihood) is the product of all of these densities (heights). This assumes that all of your observations are statistically independent of each other (see Section 2.3.2).

So, the value of the likelihood function in the left plot of Figure 2.6 at 174 cm is equal to the product of the densities over the points in the right plot (i.e. the heights of the lines in the plot). Imagine we did this for a range of values along the x-axis, sliding our

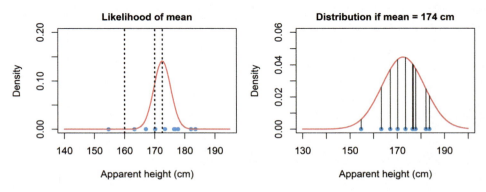

Figure 2.6 (left) The red curve indicates the likelihood of the population mean given the blue points in the figure. The vertical lines indicate three different parameter values that will be considered. (right) The red curve indicates the probability density given an assumed mean of 174 cm (the sample mean). Vertical lines highlight the density over each point.

Probabilities, likelihood, and inference   47

probability distribution along the x-axis and recording the likelihood values at each step. If we do this and then plot the product of the densities for each corresponding *x* -value the result would be a curve identical to that of the left plot in Figure 2.6.

Let's discuss what the likelihood in Figure 2.6 *means*. When you conduct an experiment, you *know* you have your data, but you don't know much else. Suppose all your data was the blue points in the figure. If someone said to you "hey do you think the mean is 140 cm?" you might respond "that is unlikely". It is unlikely because the observations you have are extremely *improbable* given a probability distribution centered at 140 cm. Since your data are incompatible with a mean of 140 cm, and you *know* you have your data, a mean of 140 cm does not seem credible given your probability model. This information is reflected by the very low value of the likelihood function at 140 cm. In contrast, based on the high value of the likelihood function, we can see that a mean of 174 cm *is* likely. This is because the data you have is very probable given a mean of 174 cm, making this parameter value consistent with our data.

The right plot of Figure 2.6 shows the probability of points assuming that the population mean is equal to the sample mean (for our tiny sample). We can see in the left plot of Figure 2.6 that this is the most likely value for the mean parameter. When we said earlier that the sample mean is the 'best' estimate of the population mean, what we really meant was that the sample mean is the **maximum-likelihood estimate** of the population mean. This means that the sample mean provides an estimate of μ that maximizes the value of the likelihood function given the data. This is related to the fact that, as mentioned in Section 2.5.1, the sample mean minimizes the variance of the sample. As a result, if you want to know which mean estimate is most likely given your data, you simply need to calculate the sample mean as in equation (2.3).

In the left plot of Figure 2.7, we see that a normal distribution with a μ of 170 cm is a reasonable fit to the data. However, several observations are very improbable and this relative lack of fit is reflected by the low value of the likelihood function at 170 in Figure 2.6. In the right plot of Figure 2.7, we see that a normal distribution with a mean of 160 is very unlikely to generate this data: Many points are extremely improbable and have densities close to zero. Correspondingly, the value of the likelihood corresponding to $\mu = 160$ in Figure 2.6 reflects a very unlikely parameter value.

We want to talk about why it makes sense to multiply densities to calculate joint probabilities. Above, we stated that probabilities relate to the area under the curve of the density function. A problem we have is that the area under the curve of a single point is always zero. This is because a single point is so thin (it's width is zero) that the area under the curve under the point will equal zero regardless of its density. Suppose that we said "ok let's agree to use a fixed width, a, around our point to calculate our area under the curve". We can make a so teeny tiny that it is almost as if we were calculating just the area under our single point. We can use $f(x)$ to represent the height of a density for a given value of x. This means that we could approximate the value of the area under the curve at x by treating it like a trapezoid and finding $f(x)*a$. If we wanted to calculate the joint probability of a number of observations, we could multiply a series of these areas, as seen in (2.11).

$$P(x_1 \& x_2 \& \dots \& x_n) = \left[f(x_1) \cdot a \right] \cdot \left[f(x_2) \cdot a \right] \cdot \dots \cdot \left[f(x_n) \cdot a \right] \tag{2.11}$$

Since each term in (2.11) contains a, this can be factored out as in (2.12).

$$P(x_1 \& x_2 \& \dots \& x_n) = \left[f(x_1) \cdot f(x_2) \cdot \dots \cdot f(x_n) \right] \cdot a^n \tag{2.12}$$

48   *Probabilities, likelihood, and inference*

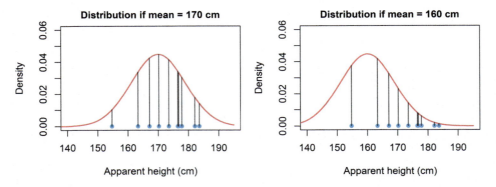

Figure 2.7 (left) The red curve indicates the probability density given an assumed mean of 170 cm (the sample mean). Vertical lines highlight the density over each point. (right) The same information as in the left plot, but given a mean of 160 cm.

At this point, we see that the joint probability of a set of values (x_n) can be thought of as the product of the densities over those values $(f(x_n))$ times some arbitrary constant a^n. If we agree to use the same constant for all our calculations, we can ignore it and use the product of the densities to evaluate the relative probabilities of different combinations of observations.

2.7.1 Characteristics of likelihoods

It's fairly important to understand at least the gist of the previous section: Likelihoods tell you which parameter values are 'likely' (i.e. credible) given the data you have. It's less important that you understand the information from here to Section 2.8. We're presenting it here to take the mystery out of it, and because in order to understand it you will probably need to read about it several times so you might as well get started now. If this is the first time you read about these topics, you should accept the fact that you may not *understand* much of this, however, given time and effort you will eventually *get used to it*.

We can think about the characteristics of the likelihood of μ to make some predictions about its expected shape given different numbers of observations and underlying data distributions. The likelihood is the joint probability of your data given some parameter values. We can calculate the joint probability of two observations x_1 and x_2 (using a comma instead of '&' to indicate 'and') by multiplying their individual densities as in equation (2.13), assuming these observations are independent.

$$f(x_1, x_2) = \left[\frac{1}{\sigma\sqrt{2\pi}}\exp\left(-\frac{1}{2\sigma^2}(x_1-\mu)^2\right)\right] \cdot \left[\frac{1}{\sigma\sqrt{2\pi}}\exp\left(-\frac{1}{2\sigma^2}(x_2-\mu)^2\right)\right] \quad (2.13)$$

Equation (2.13) defines the likelihood of μ given the data x_1 and x_2 and some σ. We will update the left-hand side to reflect this, replacing a term representing the joint probability of x_1 and x_2 ($f(x_1, x_2)$) with a term representing the likelihood of the mean given the data, $\mathcal{L}_{(\mu|x)}$. Notice that nothing has changed except our perspective. In equation (2.13), we treat the parameter μ as fixed and use it to calculate the joint probability of

Probabilities, likelihood, and inference 49

some data. In equation (2.14), we treat the data x as fixed and use it to calculate the likelihood of values of μ.

$$\mathcal{L}_{(\mu|x)} = \left[\frac{1}{\sigma\sqrt{2\pi}}\exp\left(-\frac{1}{2\sigma^2}(x_1-\mu)^2\right)\right]\cdot\left[\frac{1}{\sigma\sqrt{2\pi}}\exp\left(-\frac{1}{2\sigma^2}(x_2-\mu)^2\right)\right] \qquad (2.14)$$

2.7.2 A brief aside on logarithms

The **logarithm** (`log`) is the inverse function to exponentiation, it basically *erases* or *undoes* exponentiation. We can apply a logarithmic transformation to both sides of the density in equation (2.8), resulting in the **log density** of the normal distribution seen in equation (2.15).

$$\log(f(x)) = \log\left(\frac{1}{\sigma\sqrt{2\pi}}\right) - \frac{1}{2\sigma^2}(x-\mu)^2 \qquad (2.15)$$

Understanding logarithms and log densities is important because, in practice, much of statistics is done on the logarithms of probabilities, likelihoods, and densities. In addition, it is extremely common to log-transform probability density functions or other equations before manipulating them, making a good understanding of the properties of logarithms extremely useful. As a result, as we will see below, using logarithms can help us simplify and understand at least some probability distributions.

Before explaining equation (2.15), we will discuss some basic properties of logarithms that are useful to understand probabilities and probability distributions, as these often involve exponentiation and logarithms. The first line in (2.16) shows the basic behavior of logarithms. The next four lines pertain to the values expected, or undefined, for different x. The next two lines highlight the fact that the exponentiation of numbers is equivalent to the multiplication of their logarithms. The final two lines highlight the fact that the multiplication of two numbers is equivalent to the addition of the logarithms of the numbers.

$$\log(e^x) = x$$

$$\log(1) = 0$$
$$\text{if } x < 1, \log(x) < 0$$
$$\text{if } x > 1, \log(x) > 0$$
$$\text{if } x < 0 \, \log(x) = \text{undefined}$$

$$\log(x^y) = \log(x)\cdot y$$
$$\log(\sqrt[y]{x}) = \log(x)/y$$

$$\log(x) + \log(y) = \log(x\cdot y)$$
$$\log(x) - \log(y) = \log(x/y)$$

$$(2.16)$$

50 *Probabilities, likelihood, and inference*

Armed with knowledge of the behavior of logarithms, we can see that compared to equation (2.8), equation (2.15) reflects the following changes associated with taking the logarithm of both sides of the equation. First, we remove the exp function around the rightmost term $-\frac{1}{2\sigma^2}(x-\mu)^2$, and added the log function around all terms that were *not* previously exponentiated. Then, multiplication of the two terms on the right-hand side of the equation turns into addition, or subtraction in this case because we are adding a negative term.

The properties of logarithms presented above can be used to make the simplifications presented in (2.17). When presented in its final form, this function is that of a parabola in vertex form, $y = a(x-h)^2 + k$, where $a = -1/2\sigma^2$, $h = \mu$, and $h = -\log(\sigma\sqrt{2\pi})$. So, we can see that the density of the normal distribution is just an exponentiated parabola that is scaled by $1/\sigma\sqrt{2\pi}$ so that the area under the curve is equal to one.

$$\log(f(x)) = \log\left(\frac{1}{\sigma\sqrt{2\pi}}\right) - \frac{1}{2\sigma^2}(x-\mu)^2$$

$$\log(f(x)) = \log(1) - \log(\sigma\sqrt{2\pi}) - \frac{1}{2\sigma^2}(x-\mu)^2$$

$$\log(f(x)) = 0 - \log(\sigma\sqrt{2\pi}) - \frac{1}{2\sigma^2}(x-\mu)^2 \qquad (2.17)$$

$$\log(f(x)) = -\frac{1}{2\sigma^2}(x-\mu)^2 - \log(\sigma\sqrt{2\pi})$$

The parabola defined in (2.17) has its vertex at $(\mu, -\log(\sigma\sqrt{2\pi}))$, and opens downwards since the a term is negative. When a parabola is in vertex form, the relationship between parabola width and the value of a is inverted, its width decreases as the value of a increases. However, because $a = -\frac{1}{2\sigma^2}$, the relationship is doubly inverted. As a result, in the case of normal distributions the parabola width increases as σ grows larger, leading to wider parabolas and wider probability densities.

Equation (2.17) shows how the μ and σ parameters work to make observations further from the mean less probable. First, we know that negative logarithmic values will fall between 0 and 1, with more negative values being closer to zero (i.e. less probable). As observations (x) are further from the mean, the value of $(x-\mu)^2$ will be greater so that values further from the mean will be generally less probable. However, whether a deviation is considered 'big' or 'small' is relative, and so this distance is scaled with respect to the average expected squared deviation from the mean (i.e. the variance σ^2). Variation of 1 cm in body length means different things for an earthworm as opposed to an anaconda. As a result, large values of $(x-\mu)^2$ can be offset by large values of σ^2 when determining the probability of an outcome.

2.7.3 *Characteristics of likelihoods, continued*

We will pick up where we left off, considering the likelihood of μ given some data. This was presented in equation (2.14) and is presented again as (2.18).

$$\mathcal{L}_{(\mu|x)} = \left[\frac{1}{\sigma\sqrt{2\pi}}\exp\left(-\frac{1}{2\sigma^2}(x_1-\mu)^2\right)\right] \cdot \left[\frac{1}{\sigma\sqrt{2\pi}}\exp\left(-\frac{1}{2\sigma^2}(x_2-\mu)^2\right)\right] \qquad (2.18)$$

Probabilities, likelihood, and inference 51

We can log-transform both sides of equation (2.18) so that each bracketed element on the right-hand side of (2.18) is equal to the final version of equation (2.17). This is presented in equation (2.19).

$$\mathcal{LL}_{(\mu|x)} = \left[-\frac{1}{2\sigma^2}(x_1 - \mu)^2 - \log(\sigma\sqrt{2\pi}) \right] + \left[-\frac{1}{2\sigma^2}(x_2 - \mu)^2 - \log(\sigma\sqrt{2\pi}) \right] \quad (2.19)$$

Because they make working with likelihoods much simpler, statisticians often use the logarithms of likelihood functions, referred to as **log-likelihoods**. Log-likelihoods are denoted using the symbol $\mathcal{LL}_{(\mu|x)}$. When you see this, $\mathcal{LL}_{(\mu|x)}$, just think "the logarithm of the likelihood of the mean given the data x". In equation (2.19) we see that the log-likelihood of these two observations is the sum of two parabolas. Since the sum of parabolas will (almost always) also be a parabola, we know that the log-likelihood of the mean given these, and any number of other observations, will also be a parabola. As a result, we see that the (non-log) likelihood of the mean is an exponentiated parabola and has the same general shape as the normal distribution.

Equation (2.19) is specifically for two variables, however, Because each term is identical except for $x_n - \mu$, the log-likelihood function can be greatly simplified as in equation (2.20). In (2.20), we can see that the log-likelihood of μ given n observations of x is equal to the sum of the individual squared deviations from the mean, divided by $-1/2\sigma^2$, with the value $n \cdot \left(\log(\sigma\sqrt{2\pi}) \right)$ subtracted from it. So, we see that the log-likelihood is a parabola that has its vertex at $\left(\hat{\mu}, -n \cdot \left(\log(\sigma\sqrt{2\pi}) \right) \right)$, meaning that this parabola has its maximum value when μ is equal to the sample mean. This again reflects the fact that the sample mean is the maximum-likelihood estimate for the population mean.

$$\mathcal{LL}_{(\mu|x)} = -\frac{1}{2\sigma^2}\sum_{i=1}^{n}(x_i - \mu)^2 - n \cdot \left(\log(\sigma\sqrt{2\pi}) \right) \quad (2.20)$$

There are two mechanisms by which the likelihood function may get narrower or wider. The first was discussed in Section 2.5.3, where a smaller value of σ results in a narrower parabola and a narrower likelihood. Independently of the underlying variation in the data, likelihood functions can also become narrower when the sample size is increased. To see why this is the case, consider what happens to the relative value of our a parameter $(-1/2\sigma^2)$ as the sample size grows. Imagine that we are calculating the sum of squared deviations about our sample mean. We know that the average squared variation we expect from our mean is equal to the variance. So, let's replace $(x_i - \mu)^2$ in (2.20) with σ^2 in (2.21). Now, instead of adding n squared deviations around the mean, $\sum_{i=1}^{n}(x_i - \mu)^2$, we are multiplying our expected squared deviation by n, $n \cdot \sigma^2$.

$$\mathcal{LL}_{(\mu|x)} = -\frac{1}{2\sigma^2} \cdot \left(n \cdot \sigma^2 \right) - n \cdot \left(\log(\sigma\sqrt{2\pi}) \right) \quad (2.21)$$

We can also move the σ^2 over from under the $-1/2$ to make the following point simpler, as in (2.22).

$$\mathcal{LL}_{(\mu|x)} = -\frac{1}{2} \cdot \frac{n \cdot \sigma^2}{\sigma^2} - n \cdot \left(\log(\sigma\sqrt{2\pi}) \right) \quad (2.22)$$

52 *Probabilities, likelihood, and inference*

Multiplying the numerator of a fraction is exactly equivalent to dividing the denominator of the fraction by the same amount, e.g. $(x \cdot y) / z = x / (z / y)$. Thus, we see that calculating the likelihood using n data points is expected to have about the same effect on parabola width as dividing the data variance by n, as shown in (2.23). As a result, increasing numbers of observations reduces the uncertainty in parameter estimates by making the likelihood narrower and narrower for any given underlying σ.

$$\mathcal{LL}_{(\mu|x)} = -\frac{1}{2} \cdot \frac{\sigma^2}{(\sigma^2 / n)} - n \cdot \left(\log\left(\sigma \sqrt{2\pi} \right) \right) \tag{2.23}$$

2.8 Answering our research questions

In Section 2.6, we discussed using the normal distribution to make inferences about the probable values of a random variable. When variables are normally distributed we can use the theoretical normal distribution and functions such as `pnorm` to answer questions about values we expect, and don't expect, to see. In the same way, we can use likelihood functions to understand probable, and improbable, values of parameters given our data.

For example, suppose that you measured the heights of 100 women in a small town (pop. 1,500) and found the average height was 160 cm, with a standard deviation of 6 cm. You might accept that the *actual* population average is 161 cm, but may find it difficult to accept that it was actually 180 cm. This is because a true mean of 180 cm is *unlikely* given your observed data: The observations you have are *improbable* given a true mean of 180 cm. The logic is quite simple: A true mean of 180 cm is unlikely to result in a random selection of so many women around 160 cm. You *know* you observed the short women, therefore, you have no reason to believe that the true mean is 180 cm.

Below we calculate the likelihood of different mean parameters given our data. We do this by finding the log density of each observation and then adding the points together. Log densities are used because the likelihood is often a number so small that computers have a hard time representing them otherwise.

```
# make candidates for mean parameter
mus = seq (172.5,175, .01)

# easy way to make zero vector of same length as above
log_likelihood = mus*0

# add the log-density of all observations. Notice only the
# mean changes across iterations of the for loop.
for (i in 1:length(mus)) log_likelihood[i] =
  sum (dnorm (mens_height, mus[i], sd(mens_height), log = TRUE))
```

For example, the highest point of the probability densities in Figure 2.7 is about 0.07. Let's pretend it's 0.1 for the sake of simplicity. Recall that to find the likelihood we need to multiply the densities above each of the points. This means that the likelihood of two observations at the mean is $0.1 \cdot 0.1 = 0.001$, and the likelihood of observing n observations at the mean is equal to 0.1^n. Since we have 675 observations in our `mens_height`

Probabilities, likelihood, and inference 53

vector, the likelihood of observing every one of those at the mean, the most probable outcome, would be equal to 0.1^{675}, or a decimal point followed by 674 zeros and then a one. By relying on the logarithms of densities instead, we can accurately represent very small numbers more comfortably. This is because adding together the logarithms of two numbers is equivalent to multiplying those numbers, and multiplying a logarithm by another number is equivalent to raising it to that power (see (2.7)). For example, the number 0.1^{675} can also be expressed like $\log(0.1) \cdot 675$, which equals -1554.245 (i.e. $0.1^{675} = e^{-1554.245}$). This is obviously a much easier number to deal with than one with 675 decimal places.

In Figure 2.8, we plot the log-likelihood calculated above, and the 'scaled likelihood'. This is just the likelihood that has been scaled so that its peak is equal to one, and the peak of the log-likelihood equals zero. This allows us to actually plot and consider the likelihood function, though the values of the density no longer reflect the actual values of the likelihood. However, the *relational* characteristics are maintained by this scaling. So, a scaled likelihood value of 0.2 is still five times less likely than a value of one.

At this point we can provide answers to the questions posed in Section 2.2. The questions were:

(Q1) How tall does the average adult male sound?
(Q2) Can we set limits on credible average apparent heights based on the data we collected?

Below, we see that the **maximum-likelihood estimate**, the value of the parameter which maximizes the likelihood, for the mean corresponds to the sample mean:

```
# find index number of highest values in log-likelihood
maximum = which.max(scaled_log_likelihood)

# print and compare to sample mean
mus[maximum]
## [1] 173.8
mean (mens_height)
## [1] 173.8
```

So, we may conclude that the average male speaker is *most likely* to sound about 174 cm tall. We can also conclude informally based on Figure 2.8 that the most likely mean values fall between (approximately) 173 and 174.5 cm. This means that although the sample mean was 174 cm, it is reasonable that the true population mean might actually be 173.5 cm. This is because mean parameters in this range are also reasonably *likely* given our data. Basically, maybe our sample mean is wrong and 173.5 cm is the true population μ. This outcome is compatible with our data. However, a value of 172 cm is very *unlikely* given our data. Since we think that 172 cm is not a plausible mean parameter given our sample, we can rule it out as a credible value for the μ parameter of our variable. Using this approach, we can use the information in likelihood functions to rule out implausible values of μ based on the characteristics of our data.

54 *Probabilities, likelihood, and inference*

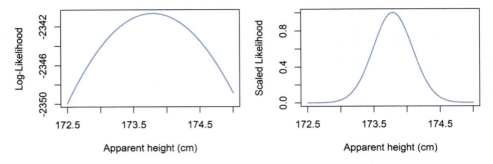

Figure 2.8 (left) The curve represents the log-likelihood for different values of our mean given our apparent height judgments and assuming a normal distribution. (right) The likelihood is implied by the log-likelihood on the left. The curve has been scaled to have a peak of 1 so that we can plot it. For example, exp (−2,300) is a value so small that it is difficult to represent in a figure axis.

2.9 Exercises

Use the techniques outlined in this chapter to start thinking about credible estimates, and bounds, of the mean apparent height for other groups of speakers. This can be done for the original or modified voice resonance conditions.

References

Ross, S. M. (2019). *A first course in probability.* Boston, MA: Pearson.
Parzen, E. (1960). *Modern probability theory and its applications.* Chichester: Wiley.
Jaynes, E. T. (2003). *Probability theory: The logic of science.* Cambridge: Cambridge University Press.

3 Fitting Bayesian regression models with *brms*

In this chapter, we're going to start answering basic research questions with Bayesian regression models using the `brms` package in R. The model we'll use initially is not 'correct' for our data, but it's simple enough to work as an introduction to Bayesian regression models. In the next chapter, we'll use `brms` to build models that are closer to 'correct' given the structure of our data. Before using a Bayesian regression model to investigate our data, we'll explain what we mean by *regression model* and what specifically makes the models in this book *Bayesian*. We'll leave a discussion of the 'multilevel' aspect of our models for the following chapter.

Throughout this book, we will present formal descriptions of our models. The relationship between statistical concepts and the formal notation used to represent them is very similar to the ability to play music and read musical notation. Someone who can play a song undoubtedly *knows* that song. However, in the absence of formal musical training, that same person might not recognize sheet music representing the song. This person may also lack the vocabulary to discuss components of the song, and may find it difficult to learn to play new pieces without instruction. In the same way, most people have an excellent intuitive understanding of many statistical concepts (to be discussed in upcoming chapters) such as slopes, interactions, errors, and so on. However, they may lack the knowledge of formal statistical notation that enables a deeper understanding of these concepts, and the ability to generalize these concepts to new situations. As a result, learning to read/write this notation will help you describe your models efficiently, and understand the models used by other people more effectively.

3.1 Chapter pre-cap

In this chapter, we introduce the concept of a regression model and explain what makes a regression model 'Bayesian'. We discuss posterior probabilities, and also `brms`, an R package that can be used to fit Bayesian regression models using the Stan programming language. After this, we fit an 'intercept-only' Bayesian regression model to our experimental data. We present topics related to model fitting such as thinning, chains, and iterations, and also discuss the specification of prior probabilities. After that, we outline the interpretation of the `brm` model print statement and introduce the concepts of errors and residuals. Finally, we provide information regarding how to work

DOI: 10.4324/9781003285878-3

56 *Fitting Bayesian regression models with* brms

directly with the model posterior samples and discuss the log prior and posterior densities of our models.

3.2 What are regression models?

It's difficult to offer a precise definition for **regression** because the term is so broad, but regression models are often models that help you understand systematic variation in the mean parameter (μ) of a normal distribution. Actually, you can model variation in other parameters and use a variety of other probability distributions, and we will do so later in this book. However, for now, we'll focus on models based on the normal distribution. Here is a general summary of the concepts underlying a regression that assumes normally distributed errors:

- You have a variable you are interested in, y, which is a vector containing n observations. We can refer to any one of these observations like this: $y_{[i]}$ for the ith observation. Although it's a bit atypical and, strictly speaking, not necessary, we're going to put the index variables associated with a trial number (i) in brackets like this $y_{[i]}$. This is just to make it easier to identify, and highlight the similarity to vectors in R (e.g. `mens_height[i]`).
- You assume that the random variation in your data is well described by a normal probability distribution centered at μ. This is a mathematical function $\left(\mathrm{N}(\mu,\sigma)\right)$ that describes what is and is not probable based on two parameters. You also assume that the random variation in each observation is independent of the random variation in each other observation. This means, for example, that you can't really say why any two observations are above or below the mean.
- The mean of this distribution is either fixed or varies in a systematic manner. The standard deviation of the error distribution is usually fixed but can vary (more on this in Chapter 8).
- The variation in the mean of this distribution can be understood using some predictor variables, and regression is a tool for modeling these relations.

We can write our model more formally as in equation (3.1). This says that we think the tokens of our dependent variable (y) are distributed according to (~) a normal distribution with parameters equal to μ and σ. Notice that y gets a subscript while μ and σ do not. That means that we are modeling all of the observations with fixed parameters, while the value of y changes for each observation based on the i subscript.

$$y_{[i]} \sim \mathrm{N}(\mu,\sigma) \tag{3.1}$$

Equation (3.1) formalizes the fact that we think the *shape* of our data distribution will be like that of a normal distribution with a mean equal to μ and a standard deviation equal to σ. When you see this, $\mathrm{N}(\mu,\sigma)$, picture in your mind the shape of a normal distribution just like if you see this $y = x^2$ you may imagine a parabola. $\mathrm{N}(\mu,\sigma)$ really just represents the shape of the normal distribution and associated expectations about more and less probable outcomes. The above relationship can also be presented as in equation (3.2).

$$y_{[i]} = \mu + \mathrm{N}(0,\sigma) \tag{3.2}$$

Fitting Bayesian regression models with brms   57

Notice that we got rid of the ~ symbol, moved μ out of the distribution function, and that the mean of the distribution function is now 0. This representation breaks up our variable into two components:

1   A systematic component, systematic variation in the *expected value* μ of the variable y.
2   A random component, the *error* $N(0, \sigma)$, that causes unpredictable variation around the expected value, often μ.

Regression models separate observed variables into their **systematic** and **random** components. In this case, the systematic component is predictable for all observations in the data. The random component represents the *noise*, or *error* in our data, random variation around our expected values that isn't explained. This doesn't mean that it's inexplicable in general, it only means that we've structured our model in a way that doesn't let us explain it. In other words, a model like this thinks all variations from the mean are noise because it is structured in such a way that treats such deviations as noise.

In regression models, we can try to understand variation in μ using predictor variables x. These predictor variables co-vary (vary with) our y variable, and, we think (or hope), help explain the variation in y. For example, in (3.3) we're saying we think μ is equal to some combination of the three predictor variables x_1, x_2, and x_3. For example, we might expect that the apparent height of a speaker is affected by their fundamental frequency (x_1), vocal-tract length (x_2), and resonance (x_1). So, when we combine these predictors we think we can come up with a pretty good estimate of how tall someone will sound.

$$\mu = x_1 + x_2 + x_3 \tag{3.3}$$

The values of the predictor variables will vary across observations and are not fixed. In fact, often the whole point of running an experiment is to predict differences in observations based on differing predictor values. If we expect our predictors to vary from trial to trial, that means that the equation above should include i subscripts indicating that the equation refers to the value of the predictors *for that trial* rather than overall. If we expect the predictors to vary across observations, naturally it's possible that μ may take on different values from trial to trial, and it therefore also needs an i subscript. This update is reflected in equation (3.4).

$$\mu_{[i]} = x_{1[i]} + x_{2[i]} + x_{3[i]} \tag{3.4}$$

The predicted value ($\mu_{[i]}$) for a given trial is very unlikely to be an equal combination of the predictors (as in equation (3.4)), so a *weighting* of the predictors will be necessary. We can use the symbol α for these weights as in equation (3.5). For example, maybe x_1 is twice as important as the other two predictors and so $\alpha_1 = 2$, while $\alpha_2 = 1$ and $\alpha_3 = 1$. Actually, maybe one predictor has a *negative* effect so that $\alpha_3 = -1$. The 'weights' associated with each predictor are the **coefficients** (or parameters) of our model. Note that the weight terms (α) do not get an i subscript. This is because they do not change from trial to trial. The values of the *predictors* change from trial to trial, but the way that

58   *Fitting Bayesian regression models with* brms

they are combined to produce an expected value for any given observation is a stable property of the model.

$$\mu_{[i]} = \alpha_1 \cdot x_{1[i]} + \alpha_2 \cdot x_{2[i]} + \alpha_3 \cdot x_{3[i]} \tag{3.5}$$

We can insert equation (3.5) into equation (3.2), resulting in equation (3.6). At this point, our model consists of an average value that has been broken up into three component parts and the random component represented by normally distributed noise.

$$y_{[i]} = \left(\alpha_1 \cdot x_{1[i]} + \alpha_2 \cdot x_{2[i]} + \alpha_3 \cdot x_{3[i]}\right) + N(0,\sigma) \tag{3.6}$$

Often, ε is used to represent the random component, the error term, as in equation (3.7). Notice that the error term *does* get an i subscript, as in $\varepsilon_{[i]}$. This is because the exact value of the error *does* change from trial to trial, even though the statistical characteristics of the error (i.e. $N(0,\sigma)$) do not. This is a typical way to express a **regression equation** or a *regression model*. **Fitting** a regression model to data basically consists of finding the 'best' values of its coefficients, α_1, α_2, and α_3 and the parameter governing the error, σ, given our data and model structure.

$$y_{[i]} = \alpha_1 \cdot x_{1[i]} + \alpha_2 \cdot x_{2[i]} + \alpha_3 \cdot x_{3[i]} + \varepsilon_{[i]} \tag{3.7}$$

Notice that according to equation (3.6), regression models do not require that our *data* (y) be normally distributed, but only that the *random error* in our data (ε) be normally distributed. In (3.8), we see the sort of representation of our model that we will use in this book.

$$y_{[i]} \sim N\left(\mu_{[i]}, \sigma\right)$$
$$\mu_{[i]} = \alpha_1 \cdot x_{1[i]} + \alpha_2 \cdot x_{2[i]} + \alpha_3 \cdot x_{3[i]} \tag{3.8}$$

This representation presents the random and systematic components of our regression model separately, and it clearly and succinctly describes the structure of our model. In plain English, this is:

> *Our observations are expected to be randomly distributed around the mean value according to a normal distribution with a standard deviation equal to sigma (σ), and a mean of mu (μ). We expect the mean of our variable to vary from trial to trial based on three predictors. The combination of these predictors is based on model-specific coefficients ($\alpha_1, \alpha_2, \alpha_3$) that are static across trials.*

By the way, the combination of parameters we use is a **linear combination**, one in which terms (x) are added together after being multiplied by a real number (a). The fact that our regression models make predictions using linear combinations is what makes them **linear regression models**. We will be focusing entirely on linear regression models in this book.

3.3 What's 'Bayesian' about these models?

In one common 'traditional' approach to statistics, model parameters are estimated by trying to find the values that maximize the value of likelihood functions based on a

Fitting Bayesian regression models with brms   59

theoretical probability distribution of interest, and given a particular model structure (i.e. maximum-likelihood estimation, as discussed in Chapter 2). We're not going to discuss this approach to statistical inference in any detail as there are hundreds, if not thousands, of books available on the subject (for recommended readings, see the preface). Rather than dwell on these 'traditional' approaches to statistical inference, we're going to talk about what makes Bayesian inference *Bayesian*, focusing on practical rather than 'philosophical' differences.

Instead of estimating parameters using only information from likelihood functions (and data), Bayesian models estimate the **posterior probabilities** of parameters. To explain what posterior probabilities are, we need to talk about joint probabilities again. We'll begin by stating something obvious: The probability of events A and B occurring is the same as the probability of B and A occurring.

$$P(A\,\&\,B) = P(B\,\&\,A) \tag{3.9}$$

Equation (3.9) can be reformulated as in (3.10) (see Section 2.3.2).

$$P(A\,|\,B) \cdot P(B) = P(B\,|\,A) \cdot P(A) \tag{3.10}$$

Recall that $P(A)$ and $P(B)$ are simply placeholders for the probability of some event. We can replace these with $P(y)$ and $P(\mu)$, which represent "the probability of observing your data" and "the probability of observing a certain parameter value" respectively. This is seen in equation (3.11), which states that "the probability of the parameter and the data is the same as the probability of the data and parameter".

$$P(\mu\,|\,y) \cdot P(y) = P(y\,|\,\mu) \cdot P(\mu) \tag{3.11}$$

We can isolate $P(\mu\,|\,y)$ on the left-hand side by dividing both sides by $P(y)$, resulting in equation (3.12). When structured in this way, this is a common formulation of **Bayes theorem**, and it underlies Bayesian statistical inference. Note, however, that all we did was state a basic principle of probability theory (equation (3.9)) and then expand and rearrange some terms.

$$P(\mu\,|\,y) = \frac{P(y\,|\,\mu) \cdot P(\mu)}{P(y)} \tag{3.12}$$

Each of the components in (3.12) has a name:

- $P(\mu)$ is the **prior probability** of the parameter μ. This is the *a priori* (before observation) probability of parameter values independent of the data y. This a priori expectation can come from world knowledge, previous experiments, common sense, or some combination thereof. For example, before you measure the height of adults in San Francisco, you know the average is not 4 feet and it is not 7 feet.
- $P(y\,|\,\mu)$ is the likelihood, discussed at length in Chapter 2. This is the product of the probability density values corresponding to the data points for a given value of μ. The likelihood reflects the probability that the data, y, would be observed or generated for particular values of μ. As a result, the likelihood tells us about the distribution of possible/credible parameter values given the data and probability model.

60 *Fitting Bayesian regression models with* brms

- $P(\mu \mid y)$ is the **posterior probability** of the parameter given the data, the probability model, and the prior. This is the **a posteriori** (after observation) probability that the parameter is μ given your data y, and the structure of your model. You get the posterior probability by combining the prior distribution and the likelihood, and in doing so incorporating your current observations into your prior beliefs.
- $P(y)$ is the **marginal probability** of the data. This is necessary to scale the numerator so that the posterior density has a total area under the curve equal to one. However, note that the marginal probability does not vary as a function of μ. As a result, this does not affect the relative posterior probability of different values of μ. For this reason, and for computational reasons described later, you don't typically need to worry about the marginal probability. In fact, you can sample from the posterior even if you don't calculate the denominator of (3.12).

As noted above, 'traditional' models focus primarily (or exclusively) on how *likely* different conclusions are given your data. In contrast, Bayesian models focus on the posterior probability of different parameter values, that is on the combination of the likelihood and prior probabilities of parameters.

3.3.1 Prior probabilities

In a Bayesian model, every parameter whose value is being estimated needs a prior probability distribution to be specified. For example, imagine you are interested in estimating the mean of a set of values, μ. You decide to use a Bayesian model and decide that μ will have a normal prior with a mean and standard deviation equal to μ_{prior} and σ_{prior}. In other words, the prior distribution of $P(\mu)$ in (3.12) is $\text{N}\left(\mu_{\text{prior}}, \sigma_{\text{prior}}\right)$ such that $\mu \sim \text{N}\left(\mu_{\text{prior}}, \sigma_{\text{prior}}\right)$. To estimate this model you would need to provide fixed values for μ_{prior} and σ_{prior}, for example we could use $\mu_{\text{prior}} = 3$ and $\sigma_{\text{prior}} = 5$ so that $\mu \sim \text{N}\left(3, 5\right)$. Note that the parameters of the prior do not get prior distributions themselves. This is because we are not *estimating* values of μ_{prior} and σ_{prior}, but are instead setting them to fixed values such as 3 and 5. Only estimated parameters need priors.

The use of prior probabilities is sometimes said to make Bayesian models inherently 'subjective', but this concern is a bit overblown in most situations. First, when there is plenty of data (as is often the case for repeated measures data), prior probabilities may have little to no effect on outcomes. This is because when you have many observations, the posterior probability of parameters is dominated by the likelihood (as will be discussed in Section 3.3.2). Second, a researcher will always use 'common sense' (i.e. their prior expectations) to interpret their data. For example, if a listener was asked to judge the apparent height of speakers and reported that all adult males were 90 cm tall, a researcher would have to wonder if this subject understands height in centimeters or if they were carrying out the experiment in good faith. So, even when they do not explicitly assign prior probabilities to parameter values, researchers still often use their expectations to 'screen' results in a manner broadly consistent with the use of prior probabilities in Bayesian reasoning. A Bayesian model requires you to build your expectations into your model. It *formalizes* them and makes them *definable* and *replicable*.

Finally, every model involves arbitrary decisions which can substantially affect our results so that the design of a model can never be said to be strictly 'objective'. As a result, there is no particular reason to worry about the objectivity involved in establishing a prior in Bayesian modeling without also worrying about the objectivity involved in model building more generally.

3.3.2 Posterior distributions

The calculation of posterior distributions involves the combination of the likelihood function with the prior probability distribution and the marginal probability. The marginal probability does not affect the 'shape' of the posterior distribution and exists to scale the posterior so that the area under the curve is equal to one (to satisfy the requirements of probability theory). As a result, we will focus on the combination of the likelihood and prior probabilities.

The combination of the likelihood and prior probability density functions is straightforward conceptually: You multiply the values of the two functions (i.e. curves) at each x-axis location. This works because we are interested in the *joint* probability of the likelihood and the prior, reformulated as the product of a conditional probability (the likelihood) and a marginal probability (the prior). The resulting curve represents the **joint density** of the two distributions. In Figure 3.1, several likelihoods and

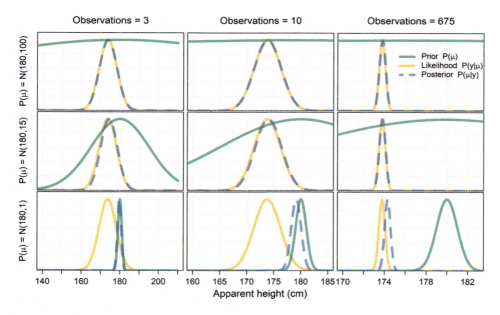

Figure 3.1 Demonstration of the effect of different prior probabilities and number of observations on resulting posterior distributions. In each case, the posterior is the product of the likelihood and the prior. All curves have been scaled to have the same height in the figure. This makes the figures visually interpretable but does not affect any of the points made in the discussion.

62   *Fitting Bayesian regression models with* brms

priors are combined, showing the effects of variations in priors, and the number of observations, on posterior distributions.

The different standard deviations used for the prior probabilities of μ encode different levels of prior belief regarding expected apparent heights for adult male speakers. Researchers often distinguish between different types of priors based on how much they are expected to affect conclusions. For example, priors are often referred to as **vague**, **weakly informative**, or **informative**. The boundaries between these categories are fuzzy, and the 'informativeness' of a prior is more continuous than discrete, therefore, we will discuss these categories in terms of how they might differently affect your models. It's important to note however, that there is no generally accepted definition for these terms and what follows is just an informal guide to thinking about these categories of priors.

Recall that the 'width' of the likelihood depends on the amount of underlying variability and the sample size. The underlying variability in a measurement or parameter determines the underlying 'width' of the likelihood. However, as the sample size increases the likelihood becomes narrower and narrower with respect to the underlying variation in the measurement/parameter (see Section 2.7.3). As a result, a prior that is wider than the underlying variability in the measurement has no chance of meaningfully affecting outcomes given even only a small number of observations. This is shown in the top row of Figure 3.1, where even three observations can overwhelm a very broad prior. As a result, we will be thinking of the 'informativeness' of priors with respect to the variation we expect in them a priori, with priors going from *vague* to *informative* as they become smaller than the expected random variation.

Each column of Figure 3.1 differs in terms of the number of observations used to calculate the likelihood (n = 3, 10, 675), and rows differ in terms of the standard deviation of the prior probabilities of the mean with μ equal to 180 cm and σ = 100, 15, 1. In each case, the calculation of the likelihood assumes that the data has the same standard deviation as our apparent height data (7.8 cm). Note that the yellow curve (the likelihood) is the same in each column. What changes is that priors become narrower across rows from top to bottom, and therefore have an increasing effect on posterior densities.

In the middle row of Figure 3.1 we see the influence of a *weakly informative* prior. This prior is a normal distribution with a mean of 180 and a standard deviation of 15 (i.e. $P(\mu) = N(180, 15)$). The standard deviation was set to twice the value of the standard deviation of adult male heights in the United States. As a result, it places reasonable constraints on our expectations but it will not strongly influence results within that reasonable range. We see that in this case, the likelihood still dominates the posterior even when only three observations are available.

In the top row of Figure 3.1, we see the influence of a *vague* or *diffuse* prior on inference. Since this distribution has a standard deviation of 100 and a mean of 180, this means that basically, all average heights from 0 to 400 cm are plausible a priori. A prior probability this wide is only going to place very minimal constraints on the posterior probabilities that fall inside this range. This is reflected in the top row of Figure 3.1 where even in the case of only three observations the posterior probability almost exactly matches the likelihood. So, in the presence of very weak prior beliefs, the most credible values for your parameters *a posteriori* (after incorporating your data) will be dominated by the most likely values. This makes sense.

Fitting Bayesian regression models with brms   63

In the bottom row of Figure 3.1, we see the influence of a *informative* prior. This distribution has a standard deviation of 1 and a mean of 180. A prior distribution this narrow basically says that we are *sure* that the average height is around 180 cm. This is because the prior probability of any value outside of 178–182 cm is nearly zero, meaning that we will be very hesitant to believe values outside this bound before collecting our data. We can see that under these conditions, the prior distribution can actually have a strong effect on the posterior, especially in cases with few observations. However, with a large enough sample size, the likelihood can still come to dominate even the narrowest prior distributions.

3.3.3 *Posterior distributions and shrinkage*

If we focus on the general characteristics of posterior distributions with respect to the characteristics of priors and likelihoods, a pattern emerges. Specifically, the posterior is a mix of the prior and likelihood which takes their relative 'variances' into account. We know that the width of the likelihood function is dependent on the underlying error in the data and on the sample size. Greater error increases the width of the likelihood since a wider spread of data will be compatible with a wider range of parameter values. On the other hand, more observations will tend to decrease the width of the likelihood, since it consists of the product of density values across all the observations in a data set. So, we see that the characteristics of the posterior distribution will depend simultaneously on the 'width' of the prior distribution, the amount of noise in your dependent variable, and the size of the sample involved in the calculation of your likelihood.

A consequence of the 'merging' of prior information with the likelihood is that posterior distributions can be **shrunk** toward the prior. Recall from Chapter 2 that the maximum-likelihood estimate of a parameter can be thought of as the 'best' parameter in that it is the parameter that makes your data as probable as it can be given the model structure. In Figure 3.1, we see that in some cases the posterior distribution is not exactly like the likelihood and has been *pulled* toward the prior. This means that the maximum *a posteriori* parameter value is not necessarily equal to the *maximum-likelihood* parameter value.

The *pull* exerted by priors is referred to as **shrinkage** because it tends to *shrink* the magnitude of effects by pulling them toward the prior mean (which is often zero). Broadly speaking, deviations from prior expectations are maintained when there is good enough evidence for them, and shrunk when there is not. What constitutes 'enough' evidence is based on the structure of the model and the nature of the data. As seen in Figure 3.1, a wide enough prior will not meaningfully affect estimates even for extremely small sample sizes. You may wonder, is shrinkage a good thing? It turns out that shrinkage can help models arrive at more reliable parameter estimates by reducing weakly supported values that deviate substantially from prior expectations. This will be discussed further in Chapter 4.

3.4 Sampling from the posterior using *Stan* and *brms*

We want to understand the posterior distribution of parameters. How do we get this information? For very simple models, posterior distributions can be derived **analytically**, that is by finding exact solutions to a series of equations. However, for more

64   *Fitting Bayesian regression models with* brms

complicated models, such as the ones we'll discuss in this book, it can be difficult (if not impossible) to understand the characteristics of the posterior distributions of parameters in this way. As a result, these questions are answered **numerically** using software that samples from posterior distributions using algorithms designed to do so as accurately and efficiently as possible. Given enough samples from the posterior distribution, we can estimate the properties of the distribution (just as we could by sampling the distribution of other variables).

Many different software approaches to sampling from posterior distributions have been developed through the years including *winBUGS*, *JAGS*, *PyMC*, and *Stan*. The software used in this book is **Stan**. We use this because it is (relatively) fast, reliable, extremely flexible, and widely adopted. However, the modeling and statistical principles explained in this book apply to all Bayesian models regardless of the software used to fit them, and the central concepts extend to linear modeling more generally.

One downside of working with *Stan* directly is that you need to write your own models. This is not too difficult, but it is not particularly *easy* either, and it can be a bit time-consuming, especially for complicated models. In this book, we will rely on the `brms` package to use *Stan*. `brms` simplifies the use of *Stan* by making the specification of highly efficient models very simple, and providing us with a great deal of flexibility in doing so. It also includes many helper functions that make working with Bayesian models very convenient. So, even though we will use `brms` for simplicity, the topics we discuss in this book could be used to directly write your own models for *Stan* (or any other statistical software).

In order to sample from the posterior distribution using software like *Stan*, the user provides data and a description of a model which specifies:

- The relations between the variables in the data. For example, what is the dependent variable? What are the independent variables? How do these relate?
- The nature of random variation in the model. To this point, we have only discussed single sources of normally distributed noise in our models.
- Prior distributions for all *estimated* parameters.

Given this information, *Stan* samples from the posterior distributions of your parameters and returns vectors containing these samples (one vector for each estimated parameter), rather than looking for the single 'best' estimate. The result of this process is a **chain** of samples from the posterior distribution for each of the parameters you are estimating in your model. Together, the samples in these chains tell us about the characteristics of the parameter they represent. Under a very reasonable set of conditions, random sampling from the posterior distribution will result in a distribution of sampled values of parameters (e.g. μ) that will converge on the posterior distribution of the parameter given your data and model structure (including prior probabilities).

3.5 Estimating a single mean with the `brms` package

3.5.1 *Data and research questions*

We're going to use the same experimental data we looked at last chapter: The height judgments collected for the adult male speakers in our experiment. For more

Fitting Bayesian regression models with brms   65

information on the experiment, see Section 1.3.2. Below we load the book package and extract only those trials including adult male speakers. In addition, we will focus only on the natural productions (contained in `exp_data`), excluding those trials involving the manipulated 'big' resonance level.

```
# load book package and brms
library (bmmb)
library (brms)

# load and subset experimental data
data (exp_data)
men = exp_data[exp_data$C_v=='m',]
mens_height = men$height
```

We're going to revisit the research questions posed at the beginning of Chapter 2:

(Q1) How tall does the average adult male sound?
(Q2) Can we set limits on credible average apparent heights based on the data we collected?

However, this time we're going to approach these questions more formally using a Bayesian regression model using brms (and *Stan*).

3.5.2 Description of the model

We're beginning with a model that treats all of our data as random deviations drawn from a single, undifferentiated normal distribution. Our model for a single group of normally distributed values can be thought of in several different ways. In (3.13), the value of your dependent variable for any given trial ($y_{[i]}$) is thought of as being a normally distributed variable with a constant mean of μ, and a fixed standard deviation σ.

$$y \sim \mathrm{N}(\mu, \sigma) \tag{3.13}$$

Our trial-specific mean will be constant across trials for now, but we introduce the formalism of the trial-dependent mean ($\mu_{[i]}$) now in (3.14) as it will be useful in our discussion below. So, we can still present our variable as coming from a trial-specific value of μ even if we expect $\mu_{[i]} = \mu_{[j]}$ for all values of i and j (some other number), i.e. that all observations share the same μ.

$$y_{[i]} \sim \mathrm{N}(\mu_{[i]}, \sigma) \tag{3.14}$$

We can also think of this model as in (3.15), which says that your dependent variable is the sum of some *expected value* for that trial, ($\mu_{[i]}$), and some specific random error for that trial ($\varepsilon_{[i]}$). The random error is expected to be normally distributed with a mean of 0 and some unknown standard deviation (as in: $\varepsilon_{[i]} \sim \mathrm{N}(0, \sigma)$).

$$y_{[i]} = \mu_{[i]} + \varepsilon_{[i]} \tag{3.15}$$

66 *Fitting Bayesian regression models with* brms

In general, we use regression models to understand orderly variation in $\mu_{[i]}$ from trial to trial by breaking it up into predictors $(x_1, x_2, ...)$ that are combined based on weights as determined by the model coefficients (e.g. $\alpha_1, \alpha_2, ...$). However, in this case we expect the value of $\mu_{[i]}$ to actually be equal for all trials. When we are only trying to estimate a single average, we don't have any predictors to explain variation in $\mu_{[i]}$. In fact, our model structure suggests we expect no variation in $\mu_{[i]}$ from trial to trial. However, mathematically we can't just say 'we have no predictor' since everything needs to be represented by a number. As a result, we use a single 'predictor' x with a value of 1 so that our regression equation is as in (3.16). Now, our model is trying to guess the value of a single coefficient (α_1), and we expect this coefficient to be equal to $\mu_{[i]}$ since it is being multiplied by a 'predictor' with a constant value of 1.

$$\mu_{[i]} = \alpha_1 \cdot 1 \tag{3.16}$$

This kind of model is called an **Intercept-only** model. Regression models are really about representing *differences*, differences between groups and across conditions. When you are encoding differences, you need an overall reference point. For example, saying that something is '5 miles north' is only interpretable given some reference point. The 'reference point' used by your model is called your 'Intercept', and it is the center of your model's universe. At this point, our model consists *only* of a single reference point, and the α_1 parameter reflects its value (as shown in equation (3.16)). As a result, the α_1 coefficient is called the 'Intercept' in our model. When a coefficient is just being multiplied by a 'fake' predictor that always equals one, we can omit it from the regression model (but it's still secretly there). So, our model investigating the apparent heights of adult males can be formalized like this:

$$\text{height}_{[i]} \sim N\left(\mu_{[i]}, \sigma\right) \tag{3.17}$$
$$\mu_{[i]} = \text{Intercept}$$

Put in plain English, each line in the model says the following:

- We expect that the apparent height for a given observation i is normally distributed according to some trial-specific expected value and some unknown (but fixed) standard deviation.
- The expected value for any given trial ($\mu_{[i]}$) is equal to the intercept of the model for all trials. This means it's fixed and we have the same expected value for all tokens.

3.5.3 *Errors and residuals*

Our model above implicitly says that the error, the random variation around μ, is drawn from a normal distribution with a mean of 0 and a standard deviation of σ. This distribution represents all deviations in apparent height around the mean apparent height for the sample ($\mu_{[i]}$). In other words, the error for this model is expected to look like:

$$\varepsilon_{[i]} \sim N\left(0, \sigma\right) \tag{3.18}$$

Fitting Bayesian regression models with brms   67

We can rearrange the terms in (3.15) to isolate the random term on the left side, as in (3.19). When we do this, we see that **error** is what we call the difference between the value of an observation and the expected value for that observation.

$$\varepsilon_{[i]} = y_{[i]} - \mu_{[i]} \tag{3.19}$$

In practice, you never know the true expected value, the *real* exact parameter for whatever distribution you are working with. Instead, you work with an estimate of the predicted value $\hat{\mu}$. As a consequence, you do not have access to the exact errors but instead to estimated errors $\hat{\varepsilon}$, as seen in (3.20). Estimated errors are called **residuals**.

$$\hat{\varepsilon}_{[i]} = y_{[i]} - \hat{\mu}_{[i]} \tag{3.20}$$

As noted in Section 3.2, regression models assume that the random error, the unpredictable deviations about the expected value across trials, are independent and identically distributed. We can now be more specific and say that we expect our *residuals* to be independent and identically distributed. This assumption is obviously violated for our experimental data since we have multiple observations from each listener, each of who had their own tendencies (as discussed in Section 2.3.1). For this reason, we can say that this model is 'wrong'; it's built in such a way that we know it is not a good fit for our data. We will discuss this, and the problems it causes, in the following chapter.

3.5.4 The model formula

Model structures are expressed in R using a very specific syntax. Think of writing a model formula as a sub-language within R. Generally, model formulas in R have the form:

```
y ~ predictors
```

The variable we are interested in understanding (`y`) goes on the left-hand side of the tilde (`~`) and our predictors go on the right-hand side. Notice that information regarding the random term (ε) is not included in the model formula. The formula above can be read as 'y is distributed according to some predictor', which really means "we think there is systematic variation in our y variable that can be understood by considering its joint variation with our predictor variable(s)."

For intercept-only models, the number `1` is included in the model formula to indicate that a single constant value is being estimated (as in (3.16)). As a result, our model formula will have the form seen below.

```
height ~ 1
```

This model formula could be said out loud like "we are trying to estimate the mean height" or "we are predicting mean height given only an intercept".

68 *Fitting Bayesian regression models with* brms

3.5.5 *Fitting the model: Calling the brm function*

The brms package contains the brm (Bayesian regression models) function, which we will use to fit our models. The brm function takes a model specification, data, and some other information, and fits a model that estimates all the model parameters. Unless otherwise specified, brm assumes that the error component (ε) of your model is normally distributed. The first argument in the function call below is the model formula, and the second argument tells the function where to find the data (a data frame called men). The other arguments tell the function to estimate a single set of samples (chains = 1) using a single core on your CPU (cores = 1). These arguments will be discussed in more detail in the next chapter.

```
model = brms::brm (height ~ 1, data = men, chains = 1, cores = 1)
## Compiling Stan program...
## Start sampling
##
## SAMPLING FOR MODEL '03859e54349182b6cd9cd51aa7ca25d3' NOW
(CHAIN 1).
## Chain 1:
## Chain 1: Gradient evaluation took 0 seconds
## Chain 1: 1000 transitions using 10 leapfrog steps per
transition would take 0 seconds.
## Chain 1: Adjust your expectations accordingly!
## Chain 1:
## Chain 1:
## Chain 1: Iteration:    1 / 2000 [  0%]  (Warmup)
## Chain 1: Iteration:  200 / 2000 [ 10%]  (Warmup)
## Chain 1: Iteration:  400 / 2000 [ 20%]  (Warmup)
## Chain 1: Iteration:  600 / 2000 [ 30%]  (Warmup)
## Chain 1: Iteration:  800 / 2000 [ 40%]  (Warmup)
## Chain 1: Iteration: 1000 / 2000 [ 50%]  (Warmup)
## Chain 1: Iteration: 1001 / 2000 [ 50%]  (Sampling)
## Chain 1: Iteration: 1200 / 2000 [ 60%]  (Sampling)
## Chain 1: Iteration: 1400 / 2000 [ 70%]  (Sampling)
## Chain 1: Iteration: 1600 / 2000 [ 80%]  (Sampling)
## Chain 1: Iteration: 1800 / 2000 [ 90%]  (Sampling)
## Chain 1: Iteration: 2000 / 2000 [100%]  (Sampling)
## Chain 1:
## Chain 1:   Elapsed Time: 0.103 seconds (Warm-up)
## Chain 1:                 0.057 seconds (Sampling)
## Chain 1:                 0.16 seconds (Total)
```

By default, brms takes 2,000 samples, throwing out the first 1,000 and returning the last 1,000. The first 1,000 samples are the **warmup**, the time the model uses to find appropriate parameter values for the model and to tune the behavior of the sampling algorithm. The output above shows you that the sampler is working, and tells you about the progress as it works. This is a small amount of data and a simple model so

Fitting Bayesian regression models with brms   69

it should fit pretty quickly. You can fit the models discussed in this book on your own computer using the code provided, or you can download them directly from the book GitHub repo using the code below.

```
# Download the model above from the GitHub page.
# File names are in the formant: 'chapterNumber_modelName'
model = bmmb::get_model ('3_model.RDS')
```

3.5.6 Interpreting the model: The print statement

Typing the model name into the console and hitting enter prints the default brms model print statement:

```
# inspect model
model
```

The first part provides you with some basic information and tells you some technical details that we don't have to worry about for now (though some are obvious).

```
## Family: gaussian
##   Links: mu = identity; sigma = identity
##Formula: height ~ 1
##    Data: men (Number of observations: 675)
##   Draws: 1 chains, each with iter = 2000; warmup = 1000; thin = 1;
##          total post-warmup draws = 1000
```

Next, we see estimated effects for our predictors, in this case only an intercept. This is an estimated **population-level effect** because it is shared by all observations in our sample, and it is not specific to any particular subset of observations.

```
## Population-Level Effects:
##           Estimate Est.Error l-95% CI u-95% CI Rhat Bulk_ESS Tail_ESS
## Intercept   173.78      0.30   173.16   174.33 1.00     1055      714
```

The information above provides the mean (Estimate) and standard deviation (Est. Error) of the posterior distribution of μ (Intercept), i.e. $P(\mu \mid y)$. The values of l-95% CI and u-95% CI represent the lower and upper 95% **credible interval** of the posterior distribution. An $x\%$ credible interval of a parameter is an interval such that the parameter has an $x\%$ chance ($0.x$ probability) of falling inside the interval. The credible intervals provided by brms are based on quantiles so that the l-95% CI and u-95% CI represent 2.5% and 97.5% quantiles of the posterior samples of a parameter. Based on its 95% credible interval, we see that there is a 95% probability that μ is between 173.2 and 174.3 cm given our data and model structure.

Our model also provides us an estimate of the error standard deviation (σ), under Family Specific Parameters: sigma. This estimate closely matches our sample standard deviation estimate of 7.77 cm. In addition, we also get a 95% credible interval

70   *Fitting Bayesian regression models with* brms

for this parameter, spanning from 2.5% = 7.37 to 97.5% = 8.21. Although our focus is often on the estimation of mean parameters, it's very important to keep in mind that our model in (3.15) involves the estimation of *two* parameters: μ and σ.

```
## Family Specific Parameters:
##        Estimate Est.Error l-95% CI u-95% CI Rhat Bulk_ESS Tail_ESS
## sigma      7.77      0.22     7.37     8.21 1.00     1139      741
```

This last section is just boilerplate and contains some basic reminders which will generally look the same.

```
## Samples were drawn using sampling(NUTS). For each parameter, Bulk_ESS
## and Tail_ESS are effective sample size measures, and Rhat is the potential
## scale reduction factor on split chains (at convergence, Rhat = 1).
```

3.5.7 Seeing the samples

In Section 3.4, we discussed that Bayesian modeling software (like *Stan*) takes *samples* of the posterior distributions of parameters given the data and model structure. It's helpful to see that our model is really just a series of **posterior samples**, that is, samples of values from the distribution of μ given your data and priors, i.e. $P(\mu \,|\, y)$.

Compact descriptions of our models, such as the one in the print described above, are just summaries of the information contained in the posterior samples. Below we get the posterior samples from the model we fit above, in the form of a data frame using the get_samples function from the bmmb package. As expected, we have 1,000 samples of each parameter. The first column represents the model intercept (b_Intercept), the second column is the error (sigma) (i.e. $P(\sigma \,|\, y)$). The third and fourth columns (lprior, lp__) are the log prior and log posterior densities, to be discussed in Section 3.8.

```
# get posterior samples from model
samples = bmmb::get_samples (model)

# check number of samples
nrow (samples)
## [1] 1000

# see first six samples
head (samples)
##    b_Intercept sigma lprior    lp__
## 1        173.2 7.518 -5.885 -2347
## 2        174.1 7.613 -5.880 -2345
## 3        173.3 7.940 -5.945 -2346
## 4        174.2 7.564 -5.872 -2346
## 5        173.7 7.879 -5.924 -2345
## 6        174.0 7.859 -5.916 -2345
```

Fitting Bayesian regression models with brms   71

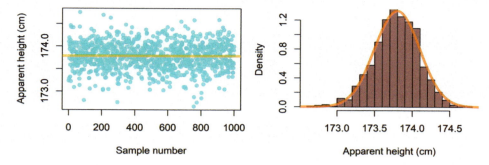

Figure 3.2 (left) Individual samples from the posterior distribution of the model intercept parameter. (right) A histogram of the samples on the left. The curve shows the density of a normal distribution with a mean of 173.8 and a standard deviation of 0.30.

We can plot the individual samples for the intercept parameter on the left in Figure 3.2, and on the right, we can see a histogram of the samples.

Recall that our model output provides information about 95% credible intervals for the mean parameter: It was expected to fall between 173.2 and 174.3 cm. We know that this interval simply corresponds to the 2.5% and 97.5% quantiles of the posterior samples. We can confirm this by checking the quantiles on the vector containing our posterior samples and see that these exactly correspond to the values of `Estimate`, `l-95% CI`, and `u-95% CI` in the model print statement above.

```
quantile (samples[,"b_Intercept"], c(.025, .975))
##  2.5%  97.5%
## 173.2 174.3
```

One of the great things about Bayesian models is that you can make your own summaries of the posterior samples, summarize them in several ways as required, and ask different questions easily. For example, there is no special status for the 2.5% and 97.5% quantiles, and we can easily check the values of other ones, such as the first and third quartiles:

```
quantile (samples[,"b_Intercept"], c(.25, .75))
##   25%   75%
## 173.6 174.0
```

We can also use the posterior distribution to find the probability that the mean parameter is over/under any arbitrary value:

```
# probability that the intercept is less than 174 cm
mean (samples[,"b_Intercept"] < 174)
## [1] 0.76
```

Let's take a second to think about why this works. Recall that the probability is the odds that something will occur, relative to all other outcomes. Our vector

72 *Fitting Bayesian regression models with* brms

`samples[,"b_Intercept"]` represents 1,000 observations of a random variable and 1,000 possible values of the posterior distribution of the mean apparent height of adult males ($P(\mu \mid y)$). If we find the total number of these observations that were below 174 cm and then divide it by the total number of observations (1,000), we are effectively calculating the probability of observing a mean estimate below 174 cm. As a result, the calculation above says that there is a 0.76 probability (a 76% chance) that the mean apparent height of adult male speakers in this population is under 174 cm, given our data and model structure. We come to this conclusion by finding that 76% of the posterior samples of the parameter of interest are below 174 cm.

3.5.8 *Getting the residuals*

We can get the model residuals using the `residuals` function. By default, it returns a data frame where one row corresponds to each observation in your data, and the different columns provide you with information about the estimate. You will notice that you also get credible intervals for each of the estimated residuals. This is because there is one prediction for each set of posterior samples. Since we have 1,000 posterior samples that means we have 1,000 slightly different predicted values for each observation and therefore 1,000 slightly different estimated errors for each observation.

```
model_residuals = residuals (model, )
head (model_residuals)
##         Estimate Est.Error      Q2.5      Q97.5
## [1,]     -3.8844    0.2988   -4.4347   -3.2638
## [2,]     -0.2844    0.2988   -0.8347    0.3362
## [3,]     -1.7844    0.2988   -2.3347   -1.1638
## [4,]    -16.0844    0.2988  -16.6347  -15.4638
## [5,]    -20.3844    0.2988  -20.9347  -19.7638
## [6,]      0.4156    0.2988   -0.1347    1.0362
```

By default, information regarding the posterior distribution of residuals for each data point is presented. However, you can get all the posterior estimates for each individual residual by setting `summary=FALSE`. When you do this, you will get a matrix of size m (rows) by n (columns) for m posterior samples and n data points. We can see below that we get 1,000 rows representing our posterior samples and 675 columns representing our data points.

```
model_residuals = residuals (model, summary=FALSE)
dim (model_residuals)
## [1] 1000   675
```

In the left plot of Figure 3.3, we show a histogram of our residuals and compare this to a normal distribution centered at zero, with a standard deviation equal to the error in our model (`sigma = 7.78`). It's no surprise that these match because this is precisely what the sigma parameter in our model is an estimate of, the standard deviation of the residuals. Since our model consists of only an intercept, a single expected value (μ) for all instances of the variable, all variation around the mean constitutes error. We

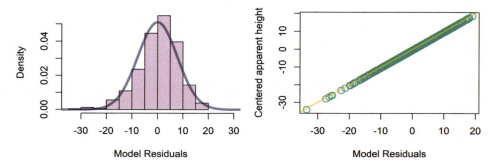

Figure 3.3 (left) Histogram of the residuals for `model`. (right) A comparison of our residuals and centered height judgments shows that these are nearly equal.

can show this by comparing our residual estimates to the centered data (right plot of Figure 3.3) and seeing that these are basically the same.

3.6 Checking model convergence

Our parameter estimates are based on a set of samples from the posterior distribution of a parameter. As with any other inference based on samples, our parameter estimates will be unreliable if we don't have enough samples, or if our samples do not represent the population we are trying to understand. For this reason, it's important to look at the **ESS** values (the *effective sample size*), and the **Rhat** values provided for `brm` model print statements.

Rhat tells you whether your chains have converged, and it basically compares how much within-chain variation there is relative to the amount of between-chain overlap. Ideally, you want your chains to overlap almost entirely in the values that they span since they are supposed to be sampling the same thing. As noted in the 'boilerplate' at the end of the `brm` model print statement, values of Rhat near 1 are good, and values higher than around 1.1 are a bad sign.

ESS tells you approximately how many *independent* samples you have taken from the posterior. Bulk ESS tells you how many samples the sampler took in the 'thick' part of the density, and Tail ESS reflects how much time the sampler spent in the 'thin' part, in the tails of the distribution. Ideally, we would like several hundred samples (at least) for mean estimates, and thousands to be confident in the 95% credible intervals. You may sometimes fit a model and get a warning message like this:

```
## Warning messages:
## 1: Bulk Effective Samples Size (ESS) is too low,
indicating posterior means and
## medians may be unreliable. Running the chains for more
iterations may help. See:
## http://mc-stan.org/misc/warnings.html#bulk-ess
## 2: Tail Effective Samples Size (ESS) is too low,
indicating posterior variances
```

```
## and tail quantiles may be unreliable.
## Running the chains for more iterations may help. See
## http://mc-stan.org/misc/warnings.html#tail-ess
```

That is brms telling you that you need to collect more samples in order to be confident in your parameter estimates. To get more samples, we can run the model for more iterations, or we can use more *chains*. Each chain is a separate set of samples for your parameter values. A model can be fit in parallel across several cores on your computer, resulting in several independent chains in roughly the same amount of computing time. Since these chains are all supposed to be sampling from the same posterior distribution, their samples can be merged across chains after sampling. There is a fixed number of samples a single core of your computer can make in a given amount of time. When you do this across *n* cores, you can get (approximately) *n* times as many samples in the same amount of time. Since many personal computers these days have 4–8 (or more) cores, we can take advantage of parallel processing to fit models faster. Before fitting a model across multiple cores, you should confirm how many you have. You can use the following command (you may need to install the parallel package):

```
parallel::detectCores()
```

The example code throughout this book will use four cores to fit models. If you only have four total cores on your computer, you should change the models to use 2–3 chains and cores so that your computer can take care of other necessary functions while you fit your model(s). One thing to keep in mind is that these models can be computationally intensive to fit. As the data sets become larger and the models become more complicated, more powerful computers are needed in order to fit a model in a reasonable amount of time. Below, we re-fit our initial model but run it on four chains, and on four cores at once.

```
# Fit the model yourself
model_multicore =
  brms::brm (height ~ 1, data = men, chains = 4, cores = 4)

# Or download it from the GitHub page:
model_multicore = bmmb::get_model ('3_model_multicore.RDS')
```

We print the model below and can see that using four chains has substantially increased our ESS, without taking up much more computing time. Toward the top of our print statement, we see that 4 chains have collected total post-warmup samples = 4000. This means our model has 4,000 samples for every parameter in the model. However, for some parameters, we have only about 3,000 'effective samples'. This means some of our samples are basically dead weight, taking up space and slowing down future computations for no good reason. The discrepancy between the number of samples and the 'effective' number of samples is due to something called **autocorrelation**, the self-similarity of nearby observations in a series of observations (discussed further in Section 5.8.2).

```
# inspect model
model_multicore
##   Family: gaussian
##    Links: mu = identity; sigma = identity
## Formula: height ~ 1
##     Data: men (Number of observations: 675)
##    Draws: 4 chains, each with iter = 2000; warmup = 1000; thin = 1;
##           total post-warmup draws = 4000
##
## Population-Level Effects:
##             Estimate Est.Error l-95% CI u-95% CI Rhat Bulk_ESS Tail_ESS
## Intercept     173.79      0.30   173.21   174.38 1.00     3139     2534
##
## Family Specific Parameters:
##         Estimate Est.Error l-95% CI u-95% CI Rhat Bulk_ESS Tail_ESS
## sigma       7.78      0.21     7.39     8.21 1.00     3671     2476
##
## Draws were sampled using sampling(NUTS). For each parameter, Bulk_ESS
## and Tail_ESS are effective sample size measures, and Rhat is the
potential
## scale reduction factor on split chains (at convergence, Rhat = 1).
```

Sometimes consecutive samples can be too similar and so don't give you that much *independent* information. When this happens you end up with less information about a parameter than you might think based on the number of samples you have. Think of it like measuring the temperature of a place to get an idea of its average annual weather. Measurements need to be well separated in order to be really independent and to give an accurate picture of the true average. If you were to measure the temperature every 5 minutes these measurements would have a high *autocorrelation*, and would not give you a good impression of the range of temperatures that place tends to experience in a calendar year.

One way to increase the ESS without increasing the final number of posterior samples is to run longer chains and keep only every n^{th} one. This strategy is called **thinning**, and it lets your models be smaller while containing approximately the same information. To do this you have to change the `iter`, `warmup` and `thin` parameters when you fit your model. The default behavior is that the models you fit keep every sample after the `warmup` is done, up to the `iter` maximum. So if `iter=3000` and `warmup=1000` you will end up with 2,000 samples. If you set `thin` to some value other than 1, you keep only one every `thin` samples. As a result, you will end up with (`iter`-`warmup`)/ `thin` samples per chain. If you are doing this across `cores` cores, then you will end up with (`iter`-`warmup`)/`thin`)$\times$ `cores` samples in total. Below, we ask for 3,000 samples per chain. Since the warmup is 1,000 this means we will keep 2,000 post warmup per chain, for 8,000 total samples across all four chains. However, since `thin=2`, we will keep only half of these of these. As a result, we will end up with 4,000 samples in total (i.e. ((3,000 − 1,000)/2) × 4).

76 *Fitting Bayesian regression models with* brms

```
# Fit the model yourself
model_thinned =
  brms::brm (height ~ 1, data = men, chains = 4, cores = 4,
       warmup = 1000, iter = 3000, thin = 2)

# Or download it from the GitHub page:
model_thinned = bmmb::get_model ('3_model_thinned.RDS')
```

We inspect the model print statement and see that despite having the same number of samples as the `model_multicore`, the ESS for this model is higher than for the previous model, in particular for the `sigma` parameter. Before moving on from ESS we just want to note that it is possible for your ESS to be *higher* than your actual (real) number of samples. This is simply due to the way that ESS is calculated and is nothing to worry about, in fact, it may mean that your model is sampling the posterior very efficiently.

```
# inspect model
model_thinned
##  Family: gaussian
##   Links: mu = identity; sigma = identity
## Formula: height ~ 1
##    Data: men (Number of observations: 675)
##   Draws: 4 chains, each with iter = 3000; warmup = 1000; thin = 2;
##          total post-warmup draws = 4000
##
## Population-Level Effects:
##           Estimate Est.Error l-95% CI u-95% CI Rhat Bulk_ESS Tail_ESS
## Intercept   173.78      0.30   173.21   174.39 1.00     3772     3556
##
## Family Specific Parameters:
##        Estimate Est.Error l-95% CI u-95% CI Rhat Bulk_ESS Tail_ESS
## sigma      7.77      0.21     7.38     8.20 1.00     3933     3568
##
## Draws were sampled using sampling(NUTS). For each parameter, Bulk_ESS
## and Tail_ESS are effective sample size measures, and Rhat is the
potential
## scale reduction factor on split chains (at convergence, Rhat = 1).
```

Before moving on we want to talk about another problem you may run into: **Divergent transitions**. When you see an error like this:

```
## There were n divergent transitions after warmup.
Increasing adapt_delta
## above 0.8 may help. See
## http://mc-stan.org/misc/warnings.html#divergent-
transitions-after-warmup`
```

Fitting Bayesian regression models with brms   77

It means your model encountered n (some integer) divergent transitions during sampling. Your model has very specific expectations regarding parameter likelihoods and samples from the posterior distribution on this basis. A *divergent transition* indicates that as it sampled, it came across things that were not as expected. The fact that there is a difference between what your model thought would happen and what actually happened then calls the reliability of the entire simulation into question. One way to fix this problem is to increase `adapt_delta` to 0.95 or 0.99. The `adapt_delta` parameter is set to 0.8 by default and has a maximum value of one. This can be done as seen below.

```
brms::brm (height ~ 1, data = men, chains = 4, cores = 4, warmup = 1000,
           iter = 3000, thin = 2, control = list(adapt_delta = 0.9))
```

Increasing the `adapt_delta` parameter results in fewer divergences and a more robust, but slower, sampler. Think of it like walking on ice taking little tiny steps; you are less likely to fall but will take longer to get there. If you raise `adapt_delta` to 0.999 or something and are still getting divergent transitions, there may be an error in your data or in the way that your model is specified. We can't really be more specific than that at this point, however, we can say that divergent transitions are often not a *Stan* problem but rather a data or model structure problem (see Section 8.8).

3.7 Specifying prior probabilities

In Section 3.3, we mentioned that in Bayesian models all estimated parameters *must* have prior probability distributions specified for them. And yet, to this point, we've been fitting models without explicitly specifying prior probability distributions for their parameters. If you don't specify prior probabilities for your parameters, `brm` will use its own default priors using the characteristics of your data. We can use the function `get_prior` in `brms` to see what the default priors are for our model and to see which parameters in our model require priors. Of course, we should know this based on the structure of our model but this method is useful to help verify our expectations.

Below we can see that our model requires priors for our two estimated parameters, the `Intercept` (μ) and `sigma` (σ) parameters, and that these have been given `default` values. The default values use a t distribution (`student_t()`), which we will discuss in Section 5.9. We've omitted a few (empty) columns below so the printout will fit on the page, but we encourage you to erase the `[,-c(7:9)]` part in the code below and run it yourself so you can see the full output.

```
brms::get_prior (height ~ 1, data = men)[,-c(7:9)]
##                      prior     class coef group resp dpar    source
##   student_t(3, 174.5, 7.1) Intercept                       default
##       student_t(3, 0, 7.1)     sigma                       default
```

`brms` makes it easy to specify prior probabilities for specific parameters or whole 'classes' of parameters. Setting priors for entire classes of parameters is faster for you

78   *Fitting Bayesian regression models with* brms

and makes the model run faster, so it is a good idea to do it where possible. Right now, our model only includes the following classes of parameters:

- `Intercept`: This is a unique class, only for intercepts.
- `sigma`: This is for the standard deviation of our error parameters. Our model only has one for now, `sigma` (σ), but it can have more.

We're going to set *weakly informative* prior probabilities for our parameters. This means we're going to set our priors to be about the same size as the variation we expect in the data itself. To set these you have to use what you know about your variables and the world in general. Since we know that the average male over 20 in the US is 176 cm tall, this seems like a reasonable prior expectation for how tall the adult males in our sample will sound. We also know that the standard deviation of adult male heights in the US is 7.5 cm, and will double this for our priors. This is to account for the fact that there may be more variation in how tall people 'sound' compared to how tall they *are*. The code to set the priors for our model looks like this:

```
prior = c(brms::set_prior("normal(176, 15)", class = "Intercept"),
          brms::set_prior("normal(0, 15)", class = "sigma"))
```

The code above tells our model to use a normal distribution with a mean of 176 and a standard deviation of 15 (`normal(176, 15)`) for the prior distribution of the intercept. Around 90%–95% of the mass of normal distributions is within two standard deviations of the mean. This means that we are saying that we expect, a priori, that the intercept should be between around 146 (176 − 15 × 2) and 206 cm (176 + 15 × 2). This is probably too broad, but it places the expected outcomes within reasonable human ranges.

The random error, `sigma`, was given a prior with a normal distribution with a mean of 0 and a standard deviation of 15 (`normal(0, 15)`). Again, this is likely an overestimation of the magnitude of the random error in this data. However, it is likely to be in the ballpark. Our prior specifies a normal distribution centered at 0 for the standard deviation. Since standard deviations, like variances, can only be positive, the sampler (*Stan*) used by `brm` ignores the negative half and uses only the positive half of the prior distribution. This prior basically says that we expect the average variation around the mean to be less than 30 cm, which it is very likely to be.

The left plot in Figure 3.4 compares the normal distribution we used (blue line) to a histogram of our height judgments. As we can see, the prior distribution we used for the intercept is much broader (more vague) than the data distribution so that it will probably have little to no practical effect on our posterior distribution (but will help our model fit properly). The right plot compares the prior for the standard deviation parameters to the absolute value of the centered apparent heights. This presentation shows how far each observation is from the mean apparent height (at 174 cm), and again we see that most of these deviations are in the thicker part of the prior density. As a result, neither of these priors is going to have much of an effect on our parameter estimates given the size of our sample (see Figure 3.1).

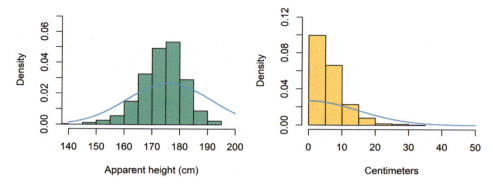

Figure 3.4 (left) The densities of the prior probability for our model intercept, compared to a histogram of height judgments for male speakers. (right) The distribution of absolute deviations from the mean height judgment, compared to the prior distribution for the error parameter (σ) in our model.

We can update the description of our model to include the specification of prior distributions for each estimated parameter, as in (3.21). In the future, our model descriptions will always include these. Our model specification now makes it clear: We expect height judgments to be normally distributed, we expect the mean to always equal the intercept, and we have specific prior distributions in mind for all estimated model parameters (Intercept and σ).

$$\text{height}_{[i]} \sim \text{N}\left(\mu_{[i]}, \sigma\right)$$
$$\mu_{[i]} = \text{Intercept}$$

$$\text{Priors:}$$
$$\text{Intercept} \sim \text{N}(176, 15)$$
$$\sigma \sim \text{N}(0, 15)$$

(3.21)

We can fit this new model below, passing the lines that specify the prior distributions for our parameters to the `prior` parameter of the `brm` function.

```
# Fit the model yourself, or
model_priors =
  brms::brm (height ~ 1, data = men, chains = 4, cores = 4,
      warmup = 1000, iter = 3500, thin = 2,
      prior = c(brms::set_prior("normal(176, 15)", class = "Intercept"),
                brms::set_prior("normal(0, 15)", class = "sigma")))

# Download the model above from the GitHub page.
model_priors = bmmb::get_model ('3_model_priors.RDS')
```

80 *Fitting Bayesian regression models with* brms

We can use the `short_summary` function in the `bmmb` package to get an abridged version of the model print statements. These shorter versions are not a replacement for the complete statement as they omit important information about our models. However, these abbreviated print statements will help us compare models while minimizing redundant information on the page, and so are useful for this book. If we compare the output of `model_thinned`:

```
# inspect model
bmmb::short_summary (model_thinned)
## Formula:   height ~ 1
## Population-Level Effects:
##             Estimate Est.Error l-95% CI u-95% CI
## Intercept     173.8        0.3    173.2    174.4
##
## Family Specific Parameters:
##         Estimate Est.Error l-95% CI u-95% CI
## sigma      7.77      0.21     7.38      8.2
```

To that of the model where we specified our own priors (`model_priors`), we see that there is no meaningful effect on our results.

```
bmmb::short_summary (model_priors)
## Formula:   height ~ 1
## Population-Level Effects:
##             Estimate Est.Error l-95% CI u-95% CI
## Intercept     173.8       0.31    173.2    174.4
##
## Family Specific Parameters:
##         Estimate Est.Error l-95% CI u-95% CI
## sigma      7.77      0.21     7.37     8.19
```

This is because the prior matters less and less when you have a lot of data, and because we have set priors that are appropriate (but vague) given our data. Although the priors may not matter much for models as simple as these, they can be very important when working with more complex data and are a necessary component of Bayesian modeling.

3.8 The log prior and log posterior densities

The information presented in this section is not strictly necessary to understand the models outlined in this book. However, it is useful information to know and so we put it here so that you will know when to find it when you want it.

When we got our posterior samples with the `get_samples` function, in addition to our mean and standard deviation estimates we got estimates of something called `lprior` and `lp__`. We can see these below:

```
samples = bmmb::get_samples (model_priors)
head (samples)
```

Fitting Bayesian regression models with brms 81

```
##    b_Intercept sigma lprior   lp__
## 1        173.4 8.041 -6.719 -2347
## 2        173.5 7.997 -6.716 -2346
## 3        173.8 8.043 -6.715 -2346
## 4        174.8 7.936 -6.704 -2351
## 5        173.4 7.630 -6.705 -2346
## 6        173.8 7.965 -6.712 -2346
```

These are the *log prior* and the (unnormalized) *log posterior* densities, respectively. To explain what these are, let's generalize equation (3.12), which presented the posterior probability of a μ parameter given your data and priors, to encompass all of our model parameters represented by θ in (3.22). Now, (3.22) represents the posterior probability of *all* our model parameters given our data.

$$P(\theta \mid y) = \frac{P(y \mid \theta) \cdot P(\theta)}{P(y)} \tag{3.22}$$

First, we can discuss `lprior`, the log prior density. This is the logarithm of the joint prior density of all of your parameters (i.e. the sum of their log densities), in other words $\log(P(\theta))$. Specifically for our model, the is equal to $\log(P(\mu \,\&\, \sigma))$. We can see the prior probabilities of our model parameters below:

```
model_priors$prior
##               prior      class coef group resp dpar nlpar lb ub source
##   normal(176, 15) Intercept                                       user
##     normal(0, 15)     sigma                               0       user
```

And we can use this information to calculate `lprior` for the first and fourth values of `lprior` seen in the samples above (-6.719 and -6.704). In the lines below we find the log density of the mean and the log density of the error term (`sigma`) for the first and fourth posterior estimates of μ and σ. For example, `dnorm (173.4,176,15,log=TRUE)` returns the log (since `log=TRUE`) density over a point at 173.4 (the first posterior sample of the mean) given a normal distribution with the characteristics of the prior of our mean (i.e. a mean of 176 cm and a standard deviation of 15 cm). Since variances are bounded by zero, *Stan* ignores the negative half of the density. As a result, we add log(2) to multiply the log density of the `sigma` term by two, and make the area under the curve still be equal to one. By adding these terms together, we can recreate the values of `lprior` above.

```
dnorm (173.4,176,15,log=TRUE) + dnorm (8.041,0,15,log=TRUE) + log(2)
## [1] -6.72
dnorm (174.8,176,15,log=TRUE) + dnorm (7.936,0,15,log=TRUE) + log(2)
## [1] -6.704
```

The **log posterior density** (`lp__`) is basically the overall posterior probability of your model parameters given your data. The *unnormalized* posterior density ignores the marginal distribution ($P(y)$) and so returns a density that is proportional to the posterior density up to some constant, as in (3.23).

82   *Fitting Bayesian regression models with* brms

$$P(\theta \mid y) \propto P(y \mid \theta) \cdot P(\theta) \tag{3.23}$$

By saying that it's defined up to a **proportional constant**, this is what we mean. We cannot, or do not bother calculating the exact posterior density. However, we can calculate a value that when multiplied by some constant C (which we happen to know is equal to $(1 / P(y))$), equals the posterior density. This value is $\left[P(y \mid \theta) \cdot P(\theta) \right]$, presented in square brackets in (3.24). When we model the unnormalized posterior density we take this approach, we try to estimate $P(\theta \mid y)$ while ignoring C (i.e. $1 / P(y)$).

$$P(\theta \mid y) = \left[P(y \mid \theta) \cdot P(\theta) \right] \cdot C \tag{3.24}$$

If we log-transform both sides of (3.24), we get the log posterior density, shown in (3.25).

$$\log\big(P(\theta \mid y) \big) = \log\big(P(y \mid \theta) \big) + \log\big(P(\theta) \big) + \log(C) \tag{3.25}$$

Let's pause to think about what (3.25) means and why it's a useful measure. First, let's talk about $P(y \mid \theta)$ which is the model likelihood: The joint density of the data given the values of the parameters. We can think about the probability of observing each of the observations in our height data given the posterior mean estimates of μ and σ provided by `model_priors`. Below, we see the values of the probability density above the first six observations, and then the logarithm of these values below.

```
# density over the first 6 observations
head (dnorm (mens_height, 173.8, 7.77))
## [1] 0.045267 0.051306 0.049985 0.006000 0.001636 0.051276

# log density over first 6 observations
head (dnorm (mens_height, 173.8, 7.77, log = TRUE))
## [1] -3.095 -2.970 -2.996 -5.116 -6.416 -2.971
```

To find the joint density of the data given the model parameters, we can sum the log densities as seen below. This provides us an estimate of the log-likelihood of the model given all parameter values $\big(\log\big(P(y \mid \theta) \big)\big)$.

```
sum (dnorm (mens_height, 173.8, 7.77, log = TRUE))
## [1] -2341
```

We can then add the logarithm of the priors for our parameters to this. By combining our priors and likelihoods in this way, we are calculating the *unnormalized* posterior density.

```
sum (dnorm (mens_height, 173.8, 7.78, log = TRUE)) + # the likelihood
  dnorm (173.8,176,15,log=TRUE) +    # prior probability of mu
  dnorm (7.77,0,15,log=TRUE) +log(2) # prior probability of sigma
## [1] -2347
```

Fitting Bayesian regression models with brms   83

We can see that our calculation is very close to the average value of the `lp__` estimates provided by our model.

```
mean (samples$lp__)
## [1] -2346
```

The log posterior density, or values related to it, will come up again in Chapter 6 when we discuss model comparison. This is because this value captures the posterior probability of the parameters given the data. Broadly speaking, models with a higher posterior probability are more believable because they are more likely to generate the observed data, and/or they have parameter values that are more probable a priori.

3.9 Answering our research questions

Finally, let's return again to the research questions we posed initially in Chapter 2, and again at the beginning of this chapter:

(Q1) How tall does the average adult male sound?
(Q2) Can we set limits on credible average apparent heights based on the data we collected?

Here's what we had to say about this at the end of Chapter 2:
"the average male speaker is *most likely* to sound about 174 cm tall. We can also conclude informally based on Figure 2.8 that the most likely mean values fall between (approximately) 173 and 174.5 cm"

We can reconsider the answers to these questions provided by our final model, `model_priors`. Usually, parameters should be reported with *at least* the mean/ median and standard deviations of the posterior distribution, in addition to some useful credible interval (e.g. 50%, 95%) around that parameter. Based on the result of our final model, an answer to each question might be something like this:

(A1) Based on our model the average apparent height for adult males is likely to be 174 cm. In a paper we might report this like: "The mean height is 174 cm (s.d. = 0.3, 95% CI = [173.2, 174.4])".

(A2) Yes we can. There is a 95% probability that the population mean is between 173.2 and 174.4 given our data and model structure. In other words, 95% of the posterior density is concentrated between the values of 173.2 and 174.4.

Notice that our answers correspond closely to what we concluded at the end of the last chapter. The reason for this correspondence is that we made our inferences at the end of Chapter 2 using only the likelihood and, due to the shape of the prior and the number of observations in our data, the posterior distribution of our model is being dominated by the likelihood. As a result, the two approaches converge on approximately the same solution in this situation.

3.10 'Traditionalists' corner

In traditionalists' corner, we're going to compare the output of `brms` to some more 'traditional' approaches. We're not going to talk about the traditional models in any

84   *Fitting Bayesian regression models with* brms

detail, the focus of this section is simply to highlight the similarities between different approaches, and to point out where to find equivalent information in the different models. If you are already familiar with these approaches, these sections may be helpful. If not, some of the information provided here may not make much sense, although it may still be helpful. If you want to know more about the statistical methods being discussed here, please see the preface for a list of suggested background reading in statistics.

3.10.1 One-sample t-*test vs. intercept-only Bayesian models*

A one-sample *t*-test helps investigate whether the mean of a set of observations is consistent with a true underlying value of zero. The *t*-test answers questions using the likelihood of parameters given the data (priors and posteriors are not involved). In addition, *t*-tests are calculated using analytic (exact) methods and do not involve sampling from distributions. The *t*-test assumes that all of your observations are independent, so it is not appropriate to use for our experimental data. However, we just want to compare it to our initial Bayesian model (which made the same assumptions). We can apply a one-sample *t*-test to our vector of apparent height judgments:

```
t.test (mens_height)
##
##   One Sample t-test
##
## data:  mens_height
## t = 582, df = 674, p-value <2e-16
## alternative hypothesis: true mean is not equal to 0
## 95 percent confidence interval:
##   173.2 174.4
## sample estimates:
## mean of x
##      173.8
```

Notice that the interval provided around the mean (`95 percent confidence interval:    173.2    174.4`) corresponds very well to the 95% credible interval around the intercept provided in `model` (`173.16,   174.33`). The reason they align so well is that both models have the same general structure and make similar mathematical assumptions. In addition, our Bayesian estimate is being dominated by the likelihood, and the more 'traditional' *t*-test *only* considers information from the likelihood.

3.10.2 *Intercept-only ordinary-least-squares regression vs. intercept-only Bayesian models*

Ordinary-least-squares (OLS) regression is an approach to fitting regression models using likelihoods (without priors or posteriors). OLS regression assumes that your

Fitting Bayesian regression models with brms   85

residuals are independent and that your error variation is normally distributed. We can fit an OLS model using the `lm` (linear model) function in R, using the same model formula we used for our Bayesian models.

```
ols_model = lm (mens_height ~ 1)
summary (ols_model)
##
## Call:
## lm(formula = mens_height ~ 1)
##
## Residuals:
##     Min      1Q Median      3Q     Max
## -34.09   -4.59   0.71    5.31   18.51
##
## Coefficients:
##             Estimate Std. Error t value Pr(>|t|)
## (Intercept)  173.788      0.299     582   <2e-16 ***
## ---
## Signif. codes:  0 '***' 0.001 '**' 0.01 '*' 0.05 '.' 0.1 ' ' 1
##
## Residual standard error: 7.76 on 674 degrees of freedom
```

Again, we see a close similarity to our initial `model`. The `Std.error` for the Intercept above (0.299) corresponds closely to the `Est.error` of the intercept below (0.30), and the `Residual standard error` above (7.76) corresponds closely to the `sigma` estimate below (7.77).

```
## Population-Level Effects:
##            Estimate Est.Error l-95% CI u-95% CI Rhat Bulk_ESS Tail_ESS
## Intercept    173.78      0.30   173.16   174.33 1.00     1055      714
##
## Family Specific Parameters:
##         Estimate Est.Error l-95% CI u-95% CI Rhat Bulk_ESS Tail_ESS
## sigma       7.77      0.22     7.37     8.21 1.00     1139      741
```

Just as with the *t*-test, these similarities are due to the models having the same general structure, making the same assumptions, and being dominated by the likelihood of the parameters.

3.11 Exercises

The analyses in the main body of the text all involve only the unmodified 'actual' resonance level (in `exp_data`). Responses for the stimuli with the simulated 'big' resonance are reserved for exercises throughout. You can get the 'big' resonance in the `exp_ex` data frame, or all data in the `exp_data_all` data frame.

86 *Fitting Bayesian regression models with* brms

Fit and interpret one or more of the suggested models:

3   Easy: Analyze the (pre-fit) model that's exactly like `model_priors`, except using the data in `exp_ex` (`bmmb::get_model("3_model_priors_ex.RDS")`).
4   Medium: Fit a model just like `model_priors`, but for the data from some other group, for either the original or big resonance levels.
5   Hard: Fit two models like `model_priors` for two arbitrary groups, and compare results across models.

In any case, describe the model, present and explain the results, and include some figures.

4 Inspecting a 'single group' of observations using a Bayesian multilevel model

In the last chapter, we built a Bayesian regression model suitable for inspecting the average of a single group of observations. However, as we noted multiple times this model was 'wrong' for the structure of our data. The reason for this is that this model did not properly account for the *the repeated measures* in our data. To properly handle repeated measures data, we need a *multilevel model*. In this chapter, we will explain what we mean by 'repeated measures' and 'multilevel', in addition to fitting our first proper multilevel Bayesian model using `brms`.

4.1 Chapter pre-cap

In this chapter we discuss the analysis of data made up of multiple observations from members of a 'single group'. We explain the 'multilevel' component of 'Bayesian multilevel models', and explain what is meant by 'repeated measures data'. We introduce the problem of estimating factors with large numbers of levels, and present three approaches: No pooling, complete pooling, and adaptive partial pooling. After this, we fit a multilevel model with a structure that is more appropriate for our repeated measures data than the models presented in the previous chapter. We introduce the concepts of 'random' and 'fixed' effects and discuss how to inspect and manipulate random effects. We then simulate some repeated-measures data based on the parameters estimated by our model and see how the exclusion of different components affects our simulated data. Finally, we fit and interpret a model with a second 'random' effect to our data, and investigate the 'shrinkage' in the estimates of our 'random' model parameters.

4.2 Repeated measures data

Depending on the field of study, experiments often produce **repeated measures data**, data where multiple observations come from the same experimental unit (e.g. individual listeners, as in the data used in this book). As a practical matter, setting up experiments is often time-consuming such that it often makes more sense to collect, for example, 100 observations from each of 50 different people, rather than 1 observation from each of 5,000 different people. In addition, collecting more than one measurement from each source can go a long way toward reducing uncertainty in a model. However, the statistical analysis of repeated measures data requires models that take the repeated nature of the measurements into account. Treating repeated measures data as if it were *not* repeated measures data can cause problems for the inferences we make using statistical models.

DOI: 10.4324/9781003285878-4

88 *Observations using a Bayesian multilevel model*

For example, in our experiment, we are interested in the average apparent height of different speakers, or categories of speakers. Imagine we had an experiment with 10,000 total observations. Would it matter how these were distributed? What if we had 5,000 observations for each of two different speakers? In this case, we would have a lot of information about the apparent height of these speakers but not much information about speakers in general. What if we had 10 observations for each of 1,000 different speakers? In this case, we would have much more information about the apparent height of speakers in general, given the same number of overall observations. However, we have a lot less information about any individual speaker in the sample. So, we see two situations with the same total number of observations but substantially different internal structures.

In general, the reason repeated measures data can cause problems when not modeled appropriately is because the observations within each experimental unit are not independent: Multiple measurements from the same person are probably going to be similar to each other. This can give us a warped perspective regarding the degree and nature of the variability in a set of observations when repeated measures data is not modeled appropriately. For example, the final model we used to analyze our data in the last chapter looked like this:

$$\text{height}_{[i]} \sim \text{N}\left(\mu_{[i]}, \sigma\right)$$
$$\mu_{[i]} = \text{Intercept}$$

$$\text{Priors:}$$
$$\text{Intercept} \sim \text{N}(176, 15)$$
$$\sigma \sim \text{N}(0, 15)$$

(4.1)

We're going to consider the same data we discussed in Chapters 2 and 3, the apparent height judgments made for the adult male speakers in our experiment in the actual, unmodified resonance condition (see Section 1.3). Below we load the data that includes only these trials (`exp_data`) and subset to include only veridical male speakers:

```
library (bmmb)
data (exp_data)
men = exp_data[exp_data$C_v=='m',]

# create vector of height judgments
mens_height = men$height
```

Figure 4.1 presents the height judgments collected for adult male speakers in our experiment, organized in two different ways. In the left plot, we see the marginal distribution of the data with no differentiation made for the data collected from different listeners. This boxplot shows the individual observations of our vector $\text{height}_{[i]}$ around the overall mean μ with a standard distribution equal to σ. In other words, the left boxplot represents the model presented in (4.1). From the perspective of this model, an observation of 181 cm is +7 above the mean, regardless of who provided it, because 174 cm is the assumed mean for all listeners. As a consequence, all variation about the mean is noise. There is no systematic structure 'inside' that single giant box of data.

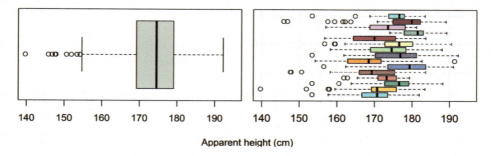

Figure 4.1 (left) Distribution of all apparent height judgments for adult male speakers. (right) Distribution of height judgments for adult male speakers, individually for each listener.

In the right plot, we see each listener's height judgments in a different boxplot. Clearly, each listener has a general tendency so that certain values are more or less surprising for individual listeners. For example, a height response of 181 cm is perfectly average for listener 6 (blue box, sixth from the bottom). Thus, if you know listener 6 provided a response, an apparent height of 181 cm should not be surprising. In fact, this would represent an error of 0 cm when provided by this listener, considered relative to their expected apparent height judgment. In contrast, a response of 174 cm, the overall average response, would be a relatively atypical response for this listener.

The failure to acknowledge the fact that listeners provided non-independent responses might not seem like a big deal but it really is. Remember from Section 2.3.2 that the calculation of joint probabilities (and densities) is 'easy' only if the model residuals are assumed to be independent. Well, on the right side of Figure 4.1, we see that all of our errors (i.e. deviations from the intercept at 174 cm) are definitely *not* independent, which means that ignoring this fact is going to lead to inaccuracies throughout our models. It's also a fact that we actually *do* have different listeners providing our data, and they do appear to vary from each other, and maybe we want to represent this in our model.

4.2.1 Multilevel models and 'levels' of variation

We can think of the repeated measures data presented in Figure 4.1 as having multiple 'levels' of variation. These levels are often referred to as *upper* and *lower* but this is entirely metaphorical/conceptual. Another way to think of them is as within-group variation (lower) and between-group variation (upper). We will describe these 'levels' of variation with respect to our repeated measures data involving the apparent heights of adult males presented in Figure 4.1.

- The 'lower' level: The data-level distribution of individual observations given a certain listener. This is the distribution of data points inside of each of the little boxes in the right plot in Figure 4.1. If not for this variation, the boxes in the plot would all be clustered about their respective listener means. So, the lower level of variation gives the listener boxes their widths and causes one response provided by a listener to differ randomly from another response from the same listener. For the

90 *Observations using a Bayesian multilevel model*

sake of simplicity, our models usually assume that the standard deviation is equal to σ for all of the listener-dependent distributions, though our models can relax this assumption (see Chapter 8).

- The 'upper' level: The distribution of *parameters* between your sources of data. The upper level of variation causes the boxes in the right plot of Figure 4.1 to not all be aligned at the grand mean. Although the listener mean is a parameter for the distribution of apparent height responses given the listener, it can also be thought of as a random variable. When we run an experiment we randomly 'sample' a small number of values of this variable by selecting a small number of humans to participate in our experiment. We might expect the average reported height for a single listener to be a relatively stable property such that a replication with the same listener should result in about the same listener mean. However, it's impossible to know any given listener's average apparent height judgment a priori. As a result, our listener means are as unpredictable to us as the individual responses provided by those listeners.

A **multilevel model** is a special kind of regression model that's able to simultaneously estimate random variation at multiple 'levels'. A multilevel model fit to our height judgments would be able to estimate the average reported by each listener, the variation in listener means, and the random within-listener variation, all at the same time. Model parameters describe some tendencies in the data. For now, we're just talking about average values. So, our model describes listeners in terms of their average response, which it encodes using parameters related to the listener means. As a result, when we say "the distribution of parameters" to refer to the distribution of listener means, we're really saying "the distribution of listener characteristics". So, when we say "multilevel models model variation at the data level and the parameter level", we're basically saying "multilevel models allow us to model the variation of data within listeners, and of parameters/characteristics between listeners".

Figure 4.2 compares visual representations of the same data, the points $y_{[1]}\cdots y_{[6]}$, represented as unilevel or multilevel models. In the unilevel model there is only one distribution, the data distribution, and a single random source of variation, the data-level error σ. Since there is no 'upper' level describing between-listener variation, our model doesn't 'know' our data contains repeated observations from a small number of listeners. In addition, our model has no mechanism by which to explain, for example, why $y_{[1]}$ and $y_{[2]}$ have such low values. This model treats all deviations from the mean as random and therefore acts as if systematic between-listener variation did not exist. It also treats all variation around the mean as totally independent, which we know it is not.

In contrast, the multilevel model in the same figure introduces an intervening second level between the observations and the grand mean μ. This level features some new symbols, these are:

1   listener-specific effects representing the difference between the listener mean and the grand mean, $L_{[j]}$ for listener j.
2   σ_L, the standard deviation of the listener effects.

Notice that we are now estimating two variance components, the data-level error (σ) and the random between-listener variation σ_L. This seemingly small difference

Figure 4.2 Comparison of the structure of a statistical model with only a single level of variation (a 'unilevel model', left), to a model with multiple levels of variation (a multilevel model, right).

in structure results in important changes in our model. For example, since the total amount of variation in the data is fixed, as variation in the second level (σ_L) grows larger, variation at the first level (σ) *necessarily* gets smaller.

We can see this happening in Figure 4.2. In the unilevel model, $y_{[1]}$ and $y_{[2]}$ where low values 'for no reason', resulting in large deviations from our expectations and a large σ (the blue distribution). Now, we know that $y_{[1]}$ and $y_{[2]}$ are low because listener 2 ($L_{[2]}$) tends to provide low values. As a result, the large deviations between $y_{[1]}$, $y_{[2]}$, and the grand mean (μ) are mainly attributed to σ_L (the green distribution) rather than σ. In the multilevel model, it is only the relatively small amount of within-listener variation that is directly attributed to σ, resulting in a substantial reduction in the data-level error.

One thing to note is that if there is no between-listener variation, i.e. if $\sigma_L = 0$, the the multilevel model above converges *structurally* on the unilevel model. For example, if σ_L is near zero all the listener effects would need to have very small values. If this occurred, all the densities at the lower level in the right plot in Figure 4.2 would overlap, and look a lot like the single density in the left side of the figure. In addition, the second level distribution would effectively be meaningless/useless since it would represent no systematic variation between listeners. This potential equivalence is a very important feature of multilevel models. Since the multilevel model *estimates* values of L and σ_L, the outcome $\sigma_L \approx 0$ is within the realm of possibility. So, fitting a multilevel model allows one to investigate the very existence of systematic variation in parameters across research units (e.g. listeners) but does not necessarily *impose* this on data if such systematic variation is not present.

4.3 Representing predictors with many levels

Before moving on to a discussion of multilevel models and parameter estimation strategies, we want to take a moment to discuss some practical and notational issues that arise when your models include factors with large numbers of levels. First, we will discuss a way to efficiently represent models including factors with many levels as predictors. After that, we will discuss some 'quirks' in the way that R names model parameters and the way that we've chosen to represent this in our model notation.

92 *Observations using a Bayesian multilevel model*

R treats nominal, categorical predictors (such as listener) as *factors* and assumes that each different label represents a different group. Each value of a factor is called a *level*. Although we can indicate listeners using numbers, we're not treating this predictor as numerical or otherwise quantitative. Instead, we treat listener (L) as a factor, and the individual listeners in the experiments are its levels. As far as our models are concerned, participant/speaker/subject/listener has no special status as a predictor and it is just a factor with (usually) many levels.

In order to estimate a separate effect for each listener, we need to add 15 parameters to our model, $L_{[1]},...,L_{[15]}$, one for each listener. In order to represent these predictors, our model descriptions could include a predictor for each listener coefficient that would equal one or zero based on whether the row was contributed by that listener (1) or not (0). For example, in (4.2) we see a line consisting of a set of 15 predictors associated with the L coefficients, all multiplied by zero save for the second one. The effect of this, seen in the second line in (4.2), is to only have the second listener coefficient contribute to the predicted value for observation i. In other words, observation i was contributed by listener 2 for this data.

$$\mu_{[i]} = \text{Intercept} + L_{[1]} \cdot 0 + L_{[2]} \cdot 1 + L_{[3]} \cdot 0 + ... + L_{[15]} \cdot 0$$
$$\mu_{[i]} = \text{Intercept} + L_{[2]}$$

(4.2)

This is actually how regression models represent these sorts of predictors 'under the hood'. However, if every single factor level were to get an independent parameter represented in the regression equations in this book, these would become very long and difficult to interpret. For example, we have 139 different speakers in our data, meaning our prediction equation would be extremely long if we included each of these predictors as separate terms. Instead, we can treat the effects associated with the levels of a factor as a vector, and just pick the correct element of this vector for each observation in our data. In order to know which listener contributed each observation, we also need an index variable, a variable that equals a number from one to 15 that indicates which listener parameter to use on that trial. This is the `L` column in our data (`exp_data`), the listener predictor.

For example, below we see that our listener predictor has a value of 1 for observation 1 and a value of 8 for observation 1,000. This tells us that the first listener provided the first observation and the eighth listener provided the 1000th observation. It tells our model to use $L_{[1]}$ for observation 1 and $L_{[8]}$ for observation 1,000. In general, we should use $L_{[j]}$ for observation i when the listener prediction is equal to j for that observation (i.e. `exp_data$L[i]=j`).

```
exp_data$L[1]
## [1] 1
exp_data$L[1000]
## [1] 8
```

Unfortunately, this leads to some notational strangeness. R names the vector of coefficients in your model using the same name as your predictor. So, the vector of listener effects in your model won't have an interpretable name like `listener_effects`. Instead, we have a predictor called `L` which represents listeners, *and*, we

Observations using a Bayesian multilevel model 93

have a set of coefficients called L in our model that represent the effects for each of our listeners. As a result, our regression equations will include terms that look like this, $L_{\left[\mathsf{L}_{[i]}\right]}$, which means: "Coefficient L, and the level is the one indicated by value of the L predictor (L) for trial i". This term is now included in our prediction equation in (4.3), which says: The expected value for any given trial is equal to the intercept, plus the listener effect (L) specific to the listener that contributed that trial as indicated by the L vector (L in our model).

$$\mu_{[i]} = \text{Intercept} + L_{\left[\mathsf{L}_{[i]}\right]} \tag{4.3}$$

We think the $L_{\left[\mathsf{L}_{[i]}\right]}$ notation is potentially confusing, and not ideal. However, the only way we can have formal model descriptions that actually match the name of our model coefficients *and* the names of the predictors they are associated with is by giving these the same names. One thing we'll do to try to make things clearer is use different font for the predictors (L) and the corresponding coefficients (L). So, when you see terms like these $L_{\left[\mathsf{L}_{[i]}\right]}$ in your models, this is nothing more than a compact way of representing the same model structure shown in (4.2).

For example, if your data contains a predictor called L (L) whose first three values are 2, 4, and 1, then we need parameters $L_{[2]}$, $L_{[4]}$, and $L_{[1]}$ for the first three trials. We can get the correct listener effect for each trial using the information in our listener predictor. We can see how this would work in the example in (4.4), showing the combination of intercepts and listener effects for the first three observations in our hypothetical example. In each case, we find the value of the predictor L for observation i and use this to fetch the correct listener effect (L) for our regression equation for that observation.

$$\mathsf{L}_{[1]} = 2, \mathsf{L}_{[2]} = 4, \mathsf{L}_{[3]} = 1,\ldots$$

$$\mu_{[i=1]} = \text{Intercept} + L_{\left[\mathsf{L}_{[i=1]}\right]} = \text{Intercept} + L_{[2]}$$

$$\mu_{[i=2]} = \text{Intercept} + L_{\left[\mathsf{L}_{[i=2]}\right]} = \text{Intercept} + L_{[4]} \tag{4.4}$$

$$\mu_{[i=3]} = \text{Intercept} + L_{\left[\mathsf{L}_{[i=3]}\right]} = \text{Intercept} + L_{[1]}$$

$$\ldots$$

The example above says: We add the intercept to the effect for listener 2 to get our expected value for observation 1 (i.e. observation 1 was contributed by listener 2), we add the intercept to the effect for listener 4 to get our expected value for observation 2 (i.e. observation 2 was contributed by listener 4), and so on, for all observations in our data.

4.4 Strategies for estimating factors with many levels

We know that the 15 values of L are related by being different listeners in our experiment. The way you tell your model that these coefficients are related is by treating them as levels of the same factor rather than as unrelated coefficients. One way to

94 *Observations using a Bayesian multilevel model*

think of factors is that they represent 'batches' of coefficients in your model that are thematically or conceptually related (more on this in Chapter 11). Once you encode the fact that there are 'batches' of parameters in your model, you have several options with respect to how these batches are estimated.

Gelman and colleagues (Gelman and Hill, 2006; Gelman et al. 2013) distinguish three general ways that parameters related to levels of a factor can be estimated: (1) *Complete pooling*, (2) *No pooling*, and (3) *Partial pooling*. The distinction between complete, no, and partial pooling is made for each factor in a model. So, one factor may be estimated using partial pooling while another may be estimated using no pooling. This makes understanding the distinction between these approaches very important.

4.4.1 Complete pooling

In the last chapter, we carried out a **complete pooling** analysis of our data, presented in (4.1). That is, we threw everything into one big pile and analyzed it as if it came from one undifferentiated group (as in the unilevel model in Figure 4.2). There are several problems with this approach when applied to our experimental data. First, the complete pooling approach does not allow us to make any statements about variation between listeners since it does not estimate values of L. In fact, this model assumes that σ_L is equal to zero (or does not exist). As noted earlier, if listeners do not differ from each other in any way, then σ_L will be equal to zero and the two models in Figure 4.2 will converge on each other. However, if σ_L is *not* zero, then this approach will miss out on important information.

There is perhaps a more serious problem with the complete pooling approach for repeated measures data. The complete pooling model assumes that all deviations from the mean are due to random error. Recall that regression models assume that all random variation around expected values (i.e. the residuals) are independent. Since independence is assumed, likelihoods are calculated the 'easy' way by multiplying individual marginal probabilities (see Sections 2.3.2 and 2.7.1). However, as we can see in Figure 4.1, each listener had a slightly different average judged height. This means that the residuals associated with each individual listener are not independent and may be related. For example, we expect almost all of listener 12's residuals to be positive (i.e. larger than average) since nearly all of this listener's responses were above the overall average μ. The violation of the assumption of independent residuals means that if we're using a complete pooling approach for our repeated measures data we are calculating likelihoods the 'wrong' way. Basically, our data has 675 rows but not 675 totally independent observations, but our model doesn't know this. As a result, the information provided by our model may not be reliable.

We've previously mentioned that our models are not exactly 'right' or 'true', so why does it matter all of a sudden that the complete pooling model is 'wrong'? Recall that in Section 2.7.1 we mentioned that the likelihood function gets narrower as a function of the sample size n. This applies only to n *independent* observations, but not necessarily to *dependent* observations. As a result, when we treat dependent observations as independent our likelihood may end up being narrower than is warranted. This gives us a false sense of security about how precise our parameter estimates are. Basically, spherical models of billiards balls are wrong but useful, while cubic models of the balls are wrong and less useful. Treating residuals both within and across listeners as independent is kind of like using a cubic model of a billiard ball.

4.4.2 No pooling

To account for systematic variation between listeners in the data we can include listener predictors (L) in our model, as in (4.5). When we estimate the levels of this factor with **no pooling**, we estimate every level of the factor totally independently. One way to model this mathematically is to think of these coefficients as coming from a uniform distribution that extends from negative to positive infinity. The uniform distribution is just a flat line, meaning any value in the interval is equally likely. So, a uniform distribution extending from positive to negative infinity places absolutely no restrictions on the possible values of a parameter and says absolutely any value is equally likely. This is equivalent to setting $\sigma_L = \infty$. As a result, we can see complete and no pooling as two extremes, in one case we assume there is no between-listener variation at all and in the other we assume that between-listener variation can potentially be infinitely large.

In (4.5) we see that in our no pooling model, the expected value (μ) for each trial is the sum of our intercept and the listener predictor, and that each of the L terms is drawn from the same uniform distribution. We introduce the notation $[\bullet]$ to represent every individual level of a factor. Below, we note that each of the 15 listener effects $\left(L_{[\bullet]}\right)$ was individually drawn from the same uniform distribution.

$$\text{height}_{[i]} \sim N\left(\mu_{[i]}, \sigma\right)$$
$$\mu_{[i]} = \text{Intercept} + L_{\left[L_{[i]}\right]}$$

$$(4.5)$$

$$\text{Priors:}$$
$$L_{[\bullet]} \sim \text{uniform}(-\infty, \infty)$$

$$\text{Intercept} \sim N(176, 15)$$

There are two main weaknesses to this approach. First, assuming that $\sigma_L = \infty$ does not allow **regularization** (also known as *shrinkage*, see Section 3.3.3) to occur across the levels of the factor. Shrinkage occurs when an estimate is pulled toward its prior mean. However, a perfectly uniform prior does not exert any influence on posterior distributions, so that these are completely reflective of the likelihood function. In the absence of shrinkage, the characteristics of each listener are estimated as if only a single listener had taken part in our experiment. But we don't have one listener, we have 15, and they all performed the experiment in quite similar ways. Clearly, it may be useful if our model could consider what it knows about the values of L in general when it estimates the value of $L_{[j]}$ for any given listener j.

The second weakness of a no pooling approach is that these models do not represent information about the range of credible values for the levels of a factor. For example, below we see some quantiles for the average apparent height reported for adult male speakers by the listeners in our experiment:

```
listener_means = tapply (men$height, men$L, mean)
quantile(listener_means)
##      0%    25%    50%    75%   100%
## 167.8 170.5 174.1 175.9 180.9
```

96 *Observations using a Bayesian multilevel model*

These listeners each carried out this experiment independently and did not know each other. Despite this, we see below that half of listeners' average height judgments are between 171 and 176 cm, and that all listener averages fell between 168 and 181 cm. The consistency of these judgments suggests a common behavior between listeners and an underlying similarity in listener characteristics and parameters. Given this, it might be surprising if a new listener carried out the experiment and provided an average height judgment of 130 cm for adult males. Although our model does include information about individual listeners, it cannot represent information about more or less likely values for listener effects.

4.4.3 (Adaptive) Partial pooling

Complete pooling and no pooling offer extremes: We either assume σ_L is zero or we assume it is infinite. Partial pooling offers a sort of middle ground between complete pooling and no pooling, a potential 'just right' compromise solution. **Partial pooling** estimates the values of L using non-zero values of σ_L, meaning that the parameters representing the levels of a factor are neither completely independent nor totally merged. This allows the parameter estimates to share information and often results in the parameters being more similar to each other compared to when they are fit using no pooling.

Technically speaking, we can fit a model with partial pooling by specifying any finite prior probability for our parameters. So, simply drawing the L parameters from any given shared distribution (e.g. $L_{[\bullet]} \sim N(0,30)$) would constitute a partial pooling estimate of the parameters. However, we know that our prior probability can help to pull parameters toward the prior mean (as discussed in Section 3.3.2), resulting in *shrinkage*. In order for this to work effectively, the variance of the prior needs to be set at a reasonable value given the amount of variation in the data. Below, we see that the standard deviation of listener means is 3.6 cm. It would be nice to be able to use a value close to this since we know this to be a good fit for our data. Unfortunately, if we did this it would not really be a *prior* probability anymore, since we would be analyzing the data, finding the most likely parameter values, and then using that to set what is supposed to be the *prior* probability.

```
sd(listener_means)
## [1] 3.594
```

Instead of doing this, we can estimate σ_L using our data. This allows us to have a prior distribution for our parameters that is tailored to the data, without us having to actually specify it a priori. When standard deviation parameters like σ_L are estimated from the data rather than specified a priori, this is called **adaptive partial pooling**. Often, the 'adaptive' part is dropped and authors may describe the method as partial pooling when they mean specifically *adaptive* partial pooling. So, when you read that a factor was estimated using 'partial pooling', most often that means that the standard deviation parameter corresponding to that factor (e.g. σ_L for L) was estimated from the data. We will refer to it as *adaptive pooling*, tending to drop the 'partial', in order to clearly communicate when we refer to parameters whose variance parameters (e.g. σ_L) are estimated from the data.

The adaptive (partial) pooling version of our model is presented in (4.6). There are two important differences with respect to the model in (4.5). First, the $L_{[\bullet]}$ terms are drawn from a normal distribution with a mean of zero and a standard deviation equal

Observations using a Bayesian multilevel model 97

to σ_L. The reason the mean of the distribution is equal to zero is that our listener coefficients only encode deviations relative to the intercept, and not the listener average. So, a listener that is perfectly average will have a coefficient equal to 0. Second, since the σ_L term is estimated from the data a prior distribution for σ_L is specified. This is because prior probabilities must be specified for all estimated parameters in our model, and σ_L is now being estimated.

$$\text{height}_{[i]} \sim N\left(\mu_{[i]}, \sigma\right)$$
$$\mu_{[i]} = \text{Intercept} + L_{\left[L_{[i]}\right]}$$

$$\text{Priors}:$$
$$L_{[\cdot]} \sim N(0, \sigma_L) \tag{4.6}$$

$$\text{Intercept} \sim N(176, 15)$$
$$\sigma \sim N(0, 15)$$
$$\sigma_L \sim N(0, 15)$$

This approach is called adaptive partial pooling because the estimate of each level of L is *partially* influenced by every other level of L by virtue of being drawn from the same distribution $N(0, \sigma_L)$. For example, we saw that half of listener mean height judgments were between 170 and 176 cm, and our model will now take that into account when estimating the individual coefficients that make up L. So, unlike the complete pooling case, we do not ignore variation between listeners, and unlike in the no-pooling case, we do not ignore the similarities between them. In addition, the amount of blending that occurs across levels is determined by the data, and so the method is 'adaptive' to the specific situation.

4.4.4 Hyperpriors

You may have noticed that in (4.6) we assign a prior distribution to σ_L. However, σ_L is a parameter in the prior distribution of our listener parameters $L_{[\cdot]}$. So actually, the prior for σ_L is the prior of a prior. We might call this a 'grand prior' (like a grandparent) but the actual term for it is **hyperprior**. One way to think of it is that in a multilevel model, each level effectively acts as the prior for the level below it. This leads to a nested or hierarchical model structure (sometimes multilevel models are called **hierarchical models** for this reason).

We're going to update the equation defining our posterior distributions (originally presented in (3.12)) to take into account the structure of our partial pooling models. Our model will now reflect not only our prior beliefs but also the information encoded in our hyperpriors, and it will estimate the distribution of σ_L from the data. We can begin with the posterior probability of observing a given value of $L_{[\cdot]}$ for a single listener in isolation. Equation (4.7) says that the posterior probability of some listener effect $\left(L_{[\cdot]}\right)$ given the data y is equal to the product of the likelihood of $L_{[\cdot]}$ given the data $\left(P\left(y \mid L_{[\cdot]}\right)\right)$ and the prior of $L_{[\cdot]}$ $\left(P\left(L_{[\cdot]}\right)\right)$, divided by the marginal probability of the data $\left(P(y)\right)$.

98 *Observations using a Bayesian multilevel model*

$$P\left(L_{[\cdot]} \mid y\right) = \frac{P\left(y \mid L_{[\cdot]}\right) \cdot P\left(L_{[\cdot]}\right)}{P(y)} \tag{4.7}$$

If we want to consider the posterior probability of σ_L given the data, we can add σ_L to every term that previously included $L_{[\cdot]}$ in (4.7). Basically, we're saying σ_L *and* $L_{[\cdot]}$, instead of just $L_{[\cdot]}$. Equation (4.8) can be read aloud as "the posterior probability of observing a certain listener effect *and* a certain amount of between-listener variation given some data $\left(P\left(L_{[\cdot]}, \sigma_L \mid y\right)\right)$ is equal to the likelihood of the data given the listener effect and the amount of variation between listeners $\left(P\left(y \mid L_{[\cdot]}, \sigma_L\right)\right)$, times the joint prior probability of the listener effect and the amount of variation between listeners $\left(P\left(L_{[\cdot]}, \sigma_L\right)\right)$, divided by the marginal probability of the data $\left(P(y)\right)$".

$$P\left(L_{[\cdot]}, \sigma_L \mid y\right) = \frac{P\left(y \mid L_{[\cdot]}, \sigma_L\right) \cdot P\left(L_{[\cdot]}, \sigma_L\right)}{P(y)} \tag{4.8}$$

We know that we can represent the joint probability of a listener effect and the listener standard deviation, $P\left(L_{[\cdot]}, \sigma_L\right)$, using normalized conditional probabilities as in $P\left(L_{[\cdot]} \mid \sigma_L\right) \cdot P(\sigma_L)$ (see Chapter 2). We can also remove the listener standard deviation (σ_L) from the likelihood of $L_{[\cdot]}$ given the data $\left(P\left(y \mid L_{[\cdot]}\right)\right)$, because we know that the probability of any given data point in a normal distribution depends only on the mean of the distribution and not the standard deviation of means *between* distributions (i.e. σ_L). These two changes are reflected in (4.9). The first term in the numerator on the right-hand side is the likelihood, this was in our original equation in (4.7). The second term is the prior distribution of listener effects. This also appeared in (4.7), however, this distribution now allows for variation in the value of σ_L. Finally, the third term $\left(P(\sigma_L)\right)$ represents the hyperprior, the prior distribution of one of the parameters of another prior distribution.

$$P\left(L_{[\cdot]}, \sigma_L \mid y\right) = \frac{P\left(y \mid L_{[\cdot]}\right) \cdot P\left(L_{[\cdot]} \mid \sigma_L\right) \cdot P(\sigma_L)}{P(y)} \tag{4.9}$$

Our posterior estimates of $L_{[\cdot]}$ may differ from our no pooling estimates of the listener effects. This is because, in addition to the individual parameter likelihoods, the posterior probability of $L_{[\cdot]}$ in (4.9) takes into account the estimates of σ_L. When our posterior estimates of the listener (or any other) effects are more similar to the population average, and to each other, than the no pooling estimates, *regularization* has occurred. Importantly, the amount of pooling/shrinkage that will occur will be determined by σ_L, which is estimated from the data itself.

4.5 Estimating a multilevel model with `brms`

We're going to fit a model to the same data we investigated in Chapter 3, however, we're going to use a multilevel model that reflects the repeated measures nature of the data.

Observations using a Bayesian multilevel model 99

4.5.1 Data and research questions

Below we load and subset our full data to only include those trials involving adult male speakers, and only when the actual resonance size was presented. This is the same data we considered in Chapters 2 and 3.

```
# load book package and brms
library (bmmb)
library (brms)

# load and subset experimental data
data (exp_data)
men = exp_data[exp_data$C_v=='m',]
```

Once again, we're going to try to address the following basic research questions:

(Q1) How tall does the average adult male sound?
(Q2) Can we set limits on credible average apparent heights based on the data we collected?

To analyze our data using `brms` in R we need it to be in a data frame with each row containing a different observation. We need one column representing our dependent variable (the variable we want to analyze) and one column that indicates the 'source' of the data. The relevant columns in our data are:

- `L`: An integer from 1 to 15 indicating which *listener* responded to the trial.
- `height`: A floating-point number representing the *height* (in centimeters) reported for the speaker on each trial.

We can see that our data satisfies these conditions below, where the relevant columns (for this model) are `L` for listeners and `height` for our dependent variable.

```
head (men)
##       L C height R  S C_v  vtl   f0 dur G A G_v A_v
## 93   1 m  169.9 a 47    m 14.8 172 339 m a   m   a
## 95   1 m  173.5 a 48    m 15.6 108 236 m a   m   a
## 97   1 m  172.0 a 49    m 15.5  96 315 m a   m   a
## 99   1 b  157.7 a 50    m 14.5 134 240 m c   m   a
## 101  1 m  153.4 a 51    m 15.0 122 241 m a   m   a
## 103  1 m  174.2 a 52    m 14.8 101 259 m a   m   a
```

Often, experiments (or data more generally) will feature a single factor that indicated the 'source' of information. However, in this experiment, we have both speakers producing our data and listeners providing judgments about our data. This leads to non-independent observations based on both speaker *and* listener. For example, a speaker who sounded tall to one person may have sounded tall to other listeners, and listeners who identified all speakers as generally tall/short would have done so in a similar way across all speakers. We'll begin by building a model that only incorporates information about listeners before discussing a model that includes information regarding both speakers and listeners later in the chapter.

100   *Observations using a Bayesian multilevel model*

4.5.2 *Description of the model*

To specify a multilevel model, you need to write a slightly more complicated model formula. This explanation assumes that you have a data frame where one column contains the variable you are interested in predicting (in this case `height`), and another column contains a vector containing unique labels for each grouping factor (e.g. speaker, listener, and participant) in this case a unique listener label `L`. Before, the model formula looked like this:

```
height ~ 1
```

Which meant 'predict height using only an overall intercept'. To indicate that your model contains an 'upper' level where you have repeated measures clusters of data coming from different sources, you have to put another model formula *inside* your main model formula. The formula corresponding to the model shown in (4.6) looks like this:

```
height ~ 1 + ( 1 | L)
```

Which means 'predict height using an overall intercept and separate intercepts for each level of the L (listener) factor'. In mathematical notation, this symbol | (called 'pipe') means "given that" or "conditional on". It can effectively be interpreted in the same way in our models: "estimate an intercept *given* each level of the L predictor". So, when you place a predictor in parenthesis on the right-hand side of a pipe |, like this `( | predictor )`, you tell `brm` that you would like to estimate separate parameters for each level of the factor. Whatever you put in the left-hand side of the parentheses `( in here | predictor )` specifies the parameters you wish to estimate for each level of the factor. In addition, any parameters specified on the left-hand side of the pipes in parentheses, `( in here | predictor )`, will be estimated using adaptive partial pooling. By convention, effects estimated using adaptive pooling are modeled as coming from a normal distribution with a mean of zero, so that aspect of the model does not need to be directly specified.

So, the model formula `height ~ 1 + ( 1 | L)` tells `brms` to build an intercept-only model with a separate intercept for each listener, and that the listener intercept terms should be estimated with adaptive pooling. This model formula specifies a subset of the information provided in our full model specification shown in (4.10) (originally (4.6)).

$$\text{height}_{[i]} \sim \text{N}\left(\mu_{[i]}, \sigma\right)$$

$$\mu_{[i]} = \text{Intercept} + L_{\left[\mathsf{L}_{[i]}\right]}$$

$$\text{Priors}:$$

$$L_{[\cdot]} \sim \text{N}\left(0, \sigma_L\right)$$

$$\text{Intercept} \sim \text{N}\left(176, 15\right)$$

$$\sigma \sim \text{N}\left(0, 15\right)$$

$$\sigma_L \sim \text{N}\left(0, 15\right)$$

(4.10)

As a reminder, we use the notation $L_{[\cdot]}$ to indicate that this prior distribution applies individually to every member of the set. In our case, each of our 15 listener effects is drawn from the same normal distribution, one at a time (i.e. $L_{[1]} \sim N(0, \sigma_L), \ldots, L_{[15]} \sim N(0, \sigma_L)$). In plain English, the model above says:

> *We expect height judgments to be normally distributed around the expected value for any given trial, $\mu_{[i]}$, with some unknown standard deviation σ. The expected value for a trial is equal to a fixed overall average (Intercept) and some value associated with the individual listener who made a perceptual judgment on the trial $\left(L_{[\mathfrak{l}_{[i]}]}\right)$. The listener coefficients $\left(L_{[\cdot]}\right)$ were modeled as coming from a normal distribution with a mean of zero and a standard deviation (σ_L) that was estimated from the data.*

There is a very important difference in how the 'unilevel' (complete pooling) model from Chapter 3, and this model partition the variance in apparent talker heights. The initial complete pooling model broke down the total variation in the data (σ_{total}) like this:

$$\sigma^2_{\text{total}} = \sigma^2 \tag{4.11}$$

In other words, all variation was error. We don't know why values vary from the mean, so all variation is just random noise. Our multilevel model views the variation in our data like this:

$$\sigma^2_{\text{total}} = \sigma^2_L + \sigma^2 \tag{4.12}$$

The total variance is equal to the within-listener variance (σ^2) plus the between-listener variance (σ^2_L). From the perspective of this model, the variation *within* a speaker's individual boxplot is (data-level) error. The differences from listener to listener represent random between-listener variation in apparent height judgments (i.e. listener-level error). To some extent, investigating the *effects* for the different listeners in our sample involves asking how much the listener averages tended to differ from the overall response. So, a crucial part of investigating the overall effect of different listeners on our results is understanding the magnitude of σ_L.

4.5.3 *Fitting the model*

We can use `brms` to fit a model that more closely resembles our model specification in (4.10). To do this we need to use the formula given above, and we also need to specify priors for three estimated parameters: Intercept, σ_L, and σ. We can confirm our expectations using the `get_prior` function as seen below. This time we use a clone of the function in the `bmmb` package simply because the output of the 'real' function sometimes doesn't like it when you omit columns from the output (which we need to do so that it will fit on the page).

```
bmmb::get_prior (height ~ 1 + (1|L), data = men) [,-c(7:9)]
##                          prior      class       coef group resp dpar    source
##   student_t(3, 174.5, 7.1) Intercept                               default
```

102 *Observations using a Bayesian multilevel model*

```
##      student_t(3, 0, 7.1)    sd                      default
##      student_t(3, 0, 7.1)    sd              L       default
##      student_t(3, 0, 7.1)    sd  Intercept   L       default
##      student_t(3, 0, 7.1)    sigma                   default
```

We see a new `class` of prior, `sd`. Our classes of priors are now:

- `Intercept`: This is a unique class, only for intercepts.
- `sd`: This is for standard deviation parameters related to 'batches' of parameters, e.g. `sd(Intercept)` for L (σ_L).
- `sigma`: The data-level error term.

The information presented by `get_prior` does not just list the priors that must be specified, but also different ways that priors can be set, so there are some redundancies. This is not so necessary for our very simple models now but it will become very useful later so it is worth understanding now while it's still relatively simple. Top to bottom, here is the information presented in the output above. First, you can specify a prior for the `Intercept`, which is its own unique class. Second, you can specify a prior for *all* `sd` parameters in your model. Third, you can specify a prior for all the `sd` parameters, specifically for your L group. The fourth line indicates that you can also specify a prior *only* for the `Intercept` for your L group (i.e. *L*) and not to any other listener-related predictors in your model (there are none for now). The fifth line lets you specify the prior for the error in the model (i.e. σ). Right now, we only have one `sd` parameter and so all this flexibility is not so useful, but later on, we might want to specify different priors for different `sd` parameters and so this will come in handy.

Below we fit a model and specify prior distributions for our intercept, for *all* variables in the `sd` class, and for the error term (basically the first, second, and fifth lines above).

```r
# Fit the model yourself
model_multilevel =  brms::brm (
  height ~ 1 + (1|L), data = men, chains = 4, cores = 4,
  warmup = 1000, iter = 3500, thin = 2,
  prior = c(brms::set_prior("normal(176, 15)", class = "Intercept"),
          brms::set_prior("normal(0, 15)", class = "sd"),
          brms::set_prior("normal(0, 15)", class = "sigma")))

# Or download it from the GitHub page:
model_multilevel = bmmb::get_model ('4_model_multilevel.RDS')
```

4.5.4 *Interpreting the model*

We can inspect the model print statement:

```r
# inspect model
bmmb::short_summary (model_multilevel)
## Formula:  height ~ 1 + (1 | L)
```

```
## 
## Group-Level Effects:
## ~L (Number of levels: 15)
##                 Estimate Est.Error l-95% CI u-95% CI
## sd(Intercept)       3.78       0.87     2.47     5.84
## 
## Population-Level Effects:
##             Estimate Est.Error l-95% CI u-95% CI
## Intercept      173.8      1.02    171.8    175.8
## 
## Family Specific Parameters:
##        Estimate Est.Error l-95% CI u-95% CI
## sigma      7.03      0.19     6.67     7.41
```

This model contains one new chunk in its print statement, the `Group-Level Effects`, which tells us the standard deviation of the listener-dependent intercepts ($sd(Intercept)$) in the sample, σ_L. Below, we calculate the listener mean height values, the standard deviation of these, and the amount of within-listener variation in apparent height judgments. We can see that these resemble the value of the analogous parameters in our model.

```
# find mean height for each listener
listener_means = aggregate (height ~ L, data = men, FUN = mean)

# find the within listener standard deviation
# This is the within-talker 'error'.
listener_sigmas = aggregate (height ~ L, data = men, FUN = sd)

# the mean of the listener means corresponds to our Intercept
mean (listener_means$height)
## [1] 173.8

# the standard deviation of the listener means corresponds
# to 'sd(Intercept)', the estimate of the standard deviation
# of listener intercepts
sd (listener_means$height)
## [1] 3.594

# the average within-listener standard deviation corresponds
# to sigma, the estimated error
mean (listener_sigmas$height)
## [1] 6.822
```

We're going to discuss the calculations we made above in terms of what they represent in the boxplot in Figure 4.3, our model coefficients in the print statement above, and in our model definition in (4.10).

104   Observations using a Bayesian multilevel model

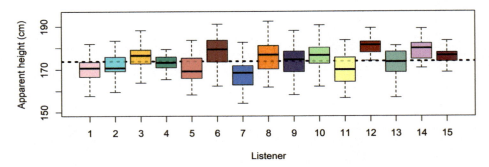

Figure 4.3 Listener-specific boxplots for apparent height judgments made for adult male speakers. The horizontal line represents the model intercept.

The overall mean height in our data (173.8) corresponds quite well to our model intercept of 173.8, seen in the horizontal line in the figure. The standard deviation of the listener means is 3.6 cm. This is very similar to our model estimate of 3.8 cm (`sd(Intercept)`). The standard deviation of the listener effects reflects the average distance from each speaker's average to the overall average and reflects σ_L in our model. Finally, the average of the within-speaker standard deviations in our data (6.8 cm) corresponds closely to our model's error estimate (`sigma` = 7.0), represented by σ in our model. This reflects the average spread of each speaker's data relative to their own mean, within their own little box in the figure. We can see that the information provided by `brms` is quite similar to what we can estimate directly using our data. However, *brms* does this all for us, in addition to giving us information regarding credible intervals for different parameters.

4.6 'Random' effects

If you have some familiarity with statistical modeling or the analysis of experimental or repeated measures data, you may have heard of **random-effects models** or **mixed-effects models**. People often distinguish the predictors in their models between those that are 'fixed' and those that are 'random'. So, a researcher might describe their model as including 'random effects' for so and so and 'fixed effects' for some other predictor. In fact, a very common way of describing our model above would be that we used a 'mixed-effect model with random intercepts by listener'. What makes a predictor fixed or random and what is the practical effect of this in our models? It turns out that although they are commonly used, the terms 'fixed' and 'random' effects do not have a single agreed-upon definition. Gelman (2005, p. 20) highlights five different definitions of the terms given in the literature:

1   Fixed effects are constant across individuals/groups, while random effects can vary across them.
2   Effects are fixed when you are interested in them specifically, but random if you are actually interested in the population.
3   When a sample represents the whole population, the effect is fixed. If the sample is a small part of the population, the effect is random.

Observations using a Bayesian multilevel model 105

4   If the effect is assumed to be an observation from a random variable, it is a random effect.
5   Fixed effects are estimated using maximum likelihood and no pooling. Random effects are estimated using partial pooling (and shrinkage).

You will note that some of these definitions would have an effect change from random to fixed based on the researcher's conception of it. Rather than focus on effects as fixed or random in *theory*, we may ask: What is the difference between these sorts of effects in *practice*? What special treatment are we referring to when we say that a certain predictor in our model is a 'random effect'? The answer is that when researchers discuss the inclusion of **random effects** in their models, what they are usually (if not always) referring to is that the effects were estimated using adaptive partial pooling. When researchers indicate that their effects were **fixed effects**, they are usually saying that they were fit with no, or at least minimal, pooling (i.e. using weak priors). This applies to both Bayesian models, and to models fit using more 'traditional' approaches such as the popular `lmer` function in the `lme4` package in R (Bates et al. 2015).

As a result, although researchers may define 'random' effects using any of the definitions above, in practice, terms labeled 'random' are usually those estimated using adaptive partial pooling. In light of this, Gelman and Hill (2006) recommend avoiding the terms 'fixed' and 'random', since these are vaguely defined and overly-broad. Although we agree with this position, the fact is that in many research areas it is still most common to refer to effects as being either fixed or random. For that reason, we will follow this convention, although we will continuously highlight the relevant underlying distinction: That so-called 'random' effects are simply those that are estimated using adaptive partial pooling.

In general, when you have many levels of a factor, it may be a good idea to include these as 'random' effects, regardless of how 'random' they might actually be. There is not much downside to it: You get more information from the model (e.g. information about $\sigma_{\text{predictor}}$), there are several modeling advantages associated with estimating large batches of coefficients with adaptive pooling (see Chapter 11), and you can always fit multiple models to see what, if any differences, exist across the two approaches. Rather than considering the more 'philosophical' position outlined in 1–5 above, some useful things to consider when deciding between fixed and random effects are: Do you believe that treating a predictor as a 'random' effect offers a modeling advantage? Does it better reflect the process/relationships you're trying to understand? Does it provide you with information you find useful? Is it realistic to fit this kind of model given the amount of data you have, and the nature of the relationships in the data? Right now the last point is not something we've talked about very much, but it is something we will need to worry about as our models become more complicated.

4.6.1 Inspecting the random effects

You may have noted that the estimates of our coefficients fit with adaptive pooling (L) do not appear in the model print statement. Instead, only the standard deviation of the effects is presented (σ_L, or `sd(Intercept)`). The reason for this is that there may sometimes be a very large number of random effects coefficients, which would result in models that are difficult to read if they were all shown. A second reason for this is that researchers are often not directly interested in the individual values of their random

106 *Observations using a Bayesian multilevel model*

effects, but rather they are usually focused on the overall effects common to all listeners such as the model intercept. For example, to this point we have been talking about "what is the average apparent height of male speakers" and never "what did listener 04 think the average height of speaker 101 is?". However, there are situations in which we may be interested in investigating the random effects, and the `brms` package has several functions to facilitate this process.

We will present two ways to consider the random listener effects using the `ranef` function, which gets information about your random effects from your `brms` model. In the first of these, you set `summary=FALSE` in the call to `ranef` as shown below. This function returns a list of three-dimensional matrices, where each list element is named after the grouping factor it represents. Below, we collect the random effects and take the element named `L`, corresponding to a matrix representing our listener factor.

```
# get random effects, without summarizing
random_effects = brms::ranef (model_multilevel, summary = FALSE)

# get only the listener random effects
listener_effects = random_effects$L
```

The matrix representing each factor has three dimensions, with individual posterior samples varying across the first dimension (rows), factor levels varying along the second dimension (columns), and parameters varying across the third dimension. Basically, `listener_effects` is a set of two-dimensional matrices stuck together, one for each random parameter. Of course, this time we only have a single random effect for listeners, so there is only one element along the third dimension.

```
str (listener_effects)
##   num [1:5000, 1:15, 1] -1.76 -2.74 -1.39 -6.66 -2.71 ...
##   - attr(*, "nchains")= int 4
##   - attr(*, "dimnames")=List of 3
##   ..$ : NULL
##   ..$ : chr [1:15] "1" "2" "3" "4" ...
##   ..$ : chr "Intercept"
```

You can select the matrix corresponding to the intercept by putting the name of the parameter in the third dimension of the matrix, as seen below. This reduces our three-dimensional matrix to a two-dimensional one representing the random listener intercepts in our model.

```
# take only the intercept along the third dimension
listener_intercepts = listener_effects[,,"Intercept"]
```

The above process results in a two-dimensional matrix representing the individual samples of our listener effects. We can see below that this matrix has 5,000 rows, corresponding to the individual samples, and 15 columns, representing the individual

Observations using a Bayesian multilevel model 107

listeners. We use the head function to see the first six samples of the listener effects. To be totally clear, each column represents the samples of $P\left(L_{[\cdot]} \mid y\right)$ for different speakers. So, the first column represents the individual posterior samples of the listener effect for listener 1 $\left(P\left(L_{[1]} \mid y\right)\right)$, and the second column represents the individual posterior samples of the listener effect for listener 2 $\left(P\left(L_{[2]} \mid y\right)\right)$,

```
# Our matrix of posterior samples showing 5000 samples
# for each of 15 listener effects
dim (listener_intercepts)
## [1] 5000    15


# the first six samples of the listener effect for 6 listeners
head ( round (listener_intercepts[,1:6], 2))
##            1     2     3     4     5    6
## [1,] -1.76 -2.12  3.24  1.29 -2.95 3.13
## [2,] -2.74 -1.65  1.84  0.00 -2.93 5.85
## [3,] -1.39 -2.99  2.47 -0.02 -5.25 2.98
## [4,] -6.66 -5.17 -2.59 -1.72 -6.98 1.72
## [5,] -2.71 -2.13  3.70 -0.83 -3.61 3.89
## [6,] -3.20 -1.86  1.96 -1.74 -3.67 5.17
```

If we were to find the average of the samples within each column, the result would be the posterior mean estimate for each of our individual listener effects.

```
colMeans (listener_intercepts)[1:10]
##     1     2     3     4     5     6     7     8     9    10
## -3.61 -2.65  1.49 -0.69 -3.80  3.81 -5.52  1.91  0.25  1.98
```

We can repeat the process above but without specifying summary=FALSE. When you do this, rather than the individual samples you get summaries of the posterior distribution of each parameter. We will still get a list of three-dimensional matrices. However, this time factor levels vary across the first dimension (rows), information about each factor level varies across columns, and parameters vary across the third dimension. We again take the list element corresponding to listeners (L) and take only the element of the third dimension corresponding to our Intercept.

```
# get random effects, *with* summarizing (by default)
random_effects = brms::ranef (model_multilevel)


# get only the listener random effects
listener_effects = random_effects$L


# along the third (coefficient) dimension, take only the intercept dimension
listener_intercepts = listener_effects[,,"Intercept"]
```

108 *Observations using a Bayesian multilevel model*

This time, the process results in a two-dimensional matrix representing a summary of the posterior, as seen below. The leftmost column of the output below represents the posterior mean effect estimated for each listener, the second column represents the standard deviation of posterior samples, and the third and fourth columns provide he 2.5% and 97.5% credible intervals for each parameter, respectively. We can see that the information in the first column below exactly matches the posterior means we calculated for each listener effect above. This is because they are the same thing. In the un-summarized representation above we were seeing the individual samples varying across columns, and we 'summarized' them by averaging across the columns. In the summarized representation we are seeing the same samples, summarized in each row.

```
listener_intercepts[1:6,]
##    Estimate Est.Error    Q2.5     Q97.5
## 1   -3.6106    1.404  -6.388  -0.88497
## 2   -2.6477    1.387  -5.419   0.07352
## 3    1.4902    1.387  -1.266   4.27533
## 4   -0.6855    1.386  -3.393   2.04369
## 5   -3.7971    1.382  -6.494  -1.11026
## 6    3.8118    1.399   1.050   6.60174
```

Notice that the listener averages vary around 0, and some are even negative. That is because the listener effects (and all random effects) are represented as deviations from the intercept, as noted above. We can verify this by calculating the average reported height for each listener and centering these values. We can then compare these centered means to our model random effects and see that they are very similar.

```
# find listener means
listener_means = tapply (men$height, men$L, mean)

# center them
listener_means_centered = listener_means - mean(listener_means)

# compare centered means to model random effects
round (rbind (listener_means_centered,
            listener_random_effects = listener_intercepts[,1]))
##                            1  2  3  4  5  6  7  8  9 10 11 12 13 14 15
## listener_means_centered   -4 -3  2 -1 -4  4 -6  2  0  2 -4  7 -1  3  2
## listener_random_effects   -4 -3  1 -1 -4  4 -6  2  0  2 -3  6 -1  3  1
```

We can use a simple plotting function included in the bmmb package (brmplot) to inspect the posterior distributions of our model coefficients. The function takes in the summary matrices made by brms and plots a point for each parameter mean/median, and lines indicating the credible intervals calculated by brm (usually 95% credible intervals). These matrices all have a standard form where parameters vary across rows, the first column is the posterior mean, the second is the posterior standard deviation (the estimated error), and the third and fourth columns are the 2.5%

and 97.5% credible intervals. If you have a matrix like this you can easily plot it with `brmplot` as shown below.

```
bmmb::brmplot(listener_intercepts)
```

We can compare the estimates of our by-listener effects to the distribution of centered height responses arranged by subject. In Figure 4.4, we plot centered listener responses using boxplots and then use `brmplot` to overlay the colored points and lines, representing the listener 'random effects', on top. We can see that the estimated listener parameters and the raw data show a close correspondence.

4.7 Simulating data using our model parameters

Regression models break up variation in the dependent variables into component parts. One way to think about what all the numbers in our model mean is to simulate the dependent variable by building it from the individual component parts indicated by the model. Our model (`model_multilevel`) has just four components we need to include, one for every estimated parameter: The intercept, the listener-dependent intercepts (L), the between-listener variation (σ_L), and the within-listener variation, the error (σ).

We do this in the code below. First we set the intercept to 174 cm. Then, we sample 15 random listener effects from a normal distribution, representing simulated listeners. The listener population has a mean of 0 and a standard deviation (σ_L) equal to 3.8 as indicated by our model. These effects are stored in a vector called `L_`, and they represent the values of L for our different listeners. After this, we create an index vector `L` that tells us which value of `L_` to apply for any given trial. This vector contains values from 1 to 15, representing each listener, repeated 45 times each in order to simulate 45 observations from each listener. Finally, we draw our error (i.e. $\varepsilon \sim N(0, \sigma)$) based on the magnitude of `sigma` in our model. Note that the error is just 45·15 random draws from this population. Since the model contains the same value of σ for all

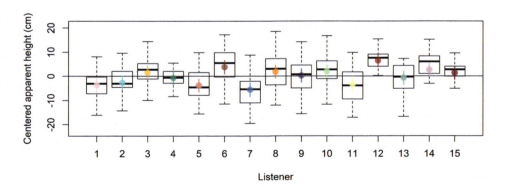

Figure 4.4 Distribution of centered apparent height, individually for each listener. Colored points and lines indicate posterior mean estimates and 95% credible intervals for the listener-specific intercept effects (i.e. the listener 'random' effects).

110 *Observations using a Bayesian multilevel model*

trials, there is no distinction between one listener and another when it comes to the magnitude of the error.

```
# skip this line if you want a new simulated data set.
set.seed(1)
# this is the value of our intercept
Intercept = 174
# this is a vector of 15 listener effects
L_ = rnorm (15, 0, 3.8 )
# vector indicating which listener produced which utterance
L = rep (1:15, each = 45)
# this vector contains the error
error = rnorm (45 * 15, 0, 7)
```

After creating our components, we add the Intercept, listener effects, and random error to make our fake 'replicated' data. Since this data has the same statistical properties as our real data, it should look a lot like it.

```
# the sum of an intercept, listener effects and random error
height_rep = Intercept + L_[L] + error
```

In Figure 4.5 we compare the results of our simulation to our real data. The are reasonably similar, which tells us that our model is a good reflection of the data.

Below we make two data sets that are 'incomplete' with respect to the variation in our data. The first contains the intercept and noise only, the second contains the intercept and listener effects only.

```
# this fake data is missing between listener variation
height_rep_1 = Intercept + error
# this fake data is missing within listener variation
height_rep_2 = Intercept +  L_[L]
```

In Figure 4.6 we compare these 'incomplete' data sets to the full simulated data. The top row contains only error (σ). As a result, height judgments vary around the

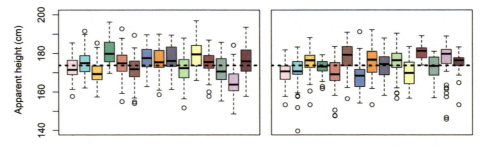

Figure 4.5 Comparison of real and simulated apparent height data. Each box represents data from one listener, the horizontal line represents the mean of the listener means. Which is the real data?

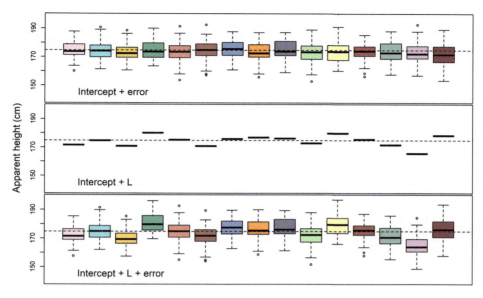

Figure 4.6: (top) Simulated data containing within-listener variation but no between-listener variation. (middle) Simulated data containing between-listener variation but no within-listener variation. (bottom) Simulated data containing both within and between-listener variation in apparent height.

intercept, but there is no listener-to-listener variation. This is what that data would look like if there is no variation in means across listeners, as is assumed by the 'uni-level' (complete pooling) model in Figure 4.2. However, notice that each little box is not centered at zero. Although we have not added any variation in listener means, a small amount of this appears to be present in our data anyways. This is because although the error distribution has a mean of zero, each of our listener boxes contains only a small sample of errors. This tiny sample of errors is *extremely* unlikely to add up to exactly zero. Whatever the errors *do* add up to, this value will contribute some unknown amount to each listener's sample mean estimate. This makes estimation of the *real* listener effects impossible in practice.

In the middle plot, the figure shows only between-listener variation (σ_L) but no within-listener variation (i.e. no σ). Now listeners vary from the intercept, and between each other, but they do not vary within themselves. We can see the effect of this, the boxes have no 'width', they are lines. That is because in this situation listeners would *always* respond at their mean, showing no internal variation in their responses. The final plot is the combination of the variation in the top two plots and shows the final simulated data: The sum of the intercept, the within-listener variation, and the between-listener variation.

As seen in the top row of Figure 4.6, the model without listener variation is unlikely to generate the substantially different listener boxplots we see in our data through noise alone. However, they do show a tiny bit of variation in the listener means due to error alone (as noted above). So, random error can give the impression of listener variation even when none exists. We can investigate how likely our error is to generate listener means as diverse as those we have observed, *by accident*. To do this, we run one more simulation,

112 *Observations using a Bayesian multilevel model*

identical in all respects except for two things: (1) We set the between-listener variance to zero, and (2) we set the noise variance to 7.8 (as in our complete pooling model). Below we generate 10,000 simulated data sets and record the standard deviation of the listener means for each one. These values will be stored in a vector called `sigma_L_rep` since we are simulating values of σ_L for our complete pooling model.

```
set.seed(1)
# do 10,000 replications
reps = 10000

# hold the replicated values of sigma_L
sigma_L_rep = rep(0,reps)
for ( i in 1:reps){
  Intercept = 173.8 # set the intercept
  L_L = rnorm (15, 0, 0)  # zero between-listener variance
  L = rep (1:15, each = 45) # 45 responses from each of 15 listeners
  epsilon = rnorm (45 * 15, 0, 7.78) # generate random noise
  height_rep = Intercept + L_L[L] + epsilon # add up to components

# get replicated listener means
  L_rep_means = tapply(height_rep, L, mean)
  sigma_L_rep[i] = sd (L_rep_means) # find sigma of listener effects
}
```

Below, we see that even in 10,000 simulations we do not see a standard deviation greater than 2.1, and that 75% are smaller than 1.3.

```
quantile(sigma_L_rep)
##      0%     25%     50%     75%    100%
## 0.4429 0.9862 1.1337 1.2810 2.0813
```

The standard deviation of the listener means in our data was 3.6 and our model estimate of σ_L was 3.8. This reinforces the idea that between-listener variation (σ_L) is a 'real' aspect of our data, which is *extremely* unlikely to arise incidentally due to random variation, and that our models will benefit from taking it into account.

4.8 Adding a second random effect

Our model is looking better but is still not 'right'. This is because, in addition to repeatedly sampling from only 15 listeners, our model also features repeated sampling from only 45 different speakers. In Figure 4.7, we see that we can recreate Figure 4.1, this time illustrating systematic variation between speakers in addition to between listeners. So, we are interested in the average apparent height of adult males overall but have only sampled 45 of them, and we need to build this information into our model.

In order to investigate this, our model will now include the following additional variable from our `exp_data` data frame:

- `S`: An integer from 1 to 139 indicating which *speaker* produced the trial stimulus.

Observations using a Bayesian multilevel model 113

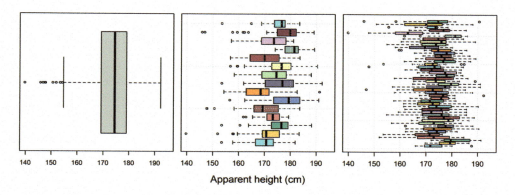

Apparent height (cm)

Figure 4.7 (left) Distribution of all apparent height judgments for adult male speakers. (middle) Distribution of height judgments for adult male speakers, individually for each listener. (right) Distribution of height judgments for adult male speakers, individually for each speaker.

4.8.1 Updating the model description

In order to model the effects of the different speakers in our data, our formula must be updated to include our S (speaker) predictor in parentheses, like this:

```
height ~ 1 + ( 1 | L) + ( 1 | S)
```

The new term in parentheses indicates a second predictor whose levels we want to estimate using adaptive pooling. Again, we include only a one on the left-hand side of the pipe indicating that we are only estimating speaker-specific intercepts. So, this formula says 'predict height using only an overall intercept, but also estimate a different intercept for each level of listener and speaker'. The regression model corresponding to the formula above now looks like this:

$$\text{height}_{[i]} \sim N(\mu_{[i]}, \sigma)$$
$$\mu_{[i]} = \text{Intercept} + L_{[\text{L}_{[i]}]} + S_{[\text{S}_{[i]}]}$$

$$\text{Priors}:$$
$$L_{[\cdot]} \sim N(0, \sigma_L)$$
$$S_{[\cdot]} \sim N(0, \sigma_S)$$

$$\text{Intercept} \sim N(176, 15)$$
$$\sigma \sim N(0, 15)$$
$$\sigma_L \sim N(0, 15)$$
$$\sigma_S \sim N(0, 15)$$

(4.13)

114 *Observations using a Bayesian multilevel model*

Just as with the listener coefficients (L), the speaker coefficients (S) represent deviations in values from the intercept and so the speaker average is set to zero. In plain English, the model description above says:

> *We expect height judgments to be normally distributed around the expected value for any given trial, $\mu_{[i]}$, with some unknown standard deviation σ. The expected value for a trial is equal to the sum of a fixed overall average (Intercept), some value associated with the individual listener $\left(L_{\left[L_{[i]}\right]}\right)$ who judged the trial, and some value associated with the individual speaker $\left(S_{\left[S_{[i]}\right]}\right)$ who produced the trial. The listener and speaker coefficients (L and S) were both modeled as coming from normal distributions whose standard deviations, σ_L and σ_S, were estimated from the data. Prior distributions for σ, σ_L, σ_S, and the intercept were all specified a priori.*

The model we fit in the last chapter only included variation due to error. The first model we fit in this chapter divided variation into random between-listener variation and random within-listener error. Now, our model breaks up the total variance in our data into three components: Between-listener variation, between-speaker variation, and random error, as seen below.

$$\sigma_{\text{total}}^2 = \sigma_L^2 + \sigma_S^2 + \sigma^2 \tag{4.14}$$

If the error was the within-listener variation before, what does it represent now? Our error is now the difference between the value we expect, given the speaker *and* listener, and the value we observe. So, it is the variation *adjusting for* the speaker and listener. In other words, if you know who the speaker is and who the listener is, and you adjust for this, how much random variability do you still have left over in your model? The answer is σ.

4.8.2 *Fitting and interpreting the model*

Below, we fit the new model using exactly the same code as for `model_multilevel`, save for the modification to the model formula. We don't need to specify a hyperprior for σ_S because this falls under the `sd` category (see Section 4.5.3). As long as we can use the same hyperprior for each factor-specific standard deviation, i.e. σ_F for factor F, we don't need to specify a prior for each parameter. We think a prior expectation of 15 cm is reasonable for the speaker standard deviation given that the standard deviation of adult male heights in the US is around 7.5 cm.

```
# Fit the model yourself
model_multilevel_L_S =  brms::brm (
  height ~ 1 + (1|L) + (1|S), data = men, chains = 4, cores = 4,
  warmup = 1000, iter = 3500, thin = 2,
  prior = c(brms::set_prior("normal(176, 15)", class = "Intercept"),
            brms::set_prior("normal(0, 15)", class = "sd"),
            brms::set_prior("normal(0, 15)", class = "sigma")))
```

Observations using a Bayesian multilevel model 115

```
# Or download it from the GitHub page:
model_multilevel_L_S = bmmb::get_model ('4_model_multilevel_L_S.RDS')
```

After fitting the model we inspect the output, some of which we include below:

```
bmmb::short_summary (model_multilevel_L_S)
## ~S (Number of levels: 45)
##              Estimate Est.Error l-95% CI u-95% CI
## sd(Intercept)    2.83      0.42      2.1     3.72
```

The model print statement should look familiar except it contains one new chunk representing information about the speaker predictor in our model (shown above). This chunk reminds us that our S predictor had 45 levels, and provides us information about the estimate of the σ_S parameter (sd(Intercept)), which is 2.83 according to our model.

4.9 Investigating 'shrinkage'

We've mentioned that multilevel models can result in *shrinkage*, that is, estimates that are smaller in magnitude (i.e. closer to the mean) than their no pooling counterparts. In the code below we extract the posterior mean estimates of our listener and speaker random effects (i.e. *L* and *S*). These estimates have been 'shrunken' by combining their likelihoods with the prior. We also calculate the no pooling estimates for the listener and speaker averages, and center these so that they will resemble their corresponding effects.

```
# these are the Bayesian 'shrinkage' estimates of
# the listener effects
L_shrunk = brms::ranef(model_multilevel_L_S)$L[,1,'Intercept']
# and the speaker effects
S_shrunk = brms::ranef(model_multilevel_L_S)$S[,1,'Intercept']

# these are the no pooling estimates
L_nopooling = tapply (men$height, men$L, mean)
S_nopooling = tapply (men$height, men$S, mean)
# and now they are centered
L_nopooling = L_nopooling - mean (L_nopooling)
S_nopooling = S_nopooling - mean (S_nopooling)
```

Figure 4.8 shows the result of shrinkage for the listener and speaker effects: Individual effects are 'pulled' toward the overall mean at zero. We can see that in all cases, the effects estimated with adaptive pooling lie closer to the mean than those estimated with no pooling. This is particularly evident for the speaker effects, and in particular, those of speaker 87, highlighted in that figure.

In the bottom row of Figure 4.8, we focus on the process by which the effect for speaker 87 gets shrunken from a no pooling value of −11.6 to a shrunken (adaptive

116   *Observations using a Bayesian multilevel model*

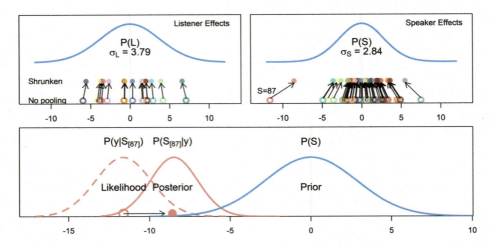

Figure 4.8 (top row) A comparison of the shrunken (i.e. adaptive pooling) and no pooling estimates of the listener and speaker effects. Curves indicate the density of the prior distribution of each set of effects. Arrows link shrunken and no pooling effects for each listener/speaker. (bottom row) An illustration of how the effect for speaker 87, highlighted in the top row, gets shrunken toward the prior through adaptive pooling.

pooling) value of −8.6. This example is simply meant to illustrate how this happens at a conceptual level, the actual calculations and processes involved are more complicated than this. Figure 4.8 is very similar to 3.1, which presented the blending of priors and likelihoods to find the posterior. The shrinkage of random effects arises from the same behavior: We combine the likelihood of a parameter in isolation with prior information about other parameters like it to arrive at a posterior estimate that blends the two.

Our 'no pooling' estimate is an estimate based solely on the individual likelihood of the parameter. The likelihood function we present in the figure is the likelihood of the speaker effect for speaker 87 given their judged height on 15 observations. To calculate this, we assume that $\sigma = 6.47$ as in our last model, and use centered height judgments. The prior density we present in the figure is based on our model parameters, it has a mean of 0 and a standard deviation of 2.83. To find the posterior distribution presented in the bottom row of Figure 4.8, we multiplied the curves representing the likelihood and the prior for each point along the x-axis. So, even in this simple demonstration, we can see how effect estimates get pulled, or shrunken, away from their no pooling values by their priors.

In Figure 4.9 we plot the no pooling estimates (x-axis) against the difference between the no pooling and shrunken estimates (y-axis). The difference between the no pooling and shrunken estimate is basically the magnitude of the horizontal arrow shown in the bottom row of Figure 4.8, for each pair of shrunken and no pooling parameters. It is the amount of tilt in the arrows in the top row of the same figure; in the absence of shrinkage, they would all be vertical. We can see that the amount of shrinkage, the difference between the no pooling and shrunken estimates, varies as a function of the

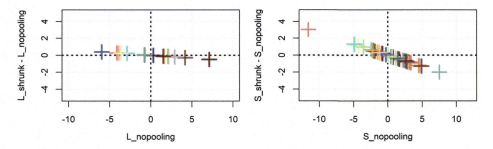

Figure 4.9 The x-axis represents the no pooling estimate for listener (L) and speaker (S) effects. The y-axis represents the difference between the shrunken and no pooling estimates of each parameter, i.e. the amount of shrinkage. Positive values indicate that the shrunken estimate was greater than the no pooling one, and vice versa. Shrunken values were more positive for negative values and more negative for positive values.

magnitude of the estimate. More deviant estimates are shrunken more, and less deviant estimates are shrunken less.

You may have noted that the listener effects exhibit less shrinkage than the speaker effects. There are two reasons for this. First, we have 45 observations for each listener but only 15 for each speaker. As a result, the likelihood functions for our listener effects will be narrower than those of our speaker effects. This makes the likelihoods for our listener parameters more resistant to the effects of the prior, and therefore more resistant to shrinkage (see Sections 3.3.2 and 2.7.3 for more information). Second, a large proportion of the speaker effects are close to zero, with only a relatively small number exhibiting large deviations from this. In contrast, the listener effects are less concentrated near the average. As a result of this $\sigma_L > \sigma_S$, which causes speaker effects to be shrunken more than listener effects, in general.

4.10 Answering our research questions

Let's return to the research questions we posed in Section 4.5.1:

(Q1) How tall does the average adult male sound?
(Q2) Can we set limits on credible average apparent heights based on the data we collected?

We can consider the answers provided to this question by the complete pooling model we fit at the end of last chapter:

```
bmmb::short_summary (model_priors)
## Formula:  height ~ 1
## Population-Level Effects:
##            Estimate Est.Error l-95% CI u-95% CI
## Intercept    173.8       0.31    173.2    174.4
##
```

118 *Observations using a Bayesian multilevel model*

```
## Family Specific Parameters:
##         Estimate Est.Error l-95% CI u-95% CI
## sigma     7.77      0.21      7.37     8.19
```

And compare this to the final model we considered above, which contained information about repeated measurements across speakers and listeners:

```
bmmb::short_summary (model_multilevel_L_S)
## Formula:  height ~ 1 + (1 | L) + (1 | S)
##
## Group-Level Effects:
## ~L (Number of levels: 15)
##              Estimate Est.Error l-95% CI u-95% CI
## sd(Intercept)    3.81      0.86      2.51     5.87
##
## ~S (Number of levels: 45)
##              Estimate Est.Error l-95% CI u-95% CI
## sd(Intercept)    2.83      0.42      2.1      3.72
##
## Population-Level Effects:
##            Estimate Est.Error l-95% CI u-95% CI
## Intercept    173.8      1.12     171.6    176.1
##
## Family Specific Parameters:
##         Estimate Est.Error l-95% CI u-95% CI
## sigma     6.47      0.19      6.11     6.85
```

Our complete pooling model from the previous chapter, `model_priors`, and our adaptive pooling model from this chapter, `model_multilevel_L_S`, agree on the average apparent height as reflected by their respective intercept terms. However, they disagree on a credible interval for the parameter, with the complete pooling model having a 95% credible interval that is nearly four times narrower (1.2 cm vs 4.4 cm). This is because the complete pooling model did not specify information about repeated measures, which caused our model to think that it had more independent observations than it did. This led the initial model to return an overly-precise estimate.

Another difference is that the final model has a smaller `sigma` parameter (7.8 vs 6.5), which indicates that the data-level error is smaller in the final model than in the initial model. Keep in mind that 'error' is just what your model can't explain at the data level. Our final model explains more (at the listener and speaker levels) and so there is less error (at the data level). The reduced error is a direct consequence of the fact that the final model splits variation in the data into several components (i.e. $\sigma_{total}^2 = \sigma_L^2 + \sigma_S^2 + \sigma^2$). Since σ_{total} is a fixed value (given the data), obviously, the larger your between-speaker and between-listener variation is, the smaller your random error (σ) *must* be.

Usually, parameters should be reported with *at least* the mean/median and standard deviations of the posterior distribution, in addition to some useful credible interval

Observations using a Bayesian multilevel model 119

(i.e. 50%, 95%) around that parameter. Based on the result of our final model, a thorough answer to our research questions might go something like:

> *Based on our model the average apparent height of adult males is likely to be 173.8 cm (s.d. = 1.1, 95% CI = [171.6, 176.1]). The estimated magnitude of the random error was 6.5 cm (s.d. = 0.2, 95% CI = [6.1, 6.9]). Systematic between-listener variation averages about 3.8 cm (s.d. = 0.9, 95% CI = [2.5, 5.8]), while systematic between-speaker variation averages about 2.8 cm (s.d. = 0.4, 95% CI = [2.1, 3.8]).*

4.11 'Traditionalists' corner

In traditionalists' corner, we compare the output of `brms` to some more 'traditional' approaches. We're not going to talk about the traditional models in any detail, the focus of this section is simply to highlight the similarities between different approaches, and to point out where to find equivalent information in the different models. If you are already familiar with these approaches, these sections may be helpful. If not, some of the information provided here may not make much sense, although it may still be helpful. If you want to know more about the statistical methods being discussed here, please see the preface for a list of suggested background reading in statistics.

4.11.1 Bayesian multilevel models vs. lmer

Here we compare the output of `brms` to the output of the `lmer` ("linear mixed-effects regression") function, a very popular function for fitting multilevel models in the `lme4` R package. We're not going to talk about `lmer` in very much detail. The focus of this section is simply to highlight the similarities between different approaches and to point out where to find equivalent information in both kinds of models. Below we use `lmer` to fit a model that is analogous to our `model_multilevel_L_S` model. The `lmer` function uses adaptive pooling to estimate its 'random effects' and no pooling to estimate its 'fixed effects'. Notice that the formulas are identical in both cases, except we do not specify priors for this model.

```
lmer_model = lme4::lmer (height ~ 1 + (1|L) + (1|S), data = men)
```

We can consider the short print statement for our Bayesian model, which we have annotated with numbers indicating where certain information can be found.

```
bmmb::short_summary(model_multilevel_L_S)
## (1) Formula:  height ~ 1 + (1 | L) + (1 | S)
##
## (2) Group-Level Effects:
##      ~L (Number of levels: 15)
##                     Estimate Est.Error l-95% CI u-95% CI
## (3) sd(Intercept)     3.81      0.86      2.51      5.87
##
##      ~S (Number of levels: 45)
##                     Estimate Est.Error l-95% CI u-95% CI
```

120 *Observations using a Bayesian multilevel model*

```
## (4)  sd(Intercept)        2.83         0.42        2.1       3.72
##
##      Population-Level Effects:
##                   Estimate Est.Error l-95% CI u-95% CI
## (5)  Intercept      173.8        1.12     171.6    176.05
##
##      Family Specific Parameters:
##              Estimate Est.Error l-95% CI u-95% CI
## (6)  sigma       6.47        0.19     6.11      6.85
```

And compare this to the print statement of our `lmer` model, annotated with the same numbers highlighting equivalent information. We see that our models provide very similar information, although it is organized (and named) in somewhat different ways. We also see that the two approaches provide us with very similar parameter estimates for our models.

```
summary (lmer_model)
##      Linear mixed model fit by REML ['lmerMod']
## (1)  Formula: height ~ 1 + (1 | L) + (1 | S)
##         Data: men
##
##      REML criterion at convergence: 4527.4
##
##      Scaled residuals:
##        Min      1Q  Median       3Q      Max
##      -4.6205 -0.4868  0.0722  0.5700  2.7179
##
## (2)  Random effects:
##       Groups    Name           Variance Std.Dev.
## (3)  S         (Intercept)   7.593    2.756
## (4)  L         (Intercept)  11.990    3.463
## (6)  Residual               41.630    6.452
##      Number of obs: 675, groups:  S, 45; L, 15
##
##      Fixed effects:
##                   Estimate Std. Error t value
## (5)  (Intercept)  173.788        1.015    171.3
```

We can get the random effects out of our `brm` model and compare them to the random effects we get from `lmer`. As seen below, the random effects estimates we get from `brm` also include credible intervals. As a result, we have some idea regarding the uncertainty in these estimates.

```
brms_ranefs = brms::ranef (model_multilevel_L_S)$L[,,"Intercept"]
head (brms_ranefs)
##    Estimate Est.Error   Q2.5    Q97.5
```

```
## 1   -3.6312       1.346  -6.366  -1.07315
## 2   -2.6594       1.371  -5.350   0.01293
## 3    1.5297       1.368  -1.158   4.23982
## 4   -0.7165       1.358  -3.380   1.95702
## 5   -3.8413       1.361  -6.472  -1.18510
## 6    3.8990       1.353   1.266   6.58467
```

In contrast, `lmer` gives you what are called **point estimates**. These are single estimates of parameter values with no intervals indicating uncertainty. Because of this, it is difficult to compare estimates for different speakers/participants in the data.

```
lmer_ranefs = lme4::ranef (lmer_model)[["L"]]
head (lmer_ranefs)
##   (Intercept)
## 1     -3.6134
## 2     -2.6726
## 3      1.5298
## 4     -0.7024
## 5     -3.8238
## 6      3.8796
```

Importantly, the values we get from both approaches are nearly identical, as seen in Figure 4.10.

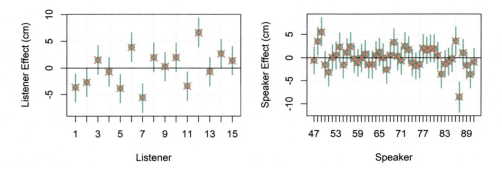

Figure 4.10 (left) In green, the random speaker intercept estimates provided by brm. The red arrows indicate the estimates of the same provided by lmer.

The *largest* difference between the two sets of coefficients is 0.05 cm for the listener effects and 0.06 cm for the speaker effects, with the average absolute difference for both being around 0.03 cm. So, as a practical matter analyzing this data using a Bayesian multilevel model provides some advantages (e.g. intervals around random effects), while still providing effectively the same 'answers' as a 'traditional' approach to the data.

122 *Observations using a Bayesian multilevel model*

4.12 Exercises

The analyses in the main body of the text all involve only the unmodified 'actual' resonance level (in `exp_data`). Responses for the stimuli with the simulated 'big' resonance are reserved for exercises throughout. You can get the 'big' resonance in the `exp_ex` data frame, or all data in the `exp_data_all` data frame.

Fit and interpret one or more of the suggested models:

1 Easy: Analyze the (pre-fit) model that's exactly like `model_multilevel_L_S`, except using the data in `exp_ex` (`bmmb::get_model("model_multilevel_L_S_ex.RDS")`).
2 Medium: Fit a model just like `model_multilevel_L_S`, but for the data from some other group, for either the original or big resonance levels.
3 Hard: Fit two models like `model_multilevel_L_S` for two groups, or for one group across resonance levels, and compare results across models.

In any case, describe the model, present and explain the results, and include some figures.

References

Bates, D., Mächler, M., Bolker, B., & Walker, S. (2015). "Fitting linear mixed-effects models using lme4." *Journal of Statistical Software*, 67(1), 1–48. doi:10.18637/jss.v067.i01.

Gelman, A. (2005). Analysis of variance—why it is more important than ever. *The Annals of Statistics*, 33(1), 1–53.

Gelman, A., & Hill, J. (2006). *Data analysis using regression and multilevel/hierarchical models*. Cambridge University Press.

Gelman, A., Carlin, J. B., Stern, H. S., Dunson, D. B., Vehtari, A., & Rubin, D. B. (2013). *Bayesian data analysis*, Third Edition. Abingdon: Taylor & Francis.

5 Comparing two groups of observations
Factors and contrasts

The models discussed in this chapter can be used for data that compares observations across two groups. In this chapter, we will ask: Are two averages different or are they the same? Comparing two groups basically means estimating a single *effect*, a single difference between groups. We do not discuss the comparison of multiple groups, i.e. the estimation of multiple fixed effects, until Chapter 7.

Research questions comparing two groups come up often in scientific research. For example, a psycholinguist may ask: Does visual information speed up speech perception or not (are two sets of reaction times the same)? A phonetician may ask: Do men and women produce vowels that are about the same duration (are two sets of speech durations the same)? A doctor may ask: Is the blood pressure of people who take some medicine the same as that of those who don't (are two sets of blood pressure measurements the same)?

5.1 Chapter pre-cap

In this chapter, we discuss models comparing two groups, and introduce the concept of between and within-subjects factors. Factor coding is presented, and treatment and sum coding are compared. We then discuss the decomposition of variation in the dependent variable into effects associated with independent variables, and the difficulty of establishing causal relationships using statistical models. We fit a sum-coded model comparing two groups and compare this to a treatment-coded model fit to the same data. We present a discussion on retrieving and manipulating the model posterior samples, including the importance of combining parameters before summarizing them. The `hypothesis` function is introduced, and the retrieval and combination of 'random effect' parameters are explained. Finally, there is a discussion of outliers and robustness, and the t-distribution is presented. We fit a model with t-distributed errors and compare this to our model assuming normal errors.

5.2 Comparing two groups

We introduce the comparison of two groups in terms of our hypothetical experiment regarding coffee and reading times (discussed in Chapter 1) where we investigate whether coffee makes people read faster. Subjects are asked to drink either a cup of decaf or a cup of regular coffee. After a 30-minute wait, they are asked to read a passage aloud and the duration of the reading time is measured. In this case, we might call the factor 'drink' and have two levels 'decaf', and 'coffee'. However, we might have

DOI: 10.4324/9781003285878-5

124 *Comparing two groups of observations: Factors and contrasts*

named them 'A1' and 'A2': The factor and factor levels are named arbitrarily by the researcher and have no real effect on the outcome of an analysis.

Every observation in our data can be assigned to a 'group' based on the value of the coffee group predictor for that observation (i.e., whether it indicates that the observation is associated with decaf or regular coffee). The values associated with each group can be thought of as realizations of two random variables: "the amount of time it takes people to read this passage of text after drinking decaf" and "the amount of time it takes people to read this passage of text after drinking regular coffee". These variables have some unknown mean parameters we can call μ_{decaf} and μ_{coffee}, respectively.

Usually, researchers don't ask if two distributions of observations are identical in absolutely all respects across the two groups, and instead, mostly focus on whether $\mu_{decaf} = \mu_{coffee}$ or not. So, when we design an experiment to test for differences between groups, what we are often really asking is: Is the mean of the distribution of these two variables the same? In other words, is "the mean of the distribution of the amount of time it takes people to read this passage of text after drinking decaf" the same as "the mean of the distribution of the amount of time it takes people to read this passage of text after drinking coffee"?

5.3 Distribution of repeated measures across factor levels

Since we are discussing repeated measures data, we necessarily have repeated observations of measurements for different sources of data (e.g. listener). The way that these repeated measurements are distributed across levels of a grouping factor affects the structure of your regression model and the efficiency of your analysis, so it is useful to be familiar with these characteristics. We will consider a situation where you have several subjects (S) distributed among levels of a predictor factor (A) with two levels. Figure 5.1 is a visual representation of three ways that the comparison of two groups can be structured: Between-subjects, within-subjects, and an unnamed but possible configuration.

We can consider the organizations in Figure 5.1 in terms of our hypothetical experiment regarding coffee and reading times described above. In the first example, factor A is a *within-subjects* factor. This is because each subject appears at both levels of A so that the grouping factor (A) varies *within* subjects. This would occur if we measured all subjects at both levels, i.e., we first ask people to read the passage after drinking decaf, then, we ask them to do the same after drinking regular coffee. Within-subject factors can usually be estimated more reliably because their effect can be measured for each person, letting you 'average out' random differences between people. For example, what if you put an extremely fast reader in the coffee group. You may think the caffeine had a huge effect but they actually just naturally read fast. If you had also observed them in the decaf group, you would know that.

Although having factors vary within-subjects has many benefits, this is not always possible or practical. For example, speakers cannot usually exist at multiple levels of the first-language factor since most have only one first language. Sometimes, practical considerations cause problems. For example, for our hypothetical experiment, we can't give people coffee first and then decaf in the same session because the caffeine would still have an effect on their performance. To solve this problem, a researcher may always ask subjects to perform the decaf round first. However, this may make the second reading faster due to rehearsal effects, making the second (caffeinated) reading

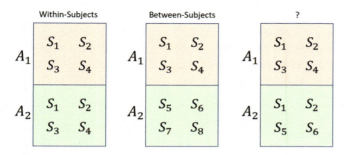

Figure 5.1 Three ways that subjects (S) can vary across levels of factor A, making two groups.

seem artificially faster. Sometimes, there is no perfect solution to a problem and a researcher will need to select the best experimental structure given the limitations of the situation.

In the second example, A is a *between-subjects* factor. This is because the factor varies *between* subjects since each subject appears at only one level of A. This would occur if we only measured subjects in either the decaf condition or the coffee condition, but not both. A design like this avoids the possible problems with within-subjects designs mentioned above. However, since different random people are in each group, finding stable differences between groups is a bit harder. As a result, the estimation of between-subjects factors will tend to be noisier than for within-subjects factors, all other things being equal.

Finally, we have a design that doesn't really have a name (labeledwith a question mark). This would arise if you tested some people in both conditions and other people in only one condition. This is not really a 'proper' design, to the extent that it cannot be analyzed with some more 'traditional' approaches to statistical inference. Although there is no particular reason that you should design an experiment like this, this sort of data can arise incidentally out of experiments or observational studies.

For example, in our experiment, we asked people to judge the height, age, and gender of all speakers. Imagine we're interested in the effect of apparent age on apparent height, we wonder, "do people sound shorter when listeners think they are children?" To investigate this question we would make two groups, one containing all rows where listeners indicated hearing a child and another with all rows where listeners indicated hearing an adult. If *all* listeners identify at least some speakers as adults and others as children, then apparent age is a *within-subject* factor. This is because in this case, all listeners would exist in both the "I think the speaker is an adult" and "I think the speaker is a child" groups (though the number of observations at each of these levels would likely vary across listeners). If all listeners identified *all* speakers as *either* children *or* adults, then apparent age would be a *between-subjects* factor. This is because there would be no speakers in *both* the "I think the speaker is an adult" and the "I think the speaker is a child group".

However, it may occur that *some* speakers report both adult and child speakers, others report only adult speakers and others report only child speakers. If this were to occur, we could end up with the unnamed organization unintentionally due to the

126 *Comparing two groups of observations: Factors and contrasts*

behavior of the listeners in the experiment. Note that in all of these cases, drawing inferences is additionally complicated by the fact that we can't randomly allocate listeners to either the "I think the speaker is an adult" or the "I think the speaker is a child" group, though we can (probably) shift the probability that a listener perceives particular speech stimuli as adult or childlike. Hence, these groups are more like groups defined by listeners' first languages than they are like decaf and coffee groups (i.e., there is a lack of *control* in their creation).

5.4 Data and research questions

In the last chapter, we focused on the apparent height of adult male speakers. The reason for this is that, because of the very low voice pitch of many adult male speakers, adult males represent the least confusable category of speakers among women, men, boys, and girls. For example, we can compare veridical (i.e. actual, C_v) to perceived (C) speaker category in what is called a **confusion matrix** below. A confusion matrix organizes responses to a classification problem in a way that makes correct classifications and confusions (i.e., errors) comparable across categories. In the matrix below, rows indicate the actual speaker category, and columns indicate the apparent speaker category. We see that boys were identified as boys 234 times in total, and as girls and adult females 133 and 32 times, respectively. So, boys were misidentified at a relatively high rate. In contrast, men were correctly identified in 626 cases and only misidentified in 49 cases, meaning their category was correctly identified in 93% of cases $(626 / (626 + 49))$.

```
xtabs ( ~ bmmb::exp_data$C_v + bmmb::exp_data$C)
##                     bmmb::exp_data$C
## bmmb::exp_data$C_v    b    g    m    w
##                   b 234  133    6   32
##                   g  79  184    0   22
##                   m  31    0  626   18
##                   w  97  109    3  511
```

In this chapter we're going to focus on *confusable* voices, so we're going to exclude adult males from our data. Below we load our packages and experimental data and create a new data frame called notmen that excludes all data associated with adult male speakers. This excludes both speech produced by adult males and stimuli identified as being produced by adult males. We also exclude the 'big' resonance level by using the exp_data data frame, focusing only on the unmodified speech.

```
# load packages and data
library (bmmb)
library (brms)
data (exp_data)
# exclude actual men and apparent men
notmen = exp_data[exp_data$C_v!='m' & exp_data$C!='m',]
```

We create a new confusion matrix that compares A_v (veridical age group, with levels a adults, and c children) and C (apparent speaker category) to see to what extent listeners confused the adult women in our sample with younger speakers (since all adults were women). We can see that although a majority of stimuli were classified correctly, there are plenty of misidentifications in the data.

```
xtabs (~ notmen$A_v + notmen$C)
##             notmen$C
## notmen$A_v   b    g    w
##           a  97  109  511
##           c 313  317   54
```

Our height responses could potentially be modeled on the basis of either an apparent age group or a veridical age group. Neither of these approaches would be *wrong* or *right* in any general, absolute sense. Rather, each can provide different information regarding our response variable, and so answer different research questions. The boxplot in Figure 5.2 presents a comparison of height judgments for our confusable speakers, organized according to perceived and veridical age. Based on this plot, we see that the apparent age of a speaker dominates their apparent height.

For example, the first two boxes from the top indicate that speakers 'sounded' shorter when they were identified as children, regardless of whether they were adults or not. Conversely, the bottom two boxes indicate that speakers 'sounded' taller when they were identified as adults, even if they were children. So, we see that what seems to determine apparent height is apparent speaker age, rather than veridical speaker age. This makes sense to some extent since listeners don't *know* how old speakers are, they just know how old they *think* speakers are. For this reason, the analysis in this chapter will focus on understanding the role of *apparent age* on the perception of speaker height.

By focusing on apparent age, we are effectively asking how apparent height is affected by whether the listener *thinks* the speaker is an adult or not. As a result, this experiment focuses on how our expectations and 'real-world knowledge' can influence how we perceive the world. This may seem unusual but it is actually a very common thing. For example, think of an image of a box of an unknown size. Your estimate of how heavy this is, or how hard it is to move, will depend on how large you think the box is and on what you think is inside of it. Historically, research on the perception of speaker size from speech has taken a very mathematical approach, assuming humans

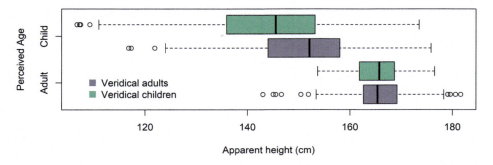

Figure 5.2 Distribution of apparent height judgments organized by apparent and veridical age. Apparent height varies a lot across levels of apparent age, but not much across levels of veridical age.

128   *Comparing two groups of observations: Factors and contrasts*

are using acoustic information in an optimal and dispassionate manner. More recent work highlights the role of 'real-world knowledge', and stereotypes about different kinds of speakers, in the determination (or reporting) of apparent speaker height (see Chapter 13 for more information on this topic).

One potential problem with using apparent age as a predictor is that this is not necessarily balanced across listeners. To investigate the distribution of levels of *A* across listeners, we can cross-tabulate age classifications by listener as seen below. Since each listener has observations at both levels of the A factor (i.e. across each column), we know that apparent age is a within-subjects factor. If *all* of the columns contained one zero and one non-zero value, this would be a *between-subjects* factor. Finally, if *some* of the columns featured one zero and others featured no zeros apparent age would vary across listeners in a manner resembling the nameless (?) design.

```
xtabs (~ notmen$A + notmen$L)
##          notmen$L
## notmen$A  1  2  3  4  5  6  7  8  9 10 11 12 13 14 15
##        a 42 35 42 20 34 37 30 48 42 46 42 44 31 36 36
##        c 52 59 50 74 58 55 64 46 49 48 52 50 63 58 58
```

We can see an example of our 'undesirable' organization when we inspect the distribution of apparent age across speakers, a subset of which is shown below. Some speakers are *never* identified as adults, some are *always* identified as adults, and some are *sometimes* identified as adults.

```
xtabs (~ notmen$A + notmen$S)[,40:50]
##          notmen$S
## notmen$A 40 41 42 43 44 45 46 92 93 94 95
##        a 11  0  0  0  0  0  0 11  7 15 14
##        c  4 15 15 15 15 15 15  4  8  0  1
```

To analyze data from two groups, we need to have it in a data frame with one row for each observation. One column should contain the dependent variable, the variable whose variation you're trying to predict. Another column should contain information about which group each observation belongs to. Finally, since we have repeated measures data, we also need a column that indicates which source (speaker/listener/participant) provided the data point. The variables from our `exp_data` data frame that we will be using are:

- `L`: An integer from 1 to 15 indicating which *listener* responded to the trial.
- `height`: A floating-point number representing the *height* (in centimeters) reported for the speaker on each trial.
- `S`: An integer from 1 to 139 indicating which *speaker* produced the trial stimulus.
- `A`: The *apparent age* of the speaker indicated by the listener, `a` (adult) or `c` (child).

In this chapter, we will build models that help us answer the following questions, among others:

(Q1) How tall do speakers perceived as adult females sound?

(Q2) How tall do speakers perceived as children sound?
(Q3) What is the difference in apparent height associated with the perception of adultness?

Figure 5.3 presents between-speaker and within-speaker variation in apparent height, according to apparent age. The answer to (Q1) above will depend on the distribution illustrated by the left boxplot of the left plot of the figure. The answer to (Q2) will depend on the distribution illustrated by the right boxplot of the left plot of the figure. The answer to (Q3) will depend on the difference between these distributions. Of course, we see that this is not the full story since there is substantial between-listener variation in the locations of these distributions, and in the differences between them, as illustrated by the pairs of boxes in the right plot. However, we will leave the discussion of between-listener variation in effects for the next chapter.

5.5 Estimating the difference between two means with 'brms'

In Chapter 4, we fit a model with the simplest possible fixed-effect structure, basically an 'intercept-only' random effects model. To estimate a difference between two group means, we need to include a 'real' predictor in our model, a variable indicating apparent age for each observation. Remember that formulas look like `y ~ predictor(s)`. Previously, our formula had no (fixed-effect) predictors and so it looked like `height ~ 1 + (1|L) + (1|S)`, where the `1` indicates that this is an intercept-only model. To predict apparent height based on whether the talker was perceived as an adult or not, our model formula would now look like this:

```
height ~ 1 + A + (1|L) + (1|S)
```

This assumes that we have a column in our data frame (`A`) that indicates whether the listener thought a data point was produced by an adult or not. This model formula basically says "we expect height to vary around the intercept based on whether

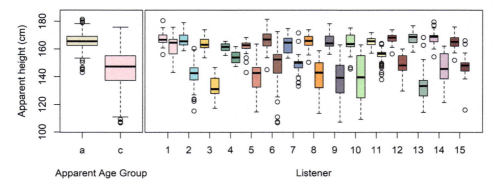

Figure 5.3 (left) Distribution of apparent heights according to apparent age group, across all listeners. (right) Same as the left plot but presented individually for each listener. In each case, the first box of each color (the higher box) represents responses for apparent adults.

130   *Comparing two groups of observations: Factors and contrasts*

the speaker was judged to be an adult, in addition to listener and speaker-specific adjustments to the intercept". When you have at least one non-intercept predictor in your model then you don't need to include a 1 in your formula, since the intercept is included in the model by default. So, your model formula can look like:

```
height ~ A + (1|L) + (1|S).
```

Since the intercept is included by default, if you want to *suppress* (omit) an intercept from your model you need to specifically indicate this in your formula. You can do this by placing a `0` in front of your model formula like this `height ~ 0 + A + (1|L) + (1|S)`.

To fit our model comparing two groups, we need to specify prior probabilities for our age predictor. We should also rethink our priors since our data has changed substantially (from *only* men to *no* men). We can do this using the information provided in `height_data`, which tells us that adult females are about 162 cm tall on average, and 11-year-old children are around 150 cm tall (our boys and girls were 10–12 years old). Based on this we can set the intercept to 156 cm, halfway between each average. We set the standard deviations for all priors to the difference between group means, 12 cm. This means that we expect that variation in the data, whether it be between groups (the *A* predictor) or within-listener error (`sigma`, σ), will be roughly on the order of the empirical group differences.

Usually, we would discuss the structure of this model now, *before* fitting. However, this time we're going to put this off for a little bit because an explanation involves some of the less intuitive concepts relating to regression. So, this time we're going to fit the model first and then get to the details of the model later in the chapter.

5.5.1 Fitting the model

Our model now includes a non-intercept term, apparent age (`A`), and so we need to specify a prior for class `b` in addition to the priors we set in Chapter 4. This is the class for all fixed-effect predictors (those fit without adaptive pooling) other than the intercept. Below we see a summary of the classes of predictors we have set priors for so far.

*   `Intercept`: this is a unique class, only for intercepts.
*   `b`: This class includes all fixed-effect predictors *apart* from the intercept.
*   `sd`: This is for standard deviation parameters related to 'batches' of parameters, e.g. `sd(Intercept)` for L (σ_L).
*   `sigma`: the error term.

Below we fit the model, using the formula discussed above.

```
# Fit the model yourself
model = brms::brm (
  height ~ A + (1|L) + (1|S), data = notmen, chains = 4, cores = 4,
  warmup = 1000, iter = 3500, thin = 2,
  prior = c(brms::set_prior("normal(156, 12)", class = "Intercept"),
            brms::set_prior("normal(0, 12)", class = "b"),
```

Comparing two groups of observations: Factors and contrasts   131

```
          brms::set_prior("normal(0, 12)", class = "sd"),
          brms::set_prior("normal(0, 12)", class = "sigma")))

# Or download it from the GitHub page:
model = bmmb::get_model ('5_model.RDS')
```

5.5.2 *Interpreting the model*

We can inspect the model print statement, which is mostly familiar by now.

```
# inspect model
bmmb::short_summary (model)
## Formula:  height ~ A + (1 | L) + (1 | S)
##
## Group-Level Effects:
## ~L (Number of levels: 15)
##                 Estimate Est.Error l-95% CI u-95% CI
## sd(Intercept)       5.24      1.11     3.54     7.85
##
## ~S (Number of levels: 94)
##                 Estimate Est.Error l-95% CI u-95% CI
## sd(Intercept)       3.59      0.43      2.8     4.51
##
## Population-Level Effects:
##             Estimate Est.Error l-95% CI u-95% CI
## Intercept     163.92      1.46   160.97   166.72
## Ac            -17.37      0.74   -18.81   -15.89
##
## Family Specific Parameters:
##         Estimate Est.Error l-95% CI u-95% CI
## sigma       8.58      0.17     8.25     8.92
```

There's a new predictor in the section on `Population-Level Effects` (i.e. the 'fixed' effects). In addition to the `Intercept` term, we now get estimates for a term called `Ac`. Admittedly, this is a strange name, but it's how R handles predictors that are words (called *factors* in R). R names predictors like this `factornameFactorlevel`. For example, a factor called `colors` with levels `red`, `green,` and `blue` would have the levels `colorsred`, `colorsgreen`, and `colorsblue`. So, the `Ac` name tells us this is the estimate for the `c` (child) level of the `A` (apparent age) factor. The `Ac` term in our model reflects something about the average apparent height of speakers identified as children. But what about this value does it reflect? Note that the 'Intercept' term in the model above corresponds to the mean apparent height for speakers perceived as adult females:

```
# calculate mean apparent height based on apparent adultness
tapply (notmen$height, notmen$A, mean)
##     a       c
## 165.5 145.4
```

132   *Comparing two groups of observations: Factors and contrasts*

What does the value of `Ac` reflect about the apparent height of speakers identified as children? It tells us the difference between the group means, which is 20.1 cm when calculating simple group means, and 17.4 cm as estimated in the model. Well, our model coefficient is actually −17.4, but since it reflects a distance we can express it as an absolute value. Ideally, it seems like our model would have three `population level` predictors, the intercept, a predictor associated with the adult response mean (i.e. `Aa`), and a predictor associated with the child response mean (`Ac`). To understand why this can't happen, we need to talk about contrasts.

5.6 Contrasts

Factors are variables like 'adult' vs. 'child' that are not inherently numerical. **Contrasts** are the numerical implementation of factors in your model. The general problem is, in many cases, that coefficients for every level of a factor cannot all be estimated. For example, if you have two groups, then you can't *independently* calculate all of the following:

1   The group 1 mean.
2   The group 2 mean.
3   The grand mean (the Intercept).

Why not? Because once you know any 2 of these quantities, you also know the third. In Section 2.5.1, we mentioned that the sum of the differences between observations and the sample mean calculated from those observations will always equal zero. When we estimate the intercept based on the group 1 and group 2 means, the intercept is analogous to a sample mean, and each group average can be thought of as an 'observation'. As a result, the deviations of the group means around the intercept (i.e. the effects) are constrained to sum to zero. Since the sum of the effect of group 1 and the effect of group 2 must equal zero, that means that the group 1 effect *must* equal the opposite of the group 2 effect. For example, if the group 1 mean is 5 and the overall mean is 6, the group 2 mean *must* be 7. This is because if the group 1 mean is 1 below the overall mean (an effect of −1), then the other group *must* be 1 above the mean (an effect of +1) in order to balance out.

The situation described above means that when we estimate the mean of the means (i.e. the intercept) based on two group means, one of the three values is always perfectly predictable based on the other two. When things are entirely predictable in this way we say they are **linearly dependent**, and regression models don't like this (for more information on linear dependence, see Section 8.8). For example, imagine you were trying to predict a person's weight from their height. You want to include height in centimeters *and* height in meters in your model, and you want to *independently* estimate effects for both predictors. Since height in centimeters = height in meters × 100, that is not going to be possible. The effect of one *must* be 100 times the effect of the other. Clearly, one value is not independent of another if it always exactly 100 times the other. This means that we can't independently estimate these two values. Even though it may be less transparent, this is the same reason why we can't estimate all the group means *and* the overall mean.

There are many different contrast coding schemes, and these reflect different ways of representing group differences, and decisions regarding which effects to estimate

Comparing two groups of observations: Factors and contrasts   133

(and which to ignore). Here we will discuss two approaches: Treatment coding and sum coding.

5.6.1 Treatment coding

The coding scheme you use determines how your model represents the differences it encodes. In the model above we used **treatment coding** (the default in R). In treatment coding, a 'reference' level is chosen to be the intercept, and all group effects reflect the difference between the mean for that group, and the value of the Intercept (i.e., the mean for the reference level). By default, R chooses the alphabetically-lowest level to be the reference level. In our model above, the `a` (adult) level was chosen as the reference level, and so the intercept represents the mean for this group. The effect for 'child' (`Ac`) represents the *difference* between the child mean and the adult mean. This means that our credible intervals also represent the difference in the means and not the means themselves. So, based on our treatment-coded model we expect the *difference* in the apparent heights of adults and children to be about 17.4 cm, and we think there is a 95% chance that the *difference* between the means is between 15.9 and 18.8 cm in magnitude.

To interpret treatment-coded coefficients in a regression model:

- The reference category mean is the 'Intercept' in the model.
- The value of the coefficients of any non-intercept group is equal to `group mean - Intercept (reference group mean)`.
- To recover the mean estimate for any non-intercept group, we add `group effect + Intercept (reference group mean)`.

Notice that under treatment coding you estimate a group mean and the differences between the group means, but you do not estimate an overall **grand mean**. Although there is potentially some variation in terminology, we will use *grand mean*, to refer to the mean of the group means. Keep in mind that this may have a different value from the overall mean of all of the observations with no group structure included in the calculations.

5.6.2 Sum coding

There are multiple options for coding schemes, and the best one for you depends on what you want to get out of your model. Changing the coding scheme may substantially change the value of your coefficients and the way they should be interpreted. However, this will not change the fundamental relationships encoded in your model. Think of it this way, you can tell someone that the library is five miles west of your house or that your house is five miles east of the library. This sounds different because you are changing the reference point (the 'intercept'), but it represents the same relationship. As a result, the selection of a coding scheme best suited for a model depends on which one results in the simplest interpretation of the model given the purpose of the research.

That being said, going forward we will focus exclusively on what is known as **sum coding**. The focus on a single coding scheme is meant to save space and minimize confusion. The reason for selecting sum coding specifically is because it has some

134   *Comparing two groups of observations: Factors and contrasts*

desirable mathematical properties and it allows models to be interpreted in a style reminiscent of a traditional analysis of variance (to be discussed in Chapter 11), which many researchers may find useful.

In sum coding, there is no reference level. Instead, the intercept represents the mean of the group means. The effect for each individual group is then represented as a deviation from the intercept, and all of these effects are constrained to sum to zero. Just like for treatment coding, you can't estimate all of your group effects *and* the overall grand mean. Since we are estimating the grand mean, that means we will not be able to estimate *one* of our group effects. When using sum coding, R selects the *alphabetically last* level of your factor, and does not estimate it. The value of the missing effect is easy to recover algebraically. Since the sum of the coefficients must equal zero, the missing factor level will always be equal to the *negative sum* of the other factors. This means that if you add up the values of the levels that *are* present and flip the sign, the outcome is the value of your missing level. If you think about it, it must be this way. This is because the final missing value must cancel out the sum of the others if the sum of all the values is to equal zero.

As discussed earlier, with only two groups if you know the grand mean and the distance between one group to the grand mean, you also know the distance of the other group to the grand mean. This can be seen quite clearly below where the difference between each group to the overall mean has a magnitude of 10.07. So, if our sum-coded model tells us that the intercept is 155.4 cm and the adult mean is 10.1 cm above this, then the child mean *must* be 10.07 cm below it.

```
# calculate group means
means = tapply (notmen$height, notmen$A, mean)
mean (means)
## [1] 155.5

# find the distances to the mean of the means
means - mean (means)
##       a       c
##   10.07 -10.07
```

To interpret sum-coded coefficients in regression models:

*   The mean of all your group means (the grand mean) is the 'Intercept' in the model.
*   The value of the coefficients of any other group mean will be equal to `group mean - Intercept (grand mean)`.
*   To recover the mean estimate for any other group, we add `group effect + Intercept (grand mean)`.

Before continuing, we want to mention two things with respect to sum coding. First, in Chapter 4 we noted that random effects are coded as deviations from the mean. Now we can be more specific and say that `brms` will use sum coding to specify all of your random effects (i.e. all terms estimated with adaptive pooling). Second, you may have noted that last chapter we did, in fact, estimate all of the levels of the listener random effects. We have 15 listeners in our data and we clearly saw 15 'random effects' for listeners at several points in the chapter. The reason for this is that unlike fixed effects, random effects are not constrained to sum to zero, and the value of the Jth factor level is not necessarily predictable given knowledge of the value of the other $J-1$ levels. As a result, in many cases, all levels of a random effect *can* be estimated.

5.6.3 Comparison of sum and treatment coding

Figure 5.4 presents a comparison of the way the two coding schemes represent the group means in a two-group model. In each case, they estimate one intercept and one effect, letting you recreate one other effect (i.e., they each omit one parameter). In treatment coding, the omitted value is the overall mean, which in the two-group case will always be `Intercept + estimatedEffect/2`. In the case of sum coding, the omitted value is the effect for the second group, which will always be the same magnitude but have the opposite sign as the effect for the first group (i.e., `-estimatedEffect` in a two-group model).

5.7 Sum coding and the decomposition of variation

Regression models try to break up the value of the dependent variable into different components. This is why effects are expressed in terms of differences to some reference value. For example, imagine we say that a speaker's apparent height is 160 cm, and under some other condition, their apparent height is also 160 cm. If this were the case, we might be inclined to say that the change in these conditions has no *effect* on their apparent height. On the other hand, something that *is* associated with a difference in apparent height *can* be said to have an effect on that variable. As a result, we can express the *effect* of something in terms of the difference it is associated with. For example, we can say that under so and so condition a person will tend to sound 17.5 cm shorter, relative to some reference value. More generally, we can think of any variable as the sum of a bunch of independent *effects*.

As discussed in Section 1.2, the term *effect* is meant to indicate that variation in the independent variable is associated with variation in the dependent variable. This term is not meant to imply that any causal relationship exists, and certainly not that such a relationship is *proven* by the model.

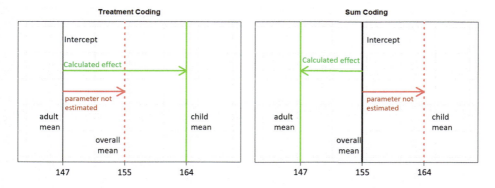

Figure 5.4 Artist's rendition of contrast and treatment coding differences for our model.

136 *Comparing two groups of observations: Factors and contrasts*

For example, since age and height are so strongly related between the ages of 2 and 18 (see Figure 1.1), you can predict the veridical height of a person between the ages of 2 and 18 from their age with good accuracy. If you build a model that predicts the height of a child based on their age you might say that in your model "age has an effect on height". A statement like this does not mean that age variation *causes* height variation in real life. Age (i.e. *time*) is a useful way to measure the progress of biological processes during childhood that themselves cause growth in body length, but age does not itself *cause* growth. Instead, a statement regarding the effect of one variable on another means that within the context of the universe you have constructed using your model, variation in body length is predictable (to some extent) based on variation in age.

The above is not to say that effects in your model will *never* reflect causal relationships, just that establishing this requires substantially more than simply finding statistical associations between variables. The decomposition of variables into a sum of effects, and the view of effects as representing predictable (maybe not causal) variation is just a way to *think* about variables, to break up observed values into their component parts. It should not be confused with the *reality* of these values and the process that underlies them (whatever that is!).

So far we've covered the fact that after picking a value to use as a reference point (the model intercept), our models:

- Represent group means as deviations from the intercept.
- Represent the listener and speaker-specific deviations from the intercept $\left(L_{[\cdot]}, S_{[\cdot]}\right)$ as being centered at 0, with standard deviations of σ_L and σ_S.
- Represent the random error (ε) as having a mean of 0 and a standard deviation of σ.

In each case, these model coefficients reflect *deviations* from some reference point. As a result, when the parameters associated with these predictors equal 0, this means that no effect is present.

- When a group coefficient is 0 the group lies exactly at the intercept. In sum coding this is the grand mean (the mean of the means) indicating that the group is basically average.
- When a listener or speaker effect is 0 this listener/speaker is exactly average with respect to their group. This means there is nothing about this speaker's average that is unpredictable given knowledge of their group.
- When an error is 0 this production is exactly as expected for a given listener/ speaker in a given group. This means that an observation contains no error since it was *exactly* predictable.

If we think of our predictors as representing deviations from some reference value, we can 'break up' any observed value into its component parts. For example, suppose that:

- The overall mean is 157 cm.
- The adult female mean is 165 cm (+8 over the intercept).
- A particular speaker has a mean apparent height of 170 cm (+5 over the adult female mean).

Comparing two groups of observations: Factors and contrasts 137

If we observe an apparent height judgment of 173 cm for this speaker, that suggests the following decomposition:

173 = 157 (Intercept) + 8 (adult female effect) + 5 (speaker effect) + 3 (error)

This reflects the following considerations:

- The average apparent height across the groups is 157 cm.
- The average for adult females is 8 cm above the overall mean (157 + 8 = 165).
- This speaker's average apparent height is 5 cm above the average for adult females (157 + 8 + 5 = 170).
- This particular production is 3 cm higher than expected for this particular speaker (157 + 8 + 5 + 3 = 173).

Another observation from this same talker might be:

164 = 157 (Intercept) + 8 (adult female effect) + 5 (speaker effect) − 6 (error)

In this case, the error is −6 since the production is now 6 cm *below* the speaker average. However, no other part of the equation has changed since this is the same speaker in the same group. Regression models basically carry out these decompositions for us and provide estimates of these components using their model parameters.

5.7.1 *Description of the model*

We're going to re-fit our treatment-coded model using sum coding and see what effect this has on the estimated coefficients. The full model specification, including prior probabilities, is presented in (5.1) below. Our model includes a new coefficient called A reflecting the effect for apparent age, but is otherwise very similar to the model described in Section 4.8.1.

$$\text{height}_{[i]} \sim N\left(\mu_{[i]}, \sigma\right)$$
$$\mu_{[i]} = \text{Intercept} + A + L_{\left[\mathsf{L}_{[i]}\right]} + S_{\left[\mathsf{S}_{[i]}\right]}$$

$$\text{Priors}:$$
$$L_{[\bullet]} \sim N(0, \sigma_L)$$
$$S_{[\bullet]} \sim N(0, \sigma_S)$$

$$\text{Intercept} \sim N(156, 12)$$
$$A \sim N(0, 12)$$
$$\sigma \sim N(0, 12)$$
$$\sigma_L \sim N(0, 12)$$
$$\sigma_S \sim N(0, 12)$$

$$(5.1)$$

We need to talk about why there is only a single A coefficient despite there being two different age groups, and why this parameter does not get a subscript. Recall that

138   *Comparing two groups of observations: Factors and contrasts*

regression models work by multiplying predictor variables with model parameters/coefficients and adding these products together to arrive at an expected value (e.g. $\mu = x_1 \cdot \alpha_2 + x_2 \cdot \alpha_2 + ...$). This means that every parameter needs to be multiplied by some number in our prediction equation. When we introduced the intercept in Section 3.5.2, we noted that the intercept is 'secretly' multiplied by a predictor equal to 1 for each observation. In order to meet this requirement, R adds a column of ones to your data to represent the intercept in your predictors.

In the case of factors with two levels (under sum coding), R adds a predictor to our data that equals 1 when A equals its first value (adult) and -1 when it has its second value (child). In this way, the single A coefficient can represent the effects for both groups, i.e. the distance between each group and the intercept. These 'hidden' predictors are how contrasts are handled mathematically. Coding schemes differ in the ways they use combinations of 1, -1, 0, and in some cases fractions, in order to mathematically represent the relations between groups. Here's how you would read the model description in (5.1) aloud in plain English:

> *Apparent speaker height is expected to vary according to a normal distribution with some unknown mean (μ) and standard deviation (σ). Means are expected to vary based on whether the listener identified the speaker as an adult or a child (A), and listener and speaker-dependent deviations from the mean (L,S). The listener and speaker effects were modeled as coming from a normal distribution with means of 0 and unknown standard deviations (σ_L, σ_S). The intercept was given a normal prior with a mean of 156 and a standard deviation of 12, and the remaining parameters were given normal priors centered at 0 with standard deviations of 12.*

5.7.2 Fitting the model

To fit a model with sum coding, we need to change the global contrast options in R. These options will be in effect until we restart R or change the contrasts to something else. If you fit a model with this coding, be sure to set this option every time you start R and want to work with this model. If there is a mismatch between your contrast settings and what the `brms` helper functions expect for your model, you may encounter problems and inscrutable error messages.

```
# to change to sum coding
options (contrasts = c('contr.sum','contr.sum'))

# to change back to treatment coding
# options (contrasts = c('contr.treatment','contr.reatment'))
```

Since the options (and our coding) have changed, but nothing else has, we can fit our sum-coded model with the same code we used above.

```
# Fit the model yourself
model_sum_coding =  brms::brm (
  height ~ A + (1|L) + (1|S), data = notmen, chains = 4, cores = 4,
  warmup = 1000, iter = 3500, thin = 2,
  prior = c(brms::set_prior("normal(156, 12)", class = "Intercept"),
```

Comparing two groups of observations: Factors and contrasts 139

```
          brms::set_prior("normal(0, 12)", class = "b"),
          brms::set_prior("normal(0, 12)", class = "sd"),
          brms::set_prior("normal(0, 12)", class = "sigma")))

# Or download it from the GitHub page:
model_sum_coding = bmmb::get_model ('5_model_sum_coding.RDS')
```

We're going to use the `fixef` (i.e. 'fixed effects') function in `brms` to inspect only the `Population-Level Effects` in our model. The `Population-Level Effects` are also sometimes called *fixed* effects in part because they are 'fixed' across the population. For example, the effect for 'child' doesn't apply only to little Susie or little Johnny in particular, but to speakers perceived as *children* more generally.

```
# inspect model fixed effects
brms::fixef (model_sum_coding)
##            Estimate Est.Error    Q2.5    Q97.5
## Intercept   155.218    1.4050 152.434 157.965
## A1            8.711    0.3602   8.003    9.416
```

An inspection of the fixed effects shows that, as expected, the `Intercept` now reflects the mean of the group means (i.e. the grand mean) and the single estimated parameter (`A1`) reflects the distance between the adult mean and the grand mean. The name of our `A1` parameter is based on how `brm` handles factors with sum coding. Predictors representing factors will be named `factornameN`, where `factorname` is the predictor name and `N` is the level number. Levels are ordered, and numbered, alphabetically starting at one, and the alphabetically last level will not be estimated. You can predict how your factor levels will be ordered by doing something like this:

```
sort (unique (notmen$A))
## [1] "a" "c"
```

So, `A1` in our model corresponds to the 'adult' level of our predictor, and `A2` *would* be the coefficient reflecting the effect for 'child'. However, this is not separately estimated by our sum-coded model since `A2 = -A1`.

5.7.3 *Comparison of sum and treatment coding*

If you compare the output of the treatment and sum coding models:

```
bmmb::short_summary (model)
bmmb::short_summary (model_sum_coding)
```

The main differences are in the population-level effects, seen below:

```
# treatment coding
brms::fixef (model)
##            Estimate Est.Error   Q2.5   Q97.5
## Intercept   163.92    1.4580 160.97  166.72
```

140 *Comparing two groups of observations: Factors and contrasts*

```
## Ac              -17.37     0.7391 -18.81 -15.89

# sum coding
brms::fixef (model_sum_coding)
##              Estimate Est.Error     Q2.5   Q97.5
## Intercept   155.218    1.4050 152.434 157.965
## A1            8.711    0.3602   8.003   9.416
```

In the treatment-coded model, the intercept represents the adult mean and the `Ac` effect reflects the difference between the intercept and the child mean. In the sum-coded model, the intercept is the overall grand mean and the `A1` effect represents the difference between the adult mean and the intercept. We can see that the information contained in the models is equivalent, just represented differently. First, we can divide the `Ac` effect by two to find half the distance between the groups, which we know must be the distance between the grand mean and the child group. This is the same magnitude as the `A1` effect in the sum-coded model (since it represents the same distance).

```
17.4/2
## [1] 8.7
```

If we subtract this value from the adult mean, we recover the intercept of the sum-coded model.

```
163.9 - (17.4/2)
## [1] 155.2
```

We can take the opposite approach and add the `A1` effect to the intercept of the sum-coded model. This allows us to recreate the intercept of the treatment-coded model.

```
155.2 + 8.7
## [1] 163.9
```

Just as half the `Ac` effect equaled the magnitude of the `A1` effect, we can take the opposite approach below. Since `A1` reflects the difference between groups and the grand mean, twice this value must equal the distance between the group means themselves.

```
8.7*2
## [1] 17.4
```

5.8 Inspecting and manipulating the posterior samples

In the examples above, we added the posterior means of our model coefficients together. What we mean by this is that we took the `Estimate` in the model print statement, and used that to recreate our parameters (e.g., `156.7 + 8.77`). This approach is fine if we intend to quickly estimate simple combinations of our parameters as we did in the section above. However, this does not allow us to estimate the intervals around parameters in a reliable way. The main issue is that this approach does not adequately

Comparing two groups of observations: Factors and contrasts 141

reflect the shared variation in the parameters we are combining, and this is a problem when estimating their credible intervals.

It's important to remember that our models are actually a series of samples from the posterior distributions of our model parameters. Each of these posterior distributions reflects a different random variable, each with its own mean and variance. When one adds or subtracts two random variables, the variance of the outcome is defined as in (5.2). The top line in (5.2) says: "The variance of the sum of the random variables x and y is equal to the sum of their individual variances (σ_x^2, σ_y^2), plus two times the product of the correlation between the variables (ρ), and their individual standard deviations (σ_x, σ_y)".

$$\sigma_{x+y}^2 = \sigma_x^2 + \sigma_y^2 + 2\rho\sigma_x\sigma_y$$
$$\sigma_{x-y}^2 = \sigma_x^2 - \sigma_y^2 - 2\rho\sigma_x\sigma_y \tag{5.2}$$

We haven't talked about *correlation* yet (we will in Section 6.3.2). Basically, the correlation is the strength of the relationship between variables, and it can greatly affect the outcome of the equations above. Consider a situation where x is very positive when y is very negative and vice versa. We show this in the code below where we make y equal the negative of x, plus a small amount of random variation. In this example, x and y exhibit a *negative* correlation, a negative association between the variables. If you were to plot these variables (`plot(x,y)`) you would see a line sloping down from left to right.

```
set.seed (1)
x = 1:10
y = -x + rnorm (10)
```

As seen in the code below, each of x and y has a variance of about 9. However, since x and y tend to have opposite values, the sum of x and y will be near zero, meaning the variance of this sum will be near zero. On the other hand, since they have opposite signs their *difference* will be large, meaning the variance of their difference may also be very large.

```
# 'marginal' variance of x
var (x)
## [1] 9.167

# 'marginal' variance of y
var (y)
## [1] 8.773

# variance of sum of x and y
var (x+y)
## [1] 0.6093

# variance of difference of x and y
var (x-y)
## [1] 35.27
```

142   *Comparing two groups of observations: Factors and contrasts*

This example shows that the sum/difference of two variables may vary substantially based on the correlation between the variables. However, this will be unpredictable if one does not take the correlation into account. Why do we care about this? Well, clearly the credible intervals describing our posterior distributions reflect the variance of these distributions; wider intervals correspond to larger variances. So, as a practical matter, the only way to ensure that we get the correct variance, and credible interval, for the combination of the intercept and the apparent age predictors (i.e., $\sigma^2_{\text{Intercept}+A}$) is to take the correlation of the predictors into account. When we summarize parameters and then combine them, we lose all information about the correlations between the parameters, making an accurate estimation of $\sigma^2_{\text{Intercept}+A}$ impossible.

On the other hand, if we add our parameters together, or find the differences between, them *before* summarizing, we don't need to worry about the correlations between them. This is because this information is directly present in the posterior samples and is preserved when we work with these directly. In our simple example above, we didn't actually calculate the correlation between x and y to find the correct variance of their sum, we simply found the sum and then calculated the variance. This is why when combining parameters, you should *always* do so with the original samples, and *then* summarize the combined samples.

We can see the individual samples for our population-level (i.e. fixed effects) parameters by calling the `fixef` function and setting `summary` to `FALSE`. Below, we see the first 6 posterior samples for each parameter.

```
samples = brms::fixef (model_sum_coding, summary = FALSE)
head (samples)
##       variable
## draw Intercept      A1
##    1      153.2 9.040
##    2      154.7 8.365
##    3      152.2 8.835
##    4      156.0 9.003
##    5      154.7 8.196
##    6      155.9 8.305
```

If we find the mean of the samples across both columns, these exactly correspond to the estimates of these parameters provided by the `fixef` function above. In fact, the `fixef` function is only doing some convenient summarizing of the samples for us and presents this to us in a nice, interpretable way.

```
colMeans (samples)
## Intercept         A1
##   155.218      8.711
```

When we fit the models above, we made certain choices regarding what information was directly represented in the model, and what was not. In other words, we made a decision regarding how to **parameterize** our model, including the selection of a coding scheme. However, the information that is not directly represented in the model can still often be recovered by combining parameter estimates in appropriate ways. For example, we know that our adult mean is equal to the sum of the intercept and the

Comparing two groups of observations: Factors and contrasts 143

`A1` parameter. If we want to know what the value of `Intercept+A1` is according to our model, all we need to do is add the values of `A1` and `Intercept`, individually for each sample, and then consider the distribution of the sum. This means we add the elements of each row together, resulting in a single vector as long as the two vectors are summed. Combining the intercept and `A1` parameters in our model is as easy as seen below, we simply add the two vectors together:

```
adult_mean = samples[,"Intercept"] + samples[,"A1"]
```

In Figure 5.5, we plot histograms and the individual posterior samples for the `Intercept` (the overall mean) and the `A1` parameter (the effect for adults). We also show how the intercept and the `A1` parameter can be combined to find the posterior estimates of our child and adult means.

We can summarize our combinations of parameters using the `posterior_summary` function from the `brms` package. This function takes in a matrix or vector and calculates the mean, standard deviation, and 95% credible interval (by default) for each column in the data. Below, we use this strategy to get information about posterior means and credible intervals for our adult and child means. Whereas the credible interval for the `A1` effect reflected uncertainty in the *difference* between the adult female mean and the Intercept, the values below provide information about the adult and child group means directly.

```
new_parameters = cbind(adult_mean = samples[,'Intercept'] + samples[,'A1'],
                       child_mean = samples[,'Intercept'] - samples[,'A1'])

# report mean and spread of samples
brms::posterior_summary (new_parameters)
##              Estimate Est.Error   Q2.5  Q97.5
```

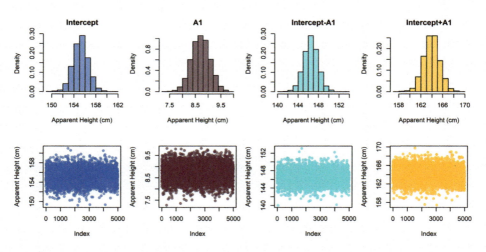

Figure 5.5 Comparison of histograms (top row) and trace plots (bottom row) of the posterior samples of selected parameters, and their combinations.

144 *Comparing two groups of observations: Factors and contrasts*

```
## adult_mean    163.9    1.465 161.1 166.8
## child_mean    146.5    1.435 143.7 149.3
```

We can also compare the intervals above to those of our intercept and effect for apparent age:

```
brms::fixef (model_sum_coding)
##              Estimate Est.Error    Q2.5   Q97.5
## Intercept   155.218    1.4050 152.434 157.965
## A1            8.711    0.3602   8.003   9.416
```

We see that the 95% credible interval for our intercept spans about 5.5 cm and our 95% credible interval for the apparent age effect (A1) spans about 1.4 cm. However, the 95% credible intervals for the adult and child means span only about 5.7 cm each, indicating that $\sigma^2_{\text{Intercept}+A} < \sigma^2_{\text{Intercept}} + \sigma^2_A$. In other words, the variance of the sum of the intercept and the apparent age effect is smaller than the sum of their individual variances. We know that this likely reflects a negative correlation between the posterior samples of the intercept and the A1 parameter, however, this is not so obvious if we only look at the summaries immediately above.

5.8.1 *Using the hypothesis function*

Working directly with the posterior samples is simple, but often not strictly necessary. The brms package contains a very useful function called hypothesis that helps us combine and manipulate parameters very easily without having to do any of the steps outlined in the previous section. The hypothesis function provides a lot of extra information and formatting which may be useful in 'real life' but is cumbersome for this book. As a result, we will be relying on the short_hypothesis function provided in the book R package (bmmb). This function is simply a wrapper for the hypothesis function that provides a more compact output while still maintaining most of the information we need. To be clear, any functionality we credit to short_hypothesis is actually a property of hypothesis and all the credit goes to the brms package.

You can ask short_hypothesis to add terms in your model (spelled just as they are in the print statement), and to compare the result to some number. If you compare the result to 0, it just tells you about the result of the terms you added. However, you can compare your parameters to any value, or to each other. For example, the line below says "test my hypothesis that the Intercept plus the A1 parameter is equal to zero". This is a slightly convoluted way of saying "tell me what the value of the adult mean is so I can see if it is different from zero". We want to be clear, however, that we're not suggesting that short_hypothesis is used to test binary true/false hypotheses with respect to the 'real' value of the parameter in question. Instead, we are simply using the short_hypothesis function as an easy way to calculate combinations of parameter values.

```
bmmb::short_hypothesis(model_sum_coding, "Intercept + A1 = 0")
##     Estimate Est.Error  Q2.5 Q97.5          hypothesis
## H1    163.9     1.465 161.1 166.8 (Intercept+A1) = 0
```

Comparing two groups of observations: Factors and contrasts 145

You will notice that the mean, error, and credible intervals correspond to the values obtained by calculating our `new_parameters` above. We can also check several parameter combinations simultaneously. Below we use the information provided in Section 5.6 to recreate all our mean estimates of interest, first for the sum coding model:

```
short_hypothesis(model_sum_coding,
                 c("Intercept = 0",          # overall mean
                   "Intercept + A1 = 0",     # adult mean
                   "Intercept - A1 = 0"))    # child mean
##    Estimate Est.Error   Q2.5 Q97.5          hypothesis
## H1    155.2     1.405  152.4 158.0     (Intercept) = 0
## H2    163.9     1.465  161.1 166.8  (Intercept+A1) = 0
## H3    146.5     1.435  143.7 149.3  (Intercept-A1) = 0
```

And then for the treatment coding model:

```
short_hypothesis(model,
                 c("Intercept + Ac/2 = 0",   # overall mean
                   "Intercept = 0",          # adult mean
                   "Intercept + Ac = 0"))    # child mean
##    Estimate Est.Error   Q2.5 Q97.5           hypothesis
## H1    155.2     1.399  152.4 157.9 (Intercept+Ac/2) = 0
## H2    163.9     1.458  161.0 166.7      (Intercept) = 0
## H3    146.5     1.436  143.7 149.4   (Intercept+Ac) = 0
```

As noted earlier, these models clearly contain the same information, just represented in different ways.

5.8.2 Working with the random effects

Both ways of adding fixed effects presented above will also work for combining and manipulating our random effects. For example, we can get our listener random intercept using the `ranef` function (as discussed in Section 4.6.1) using the code below:

```
listener_effects_hat =
  ranef(model_sum_coding, summary = FALSE)$L[,,"Intercept"]

str (listener_effects_hat)
##  num [1:5000, 1:15] 13.17 9.58 12.68 9.24 9.55 ...
##  - attr(*, "dimnames")=List of 2
##   ..$ : NULL
##   ..$ : chr [1:15] "1" "2" "3" "4" ...
```

The _hat suffix represents the 'hat' ($\hat{x}$) diacritic (i.e. little symbol) in mathematical notation, which goes above variables to indicate that they represent modeled quantities

146 *Comparing two groups of observations: Factors and contrasts*

rather than (unknown) population quantities. We can get the intercept from the model using the `fixef` function and asking for the column called 'Intercept' from the output.

```
Intercept_hat =
  fixef(model_sum_coding, summary = FALSE)[,"Intercept"]

str (Intercept_hat) ##  Named num [1:5000] 153 155 152 156 155 ...
##  - attr(*, "names")= chr [1:5000] "1" "2" "3" "4" ...
```

We can combine the above samples and summarize these to get the conditional means and the listener effects, according to our model.

```
# add the intercept and listener random effects, and summarize
listener_means_hat =
  brms::posterior_summary (Intercept_hat + listener_effects_hat)

# summarize listener effects
listener_effects_hat = brms::posterior_summary (listener_effects_hat)
```

We can calculate analogous values directly from the data, as seen below. First, we find the average for each listener across each adult and child groups, and then we find the average of that. The reason for this is to control for the fact that adult and child responses may not be balanced within listeners, and we want the listener average to be halfway between the adult and child *category means* rather than simply reflecting the distribution of responses overall. For example, if a listener identified 90% of speakers as adults, their overall mean would obviously be closer to their adult responses than their child responses.

```
# find average apparent height for each listener and apparent age
listener_means = tapply (notmen$height, notmen[,c('A','L')], mean)
# find average apparent height for each listener
listener_means = colMeans (listener_means)
```

After finding the listener means we calculate the mean of the means (the `Intercept`), and subtract this from the listener means to get the listener effects (i.e., the listener-dependent deviations from the intercept).

```
Intercept = mean (listener_means)
listener_effects = listener_means - Intercept
```

The above values represent the no pooling estimates of the listener means and effects since these values were each estimated entirely independently for each listener. In Figure 5.6, we plot the listener effects and means estimated using adaptive pooling with `brms` (`listener_effects_hat`, `listener_means_hat`) and compare these to the equivalent values we calculated directly from the data (`listener_effects`, `listener_means`). Clearly, these are a good match. A benefit of using the modeled parameters is that these come with credible intervals so that we can make statements about likely bounds for values in addition to providing point estimates.

Random effects can be investigated using the `hypothesis` (or `short_hypothesis`) function by setting appropriate values for the `scope` and `group` parameters. For example, below we repeat the code to test the hypothesis that the overall, fixed-effect intercept is equal to zero.

```
short_hypothesis(model_sum_coding, "Intercept = 0")
##    Estimate Est.Error   Q2.5  Q97.5       hypothesis
## H1    155.2     1.405  152.4    158  (Intercept) = 0
```

However, if we set `scope=ranef` we tell the function to check for intercepts in the random effects, rather than our `population level` intercept. In addition, by setting `group=L` we tell the function to check for the random intercepts of the `L` factor specifically. Below we compare this output:

```
short_hypothesis(model_sum_coding, "Intercept = 0",
                 scope = "ranef",group="L")[1:5,]
##    Estimate Est.Error      Q2.5    Q97.5       hypothesis group
## H1    9.690     1.585     6.603   12.832  (Intercept) = 0     1
## H2   -1.792     1.597    -4.941    1.297  (Intercept) = 0     2
## H3   -7.376     1.602   -10.636   -4.255  (Intercept) = 0     3
## H4    5.121     1.566     2.104    8.283  (Intercept) = 0     4
## H5   -4.393     1.570    -7.598   -1.383  (Intercept) = 0     5
```

With those calculated 'manually' above, and see that they are the same.

```
listener_effects_hat[1:5,]
##    Estimate Est.Error   Q2.5  Q97.5
## 1     9.690     1.585  6.603 12.832
## 2    -1.792     1.597 -4.941  1.297
```

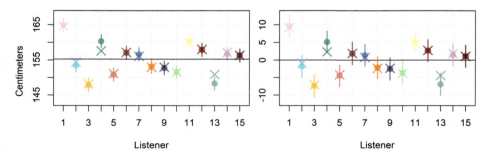

Figure 5.6 (left) Estimated listener means and 95% credible intervals. Crosses indicate no pooling estimates. (right) Estimated listener effects and 95% credible intervals. Crosses indicate centered no pooling estimates.

148 *Comparing two groups of observations: Factors and contrasts*

```
## 3    -7.376    1.602 -10.636 -4.255
## 4     5.121    1.566   2.104  8.283
## 5    -4.393    1.570  -7.598 -1.383
```

Setting `scope=ranef` returns the random effects themselves. By changing the `scope` parameter to `coef` rather than `ranef`, we tell `hypothesis` to consider the value of the intercept coefficient (i.e., Intercept + random effect) rather than the random effect itself. Since `group=L`, this is done for the grouping factor `L` (i.e. across listeners). Below, we see that this approach:

```
short_hypothesis(model_sum_coding, "Intercept = 0",
                 scope = "coef",group="L")[1:5,]
##      Estimate Est.Error   Q2.5 Q97.5       hypothesis group
## H1      164.9    0.9516  163.1 166.8  (Intercept) = 0     1
## H2      153.4    0.9438  151.6 155.3  (Intercept) = 0     2
## H3      147.8    0.9585  146.0 149.8  (Intercept) = 0     3
## H4      160.3    0.9556  158.5 162.2  (Intercept) = 0     4
## H5      150.8    0.9475  149.0 152.7  (Intercept) = 0     5
```

Also yields identical results to obtaining the individual samples, and adding and summarizing those (as we did above).

```
listener_means_hat[1:5,]
##    Estimate Est.Error   Q2.5 Q97.5
## 1     164.9    0.9516  163.1 166.8
## 2     153.4    0.9438  151.6 155.3
## 3     147.8    0.9585  146.0 149.8
## 4     160.3    0.9556  158.5 162.2
## 5     150.8    0.9475  149.0 152.7
```

Finally, in Section 5.8 we combined fixed-effect parameters, adding and subtracting these to answer specific questions. In our Bayesian models, we can do this same thing using our random effects, and in fact, we just did so to recover our listener means above. However, we can also do this to compare levels of our random effects among themselves. For example, in Figure 5.6 we see that listeners two and three appear to have reported different average apparent heights. Is this conclusion supported by our model? To answer this question we can subtract the samples corresponding to the two parameters, and then summarize the distribution of the difference, as seen below.

```
# get listener effects
listener_effects_hat =
  ranef(model_sum_coding, summary = FALSE)$L[,,"Intercept"]

# find the difference between the second and third listener effect
difference_2_3 = listener_effects_hat[,2] - listener_effects_hat[,3]
```

Comparing two groups of observations: Factors and contrasts 149

```
# summarize the difference
posterior_summary (difference_2_3)
##        Estimate  Est.Error   Q2.5  Q97.5
## [1,]     5.585        1.234 3.188   7.95
```

We see that the average difference is 5.6 cm and the 95% credible interval is between 3.2 and 8.0 cm. Based on this, it seems likely that listener 2 *really does* rate speakers as taller overall relative to listener 3. A minimum difference of 3.2 cm may seem odd if we look at the intervals of the effects for listeners two and three in the right plot in Figure 5.6, which seem to overlap. The mismatch is related to the difference between summarizing and then comparing and comparing and then summarizing.

Imagine listeners 2 and 3 have average apparent height judgments of 162 and 164 cm, and that the intercept is 156 cm. If for some sample the intercept is 157, then the listener effects for that sample would need to be +5 (157 + 5 = 162) and +7 (157 + 7 = 164). If, for the next sample the intercept were 153, now the listener effects would need to be +9 (153 + 9 = 162) and +11 (153 + 11 = 164). In this way, model parameters (including random effects) can rise and fall together across posterior samples. This 'rising and falling together' can result in a *correlation* between parameters which, as noted above, can affect the credible intervals around combinations of parameters.

Note that in our example above, the range for the first listener spanned from +5 to +9 across samples, and the second range spanned from +7 to +11. This gives the impression that these parameters overlap, but we know that this is somewhat artificial. The listeners in our hypothetical example above had varying effect estimates across samples, however, the difference between the parameters was 2 *within* each sample. In the right plot of Figure 5.6, we are showing the marginal distributions of the listener effects. This provides information about the individual credible range of these parameters but makes it difficult to consider the distribution of the *differences* between pairs of parameters. In this case, it obscures the fact that the effects for listeners 2 and 3 are more dissimilar than they appear.

Instead, we can consider the distribution of the differences in listener effects directly as we did in `difference_2_3` above. This gives us information about the difference between these parameters and correctly calculates the credible interval around this difference, however, information about the ranges of the individual parameters is obviously lost. So, we effectively represent different information when we plot (or summarize) marginal parameter distributions as opposed to combinations (including differences) of these. If we are interested primarily in highlighting the difference between parameters, focusing on the marginal distribution of each parameter may paint a misleading picture for the reader.

5.9 Making our models more robust: The (non-standardized) t-distribution

By almost any objective measure, a Ferrari is a 'good' car. A Ferrari will be fast, beautiful, and precisely made. And yet a Ferrari will not do well on a bumpy dirt road or even over speed bumps. You could say that the design of the Ferrari assumes that it will be used on flat, clean(ish) roads. Someone who damaged their Ferrari driving fast on a bumpy dirt road would be foolish to blame the car, they used it 'incorrectly' by violating the assumptions implicit in the design of a Ferrari. You don't buy a Ferrari to drive it down dirt roads, because that's not what it was designed for.

150 *Comparing two groups of observations: Factors and contrasts*

However, not everything breaks just because you use it for something it wasn't designed for. One way to think of this is that a Ferrari is not very *robust*, it only works well if you stick to its design assumptions. A more robust car, like a reasonably-priced mid-sized sedan, may not be as 'good' a car as the Ferrari, however, it can be used successfully in a very wide range of circumstances. Similarly, a statistical model is **robust** when it provides useful, reliable results in a wide range of situations. If we think of robustness as a continuous (rather than discrete) property, more robust statistical models are more reliable in a wider range of situations than less-robust statistical models. Since all statistical models rely on certain assumptions implicit in their structure, more robust statistical models are those which are either more tolerant of violations of their assumptions, or those that make assumptions that are violated in a smaller number of cases.

One of the simplest ways for us to increase the robustness of our models is to think about their **distributional robustness**, that is robustness related to the distributional assumptions made by the model. For example, using **t-distributions** in place of normal distributions can lead to more robust models in many situations. This is because the t-distribution is substantially more tolerant to outliers than the normal distribution, and thus can be substantially more robust in the presence of outliers.

Rather than focusing on the mathematical properties of priors in the abstract, it's more useful to focus on whether or not the *shapes* of their densities reflect the distributions of interest. This is because, ultimately, any distribution you choose is at best an approximation and will not exactly correspond to the *true* underlying distribution (which we can never know anyway), and the characteristics of the shape of the distribution can have a *direct* and practical effect on your outcomes.

The shape of the **t-distribution** is broadly similar to the standard normal distribution. It is symmetrical about its mean and has a similar 'bell' shape to it. However, the t-distribution has a *degrees of freedom* parameter (v, nu pronounced "noo") that affects the shape of the distribution. Lower values of v result in 'pointier' distributions that also have more mass in the 'tails', far away from the mean of the distribution. We can see the effect of v on the shape of the t-distribution in Figure 5.7. When $v = \infty$, the t-distribution converges on the normal distribution. As v decreases in value, the t-distribution becomes less like the normal distribution and more distinctively 't like'.

In the middle plot of Figure 5.7, we see that, apart from when $v = 1$, the shape of the distributions are all pretty similar within about two standard deviations of the mean. Since we expect the large majority of our observations to fall inside this area, this

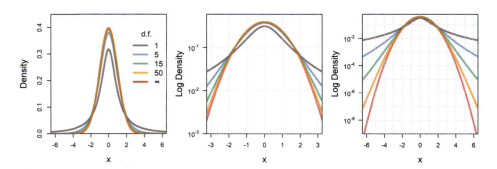

Figure 5.7 (left) A comparison of the density of a standard normal distribution (red curve) with the densities of t-distributions with different degrees of freedom. (middle) The log densities of the distributions in the left plot. (right) The same as the middle plot, except across a wider domain.

Comparing two groups of observations: Factors and contrasts   151

means that v is not expected to have a large effect on inference in many cases where data falls within 'typical' ranges (when $v > 1$). In contrast, in the right plot we see that the differences can be quite large in the 'tails' of the distributions, the areas outside of three standard deviations or so.

The most common implementation of the t-distribution has only one parameter, v. This *standardized* t-distribution always has a mean equal to zero and a variance equal to exactly $v/(v-2)$. In this way, the standard t-distribution is similar to the standard normal distribution, discussed in Section 2.5.4. In order to use the t-distribution for variables with other means and variances, we need to refer to the **non-standardized t-distribution**, a three-parameter distribution consisting of mean (μ), scale (s), and degrees of freedom (v). The non-standardized t-distribution consists of a (standard) t-distributed variable (t) that has been scaled up by some value s and then has had some value μ added to it, as in (5.3). Compare the equation below to the way that we turn the standard normal into a wide range of normal distributions, presented in equation (2.9).

$$x = \mu + s \cdot t$$

(5.3)

The μ parameter allows for the probability distribution to be centered at different locations along the number line and represents the population mean. The s parameter allows the distribution to have wider/narrower distributions than those seen in Figure 5.7, but does *not* represent the standard deviation. Since we know that the variance of the (standardized) t-distribution is $v/(v-2)$, the standard deviation must be $\sqrt{v/(v-2)}$. Since the s parameter simply scales the standard deviation up or down, the relation of s to the standard deviation and variance of the non-standardized t are presented in (5.4).

$$\sigma = s \cdot \sqrt{v/(v-2)}$$

(5.4)

$$\sigma^2 = s^2 \cdot v/(v-2)$$

5.10 Re-fitting with t-distributed errors

Eagle-eyed readers may have noticed the presence of many outliers in some of our boxplots, which are not in line with a normal distribution. Below we get the residuals from our sum-coded model and take only the first column (the posterior estimates).

```
resids = residuals (model_sum_coding) [,1]
```

We scale our data, which means we subtract the mean and divide by the standard deviation. This makes the distribution of our residuals resemble a standard normal distribution, and expresses all deviations from the mean in units of standard deviations. We do this because we know that the standard normal distribution has very little of its mass beyond three standard deviations from the mean. This means scaled residuals with magnitudes greater than three should be relatively rare. When we check the range of our scaled residuals we see that our smallest value is 4.1 standard deviations from the mean, while our largest value is 3.4 standard deviations from the mean.

```
range (scale(resids))
## [1] -4.144  3.471
```

152 *Comparing two groups of observations: Factors and contrasts*

Below, we see that this is not just two very deviant outliers, since there are several between −4 and −3.5 standard deviations from the mean.

```
head (sort(scale(resids)))
## [1] -4.144 -3.846 -3.785 -3.679 -3.668 -3.613
```

We can use the pnorm function to consider how likely these observations are given our model. The pnorm function takes in an x-value, values of μ and σ, and tells you how much of the mass of the probability density is to the *left* of the value x (see Figure 2.5). So, the code below tells us that the probability of finding a value smaller than our furthest outlier is only 0.000017.

```
mu = mean(resids)
sigma = sd(resids)

# probability of value smaller than smallest outlier
pnorm (min (resids),mu,sigma)
## [1] 1.704e-05
```

We can use this probability to estimate the sample size we would expect before seeing an outlier this far out by inverting it. For example, imagine the probability was 1/10, meaning about one-tenth of the population is as extreme as our observation. If we invert that we get 10, meaning that a sample of 10 can reasonably be expected to contain an observation as extreme as this, on average. When we do this for our probability above (0.000017), we see that the furthest outlier is extremely improbable, and would be expected in a sample of about 58,680 observations (we have 1,401).

```
# sample size before outlier this big expected
1/pnorm (min (resids),mu,sigma)
## [1] 58680
```

If this were the only outlier this extreme, we might adopt an "outliers happen" attitude and leave it at that. However, the fact that we have several such improbable outliers suggests three possibilities: (1) Our data is from a distribution with more of its density in its tails, (2) the real standard deviation of the error is much larger than we think it is, and (3) something else is wrong with our model or data. We can use the fitdistr function from the MASS package to get maximum-likelihood estimates for $v, s,$ and μ given our data, and assuming a non-standardized t-distribution. We can see that the estimate for v is a relatively small number, suggesting substantial deviations from a normal distribution in the tails of the data.

```
# get maximum likelihood estimates of t parameters
# the 'lower' bounds are for the sd and df respectively
tparams = MASS::fitdistr (resids, 't', lower = c(0,1))
# check out mean, scale and nu. bottom row is standard errors
tparams
##        m         s         df
##    0.2902    7.1651    7.5753
```

```
##   (0.2160)  (0.2335)  (1.5075)
```

Just to show that this is not always the case, below we generate 1,401 samples from a standard normal distribution, and then estimate its t parameters. We can see that the v (df, degrees of freedom) estimate is a very large number (3,607), indicating that the shape of the distribution is very much like a normal distribution.

```
set.seed(1)
# generate standard normal data
x_norm = rnorm (1401)
norm_params = MASS::fitdistr (x_norm, 't', lower = c(0,1))

# nu is very large
norm_params
##           m              s            df
##     0.000e+00    1.025e+00    3.607e+03
##    (2.740e-02)  (1.043e-04) (       NaN)
```

We can use the t parameters estimated for our residual distribution to find the probability of observing outliers as extreme as those seen above from a t-distribution. We do this with the `ptns` function which works very much like the `pnorm` function, except for non-standardized t-distributions. This function takes in an x-value, and values of `m` (μ), `s`, and `df` (i.e., v), and tells you how much of the mass of the probability density is to the *left* of the value x. So, the function below tells us what the probability is of finding a value smaller than our furthest outlier from a t-distribution. As we can see, the outliers in our height judgments are unlikely but not *too* unlikely given a t-distribution with $v = 7.58$. For example, our sample size is 1401 and we would expect to see an observation as unusual as our furthest outlier about one in every 1354 samples.

```
m = tparams [[1]] [1]
s = tparams [[1]] [2]
df = tparams [[1]] [3]

# probability of value smaller than smallest outlier
bmmb::ptns (min (resids),m, s, df)
##           m
## 0.0007384

# sample size before outlier thie big expected
1/bmmb::ptns (min (resids),m, s, df)
##       m
## 1354
```

Below, we see that our largest outlier is about 43 times more likely in the t-distribution with $v = 7.58$ than in the normal distribution.

```
ptns (min (resids),m, s, df) /
  pnorm (min (resids),mu,sigma)
##       m
## 43.33
```

154 *Comparing two groups of observations: Factors and contrasts*

The benefit of using t-distributions is that they allow for outliers, that is observations that are very unlike the 'typical' observation in a normal model, without such a strong effect on your analysis. Basically, the normal distribution doesn't like extreme events. When an extreme event *does* occur, this will result in an increase in your standard deviation estimate so that the extreme event seems less extreme. Since the t-distribution encompasses more extreme events, these do not have such a strong effect on estimates of the distribution scale parameter.

5.10.1 *Description of the model*

We update the first line of our model description to show that we are now modeling our height responses using a t-distribution. We also add the prior for the v (degrees of freedom) parameter in the last line of the model. In addition, we are going to begin using t-distributions for our priors instead of normal distributions. This is the default in brms (as noted in Section 3.7), and serves to allow possible 'outliers' that are well-supported by data, while still having a majority of their mass within 2–3 standard deviations from the mean. We're going to keep using σ to represent the model error parameter, even though this represents the *scale* and not the standard deviation of the distribution. We do this for consistency, and because `brms` keeps referring to it as `sigma`, but it's important to keep in mind the different roles this parameter plays in the normal and t-distributions.

$$\text{height}_{[i]} \sim t\left(v, \mu_{[i]}, \sigma\right)$$
$$\mu_{[i]} = \text{Intercept} + A + L_{\left[\mathsf{L}_{[i]}\right]} + S_{\left[\mathsf{S}_{[i]}\right]}$$

$$\text{Priors}:$$
$$L_{[\cdot]} \sim N\left(0, \sigma_L\right)$$
$$S_{[\cdot]} \sim N\left(0, \sigma_S\right)$$

$$\text{Intercept} \sim t\left(3, 156, 12\right)$$
$$A \sim t\left(3, 0, 12\right)$$
$$\sigma \sim t\left(3, 0, 12\right)$$
$$\sigma_L \sim t\left(3, 0, 12\right)$$
$$\sigma_S \sim t\left(3, 0, 12\right)$$
$$v \sim \text{gamma}\left(2, 0.1\right)$$

(5.5)

We are using the default prior for v set by `brms` but we are explicitly stating it just to be transparent. We can see what this prior looks like using the `dgamma` and `curve` functions to draw the density of a gamma distribution with those parameters. For example, the code below will draw the density of the default prior for v:

```
curve (dgamma(x,2,0.1), xlim = c(1,250), xaxs='i', ylab="Density",
       xlab="", lwd=4, yaxs='i', ylim = c(0,0.045))
```

This approach can also be used to investigate the consequences of tweaking the distributional parameters. In the first two plots of Figure 5.8, we show the density and log density of the curve generated by `dgamma(x,2,0.1)` (the default), and in the second two plots, we see the same for `dgamma(x,2,0.02)`. For most people, this approach will be more convenient for understanding the relations between parameter setting and density shapes than reading equations. Remember that it is not so important if the prior of *v really* has the shape of a gamma distribution with those parameters. Instead, we need to worry about whether the density distributed credibility in the right places, and the default one basically does.

5.10.2 Fitting and interpreting the model

Below we fit the new model described in (5.5). This model is exactly like our `model_sum_coding` model save for three differences. First, we specify that our error distribution is a t-distribution rather than Gaussian by setting `family="student"`. Second, we set the prior probability for a new special class of parameter (`nu`) that is specific to the t-distribution. We use the default prior for `nu` used by `brm`, but we explicitly state it in the model for clarity. Third, we are now using `student_t` for our priors for all of our other classes of parameters where we previously used `sigma`.

```
# Fit the model yourself
options (contrasts = c('contr.sum','contr.sum'))
model_sum_coding_t =   brms::brm (
  height ~ A + (1|L) + (1|S), data = notmen, chains = 4,
  cores = 4, warmup = 1000, iter = 3500, thin = 2, family="student",
  prior = c(brms::set_prior("student_t(3, 156, 12)", class = "Intercept"),
    brms::set_prior("student_t(3, 0, 12)", class = "b"),
    brms::set_prior("student_t(3, 0, 12)", class = "sd"),
    brms::set_prior("gamma(2, 0.1)", class = "nu"),
    brms::set_prior("student_t(3, 0, 12)", class = "sigma")))

# Or download it from the GitHub page:
model_sum_coding_t = bmmb::get_model ('5_model_sum_coding_t.RDS')
```

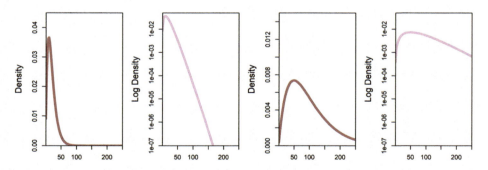

Figure 5.8 (left) The density of a gamma distribution with the parameters specified in our model (`dgamma(x,2,0.1)`). (left middle) The log density of the distribution in the left plot. (right middle) The density of a gamma distribution with alternate parameters (`dgamma(x,2,0.02)`). (right) The log density of the distribution in the right-middle plot.

156 *Comparing two groups of observations: Factors and contrasts*

We inspect the short summary:

```
# inspect model
bmmb::short_summary (model_sum_coding_t)
## Formula:  height ~ A + (1 | L) + (1 | S)
##
## Group-Level Effects:
## ~L (Number of levels: 15)
##                Estimate Est.Error l-95% CI u-95% CI
## sd(Intercept)      5.08      1.12     3.46     7.81
##
## ~S (Number of levels: 94)
##                Estimate Est.Error l-95% CI u-95% CI
## sd(Intercept)      3.36      0.42      2.6     4.21
##
## Population-Level Effects:
##            Estimate Est.Error l-95% CI u-95% CI
## Intercept    155.59      1.38   152.85   158.31
## A1             8.44      0.34     7.78     9.12
##
## Family Specific Parameters:
##        Estimate Est.Error l-95% CI u-95% CI
## sigma      7.23      0.27     6.71     7.76
## nu         6.90      1.52     4.72    10.40
```

And see that there is a new line in the family-specific parameters corresponding to our estimate of v, and we get a mean and credible interval for this parameter. As noted above, the `sigma` parameter reported by this model corresponds to the scale parameter of the non-standardized t-distribution, and not the standard deviation. To recover the standard deviation, we can carry out the operation given in (5.4). The result of this is that our model is actually estimating a very similar standard deviation to what we find using a normal error (8.58 in `model_sum_coding`).

```
nu = 6.90
sigma = 7.23
sigma * sqrt (nu / (nu-2))
## [1] 8.58
```

If we compare the means and intervals around our fixed effects, we see that the two models provide very similar conclusions.

```
fixef (model_sum_coding)
##            Estimate Est.Error      Q2.5     Q97.5
## Intercept   155.218    1.4050  152.434  157.965
## A1            8.711    0.3602    8.003    9.416
fixef (model_sum_coding_t)
##            Estimate Est.Error      Q2.5     Q97.5
## Intercept   155.588    1.3803   152.85  158.311
## A1            8.443    0.3386     7.78    9.119
```

Comparing two groups of observations: Factors and contrasts 157

We may wonder, is it worth using t-distributed errors? On the one hand, we know that our error residuals don't seem to be normally distributed, which suggests that an important assumption of the model we used in `model_sum_coding` is being violated. On the other hand, we know that no model is perfect and that we should never expect that our model will exactly match an underlying process. As a result, we may often have to accept slight misalignments between our model and 'reality'. So, when do we care that a model is 'wrong' and when do we not care that it's wrong? We need a principled way to think about whether an addition to a model is 'worth it', and our approach will have to be more sophisticated than glancing at the model output and seeing if things have changed. We will return to this topic in the next chapter.

5.11 Simulating the two-group model

As in the last chapter, we're going to make fake data that has the same properties as our real data by adding up its component parts. We're going to base this on the parameters of `model_sum_coding` because t-distributed errors can sometimes be quite large.

First, there is an intercept equal to 155 cm. The next step is to create a vector of length two that contains the effects for the adult and child groups (`A1` and `-A1`). Notice that we are *not* drawing these values from a probability distribution. Instead we are treating these effects as fixed for all speakers, for future experiments, etc. (hence the 'fixed effects' nomenclature). For the purposes of our simulated data, this means that these effects will be consistent across any number of simulations you run. In contrast, the `L_` and `S_` values (representing $L_{[\bullet]}$ and $S_{[\bullet]}$) *are* drawn from probability distributions. This is because every time we simulate our data (or re-run our experiment), we may encounter different speakers and listeners, and these may vary in unpredictable ways.

```
n_listeners = 15
n_speakers = 94 # must be even!

# don't run this line if you want a new simulated dataset.
set.seed(1)

# this is the value of our intercept
Intercept = 155

# this is a vector of adultness fixed effects
A_ = c(8.7, -8.7)

# this is a vector indicating the adultness group
A = rep(1:2, (n_listeners*n_speakers/2))

# this is a vector of 15 listener effects
L_ = rnorm (n_listeners, 0, 5.2)
```

158 *Comparing two groups of observations: Factors and contrasts*

```
# this is a vector indicating the listener
L = rep (1:n_listeners, each = n_speakers)

# this is a vector of 94 speaker effects
S_ = rnorm (n_speakers, 0, 3.6)

# this is a vector indicating the speaker
S = rep (1:n_speakers, each = n_listeners)

# this vector contains the error
epsilon = rnorm (n_speakers*n_listeners, 0, 8.6)

# the sum of the above components equals our observations
height_rep = Intercept + A_[A] + L_[L] + S_[S] + epsilon
```

We need to highlight something that's very important about the way we are simulating our speaker and listener effects. When we simulated data last chapter, we saw that the error (ε) does not distinguish between listeners. Instead, our error variable is 'the same' across groups and is divided arbitrarily among them. In the same way, our draws of $S_{[\cdot]}$ do not distinguish between our child and adult groups. Notice that all 94 speaker effects are drawn from the same distribution of speakers. We can see this same behavior reflected in the print statement of our `model_sum_coding` model, which contains this text:

```
## ~S (Number of levels: 94)
##        Estimate Est.Error l-95% CI u-95% CI Rhat Bulk_ESS Tail_ESS
## sd(Intercept)    3.58    0.42    2.82    4.45 1.00    2878    4054
```

We know that these speakers are divided into two groups, adults and children. However, our model is treating these as 94 observations from a single group with a standard deviation of 3.58 and a mean of zero. Rather than reflect differences between adult and child speakers in the characteristics of the random effects, our model does so with its fixed-effect structure. What we mean by this is that our model represents differences between apparent children and adults using the `A1` parameter, and so does not need to do so using the random effects. This is analogous to the way in which we draw our random error around 0, and then move these errors around the number line by adding them to (for instance) our listener effects.

Below we make five data sets that are 'incomplete': The first contains the intercept and noise only, the second contains the intercept and adultness effects only, the third contains the intercept and listener effects, and the fourth contains the intercept, adultness effect, and the error. The fifth 'incomplete' data set is *almost* complete, it contains everything in our full model save for the speaker effects.

```
# only intercept and error
height_rep_1 = Intercept + epsilon
# only intercept and adultness
height_rep_2 = Intercept + A_[A]
```

```
# only intercept and speaker
height_rep_3 = Intercept + L_[L]

# intercept, adultness and error
height_rep_4 = Intercept + A_[A] + epsilon

# intercept, adutlness and speaker
height_rep_5 = Intercept + A_[A] + L_[L] + epsilon
```

In Figure 5.9, we compare our incomplete, simulated data to our real data. In each of the figures, we can see what each source of variance contributes to the data by seeing how the figures change when the source is omitted from the replicated data.

5.12 Answering our research questions

We've fit and interpreted a model, discussed the details of the results, and seen several representations of the data. At this point we need to think about what it all 'means' in terms of our research questions:

(Q1) How tall do speakers perceived as adult females sound?
(Q2) How tall do speakers perceived as children sound?
(Q3) What is the difference in apparent height associated with the perception of adultness?

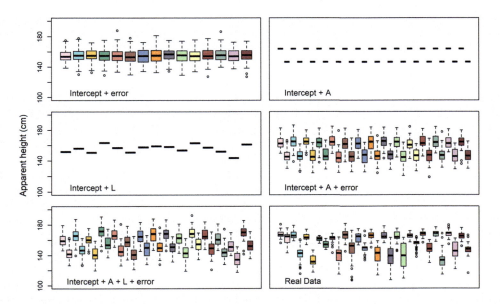

Figure 5.9 Boxplots comparing different simulated datasets to the real data. Each color represents a different simulated listener.

160 *Comparing two groups of observations: Factors and contrasts*

Although these questions are framed in terms of differences between means, a full accounting of the patterns in our data will also discuss the random and systematic variation found therein. In Figure 5.10, we consider the distribution of height judgments across listeners and age groups, as in Figure 5.1. However, this time information about the grand mean and the expected adult and child average apparent heights is presented in the figure.

A look at `model_sum_coding_t` (and Figure 5.10) suggests that:

- The magnitude of between-listener and speaker variation is much smaller than the difference between the adult mean and the child mean (5.1 and 3.4 cm, vs 17 cm). This means that the effect of apparent age on apparent height is not overwhelmed by random variation due to differences between the characteristics of speakers and the tendencies of listeners.
- The magnitude of the random error, i.e. the variation given in a certain listener, speaker, *and* apparent age judgment, is 8.6 cm (`sqrt(6.90/(6.90-2))*7.23`). This is larger than the between-listener and between-speaker variation in our data. This means that for any two adults or children selected at random, the expected difference between them will be smaller than the variability in repeated height estimation for any given voice. So, we see that our height judgments are noisy and that this noisiness can potentially overwhelm at least some of the systematic variation in our data.
- However, the difference in apparent height due to apparent age (17 cm in total) is twice as large as the random error and larger than the between-speaker and between-listener variation. This means that the systematic variation in apparent height due to apparent age is expected to be quite salient even in the face of the noisiness of our data.

If we were reporting this in a paper, based on the sum-coded model we might say something like:

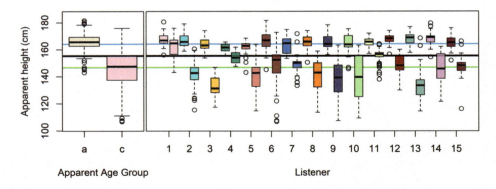

Figure 5.10 (left) Distribution of apparent heights according to apparent age group, across all speakers. (right) Same as the left plot but presented individually for each listener. In each case, the first box of each color (the upper box) indicates responses for apparent adults. The horizontal lines running through the plots represent the grand mean (black), the adult mean (blue), and the child mean (green).

The overall mean apparent height across all speakers was 156 cm (s.d. = 1.38, 95% C.I = [152.85, 158.31]). We found a difference of 17 cm (s.d. = 0.68, 95% C.I = [15.56, 18.24]) in apparent height associated with the perception of adultness in speakers. The standard deviation of the listener and speaker effects were 5.1 cm (s.d = 1.1, 95% CI = [3.5, 7.8]) and 3.4 cm (s.d = 0.4, 95% CI = [2.6, 4.2]) respectively. Overall, results indicate a reliable difference in apparent speaker height due to apparent age, which is larger than the expected random variation in apparent height judgments due to variation between speakers and listeners.

Notice that to report the difference between groups, we just double the value of the estimated effect for A1. This is because the A1 coefficient reflects the distance between each group mean and the intercept, and therefore *half* of the distance between the two groups.

5.13 'Traditionalists' corner

In traditionalists' corner, we compare the output of `brms` to some more 'traditional' approaches. We're not going to talk about the traditional models in any detail, the focus of this section is simply to highlight the similarities between different approaches, and to point out where to find equivalent information in the different models. If you are already familiar with these approaches, these sections may be helpful. If not, some of the information provided here may not make much sense, although it may still be helpful. If you want to know more about the statistical methods being discussed here, please see the preface for a list of suggested background reading in statistics.

5.13.1 *Bayesian multilevel models vs. lmer*

Here we compare the output of `brms` to the output of the `lmer` ("linear mixed-effects regression") function, a very popular function for fitting multilevel models in the `lme4` package in R. Below we fit a model that is analogous to `model_sum_coding`. Since we set contrasts to sum coding using the options above, this will still be in effect for this model. If you have not done so, run the line:

```
options (contrasts = c("contr.sum","contr.sum"))
```

Before fitting the model below so that its output looks as expected.

```
library (lme4)
lmer_model = lmer (height ~ A + (1|L) + (1|S), data = notmen)

summary (lmer_model)
## Linear mixed model fit by REML ['lmerMod']
## Formula: height ~ A + (1 | L) + (1 | S)
##    Data: notmen
##
## REML criterion at convergence: 10161
##
```

162 *Comparing two groups of observations: Factors and contrasts*

```
## Scaled residuals:
##     Min      1Q Median      3Q     Max
## -4.023 -0.562   0.058   0.603   3.364
##
## Random effects:
##  Groups    Name          Variance Std.Dev.
##  S         (Intercept) 12.4        3.52
##  L         (Intercept) 22.9        4.79
##  Residual                73.5        8.57
## Number of obs: 1401, groups:  S, 94; L, 15
##
## Fixed effects:
##                 Estimate Std. Error t value
## (Intercept)    155.193        1.310   118.5
## A1               8.729        0.312    27.9
##
## Correlation of Fixed Effects:
##     (Intr)
## A1 0.046
```

We can see that this contains estimates that are very similar to those of our model. The 'fixed' effects above correspond closely to their 'Population-Level' counterparts, and the rest of the information provided by the models (see Section 4.11.1) is also a reasonable match.

```
## Population-Level Effects:
##              Estimate Est.Error l-95% CI u-95% CI Rhat Bulk_
ESS Tail_ESS
## Intercept    155.22        1.41   152.43   157.96 1.00
1687      2492
## A1             8.71        0.36     8.00     9.42 1.00
3883      4065
```

5.14 Exercises

The analyses in the main body of the text all involve only the unmodified 'actual' resonance level (in `exp_data`). Responses for the stimuli with the simulated 'big' resonance are reserved for exercises throughout. You can get the 'big' resonance in the `exp_ex` data frame, or all data in the `exp_data_all` data frame

Fit and interpret one or more of the suggested models:

1 Easy: Analyze the (pre-fit) model that's exactly like `model_sum_coding_t`, except using the data in `exp_ex` (`bmmb::get_model("5_model_sum_coding_t_ex.RDS")`).

2 Medium: Fit a model like `model_sum_coding_t`, but comparing any two groups across resonance levels.

Comparing two groups of observations: Factors and contrasts 163

3 Hard: Fit two models like `model_sum_coding_t`, but compare any two groups across resonance levels. Compare results across models to think about group differences.

In any case, describe the model, present and explain the results, and include some figures.

6 Variation in parameters ('random effects') and model comparison

In Chapter 4, we introduced 'random effects'. These were intercept terms that were specific to 'sources' of data (e.g. listener, speaker), and fit using adaptive partial pooling. We used speaker and listener-dependent intercepts because we know that each listener, and each speaker, in our data can be associated with unpredictably different average apparent heights. In Chapter 5, we built models that compared two groups of measurements by including a single predictor that distinguished the groups. However, our models assumed that the difference between the groups, the effect of the single predictor, was fixed across all listeners. In this chapter, we will build models that allow for listener-specific variation in fixed-effects predictors in addition to the intercept. Then, we will discuss how to evaluate whether the increasing complexity of our model is making our model 'better' and whether it's justified by our data.

6.1 Chapter pre-cap

In this chapter, we introduce interactions as conditional effects, and marginal (average) effects are introduced as 'main' effects. The concepts of crossing and nesting are presented and the importance of crossing for the estimation of interactions is discussed. We then outline models with multiple group-dependent parameters ('random effects') and the interpretation of these as interactions. We introduce the multivariate normal distribution, in addition to the concepts of multidimensionality and correlation. The fact that random effects are drawn from multivariate normal distributions is discussed, as are related topics for multilevel models (e.g. the specification of priors for correlation matrices). After that, this chapter focuses on model comparison. We contrast in-sample and out-of-sample prediction and discuss the bias-variance trade-off. Finally, we present the widely applicable information criterion (WAIC) and leave-one-out cross-validation, and discuss model selection.

6.2 Data and research questions

We're going to use the same data from the last chapter, again excluding adult males and focusing only on the apparent height of adult females, girls and boys. We're going to build models that expand on those of the last chapter to ask the same questions:

(Q1) How tall do speakers perceived as adult females sound?
(Q2) How tall do speakers perceived as children sound?
(Q3) What is the difference in apparent height associated with the perception of adultness?

DOI: 10.4324/9781003285878-6

Variation in parameters ('random effects') and model comparison 165

Below we load the data and exclude all apparent and veridical adult males.

```
# load packages and data
library (bmmb)
library (brms)
data (exp_data)

# exclude actual men and apparent men
notmen = exp_data[exp_data$C_v!='m' & exp_data$C!='m',]
```

The relevant variables in our data frame are:

- `L`: An integer from 1 to 15 indicating which *listener* responded to the trial.
- `height`: A floating-point number representing the *height* (in centimeters) reported for the speaker on each trial.
- `S`: An integer from 1 to 139 indicating which *speaker* produced the trial stimulus.
- `A`: The *apparent age* of the speaker indicated by the listener, `a` (adult) or `c` (child).

We recreate Figure 5.9 as Figure 6.1 below to show the distribution of apparent height by listener and across apparent ages. In the last chapter, we focused on 'the difference' between height judgments for apparent adults and apparent children as a singular thing. This is a bit like focusing only on the difference between the boxes in the left plot of Figure 6.1. However, if we instead focus on the right plot in Figure 6.1, we see that there is not a *single* difference in apparent heights between apparent children and adults, but rather a *set* of listener-specific differences. The model we will introduce in this chapter will be able to represent this information.

6.3 Variation in parameters across sources of data

The models we fit in Chapter 5 included a predictor representing the apparent age of the speaker. However, this was only a `population-level parameter` (i.e. a 'fixed'

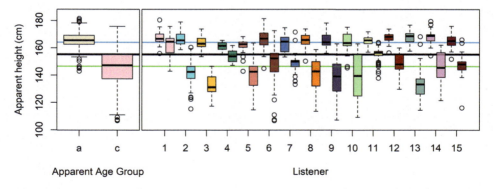

Figure 6.1 (left) Distribution of apparent heights according to apparent age group. (right) Same as the left plot but presented individually for each listener. In each case, the first box of each color (the upper box) indicates responses for apparent adults. The horizontal lines running through the figures represent the grand mean (black), the adult mean (blue), and the child mean (green).

166   *Variation in parameters ('random effects') and model comparison*

effect) meaning that it had the same value for all listeners. Another way to think about this is that our model included only the *marginal* effect for apparent age. This is the effect of apparent age on average across all listeners, *independent* of listener. This sort of effect is often referred to as a **main effect**. Someone might ask "what is the average apparent height difference between apparent children and adult females?" and you might say "about 20 cm". Which listener exactly does this statement apply to? To all of them, this is the average *overall* effect.

In contrast, we may want to think about the effect of apparent age *conditional* on the listener. For example, imagine that this effect varies conditionally based on the listener such that it is large for some listeners and small for others. In this case, if someone asks "what is the apparent height difference between apparent children and adult females?" you may have to answer "well it depends on the listener". When the effect of one predictor varies based on the value of another predictor, these predictors are said to **interact** or to have an **interaction**. The parameters in your model that help you capture these conditional effects are referred to as interactions or **interaction effects**. The 'fixed' effect for A1 we included in our models in the last chapter really represents the marginal (overall) effect for the predictor. To investigate the values of this predictor *conditional* on the listener, we need to include the listener by A1 *interaction* in our model. We denote interaction terms in our models using a colon (:) where A:B can be read 'A given B' or 'A conditional on B'.

We can find the average apparent height reported by each listener for each apparent age (a adult, or c child) using the code below:

```
round ( tapply (notmen$height, notmen[,c("A","L")], mean) )
##      L
## A      1    2    3    4    5    6    7    8    9   10   11   12   13   14   15
##    a  167  167  164  161  162  166  163  165  166  165  165  168  168  168  165
##    c  162  142  132  154  141  148  149  140  140  138  155  148  134  146  148
```

The average of each column is the average apparent height reported by each listener across both apparent ages. The average across each row is the average apparent height reported for each apparent age, across all listeners. Each individual cell represents the average apparent height reported by each listener for each apparent age, and the mean of all cells represents the overall grand mean.

In the left plot of Figure 6.2, we present the average height reported by each listener. The variation seen along the line is a result of non-zero listener effects: In the absence of listener effects, the line would be flat and horizontal at the grand mean. So, it is the listener effect (L) that gives the line its specific shape. In the middle plot, we see the average apparent height reported by each listener for each apparent age. Each line has an unpredictably different shape, and since the shape reflects the listener effect, this means that listener (L) has an unpredictable effect across the levels of apparent age (A). This suggests that our data has a meaningful interaction between listener and apparent age, L:A, which can be read as 'the effect of listener given the level of apparent age'.

In the middle plot of Figure 6.2, the broken lines represent the mean apparent heights for apparent adults and apparent children. The average (main) effect for apparent age is equal to the difference between these broken lines and the solid line representing the grand mean (or half the distance between the broken lines). This effect has an average magnitude of 10.1 cm, which we can see in the right plot of the figure. However, each

Variation in parameters ('random effects') and model comparison

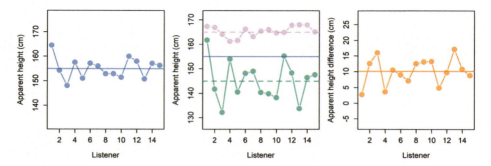

Figure 6.2 (left) Average height reported by each listener overall. The horizontal line represents the grand mean. (middle) Age-dependent listener effects for apparent children (lower line) and apparent adults (upper line). The horizontal lines indicate the grand mean (solid), and the average means for apparent adults (upper dotted) and apparent children (lower dotted). (right) Listener-dependent age effects, the difference between the adult and child means reported by each listener (i.e. the difference between the lines in the middle plot). The horizontal line represents the average age effect across listeners.

listener has an unpredictable difference between their points on each line and a correspondingly unpredictable effect for apparent age in the right plot in Figure 6.2. Since the distance between the lines determines the effect for apparent age, this represents listener-dependent variation in A and a meaningful interaction between apparent age and listener (A:L) in our data.

Actually, the L:A interaction *entails* an A:L interaction (and vice versa): In the process of adding an A:L interaction in your data you also necessarily add an L:A interaction to your data. Imagine the middle plot in Figure 6.2 contained two flat parallel lines, separated by some amount (the effect for A). In order to add a listener-dependent age effect (A:L) to these lines, we would need to make the separation between the lines unpredictably different for each listener. However, in doing so we *necessarily* also make the shapes of the two lines unpredictably different. This is the only way to make the separation between the lines different for each listener. Since the shape of the line is the listener effect, by giving each line a different shape we also necessarily add an age-dependent effect for listener to our data. As a result of this, the A:L interaction is *the same thing* as the L:A interaction, and the notational difference between them is only superficial.

Although we can think of interactions either way, conceptually it may be useful to think of them primarily from one perspective or another. In our case, we will focus on the listener-dependent effect for apparent age, presented in the right plot of Figure 6.2. The value of each point along the line in the right plot reflects the spacing of the two lines in the middle plot of the same figure. In the complete and total absence of an interaction between listener and age, the orange line in the figure would be horizontal at 10.1 (the marginal difference). In the presence of an interaction, our marginal and listener-dependent effects may diverge in a seemingly random manner, as seen in the figure.

Before moving on, we need to discuss the concepts of **crossing** and **nesting**, and how these relate to interactions. When two factors are **crossed**, this means that all levels of one factor appear at all levels of the other factor. When levels of one factor appear

168   *Variation in parameters ('random effects') and model comparison*

exclusively at specific levels of the other factor they are said to be *nested*. To estimate the interaction between two factors, the factors should be crossed. Since our 'random effects' are just interactions, this means that to include a random effect for a predictor given some grouping factor (like listener), it needs to be crossed with that factor.

For example, consider a situation where (monolingual) listeners are divided into groups according to their native languages. We might imagine a model like this that tries to estimate height based on the native language (`NatLang`) of the listeners to see if there are reliable cross-language differences in listener's opinions:

```
height ~ NatLang + (1|L)
```

In such an experiment, the listener factor will be nested within first language because each listener only speaks one language. As a result, in such a situation a model *can* estimate the 'fixed', marginal effect of native language on apparent height. However, this model can *not* estimate the listener-dependent effect of first language, i.e. the first language 'random effect' for listeners *or* the listener by native language interaction. This means that neither of the following models is possible:

```
height ~ NatLang + (NatLang|L)
height ~ NatLang + L + NatLang:L
```

The reason for this is very straightforward. If we do not observe the effect of first language for each level of listener, we are not in a position to say anything about the *listener-dependent* effect of first language (i.e. the conditional effect of native language for every individual listener). For example, if the first listener is an English speaker, how can you possibly estimate the conditional effect for when that listener is a Mandarin speaker? What would that even mean?

In terms of our data, this means that to estimate listener-dependent effects for apparent age we need to make sure listener is *crossed* with apparent age. We can do this by, for example, cross tabulating our observations of apparent age with listener (`table(notmen$A, notmen$L)`) and making sure that we have more than zero observations for every combination of listener and apparent age (which we do). As a result, it's possible to estimate the interaction between these in our model. In contrast, speakers are not crossed with apparent age. If we tabulate apparent age by speakers (`table(notmen$A, notmen$S)`), we see a lot of cells with zero observations. This is because some speakers were just not very confusable: Some children were never identified as adults and some adults were never identified as children. As a result, our model may run into problems if it tries to estimate the interaction between speaker and apparent age, or the random effect of apparent age for each speaker.

6.3.1 Description of our model

Before including interactions in our model, let's take a step back and consider the model formula we used in the last chapter. Below, we explicitly include the leading one (indicating the intercept) to make the following discussion simpler.

```
height ~ 1 + A + (1|L) + (1|S)
```

Variation in parameters ('random effects') and model comparison 169

This formula told our model to draw the parameter related to `A` from a fixed prior distribution and to draw the `L` and `S` terms from distributions whose standard deviations were estimated from the data (i.e. using adaptive partial pooling). We did this by adding `L` and `S` to the right of a pipe inside parentheses (like this `(1|L)`) and putting a `1` to the left of the pipe. Recall that the `|` symbol means 'given' so that the notation `(1|L)` says "estimate an intercept given listener" or "estimate a different intercept effect for each level of the factor listener".

We can imagine an analogous model formula that uses only 'fixed effects', meaning it uses no pooling to estimate all of the listener and speaker effects. The formula for such a model would look like this:

```
height ~ 1 + A + L + S
```

As discussed above, we seem to have listener-dependent age effects in our model, suggesting that we want to include the interaction of apparent age and listener in our model. Interactions between combinations of fixed effects can be denoted using `:`. For example, the formula below says "include the main effect for A and L, and the interaction between A and L". The `:` symbol can also be read as "given", which helps to highlight that these represent conditional effects. So `A:L` can be read out loud as "A given L" or "the effect of A given the value of L".

```
height ~ 1 + A + L + A:L + S
```

As a shortcut, we can use the symbol `*` which means "include the main effects for these predictors and all interactions between them."

```
height ~ 1 + A * L + S
```

The previous two formulas include the marginal effects of age and listener and the interaction between them. However, they estimate all these without adaptive pooling. We know that it is advisable to estimate factors with large numbers of levels using adaptive pooling, regardless of how 'random' the effect may be (see Section 4.4). This applies not only to the marginal effects of predictors such as listeners but also to the interactions between these 'random' effects and our 'fixed' effects. In order to estimate listener-dependent age effects in our model using adaptive pooling, we include these inside the parentheses belonging to the listener predictor, like so:

```
height ~ 1 + A + (1 + A|L) + (1|S)
```

The formula above tells `brms`: "Height varies as a function of an intercept and an age effect, a listener-specific intercept and age effect, and a speaker specific intercept". It also tells `brms` to estimate the listener intercepts, the listener age effects, and the speaker intercepts as random effects, i.e. using adaptive pooling. Notice the parallel structure between our models with and without random effects:

```
height ~ 1 + A +  L +  A:L      + S
height ~ 1 + A + (1 +   A |L) + (1 |S)
```

170 *Variation in parameters ('random effects') and model comparison*

These models have equivalent parameters, which have been horizontally aligned in the two formulas above. The L term in the top model is represented by the 1 in (1 + A|L) in the bottom model (the listener-dependent intercept effect), and the A:L term in the top model is represented by the A in (1 + A|L) in the bottom model (the listener-dependent age effect). The main difference between L and A:L on one hand and (1 + A|L) on the other, is that the latter notation tells your model to estimate these listener-dependent predictors using adaptive pooling. When our formula has non-intercept predictors, we can omit the 1 and write it as seen below:

```
height ~ A + (A|L) + (1|S)
```

Our model formula might specify a model as in (6.1). Compared to the t-distributed model we fit at the end of Chapter 5, the only changes have been the addition of a new term, $A:L$, and its associated priors $A:L_{[\cdot]} \sim t(3,0,\sigma_{A:L})$, and $\sigma_{A:L} \sim t(3,0,12)$. Note that although the A predictor does not need a subscript, the $A:L$ term (the by-listener random effect for age) does. This is because although we only have a single age predictor, the interaction term estimates a different one of these for each listener, which requires the estimation of 15 such parameters in our model.

$$\text{height}_{[i]} \sim t\left(v,\mu_{[i]},\sigma\right)$$
$$\mu_{[i]} = \text{Intercept} + A + L_{\left[\mathsf{L}_{[i]}\right]} + A:L_{\left[\mathsf{L}_{[i]}\right]} + S_{\left[\mathsf{S}_{[i]}\right]}$$

$$\text{Priors}:$$
$$L_{[\cdot]} \sim N\left(0,\sigma_L\right)$$
$$A:L_{[\cdot]} \sim N\left(0,\sigma_{A:L}\right) \qquad\qquad (6.1)$$
$$S_{[\cdot]} \sim N\left(0,\sigma_S\right)$$

$$\text{Intercept} \sim t(3,156,12)$$
$$A \sim t(3,0,12)$$
$$\sigma_L,\sigma_S,\sigma_{A:L} \sim t(3,0,12)$$
$$v \sim \text{gamma}(2,0.1)$$
$$\sigma \sim t(3,0,12)$$

For the sake of comparison, (6.2) presents the model structure associated with the following formula:

```
height ~ 1 + A + L + A:L + S
```

We can see that (6.1) and (6.2) are nearly identical. The only difference between the two models is whether the standard deviations of the prior distributions of the listener and speaker-related parameters (e.g. $L_{[\cdot]}$) are estimated from the data (as in (6.1)), or specified a priori (as in (6.2)).

Variation in parameters ('random effects') and model comparison

$$\text{height}_{[i]} \sim t(v, \mu_{[i]}, \sigma)$$

$$\mu_{[i]} = \text{Intercept} + A + L_{[L_{[i]}]} + A : L_{[L_{[i]}]} + S_{[S_{[i]}]}$$

Priors:
$$L_{[\bullet]} \sim N(0, 12)$$
$$A : L_{[\bullet]} \sim N(0, 12) \quad (6.2)$$
$$S_{[\bullet]} \sim N(0, 12)$$

$$\text{Intercept} \sim t(3, 156, 12)$$
$$A \sim t(3, 0, 12)$$
$$v \sim \text{gamma}(2, 0.1)$$
$$\sigma \sim t(3, 0, 12)$$

The model in (6.1) is often preferable over the one in (6.2) because it will use information about the distribution of L, $A:L$, and S to estimate the associated effects. However, one potential problem is that the model in (6.1) draws each of the listener-dependent effects (L, $A:L$) from independent distributions as if these were totally unrelated, and they may not be.

6.3.2 Correlations between random parameters

In Figure 6.3, we plot the listener effects, and the listener-dependent age effects originally presented in Figure 6.2. However, this time they have both been sorted based on the value of the listener effects. We can see clearly that as the listener effects increase, the age effects decrease. In the rightmost plot, we present a scatter plot of these two variables, which reinforces the fact that these variables have a negative relationship: Smaller values of apparent height tend to be associated with larger apparent age

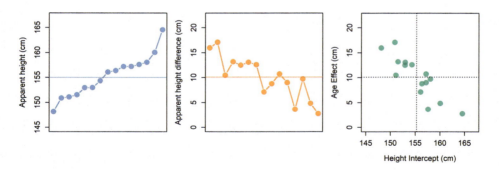

Figure 6.3 (left) Average reported height by each listener, sorted by magnitude. (middle) The magnitude of the age effect for each listener, sorted by that listener's effect in the left plot. (right) Listener average reported height plotted against listener age effects.

172   *Variation in parameters ('random effects') and model comparison*

effects. This is important because, if this is true, it suggests that we are unlikely to observe listeners who reported tall speakers on average *and* had large age effects on height (or vice versa). This is because as seen in Figure 6.3, listeners who reported tall speakers on average tended to exhibit small age effects.

The **linear correlation** between two variables (often referred to simply as the **correlation**) is a measure of the **linear relationship** between the variables. An informal (but accurate) way to think of a linear relationship is that when you make a scatter plot using two variables (as in the right plot of Figure 6.3), the organization of the points should resemble a line if there is a strong linear relationship between them. The more the dots form a single perfect line, the closer the magnitude of the correlation gets to 1. Whether the value of a perfect correlation is 1 or −1 depends on if the line is sloped up (1) or down (−1) from left to right. A correlation of 0 means there is no linear relationship between the variables. So, if two variables have a correlation of 0 you would be hard-pressed to draw any kind of *line* that captured the relationship between the variables (though some other curve might work). Figure 6.3 suggests that listener means and age effects are *negatively correlated*.

There are many ways to measure correlation, but the most common way is by using **Pearson's correlation coefficient**, defined in equation (6.3) for variables x and y. We use the little hat, like this $\hat{r}$, because this is an estimate of the correlation between our variables. Equation (6.3) introduces a term we have not seen yet, $\sigma_{x,y}$, corresponding to the *covariance* between x and y (often denoted by $\text{cov}(x,y)$). We can see below that the correlation between two variables is the covariance divided by the product of their individual standard deviations $(\hat{\sigma}_x$ and $\hat{\sigma}_y)$.

$$\hat{r} = \frac{\hat{\sigma}_{x,y}}{\hat{\sigma}_x \hat{\sigma}_y} \tag{6.3}$$

The variance of a variable is the expected value of squared deviations from the mean. The **covariance** of two variables is the expected value of the product of their deviations from each from their respective means. The covariance of two variables of length n can be estimated by calculating the sum of the product of deviations from the mean and dividing by the number of observations minus one, as seen in (6.4).

$$\hat{\sigma}_{x,y} = \frac{\Sigma\left(x_{[i]} - \bar{x}\right)\left(y_{[i]} - \bar{y}\right)}{(n-1)} \tag{6.4}$$

Replacing $\hat{\sigma}_{x,y}$ in (6.3) with (6.4) yields (6.5), an estimate of the correlation (r) between x and y.

$$\hat{r} = \frac{\Sigma\left(x_{[i]} - \bar{x}\right)\left(y_{[i]} - \bar{y}\right)}{(n-1)\cdot\hat{\sigma}_x\hat{\sigma}_y} \tag{6.5}$$

Using equation (6.5), we can calculate Pearson's correlation coefficient for two variables. We can do this for any two vectors in R using the `cor` function. Below we find the average apparent height reported by each listener, and then half the difference in apparent height reported by each listener for each apparent age (i.e. the effect for apparent age). As seen below, this tells us that the correlation between the listener

Variation in parameters ('random effects') and model comparison　173

means and apparent age effects is −0.85, representing a strong negative correlation between these two variables.

```
# find means for each listener for each apparent age
listener_age_means = tapply (notmen$height, notmen[,c("A","L")], mean)

# average of each column = listener means
listener_effects = colMeans (listener_age_means)

# half the difference across rows = listener age effects
listener_age_effects = (listener_age_means[1,] - listener_age_means[2,]) / 2

# correlation between listener means and age effects
cor (listener_effects, listener_age_effects)
## [1] -0.8691
```

We can develop some intuitions regarding correlations by considering the very simple vectors seen below. The elements of the second vector are exactly equal to twice every element of the first vector: They are perfectly predictable one from the other. As a result, these two vectors have a correlation of 1.

```
x1 = c(-1, -1, 1, 1)
y1 = c(-2, -2, 2, 2)
cor (x1, y1)
## [1] 1
```

Below we see the opposite situation. The second vector is still twice the first vector, but now every sign differs across the two vectors. These are still perfectly predictable, just backward. For example, if a gambler were wrong 100% of the time, anyone who did the opposite would win every bet. Below, we see that these vectors have a correlation of −1.

```
x1 = c(-1, -1,  1,  1)
y1 = c( 2,  2, -2, -2)
cor (x1, y1)
## [1] -1
```

In the next example, we see that the signs of each element of the second vector are totally *unpredictable* based on the corresponding element in the first vector. In half the cases the signs match and in half the cases they do not. This results in a correlation of 0 between the vectors.

```
x1 = c(-1, -1,  1, 1)
y1 = c(-2,  2, -2, 2)
cor (x1, y1)
## [1] 0
```

174   *Variation in parameters ('random effects') and model comparison*

Finally, we see a situation where the vectors *almost* match. In the example below, three of the four elements match in sign, resulting in a positive correlation between 0 and 1.

```
x1 = c(-1, -1,  1, 1)
y1 = c(-2, -2, -2, 2)
cor(x1, y1)
## [1] 0.5774
```

6.3.3 Random effects and the multivariate normal distribution

The **multivariate normal** distribution is a straightforward and very useful generalization of the normal distribution. A multivariate normal variable is a set of variables that are each normally distributed, *and* that result in another normally distributed variable when linearly combined. Each individual variable that makes up the multivariate normal represents a **dimension** of the multivariate normal. So, if we have a three-dimensional normal distribution with dimensions x_1, x_2, and x_3, this implies that: (1) Each of x_1, x_2, and x_3 is normally distributed, and (2) If we define a new variable x_4 such that $x_4 = a \cdot x_1 + b \cdot x_2 + c \cdot x_3$, where a, b, and c can take any scalar value, then x_4 will be normally distributed.

When our models feature multiple predictors for a factor whose levels are estimated with adaptive pooling (e.g. speaker, listener), we model the coefficients with a multivariate normal distribution. In doing so, we estimate the standard deviation of each dimension *and* the correlation between all pairs of dimensions. The easiest way to see why the correlation between dimensions matters is by drawing bivariate (two-dimensional) normal variables with different correlations and plotting the results.

The dimensions of the multivariate normal can have arbitrarily different means and standard deviations, but their marginal distributions will always be a (univariate) normal. In Figure 6.4, we plot randomly-generated samples from three different bivariate normal distributions differing in the correlation between their dimensions, one variable presented in each row. The variables all have means and standard deviations that reflect the distribution of listener means (first column), and the listener-dependent age effects (second column). So, the first dimension has a mean and standard deviation equal to 154 and 4.8 cm, and the second dimension has a mean and standard deviation equal to 10.1 and 4.2 cm, respectively.

We can use the simulated variables presented in Figure 6.4 to imagine possible relationships between listener means and age effects across a large sample of listeners. In the absence of any correlation between variables (top row), the distribution will resemble a circle in two dimensions (if the standard deviations are equal). When there is a positive correlation between the two dimensions (middle row), the joint distribution looks like an ellipse tilted up (moving from left to right). When there is a negative correlation (bottom row), the ellipse is tilted down moving left to right. Note, however, that the marginal distributions of the variables (illustrated in the left and middle columns) don't change as the correlation changes. The correlation is a reflection of the *joint* variation in the two variables and will not be evident in the marginal distributions of each variable.

Understanding the correlations between your 'random effect' parameters is important because it helps you understand which combinations of parameter values are

Variation in parameters ('random effects') and model comparison 175

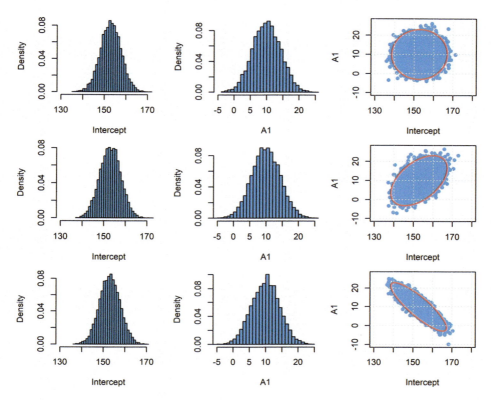

Figure 6.4 Marginal distributions of 10,000 bivariate normal draws of simulated listener intercepts (left column) and listener-dependent A1 coefficients (middle column) from distributions with means and standard deviations based on our listener data. The right column presents both variables together. The correlation of the variables is 0 (top), 0.5 (middle), and −0.85 (bottom).

more or less likely. When our dimensions are uncorrelated it is difficult (if not impossible) to make useful predictions from one dimension to the other. For example, in the top row, we see that a mean height of 140 cm is about equally likely to be paired with apparent age affects (`A1`) of 0 or 20 cm. As a result, knowing that the speaker mean is 140 cm does not provide you much information about whether the age effect for that listener is likely to be large or small, positive or negative.

However, when the dimensions *are* correlated we can use this to make better predictions using our data. For example, in the bottom row, we see a strong negative correlation between our dimensions. As a result, an average height of 140 cm is very likely when age effects are 20 cm, but *extremely* unlikely to be seen with an age effect of 0 cm. So, in this case, knowing the speaker mean would actually help you narrow down the range of plausible listener effects. For this reason, when more than one random effect is estimated for each grouping factor, these are usually treated as a *multivariate normal* variable rather than as a set of independent normal distributions (as in our model in (6.1)).

176   *Variation in parameters ('random effects') and model comparison*

6.3.4 *Specifying priors for a multivariate normal distribution*

The shape of the multivariate normal distribution (i.e. how much it looks like a circle vs a tilted ellipse in the bivariate case) is determined by a covariance matrix, often represented by a capital sigma (Σ). A covariance matrix will be a square $n \cdot n$ matrix for a variable with n dimensions. In equation (6.6), we see an example of a covariance matrix for variables x, y, and z. The elements on the main diagonal of the covariance matrix represent the variances of each dimension, while the off-diagonal elements represent the co-variances of the variables (where $\sigma_{x,y} = \sigma_{y,x}$).

$$\Sigma = \begin{bmatrix} \sigma_x^2 & \sigma_{x,y} & \sigma_{x,z} \\ \sigma_{y,x} & \sigma_y^2 & \sigma_{y,z} \\ \sigma_{z,x} & \sigma_{z,y} & \sigma_z^2 \end{bmatrix} \tag{6.6}$$

Consider two random effects, a random by-subject intercept L, and a random by-listener apparent age effect called $A:L$. If we assumed these came from a bivariate normal distribution, the covariance matrix associated with this distribution might be:

$$\Sigma = \begin{bmatrix} \sigma_L^2 & \sigma_{L,A:L} \\ \sigma_{A:L,L} & \sigma_{A:L}^2 \end{bmatrix} \tag{6.7}$$

When we dealt with unidimensional normal distributions for our previous random effects, we specified priors for the (unidimensional) standard deviations using t (or normal) distributions. The specification of priors for our covariance matrix is only slightly more complicated. Rather than specify priors for Σ directly, `brms` (and *Stan*) builds up Σ from some simpler components that we specify. The covariance matrix for our random effects is created by multiplying the standard deviations of our individual dimensions by a correlation matrix (R) specifying the correlations between each dimension. The operation is presented in (6.8).

$$\Sigma = \begin{bmatrix} \sigma_L^2 & \sigma_{L,A:L} \\ \sigma_{A:L,L} & \sigma_{A:L}^2 \end{bmatrix} = \begin{bmatrix} \sigma_L & 0 \\ 0 & \sigma_{A:L} \end{bmatrix} \cdot R \cdot \begin{bmatrix} \sigma_L & 0 \\ 0 & \sigma_{A:L} \end{bmatrix} \tag{6.8}$$

The non-zero values in the outside matrices are the (marginal, univariate) standard deviations of the random intercepts (σ_L) and age effects ($\sigma_{A:L}$). The correlation matrix R contains information about the correlation between the dimensions of the variable (e.g. $r_{L,A:L}$). The correlation matrix R will look like (6.9) for a two-dimensional variable. In a correlation matrix, each row gives you information about the correlation of one dimension with the others. For example, the first row represents the correlation of the first dimension to itself (first column) and the second dimension (second column). Correlation matrices contain only values of 1 on the main diagonal since the correlation of something with itself is one. Since the correlation of x and y equals the correlation of y and x, correlation matrices are symmetric. This means that in the two-dimensional case $r_{1,2} = r_{2,1}$, or, more generally, $r_{i,j} = r_{j,i}$.

$$R = \begin{bmatrix} 1 & r_{L,A:L} \\ r_{A:L,L} & 1 \end{bmatrix} \tag{6.9}$$

When we have multiple random effects that we are modeling as a multivariate normal, we need to specify priors for the standard deviations of each individual dimension and for the correlations between each pair of dimensions (i.e. for the correlation matrix), but not for the covariance matrix Σ directly. We provide priors for the standard deviations of the individual dimensions in the same way as we do for 'unidimensional' random effects. We specify priors for correlation matrices using the LKJCorr (Lewandowski-Kurowicka-Joe) distribution in `brms`.

$$R \sim \text{LKJCorr}(\eta) \tag{6.10}$$

This distribution has a single parameter (eta, η) that determines how peaked the distribution is around 0 (seen in Figure 6.5). Basically, higher numbers make it harder to find larger correlations (and therefore yield more conservative estimates).

The above was a full explanation of what information the model needs and why it needs it. You don't need to *understand* any of the above to use random effects correctly. The important take away is that whenever you are estimating any random effects above and beyond a random intercept, you need to:

1 Specify priors for the standard deviation of each dimension.
2 Specify a prior for the correlation matrix for the multivariate normal used for the random parameters.

And `brm` (and *Stan*) will do the rest.

6.3.5 Updating our model description

Now that we've discussed using multivariate normal distributions for our random effects, we can update our model formula as in (6.11). Only two things have changed with respect to the description in (6.1). First, the listener random effects are drawn from a multivariate normal distribution (MVNormal) rather than as independent univariate normal variables. Second, we specify a prior for our correlation matrix (LKJCorr). Notice that we do not directly specify a prior for the multivariate normal covariance matrix Σ. This is because, as noted above, *Stan* constructs Σ by multiplying

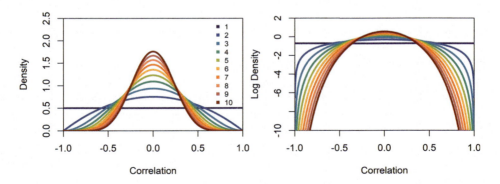

Figure 6.5 (left) Density of different correlation parameters for a two-dimensional correlation matrix, according to LKJ distributions with varying eta parameters. (right) Log densities of the densities in the left plot.

178 *Variation in parameters ('random effects') and model comparison*

the standard deviation for each dimension ($\sigma_{A:L}$ and σ_L) by the correlation matrix (R) as in equation (6.8). We include this in the final line of the model for completeness but will be excluding it from future model specifications. This is because this element is not specified by the user, and becomes increasingly bulky as our models become more complicated.

$$\text{height}_{[i]} \sim t\left(v, \mu_{[i]}, \sigma\right)$$

$$\mu_{[i]} = \text{Intercept} + A + L_{\left[L_{[i]}\right]} + A : L_{\left[L_{[i]}\right]} + S_{\left[S_{[i]}\right]}$$

$$\text{Priors}:$$

$$S_{[\bullet]} \sim N\left(0, \sigma_S\right)$$

$$\begin{bmatrix} L_{[\bullet]} \\ A : L_{[\bullet]} \end{bmatrix} \sim \text{MVNormal}\left(\begin{bmatrix} 0 \\ 0 \end{bmatrix}, \Sigma\right)$$

$$\text{Intercept} \sim t\left(3, 156, 12\right) \quad\quad (6.11)$$
$$A \sim t\left(3, 0, 12\right)$$
$$\sigma, \sigma_L, \sigma_{A:L}, \sigma_S \sim t\left(3, 0, 12\right)$$
$$v \sim \text{gamma}\left(2, 0.1\right)$$
$$R \sim \text{LKJCorr}\left(2\right)$$

$$\Sigma = \begin{bmatrix} \sigma_L & 0 \\ 0 & \sigma_{A:L} \end{bmatrix} \cdot R \cdot \begin{bmatrix} \sigma_L & 0 \\ 0 & \sigma_{A:L} \end{bmatrix}$$

Here's a plain English description of the model specification in (6.11):

We are modeling apparent height as coming from a t distribution with unknown nu (v), mean (μ), and scale (σ) parameters. The expected value for any given trial (μ) is modeled as the sum of an intercept, an effect for apparent age (A), a listener effect (L), a listener dependent effect for apparent age (A : L), and a speaker effect (S). The speaker effects were drawn from a univariate normal distribution with a standard deviation (σ_S) estimated from the data. The two listener effects were drawn from a bivariate normal distribution with standard deviations ($\sigma_L, \sigma_{A:L}$) and a correlation matrix (R) that was estimated from the data. The remainder of the 'fixed' effects and the bivariate correlation were given prior distributions appropriate for their expected range of values.

6.3.6 *Fitting and interpreting the model*

Below we fit a model where age coefficients vary across listeners. Notice that the only change in the formula is the inclusion of the A predictor on the left-hand side of the pipe in (A|L). We now include a prior for a new class of parameter cor which applies to the correlation matrices for our multivariate normal variables. In addition, we specify the priors *outside* the brm function call and pass this to the function.

```
# Fit the model yourself
priors = c(brms::set_prior("student_t(3,156, 12)", class = "Intercept"),
    brms::set_prior("student_t(3,0, 12)", class = "b"),
```

Variation in parameters ('random effects') and model comparison **179**

```r
    brms::set_prior("student_t(3,0, 12)", class = "sd"),
    brms::set_prior("lkj_corr_cholesky (2)", class = "cor"),
    brms::set_prior("gamma(2, 0.1)", class = "nu"),
    brms::set_prior("student_t(3,0, 12)", class = "sigma"))

model_re_t =
  brms::brm (height ~ A + (A|L) + (1|S), data = notmen, chains = 4,
            cores = 4, warmup = 1000, iter = 5000, thin = 4,
            prior = priors, family = "student")

# Or download it from the GitHub page:
model_re_t = bmmb::get_model ('6_model_re_t.RDS')
```

We can check out the summary of our model:

```r
bmmb::short_summary (model_re_t)
```

And see that although many parameter values may have changed with respect to `model_sum_coding_t` from Chapter 5, the only new information is in the `L` group-level effects:

```r
## Group-Level Effects:
## ~L (Number of levels: 15)
##                       Estimate Est.Error l-95% CI u-95% CI
## sd(Intercept)            4.34      0.84      3.05      6.29
## sd(A1)                   4.26      0.85      2.96      6.25
## cor(Intercept,A1)       -0.80      0.12     -0.95     -0.51
```

This section of the model summary now includes an estimate of the standard deviation of the by-listener effect for age (`sd(A1)`, i.e. the standard deviation of the listener by age interaction, $\sigma_{A:L}$ in (6.11)), and the correlation between our listener-dependent intercept and age-effect terms (`cor(Intercept,A1)`). We can see that the estimate of this correlation (-0.80) is very similar to the 'simple' estimate we found above (-0.85).

You can get information about the variance, correlation, and covariance parameters using the `VarCorr` function in the `brms` package. As with the `fixef` and `ranef` functions, this function returns summaries of these samples by default but you can set `summary=FALSE` to get the individual samples for these parameters. We're not going to talk about the structure of this output, but we encourage you to investigate it using the `str` function.

```r
varcorr_information = brms::VarCorr (model_re_t)
str (varcorr_information)
```

You can also use the `get_corrs` and `get_sds` functions in the `bmmb` package to get summaries of your model standard deviations (including the error term):

```r
bmmb::get_sds (model_re_t)
##           Estimate Est.Error   Q2.5 Q97.5 group
## Int.L        4.338    0.8356  3.050 6.289     L
```

```
## A1          4.258       0.8463 2.964 6.248        L
## Int.S       3.057       0.3594 2.398 3.808        S
## sigma       5.354       0.2057 4.958 5.770    sigma
```

And correlations:

```
# specify that we want the correlations for L
bmmb::getcorrs (model_re_t, factor="L")
##            Estimate Est.Error      Q2.5    Q97.5
## A1, Int.    -0.8018    0.1151   -0.9491  -0.5087
```

Below we load the sum-coded, t-distributed model we fit in the last chapter. This model contained an identical fixed-effects structure to `model_re_t`, but does not include listener-dependent age effects (and associated parameters).

```
model_sum_coding_t = bmmb::get_model ('5_model_sum_coding_t.RDS')
```

Figure 6.6 presents a comparison of the two models, for selected model parameters. Despite clear similarities between the models, there are some changes to the credible intervals around the parameters that are shared across both models (presented in Figure 6.6). It can be risky to make up explanations for things after the fact (**post hoc**), but we can try to think about why these changes may have occurred. The change in the interval around the intercept is very small, and likely reflects our (slightly) better overall understanding of the data. In contrast, the interval around `A1` has grown substantially. This is likely because we are now acknowledging between-listener variation in the `A1` parameter, which `model_sum_coding_t` ignored (or treated as zero). `model_re_t` predicts a standard deviation of 4.3 cm in the `A1` effect between listeners, and our data includes judgments from only 15 unique listeners. This limits how precise our `A1` estimate can/should be.

The standard deviation of our listener intercepts (σ_L, 'sigma_L' in the figure) appears to decrease slightly at the inclusion of random effects for age. This is likely because what previously seemed like variation in listener averages may have actually been variation in listener age effects. The separation of this into two separate predictors may lead to the magnitude of variation in one being diminished. Finally, the decrease in

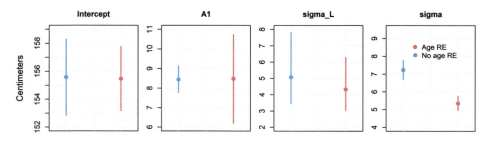

Figure 6.6 A comparison of estimates of the same parameters across our models with and without random effects (RE) for apparent age.

Variation in parameters ('random effects') and model comparison 181

the data-level error (σ, 'sigma' in the figure) is due to the inclusion of the listener random effects for `A1`, and the fact that including listener-dependent values for `A1` helped explain our variable. The error is just what the model can't explain, so as our models explain more, the error will tend to get smaller.

6.4 Model comparison

Bayesian models allow you to fit rather complicated 'bespoke' models to your data. A potential problem with this is that at some point your model may be 'good enough' such that, although further tweaks could be made, they are no longer contributing any practical benefit to your model. In fact, you can build a model that is so good at predicting your data that it can actually become bad at understanding the subject of your investigation more generally.

An analogy can be made between model fitting and clothing made by a tailor for an individual. You can go to a tailor and get a shirt made that exactly fits your body proportions. Imagine that tailoring the perfect shirt for a human body usually involved adjusting ten 'shirt parameters' (e.g. torso circumference, torso to sleeve ratio, etc.) to ensure a perfect fit for an individual. Despite this, when you go to a store to buy a shirt, there is usually one 'parameter', size, and it often comes in a small number of variants (e.g. small, medium, large). Since the shirts vary only in a small number of ways, they are very unlikely to fit any individual perfectly.

Why do stores intentionally sell clothing that doesn't fit people as well as they could? Because the store is interested in selling clothes that fit everyone *pretty well*, rather than selling clothes that fit everyone perfectly. If stores sold shirts that fit everyone perfectly, each shirt model would only be useful to a very small number of people and would be useless for a large number of people. In contrast, by having a small number of shirts that fit most people 'pretty well', the store can carry a small number of models and apply them successfully to customers in general.

This problem is sometimes referred to as the **bias-variance trade-off**. In this case, *bias* refers to the model's ability to accurately represent the patterns in the data, and variance refers to the degree to which the model is stable across data sets. Models that fit data very well (i.e. they have a low bias) often change substantially when fit to new data sets (i.e. they have a high variance). This is analogous to the fact that the shape of two shirts perfectly tailored (low bias) for two different people will potentially be very different from each other (high variance). On the other hand, models that do not fit the data *too* well (higher bias) often also have more consistent properties across new data sets (lower variance). This is analogous to the fact that shirts that vary in terms of small, medium, and large don't fit many people perfectly, but manage to fit everyone pretty well while varying only slightly.

The bias-variance trade-off can be understood in terms of the prediction of in-sample and out-of-sample data. Your **in-sample** data is the data you used to fit your model, and the **out-of-sample** data is other data that you do not have access to. A statistical model is **overfit** when it corresponds too closely to your in-sample data to the detriment of its ability to explain out-of-sample data. Recall that our models are usually used to carry out inductive reasoning: Going from a limited number of observations to the general case. In light of this, overfitting a model is exactly contrary to the goals of inductive inference. A model that does a poor job of generalizing to new observations is not useful to carry out induction. Further, a model that cannot explain

182 *Variation in parameters ('random effects') and model comparison*

out-of-sample data will not hold up to replication, which should be a concern for any researcher. This is because a researcher carrying out a replication of your work will necessarily be working with data that, from your perspective, is *out-of-sample* data.

In this section, we will offer a high-level conceptual understanding of Bayesian model comparison, along with an explanation of how to carry this out. For more information on the subject, we recommend reading Chapter 7 of the excellent *Statistical Rethinking* (McElreath, 2020). Much of the information provided in this section is provided in more detail in Gelman et al. (2014) and Vehtari et al. (2017).

6.4.1 In-sample and out-of-sample prediction

In order to compare models in a quantitative way, we need some value that can be calculated for different models that captures how 'good' the model is. For Bayesian models, we begin with what is called the **log pointwise predictive density**, abbreviated lpd (or lppd). The lpd can be calculated in several ways, but equation (6.12) presents an example of the general case. The lpd is the sum of the logarithm of the density for each of your data points. The symbol θ represents posterior estimates of all of the estimated parameters necessary to determine the probability density over each data point. This can be thought of as the general case of the log-likelihood outlined for the normal distribution in Section 2.7.1.

$$\widehat{\text{lpd}} = \sum_{i=1}^{N} \log\left(p\left(y_{[i]} \,|\, \theta \right) \right) \tag{6.12}$$

The definition of $\widehat{\text{lpd}}$ bears a strong resemblance to the log posterior density, discussed in Section 3.8. Since we are adding logarithmic values, we know we are multiplying the underlying probabilities. If the data points are independent given our parameter values, then lpd represents the joint density of observing the data given the model structure and the parameter estimates (θ). Although prior probabilities are not included in this calculation, they do factor into the estimation of θ, and as a result, do have an effect on values of lpd.

Because lpd is a logarithmic value, large negative values are closer to zero on the original scale. So, values of lpd closer to (or above) zero represent models that are more likely given the data. As a result, we might think that we should simply select the model with the highest lpd as our 'best' model. However, lpd does not tell us directly about expected out-of-sample prediction, which is what we often care about.

We can think about out-of-sample prediction in terms of the **expected log pointwise predictive density**, abbreviated elpd (or elppd), presented in (6.13). Unlike the lpd, the elpd is defined in terms of hypothetical out-of-sample data ($\tilde{y}$) instead of the in-sample data (y). The $\mathbb{E}$ below represents the expected value function (discussed in Section 2.5.1). So, the elpd represents the expected value of lpd for out-of-sample data.

$$\text{elpd} = \sum_{i=1}^{N} \mathbb{E}\left(\log\left(p\left(\tilde{y}_{[i]} \,|\, \theta \right) \right) \right) \tag{6.13}$$

Of course, you can't actually know the value of $\mathbb{E}(\log\left(p\left(\tilde{y}_{[i]} \,|\, \theta \right) \right)$ because you do not have access to the true properties of the out-of-sample data ($\tilde{y}$). As a result, you must

Variation in parameters ('random effects') and model comparison 183

settle for an estimate of elpd, $\widehat{elpd}$. The simplest, and worst, way to estimate out-of-sample prediction is by simply looking at the in-sample prediction. One of the reasons that this does not really work is because making models more and more complicated will *always* improve in-sample prediction, at least a little. However, if the predictors are not related to the true characteristics of the processes underlying the data, they will also tend to decrease the fit of the model to *new* data generated by the same process. Returning to the analogy of shirt fits discussed above. You can buy a shirt from the store and take it to a tailor to get it customized. The more the tailor changes this from the 'standard' shape, the better the shirt will fit you, and the worse it will fit everyone else. Only alterations which conform to the 'true' average torso shape will increase the fit for people in general (and may in fact reduce the fit for you).

We can demonstrate this for some very simple models using simulations. In the code below, we generate three random variables consisting only of the values −1 and 1. We then use only the first variable (x1), and random normally distributed error, to simulate two sets of random data: Our in-sample (y) data, and our out-of-sample data (y_tilde). We then fit three models to *only* the in-sample data. These models include increasingly more predictor variables (x_1, x_2, x_3); however, we know that only x_1 is useful to understand the underlying process. Finally, we tried to predict the in-sample data *and* the out-of-sample data using the parameters estimated for each model using only the in-sample data.

```
n = 50          # how many observations
iter = 1000     # how many simulations

# these will hold the model log likelihoods for each iteration
lpd_hat = matrix (0, iter, 3)
elpd_hat = matrix (0, iter, 3)

set.seed(1)
for (i in 1:iter){
  # create 3 random predictors
  x1 = sample (c(-1,1), n, replace=TRUE)
  x2 = sample (c(-1,1), n, replace=TRUE)
  x3 = sample (c(-1,1), n, replace=TRUE)

  # generate the observed (in sample) data with an
  # underlying process that only uses the x1 predictor
  y = 1 + x1 + rnorm (n, 0, 1)
  # use the same process to simulate some "out-of-sample" data
  y_tilde = 1 + x1 + rnorm (n, 0, 1)

  for (j in 1:3){
    # fit three models, the first using the real underlying model
    if (j==1) mod = lm (y ~ 1+x1)
    # the next two include random useless predictors
    if (j==2) mod = lm (y ~ 1+x1 + x2)
    if (j==3) mod = lm (y ~ 1+x1 + x2 + x3)
```

184 *Variation in parameters ('random effects') and model comparison*

```
    # find the predicted value (mu) for each data point
    mu = mod$fitted.values
    # and the estimated sigma parameter
    sigma = summary(mod)$sigma

    # equivalent to equation 6.10
    lpd_hat[i,j] = sum (dnorm (y, mu, sigma, log = TRUE))
    # equivalent to equation 6.11
    elpd_hat[i,j] = sum (dnorm (y_tilde, mu, sigma, log = TRUE))
  }
}
```

The models above are fit using a function that we have not discussed to this point. The `lm` (linear model) function uses maximum-likelihood estimation (see Section 2.8) to fit regression models with relatively simple ('unilevel', see Figure 4.2) structures. We use it here because it estimates regression parameters very quickly and therefore is reasonable to use when we want to fit 3,000 models in five seconds or so.

For each of our three candidate models, we use the predicted values (`mu`, μ) and error estimates (`sigma`, σ) obtained using our in-sample data to estimate $\widehat{\text{lpd}}$ using the in-sample data:

$$\widehat{\text{lpd}} = \sum_{i=1}^{N} \log\left(\text{N}\left(y_{[i]} \mid \mu, \sigma \right) \right) \tag{6.14}$$

And $\widehat{\text{elpd}}$ using our out-of-sample data:

$$\widehat{\text{elpd}} = \sum_{i=1}^{N} \log\left(\text{N}\left(\tilde{y}_{[i]} \mid \mu, \sigma \right) \right) \tag{6.15}$$

In the formulas above, we replace $p\left(y_{[i]} \mid \theta \right)$ with $\text{N}\left(y_{[i]} \mid \mu, \sigma \right)$ because the simulations generate normally distributed data. Our simulations result in three sets of $\widehat{\text{lpd}}$ and three sets of $\widehat{\text{elpd}}$, a pair of each for each of the models above. The average of each of these six sets of values is presented in the left plot of Figure 6.7. Since logarithmic values closer to zero are closer to one on the original scale, *more negative* log-likelihood values indicate a *less likely* outcome. We can see that the $\widehat{\text{lpd}}$ improves as the model becomes more complicated, despite the fact that the x_1 and x_2 had absolutely no relationship to the data generating process or to the dependent variable.

Why does this happen? One way to think about it is that the tallest person in California *and* Arizona will be *at least* as tall as the tallest person in Arizona. By increasing the number of ways it can explain your data, your more complex model will do *at least as well* as the model with fewer possible explanations. However, although the extra parameters increase the $\widehat{\text{lpd}}$ estimate, they actually *decrease values* of $\widehat{\text{elpd}}$, indicating a worse out-of-sample fit. Why? Because since the extra predictors included in our model in no way relate to our data, the 'answers' they provide can only be due to *overfitting*, the learning of characteristics that are specific to the in-sample data rather than consistent properties of the out-of-sample data.

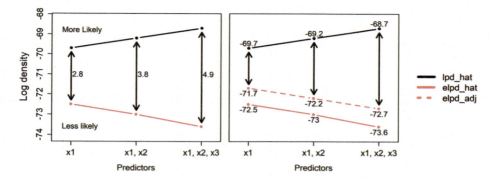

Figure 6.7 (left) Average value of lpd and elpd estimates for each model in our simulated example. (right) The same values as on the left, however, now elpd estimates are adjusted (`elpd_adj`) based on the number of predictors in the model, as discussed in the text.

So, we see that adding 'unnecessary' predictors can decrease our out-of-sample performance. Ok, maybe we should just not ever include any 'unnecessary' predictors in our models? This is a bit like suggesting that since putting is hard, one should try to get a hole-in-one whenever possible. Obviously this would be ideal, however, there are some complications. In the example in Figure 6.7, we knew the true underlying model and generated out-of-sample data that exactly conformed to the characteristics of our in-sample data. In real life, researchers do not usually have access to out-of-sample data, they do not know the characteristics of the 'true' model that underlies their data, nor can they confirm that any out-of-sample data shares the exact underlying process as their in-sample data. As a result, we can never *really* know what the difference is between in-sample and out-of-sample prediction for our models.

Despite these complications, you may have noticed that: (1) The slopes of the lines representing $\widehat{elpd}$ and $\widehat{lpd}$ in Figure 6.7 seem to have predictable slopes, and (2) The lines diverge from each other at predictable rates based on the complexity of the models. Statisticians have noticed this too, and have used this to *adjust* $\widehat{lpd}$ in order to estimate values of $\widehat{elpd}$ for out-of-sample data.

6.4.2 Out-of-sample prediction: Adjusting predictive accuracy

The logic of adjusting $\widehat{lpd}$ based on model complexity can be understood with reference to Figure 6.7. Our goal is to select the model with the best out-of-sample prediction (i.e. the highest value on the red line), given only knowledge of the in-sample prediction (the values on the black line). In the left plot we can see that the difference between the black and red lines for each model increases by approximately one for every parameter we add. Let's assume for the time being that this is a general property of all models. Since our models had two, three, and four parameters (including the intercept) respectively let's subtract two, three and four from their respective $\widehat{lpd}$ estimates to arrive at *adjusted* $\widehat{elpd}$ estimates for each model. We can think of this as

penalizing the value of $\widehat{\text{lpd}}$ based on some penalty value p as in (6.16). Different ways to estimate $\widehat{\text{elpd}}$ differ in terms of how they estimate $\widehat{\text{lpd}}$ and p.

$$\widehat{\text{elpd}} = \widehat{\text{lpd}} - p \tag{6.16}$$

You may have noticed that our penalization does not exactly recreate the line reflecting elpd in Figure 6.7, but rather results in a line (roughly) parallel to it. We can never know the real distance between lpd and elpd, the solid red and black lines in Figure 6.7, because we can never know the 'true' properties of out-of-sample data. Despite this, penalization allows us to estimate a line *parallel* to elpd (the broken red line in Figure 6.7), and base our inference on this line. In the simple example we are discussing here, we are setting $p = k$, where k is the number of parameters estimated by the model. If we carry out the operation in (6.16) using the values in Figure 6.7, we arrive at values of elpd of −71.7 (−69.7−2) and −72.7 (−68.7−4) for the least and most complex models. Based on these estimates of $\widehat{\text{elpd}}$, we expect that the model with the worst $\widehat{\text{lpd}}$ actually has the best elpd.

In fact, we know that in this case, the 'best' model corresponds *exactly* to the true data generating process. However, penalization will not always result in the highest values of $\widehat{\text{elpd}}$ for the simplest model. In Figure 6.8, we simulate new fake data, except now we include x_2 in the 'real' underlying data generating process (i.e. `y = x1 + x2 + rnorm (n, 0, 1)`). As a result, for this data, we actually *do* need both x_1 and x_2 in the model. As seen below, penalization does not obscure the benefit of adding x_2 to our model when it is warranted. This is because the relatively small penalty associated with the increased model complexity does not overwhelm the large benefit due to the inclusion of a predictor that is actually related to our dependent variable.

Two aspects involved in the traditional estimation of $\widehat{\text{elpd}}$ need to be updated to use these measures for multilevel Bayesian models. The first of these is the way that models are penalized based on their complexity. Historically, the p term is related to the number of *independent* parameters estimated by the model. Estimated parameters

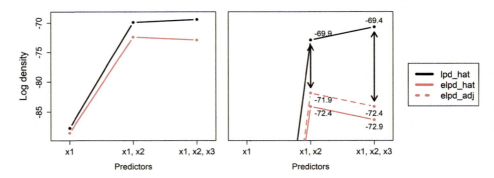

Figure 6.8 (left) Average value of lpd and elpd for each model in our simulated example, modified to also include the second predictor (x2) in the data generating process. (right) The same values as on the left, however, now elpd is estimated based on adjusting the lpd using the number of model parameters. The y-axis range intentionally omits the first model so that the information for the second and third models can be seen clearly.

Variation in parameters ('random effects') and model comparison   187

are those that are not specified a priori but instead depend on the data and structure of the model. Unfortunately, counting the number of independent parameters is not so straightforward in our multilevel models since parameters estimated with adaptive pooling (and shrinkage) are not fully independent. For example, a set of ten 'random effects' that have all been pulled slightly toward their shared mean can hardly be considered totally independent. On the other hand, they do vary from each other in unpredictable ways. As a result, it seems like a random effect with ten levels may represent somewhere between zero and ten independent parameters, based on how much they have been *shrunk* toward their mean. Our estimate of $\widehat{\text{elpd}}$ will need a way to estimate model complexity that takes this into account.

Second, lpd and p have traditionally been *point estimates*, single values often based on maximum-likelihood estimation. Since our models consist of posterior distributions of parameters, we instead have *distributions* of $\widehat{\text{lpd}}$ and p. This means that we also have a distribution of values of $\widehat{\text{elpd}}$, and it would be useful to take this into account.

In this section we're only going to discuss the **widely available information criterion** (WAIC) as calculated using the `brms` package. For a more complete treatment of other methods (and historical approaches), please see Gelman et al. (2014). To calculate WAIC we first find the average density of each data point (i) given our model parameters $\left(p\left(y \mid \theta^s\right)\right)$ across all posterior samples (S). This is presented for data point 1 in (6.17). For example, imagine a case where we have 5,000 posterior draws so that $S = 5000$. To calculate the value below for our first data point $\left(y_{[1]}\right)$, we would find the density for every one of the 5,000 posterior draws based on the changing values of θ^s across our draws. The average of these values is represented in (6.17).

$$\frac{1}{S} \sum_{s=1}^{S} p\left(y_{[1]} \mid \theta^s\right) \tag{6.17}$$

To estimate $\widehat{\text{lpd}}$ for a set of n data points, we take the logarithm of the value in (6.17) and add this up across all of our observations. This is presented in equation (6.18).

$$\widehat{\text{lpd}} = \sum_{i=1}^{n} \log\left(\frac{1}{S} \sum_{s=1}^{S} p\left(y_{[i]} \mid \theta^s\right)\right) \tag{6.18}$$

Rather than count the number of parameters in our model, WAIC estimates the penalty term based on the characteristics of the predictive density. First, you find the log density for each individual data point across all posterior draws, and then find the variance of this. Equation (6.19) shows an example of this for the first data point. The $Var_{s=1}^{S}$ term indicates that we are finding the variance of $\log\left(p\left(y_{[1]} \mid \theta^s\right)\right)$ across values of S (i.e., for individual samples).

$$\text{Var}_{s=1}^{S}\left(\log\left(p\left(y_{[1]} \mid \theta^s\right)\right)\right) \tag{6.19}$$

To estimate the penalty terms for WAIC, PWAIC, the value in (6.19) is added up for all n data points as in (6.20).

$$\text{PWAIC} = \sum_{i=1}^{n} \text{Var}_{s=1}^{S}\left(\log\left(p\left(y_{[i]} \mid \theta^s\right)\right)\right) \tag{6.20}$$

188 *Variation in parameters ('random effects') and model comparison*

Why does this work? This is one of those things that one needs to *get used to* rather than *understand*, although more information can be found in Vehtari et al. (2017). The short, conceptual explanation is that more complex (and flexible) models exhibit more variation in their posterior probabilities. As a result, the variance of the log density across the posterior samples is a general way to estimate model complexity that avoids issues related to how many truly independent parameters a model estimates. Given our estimate of $\widehat{\text{lpd}}$ and P_{WAIC}, we can now estimate $\widehat{\text{elpd}}_{WAIC}$ as in (6.21).

$$\widehat{\text{elpd}}_{WAIC} = \widehat{\text{lpd}} - p_{WAIC} \tag{6.21}$$

Below we load the sum-coded models we fit in the last chapter:

```
model_sum_coding = bmmb::get_model ('5_model_sum_coding.RDS')
model_sum_coding_t = bmmb::get_model ('5_model_sum_coding_t.RDS')
```

And set our options to sum coding to match the coding we used when we fit the models:

```
options (contrasts = c('contr.sum','contr.sum'))
```

We can use the `add_criterion` function in `brms`, and specify `criterion="waic"` to add the `waic` criterion to our model object. We do this for both of our models.

```
model_sum_coding =
  brms::add_criterion (model_sum_coding, criterion="waic")

model_sum_coding_t =
  brms::add_criterion (model_sum_coding_t, criterion="waic")
```

Adding the `waic` criterion to our model with Gaussian errors (`model_sum_coding`) returns an error message. To understand why we get these errors we can investigate the model `waic` information, which we can see below:

```
model_sum_coding$criteria$waic
##
## Computed from 5000 by 1401 log-likelihood matrix
##
##             Estimate    SE
## elpd_waic   -5042.3 32.5
## p_waic         81.8  3.7
## waic        10084.6 65.0
##
## 27 (1.9%) p_waic estimates greater than 0.4. We recommend trying loo instead.
```

The first two rows represent the expected log pointwise predictive density ($\widehat{\text{elpd}}_{WAIC}$, `elpd_waic`), and the penalty related to the flexibility of the model (p_{WAIC}, `p_waic`). The third column is the information criterion WAIC which is just -2 times the first row.

Variation in parameters ('random effects') and model comparison   189

The p_{WAIC} penalty term is sometimes referred to as the **effective number of parameters**, but Vehtari et al. (2017) caution that this usage is somewhat figurative and should not be 'over-interpreted'. The effective number of parameters relates to the complexity and flexibility of the model and its ability to adapt to new data. Our sum coding model has 114 estimated parameters: 15 listener means, 1 listener standard deviation, 94 speaker means, 1 speaker standard deviation, 2 fixed-effects terms, and 1 error standard deviation. Despite this, we see that our effective number of parameters is just 81.8.

The statistics provided above are calculated individually for each data point. We can get the pointwise information as seen below:

```
model_waic_info = model_sum_coding$criteria$waic$pointwise
model_t_waic_info = model_sum_coding_t$criteria$waic$pointwise
```

There will be one row for each data point used to fit the model. Below we can have a look at the first six values:

```
# first six data points
head (model_waic_info)
##        elpd_waic   p_waic     waic
## [1,]     -5.108 0.234948 10.216
## [2,]     -3.116 0.004170  6.232
## [3,]     -4.431 0.153398  8.862
## [4,]     -3.109 0.003014  6.217
## [5,]     -4.139 0.116198  8.279
## [6,]     -3.104 0.002666  6.208
```

The estimates above simply correspond to the sum of each column. The standard error (SE) corresponds to the variance of the column times the square root of the number of rows (since the statistics are sums and not means). Based on this, we can recreate the summary values seen above:

```
# the sum of each column
colSums (model_waic_info)
## elpd_waic     p_waic         waic
##   -5042.3       81.8      10084.6
```

```
# the standard deviation of each column
apply (model_waic_info,2,sd) * sqrt (1401)
## elpd_waic     p_waic         waic
##    32.511      3.742       65.021
```

Now we can return to the issue of the error message, which said that "27 (1.9%) p_waic estimates greater than 0.4". Large values of p_waic suggest a poor fit between a data point and the model. To investigate this we can get the posterior mean residuals from each of the models we are considering:

```
resids = scale (residuals (model_sum_coding) [,1])
resids_t = scale (residuals (model_sum_coding_t) [,1])
```

We scale our residuals so that they are represented in terms of standard deviations from the mean, and plot these against the p_waic values calculated for each data point by each model. Clearly, large residuals relate to large p_waic values. In other words, large p_waic values are related to data points that are a very poor fit for our model. In our model with Gaussian errors, this relationship is very predictable and quickly leads to large values in p_waic. However, for our model with t-distributed errors (model_sum_coding_t), residuals beyond two standard deviations do not strongly affect p_waic. These differences are due to the different behaviors of the normal and t-distributions in their tails, as discussed in Section 5.9.

The warning message suggest that we use loo (discussed in the next section) rather than waic because some p_waic values are too large. Why is this bad? Because the theory underlying the use of $\widehat{elpd}_{WAIC}$ basically assumes that there will *not* be large values of p_waic. So, if there *are* large values of p_waic that suggests that something is wrong and $\widehat{elpd}_{WAIC}$ may no longer be reliable. When this occurs, as the error message suggests, you shouldn't use $\widehat{elpd}_{WAIC}$ even if it seems reliable and looks 'fine'. Think of it this way, if a bridge says it has a weight limit of three tonnes and you're driving a truck that weighs four tonnes, should you drive across the bridge? Maybe you get across safely and save some time. Maybe you crash off the bridge into the river. When you use something like this despite being warned not to, you run the same risk: Maybe what you report is a true and reliable analysis, and maybe it's not and you are reporting nonsense (the academic equivalent of crashing into the river).

6.4.3 Out-of-sample prediction: Cross-validation

The last way to evaluate models that we'll be discussing is called **cross-validation**. Cross-validation consists of dividing your data into two groups. You use one group to fit a model (i.e. your in-sample, or **training data**), and then use this model to predict the other group of data (i.e. the out-of-sample, or **testing data**). In this way, cross-validation is a way to simulate out-of-sample prediction using only the data you actually have.

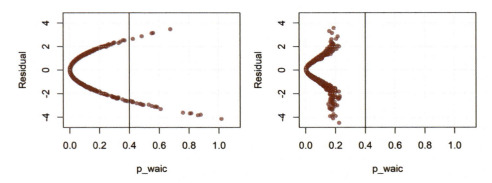

Figure 6.9 (left) Standardized model residuals plotted against values of the WAIC penalty term (p_waic) for each data point for the model with Gaussian errors, model_sum_coding. (right) The same as on the left but for the model with t-distributed errors, model_sum_coding_t.

Variation in parameters ('random effects') and model comparison **191**

There are many ways to carry out cross-validation, and these mostly differ in the way that data is divided into training and testing groups. **Holdout** cross-validation makes one single partition and uses one group to test and the other to train. Obviously, this is not ideal because the results will be highly dependent on the specific groups you made. In **k-fold** cross-validation, you split your data into k equal parts. You then train on parts k_{-i} for iteration i, and predict the ith group using that model. This approach can minimize the problems of holdout cross-validation since it uses k, rather than one, estimates of the out-of-sample performance.

The logical endpoint of k-fold cross-validation is **leave-one-out** cross-validation, sometimes referred to as LOO. In leave-one-out cross-validation, you leave out a single observation at a time. So, if you have n observations you train the model on all observations but i (i.e. $y_{[-i]}$), and then predict the lone held-out point $(y_{[i]})$. Although LOO provides excellent estimates of out-of-sample prediction, this approach can be computationally intensive since it involves fitting n models for n data points. For example, our relatively small data set (`notmen`) has 1,401 observations, potentially requiring 1,401 models.

Luckily, recent advances have resulted in fast ways to approximate $\widehat{elpd}_{LOO}$, i.e. estimates of elpd based on LOO, without having to refit models repeatedly. The `loo` package (Vehtari et al. 2022) in R and the associated functions implemented in `brms` make it easy to estimate $\widehat{elpd}_{LOO}$ in a very fast and efficient manner. In addition, LOO works in many cases where WAIC does not, hence the suggestion in the error message above to use LOO for model comparison.

The calculation of $\widehat{elpd}_{LOO}$ is more complicated than what we can explain here, however, we can provide an approximate definition. In (6.22), we use the $\approx$ symbol because we are not providing an exact definition of how $\widehat{elpd}_{LOO}$ is calculated in practice, but only in principle. Equation (6.22) states that the estimate of elpd provided by LOO cross-validation is approximately equal to the sum of the log density of each data point $(y_{[i]})$ based on parameters estimated using all the data *except* for that point $(\theta_{y_{[-i]}})$.

$$\widehat{elpd}_{LOO} \approx \sum_{i=1}^{n} \log\left(p\left(y_{[i]} \mid \theta_{y_{[-i]}} \right) \right) \tag{6.22}$$

We define the relationship between $\widehat{elpd}_{LOO}$ and $\widehat{lpd}$ using the same general relationship outlined above, updated for LOO in (6.23).

$$\widehat{elpd}_{LOO} = \widehat{lpd} - p_{LOO} \tag{6.23}$$

Based on this, we can estimate p_{LOO} by rearranging the terms of the equation as seen in (6.24). Just as with p_{WAIC}, p_{LOO} reflects the effective number of parameters, an estimate of model complexity.

$$p_{LOO} = \widehat{lpd} - \widehat{elpd}_{LOO} \tag{6.24}$$

Estimates of $\widehat{elpd}_{LOO}$ and associated statistics can be added to our models using the code below. We will now include our model with random effects for apparent age in our comparison.

```
model_sum_coding =
  brms::add_criterion (model_sum_coding, criterion="loo")
```

192 *Variation in parameters ('random effects') and model comparison*

```
model_sum_coding_t =
  brms::add_criterion (model_sum_coding_t, criterion="loo")

model_re_t =
  brms::add_criterion (model_re_t, criterion="loo")
```

We can see our new criteria using the code below. Notice that we no longer see the error message we got with WAIC.

```
model_sum_coding$criteria$loo
##
## Computed from 5000 by 1401 log-likelihood matrix
##
##          Estimate   SE
## elpd_loo  -5042.7 32.5
## p_loo        82.2  3.8
## looic     10085.4 65.1
## ------
## Monte Carlo SE of elpd_loo is 0.2.
##
## All Pareto k estimates are good (k < 0.5).
## See help('pareto-k-diagnostic') for details.
```

Since we no longer have warnings, we can compare our models as seen below. This comparison contrasts the values of $\widehat{elpd}_{LOO}$ for each data point across all our models. It presents the sum of the difference, and the standard error of that sum, relative to the best-performing model. Below, `model_re_t` has an `elpd_diff` of 0, indicating that this is the best model according to this measure.

```
brms::loo_compare (model_sum_coding,
                   model_sum_coding_t,
                   model_re_t, criterion = "loo")
##                        elpd_diff se_diff
## model_re_t                  0.0     0.0
## model_sum_coding_t       -204.4    19.2
## model_sum_coding         -224.1    19.6
```

What does the value of zero mean? It only means that this is our 'reference point'. The value of $\widehat{elpd}_{LOO}$ for our best model is:

```
model_re_t$criteria$loo$estimates[1,]
## Estimate       SE
## -4818.63    37.15
```

So, if we set this value to zero then we can express the corresponding estimates for the other models relative to this value. Values of `elpd_diff` for `model_sum_coding_t` and `model_sum_coding` are −204 and −222, respectively, indicating substantial

Variation in parameters ('random effects') and model comparison 193

differences in $\widehat{elpd}_{LOO}$ between our models. Specifically, they are around 200 less than our best model (so around −5,000, as seen above). We can explore where these values come from by extracting the pointwise information from our models just as we did for WAIC.

```
model_loo_info = model_sum_coding$criteria$loo$pointwise
model_t_loo_info = model_sum_coding_t$criteria$loo$pointwise
model_re_t_lo_info = model_re_t$criteria$loo$pointwise
```

We can see that the `elpd_diff` is just the sum of the difference in `elpd` estimates across the two models:

```
sum(model_t_loo_info[,1]-model_re_t_lo_info[,1])
## [1] -204.4
```

The standard error of the difference is simply the standard deviation of the difference times the square root of the number of observations.

```
sd(model_t_loo_info[,1]-model_re_t_lo_info[,1]) * sqrt(1401)
## [1] 19.21
```

We can use this knowledge to calculate the difference between our two worst-performing models since these are not directly compared above:

```
sum(model_loo_info[,1]-model_t_loo_info[,1])
## [1] -19.64
sd(model_loo_info[,1]-model_t_loo_info[,1]) * sqrt(1401)
## [1] 7.578
```

And see that these values correspond to those obtained using the 'official' comparison function as seen below:

```
brms::loo_compare (model_sum_coding, model_sum_coding_t,
criterion = "loo")
##                          elpd_diff se_diff
## model_sum_coding_t    0.0         0.0
## model_sum_coding     -19.6         7.6
```

Finally, we can check out the estimated number of parameters by summing the third column of our pointwise information, which contains information about p_{LOO} for each model. We can compare this to the actual number of parameters estimated by our models. An easy way to find the number of estimated parameters is to get the posterior draws for a model using the `get_samples` function from `bmmb`. This will return a data frame that contains one column for each estimated parameter, plus two columns for the `lp` and `lprior` (discussed in Section 3.8). So, if we find the number of columns minus two, we can quickly count the number of estimated parameters for most kinds of models. However, keep in mind that this works as of the writing of this sentence (October 14th, 2022), and the output of software can change. It's worth checking your expectations before taking shortcuts

194   Variation in parameters ('random effects') and model comparison

like this, for example by confirming the number of columns and seeing the information contained in each column before using this method to report the number of parameters.

Below, we compare the actual number of parameters for each model with our effective number of parameters. For example, we can see that going from Gaussian to t-distributed errors results in the estimation of one additional 'real' parameter (v), but the number of 'effective' parameters goes up by about 3. Adding random effects for apparent age to our model required the addition of 17 parameters: 15 listener-specific age effects, a standard deviation for these effects, and the correlation between the listener-specific age and intercept effects. However, we can see that this has led to an increase of about 24 effective parameters. We can potentially explain this by thinking about how the inclusion of random effects for apparent age may have affected the estimation of the other random effects already included in the model. However, we are not going to worry too much and 'over-interpret' the effective number of parameters.

```
# Actual and effective number of parameters
# for simplest model
ncol(bmmb::get_samples(model_sum_coding))-2
## [1] 114
sum(model_loo_info[,'p_loo'])
## [1] 82.17

# for t model
ncol(bmmb::get_samples(model_sum_coding_t))-2
## [1] 115
sum(model_t_loo_info[,'p_loo'])
## [1] 85.23

# for 'random effects' model
ncol(bmmb::get_samples(model_re_t))-2
## [1] 132
sum(model_re_t_lo_info[,'p_loo'])
## [1] 109.1
```

6.4.4 Selecting a model

Which model should we use? Based on the comparison above, we see that `model_re_t` has an elpd that is 204 greater than the next best model. How large does an elpd difference need to be in order to be meaningful? There are two things that need to be taken into account: The magnitude of a difference and the uncertainty in the difference. A general rule of thumb seems to be that a difference of around 4 in elpd suggests a meaningful difference between the models (Vehtari et al. 2017). However, this is simply a general guideline and doesn't mean that a difference of 3.99 does not matter and a difference of 4.01 does. On the other hand, even large differences between models may not be reliable in the presence of large standard errors (i.e. large amounts of variation in

Variation in parameters ('random effects') and model comparison 195

the difference). For example, below we see the difference between our two smaller models:

```
brms::loo_compare (model_sum_coding, model_sum_coding_t,
criterion = "loo")
##                      elpd_diff se_diff
## model_sum_coding_t    0.0       0.0
## model_sum_coding    -19.6       7.6
```

The difference is 19.6, which is obviously large enough to be considered a meaningful improvement in the model. However, the standard error is 7.6. This means that the difference is only about 2.6 standard errors from zero. How many standard errors away from zero does a difference need to be in order to be 'real'? This is impossible to say, and in fact, the 'reality' of any given model can not be definitively established by any statistical test. Ok, so how many standard errors from zero should it be before we make a fuss about it? The answer to this seems to be somewhere in the neighborhood of 2–4 at least. If we think of improvements to our model as continuous, we can think of differences that are two standard errors away as potentially 'less reliable' and differences that are >5 standard errors away as 'more reliable'.

However, elpd is just a tool and is not really meant to be used to select the 'best' or 'real' model from a set of alternatives. The decision about which model to use is up to the researcher and can't be handed off to the models themselves. In addition to considering differences in elpd in isolation, the researcher should also consider how theoretically or practically warranted differences in their models are. For example, we know that our data contains way too many outliers to have proper normally distributed errors. Based on previous experience, we knew a priori that outliers are typical for listener judgments of things like apparent height. As a result, although the improvement provided by using t-distributed errors is not large, we may choose to keep using t-distributed errors in our model anyways. On the other hand, given the small difference between the estimates provided by both models and the not-huge difference in elpd between the models, a researcher may be warranted in simply using normally distributed errors in their model.

In contrast to these small differences, we see a difference of 204 in elpd due to the addition of random effects for apparent age, 10.7 standard errors away from zero. Keep in mind this does not mean that a researcher *must* include this predictor nor that this structure will necessarily be an aspect of the *real* model. What it *does* mean is that: (1) The addition of random effects for apparent age greatly improves the fit of our model to our data, (2) This increase in fit is likely to extend to the data we did *not* observe, and (3) We have pretty good evidence that the difference between the models is reliable. We could add to this: (4) It makes *sense* that there would be listener-dependent variation in the effect for apparent age, for many reasons, and we might be interested in measuring and reporting this variation. As a result, in this situation, it seems that random age effects should be included in our model.

Before finishing our discussion of model comparison, we want to show an example of a situation where adding a predictor does *not* help. To do this, we add a useless predictor to our data frame, as below. This predictor is a random sample of −1 and 1 with no relationship to our height judgments. We can see below that the average reported height is basically the same for both values of our useless predictor.

196 *Variation in parameters ('random effects') and model comparison*

```
set.seed(1)
notmen$useless = sample (c(-1,1),nrow(notmen), replace = TRUE)
tapply (notmen$height, notmen$useless, mean)
##   -1    1
## 153  154
```

Below we fit our t-distributed random effects model again, however, this time we include the useless predictor in the model formula, and even include a random effect for it:

```
height ~ A + useless + (A + useless|L) + (1|S)
```

We haven't discussed including multiple predictors in our formulas yet, and in fact, we will do so in the following chapter. For now, we are only interested in considering how this useless predictor affects our model comparisons. We fit this model below:

```
# Fit the model yourself
options (contrasts = c('contr.sum','contr.sum'))
priors = c(brms::set_prior("student_t(3,156, 12)", class = "Intercept"),
           brms::set_prior("student_t(3,0, 12)", class = "b"),
           brms::set_prior("student_t(3,0, 12)", class = "sd"),
           brms::set_prior("lkj_corr_cholesky (2)", class = "cor"),
           brms::set_prior("gamma(2, 0.1)", class = "nu"),
           brms::set_prior("student_t(3,0, 12)", class = "sigma"))

model_re_t_tooBig =
  brms::brm (height ~ A + useless + (A + useless|L) + (1|S), data = notmen,
             chains = 4, cores = 4, warmup = 1000, iter = 5000, thin = 4,
             prior = priors, family = "student")
```

And add the `loo` criterion to it.

```
model_re_t_tooBig = brms::add_criterion (model_re_t_tooBig,
criterion="loo")
```

Finally, we compare this to our equivalent model, minus the useless predictor.

```
brms::loo_compare (model_re_t, model_re_t_tooBig)
##                       elpd_diff se_diff
## model_re_t_tooBig  0.0           0.0
## model_re_t        -0.7           2.8
```

The more complex model has a slightly higher elpd, but this difference is only 1/4 the magnitude of the standard error. In addition, we can look at a summary of the fixed effects and see that the value of the useless predictor is near zero (0.3), and the 95% credible interval is wide relative to this value and includes zero and very small values ([−.2, .8]).

Variation in parameters ('random effects') and model comparison 197

```
brms::fixef(model_re_t_tooBig)
##               Estimate  Est.Error      Q2.5      Q97.5
## Intercept     155.4454     1.1583  153.1882   157.7513
## A1              8.5267     1.1226    6.2757    10.7094
## useless         0.3362     0.2522   -0.1688     0.8357
```

So, does this mean that this predictor should be excluded from the model? We would be justified in doing so, but may not necessarily want to. For example, if one of our important research questions centered on the value of the useless predictor, the fact that it is around zero and not some other value (e.g. −100) may be useful information. For example, we might want to keep the predictor in the model so we can say something like "So & So (2007) reported a value of −100 for the useless predictor. However, our results suggest that the effect of this predictor is likely to be near zero [mean = 0.34, sd = 0.25, 95% CI = [−0.17, 0.84])".

6.5 Answering our research questions

We've selected the model with random effects as the 'best' model and are ready to revisit our research questions from the last chapter again:

(Q1) How tall do speakers perceived as adult females sound?
(Q2) How tall do speakers perceived as children sound?
(Q3) What is the difference in apparent height associated with the perception of adultness?

Our answers to the main research questions are largely unchanged from the previous chapter (Section 5.12), however, there have been some changes that highlight interesting aspects of our data. We're going to focus on what our model tells us about the listener-dependent intercepts and effects for apparent age.

We saw that there was a strong negative correlation between the listener means and age effects. The reason for this is clearly evident in Figure 6.1. Listeners generally provided quite stable estimates for adult speakers. However, they exhibited substantial variation in their average judged height for child speakers. This makes sense. Most people probably have a good sense of approximately how tall adult females are on average. However, how tall are children 10–12? This is harder to answer for the average person. Not only is there more variability in height for children in these age ranges, but in addition, most people are not around large numbers of children 10–12 and so may not have a good sense of how tall they are on average. Since reported adult heights are more or less fixed across listeners, listeners that indicated shorter children necessarily indicated shorter speakers overall. In addition, listeners that indicated shorter children also would tend to exhibit larger age effects. In this way, the listener means and age effect become negatively correlated.

Although we said we would stick to sum coding for this book, it is worth noting that this is actually a situation where it might make sense to use treatment coding, using adult as the reference level (see Section 5.6.1). This would not affect our answers to the questions above but it would make the structure of the model more closely reflect the structure of the data, and it would decrease the correlation

198 *Variation in parameters ('random effects') and model comparison*

between the listener-dependent random effects. Why? Because when the listener intercepts correspond to their adult means (and not the grand mean), the intercept no longer helps you predict their age effect. As we can see in Figure 6.1, all listeners rate adult speakers about the same height regardless of how tall/short they think the children are.

6.6 'Traditionalists' corner

In traditionalists' corner, we compare the output of `brms` to some more 'traditional' approaches. We're not going to talk about the traditional models in any detail, the focus of this section is simply to highlight the similarities between different approaches, and to point out where to find equivalent information in the different models. If you are already familiar with these approaches, these sections may be helpful. If not, some of the information provided here may not make much sense, although it may still be helpful. If you want to know more about the statistical methods being discussed here, please see the preface for a list of suggested background reading in statistics.

6.6.1 Bayesian multilevel models vs. lmer

Here we compare the output of `brms` to the output of the `lmer` (linear mixed-effects regression) function, a very popular function for fitting multilevel models in the `lme4` package in R. Below we fit a model that is analogous to our `model_re_t` model, save for the use of Gaussian rather than t-distributed errors. Since we set contrasts to sum coding using the options above, this will still be in effect for this model. If you have not done so, run the line:

```r
options (contrasts = c("contr.sum","contr.sum"))
```

Before fitting the model below so that its output looks as expected. We can fit a model with random age effects using `lmer` with the code below, and check out the model print statement.

```r
# get data
notmen = bmmb::exp_data[exp_data$C_v!='m' & exp_data$C!='m',]

lmer_model = lme4::lmer (height ~ A +  (A|L) + (1|S), data = notmen)

lmer_model
## Linear mixed model fit by REML ['lmerMod']
## Formula: height ~ A + (A | L) + (1 | S)
##    Data: notmen
## REML criterion at convergence: 9890
## Random effects:
##  Groups   Name          Std.Dev. Corr
##  S        (Intercept)  3.53
##  L        (Intercept)  4.12
```

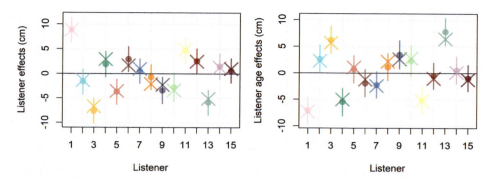

Figure 6.10 (left) Listener-dependent intercept effects and 95% credible intervals estimated using brms models. Crosses indicate random effects estimated by lmer. (right) Same as the left plot but showing the listener-dependent age effects.

```
##                  A1          3.98        -0.92
##   Residual                   7.67
## Number of obs: 1401, groups:  S, 94; L, 15
## Fixed Effects:
## (Intercept)           A1
##      155.05         8.64
```

The model now includes estimates of the correlation between the listener random effects, and of the standard deviation of the listener-dependent age effects. Figure 6.10 is a comparison of the listener means and age effects fit by both approaches. Clearly, the results are very similar save for the fact that just as with our correlations and standard deviations, `brms` gives us intervals while `lmer` only gives us point estimates.

6.7 Exercises

The analyses in the main body of the text all involve only the unmodified 'actual' resonance level (in `exp_data`). Responses for the stimuli with the simulated 'big' resonance are reserved for exercises throughout. You can get the 'big' resonance in the `exp_ex` data frame, or all data in the `exp_data_all` data frame.

Fit and interpret one or more of the suggested models:

1. Easy: Analyze the (pre-fit) model that's exactly like `model_re_t`, except using the data in `exp_ex` (`bmmb::get_model("6_model_re_t_ex.RDS")`).
2. Medium: Fit a model like `model_re_t`, but compare any two groups across resonance levels.
3. Hard: Fit two models like `model_re_t`, but compare any two groups across resonance levels. Compare results across models to think about group differences.

In any case, describe the model, present and explain the results, and include some figures. This time, also talk about the relationships between the random effects and any possible correlation between them.

References

Gelman, A., Hwang, J., & Vehtari, A. (2014). Understanding predictive information criteria for Bayesian models. *Statistics and computing*, 24(6), 997–1016.

McElreath, R. (2020). *Statistical rethinking: A Bayesian course with examples in R and Stan.* Abingdon: CRC Press.

Vehtari, A., Gelman, A., & Gabry, J. (2017). Practical Bayesian model evaluation using leave-one-out cross-validation and WAIC. *Statistics and computing*, 27(5), 1413–1432.

Vehtari A, Gabry J, Magnusson M, Yao Y, Bürkner P, Paananen T, Gelman A (2022). "loo: Efficient leave-one-out cross-validation and WAIC for Bayesian models." R package version 2.5.1, https://mc-stan.org/loo/.

7 Comparing many groups, interactions, and posterior predictive checks

We've been making our models more and more complicated, but we've still only fit models with extremely simple fixed-effects structures. For example, in the last two chapters, we talked about comparing only two groups. Although the comparison of two groups is very simple, it also comes up often. In addition, more complicated problems are often broken down into several two-group questions in the course of understanding a data set. However, real-world experiments don't usually *begin* as two-group questions. In this chapter, we're going to talk about the comparison of observations across multiple groups and using multiple factors.

7.1 Chapter pre-cap

In this chapter, we introduce models that include factors with many levels, and multiple different factors. After that, we discuss the concepts of within and between-subjects factors with respect to factorial designs, orthogonality, and interactions. We then introduce posterior prediction, and the use of this for model checking. Interactions and interaction plots are discussed, as is the way that these can be used to understand main effects and simple main effects. A model with two factors and an interaction, and random effects for all predictors, is fit, and the model is discussed and interpreted. We then present Bayesian R^2 as a simple measure of model fit, useful for getting an indication of how much two models actually differ. Finally, we discuss type S and type M errors, regions of practical equivalence, and the problem of how to know when effects are 'real'.

7.2 Comparing four (or any number of) groups

First, we're going to discuss models that compare observations across any number of groups (i.e. levels of a single factor). A model that can be used to compare multiple groups might have just one predictor factor, but that factor can have any number of levels. Although it's not very common to have a study design or model that *only* consists of a single multi-group comparison, the inclusion of multi-group comparisons is ubiquitous in many disciplines (including linguistics). Examples of predictors with multiple levels are language (e.g. participants' first languages), word category (e.g. part of speech, or usage frequency bins), and age groups (e.g. infant, child, teen, and adult).

In Figure 7.1, we see two ways that subjects (or listeners, or the levels of any grouping factor) can be arranged into groups. In the *within-subjects* version of this design,

DOI: 10.4324/9781003285878-7

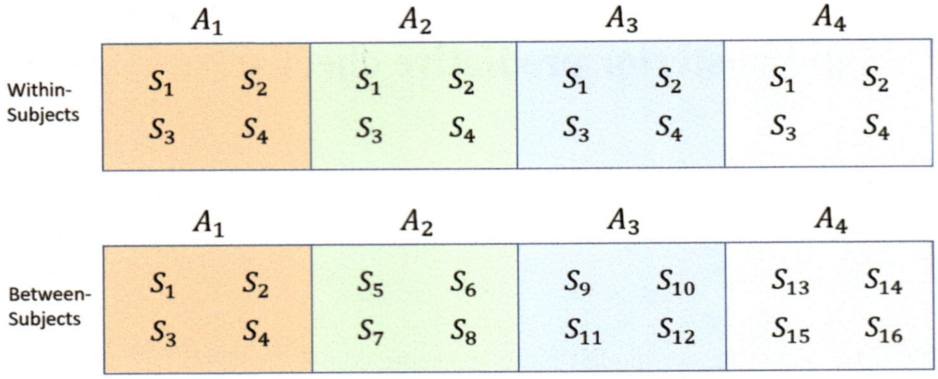

202 *Comparing many groups, interactions, and posterior predictive checks*

	A_1		A_2		A_3		A_4	
Within-Subjects	S_1	S_2	S_1	S_2	S_1	S_2	S_1	S_2
	S_3	S_4	S_3	S_4	S_3	S_4	S_3	S_4

	A_1		A_2		A_3		A_4	
Between-Subjects	S_1	S_2	S_5	S_6	S_9	S_{10}	S_{13}	S_{14}
	S_3	S_4	S_7	S_8	S_{11}	S_{12}	S_{15}	S_{16}

Figure 7.1 Data from a single group of subjects (S) divided according to a single grouping factor A.

each subject is tested at each level of *A*. In the *between-subjects* version of the design, different subjects are tested at every level of *A*. Here we omit the more complicated design discussed in Chapter 5, in which some subjects appear at all levels of *A* and others don't. Such designs are definitely analyzable with `brms`, and sometimes they may be unavoidable. However, they are not included in Figure 7.1 because there are a large number of possible configurations of this, and because the additional complexity of such designs can make them extremely challenging to use effectively, so we are typically better off not using such designs if at all possible.

7.2.1 Data and research questions

Below we load the data for our experiment investigating apparent speaker height, in addition to the `brms` and `bmmb` packages. For the first time, we're going to analyze productions from all speaker categories at the same time (i.e. boys, girls, men, and women).

```
library (brms)
library (bmmb)
options (contrasts = c('contr.sum','contr.sum'))
data (exp_data)
```

In Figure 7.2, we see that the distribution of apparent height with respect to the apparent speaker category is very similar to its distribution with respect to the veridical speaker category.

This is not terribly surprising since as we can see below, listeners identified speaker category correctly in 75% of cases. In addition, errors were most common for boys and girls, speakers that are expected to be approximately the same size.

```
# overall average correct category identification

mean(exp_data$C == exp_data$C_v)
## [1] 0.7458
```

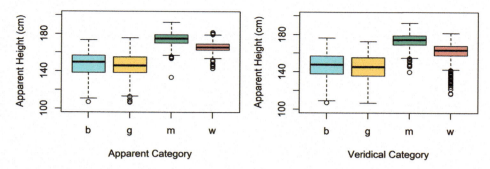

Figure 7.2 Distribution of apparent height judgments for boys (b), girls (g), men (m), and women (w) based on apparent speaker category (left) and veridical speaker category (right).

```
# average correct category identification by category
tapply(exp_data$C == exp_data$C_v, exp_data$C_v, mean)
##      b      g      m      w
## 0.5778 0.6456 0.9274 0.7097
```

In this chapter, we're going to focus on the effect of the *apparent* speaker category on apparent height. This is because we want to understand how listener's assumptions about the speaker affect their height judgments, and listeners did not know the veridical speaker category. We're first going to treat the four groups as if they had no internal relationships between the groups. This means we will be ignoring the fact that we might expect some degree of similarity in the relationships between women and girls, on the one hand, and men and boys, on the other. This may not be the best approach for this data since we know there are logical ways to group boys, girls, men, and women. However, this is a good starting point since in many cases you will have levels of a factor with no logical internal divisions.

Even with only four different groups our potential research questions are substantially more complicated than in the two-group case. First, there are four groups now, meaning we could potentially make six two-group comparisons. Second, the groups differ along multiple dimensions, making it more difficult to make two-group comparisons that answer a single question. For example, the 'man' and 'girl' groups differ according to apparent adultness *and* apparent gender. The presence of a difference between groups makes it difficult to isolate the contribution of each characteristic to the difference in apparent height. For now, we're going to keep things simple and just build a model that can tell us about our average group values.

To analyze data like this it should be in a data frame with one row for each observation. One column should contain the dependent variable, the variable whose values and variation you're trying to predict. Another column should contain the fixed effect predictor determining which group each observation belongs to. Finally, you need one or more columns indicating the sources of data in your experiment. The model in this section will use the following variables from our data frame:

- L: A number from 1 to 15 indicating which *listener* responded to the trial.
- C: A letter representing the speaker *category* (b = boy, g = girl, m = man, w =woman) reported by the listener for each trial.

204 *Comparing many groups, interactions, and posterior predictive checks*

- `height`: A number representing the *height* (in centimeters) reported for the speaker on each trial.
- `S`: A number from 1 to 139 indicating which *speaker* produced the trial stimulus.

And we are going to ask the following basic question:

(Q1) Does apparent speaker height vary systematically across apparent speaker categories?

7.2.2 Description of our model

In the last two chapters, we discussed the inclusion of a single factor with two levels in our models. Our model formula does not change in structure to include predictors with many levels. The formula to fit our model will be:

```
height ~ C + (C|L) + (1|S)
```

Where `C` is the apparent speaker category indicated by the listener for each trial, a factor with four levels (see above). Since we include `C` on the left-hand-side of the pipe of `L`, we know that we are estimating the category by listener interaction using adaptive partial pooling. At this point, we have to make a decision regarding how we represent our models in a more formal notation and striking a balance between readability and models that are directly analogous to the output in R.

Each level of the category predictor that we are estimating needs to be represented by a model parameter. Since we are using sum coding for all our factors (see Section 5.6.2), our model will estimate three of the four-group effects, omitting the alphabetically last level (in this case 'woman'). As a result, the formula above is analogous to:

```
height ~ C1 + C2 + C3 + (C1 + C2 + C3|L) + (1|S)
```

where `C1`, `C2`, and `C3` are parameters associated with the first three levels of apparent speaker category. In Section 4.3, we noted that each parameter in our model needs to be associated with a predictor. If we call the predictors `x1`, `x2`, and `x3`, our model formula could sort of be thought of as seen below. Of course, this is no longer a real or working model formula, and we're just trying to show how *C* might actually be included in our model.

```
height ~ x1*C1 + x2*C2 + x3*C3 + (x1*C1 + x2*C2 + x3*C3|L) + (1|S)
```

When a factor has only two levels, the effect for one level must equal the negative of the effect for the other level. As a result, group membership for observations can be represented using a single predictor equal to either -1 or 1 (for sum coding, discussed in Section 5.7.1). When the observation is associated with one level of the factor the predictor is 1, and when the observation is associated with the other level the predictor is -1. In that way, a single predictor and coefficient can reflect two different levels of the factor.

When there are more than two levels, each level that is being estimated is associated with a predictor variable, meaning that we expect $J-1$ estimated coefficients for a

Comparing many groups, interactions, and posterior predictive checks   205

factor with J levels in the absence of additional constraints. An example of this is seen below, where we generate three 'fake' predictors to represent four groups. Imagine the tiny matrix below represents the numerical predictors for our C parameters so that the first, second, and third columns represent x1, x2 and x3 respectively. Each row is represented by a single 1 save for the final row which is represented by -1 in *all other predictors* for that factor.

```
contr.sum(1:4)
##      [,1] [,2] [,3]
## 1     1    0    0
## 2     0    1    0
## 3     0    0    1
## 4    -1   -1   -1
```

Our tiny data matrix above suggests that the first observation (row) belongs to the first group (boy). This is because our data results in the $C1$ parameter being multiplied by one, and $C2$ and $C3$ being zeroed out (see Section 4.3). The same logic suggests the second row is an observation from the second group and the third from the third. For example, in (7.1) we imagine that the first four values of our C predictor are 1, 2, 3, and 4, meaning that the apparent speaker category indicated for the first four trials were boy, girl, man, and woman. We also imagine that our predicted value (μ) is a combination of our estimated parameters $C1, C2$ and $C3$ with the 'secret' predictors in our matrix above. We can see that multiplying our coefficients with our predictors has the effect of 'erasing' the unwanted coefficients for a given row leaving only the one associated with the observation.

$$C_{[1]} = 1, C_{[2]} = 2, C_{[3]} = 3, C_{[4]} = 4...$$
$$\mu_{[i]} = x_1 \cdot C1 + x_2 \cdot C2 + x_3 \cdot C3$$

$$\mu_{[1]} = 1 \cdot C1 + 0 \cdot C2 + 0 \cdot C3 = C1 \qquad (7.1)$$
$$\mu_{[2]} = 0 \cdot C1 + 1 \cdot C2 + 0 \cdot C3 = C2$$
$$\mu_{[3]} = 0 \cdot C1 + 0 \cdot C2 + 1 \cdot C3 = C3$$
$$\mu_{[4]} = -1 \cdot C1 - 1 \cdot C2 - 1 \cdot C3 = -(C1 + C2 + C3) = C4$$

Since $C4$ is equal to $-(C1 + C2 + C3)$ (under sum coding), adding the negative of $C1$, $C2$, and $C3$ to the prediction is equivalent to adding the value of $C4$. As a result, the fourth row of our tiny matrix represents an observation from the fourth group, and encodes the effect for $C4$, even without directly estimating this value. As a result, even though our model only directly estimates three parameters for our C predictor, we could think of our model as tacitly representing four parameters for this factor: $C1, C2, C3$, and $-(C1 + C2 + C3)$.

Even though the inclusion of C in our model requires the addition of three separate parameters, we're going to represent these with a single term like $C_{\left[c_{[i]}\right]}$ in our formal model descriptions. This term selects the value of C for trial i based on the value of the C (apparent category) predictor, which is consistent with the way we've been representing our listener and speaker-dependent intercepts. However, there appears to be a problem. The subscript of the term is a predictor which has four levels (C, or C). When

206 *Comparing many groups, interactions, and posterior predictive checks*

the `C` predictor is equal to its fourth level (`C = w`), the model seems to want to select the fourth C predictor, i.e. $C_{[4]}$. However, our C predictor vector does not contain four elements because the fourth level of the `C` predictor is not estimated (i.e. there is no x_4 predictor in (7.1)). So, when this occurs we can just imagine that our model reconstructs the missing parameter using the ones that *are* estimated, and then uses this value for $C4$.

Since we are including adult male speakers in our data we should also reconsider our priors. Based on the information in `height_data` we expect average apparent heights of around 176, 162, 150, and 150 cm respectively for men, women, girls, and boys. These four groups have an average of 159 cm and a standard deviation of 12 cm. Based on this, and especially given that we are investigating *apparent* and not *veridical* height, the priors we used in the last chapter still seem appropriate. The formal description of our model is given below. We omit the deterministic equation building up Σ from the correlation matrix (R) and the individual standard deviations (shown in (6.11)) since this does not involve the user, and it makes the model description needlessly bigger.

$$\text{height}_{[i]} \sim t\left(\nu, \mu_{[i]}, \sigma\right)$$

$$\mu_{[i]} = \text{Intercept} + C_{\left[C_{[i]}\right]} + L_{\left[L_{[i]}\right]} + C_{\left[C_{[i]}\right]} : L_{\left[L_{[i]}\right]} + S_{\left[S_{[i]}\right]}$$

$$\text{Priors}:$$
$$S_{[\cdot]} \sim \text{N}\left(0, \sigma_S\right)$$

$$
\begin{bmatrix} L_{[\cdot]} \\ C_{[1]} : L_{[\cdot]} \\ C_{[2]} : L_{[\cdot]} \\ C_{[3]} : L_{[\cdot]} \end{bmatrix}
\sim \text{MVNormal}\left(\begin{bmatrix} 0 \\ 0 \\ 0 \\ 0 \end{bmatrix}, \Sigma \right)
\tag{7.2}
$$

$$\text{Intercept} \sim \text{N}(156, 12)$$
$$C_{[\cdot]} \sim \text{N}(0, 12)$$
$$\sigma_L, \sigma_{C_{[1]}:L}, \sigma_{C_{[2]}:L}, \sigma_{C_{[3]}:L}, \sigma_S \sim \text{N}(0, 12)$$
$$\nu \sim \text{gamma}(2, 0.1)$$
$$R \sim \text{LKJCorr}(2)$$

Structurally, this model is extremely similar to the one described in (6.11) in the last chapter with $C_{\left[C_{[i]}\right]}$ replacing A, and $C_{\left[C_{[i]}\right]} : L_{\left[L_{[i]}\right]}$ replacing $A : L_{\left[L_{[i]}\right]}$. Note that since we are estimating three parameters for `C`, our listener-dependent 'random effects' come from a four-dimensional normal distribution which considers the relationships between the intercepts and category effects for individual listeners. Here is a plain English description of the model in (7.2):

> *We are modeling apparent height as coming from a t distribution with unknown nu (ν), mean (μ), and scale (σ) parameters. The expected value for any given trial (μ)*

Comparing many groups, interactions, and posterior predictive checks 207

is modeled as the sum of an intercept, an effect for apparent speaker category (C), a listener effect (L), listener dependent effects for apparent category (e.g. $C_{[1]} : L$), and a speaker effect (S). The speaker effects were drawn from a univariate normal distribution with a standard deviation (σ_S) estimated from the data. The four listener effects were drawn from a multivariate normal distribution with individual standard deviations ($\sigma_L, \sigma_{C_{[1]}:L}, \sigma_{C_{[2]}:L}, \sigma_{C_{[3]}:L}$) and a correlation matrix (R) that was estimated from the data. The remainder of the 'fixed' effects and correlations were given prior distributions appropriate for their expected range of values.

7.2.3 Fitting and interpreting the model

We fit the four-group model below:

```
# Fit the model yourself
priors = c(brms::set_prior("student_t(3,156, 12)", class = "Intercept"),
           brms::set_prior("student_t(3,0, 12)", class = "b"),
           brms::set_prior("student_t(3,0, 12)", class = "sd"),
           brms::set_prior("lkj_corr_cholesky (2)", class = "cor"),
           brms::set_prior("gamma(2, 0.1)", class = "nu"),
           brms::set_prior("student_t(3,0, 12)", class = "sigma"))


model_four_groups =
  brms::brm (height ~ C + (C|L) + (1|S), data = exp_data, chains = 4,
             cores = 4, warmup = 1000, iter = 5000, thin = 4,
             prior = priors, family = "student")

# or download it from the GitHub page:
model_four_groups = bmmb::get_model ('7_model_four_groups.RDS')
```

We'll focus on the fixed effects, seen below:

```
brms::fixef(model_four_groups)
##             Estimate Est.Error    Q2.5    Q97.5
## Intercept    158.581    1.083  156.41  160.685
## C1            -9.318    1.310  -11.87   -6.682
## C2           -12.082    1.494  -15.07   -9.110
## C3            15.286    1.327   12.59   17.950
```

It's always a good idea to make sure your model coefficients make sense given your data. Doing things like this will help minimize mistakes and make sure that you really understand your model. We can see that the intercept corresponds to the average of the group means, and our `C` coefficients correspond reasonably to, but don't exactly match, the centered group means.

```
# group means
means = tapply (exp_data$height, exp_data$C, mean)
```

208 *Comparing many groups, interactions, and posterior predictive checks*

```
# Intercept = mean of means
mean (means)
## [1] 158


# Group effects = centered group means
means - mean (means)
##       b       g       m       w
## -11.12 -13.03   16.56    7.59
```

There are many possible reasons for this including the fact that the group means don't account for repeated measures, a lack of balance in the data, or the way that outliers can unduly influence sample mean estimates. That being said, it's useful to see that our model coefficients seem to reflect the data and we should be concerned if these diverged wildly. Note that, as discussed above, we're missing the `C4` coefficient. We can use the `short_hypothesis` function to easily recover the final group coefficient by finding the negative sum of the coefficients that *were* estimated. An example of this is shown below.

```
# missing group effect
bmmb::short_hypothesis (model_four_groups, c("-(C1+C2+C3) = 0"))
##      Estimate Est.Error   Q2.5 Q97.5        hypothesis
## H1      6.114     1.216  3.686 8.543  (-(C1+C2+C3)) = 0
```

Clearly, there are differences in apparent height across groups. If someone asked you "please describe the differences to me", you might begin by saying something like "there doesn't seem to be too much difference in apparent height between apparent boys and girls", or "apparent men are identified as taller than apparent women". In each case, these statements reduce a multi-group model to focus on a single difference between groups at a time. We can use `short_hypothesis` to help us compare different combinations of our fixed effects. Using the code below we test for a difference in group means between the first and second groups (boys and girls), and between the third and fourth groups (men and women).

```
# find differences between groups
comparisons = bmmb::short_hypothesis (model_four_groups,
                          c("C1 = C2", "C3 = -(C1+C2+C3)"))
```

We can use `brmplot` from the `bmmb` package to easily make plots showing means and credible intervals for our fixed effects, including the recovered coefficient. We also plot the two comparisons we made using the `short_hypothesis` function above, presented in Figure 7.3.

The distributions in the left plot of the figure tell us about probable values for our category parameters: Given our data and model structure, there is a 95% probability that the parameter value falls within this interval. Our category effects reflect the expected difference between our model intercept, the overall grand mean, and each category mean. So, the intervals on the left of Figure 7.3 tell us that there is a 95% probability (given our data and model structure) that the actual difference between the

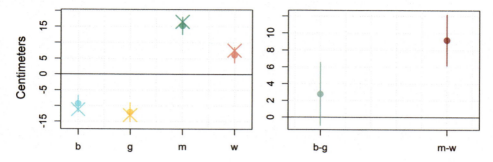

Figure 7.3 (left) Means and 95% credible intervals for boy (b), girl (g), man (m), and woman (w) effects for our four-group model. (right) Means and 95% credible intervals for differences between boys and girls, and men, and women.

grand mean and each group mean falls within that range. What do the distributions in the right plot in Figure 7.2 tell us? They represent the posterior distribution of the *difference* between category means directly, without involving the intercept.

Conceptually, finding the difference between the intercept and a group mean is no different than finding the difference between individual group means. Consider the example of providing directions with respect to your house. If the library is 5 miles west and the park is 3 miles west, you could refer to these as −5 and −3 miles from your house, west to east. However, you could also express the difference between one and the other directly as 2 (or −2). The left plot in Figure 7.2 expresses all distances with respect to the intercept (your house) while the right plot expresses differences with respect to individual category means directly (the library and park).

7.3 Investigating multiple factors simultaneously

Our model above had a single factor with four groups/levels. Another way to look at it is that the model predicted variation along a single **dimension**, which is a single piece of information that can be used to distinguish our groups. However, we can usually categorize people (or observations) along multiple dimensions simultaneously – there is more structure in the data than a single dimension captures. So, a speaker may be an adult *and* female or adult *and* male, child *and* female or child *and* male, and not just adult or child, male or female. This is because adultness and gender are separate characteristics (dimensions) and the value of one does not determine the value of the other. In our height experiment, we effectively asked listeners to make two binary classifications: Is the listener an adult or a child? Is the listener female or male? This means we can think of our four groups as varying along two dimensions, each represented by a different factor. However, although we know this, our previous model didn't: It thinks we just have four groups that have no logical internal distinctions.

To include multiple predictors in our model and inspect the effect of all combinations of factor levels on our dependent variable, we must *cross* our predictors. This means that we observe each level of one factor at every level of the other factor (and vice versa). For our data, this means that we observe both male and female children,

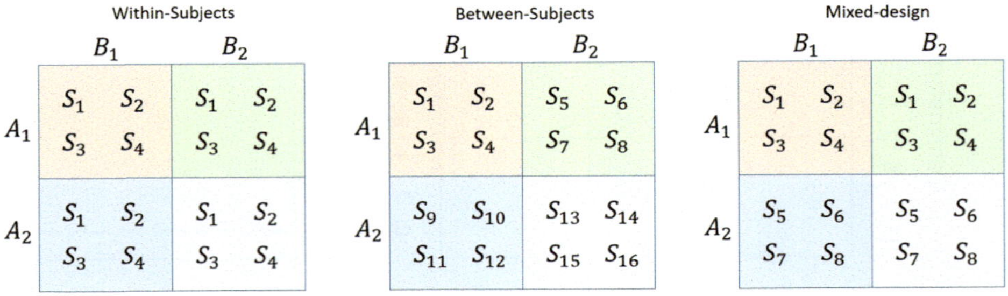

210 *Comparing many groups, interactions, and posterior predictive checks*

Figure 7.4 Data from groups of subjects (S), divided according to two grouping factors A and B.

and male and female adults. Crossing factors results in $n_A \cdot n_B$ individual groups for two factors (A and B) with n_A and n_B number of levels each. Since we have two factors with two levels each, crossing apparent age and gender results in four unique groups: Boys (male child), girls (female child), men (male adult), and women (female adult). Designs. where all the factors are crossed, are sometimes called **factorial** or **orthogonal** designs.

When you have orthogonal designs, that means that the effect of your 'dimensions' (i.e. factors) can be estimated separately. For example, if you want to know the difference in apparent height across levels of apparent gender, it helps to have observed both adults and children for each gender. A comparison of boys and women will conflate gender and age differences, thereby making it difficult to understand the independent effect of apparent gender. By balancing factors across each other, orthogonal designs allow us to *decompose* the variation in our data using different factors more effectively. This allows us to attribute the variation in our observations to the different factors in our design (we will return to this idea in Chapter 11).

Figure 7.4 presents a few ways that subjects can be combined with two two-level factors, A and B, whose combination can represent four groups. First, we can see that factors A and B are crossed with each other since there are subjects, and presumably observations, in each little **cell** (i.e. combination of factor levels). What would it look like for these factors to not be crossed? Well, one of the 'cells' (boxes) would be completely missing observations. If this were to happen, we would obviously lose the ability to make comparisons across groups involving the values in that cell. If your subjects factor is fully crossed with your fixed-effects factors (in this case A and B) then you have a fully *within-subjects* design. If you only observe certain subjects for specific combinations of fixed effects, you have a fully *between-subjects* design.

Finally, we see a new possibility, a **mixed design**. In a mixed design, one or more factors are between-subjects, and the others are within-subjects. In the example below, A is between-subjects but B is within-subjects. This means that each level of A has different subjects but each level of B has the same subjects. An example of a mixed design would arise if, for example, we wanted to run our coffee and reading time experiment (discussed in Chapter 5) on multiple first languages. Each subject could be tested at both coffee and decaf, making that factor within subjects; however, each subject would only be observed within a single first language group, making that factor between subjects.

Comparing many groups, interactions, and posterior predictive checks 211

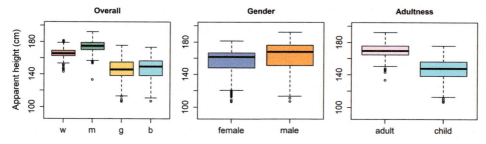

Figure 7.5 (left) Distribution of apparent height judgments for apparent boys (b), girls (g), men (m), and women (w). (middle) Comparison of distributions based on whether the speaker is female or male. (right) Comparison distributions based on whether the speaker is an adult or child.

Our model contains two predictors with two levels each, leading to four groups. Height judgments for these four groups are presented in Figure 7.5. These four boxes correspond to the four cells in Figure 7.4. The middle plot in 7.5 compares height judgments across levels of gender (male vs. female). Since we have both adults and children within each gender group, each box in the plot is really the average of two of the boxes from the left plot in 7.5 (boxes 1 and 3 vs. 2 and 4). This is equivalent to finding the average of one row in 7.4 and comparing it to the average of the other row.

Similarly, the right plot in 7.4 compares height judgments across levels of age (adult vs. child). Since we have both males and females within each gender group, each box in the plot is really the average of two of the boxes from the left plot in 7.5 (boxes 1 and 2 vs. 3 and 4). This is equivalent to finding the average of one column in 7.4 and comparing it to the average of the other column. In this way, our model including two fixed effect predictors can use four groups to answer two questions simultaneously: What is the effect of apparent age on apparent height? What is the effect of apparent gender on apparent height?

7.3.1 Data and research questions

We load our data and packages again just in case:

```
library (brms)
library (bmmb)
options (contrasts = c('contr.sum','contr.sum'))
data (exp_data)
```

We're going to use a slightly different set of columns from our data this time, this time using `A` and `G` rather than `C`. The model in this section will use the following variables from our data frame:

- `L`: A number from 1 to 15 indicating which *listener* responded to the trial.
- `height`: A number representing the *height* (in centimeters) reported for the speaker on each trial.

212 *Comparing many groups, interactions, and posterior predictive checks*

- S: A number from 1 to 139 indicating which *speaker* produced the trial stimulus.
- G: The *apparent gender* of the speaker indicated by the listener, f (female) or m (male).
- A: The *apparent age* of the speaker indicated by the listener, a (adult) or c (child).

And we're going to split the question we posed above into two questions:

(Q1) Does average apparent height differ across levels of apparent age?
(Q2) Does average apparent height differ across levels of apparent gender?

7.3.2 Description of the model

In our previous model, we acted like we just had four different groups with no internal structure. Of course, we know that our groups differ systematically from each other in meaningful ways. For example, we might have chosen to fit two separate models investigating age and gender like this:

```
brm (height ~ A + (A|L) + (1|S)
brm (height ~ G + (G|L) + (1|S)
```

For several reasons (some of which we'll see very soon), it's preferable to fit a single model with both predictors at once, rather than fitting separate models for each one. Our model formula will now look like this, reflecting the influence of both predictors simultaneously:

```
height ~ A + G + (A + G|L) + (1|S)
```

This can be read like "apparent height is distributed according to effects for apparent adultness and gender, with random intercepts, age, and gender effects for each listener, and random intercepts for each speaker". You may have noticed that our model no longer includes the C predictor. This is because the C label is perfectly predictable on the basis of A and G (i.e. as a female child, a member of the g group must have values of f and c for their G and A predictors). Basically, we have *decomposed* the four categories into two components to help us understand the effect of each. For example, the fixed effect predictors in our model were previously:

$$\mu_{[i]} = \text{Intercept} + \left(C_{\left[C_{[i]} \right]} \right) \tag{7.3}$$

We can expand the term in parentheses as seen below. Since a group can be exactly represented by combinations of gender and adult, our model sort of 'secretly' contained this more complicated model inside of it.

$$\mu_{[i]} = \text{Intercept} + \left(A_{\left[A_{[i]} \right]} + G_{\left[G_{[i]} \right]} \right) \tag{7.4}$$

The above can be thought of as a 'decomposition' of the variance in your model by breaking it up into parts and assigning them to different sources. We have actually been doing this from the start by making more and more complicated models. Recall

Comparing many groups, interactions, and posterior predictive checks 213

that our very first approach (in Chapter 3) to understanding variation in apparent height treated all variation as error, and so did not 'decompose' anything. In Chapter 4 we added between-listener and speaker variation to the model, and in Chapter 5 we added apparent age. Now we include apparent age and gender, listener specific effects and intercepts, and speaker-specific intercepts. There is a fixed amount of variation in our dependent variable. Every tiny bit of variance that these added components explain takes away from the data-level error variance (σ), and potentially also from the other components that had previously been in the model. Our updated model description is provided in (7.5), again omitting the deterministic equation 'building' up Σ.

$$\text{height}_{[i]} \sim t\left(v, \mu_{[i]}, \sigma\right)$$

$$\mu_{[i]} = \text{Intercept} + A + G + L_{\left[L_{[i]}\right]} + A : L_{\left[L_{[i]}\right]} + G : L_{\left[L_{[i]}\right]} + S_{\left[S_{[i]}\right]}$$

$$\text{Priors}:$$
$$S_{[\bullet]} \sim N\left(0, \sigma_S\right)$$

$$\begin{bmatrix} L_{[\bullet]} \\ A : L_{[\bullet]} \\ G : L_{[\bullet]} \end{bmatrix} \sim \text{MVNormal}\left(\begin{bmatrix} 0 \\ 0 \\ 0 \end{bmatrix}, \Sigma\right) \tag{7.5}$$

$$\text{Intercept} \sim N(156, 12)$$
$$A, G \sim N(0, 12)$$
$$\sigma_L, \sigma_{A:L}, \sigma_{G:L}, \sigma_S \sim N(0, 12)$$
$$\sigma \sim N(0, 12)$$
$$v \sim \text{gamma}(2, 0.1)$$
$$R \sim \text{LKJCorr}(2)$$

Our models have increasingly large numbers of priors, and many of these are the same. As a result, going forward we will place these on the same line when they have the same prior and represent the same sorts of parameters (in much the same way they are specified by the `class` parameter in the `set_prior` function). For example, the line $\sigma_L, \sigma_{A:L}, \sigma_{G:L}, \sigma_S \sim N(0, 12)$ specifies the prior probability of all standard deviation terms individually, but at the same time. In plain English this says:

We are modeling apparent height as coming from a t distribution with unknown nu (v), mean (μ), and scale (σ) parameters. The expected value for any given trial (μ) is modeled as the sum of an intercept, an effect for apparent speaker age (A) and gender (G), a listener effect (L), a listener dependent effect for apparent age (A : L) and apparent gender (G : L), and a speaker effect (S). The speaker effects were drawn from a univariate normal distribution with a standard deviation (σ_S) estimated from the data. The three listener effects were drawn from a multivariate normal distribution with individual standard deviations (σ_L, σ_{A:L}, σ_{G:L}) and a correlation matrix (R) that was estimated from the data. The remainder of the 'fixed' effects and correlations were given prior distributions appropriate for their expected range of values.

7.3.3 Fitting and interpreting the model

Below we fit a model with the structure outlined in (7.5). We don't need to change our priors because our new predictors are all covered by the classes of priors we have specified so far, and we think the priors we have been using thus far are still a good fit for our data.

```
# Fit the model yourself
priors = c(brms::set_prior("student_t(3,156, 12)", class = "Intercept"),
           brms::set_prior("student_t(3,0, 12)", class = "b"),
           brms::set_prior("student_t(3,0, 12)", class = "sd"),
           brms::set_prior("lkj_corr_cholesky(2)", class = "cor"),
           brms::set_prior("gamma(2, 0.1)", class = "nu"),
           brms::set_prior("student_t(3,0, 12)", class = "sigma"))


model_both =
  brms::brm (height ~ A + G + (A + G|L) + (1|S), data = exp_data,
             chains = 4, cores = 4, warmup = 1000, iter = 5000,
             thin = 4, prior = priors, family = "student")

# Or download it from the GitHub page:
model_both = bmmb::get_model ('7_model_both.RDS')
```

We can inspect the model fixed effects:

```
# inspect the fixed effects
brms::fixef (model_both)
##              Estimate Est.Error     Q2.5    Q97.5
## Intercept    158.654    1.1947  156.319  161.025
## A1             9.979    1.2107    7.562   12.282
## G1            -2.205    0.5524   -3.288   -1.124
```

We now have two non-Intercept 'Population-Level' effects: A1 and G1, representing the categories 'adult' and 'female' respectively. Remember that since we used sum coding and have only two levels for each factor, the effects for the groups that are not represented ('child', 'male') are just the opposite sign of the groups that *are* represented. Below, we calculate the mean apparent height of the four groups and find the grand mean of the four groups. We can see that this is very similar to our intercept.

```
# Intercept
mean (tapply (exp_data$height, exp_data$C, mean))
## [1] 158
```

Next, we find the average apparent height for each level of adultness, find the difference between these, and divide it by negative two (just to flip the sign to match our effects). We also do the same for the levels of age. This tells us half the difference

Comparing many groups, interactions, and posterior predictive checks 215

between our group means, and we can see that these values are reasonably similar to the estimated `A1` and `G1` predictors.

```
# Age effect
diff (tapply (exp_data$height, exp_data$A, mean) ) / -2
##     c
## 12.16

# Gender effect
diff (tapply (exp_data$height, exp_data$G, mean) ) / -2
##       m
## -3.166
```

We can recover the four original group means by adding up individual fixed effect coefficients. This can sometimes be tedious and requires you to be careful and methodical, but isn't actually difficult. Remember that each of the four groups is uniquely identified by a combination of gender and adultness. This means that to recover the expected group means, we need to add the right combination of coefficients to the intercept. For example, the first hypothesis we test below (`Intercept + -A1 + -G1 = 0`) takes the intercept and adds the effect for 'child' (`-A1`). We use `-A1` and not `A2` (i.e. the second level of `A`) because our model does not contain a parameter called `A2`. This parameter is not estimated in our model because `-A1=A2`. So, if we want the value of `A2` we use `-A1`. Similarly, we add the effect for 'male' using `-G1`. Since we started with the overall mean apparent height (the intercept) and add the effects for 'child' and 'male', the hypothesis `Intercept + -A1 + -G1 = 0` estimates the group mean for 'boys'.

```
means_pred = bmmb::short_hypothesis (model_both,
                    c("Intercept + -A1 + -G1 = 0",  # boys
                      "Intercept + -A1 +  G1 = 0",  # girls
                      "Intercept +  A1 + -G1 = 0",  # men
                      "Intercept +  A1 +  G1 = 0"))  # women

means_pred
##     Estimate Est.Error   Q2.5 Q97.5              hypothesis
## H1    150.9    2.2410  146.6 155.3  (Intercept+-A1+-G1) = 0
## H2    146.5    2.3680  142.0 151.2   (Intercept+-A1+G1) = 0
## H3    170.8    1.2988  168.2 173.4   (Intercept+A1+-G1) = 0
## H4    166.4    0.6901  165.0 167.8    (Intercept+A1+G1) = 0
```

Below we compare our recreated group means with our average height judgment for each group. There is a reasonable similarity, however, there also appear to be some important mismatches.

```
tapply (exp_data$height, exp_data$C, mean)
##     b     g     m     w
## 146.9 145.0 174.5 165.6
```

216 *Comparing many groups, interactions, and posterior predictive checks*

For example, we see that adult women and men differ in height by 9 cm in our data, while boys and girls by only 2 cm. So, it seems like the difference between males and females is smaller for children than for adults. However, according to our model men and women differ by about 4.4 cm, and so do boys and girls. This discrepancy suggests that our model is potentially missing important information about our data.

7.4 Posterior prediction: Using our models to predict new data

So far we've been working with very simple models and so we haven't worried very much about how well they *fit* or represent our data. Our reconstruction of the group means above suggests our current model may have some issues and that we should be concerned about its ability to accurately capture the patterns in the data. So far we've only been discussing modeling in one direction, going from data to abstract, reduced representations (i.e. regression models). However, it's also worth considering going in the other direction, from the abstract representation back toward data.

One way to see how well our model represents our data is to consider what data would be *generated* by the relationships represented in our model. Using your model in this way is called **prediction**, and you can use prediction to evaluate the fit of your model. The reasoning is basically, if your model is a good representation of the data, the 'fake' data it generates should look very much like your real data. If the fake data it generates doesn't look like your real data, something about your model is slightly 'off'. The discussion of prediction presented here will involve dependent variables that do not require a link function (discussed in Chapter 10). Some of the details discussed here, in particular those involving expected values, do not exactly apply to models that require a link function.

All our models so far have contained lines like those seen in (7.6). These lines tell our models that: (1) We expect our data to be normally distributed given some mean and standard deviation, and (2) The mean for a given trial can be predicted using some combination of the independent variables.

$$y_{[i]} \sim N\left(\mu_{[i]}, \sigma\right)$$
$$\mu_{[i]} = \text{Intercept} + A_{\left[A_{[i]}\right]} + B_{\left[B_{[i]}\right]} + C_{\left[C_{[i]}\right]} \tag{7.6}$$

The value of μ above is the expected value for a given trial. This is also sometimes called the **linear predictor**, or the **conditional expectation function** (in econometrics). Since the linear predictor is the value you expect for a trial, it's obvious that there should be a reasonable correspondence between the linear predictor and your dependent variable. If what your model tells you to expect is not like what you actually observe, then what good is the model? One shortcoming of the linear predictor is that this does not incorporate the random trial-to-trial error (i.e. σ) that you know is a part of your data. As a result, the linear predictor is constant for any single combination of dependent variables, and undersells the amount of variation that can be expected in a given data set.

The **posterior predictive distribution** is the distribution of possible data given your parameter estimates and probability model. In other words, the posterior predictive distribution uses your linear predictor, but also includes the data-level noise implied by the structure of your model. For normally distributed data, our posterior predictive distribution is the distribution of generated values of $\bar{y}$ given estimates of μ and σ

Comparing many groups, interactions, and posterior predictive checks 217

as in (7.7). We use $\tilde{y}$ to represent *new* observations, as opposed to $\hat{y}$ which represents estimates of current data.

$$\tilde{y}_{[i]} \sim N\left(\mu_{[i]}, \sigma\right) \tag{7.7}$$

A *posterior predictive check* samples from the posterior predictive distribution with the intention of comparing these samples of $\tilde{y}$ to your original data y. Posterior prediction can be used to assess how well your model fits your data. If your model really 'gets' your data, the fake data it generates ($\tilde{y}$) will have similar characteristics to your real data (y). If the fake data your model generates looks substantially different from your real data, that suggests a fundamental misalignment between your model and your data.

You can get simple representations of your posterior predictive distribution using the `pp_check` function in `brms` as seen below. This function will compare the distribution of your new data ($\tilde{y}$) to the distribution of your actual data. It compares density plots by default, though the user can select other sorts of plots.

```
brms::pp_check(model_both)
```

You can also use the `p_check` (predictive check) function in `brms` to make the same sorts of comparisons, though this function only compares densities. This function lets you hide or show your data in the plot, lets you specify the number of posterior samples you want, and also lets you specify the random effects formula when predicting. This function also returns a matrix containing the posterior predictions (`y_pred` below) where each row represents a different observation and each column represents a different posterior sample.

```
y_pred = bmmb::p_check(model_both, show_data = TRUE)
```

The functions above are good for a '30,000-foot view' of our posterior predictions. They show you when something big has gone wrong but may not let you see if something small goes wrong. To investigate nuances in your predictions, you may need to consider these using the same sort of plots you would use to interpret your real data, for example using a representation as seen in Figure 7.5. The generic functions `fitted` and `predict` will help you get linear and posterior predictions from your `brm` model.

```
# linear predictor
y_lin_pred = fitted (model_both)

# posterior prediction
y_post_pred = predict (model_both)
```

In both cases the functions return four-column data frames with as many rows as the number of observations in the data. These data frames contain columns representing the mean, standard deviation, and the upper and lower 95% credible intervals for each one of our data points. The reason we get intervals for our posterior predictions is that our model has a different prediction for each set of posterior samples. This means

218 *Comparing many groups, interactions, and posterior predictive checks*

that if we have 4,000 samples we actually have 4,000 slightly different sets of parameter estimates and so 4,000 slightly different predictions. So, in addition to information about the average prediction for each data point, we get information about variation around these estimates. We can see the (summarized) data frame representing our linear predictors.

```
# linear predictions
head (y_lin_pred)
##        Estimate Est.Error  Q2.5 Q97.5
## [1,]    156.8      2.182 152.5 161.0
## [2,]    161.7      2.059 157.6 165.6
## [3,]    160.6      1.983 156.6 164.3
## [4,]    162.3      1.846 158.5 165.9
## [5,]    163.0      1.992 159.0 167.0
## [6,]    155.7      2.371 151.1 160.5
```

And below we see the data frame corresponding to our posterior predictions. Note that although the means of the linear and posterior predictions are very similar, the intervals around the posterior predictions are noticeably wider. This is because the posterior predictions incorporate the data-level error (σ) in their predictions. Another difference between the linear and posterior predictions is that the linear predictors are fixed for a given set of posterior samples. In contrast, every time you run the command `predict(model)` you will get slightly different results because these incorporate random error.

```
# posterior predictions
head (y_post_pred)
##         Estimate Est.Error  Q2.5 Q97.5
## [1,]     157.0      7.915 141.3 172.2
## [2,]     161.7      9.137 146.3 177.2
## [3,]     160.5      8.210 144.8 175.9
## [4,]     162.1      8.312 146.4 177.0
## [5,]     162.8      7.639 147.8 177.9
## [6,]     155.7      7.708 140.0 170.8
```

For both kinds of predictions, you can also set `summary=FALSE` to get the individual (unsummarized) predictions. If you do this you get individual predictions for every set of posterior samples for your parameters, for every data point. So, if you have 1500 data points and 4000 posterior samples, the unsummarized output of these functions would be a matrix with 4000 rows and 1500 columns.

There's a parameter for the `predict` function, `re_formula`, that determines which random effect terms are included in your prediction. By default, this parameter is set to `NULL` meaning that your predictions will be made using your complete model formula. For example for our last model this means our posterior predictions reflect this model formula:

```
height ~ A + G + (A + G|S) + (1|L)
```

Comparing many groups, interactions, and posterior predictive checks 219

We can instead set `re_formula=NA` to make predictions using only the fixed effects as seen below.

```
y_post_pred_no_re = predict (model_both, re_formula = NA)
```

This corresponds to the predictions made by this model:

```
height ~ A + G
```

We could also include a subset of random effects, for example including only the listener random intercepts as seen below:

```
y_post_pred_some_re = predict (model_both, re_formula = "~(1|L)")
```

This would generate predictions made by the following model:

```
height ~ A + G + (1|L)
```

Below we sample from the posterior distribution but ask for only a single (randomly chosen) prediction. We do this for our full model and for a model that makes only fixed-effects predictions.

```
y_hat = predict (model_both, ndraws = 1)
y_hat_no_re = predict (model_both, re_formula = NA, ndraws = 1)
```

In Figure 7.6 we compare the distribution of our data to our posterior predictive distributions, without and with the inclusion of random effects.

There are some differences in the 'widths' of the boxes, but we will not discuss this for now. Instead, we would like to highlight differences in the relative positions of the boxes representing the four groups across the plots. Our data show different average

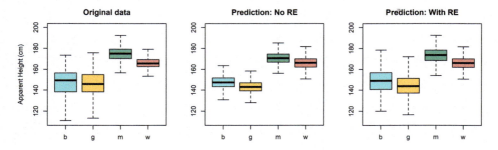

Figure 7.6 (left) Distribution of apparent height judgments according to apparent speaker category (boy, girl, man, woman) for our real data. (middle) Posterior predictions made by `model_both` without random effects (RE). (right) Posterior predictions made by `model_both` with random effects (RE).

heights for men and women but no noticeable height difference between boys and girls. Despite this, both sets of our posterior predictions show a difference in height between boys and girls. This is particularly evident in our fixed-effects predictions since the random effects can help represent many of the idiosyncrasies of any given data set. As we will discuss in the following section, the structure of our data (and our world knowledge) suggests that there is an *interaction* between apparent gender and apparent age, meaning that we should include the interaction between these predictors in our model.

7.5 Interactions and interaction plots

We can think of a single effect representing a difference between groups/conditions/levels as a slope. For example, in the left plot in Figure 7.7 we plot the mean apparent height for apparent females and males at arbitrary x-axis locations. The difference in the group means is 6 cm (females 157 cm, males 163 cm). We can use any arbitrary x-axis distance to calculate slopes, as long as we are consistent. However, there are obvious practical advantages to choosing to calculate these slopes over the arbitrary 'distance' of 1. To do this, we can imagine that we plot the first level (female) at 0 and successive levels at sequential integer values along the x-axis (i.e. 1, 2, 3, ...). When we do this, the line formed by joining the averages of these groups has a slope of 6 (i.e. it rises 6 cm from 0 to 1, from one group to another, for a slope of 6/1).

The plot highlighting the effect of apparent gender on apparent height in Figure 7.7 is a *main effects* plot. Main effects (discussed in Chapter 6) are the effects of one predictor averaged across everything else. Saying 'averaged across everything else' basically means we are ignoring everything else in our model. A person looking only at the left plot in Figure 7.7 would have no idea our data also investigates the effect of apparent adultness. We have 'erased' the differences in apparent adultness from our data by averaging across all levels of that factor. Another way to think of main effects is that they are *marginal effects*, the overall, average, *unconditional* differences between the levels of the factor. So, if someone asks you "whats the average difference in apparent height between apparent males and females?" you can respond "about 6 cm". However, as noted in the previous chapter, sometimes the answer is not so simple, and it starts more like: "well... it depends". Interactions represent situations like these, where the effect of one variable depends on, or is *conditional* on, the value of some other variable.

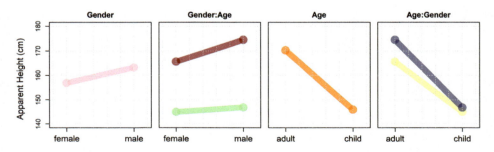

Figure 7.7 Plots showing different ways to consider average apparent height judgments across levels of apparent age and gender.

Comparing many groups, interactions, and posterior predictive checks 221

The idea of conditional effects (interactions) may *feel* complicated, but it is something we all understand intuitively. For example, how much will a given person grow in height in the next five years? What if I told you that one person is 1 and the other is 60? You *know* that makes a difference, which is to say, that you *know* there is an interaction between age and rate of growth. In other words, the expected relationship between time and growth is different for young children and grown adults. Anyone who understands these varying effects *understands* interactions, whether or not they know how to relate this concept to the mathematical formalisms used to implement these in regression models.

To understand interactions we need to talk about **simple effects** or **simple main effects**, the effects of a factor at one specific level of another factor. Basically, main effects show you the overall effect of a factor and simple effects show you the effects of the factor *depending* on the value of other things. We split the single (main) effect for gender into two simple (main) effects of gender across the levels of apparent age, presented in the second plot in Figure 7.7. We can see clearly that the lines do not have the same slope, indicating the effect for gender varies across the levels of apparent age.

The second and fourth plots in Figure 7.7 are sometimes called **interaction plots**. Knowing how to interpret interaction plots is extremely useful because they help you quickly understand the nature of any interactions in your data. Interaction plots show you the simple main effects of one predictor across the levels of the other. They do this by having one factor which varies across the x-axis and using different lines for the levels of the other factor. For example in the second plot gender varies across the x-axis and different lines are used for the levels of age, and in the fourth plot age varies across the x-axis and different lines are used for gender. Note however that the same information is presented in the two interaction plots in Figure 7.7, it is just presented differently in each case. In fact, we can see that the y-axis values of the four-line endpoints are equal across the two plots. The slopes of the lines in the second plot correspond to the differences between line endpoints in the fourth plot; one is small and one is near zero. The differences between the line endpoints in the second plot are the slopes of the fourth plot, both are large but one is larger.

Imagine what would happen if we began with a main effect plot like the first plot in Figure 7.7, and added/subtracted a single value to each end of the line segment. This single value could represent the main effect of some other factor, for example, the main effect of apparent age. Since a single number would be added to both points on the line, the line representing the effect of apparent gender would *slide* up/down the y-axis, however, the line would not change its slope. We might imagine trying to slide the line in the first plot in Figure 7.7 up and down the y-axis to try to get it to match the simple effects presented in the second plot of the same figure. However, we will not be successful because these two lines do not share a slope. In order to make the lower and upper lines *not* parallel, we need to add different values to each side of the main effects line.

The varying effect for apparent gender at different levels of apparent age indicates that these effects *interact* in our data. Interactions between our factors are detectable visually in the form of a lack of parallel lines in interaction plots (i.e. varying slopes in the simple effects). In the absence of an interaction, all lines in such a plot should be parallel, save for variation due to random error. We can see that the lines in the second and fourth plots in Figure 7.7 are *not* parallel, suggesting an interaction between apparent age and gender in our data. In the absence of an interaction, we could just answer the question "whats the average difference between apparent height between males and females?" with a number like 6 cm. In the presence of an interaction, we need to consider the *conditional effects* of each predictor at the levels of the other predictors (i.e. the simple effects). So, the most important thing to remember about interpreting main effects is:

- If there are no interactions between factors, focus on the main effects.
- If there are interactions between factors, you must inspect the simple effects to understand the nature of the interaction.

7.6 Investigating interactions with a model

In Figure 7.6 we made posterior predictions of our data with and without the inclusion of the speaker random effects and presented these as boxplots. We present these same predictions as interaction plots in Figure 7.8. We can see in Figure 7.8 that the predictions made using only fixed effects (middle plot) are systematically wrong, and that the problem with our predictions is that our predicted lines are parallel, while those for our real data are not. As we've just discussed, in the absence of interactions, interaction plots contain only parallel lines. Since our model (`model_both`) does not include interaction terms it cannot represent interactions, and so is only capable of making predictions along parallel lines. This means our model is not capable of representing the pattern in our data using only fixed effects.

We can see that when random effects are included, prediction is better. This is not surprising since the listener and speaker-specific intercept adjustments allow for deviations from the predictions made by the fixed effects to still be captured by the model. However, if accurate prediction is only possible using random effects, that limits the generalizability of our model to new levels of the grouping variable, e.g. subject or listener. In other words, the absence of good fixed-effects prediction limits the generalizability of our model and may be a cause for concern.

Our model is a little universe we made up, and it only includes the information, and structures, we included in it. This 'universe' only contains parallel lines because we only gave it that capability. So, the fact that our model generates parallel lines does not in any way 'prove' that the lines are parallel because they were bound to be. This is a little bit like taking black and white photographs and then using this as evidence that the scene does not contain color. In order to properly investigate whether the lines are

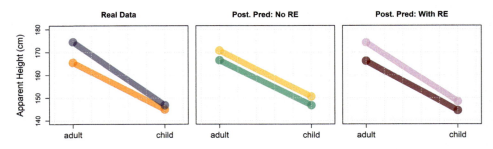

Figure 7.8 Interaction plots comparing our real data to posterior predictions, with and without random effects (RE). In each case, the top line represents height judgments for apparent males.

Comparing many groups, interactions, and posterior predictive checks **223**

parallel, the model must be built in a way that allows it to (at least potentially) represent the interactions in our data, i.e. to represent lines that are *not* parallel.

Before fitting a model with an interaction term we want to remind you that you cannot estimate interactions between factors that are not crossed: If you did not observe all combinations of factor levels, you are not in a position to talk about how effects vary for those combinations. So, it is extremely important to be sure to only include interactions in your model when these predictors are *crossed*, or your model may run into all sorts of problems.

7.6.1 Data and research questions

We load our data and packages again (again) just in case:

```
library (brms)
library (bmmb)
options (contrasts = c('contr.sum','contr.sum'))
data (exp_data)
```

We're going to use the very same variables from our data frame that we used in the previous model. These are:

- `L`: A number from 1to 15 indicating which *listener* responded to the trial.
- `height`: A number representing the *height* (in centimeters) reported for the speaker on each trial.
- `S`: A number from 1 to 139 indicating which *speaker* produced the trial stimulus.
- `G`: The *apparent gender* of the speaker indicated by the listener, `f` (female) or `m` (male).
- `A`: The *apparent age* of the speaker indicated by the listener, `a` (adult) or `c` (child).

And we're going to address our two previous research questions, and add one more:

(Q1) Does average apparent height differ across levels of apparent age?
(Q2) Does average apparent height differ across levels of apparent gender?
(Q3) Is there an interaction between the effects of apparent gender and age on apparent height?

7.6.2 Model formulas

The model presented above (`model_both`) requires only a slight tweak to include the interaction in our data. There are two ways to include interactions in R model formulas, either:

```
height ~ A + G + A:G + (A + G + A:G|L) + (1|S)
```

Or:

```
height ~ A * G + (A * G|L) + (1|S)
```

224 *Comparing many groups, interactions, and posterior predictive checks*

The first way includes an explicit interaction term, `A:G`. The syntax for these is `X:Z` for an interaction between effects `X` and `Z`, `W:X:Z` for a three-way interaction, and so on. The second way uses `*` between our two predictors. This tells R to include those predictors and all the interactions between them. This can be much faster than specifying all interactions, but you lose control over which ones you include. For example, this formula:

```
y ~ Z * X * W
```

Implies this one:

```
y ~ Z + X + W + Z:X + Z:W + X:W + Z:X:W
```

But cannot represent this one (since it omits the `Z:W` interaction):

```
y ~ Z + X + W + Z:X + X:W + Z:X:W
```

Actually, we could represent the model above using the following formula:

```
y ~ Z * X * W - Z:W
```

Where we use `-` to remove specific terms from the model formula. We can also use parentheses in model formulas to organize our interactions as in the following formula:

```
y ~ (Z + X) * W
```

Which is equivalent to:

```
y ~ Z + X + W + Z:W + X:W
```

We can also use `^` to find all interactions up to a certain order/degree, as in:

```
y ~ (Z + X + W)^2 y ~ (Z + X + W)^3
```

Which are equivalent to:

```
y ~ Z + X + W + Z:X + Z:W + X:W y ~ Z + X + W + Z:X + Z:W + X:W + Z:X:W
```

Finally, all of this applies to both our fixed and random effects predictors as in the following possible formula:

```
y ~ (Z + X) * W * V - W:V:X + ((Z + X) * W * V - W:V:X|L)
```

In our formulas, the `:` and `|` both basically mean *given* and indicate that conditional effects are being estimated. The difference between these is syntactic, much like the difference in R between `[]` and `()`. A colon (`:`) is used to indicate interactions between

Comparing many groups, interactions, and posterior predictive checks 225

'fixed' effects, that is effects estimated using fixed prior distributions. The pipe (`|`) indicates that the formula to its left is being estimated for each level of the predictor to the right of the pipe, and that this estimation is being carried out using adaptive partial pooling. In the formula above, the use of `:` and `|` for different purposes makes `((Z + X) * W * V - W:V:X|L)` interpretable: It means that, effectively, sub-models equivalent to `(Z + X) * W * V - W:V:X` will be fit for each level of `L`.

7.6.3 Description of our model

Our full model specification is presented in (7.8), once again omitting the equation specifying Σ. The model now includes an *interaction* term ($A:G$) that can help explain variation that cannot be explained by the independent effects of adultness and gender. This interaction term helps us model the *conditional* effect of one predictor given the other. Our model also actually contains a three-way interaction as well $\left(A:G:L_{\left[L_{[i]} \right]} \right)$, though it may not seem that way to us superficially. This is the 'random' effect of the interaction between A and G for each level of listener, `(A:G|L)` in our model. This is a three-way interaction because it represents the interaction between the two-way interaction of A and G with our listener factor: The listener-dependent two-way interaction between A and G.

$$\text{height}_{[i]} \sim t\left(v,\mu_{[i]},\sigma\right)$$
$$\mu_{[i]} = \text{Intercept} + A + G + A:G +$$
$$L_{\left[L_{[i]} \right]} + A:L_{\left[L_{[i]} \right]} + G:L_{\left[L_{[i]} \right]} + A:G:L_{\left[L_{[i]} \right]} + S_{\left[S_{[i]} \right]}$$

$$\text{Priors}:$$
$$S_{[\cdot]} \sim t\left(3,0,\sigma_S\right)$$

$$\begin{bmatrix} L_{[\cdot]} \\ A:L_{[\cdot]} \\ G:L_{[\cdot]} \\ A:G:L_{[\cdot]} \end{bmatrix} \sim \text{MVNormal}\left(\begin{bmatrix} 0 \\ 0 \\ 0 \\ 0 \end{bmatrix}, \Sigma \right) \tag{7.8}$$

$$\text{Intercept} \sim t\left(3,156,12\right)$$
$$A,G,A:G \sim t\left(3,0,12\right)$$
$$\sigma_L,\sigma_{A:L},\sigma_{G:L},\sigma_{A:G:L},\sigma_S \sim t\left(3,0,12\right)$$
$$\sigma \sim t\left(3,0,12\right)$$
$$v \sim \text{gamma}\left(2,0.1\right)$$
$$R \sim \text{LKJCorr}\left(2\right)$$

Our updated plain English description now says:

We are modeling apparent height as coming from a t distribution with unknown nu (ν), mean (μ), and scale (σ) parameters. The expected value for any given trial (μ) is modeled as the sum of an intercept, an effect for apparent speaker age (A), gender

226   *Comparing many groups, interactions, and posterior predictive checks*

(G), and their interaction (A:G), a listener effect (L), a listener dependent effect for apparent age (A:L), apparent gender (G:L), their interaction (A:G:L), and a speaker effect (S). The speaker effects were drawn from a univariate normal distribution with a standard deviation (σ_S) estimated from the data. The four listener effects were drawn from a multivariate normal distribution with individual standard deviations ($\sigma_L, \sigma_{A:L}, \sigma_{G:L}, \sigma_{A:G:L}$) and a correlation matrix (R) that was estimated from the data. The remainder of the 'fixed' effects and correlations were given prior distributions appropriate for their expected range of values.

Before continuing, we want to address the fact that we've included the same structure in our 'fixed effects' as for our listener 'random effects'. We will do this for all the models we fit in this book whenever possible. There are a couple of reasons for this, and we will discuss these with respect to the 'random effect' of apparent age for each listener (i.e. the $A:L$ interaction). Not including this predictor is equivalent to setting it to zero for all listeners (and setting $\sigma_{A:L} = 0$), meaning we expect the effect for apparent age to be the same across all levels of the listener factor. However, we saw in the previous chapter that this is not the case and that there is substantial variation in the effect for apparent age across listeners. So, omitting random effects relies on the assumption that the variation across listeners (or whatever variable defines the random effects) is equal to zero, which may not be well founded a priori.

Furthermore, in Chapter 6 we fit models with and without random effects and saw that the model *with* random effects produced substantially wider credible intervals for the apparent age 'fixed' effect, reflecting increased uncertainty in the parameter estimate. In that case, assuming listener-variation in the parameter was zero when it was not, resulted in an overly precise estimate of the apparent age parameter. So, we see that omitting random effects means assuming they are equal to zero and can affect the amount of uncertainty we get in our resulting parameter estimates. The only way to know whether a listener-dependent parameter shows substantial variation or not is to include the possibility for listener-dependent variation in your model, at least initially. Of course, the inclusion of any 'random effect' in your model assumes that: (1) Your model is designed in a way that the 'random' effect can be estimated, and (2) You have enough data to estimate those parameters. These issues will be discussed further in Chapter 11.

7.6.4 *Fitting and interpreting the model*

Below we fit the model including an interaction term. Remember that the line `set_prior("student_t(3, 0, 12)", class = "b")` sets the prior for all non-intercept 'Population-Level' predictors (i.e. fixed effects). This includes all of our main effects predictors and our interaction terms.

```
# Fit the model yourself
priors = c(brms::set_prior("student_t(3,156, 12)", class = "Intercept"),
           brms::set_prior("student_t(3,0, 12)", class = "b"),
           brms::set_prior("student_t(3,0, 12)", class = "sd"),
           brms::set_prior("lkj_corr_cholesky (2)", class = "cor"),
           brms::set_prior("gamma(2, 0.1)", class = "nu"),
```

Comparing many groups, interactions, and posterior predictive checks 227

```
                brms::set_prior("student_t(3,0, 12)", class = "sigma"))

model_interaction =
  brms::brm (height ~ A + G + A:G + (A + G + A:G|L) + (1|S),
            data = exp_data, chains = 4, cores = 4, warmup = 1000,
            iter = 5000, thin = 4, prior = priors, family = "student")

# Or download it from the GitHub page:
model_interaction = bmmb::get_model ('7_model_interaction.RDS')
```

We are primarily interested in discussing interactions, but we want to spend a moment looking at the listener random effects in our model since there are now several.

```
# inspect fixed effects
bmmb::short_summary (model_interaction)
## Formula:  height ~ A + G + A:G + (A + G + A:G | L) + (1 | S)
##
## Group-Level Effects:
## ~L (Number of levels: 15)
##                          Estimate Est.Error l-95% CI u-95% CI
## sd(Intercept)                4.24      0.79     2.96     6.03
## sd(A1)                       4.47      0.85     3.13     6.42
## sd(G1)                       2.10      0.49     1.37     3.22
## sd(A1:G1)                    1.34      0.36     0.76     2.13
## cor(Intercept,A1)           -0.71      0.13    -0.90    -0.38
## cor(Intercept,G1)           -0.20      0.22    -0.59     0.24
## cor(A1,G1)                  -0.24      0.21    -0.62     0.20
## cor(Intercept,A1:G1)         0.17      0.23    -0.29     0.58
## cor(A1,A1:G1)               -0.02      0.23    -0.46     0.43
## cor(G1,A1:G1)               -0.34      0.24    -0.74     0.18
##
## ~S (Number of levels: 139)
##                 Estimate Est.Error l-95% CI u-95% CI
## sd(Intercept)       2.36      0.31     1.79     2.99
##
## Population-Level Effects:
##             Estimate Est.Error l-95% CI u-95% CI
## Intercept     158.46      1.12   156.22   160.62
## A1             10.78      1.21     8.39    13.15
## G1             -2.87      0.60    -4.07    -1.72
## A1:G1          -1.64      0.41    -2.44    -0.81
##
## Family Specific Parameters:
##        Estimate Est.Error l-95% CI u-95% CI
## sigma      5.01      0.16     4.70     5.34
## nu         3.44      0.33     2.87     4.15
```

228   *Comparing many groups, interactions, and posterior predictive checks*

We can see in the short model summary above that we've estimated four standard deviation terms for our listener-dependent predictors. These correspond to σ_L (sd(Intercept)), $\sigma_{A:L}$ (sd(A1)), $\sigma_{G:L}$ (sd(G1)), and $\sigma_{A:G:L}$ (sd(A1:G1)). We've also estimated six correlation terms for our listener random effects. Recall that our random effects are drawn from a multivariate normal distribution. We have four terms which means this four-dimensional distribution is associated with a 4$$4 correlation matrix and 16 correlation terms. Of the correlations, four (on the main diagonal) equal one and can be ignored. This leaves 12 terms. Of these, only half are unique because the correlation of x and y equals the correlation of y and x. This is how we end up with six estimated correlations for our four listener-dependent predictors.

We can now focus on the fixed effects (Population-Level Effects), of which there are four: An intercept, two main effects terms, and an interaction. The interaction term is just another element of your prediction equation intended to help explain variation that can't be predicted by the main effects of predictors involved in the interaction. If there is no interaction in your data, then the value of the interaction term will be close to zero and your model will look just as if you had not included the interaction at all. A look at the model output above indicates that our interaction is much smaller than the age effect, but not much smaller than the gender effect. This suggests it has the potential to influence our conclusions about gender more than our conclusions about age.

Why is there only a single interaction? Basically for the same reason that we can only estimate a single effect for apparent age and gender (i.e. linear dependence, discussed in Sections 5.6 and 8.8). The number of levels of a factor that you can estimate is generally one fewer than the number of levels in the factor. For interaction terms, the number of parameters you can estimate is equal to (number of levels of factor A − 1) × (number of levels of factor B − 1) for two factors. Since each of our factors has two levels, we can only estimate one parameter, $(2-1)\times(2-1)=1$.

The A1:G1 term can be read aloud as "the effect of A1 given (conditional on) the level of G1". For individual factors, our models cannot estimate A2 because -A1 = A2. For interactions between factors with two levels, the model cannot estimate A2:G1 because -A1:G1 = A2:G1. For interactions between factors with two levels, every time you want to change A1 or G1 to A2 or G2 you flip the sign of the A1:G1 term instead. As a result, going left to right and changing one level at a time we get A1:G1 = -A2:G1 = A2:G2 = -A1:G2, which is precisely why we can't estimate more than one interaction for this model. Why does this happen? Looking at how interaction plots are built up out of main effects and interactions may help illustrate the reason for this.

Figure 7.9 presents an example of how our interaction plot can be built up from the components in our fixed effects above and is very useful for understanding the geometry of main effects and interactions. In the top left plot, we see that the intercept lifts up a line from 0 to the level of the overall mean apparent height of 158 cm. Then, the effect for A1 (adult, +11 cm) and -A1 (children, −11 cm) are added to this value, causing the separation between the lines indicating a 'main effect' for adultness. Notice that the lines are parallel with respect to each other, and also parallel to the x-axis. This is because we have not added an effect for gender, which will be indicated as a slope along the x-axis. In the middle plot in the top row, we see the addition of the gender effect: G1 (female, −2.8 cm), and -G1 (male, 2.8 cm). Notice that the effect is added to one end of each line segment and subtracted from the other end of the line segment. This is what causes a (single) slope along the x-axis for both lines. The right

Comparing many groups, interactions, and posterior predictive checks 229

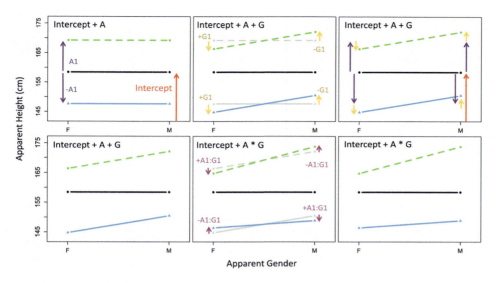

Figure 7.9 An interaction plot built up from its individual components.

plot in the top row shows the addition of all of the effects shown in the top row, the result of a model that includes both main effects but the same non-zero slope for both lines (i.e. no interaction yet).

In the middle plot in the bottom row of Figure 7.9, we add the gender interaction `A1:G1`, which was −1.6 cm, to each end point for both lines. Notice that the interaction effect has different signs when added to the same line, and also for each end of each line segment. In each case, the sign is determined by the specific speaker category it is applied to. For example, we know that `A1:G1` represents female adults (top left point). So, we flip the sign for adult children in the bottom-left point (i.e. `-A1:G1 = A2:G1`), and we flip the sign again for male children in the bottom right point (i.e. `A1:G1 = A2:G2`). The sign flips result in opposing interactions at each x-axis position across lines, but also for different endpoints along the same line. We can see that beginning with the parallel lines in the bottom-left, the interaction added in the bottom-middle plot constitutes an equal 'pinch' of one end of the lines and a spreading of the other side of the lines. This equal pinch and spreading are necessary in order to maintain the same average slope across both lines (the gender main effect) and the same average spacing between both ends of the lines (the age main effect). This is effectively why we get only a single interaction term in a model with this fixed effects structure.

7.6.5 Caulculating group means in the presence of interactions

Recovering the predicted group means using the model coefficients is straightforward, but can be tedious for larger models: We must now either add or subtract the value of the interaction term (`A1:G1`) from each group as determined by the combination of main effects. We can easily determine what to do for this model because the sign on the interaction term is the product of the signs on the relevant 'main effects' terms. So, two positive or negative main effects result in a positive interaction term, while mismatched positive and negative main effects result in a negative interaction.

230   *Comparing many groups, interactions, and posterior predictive checks*

Below, we use `short_hypothesis` to reconstruct expected group means given the model fixed effects. The fourth hypothesis we're testing below is the simplest to understand, so we will start there. This hypothesis asks whether the sum of the `Intercept`, `A1` (the effect of apparent adultness), `G1` (the effect of apparent femaleness), and `A1:G1` (the interaction of adult and female), is equal to zero. Because of the specific parameters we combined, this results in the comparison of the mean height for women to zero. The first hypothesis below says `Intercept + -A1 + -G1 + A1:G1 = 0`. Since we flipped the sign on `A1` and `G1`, these now correspond to the effects of 'child' and 'male' (i.e. boy). Since both `A1` and `G1` are negative, we flip the sign on the interaction term twice and it remains positive. Note that for all of our hypotheses below, the sign on the interaction terms always depends on the signs of the corresponding main effects terms.

```
# intercept, boys, girls, men, women
means_pred_interaction = bmmb::short_hypothesis (
  model_interaction,
  c("Intercept + -A1 + -G1 +  A1:G1 = 0",   # boys
    "Intercept + -A1 +  G1 + -A1:G1 = 0",   # girl
    "Intercept +  A1 + -G1 + -A1:G1 = 0",   # men
    "Intercept +  A1 +  G1 +  A1:G1 = 0"))  # women
```

Below we compare the actual mean apparent height for each group to the predictions made without and with an interaction term. We can see that in each case, the prediction made by the model with an interaction are closer to the data means than those made by the model without an interaction. In addition, the predictions made including an interaction finally do reflect the fact that the difference in apparent height between apparent boys and girls is much smaller than that between apparent men and women.

```
# actual data means
tapply (exp_data$height, exp_data$C, mean)
##     b     g     m     w
## 146.9 145.0 174.5 165.6

# predictions with no interaction term
means_pred[,1]
## [1] 150.9 146.5 170.8 166.4

# predictions with interaction term
means_pred_interaction[,1]
## [1] 148.9 146.4 173.8 164.7
```

7.6.6 Calculating simple effects in the presence of interactions

We know that we have an interaction in our data, and that this interaction needs to be investigated by considering the simple effects for each factor. Below we use `short_hypothesis` to find the simple effects of age across levels of gender, and of gender

Comparing many groups, interactions, and posterior predictive checks 231

across levels of age. To recover the simple effect for a predictor, we add the main effect term to the appropriate interaction term (including the appropriate sign). To figure out which sign to use, you just need to think about which group is referred to by each interaction. For example, in the first line below we add `A1`, the age main effect, to `A1:G1`. Since it has a `G1` in it and we are adding and not subtracting, we know this refers to female speakers. As a result, `A1 + A1:G1` results in the simple effect for apparent age for apparent females. In the second line, we again use `A1` but now add `-A1:G1`, which we know is equal to `A1:G2` (which does not exist). As a result, `A1 - A1:G1` results in the simple effect of apparent age for apparent males.

```
# intercept, boys, girls, men, women
simple_effects = bmmb::short_hypothesis (
  model_interaction,
  c("A1 + A1:G1 = 0",   # effect for apparent age for adults (G1)
    "A1 - A1:G1 = 0",   # effect for apparent age for children (-G1)
    "G1 + A1:G1 = 0",   # effect for apparent gender for adults (A1)
    "G1 - A1:G1 = 0"))  # effect for apparent gender for children (-A1)

# predictions with interaction term
simple_effects
##      Estimate Est.Error    Q2.5   Q97.5       hypothesis
## H1      9.142    1.2792   6.639 11.5977 (A1+A1:G1) = 0
## H2     12.424    1.2707   9.938 14.9913 (A1-A1:G1) = 0
## H3     -4.514    0.6174  -5.731  -3.3177 (G1+A1:G1) = 0
## H4     -1.232    0.8192  -2.860   0.3919 (G1-A1:G1) = 0
```

We will provide a verbal description of the calculations involved in estimating simple effects. We will use our fixed-effects estimates, rounded to make the discussion easier to follow. We've previously warned against averaging the parameters first and then combining them second. However, this approach can be useful for a quick investigation of our model parameters and is fine for our purposes.

```
round (brms::fixef (model_interaction))
##             Estimate Est.Error Q2.5 Q97.5
## Intercept        158         1  156   161
## A1                11         1    8    13
## G1                -3         1   -4    -2
## A1:G1             -2         0   -2    -1
```

First, we will calculate the simple effects for apparent age at the levels of apparent gender. The average apparent height across all groups is 158 cm. There is an age-based 11 cm deviation from the intercept, meaning the difference between apparent adults and children is 22 cm ($11 \cdot 2$). This means that the averages for apparent adults and children are about 169 and 147 cm (158 ± 11). However, the `A1:G1` interaction is −2 cm. This means that when the speaker was identified as female (`G1`), the effect for adultness decreased from 11 cm to 9 cm (11 −2, `A1+A1:G1`), meaning the difference across women and girls was 18 cm ($2 \cdot 9$). In contrast, when the speaker was identified as male (`-G1`), the affect for adultness increased from 11 cm to 13 cm (11+2, `A1-A1:G1`), meaning the

232 *Comparing many groups, interactions, and posterior predictive checks*

difference between boys and men was about 26 cm. Notice that in the calculations above, the effect for apparent age would be equal across apparent genders in the case that there is no interaction (i.e. `A1:G1=0`).

We could instead consider the simple effects for apparent gender given apparent age. There is a gender-based 3 cm deviation from the intercept, meaning the difference between apparent adults and children is −6 cm (−3 · 2). This means that, overall, the female and male averages are about 155 and 161 cm respectively (158 ± −3). However, the `A1:G1` interaction is −2 cm. This means that when the speaker was an adult (`A1`) the effect for gender increased in magnitude from −3 cm to −5 cm (−3 + −2, `G1+A1:G1`), resulting in a difference between groups of 10 cm (−5 · 2). However, when the speaker was a child (`-A1`), the effect for gender decreased in magnitude from −3 cm to 1 cm (−3+2, `G1-A1:G1`), resulting in a difference in groups of 2 cm based on apparent gender (1 · 2).

7.6.7 *Assessing model fit: Bayesian R^2*

We can assess the fit for our model including interaction terms by making more posterior predictions with our new model. We will focus on the average predictions for each data point since our objective is to see to what extent the fixed effects can represent the patterns in the data.

```
y_post_pred_int = predict (model_interaction)
y_post_pred_no_re_int = predict (model_interaction, re_formula = NA)
```

In Figure 7.10 we compare our data, the predictions of our original model, and the predictions of our model that includes interactions (both models with and without random effects). Whereas the model with no interactions enforced parallelism on the simple effects, our new model is able to capture the interaction in our data by representing different effects for gender at different levels of age (and vice versa). Although both of our models are able to capture the pattern in the data when random effects are included, only one of these is able to do so with its fixed effect structure.

We can compare the models with and without the interaction term using leave one out cross-validation, discussed in Section 6.4.3.

```
model_both = brms::add_criterion (model_both, criterion="loo")
model_interaction = brms::add_criterion (model_interaction, criterion="loo")
```

The comparison not only suggests a large difference between the models but also some uncertainty regarding the difference.

```
brms::loo_compare (model_both, model_interaction)
##                      elpd_diff se_diff
## model_interaction     0.0        0.0
## model_both          -29.1       11.2
```

To some extent, the difference may appear to be smaller than it is because our random effects do a good job of explaining listener and speaker-dependent deviations from the expectations set out by the fixed effects. Explaining things with 'random'

Comparing many groups, interactions, and posterior predictive checks   233

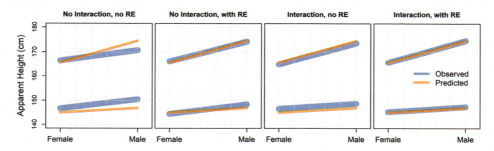

Figure 7.10 Interaction plots comparing observed apparent height judgments to different posterior predictions. Posterior predictions with no interaction come from `model_both` and predictions with interactions come from `model_interaction`. With RE (random effects) refers to predictions made using random effects, and no RE refers to predictions made without random effects.

effects is less useful for understanding the out-of-sample characteristics of your data. If we were to replicate this experiment with new speakers and listeners, we would expect all the random effects to change. However, if the relations between apparent age and gender and apparent height expressed in our model are 'true', we would expect the 'fixed' effects in the replication to be about the same. For this reason, it is extremely useful to consider fixed-effects prediction in addition to the predictive power of a complete model including both fixed and random effects.

To quantify how well our models fit our data we can also use **Bayesian** R^2. There are potentially several ways to define R^2 in a Bayesian context. The account of Bayesian R^2 presented here is a summary of the proposal outlined in Gelman et al. (2019). In addition, the discussion of R^2 to follow assumes that your model involves either Gaussian or t-distributed errors and a continuous dependent variable.

R^2 is a measure of model fit that breaks down the total variance in your dependent variable into two parts: (1) The variance that your model *can* explain, and (2) the variance that your model *cannot* explain (the residual error, which we've been calling σ). This is shown in (7.9).

$$\sigma^2_{total} = \sigma^2_{explained} + \sigma^2_{error} \tag{7.9}$$

R^2 is the ratio of the explained variance to the total variance, as seen in (7.10). Since the explained variance cannot be less than zero nor can it be greater than the total variance, values of R^2 range from zero to one. As a result, R^2 can be interpreted as the proportion of variance in the dependent variable that is explained by the model

$$R^2 = \frac{\sigma^2_{explained}}{\sigma^2_{total}} = \frac{\sigma^2_{explained}}{\sigma^2_{explained} + \sigma^2_{error}} \tag{7.10}$$

To make R^2 a *Bayesian* R^2, we need to incorporate the posterior distribution of parameter values into our estimation. This is done, in part, by calculating a value of R^2 for every individual set of posterior samples, as shown in (7.11). For every posterior sample of parameter values s (from S total samples), we calculate: (1) The variance in the

234 *Comparing many groups, interactions, and posterior predictive checks*

predicted values ($\hat{y}$) of the dependent variable for our n data points ($V_{i=1}^{n} \hat{y}_n^s$), and (2) the variance of the residual error for our n data points ($V_{i=1}^{n} \hat{e}_i^s$).

$$R_s^2 = \frac{V_{i=1}^{n} \hat{y}_i^s}{V_{i=1}^{n} \hat{y}_i^s + V_{i=1}^{n} \hat{e}_i^s} \tag{7.11}$$

The residual error is the difference between predicted ($\hat{y}$) and observed (y) values for each data point, shown in (7.11). Notice that the predictions and residuals vary across the s samples, but our observed data does not.

$$\hat{e}_i^s = \hat{y}_i^s - y_i \tag{7.12}$$

This results in a *distribution* of R^2 values, unlike more 'traditional' estimates of R^2 that result in point estimates. The `brms` package includes a function called `bayes_R2` that helps you calculate Bayesian R^2 for `brm` models. However, we're going to use the `r2_bayes` function from the `bmmb` package instead because this function allows you to modify (or omit) the fixed effects included in the prediction. Below we calculate R^2 for the models we fit in this chapter, including all random effects.

```
r2_both = r2_bayes(model_both)
r2_interaction = r2_bayes(model_interaction)
```

We can inspect the output and see that they have very similar values. This is not surprising given their similarities seen in Figure 7.10.

```
r2_both
##        Estimate Est.Error   Q2.5   Q97.5
## [1,]    0.7755  0.005566 0.7641  0.7858


r2_interaction
##        Estimate Est.Error   Q2.5   Q97.5
## [1,]    0.7802  0.005347 0.7694  0.7901
```

Just as we can omit the random effects when we use `predict`, we can omit random effects from our calculations of R^2 by setting `re_formula = NA`.

```
r2_both_no_re = r2_bayes(model_both, re_formula = NA)
r2_interaction_no_re = r2_bayes(model_interaction, re_formula = NA)
```

Now a comparison reveals a more substantial difference in explanatory power between the models.

```
r2_both_no_re
##        Estimate Est.Error   Q2.5   Q97.5
## [1,]    0.503   0.07258 0.3411  0.6216
```

Comparing many groups, interactions, and posterior predictive checks 235

```
r2_interaction_no_re
##          Estimate Est.Error    Q2.5   Q97.5
## [1,]      0.5732    0.05909   0.4389  0.6678
```

We would rather explain as much variation as possible using fixed as opposed to random effects. In addition, the interactions 'makes sense' given our domain knowledge. What we mean by this is that we know that the difference in veridical height between boys and girls 10–12 years old is inconsistent and may be about zero on average. So, we should not be too surprised if the effect of apparent gender on apparent height is small for apparent children. However, there is a larger and more consistent difference in average veridical height between adult males and females. As a result, we *do* expect a meaningful effect of apparent gender on the apparent heights of adults. For these reasons, it would be surprising if there were *not* an interaction, and we prefer the model with the interaction despite the middling support provided by our cross-validation model comparison.

R^2 is not really going to prove anything, and shouldn't form the basis of your model selection. We believe that it is a useful method to be aware of in addition to, and not instead of, other approaches such as elpd). The primary utility of R^2 is that since it reflects a proportion between 0 and 1, it is more easily interpretable for humans. For example, the difference in elpd between `model_both` and `model_interaction` is about 29, which is large enough to be statistically meaningful. However, how much does this difference actually matter at the level of our dependent variable? Well, the proportion of variance explained by the two models is only different by about 0.5%, suggesting that these models do not offer substantially different predictions. In contrast, we might imagine the same difference in elpd being associated with a 10% change in the variance explained, which will likely be a noticeable difference. In this way, R^2 can be a useful indicator of how much our predictions are really changing, provided in a measure that many readers will find relatively intuitive.

7.7 Answering our research questions

We will answer our research questions based on `model_interaction`. In addition, we used the `forpaper` function, like this `forpaper(fixef(model_interaction))` to generate a standard output of the form `(mean = --, s.d. = --, 95% C.I = [--, --])` from the typical `brms` coefficient table output.

Results indicate that the average apparent height across all speaker groups (i.e. the intercept) was 158.5 (s.d. = 1.12, 95% C.I = [156.22, 160.62]). We also found an average effect of 10.8 cm for apparent speaker age (s.d. = 1.21, 95% C.I = [8.39, 13.15]) and −2.9 cm for apparent speaker gender (s.d. = 0.6, 95% C.I = [−4.07, −1.72]). In addition, we found an interaction between the effects of apparent age and apparent gender on apparent heights (mean = −1.64, s.d. = 0.41, 95% C.I = [−2.44, -0.81]). The result of these effects is that apparent adults were perceived as taller than apparent children and apparent males were perceived as taller than apparent females. However, the difference in apparent height due to apparent gender was larger for adults than for children (and the effect for apparent age was larger for males than for females). Figure 7.11 presents the model's fixed effects other than the intercept (whose value is too large to plot in this range).

236 *Comparing many groups, interactions, and posterior predictive checks*

The fixed effects all have 95% credible intervals that do not overlap with zero. Historically, this sort of result has been thought of as indicating that the effect is 'real', as in not equal to zero. In contrast, when the 95% (or some other) credible interval of an effect overlaps with zero, researchers will often conclude that this effect is not 'real', i.e. that it is exactly equal to zero. Gelman et al. (2012) note that effects are rarely exactly equal to zero, and that an inability to conclusively distinguish the value of an effect from zero is not the same thing as thinking that the most probable value of an effect is exactly zero.

As a result, rather than focusing on whether any given interval crosses zero or not, Gelman and Carlin (2014) recommend thinking about data analysis in terms of avoiding **type S** and **type M** errors. Type S (sign) errors occur when you think an effect is negative but it's actually positive (or vice versa). A type M (magnitude) error is when you think an effect is large but it's actually small (or vice versa). Focusing on type M and S errors rather than whether an interval crosses zero forces researchers to focus on the magnitude of the predictor, its practical importance, and the uncertainty involved in the estimate. That being said, if a parameter has a 'large' magnitude (in the context of the dependent variable) and a 'small' amount of uncertainty (relative to the magnitude), this predictor is likely to be important for understanding the dependent variable in the context of your model.

Figure 7.11 also presents the pairwise difference between all four apparent speaker groups (boys, girls, women, and men). The difference between pairs of group means is calculated by extracting the samples from the group means we reconstructed in Section 7.6.5 (`means_pred_interaction`). The result of this is a matrix with four columns, each representing a group effect, with individual posterior samples differing along rows. To find the difference between group means between each pair of groups, we subtract the columns representing the group effects and inspect the distribution of the differences. This process is shown below and the distribution of pairwise group differences is presented in the right plot of Figure 7.11.

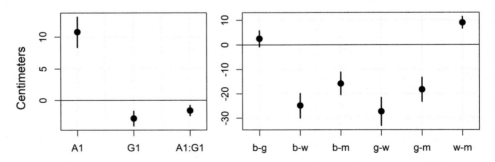

Figure 7.11 (left) Fixed effect means and 95% credible intervals (minus the intercept) for `model_interaction`. (right) Means and 95% credible intervals for the pairwise differences between predicted means for different apparent speaker categories (boys, girls, men, and women).

Comparing many groups, interactions, and posterior predictive checks 237

```r
# get group mean predictions
C = attributes(means_pred_interaction)$samples

# find pairwise differences
pairwise_diffs = cbind("b-g"=C[,1]-C[,2], "b-w"=C[,1]-C[,3],
                       "b-m"=C[,1]-C[,4], "g-w"=C[,2]-C[,3],
                       "g-m"=C[,2]-C[,4], "w-m"=C[,3]-C[,4])

# summarize these
pairwise_diffs_summary = posterior_summary(pairwise_diffs)
```

We can think about these differences in the context of our type M and S errors. All of the group differences (save for boy-girl) have values of about 10 cm (or more), which is a meaningful (and noticeable) difference in human height. In addition, the credible intervals around these differences are small relative to their magnitudes. From this, we can conclude that these differences are unlikely to *really* be the opposite sign (a type S error). In addition, since the group differences (save for boy-girl) are mostly large and the credible intervals do not go anywhere near zero, these differences seem unlikely to actually be some small and insignificant value near zero (a type S error).

But what about the boy-girl difference? The 95% credible interval of the difference between groups overlaps with zero. Does this mean there is no difference between the groups, i.e. $\mu_{\text{boy}} = \mu_{\text{girl}}$ and $\mu_{\text{boy}} - \mu_{\text{girl}} = 0$? No, it doesn't. It just means that 0 is a value that is not so implausible for the difference between groups. The most probable difference is still 2.5. Consider a replication that found a group difference with a mean and 95% credible interval of 2.6 and [0.1, 5.1] respectively, rather than our values of 2.5 and [−0.8, 5.7]. Would such a difference constitute a successful replication or an opposing finding? If we focus on whether intervals cross zero to decide if effects are 'real', we might decide that these experiments do not agree: We found no difference in our first experiment but the replication *did* find a difference. In contrast, if we focus on the sign and magnitude of the effects and the uncertainty around their estimates, the two experiments have extremely compatible results and constitute a successful replication.

```r
# summary of difference between boy and girl means
pairwise_diffs_summary[1,]
##   Estimate Est.Error      Q2.5      Q97.5
##     2.4643    1.6384   -0.7837     5.7199
```

We might wonder, under what conditions can we accept that an effect or group difference is *actually* equal to zero? If the 95% (or some other high number) credible interval is relatively narrow and (more or less) centered around zero, the parameter value may very well be zero. It may also be a small number that has no practical effect on your dependent variable, so it doesn't really matter what it is even if it's not exactly equal to 0.0000000… . In either case, a coefficient with a narrow interval (roughly) centered at zero may not have an important role in the way you interpret your model in order to tell the 'story' of your data. However, it is extremely important to keep in

238 *Comparing many groups, interactions, and posterior predictive checks*

mind that under a different parametrization of your model, or given a slightly different experimental design, it's possible that an equivalent parameter may exhibit a clearly non-zero value.

Another thing to think about is, how large does an effect need to be before it matters, even if it is not zero? This is a similar approach to Kruschke's **Region of Practical Equivalence** (ROPE, Kruschke, 2018). Rather than worrying about whether things are exactly zero or not, Kruschke suggests we think about when things are so small that they may as well be zero. For human height, apparent and veridical, we define meaningful differences as those that (1) are likely to be different from zero, *and* (2) have magnitudes of at least around 1 cm (about 0.5 inches). We establish this lower limit simply based on the fact that people may describe themselves as 175 cm (or 5'10.5") but rarely make distinctions smaller than that (e.g. people rarely distinguish 175 cm and 175.2 cm). In addition, governments, doctors, and even institutions like the NBA which are extremely interested in height will rarely measure to within less than 1 cm (half an inch). As a result, although a difference of 0.1 cm may very well be consistently different from zero, in the context of human height a difference of this magnitude has little to no practical significance in most situations.

In our case, we will conclude that the difference in apparent height between boys and girls may very well be 'real' and may reflect stereotypes that male speakers are generally taller than female speakers, whether or not this is actually true for speakers of this age. We might also suggest that if we want to know more about the precise value of this difference, future research might investigate this question with a larger number of speakers, listeners, or repetitions. By increasing the sample size, researchers would narrow the parameter likelihoods (discussed in Section 2.7.3), thereby narrowing their posterior credible intervals (given new data that's roughly the same as the data we have).

Finally, we want to directly address the fact that our discussion above regarding accepting effects as 'real' or as 'zero' may seem to be full of vagueness and equivocation. This is by design. Sometimes, researchers want to wash their hands of a difficult decision and let the model decide. However, the researcher cannot 'pass the buck' and let the model 'prove' that something is zero or non-zero. The model can certainly tell you that, given your data and model structure, something is likely to be zero or non-zero. However, transferring that knowledge to the 'real world' is an epistemological or ontological claim (or both), and *not* a statistical one. To some extent, the statistical claim underlies the claim about the real world, but it is not enough on its own. To *really* make a claim about an effect being zero or not, the researcher requires statistical evidence in addition to domain knowledge about the real world. As a result, we can give general (vague) guidelines about situations when your models suggest something is zero or non-zero, but we cannot say with certainty that in such and such a situation you can always make claims about the real world based *solely* on your statistical model.

For example, because of the relationship between sample size, likelihoods, and credible intervals, any arbitrarily small effect will be distinguishable from zero given a large enough sample. Imagine a situation where we have an effect of 0.1 cm that has a 95% credible interval of [0.09, 0.11]. Our model is telling us that this effect is extremely unlikely to equal zero, and yet we are unlikely to care much about an effect this small. However, we can only know this by knowing something about human height and meaningful variation therein, and this is domain-specific knowledge that must come from the researcher interpreting the model.

Comparing many groups, interactions, and posterior predictive checks 239

7.8 Factors with more than two levels

Before moving on, we want to provide an example of how to recover interaction terms that are not estimated by your model when you have factors with more than two levels. This is a modest extension of the principles we have discussed so far, however, it's useful to provide an explicit example. Below, we generate some toy data that includes two factors with four levels each (A,B), and an interaction between them (AB).

```
A = rep (factor(1:4), each = 60)
B = rep (factor(1:4), 60)

A_ = c(-2,1,2,-1)
B_ = c(4,2,-3,-3)
AB_ = matrix (c(-1,1,-1,1,
                1,-1,1,-1,
                -1,1,-1,1,
                1,-1,1,-1),4,4)

error = rnorm(240)

y = A_[A] + B_[B] + AB_[cbind(A,B)] + error

toy_data = data.frame (y, A, B)
```

We use this to fit a simple model with brms:

```
toy_model = brm (y ~ A*B, data = toy_data)
## Compiling Stan program...
## Start sampling
```

And inspect the fixed effects:

```
fixef (toy_model)
##             Estimate Est.Error     Q2.5     Q97.5
## Intercept    0.02768   0.06593  -0.1049    0.1569
## A1          -2.10172   0.11882  -2.3394   -1.8672
## A2           1.09184   0.11453   0.8710    1.3232
## A3           1.92469   0.11882   1.6963    2.1542
## B1           4.02158   0.11775   3.7847    4.2484
## B2           2.08544   0.11764   1.8567    2.3178
## B3          -3.11586   0.11982  -3.3485   -2.8756
## A1:B1       -1.13546   0.20105  -1.5227   -0.7469
## A2:B1        1.22386   0.20184   0.8174    1.6255
## A3:B1       -1.20820   0.20252  -1.5987   -0.8064
## A1:B2        0.86307   0.19948   0.4691    1.2506
## A2:B2       -0.85335   0.20244  -1.2481   -0.4599
## A3:B2        0.75987   0.20433   0.3672    1.1688
## A1:B3       -0.77577   0.20288  -1.1653   -0.3664
## A2:B3        0.74222   0.20478   0.3327    1.1433
## A3:B3       -0.82375   0.20784  -1.2436   -0.4235
```

240   *Comparing many groups, interactions, and posterior predictive checks*

As expected, we see that we estimate 3 of 4-factor levels for the A and B factors respectively. This means that we will be missing the fourth level of each factor. Below, we present factor levels in a grid, and indicate the missing level in parentheses.

$$
\begin{bmatrix} A1 & A2 & A3 & (A4) \end{bmatrix}
$$

$$
\begin{bmatrix} B1 & B2 & B3 & (B4) \end{bmatrix}
$$
(7.13)

In order to recover the missing levels of A and B (under sum coding), we have to find the negative sum of the estimated levels. We place this value in the corresponding grid location seen below.

$$
\begin{bmatrix} A1 & A2 & A3 & -(A1+A2+A3) \end{bmatrix}
$$

$$
\begin{bmatrix} B1 & B2 & B3 & -(B1+B2+B3) \end{bmatrix}
$$
(7.14)

As noted above, the number of interaction terms we can estimate will generally be equal to (the number of levels in $A - 1$) × (the number of levels in $B - 1$). As a result, we know that we will only be able to estimate 9 out of the 16 total interaction terms. We have arranged these terms in a similar grid as seen above and again placed the missing terms in parentheses. In the grid below, levels of A vary across columns and levels of B vary across rows.

$$
\begin{bmatrix}
A1:B1 & A2:B1 & A3:B1 & (A4:B1) \\
A1:B2 & A2:B2 & A3:B2 & (A4:B2) \\
A1:B3 & A2:B3 & A3:B3 & (A4:B3) \\
(A1:B4) & (A2:B4) & (A3:B4) & (A4:B4)
\end{bmatrix}
$$
(7.15)

Recovering missing interaction values is no more complicated but can be a bit tedious for large numbers of missing interactions. The missing values at the end of each row are simply the negative sum of the elements present in the row, and the missing values at the end of each column are simply the negative sum of the elements present in the column. We show this for only one row and one column so that the matrix will fit on the page, but the same process can be applied to all rows and columns in the matrix.

$$
\begin{bmatrix}
A1:B1 & A2:B1 & A3:B1 & -(A1:B1+A2:B1+A3:B1) \\
A1:B2 & A2:B2 & A3:B2 & (A4:B2) \\
A1:B3 & A2:B3 & A3:B3 & (A4:B3) \\
-(A1:B1+A1:B2+A1:B3) & (A2:B4) & (A3:B4) & (A4:B4)
\end{bmatrix}
$$
(7.16)

You can get the missing element in the bottom right corner above by following the same process once you have recovered the remaining elements from the final row or

Comparing many groups, interactions, and posterior predictive checks 241

column. For example, the interaction in the bottom corner is the negative sum of the other three terms in the final column *and* in the final row.

$$A4 : B4 = -(A4 : B1 + A4 : B2 + A4 : B3)$$
$$A4 : B4 = -(A1 : B4 + A2 : B4 + A3 : B4)$$

(7.17)

Of course, these values can all be recovered easily using the `hypothesis` (or `short_hypothesis`) function.

7.9 'Traditionalists' corner

In traditionalists' corner, we compare the output of `brms` to some more 'traditional' approaches. We're not going to talk about the traditional models in any detail, the focus of this section is simply to highlight the similarities between different approaches, and to point out where to find equivalent information in the different models. If you are already familiar with these approaches, these sections may be helpful. If not, some of the information provided here may not make much sense, although it may still be helpful. If you want to know more about the statistical methods being discussed here, please see the preface for a list of suggested background reading in statistics.

7.9.1 Bayesian multilevel models vs. lmer

This is going to be a short one. One shortcoming when it comes to using `lmer` to fit models including factors with many levels is that there is no easy way to compare group effects solely based on the information contained in the model. For example, we can fit the model below which encodes the difference between each group mean and the overall mean.

```
lmer_four_groups = lme4::lmer (height ~ C + (C|L) + (1|S),
data = exp_data)
summary (lmer_four_groups)$coefficients
##                   Estimate Std. Error t value
## (Intercept)        158.344     1.040  152.228
## C1                  -9.543     1.300   -7.341
## C2                 -11.126     1.332   -8.355
## C3                  14.604     1.371   10.655
```

The results provided by `lmer` are very similar to those provided by `brm`:

```
brms::fixef (model_four_groups)
##               Estimate Est.Error    Q2.5    Q97.5
## Intercept      158.581     1.083  156.41  160.685
## C1              -9.318     1.310  -11.87   -6.682
## C2             -12.082     1.494  -15.07   -9.110
## C3              15.286     1.327   12.59   17.950
```

However, it is not as straightforward to test for differences between parameter values in our `lmer` models. The same could be said for the combination of parameters as

Comparing many groups, interactions, and posterior predictive checks

is necessary for the investigation of group means and simple effects. The investigation of differences and combinations of parameters is definitely possible in `lmer` for many cases, however, this will involve either the re-parametrization of the model or the use of additional packages that allow for these sorts of questions to be asked. As a result, the comparisons or transformations that can be carried out is limited by the functionalities of the packages that carry out this comparison This can be contrasted with the ease and flexibility with which we can compare parameter estimates using Bayesian models.

7.10 Exercises

The analyses in the main body of the text all involve only the unmodified 'actual' resonance level (in `exp_data`). Responses for the stimuli with the simulated 'big' resonance are reserved for exercises throughout. You can get the 'big' resonance in the `exp_ex` data frame, or all data in the `exp_data_all` data frame.

Fit and interpret one or more of the suggested models:

1   Easy: Analyze the (pre-fit) model that's exactly like `model_interaction`, except using the data in `exp_ex` (`bmmb::get_model("7_model_interaction_ex.RDS")`).
2   Medium: Fit a model like `model_interaction`, but replace either apparent gender or apparent age with the resonance factor.
3   Hard: Fit a model including apparent age, apparent gender, and resonance. Include all interactions between these factors for both fixed and random effects.

In any case, describe the model, present and explain the results, and include some figures.

References

Gelman, A., Hill, J., & Yajima, M. (2012). Why we (usually) don't have to worry about multiple comparisons. *Journal of Research on Educational Effectiveness*, 5(2), 189–211.

Gelman, A., & Carlin, J. (2014). Beyond power calculations: Assessing type S (sign) and type M (magnitude) errors. *Perspectives on Psychological Science*, 9(6), 641–651.

Gelman, A., Goodrich, B., Gabry, J., & Vehtari, A. (2019). R-squared for Bayesian regression models. *The American Statistician*, 73(3), 307–309.

Kruschke, J. K. (2018). Rejecting or accepting parameter values in Bayesian estimation. *Advances in Methods and Practices in Psychological Science*, 1(2), 270–280.

8 Varying variances, more about priors, and prior predictive checks

So far, our models have been a bit 'old-fashioned' in one important way: They have featured a single error term (σ) for all of our observations. This means that σ is the same for all speakers, listeners, and conditions in our experiment. However, we might imagine a situation where one listener's responses (and residuals) are more widely distributed than another, resulting in a situation where, for example, $\sigma_{\left[L_{[i]}=1\right]} \neq \sigma_{\left[L_{[j]}=2\right]}$ for observations i and j contributed by listeners one and two. In such a situation, we may not want to use a single value of σ for all listeners and may instead prefer to use a different value for each listener, e.g. $\sigma_{[i]}$ for listener i. In this chapter, we're going to discuss models that allow for more variation in their σ parameters. In addition, we're going to go into more detail about setting priors for our models, and the use of prior predictive checks.

8.1 Chapter pre-cap

In this chapter, we introduce prior predictive checks and talk about the importance of these for model building. Then, examples of the results of different prior settings for models are provided. After that, we discuss how to specify more specific prior probabilities for individual model parameters. We then introduce heteroscedastic models, that is, models with error terms that vary from observation to observation. First, we present a 'simple' model that includes only variation in the error term across two conditions. Following that, we present a 'complex' model that features listener-dependent error terms fit using shrinkage, in addition to the equivalent of listener 'random effects' for the error term. Finally, we discuss building identifiable models, and models supported by the available data, and describe the problems of collinearity, linear dependence, and saturated models.

8.2 Data and Research questions

Below we load the data for our experiment investigating apparent speaker height, in addition to the `brms` and `bmmb` packages.

```
library (brms)
library (bmmb)
data (exp_data)
options (contrasts = c('contr.sum','contr.sum'))
```

DOI: 10.4324/9781003285878-8

244 *Varying variances, more about priors, and prior predictive checks*

The models we will consider below use the following variables from our data frame:

- `L`: A number from 1 to 15 indicating which *listener* responded to the trial.
- `height`: A number representing the *height* (in centimeters) reported for the speaker on each trial.
- `S`: A number from 1 to 139 indicating which *speaker* produced the trial stimulus.
- `G`: The *apparent gender* of the speaker indicated by the listener, `f` (female) or `m` (male).
- `A`: The *apparent age* of the speaker indicated by the listener, `a` (adult) or `c` (child).

We're going to use models whose structure is similar to the final model we fit in Chapter 7 (`model_interaction`). However, in this chapter we're going to focus on questions related to variation in our standard deviation parameters. We would like to know three things:

(Q1) Does our error standard deviation vary as a function of apparent speaker age?
(Q2) Does our error standard deviation vary as a function of the listener?

8.3 More about priors

To this point, our focus has been on understanding the components that make up our models, and how these are represented using our model parameters. Now that we've covered most of the essentials of using categorical predictors, we can focus a bit more on the prior distributions of the parameters in our models. The reason we've been able to get away with not talking about priors very much is that we have substantial **domain knowledge** regarding the distribution of human height as a function of age and gender. In addition, our models thus far have been fairly simple, making the consideration of prior distributions relatively straightforward.

For example, we will lay out some expected coefficient values based on the assumption that apparent height basically corresponds to veridical height, on average. Based on the information in `height_data`, we know that 11-year-old boys and girls are about 150 cm tall, and women and men are 163 and 176 cm tall, respectively, on average. This means that there is a difference of 19.5 cm ((13 + 26)/2) on average between adults and children between 11 and 12 years of age. A difference of 19.5 cm between age groups suggests about a 10 cm distance (half the group difference) between each age group and the overall intercept. In other words, if apparent height is similar to veridical height, we expect an apparent age (*A*) predictor of about 10 cm in magnitude given sum coding. In contrast, we have an expected height difference of 0 cm across genders for children, and 12 cm across genders for adults. This is an average difference of 6 cm between males and females across both ages. As a result, we expect an effect of about 3 cm for gender averaged across ages. Based on this, our prior standard deviation of 12 cm for our `b` (fixed-effects) parameters seems very reasonable, although perhaps a bit large for some effects.

Are they *too* large? An effect of 12 cm is reasonable for something related to the perception of human height. If we were astronomers, our priors might be on the order of 12 light-years rather than cm, where a light year is equal to $9.461 \cdot 10^{17}$ cm. If we were studying variation in the size of *E. coli* bacteria, our priors might be on the order of 0.2 micrometers, or about $2 \cdot 10^{-5}$ cm. When viewed from this perspective, worrying about a prior standard deviation of 12 cm vs. 6 cm is less important than providing

Varying variances, more about priors, and prior predictive checks   245

your model with information about the general magnitude of variation it can expect in your data and in parameter estimates. Furthermore, in many situations involving repeated measures data, you will have enough observations that slight differences in the settings of the priors will not have much noticeable effect on the posterior distributions of the model parameters (see Figure 3.1). This fact makes arguments regarding which prior is 'better' in many situations more *philosophical* than *practical*. That being said, it is still useful and important to provide priors that conform to plausible ranges of expected parameter values.

As we noted above, this is generally straightforward for our experiment involving the perception of apparent height. However, imagine a situation where there was less certainty about reasonable values for our priors. This can happen for many reasons. For example, imagine you carry out a lexical decision task where participants listen to a combination of 'real' (e.g. 'map') and 'fake' words (e.g. 'marp') and have to decide if the word they heard is 'real' or not. You divide your real words into five groups based on a numerical measure of their frequency (how often they tend to appear in speech). To complicate matters further, you see that your reaction times are heavily skewed and so decide to model the logarithm of the reaction times. What should your priors be for your frequency groups? The prior distribution of a parameter represents the expected distribution of your parameters *a priori*. So what do we think are reasonable group differences in this situation? Even in this relatively simple case, setting prior distributions using only your intuitions would require understanding plausible variation in the *logarithm* of reaction times across word groups. This may not be realistic in this situation nor in many others.

8.3.1 Prior predictive checks

A **prior predictive check** can help understand the consequences of the prior distributions of our parameters, especially in situations where they are otherwise difficult to understand. The prior predictive check consists of generating fake data (i.e. $\tilde{y}$) based on linear predictors (i.e. μ) simulated by sampling *only* from the prior. Conceptually, this is very similar to a posterior predictive check (discussed in Section 7.4), save for the fact that prior predictive checks are not influenced by the model likelihood (or the data). To carry out a prior predictive check using `brms` you fit your model in the same way you normally would, except for setting `sample_prior="only"`. When you do this, your model knows to generate parameter estimates and expected values (e.g. μ) based only on the prior distributions of the model parameters.

Below we fit `model_interaction` from Chapter 7 again, except this time we sample only from the prior. Imagine that we did not have much knowledge about speaker heights other than that humans tend to be between 1 and 2 meters tall. Based on this we decided to be cautious and use relatively *uninformative* priors and set all prior standard deviations to 1,000 cm (10 meters).

```r
# Fit the model yourself
priors = c(brms::set_prior("student_t(3,156, 1000)", class = "Intercept"),
           brms::set_prior("student_t(3,0, 1000)", class = "b"),
           brms::set_prior("student_t(3,0, 1000)", class = "sd"),
           brms::set_prior("lkj_corr_cholesky(1000)", class = "cor"),
           brms::set_prior("student_t(3,0, 1000)", class = "sigma"))
```

246 *Varying variances, more about priors, and prior predictive checks*

```
prior_uninformative =
  brms::brm (height ~ A + G + A:G + (A + G + A:G|L) + (1|S),
            sample_prior="only", data = exp_data, chains = 4, cores = 4,
            warmup = 1000, iter = 5000, thin = 4, prior = priors)

# Or download it from the GitHub page:
prior_uninformative = bmmb::get_model ('8_prior_uninformative.RDS')
```

We can use the `predict` function to get the prior predictions made by our model.

```
pp_uninformative = predict (prior_uninformative, summary = FALSE)
```

When we get 'unsummarized' predictions we get a prediction for each set of sampled parameters in our model. These predictions vary across samples by row and across data points by column. So, to get predictions for a single posterior sample we need to observe a single row of this matrix. This could be done using a histogram, as below:

```
hist (pp_uninformative[1,])
```

However, the `bmmb` package has a simple function called `p_check` that can be used to consider the density of multiple samples at once. By default this compares 10 random predictions, however, the number of predictions can be changed, and the user may also specify specific samples to consider.

```
bmmb::p_check (pp_uninformative)
```

In the left plot of Figure 8.1, we see the result of using `p_check` in ten random samples from our 'uninformative' prior prediction. As can be seen, our 'cautious' approach results in a range of simulated heights that make no sense even given our relatively limited prior knowledge, in this case, that most humans are between 100 and 200 cm tall. In fact, our simulated data contains not only large negative values, which make no sense in the context of height, but also substantial values above 5,000 cm, which is about the size of a ten-story office building.

It is difficult to *prove* that such a wide prior is 'bad', and in fact some authors have recommended the use of very uninformative priors (Kruschke, 2014). However, it's difficult to deny that a prior that results in prior predictions that are more in line with our domain knowledge is generally better for at least two reasons. First, more informative priors can help the model converge on credible parameter values, especially for complicated models with many parameters. Second, more informative priors can help improve out-of-sample prediction by providing actual information about plausible parameter values for our model. Basically, no fancy statistical model is going to convince anyone that 50 meters tall is a plausible apparent height for human speakers because human speakers are simply not nearly that tall. As a result, a model that acts as if 50 meters is a plausible apparent height for human speakers is likely to offer worse out-of-sample prediction than a model that correctly assigns little to no prior belief to this range of apparent heights. For a more in-depth

Varying variances, more about priors, and prior predictive checks 247

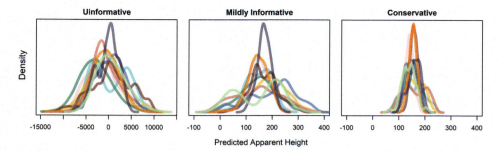

Figure 8.1 Densities of ten prior predictions of apparent height for the uninformative, mildly informative, and conservative priors.

discussion on the role and function of prior probabilities in multilevel Bayesian models, see Gelman et al. (2017).

Below we again sample from the prior using the setting we've been using so far, and that we used in the previous chapter.

```
# Fit the model yourself
priors = c(brms::set_prior("student_t(3,156, 12)", class = "Intercept"),
           brms::set_prior("student_t(3,0, 12)", class = "b"),
           brms::set_prior("student_t(3,0, 12)", class = "sd"),
           brms::set_prior("lkj_corr_cholesky (12)", class = "cor"),
           brms::set_prior("student_t(3,0, 12)", class = "sigma"))

prior_mildly_informative =
  brms::brm (height ~ A + G + A:G + (A + G + A:G|L) + (1|S),
             sample_prior="only", data = exp_data, chains = 4, cores = 4,
             warmup = 1000, iter = 5000, thin = 4, prior = priors)

# Or download it from the GitHub page:
prior_mildly_informative =
  bmmb::get_model ('8_prior_mildly_informative.RDS')
```

We can use the `p_check` function again to make plots of our prior predictions, as shown in the middle plot of Figure 8.1. As we can see, the priors we've been using allow for some implausibly large or small apparent height judgments. However, they are constraining the bulk of these to values between 100 and 200 cm, which is our approximate target. In our opinion, these priors are 'good enough'. However, we may be unhappy that even some implausible values are being generated and want to test out even tighter priors. Below, we sample from priors that are half as wide as those of our mildly informative model above.

```
# Fit the model yourself
priors = c(brms::set_prior("student_t(3,156, 6)", class = "Intercept"),
           brms::set_prior("student_t(3,0, 6)", class = "b"),
```

248 *Varying variances, more about priors, and prior predictive checks*

```
        brms::set_prior("student_t(3,0, 6)", class = "sd"),
        brms::set_prior("lkj_corr_cholesky (2)", class = "cor"),
        brms::set_prior("student_t(3,0, 6)", class = "sigma"))

prior_conservative =
  brms::brm (height ~ A + G + A:G + (A + G + A:G|L) + (1|S),
            sample_prior="only", data = exp_data, chains = 1, cores = 1,
            warmup = 1000, iter = 5000, thin = 1, prior = priors)

# Or download it from the GitHub page:prior_conservative = bmmb::get_
model ('8_prior_conservative.RDS')
```

The prior predictions made by this model are presented in the right plot of Figure 8.1. This time, we see that our prior predictions are even more tightly clustered within our desired range. For the sake of comparison, we fit the three models specified above by erasing `sample_prior="only"` from the respective function calls. We've named these models `model_uninformative`, `model_mildly_informative`, and `model_conservative` respectively. Below we load the models:

```
model_uninformative =
  bmmb::get_model ("8_model_uninformative.RDS")

model_mildly_informative =
  bmmb::get_model ("8_model_mildly_informative.RDS")

model_conservative =
  bmmb::get_model ("8_model_conservative.RDS")
```

We use `brmplot` to compare the fixed-effects estimates for the three models. As can be seen, there is little to no difference in parameter estimates or the credible intervals around them as a function of our prior probabilities. For example, although it may seem that there is a reduction in the `A1` effect based on the prior, the posterior means of these effects differ by less than 0.2 cm across the three models. This is in part due to the large amount of data we have, and the fact that our model is fairly simple relative to the information contained in our data.

8.3.2 *More specific priors*

The final model above was named `conservative` because its priors may have been *too* small. As noted above we actually expect an effect for the age of about 10 cm based on variation in veridical height between children and adults, and about 3 cm for the gender effect. When we set our priors using the `class` parameter in the `prior` function, we can reduce the time our models take to fit, but we lose the ability to fine-tune priors for specific parameters. For example, we might want a model with a standard deviation of 10 cm for the prior of the age effect, and a standard deviation of 3 cm for the prior of the gender effect. We can use the `prior_summary` function in `brms` to see what priors we can set for our model. The output of this function is formatted in the same way as that of the `get_priors` function, discussed in Sections 3.7 and 4.5.3.

Varying variances, more about priors, and prior predictive checks 249

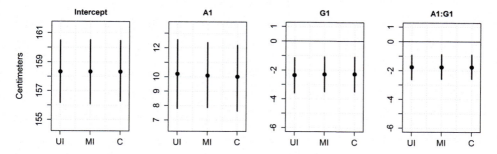

Figure 8.2 Comparison of fixed-effects estimates and 95% credible intervals for the uninformative (UI), mildly informative (MI), and conservative (C) models.

Actually, we're going to use a clone of `get_prior` in the `bmmb` package just because the one in `brms` doesn't like it when you omit columns from the output when printing.

```
# we omit empty columns to let the output fit on the page
bmmb::prior_summary(model_mildly_informative)[,-c(5:9)]
##                      prior     class       coef  group    source
##        student_t(3,0, 12)         b                          user
##        student_t(3,0, 12)         b         A1             default
##        student_t(3,0, 12)         b      A1:G1             default
##        student_t(3,0, 12)         b         G1             default
##     student_t(3,156, 12) Intercept                           user
##     lkj_corr_cholesky (2)         L                          user
##     lkj_corr_cholesky (2)         L               L        default
##        student_t(3,0, 12)        sd                          user
##        student_t(3,0, 12)        sd               L        default
##        student_t(3,0, 12)        sd         A1    L        default
##        student_t(3,0, 12)        sd      A1:G1    L        default
##        student_t(3,0, 12)        sd         G1    L        default
##        student_t(3,0, 12)        sd Intercept    L        default
##        student_t(3,0, 12)        sd               S        default
##        student_t(3,0, 12)        sd Intercept    S        default
##        student_t(3,0, 12)     sigma                          user
```

By the way, you can get the same information from your models by running the command `model_mildly_informative$prior`. We can copy the values of the `class`, `coeff`, and `group` columns in the output above to set more specific prior probabilities for the different parameters in our model. Below, We set some arbitrarily selected priors just to show an example of how these can be set for more specific groups of parameters.

```
# we omit the 'brms::' part so that the lines below will fit on the page
priors = 
  c(set_prior("student_t(3,156, 6)", class = "Intercept"),
    set_prior("student_t(3,0, 6)", class = "b"),
    set_prior("student_t(3,0, 10)", class = "b", coef = "A1"),
```

250 *Varying variances, more about priors, and prior predictive checks*

```
    set_prior("student_t(3,0, 3)", class = "b", coef = "G1"),
    set_prior("student_t(3,0, 10)", class = "sd"),
    set_prior("student_t(3,0, 5)", class = "sd", coef = "A1", group="L"),
    set_prior("student_t(3,0, 1.5)", class = "sd", coef = "G1", group="L"),
    set_prior("lkj_corr_cholesky(2)", class = "cor"),
    set_prior("student_t(3,0, 6)", class = "sigma"))

options (contrasts = c('contr.sum','contr.sum'))
prior_informative =
  brms::brm (height ~ A + G + A:G + (A + G + A:G|L) + (1|S),
          sample_prior = "only", data = exp_data, chains = 1, cores = 1,
          warmup = 1000, iter = 5000, thin = 1, prior = priors)
```

If we inspect the priors for this model and compare this to the previous one, we can see that now there is between-parameter variation in our priors.

```
bmmb::prior_summary(prior_informative)[,-c(5:8)]
##                      prior      class      coef group   source
##         student_t(3,0, 6)          b                     user
##        student_t(3,0, 10)          b        A1            user
##        student_t(3,0, 10)          b     A1:G1         default
##         student_t(3,0, 3)          b        G1            user
##       student_t(3,156, 6)  Intercept                     user
##    lkj_corr_cholesky(2)          L                        user
##    lkj_corr_cholesky(2)          L               L    default
##        student_t(3,0, 10)         sd                      user
##        student_t(3,0, 10)         sd               L    default
##         student_t(3,0, 5)         sd        A1      L      user
##         student_t(3,0, 5)         sd     A1:G1      L    default
##        student_t(3,0, 1.5)         sd        G1      L      user
##        student_t(3,0, 1.5)         sd Intercept      L    default
##        student_t(3,0, 1.5)         sd               S    default
##        student_t(3,0, 1.5)         sd Intercept      S    default
##         student_t(3,0, 6)      sigma                     user
```

8.4 Heteroskedasticity and distributional models

Most 'typical' regression models assume that the error variance is the same for all observations, all conditions, all listeners, etc. The property of having a homogeneous variance is called **homoskedasticity**, and models that make this assumption are **homoskedastic**. Historically, the homogeneity of error variance has been assumed in models because it makes them simpler to work with and understand, and not because it is 'true' for all (or any) data. With Bayesian models, it is straightforward to relax and test this assumption, and to build models that exhibit **heteroskedasticity**, differences in the error variance across different subsets of data. These sorts of models are sometimes called **distributional models** because they allow us to model variation in all of the parameters of the data distribution (e.g. σ in addition to μ).

Varying variances, more about priors, and prior predictive checks 251

Consider the residuals for the random effects model we fit in Chapter 7, which we can get from the model using the `residuals` function:

```
# download model
model_interaction = bmmb::get_model ('7_model_interaction.RDS')

# get residuals
residuals_interaction = residuals (model_interaction)
```

If we inspect the residuals we see that the distribution of these is not exactly equal for all listeners, and also appears to vary based on apparent speaker age. For example, the interquartile range for listener 9 is nearly as wide as the entire distribution of residuals for listener 12. In this section, we will fit models with age and listener-specific error variances (σ). By allowing the random error to vary as a function of the listener and apparent age, our model may be able to provide more reliable information regarding our data, in addition to letting us ask questions like "is listener 12's error variance actually smaller than listener 9's, or does it just seem that way?" in a more formal manner.

To this point, our models have all looked something like (8.1), with the generic predictors x_p. In these models, μ got a subscript because it varied from trial to trial and was being predicted, but σ has never received a subscript because it hasn't varied in our models.

$$\text{height}_{[i]} \sim \text{N}\left(\mu_{[i]}, \sigma\right)$$
$$\mu_{[i]} = x_1 + x_2 + \ldots + x_p \tag{8.1}$$

Instead, we can fit models that help us understand systematic variation in both the mean *and* the σ parameters in our data. We can imagine this by adding a subscript to σ and predicting its value from trial to trial using variables, as seen in (8.2). We've given these predictor variables little σ subscripts just to distinguish them conceptually from those predicting μ, but they could be the same variables used to understand μ or a different set.

$$\text{height}_{[i]} \sim \text{N}\left(\mu_{[i]}, \sigma_{[i]}\right)$$
$$\mu_{[i]} = x_1 + x_2 + \ldots + x_p \tag{8.2}$$
$$\sigma_{[i]} = x_{\sigma 1} + x_{\sigma 2} + \ldots + x_{\sigma p}$$

8.5 A 'simple' model: Error varies according to a single fixed effect

We'll begin with a 'simple' heteroskedastic model that allows for variation in σ based on apparent age. After this, we'll fit a model that includes listener-dependent variation in σ as well.

8.5.1 Description of our model

The `brms` package makes it easy to fit heteroscedastic models by letting you write formulas for the error just as you do for the mean. For example, the model formula for the last model we fit in Chapter 7 (`model_interaction`) was:

```
height ~ A + G + A:G + (A + G + A:G|L) + (1|S)
```

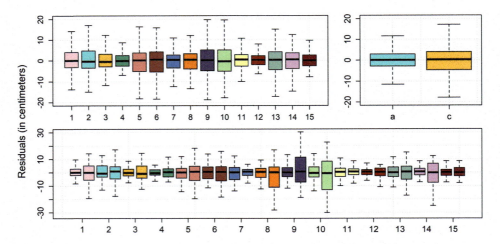

Figure 8.3 (top left) Distribution of residuals for each listener. (top right) Distribution of residuals for apparent adults (a) and apparent children (c). (bottom) Distribution of residuals for each listener, divided according to apparent children and apparent adults. Each color represents a different listener and the left box in each pair represents apparent adults.

This told `brms` "model apparent height as a function of an intercept, an effect for apparent age, an effect for apparent gender, the interaction of the two, listener-specific adjustments to all predictors, and speaker-specific intercepts". Implicitly, we know that this formula models variation in the μ parameter of a normal distribution with a fixed σ. We want our model to consider the possibility that the value of σ may vary based on whether the speaker is judged to be an adult or a child. We can do this by including a separate formula for our error (called `sigma` by `brms`) using the following formula:

```
sigma ~ A
```

This formula tells `brms` "model the standard deviation of the error as varying around an overall intercept and deviations of this based on `A`, a predictor indicating apparent age". We can 'stick' our two model formulas together using the `bf` (`brmsformula`) function as shown below:

```
model_formula = brms::bf(height ~ A + (A|L) + (1|S),
                         sigma ~ A)
```

The problem with modeling the standard deviation parameter directly is that negative values are impossible, so that standard deviations are bounded by zero. To deal with this, `brms` models `log(sigma)`, the logarithm of the error standard deviation, rather than `sigma` directly. Logarithms help model standard deviations because they map all numbers from 0 to 1 to values between negative infinity and 0. This allows one to model very small values of σ while at the same time never worrying about estimating a negative standard deviation (for more on logarithms see Section 2.7.2).

Varying variances, more about priors, and prior predictive checks 253

Since we're modeling log-transformed sigmas, we now specify the priors for sigma in logarithmic values. Previously, our prior for sigma was a t-distribution with a standard deviation of 12. This meant that the majority of the mass of the distribution was going to be between 0 and 24 cm (two standard deviations from the mean). Now, we set the distribution to 1.5, meaning that we expect most predictors related to σ to be between $\exp(-3) = 0.05$ and $\exp(3) = 20.1$. The full model specification is provided below (omitting the 'construction' of the Σ term):

$$\text{height}_{[i]} \sim t\left(v, \mu_{[i]}, \sigma_{[i]}\right)$$
$$\mu_{[i]} = \text{Intercept} + A + G + A:G +$$
$$L_{\left[L_{[i]}\right]} + A:L_{\left[L_{[i]}\right]} + G:L_{\left[L_{[i]}\right]} + A:G:L_{\left[L_{[i]}\right]} + S_{\left[S_{[i]}\right]}$$

$$\log\left(\sigma_{[i]}\right) = \text{Intercept}_\sigma + A_\sigma$$

$$\text{Priors}:$$
$$S_{[\cdot]} \sim t\left(3, 0, \sigma_S\right)$$

$$\begin{bmatrix} L_{[\cdot]} \\ A:L_{[\cdot]} \\ G:L_{[\cdot]} \\ A:G:L_{[\cdot]} \end{bmatrix} \sim \text{MVNormal}\left(\begin{bmatrix} 0 \\ 0 \\ 0 \\ 0 \end{bmatrix}, \Sigma \right) \tag{8.3}$$

$$\text{Intercept} \sim t(3, 156, 12)$$
$$A, G, A:G \sim t(3, 0, 12)$$
$$\sigma_L, \sigma_{A:L}, \sigma_{G:L}, \sigma_{A:G:L}, \sigma_S \sim t(3, 0, 12)$$
$$v \sim \text{gamma}(2, 0.1)$$
$$R \sim \text{LKJCorr}(2)$$
$$\text{Intercept}_\sigma \sim N(0, 1.5)$$
$$A_\sigma \sim N(0, 1.5)$$

A plain English description of this model is:

We are modeling apparent height as coming from a t-distribution with unknown nu (v), mean (μ), and scale (σ) parameters. The expected value for any given trial (μ) is modeled as the sum of an intercept, an effect for apparent speaker age (A), gender (G), and their interaction (A:G), a listener effect (L), a listener-dependent effect for apparent age (A:L), apparent gender (G:L), their interaction (A:G:L), and a speaker effect (S). The expected value of the logarithm of the error standard deviation (σ) is modeled as the sum of an intercept (Intercept$_\sigma$) and an effect for apparent age (A$_\sigma$) that are specific to the error. The speaker effects were drawn from a univariate normal distribution with a standard deviation (σ$_S$) estimated from the data. The four listener effects were drawn from a multivariate normal distribution with individual standard deviations (σ$_L$, σ$_{A:L}$, σ$_{G:L}$, σ$_{A:G:L}$) and a correlation matrix (R) that was estimated from the data. The remainder of the 'fixed' effects

254 *Varying variances, more about priors, and prior predictive checks*

and correlations were given prior distributions appropriate for their expected range of values, including the terms related to the error (Intercept$_\sigma$, and A_σ).

This model is quite large, but it only contains four new (or modified) lines compared to the model presented in (7.8). These lines are presented in (8.4), and effectively represent a simple two-group model for our σ parameter, which has been added to our model predicting μ. Our model now uses a trial-specific error term for trial i ($\sigma_{[i]}$), whereas it previously always used a constant standard deviation. Further, we are now modeling this trial-specific σ parameter using an intercept specific to our sigma term (Intercept$_\sigma$), and a deviation from this base on apparent age (A_σ).

$$\text{height}_{[i]} \sim t\left(v, \mu_{[i]}, \sigma_{[i]}\right)$$
$$\sigma_{[i]} = \text{Intercept}_\sigma + A_\sigma$$

(8.4)

$$\text{Intercept}_\sigma \sim t(3, 0, 1.5)$$
$$A_\sigma \sim t(3, 0, 1.5)$$

8.5.2 Prior predictive checks

Recall that when we use the `set_prior` function we can use the `class` parameter to specify priors for whole classes of parameters at a time. The classes we have discussed so far are:

- `Intercept`: this is a unique class, only for intercepts.
- `sd`: this is for our standard deviation parameters that relate to 'batches' of parameters, e.g. `sd(Intercept)` for `L` (σ_L).
- `sigma`: the error term.
- `cor`: priors for 'random effect' correlation terms.

For the first time, we need to specify priors for terms for σ rather than μ. We can do this by setting `dpar="sigma"` in the `set_prior` function. As noted just above, you can see which priors need setting, and which parameters need to be specified for a model, by using the `get_prior` function and providing your formula, data, and family.

```
brms::get_prior (brms::bf(height ~ A*G + (A*G|L) + (1|S),
                          sigma ~ A),
                 data = exp_data, family="student")
```

If you run the command above you will see output that includes the lines below:

```
##                          prior     class     coef group resp  dpar
##                         (flat)         b                      sigma
##                         (flat)         b              A1      sigma
##         student_t(3, 0, 2.5) Intercept                        sigma
```

Varying variances, more about priors, and prior predictive checks 255

We have two parameters where `dpar=sigma`: An overall intercept (`class = "Intercept"`, `dpar = "sigma"`), and an age term for sigma (`class = "b",coef="A1",dpar="sigma"`). We can set priors for these elements using the lines:

```
brms::set_prior("normal(0, 1.5)", class = "Intercept", dpar = "sigma")
brms::set_prior("normal(0, 1.5)", class = "b", dpar = "sigma")
```

Notice that we set these priors using the classes we have already discussed, `Intercept` and `b` respectively. However, now we set `dpar` (distributional parameter) to `sigma` to tell `brm` that these priors are specifically for parameters related to the model error term, and not to variation in predicted values (i.e. μ). Below we fit the model sampling only from our priors:

```
# Fit the model yourself
model_formula = brms::bf(height ~ A*G + (A*G|L) + (1|S),
                         sigma ~ A)

priors =
  c(set_prior("student_t(3, 156, 12)", class = "Intercept"),
    set_prior("student_t(3, 0, 12)", class = "b"),
    set_prior("student_t(3, 0, 12)", class = "sd"),
    set_prior("gamma(2, 0.1)", class = "nu"),
    set_prior("normal(0, 1.5)", class = "Intercept", dpar = "sigma"),
    set_prior("normal(0, 1.5)", class = "b", dpar = "sigma"),
    set_prior("lkj_corr_cholesky (2)", class = "cor"))

prior_A_sigma =
  brms::brm (model_formula, data = exp_data, chains = 4, cores = 4,
             warmup = 1000, iter = 3500, thin = 2, family="student",
             prior = priors, sample_prior = "only")

# Or download it from the GitHub page:
prior_A_sigma = bmmb::get_model ('8_prior_A_sigma.RDS')
```

We can investigate our prior predictions using the code below. We don't plot them here, but we think the predictions are reasonable.

```
p_check (prior_A_sigma)
```

8.5.3 Fitting and interpreting the model

For the first time below, we specify both the model formula (using the `bf` function) and the priors (using the `set_prior` function) outside of the call to `brm`. We do this to preserve the legibility of the code in general.

256 *Varying variances, more about priors, and prior predictive checks*

```
# Fit the model yourself
model_formula = brms::bf(height ~ A*G + (A*G|L) + (1|S),
                         sigma ~ A)


priors =
  c(set_prior("student_t(3, 156, 12)", class = "Intercept"),
    set_prior("student_t(3, 0, 12)", class = "b"),
    set_prior("student_t(3, 0, 12)", class = "sd"),
    set_prior("gamma(2, 0.1)", class = "nu"),
    set_prior("normal(0, 1.5)", class = "Intercept", dpar = "sigma"),
    set_prior("normal(0, 1.5)", class = "b", dpar = "sigma"),
    set_prior("lkj_corr_cholesky(2)", class = "cor"))


model_A_sigma =
  brms::brm (model_formula, data = exp_data, chains = 4, cores = 4,
             warmup = 1000, iter = 3500, thin = 2, family="student",
             prior = priors)


# Or download it from the GitHub page:
model_A_sigma = bmmb::get_model ('8_model_A_sigma.RDS')
```

If we look at the model 'fixed' (`population-Level) effects:

```
fixef (model_A_sigma)
##                      Estimate  Est.Error     Q2.5      Q97.5
## Intercept             158.383    1.10922  156.193   160.6196
## sigma_Intercept         1.724    0.03265    1.659     1.7881
## A1                     11.271    1.19021    8.915    13.6901
## G1                     -3.067    0.59091   -4.271    -1.9084
## A1:G1                  -1.528    0.43464   -2.403    -0.6654
## sigma_A1               -0.247    0.02199   -0.290    -0.2036
```

We see two new lines reflecting our new model parameters, both in the 'Population-level effects': `sigma_Intercept` and `sigma_A1`. These terms represent the intercept of our `sigma`, term and the effect for apparent adultness on `sigma`. These effects can be interpreted in a very similar way as we interpret the corresponding effects for μ: `Intercept` and `A1`. The value of `sigma_Intercept` represents the grand mean for our `sigma` term. The value of `sigma_A1` reflects the difference in `sigma` between the intercept and the value when speakers were perceived as adults. Since we are using sum coding `A2`, the effect for apparent children is not estimated. However, we can recover `A2` since `A1 = -A2`. One easy way to do this is using the `hypothesis` function (or its clone in `bmmb`) as follows:

```
sigmas = short_hypothesis(
  model_A_sigma,
  c("exp(sigma_Intercept) = 0",                   # overall sigma
    "exp(sigma_Intercept + sigma_A1) = 0",        # adult sigma
    "exp(sigma_Intercept - sigma_A1) = 0"))       # child sigma
```

Varying variances, more about priors, and prior predictive checks 257

```
sigmas[,-5]
##     Estimate Est.Error  Q2.5 Q97.5
## H1     5.609    0.1830 5.253 5.978
## H2     4.382    0.1526 4.085 4.680
## H3     7.184    0.3115 6.573 7.793
```

Since our model estimates `log(sigma)` and not `sigma` directly, to get our values of sigma we need to exponentiate our parameter estimates in order to recover our actual model error. We can do this directly in `short_hypothesis` as seen above. The three estimated error terms are presented in Figure 8.4. Clearly, there are substantial differences in the value of σ based on the perceived adultness of the speaker: The value of σ was 61% greater (7.1/4.4) when listeners identified the speaker as a child.

We might wonder two things about this new model. First, is there any difference in our fixed-effect parameters? Second, is the additional model complexity justified? We can compare this heteroskedastic model to the equivalent homoskedastic model we fit in Chapter 7 (`model_interaction`, loaded above). We can assess the first question visually using the `brmplot` function as seen in the right plot of Figure 8.4. It doesn't seem like the change has had much impact on our parameter estimates or the intervals around them. We can make a more formal comparison using cross-validation (discussed in Section 6.4.3). We add the `loo` (leave one out) criterion to each model and make a comparison.

```
model_interaction = add_criterion(model_interaction,"loo")
model_A_sigma = add_criterion(model_A_sigma,"loo")
loo_compare (model_interaction, model_A_sigma)
##                       elpd_diff se_diff
## model_A_sigma              0.0     0.0
## model_interaction        -53.7    12.8
```

We can see that there is a substantial difference in elpd between models, and that this difference is just over four times the size of the standard deviation. Based on this, it would seem that using the more complex model is justifiable. We will leave a discussion of whether the difference *makes sense* or *matters* for the section on answering our research questions.

8.6 A 'complex' model: Error varies according to fixed and random effects

In the previous section we fit a relatively 'simple' heteroscedastic model. This model allowed for error variances to differ based on the perceived adultness of the speaker, and so was very similar to the models we fit in Chapter 5. Here, we're going to fit a substantially more complex model that predicts variation in σ using listener-dependent 'random effects' in the same way we would for our prediction of μ.

8.6.1 Description of our model

Our previous model had the following formula for the `sigma` term:

```
sigma ~ A
```

258   *Varying variances, more about priors, and prior predictive checks*

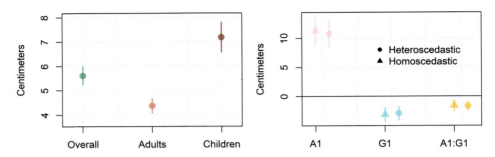

Figure 8.4 (left) Estimates of overall data-level error (σ), to estimates of this for apparent adults and for apparent children. (right) Comparison of some fixed-effects parameters shared by our heteroscedastic and homoscedastic models.

This told `brms` "model `sigma` as a function of an intercept and an effect for apparent age". We can add to our formula by specifying a 'random effect' term for listeners, and a 'random slope' for age (i.e. an interaction between apparent age and listener), both estimated using adaptive pooling.

```
sigma ~ A + (A|L)
```

This formula tells `brms` "model `sigma` as varying around an overall intercept, an effect for apparent age, listener-specific deviations, and the interaction of apparent age and listener". Effectively, we have two separate model formulas: One for a model with two categorical predictors and an interaction (like those in Chapter 7), and one for a model comparing two groups (like those in Chapter 6). We can 'stick' our two model formulas together using the `bf` (or `brmsformula`) function as shown below:

```
model_formula = brms::bf(height ~ A*G + (A*G|L) + (1|S),
                         sigma ~ A + (A|L))
```

If we were to fit the model using the formula above, our model would include independent multivariate normal distributions for the listener effects related to the mean and those related to the error term. So, we would have a four-dimensional normal distribution relating to the expected mean (μ), representing the listener intercept, the listener-dependent effects for apparent age and gender, and the listener-dependent interaction between the two. We would then have a separate two-dimensional normal distribution representing the listener-dependent intercepts and effects for apparent age relating to the error term (σ). This may be desirable in some situations, however, it may also be useful to estimate all of these listener-dependent coefficients from a single six-dimensional multivariate normal.

Right now, our model formula consists of two separate sub-formulas, each of which contains a term representing listeners (`L`). If we want our model to know that the `L` term predicting the mean is related to the `L` term predicting our error, then we can do this by adding the same label in each corresponding random effects term in parentheses, in between two pipes. Below, we use the label |x| to tell `brms` to estimate all six listener-dependent parameters jointly. The label can be almost any string, it just needs to be the same thing for every batch of random effects terms that you want to estimate together.

Varying variances, more about priors, and prior predictive checks 259

```
model_formula = brms::bf(height ~ A*G + (A*G|x|L) + (1|S),
                         sigma ~ A + (A|x|L))
```

Just keep in mind, you should *not* use the same label for things you do not want to be grouped together. So, if we wanted to estimate speaker effects for our error and wanted to associate these with the speaker effects for our means, we should use different labels as seen below.

```
model_formula = brms::bf(height ~ A*G + (A*G|x|L) + (1|y|S),
                         sigma ~ A + (A|x|L) + (1|y|S))
```

We're not actually going to fit a model like that, as we don't think we have enough observations per speaker (15) to justify the estimation of speaker-dependent errors given the complexity of our model. However, we wanted to provide an example of how this would be done. The full model specification is provided below:

$$\text{height}_{[i]} \sim \text{N}\left(\mu_{[i]}, \sigma_{[i]}\right)$$

$$\mu_{[i]} = \text{Intercept} + A + G + A:G +$$

$$L_{\left[\mathsf{L}_{[i]}\right]} + A:L_{\left[\mathsf{L}_{[i]}\right]} + G:L_{\left[\mathsf{L}_{[i]}\right]} + A:G:L_{\left[\mathsf{L}_{[i]}\right]} + S_{\left[\mathsf{S}_{[i]}\right]}$$

$$\log\left(\sigma_{[i]}\right) = \text{Intercept}_\sigma + A_\sigma + A_\sigma : L_{\sigma\left[\mathsf{L}_{[i]}\right]} + L_{\sigma\left[\mathsf{L}_{[i]}\right]}$$

Priors:

$$\begin{bmatrix} L_{[\cdot]} \\ A:L_{[\cdot]} \\ G:L_{[\cdot]} \\ A:G:L_{[\cdot]} \\ L_{\sigma[\cdot]} \\ A_\sigma:L_{\sigma[\cdot]} \end{bmatrix} \sim \text{MVNormal} \left(\begin{bmatrix} 0 \\ 0 \\ 0 \\ 0 \\ 0 \\ 0 \end{bmatrix}, \Sigma \right) \tag{8.5}$$

$$S_{[\cdot]} \sim \text{N}\left(0, \sigma_S\right)$$

$$\text{Intercept} \sim t\left(3, 156, 12\right)$$
$$A \sim t\left(3, 0, 12\right)$$
$$\sigma, \sigma_L, \sigma_{A:L}, \sigma_S \sim t\left(3, 0, 12\right)$$

$$\text{Intercept}_\sigma \sim \text{N}\left(0, 1.5\right)$$
$$A_\sigma \sim \text{N}\left(0, 1.5\right)$$
$$\sigma_{L_\sigma}, \sigma_{A_\sigma:L_\sigma} \sim \text{N}\left(0, 1.5\right)$$

$$R \sim \text{LKJCorr}\left(2\right)$$

260   *Varying variances, more about priors, and prior predictive checks*

Since our plain English description is nearly identical to the one provided for our previous model, the description below focuses on the components related to our error term σ:

> *We are modeling apparent height as coming from a t-distribution with unknown nu (ν), mean (μ), and scale (σ) parameters. The expected value of the logarithm of the error standard deviation (σ) is modeled as the sum of an intercept (Intercept$_\sigma$), an effect for apparent age (A_σ), an effect for listener (L_σ), and the interaction between apparent age and listener ($A_\sigma : L_\sigma$). The two listener effects related to the error term were drawn from a multivariate normal distribution with individual standard deviations ($\sigma_{L_\sigma}, \sigma_{A_\sigma:L_\sigma}$) and a correlation matrix (R) that was estimated from the data. The remainder of the 'fixed' effects and correlations were given prior distributions appropriate for their expected range of values.*

8.6.2 *Fitting and interpreting the model*

We need to specify a prior distribution for the standard deviation of our listener-dependent `sigma` parameters, σ_{L_σ} and $\sigma_{A_\sigma:L_\sigma}$. We can do this by specifying a prior for `class = "sd"` and `dpar = "sigma"`. Note that this is very similar to the way we fit priors for the intercept and fixed effects for `sigma`.

```
# Fit the model yourself
model_formula = brms::bf(height ~ A*G + (A*G|x|L) + (1|S),
                         sigma ~ A + (A|x|L))

priors =
  c(set_prior("student_t(3, 156, 12)", class = "Intercept"),
    set_prior("student_t(3, 0, 12)", class = "b"),
    set_prior("student_t(3, 0, 12)", class = "sd"),
    set_prior("gamma(2, 0.1)", class = "nu"),
    set_prior("normal(0, 1.5)", class = "Intercept", dpar = "sigma"),
    set_prior("normal(0, 1.5)", class = "b", dpar = "sigma"),
    set_prior("normal(0, 1.5)", class = "sd", dpar = "sigma"),
    set_prior("lkj_corr_cholesky (2)", class = "cor"))

model_A_L_sigma =
  brms::brm (model_formula, data = exp_data, chains = 4, cores = 4,
             warmup = 1000, iter = 3500, thin = 2, family="student",
             prior = priors)
```

Below we print an abridged model summary. The only change is that there are a few new lines in the listener `Group-Level  Effects`. First, we see `sd(sigma_Intercept)` and `sd(sigma_A1)`, which represent the standard deviations of the listener-specific intercepts and of the age effects (for `sigma`). Second, we see the correlations between our new random effects (i.e. `cor(sigma_Intercept,sigma_A1)`).

Varying variances, more about priors, and prior predictive checks 261

```
bmmb::short_summary (model_A_L_sigma)
## ...
## sd(sigma_Intercept)                     0.36      0.08      0.24      0.54
## sd(sigma_A1)                            0.17      0.04      0.10      0.27
## ...
## cor(A1,sigma_A1)                       -0.29      0.22     -0.67      0.16
## cor(G1,sigma_A1)                        0.22      0.24     -0.27      0.65
## cor(A1:G1,sigma_A1)                     0.12      0.24     -0.35      0.58
## cor(sigma_Intercept,sigma_A1)          -0.44      0.21     -0.79      0.05
## ...
##
## Population-Level Effects:
##                   Estimate Est.Error l-95% CI u-95% CI
## Intercept           158.29      1.10   156.15   160.51
## sigma_Intercept       1.74      0.10     1.55     1.93
## A1                   11.28      1.18     8.98    13.64
## G1                   -2.92      0.57    -4.06    -1.80
## A1:G1                -1.63      0.42    -2.47    -0.77
## sigma_A1             -0.23      0.05    -0.33    -0.14
##
## Family Specific Parameters:
##      Estimate Est.Error l-95% CI u-95% CI
## nu       8.07      1.54     5.71    11.72
```

Our listener-specific adjustments to the sigma intercept were fit with adaptive pooling, i.e. they are 'random' effects. As such, we can get these in the same way as other random effects terms (see Section 5.8.2). Below, we use `short_hypothesis` to get the listener random effects for sigma (L_σ) by setting `scope=ranef`. We get the sum of the listener sigma effects and the sigma intercept, $\text{Intercept}_\sigma + L_{\sigma[i]}$ for listener i, by setting `scope=coef`.

```
# listener random effects for sigma
log_sigmas_centered = short_hypothesis(model_A_L_sigma, "sigma_Intercept=0",
                       scope = "ranef",group="L")


# the sum of the sigma intercept and the listener sigma random effect
log_sigmas = short_hypothesis(model_A_L_sigma, "sigma_Intercept=0",
                       scope = "coef",group="L")


# the exponent of the sum of the sigma intercept
# and the listener sigma random effect
sigmas = short_hypothesis(model_A_L_sigma, "exp(sigma_Intercept)=0",
                       scope = "coef",group="L")
```

262 *Varying variances, more about priors, and prior predictive checks*

The `log_sigmas` calculated above represent the logarithm of the listener-specific error parameter. We can get the error terms themselves by exponentiating the parameter within the hypothesis function as shown for the calculation of `sigmas` above. Figure 8.5 compares the listener-dependent error effects (`log_sigmas_centered`) to the listener-dependent error terms, in their original scale (`sigmas`).

It certainly seems as though there is legitimate between-listener variation in the size of σ. We might wonder, is this added complexity a good thing? We can add the `loo` criterion to our model:

```
model_A_L_sigma = add_criterion(model_A_L_sigma, "loo")
```

And compare this model, the previous 'simple' heteroscedastic model (`model_A_sigma`), and the homoscedastic model we fit in the previous chapter (`model_interaction`).

```
loo_compare (model_interaction, model_A_sigma, model_A_L_sigma)
##                        elpd_diff se_diff
## model_A_L_sigma         0.0       0.0
## model_A_sigma        -122.1      15.6
## model_interaction    -175.8      20.8
```

This time we find a very large difference in elpd that is 7.8 times greater than the standard error of the difference. Again, it seems like the more complex model is justified and arguably 'better'.

8.7 Answering our research questions

The research questions we posed above were:

(Q1) Does our error standard deviation vary as a function of apparent speaker age?
(Q2) Does our error standard deviation vary as a function of the listener?

Based on the information we've already provided, we can answer these questions: Yes and yes. Further, we think these results are reasonable based on what we know about the heights of adults and children, and about the average speaker's knowledge of the heights of adults and children. For example, we think most people have a good handle on how tall adults tend to be. Does the average person know how tall 10–12-year-old children tend to be? We don't think so. In addition, 10–12-year-old children can show substantial variation in height based on differences in growth rates, which might also lead people to provide more variable estimates for the height of children. We think it also 'makes sense' that different listeners could be more or less systematic (i.e. predictable) than others, for many reasons.

We're going to add another, more meta, question: Which model should we report? We can approach this from the perspective that the best model according to elpd is the 'real' model. Based on the comparison of elpd above, it seems that the last model we fit (`model_A_L_sigma`) is the 'best' model. Does this mean it is the 'real' model? And does it mean that this is the one we must report? The short answers to these questions are no and no. The fit between a model and data can't 'prove' that the model represents the 'real' relationship underlying the data. The reason for this is that there are potentially a large number of other, slightly different, models that provide just about

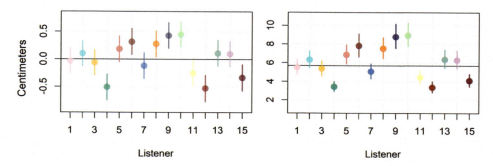

Figure 8.5 (left) Values of L_σ, listener-dependent variations from the `sigma` intercept (expressed as a logarithm). (right) Listener-specific sigma parameters. The result of $\exp\left(\text{Intercept}_\sigma + L_{\sigma[i]}\right)$ for listener i. We exponentiate the value in the plot so it reflects `sigma` rather than `log(sigma)`.

as good a fit to the data, or perhaps even a better one. This problem is called the **underdetermination** of theory with respect to data, basically that there are often (or always) multiple compatible interpretations of a set of observations, and that our observations alone are not enough to distinguish these.

Specifically with respect to our data, if the best model is the real one, how can we ever know we have the best model? How many did we try before settling on the 'best' one? Further, even if we did somehow find the best model for the data we *do* have, how could we guarantee that it will also be the best model for the data we *don't* have? It's impossible to know if some new data might come along that will not fit your model as well as one of the other models, making the 'best' model contingent on the data we have seen so far.

Ok, so we can't prove that our best model is the real one, fine. But it's still the best one we have. Do we necessarily need to report the 'best' model? This sort of reasoning can lead to serious problems because there is almost always a better model out there, and we often don't try to find it. For example, many people would never think to fit a heteroscedastic model and so would not even worry about reporting it. Does the existence of a hypothetical better model mean that the model they report is invalid? We don't think so. If it doesn't invalidate *their* simpler model, then why should this be the case for the researcher that *did* think to try the heteroscedastic model? This would seem to penalize people for bothering to look for such variation in their data, or for knowing how to fit heteroscedastic models.

In general, we can imagine that ten people might approach any given research question in ten different ways, a concept sometimes referred to as **researcher degrees of freedom** (Gelman and Loken, 2013) since it reflects model variation due to variation in researcher decisions rather than the data. Slight differences in model structure and data processing results in slight differences in model outputs, resulting in a sort of 'distribution' for any given result. How can a fixed underlying reality result in a distribution of results? When they are all slightly wrong. Rather than think of our models as representations of *reality*, we can think of them as mathematical implementations of our research questions. The model we report should include the information and structure that we think is necessary to represent and investigate our research questions. Using a different model can result in different results given the same data, but asking a different question can also lead to different results given the same data. When interpreting a statistical analysis, it is very useful to keep in mind that results are contingent on:

1. The data you collected. Given other data, you may have come to different conclusions.
2. The model you chose. Given another model you may have come to different conclusions.

So which model should we report? One way to think about our models is that they provide different *information* about our data. If we are primarily interested in the fixed effects then maybe we are not interested in additional information related to the error term. However, if we want to know about differences in error variation then we need one of the more complicated models. It's also worth considering how the differing model structures might affect the information they share in common. Figure 8.6 compares the fixed effects, random effects, and predicted values made by three models: `model_interaction` from Chapter 7, `model_A_sigma`, and `model_A_L_sigma` from this chapter.

These three models have the same structure when it comes to the prediction of the expected value of the normal distribution (μ), however, they differ in terms of the prediction of the error term. The prediction equation for `sigma` for each model is presented below. We didn't actually have a prediction equation for `sigma` in `model_interaction`, but this is equivalent to using the same `sigma` for each observation as would be done by the formula. As we can see below, these formulas correspond to 'intercept only' (Chapters 3–4), two-group fixed effects (Chapter 5), and two-group random effects (Chapter 6) structures for our error term.

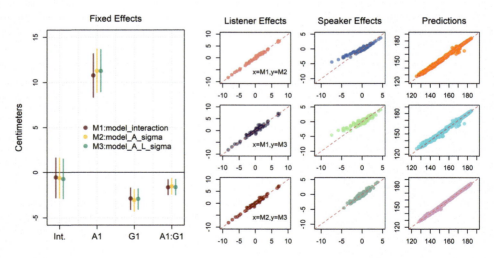

Figure 8.6 (left) Comparison of fixed effect estimates and 95% credible intervals for three models. We subtracted 159 from the model intercept (Int.) so that it would fit on the same scale as the other parameters. (right) Plots comparing parameter estimates, or predictions, for pairs of the models are presented in the left plot. Each row compares a different pair of models and each column presents a different set of parameters.

Varying variances, more about priors, and prior predictive checks 265

```
sigma ~ 1                    # model_interaction
sigma ~ A                    # model_A_sigma
sigma ~ A + (A|L)            # model_A_L_sigma
```

We can see in Figure 8.6 that the differences in the fixed effects are so small as to be largely meaningless. The three models also provide nearly identical listener 'random effects' and predicted values. Based on this, if we care primarily about the fixed effects and understanding apparent height judgments, any of the three models will work equally well. Where the models differ is in their estimates of the speaker effects. The inclusion of heteroscedasticity seems to reduce the magnitude of the speaker effects relative to the homoscedastic model (`model_interaction`). If we were specifically interested in these effects then we would need to take the time to understand the source, and meaning, of these differences. Of course, the experiment we ran was not designed to investigate speaker differences, so it does not make much sense to delve too far into these in our analysis. Our experiment was designed to investigate the perception of apparent height and the role of apparent speaker age and gender in these judgments. From this perspective, it seems that either of the three models is suitable.

8.8 Building identifiable and supportable models

Before finishing this chapter we want to talk about an extremely important issue that we have not discussed yet: Whether you *can*, or *should*, fit the complex model you are thinking of for your data. To this point, we haven't discussed this, but as our models get more and more complicated it is something we need to think about. There are generally two constraints on the sorts of models you can fit to your data.

The first of these are issues related to the **identifiability** of different model parameters, that is, the ability of your model to estimate unique and independent values for each of your model parameters. When model parameters are not **identifiable**, that means that these parameters cannot be estimated no matter how much data you have available. We have actually seen several examples of this issue already. When we discussed contrasts (Section 5.6), and when we introduced modeling factors with many levels (Section 7.2.2), we talked about the fact that you can't estimate all levels of a factor. The cause of these problems is a lack of *identifiability* of the parameters.

The second general constraint is related to whether your model is **supported** by your data, meaning you have enough data to realistically estimate all of your model parameters. In many cases involving repeated measures data this will not be an issue as there may be a large number of observations for each group (e.g. subject), and a medium to large number of groups (>30) in the experiment. However, it is still necessary to be aware of the limitations and the problems that (a lack of) support can cause for model fitting.

Because of the incredible array of regression models that can be designed, it's very difficult to give a 'high-level' set of guidelines that will ensure that any particular model will be identifiable and supported by your data. In addition, it's difficult to really explain model identifiability without talking in detail about matrix algebra (in addition to other mathematical topics). However, we will provide some examples of general cases that we hope are illustrative. You can get the models presented below by running the following line:

```
bmmb::get_model ('8_badmodels.Rda')
```

266 *Varying variances, more about priors, and prior predictive checks*

8.8.1 Collinearity

We've referenced the idea of *linear dependence* before, and we can provide a more formal definition of this now. Each of your predictors is a vector, a sequence of n values that predict your dependent variable for observation i. A set of predictor vectors $(x_1, x_2, ..., x_p)$ is linearly independent when there is no vector of non-zero real numbers $(a_1, a_2, ..., a_p)$ that can be multiplied by our vectors such that the sum of the vectors equals zero for all elements of the vector. This is presented below:

$$0 = x_1 \cdot a_1 + x_2 \cdot a_2 + ... + x_n \cdot a_n \tag{8.6}$$

Basically, if the vectors $(x_1, x_2, ..., x_p)$ are linearly independent, the values of the a variables above need to all be zero for the equation to be true. Including linearly dependent predictors in our models can cause serious problems. For example, imagine we wanted to predict apparent height based on speaker vocal-tract length (VTL) measured in centimeters (cm) and in meters (m). We only introduce the use of quantitative predictors (such as VTL) in the next chapter, but we can still show how including both of these predictors will cause problems for your model.

We can add a new predictor to our data, speaker VTL specified in meters rather than centimeters.

```
exp_data$vtl_m = exp_data$vtl / 100
```

Since this new variable equals 100 times our original VTL predictor, it's clear that the following operation will result in a string of zeros (or values near zero because of rounding errors).

```
exp_data$vtl + exp_data$vtl_m * -100
```

In other words, $\text{vtl}_{cm} - (-100 \cdot \text{vtl}_m) = 0$, meaning that vtl_{cm} and vtl_m are *linearly dependent*. We can fit a model including both of these predictors, as shown below.

```
model_bad_1 =
  brms::brm (height ~ vtl_m + vtl, data = exp_data, chains = 4, cores = 4,
      warmup = 1000, iter = 3500, thin = 2,
      prior = c(brms::set_prior("normal(176, 50)", class = "Intercept"),
              brms::set_prior("normal(0, 15)", class = "sigma")))
```

However, our model will not be able to find a satisfactory solution, and you will see a large list of warnings when trying to fit it. If you check out the model print statement you will see strange things in the population-level effects:

```
## Population-Level Effects:
##              Estimate Est.Error    l-95% CI    u-95% CI Rhat Bulk_ESS Tail_ESS
## Intercept      45.69      2.37       41.17       50.47 1.00     4031     4425
## vtl_m        1383.91 246800.93 -531293.80   343951.54 2.12        5       13
## vtl            -5.28   2468.01   -3430.88     5321.56 2.12        5       13
```

Varying variances, more about priors, and prior predictive checks 267

Above we see comically small effective sample sizes (ESS) indicating that we have basically no information about our parameters, and large Rhat values indicating that our chains have not converged. We also see an astronomically large standard error for our `vtl_m` predictor, especially given the knowledge that human speaker height tends to range from 100 to 200 cm at most. Also, what does it mean that the predictors for VTL in meters and VTL in centimeters differ in sign? How can one be positively related and the other be negatively related to apparent height? Obviously, there are serious problems with these parameter estimates.

Linear dependence is binary, a set of vectors is linearly dependent or it is not. However, we can also talk about the degree to which vectors are linearly *related*, with linear dependence being one extreme. We measure linear relatedness using correlation coefficients (Section 6.3.2) where correlations of 1 or −1 indicate linear dependence. Our model above failed because our two predictors are linearly dependent, they have a correlation of 1.

```
cor (exp_data$vtl_m, exp_data$vtl)
## [1] 1
```

In the code below, we add a small amount of random error to our VTL predictor (in meters). This is set to 1/10th the value of the standard deviation of the predictor itself. This small amount of random noise reduces the correlation between VTL in meters and VTL in centimeters to 0.9946, almost perfectly correlated but *not*, strictly speaking, linearly dependent.

```
set.seed(1)
exp_data$vtl_m_noise = exp_data$vtl_m +
  rnorm (length(exp_data$vtl_m),0,sd(exp_data$vtl_m)/10)

cor (exp_data$vtl, exp_data$vtl_m_noise)
## [1] 0.9946
```

We can fit the model with the new predictor:

```
model_bad_2 =
  brms::brm (height ~ vtl_m_noise + vtl, data = exp_data, chains = 4,
        cores = 4,warmup = 1000, iter = 3500, thin = 2, prior = priors)
```

If we inspect the population-level effects we see that this tiny change has made our model substantially better. We get no warnings or error messages when we try to fit this model, and we have a very respectable ESS for our parameters.

```
## Population-Level Effects:
##                 Estimate Est.Error l-95% CI u-95% CI Rhat Bulk_ESS Tail_ESS
## Intercept          45.75      2.36    41.16    50.35 1.00     4523     4087
## vtl_m_noise      -201.86    175.11  -544.11   139.03 1.00     3504     3697
## vtl                10.57      1.76     7.14    14.01 1.00     3439     3866
```

268 *Varying variances, more about priors, and prior predictive checks*

At this point, our model might not seem that bad except for the large effect (and huge interval) around `vtl_m_noise` (VTL in meters, plus noise). The estimate for `vtl`, and the interval around it, may seem plausible, especially in comparison to our last model. However, we might also consider the estimate for our `vtl` predictor in a model without this redundant parameter:

```
model_good =
  brms::brm (height ~ vtl, data = exp_data, chains = 4, cores = 4,
       warmup = 1000, iter = 3500, thin = 2,
       prior = c(brms::set_prior("normal(176, 50)", class = "Intercept"),
                 brms::set_prior("normal(0, 15)", class = "sigma")))
```

We see that we get a much narrower credible interval around the VTL parameter.

```
## Population-Level Effects:
##             Estimate Est.Error l-95% CI u-95% CI Rhat Bulk_ESS Tail_ESS
## Intercept     45.72      2.38    41.04    50.40 1.00     5052     4679
## vtl            8.55      0.18     8.21     8.90 1.00     5072     4831
```

The above is not to say that correlated quantitative predictors should never be included in the same regression model. However, it's important to think about the consequences of doing this. In addition, when possible, it's a good idea to not paint yourself into a corner by designing an experiment that will specifically lead to, or require, highly correlated predictors.

8.8.2 *Predictable values of categorical predictors*

Linear dependence can cause other sorts of problems that are less obvious when making predictions using categorical variables. Your model parameters will also not be identifiable if you include categorical predictors whose values can be predicted based on the value of other categorical predictors you include in your model. For example, we know that we can't estimate both group means *and* the intercept in two-group models. We can now say that this is because if you know that an observation is not in the first group, you *know* it must be in the second. This is, once again, the problem of linear dependence.

For example, below we make a small matrix representing predictor variables in a simple regression comparing two groups. The first column represents the intercept for every observation (Section 3.5.2). The second column is a variable equal to 1 when the observation was in the first group and 0 if not. The third column is equal to 1 when the observation was in the second group and 0 if not. Obviously, the second column will equal 1 if the third column is zero and 0 if the third column is 1.

```
x = cbind (intercept=rep(1,4), x1=rep(c(1,0),2),
x2=rep(c(0,1),2))
x
##      intercept x1 x2
## [1,]         1  1  0
## [2,]         1  0  1
## [3,]         1  1  0
## [4,]         1  0  1
```

Varying variances, more about priors, and prior predictive checks 269

If we look at the numbers above, we can take the first column and add it to the negative of the second and third columns and this will always equal zero.

```
x[,1] + x[,2]*(-1) + x[,3]*(-1)
## [1] 0 0 0 0
```

That means that these three predictors are linearly dependent, and that's why we can't include separate predictors for the intercept and each group in a two-group model. This also explains why we can't estimate all four levels of our C (apparent category) parameter, as we discussed in the previous chapter. Below we make a small matrix of 'predictors' for each of our four categories and the intercept. The predictors with C in their name equal 1 when the observation belongs to the first, second, third, and fourth groups, respectively.

```
x = cbind (intercept=rep(1,4), C1=c(1,0,0,0), C2=c(0,1,0,0),
           C3=c(0,0,1,0),C4=c(0,0,0,1))
x
##         intercept C1 C2 C3 C4
## [1,]            1  1  0  0  0
## [2,]            1  0  1  0  0
## [3,]            1  0  0  1  0
## [4,]            1  0  0  0  1
```

We can see that the same approach can be used to make all rows add up to zero, indicating that these predictors are linearly dependent. The predictors cannot be made to sum to zero if we omit the fifth column of the matrix above, which is why our models will not estimate C4 when C is included as a predictor in our models.

```
x[,1] + x[,2]*(-1) + x[,3]*(-1) + x[,4]*(-1) + x[,5]*(-1)
## [1] 0 0 0 0
```

This sort of thing also causes problems when you include multiple different factors that mutually explain each other. For example, in the last chapter we initially fit a model using C, apparent speaker category, as a predictor. We then fit models using A and G, apparent age and gender as predictors. However, we did not fit models that included apparent age, gender, *and* speaker category. This is because if a speaker is a woman, they are an adult female. If they are a male child, they are a boy, and if they are a female child, they are a girl. So, given combinations of some categorical predictors, we have perfect knowledge of the values of *other* categorical predictors. Mathematically, this means that the 'secret' predictors representing each category are linearly dependent. Below we make our small predictor matrix containing predictors for apparent category, apparent age and gender, and their interaction.

```
x = cbind (intercept=rep(1,4), C1=c(1,0,0,0), C2=c(0,1,0,0),
           C3=c(0,0,1,0),A1=c(0,0,1,1), G1=c(0,1,0,1),A1G1=c(1,0,0,1))
```

270 *Varying variances, more about priors, and prior predictive checks*

```
X
##          intercept C1 C2 C3 A1 G1 A1G1
## [1,]            1  1  0  0  0  0    1
## [2,]            1  0  1  0  0  1    0
## [3,]            1  0  0  1  1  0    0
## [4,]            1  0  0  0  1  1    1
```

This matrix actually features several different combinations of predictors that can be combined to equal zero. For example, we can combine the first, second, third, and fifth predictors:

```
x[,1]*1 + x[,2]*(-1) + x[,3]*(-1) + x[,5]*(-1)
## [1] 0 0 0 0
```

Or the first, third, fourth, and seventh:

```
x[,1]*1 + x[,3]*(-1) + x[,4]*(-1) + x[,7]*(-1)
## [1] 0 0 0 0
```

If we try to fit a model that includes all of these predictors:

```
model_bad_3 =
    brms::brm (height ~ C + A*G, data = exp_data, chains = 4, cores = 4,
        warmup = 1000, iter = 3500, thin = 2,
        prior = c(brms::set_prior("normal(176, 15)", class = "Intercept"),
                  brms::set_prior("normal(0, 15)", class = "sigma")))
```

We get a model with the low ESS values, the large Rhat values, and the very large coefficient values and intervals that we saw in our model featuring linearly dependent predictors above.

```
## Population-Level Effects:
##            Estimate Est.Error l-95% CI u-95% CI Rhat Bulk_ESS Tail_ESS
## Intercept    157.98      0.20   157.57   158.35 1.06       61       78
## C1          1066.31   2604.72 -4431.79  5158.68 2.07        5       18
## C2           496.91   1751.32 -2543.19  3708.83 1.87        6       13
## C3            74.39   2086.76 -4113.31  2801.74 1.99        5       21
## A1           793.68   1363.24 -2383.78  3019.96 1.90        6       12
## G1           567.63   2171.69 -4107.90  3364.23 2.04        5       18
## A1:G1        283.89   1112.60 -2295.30  2141.73 2.26        5       18
```

This concludes our discussion of linear dependence and some of the many ways it can cause problems for your models. If you try to fit a model and you get errors, divergent transitions, low ESS values, and high Rhats, you *may* have a problem with linear dependencies in your predictors, and it is worth carefully considering this possibility. In addition, a better understanding of model identifiability and linear dependence can be gained by learning a little linear algebra.

Varying variances, more about priors, and prior predictive checks 271

8.8.3 Saturated, and 'nearly saturated', models

The models in this chapter sought to estimate five parameters for each listener (Intercept, $A, G, A:G, \sigma$) based on 139 observations for each listener. This seems like a reasonable ratio of observations to parameters. If we had only 10 observations per listener, this model may still be identifiable. However, it might still not be such a good idea to fit a model with so many listener-dependent parameters given so little data. In general, before fitting a model that you *can* fit, it's a good idea to think about whether you *should* fit it given the nature of your data and the number of observations you have overall (and in different relevant subsets).

We can think of the logical extreme of a model with too many parameters and too little data. Imagine we wanted to fit a model with speaker effects, listener effects, *and* the interaction between the two. This model will be able to represent the 15 listener effects, 139 speaker effects, and all of the listener-dependent speaker effects. This means that at a minimum, this model would require $15 \cdot 139 = 2,085$ parameters to represent these effects. However, we only have 2,085 data points, one observation per speaker per listener. As a result, we would have a different parameter for every single observation leading to what's known as a **saturated model**.

In a model without shrinkage, saturated models lead to the perfect prediction of data. This means that there is no data-level error (σ), or in fact, any random variation at all. This is problematic because the existence of a non-zero σ is a pre-requisite for the calculation of the likelihood function of our regression parameters (see Chapter 2). For example, the model below doesn't report errors because it doesn't fit at all, it repeatedly crashed R and *Stan* when we attempted to fit it.

```
exp_data$S = factor (exp_data$S)
exp_data$L = factor (exp_data$L)


model_bad_4  =
  brms::brm (height ~ S*L, data = exp_data, chains = 4, cores = 4,
      warmup = 1000, iter = 3500, thin = 2,
      prior = c(brms::set_prior("normal(176, 15)", class = "Intercept"),
            brms::set_prior("normal(0, 15)", class = "sigma")))
```

This may be easier to conceive of if we use a much smaller example. Imagine two people carry out the coffee and reading times experiment we discussed in earlier chapters. Two speakers read a passage after drinking decaf, and another after drinking coffee. This results in four observations. We can estimate the speaker effect, this will be the average of the reading times for each speaker across both drink conditions. The error for this estimate will be the distribution of the coffee and decaf reading times around the speaker average. We can also estimate the effect for drink condition, the average of both speaker reading times within each condition. The error for this will be the distribution of speaker reading times around the mean for each drink condition. However, we cannot estimate the speaker by drink condition interaction. This is because once we know the mean reading time for each speaker for each drink condition, *there is no error*. We only have one observation within this condition so that observation *is* the mean. There is no error distribution because we have no other observations.

272 *Varying variances, more about priors, and prior predictive checks*

Ok, so what if we had not one but two observations per speaker per drink condition? This would not be a saturated model, but we could think of it as a **nearly saturated model**, a term that may not have a formal definition but gets the point across. A model with only two observations per person per drink condition may technically allow us to model the listener by drink condition interaction, however, each of the interaction parameters would be based on only two observations.

Back to our example of estimation of the speaker effects. We have 139 observations per listener but only one per listener per speaker. Rather than think of our n (number of observations) as a single value, we can think of our effective n for different parameters. If we plan to investigate the effect of apparent age on apparent height, we have >40 observations per listener per apparent age group (`table (exp_data$A, exp_data$L)`). We can think of our n per listener for the estimation of the apparent age parameter as >40, a reasonable amount of data. On the other hand, our n for the estimation of the listener by speaker interaction is only 1 (`table (exp_data$S, exp_data$L)`), regardless of whether we have 139 observations per listener.

If we wanted to make claims about listener-dependent judgments of individual speakers and variation in these, we would need to design an experiment that featured a 'reasonable' number of observations per listener per speaker. Establishing a 'reasonable' number of repetitions depends on the amount of variation, the type of variation, and the number of groups in your data, among other things. In general, the noisier your data the more observations you will need to get precise (and useful) estimates for your parameters.

8.9 Exercises

The analyses in the main body of the text all involve only the unmodified 'actual' resonance level (in `exp_data`). Responses for the stimuli with the simulated 'big' resonance are reserved for exercises throughout. You can get the 'big' resonance in the `exp_ex` data frame, or all data in the `exp_data_all` data frame.

Fit and interpret one or more of the suggested models:

1   Easy: Analyze the (pre-fit) model that's exactly like `model_A_L_sigma`, except using the data in `exp_ex` (`bmmb::get_model("8_model_A_L_sigma_ex.RDS")`).
2   Medium: Fit a model like `model_A_L_sigma`, but replace any of the predictors in the model with the resonance factor.
3   Medium: Fit a model like `model_A_L_sigma`, but add another predictor to the prediction equation for `sigma`, possibly with an interaction with apparent age.
4   Hard: Fit a model like `model_A_L_sigma` but include apparent age, apparent gender, and resonance. Include all interactions between these factors for both fixed and random effects.

In any case, describe the model, present and explain the results, and include some figures.

References

Gelman, A., Simpson, D., & Betancourt, M. (2017). The prior can often only be understood in the context of the likelihood. *Entropy*, 19(10), 555.

Kruschke, J. (2014). *Doing Bayesian data analysis: A tutorial with R, JAGS, and Stan*. Frankfurt: Elsevier Science.

9 Quantitative predictors and their interactions with factors

So far, we've only discussed models that include categorical predictors (factors), predictors that split up our observations into a number of discrete groups or categories. In this chapter, we're going to talk about the inclusion of quantitative predictors in our model that can explore the *linear relationship* (i.e. variation along lines) between a quantitative predictor and the dependent variable. We're going to focus on the interpretation of model coefficients and what these mean for the geometry of the lines we make. The geometric interpretations of the different model structures we will discuss in this chapter are not specifically *Bayesian*, and in fact, are shared by any approach to linear regression.

9.1 Chapter pre-cap

In this chapter, we introduce the use of quantitative predictors to model variation along lines, with a special focus on how the structure of our models affects the geometry of the lines implied by our model. First, a model with only a single slope and intercept is introduced. Then, models with a single quantitative predictor and a single categorical predictor, but no interaction, are introduced. These models predict variation along group-specific, but parallel, lines. After this, we describe models with an interaction between a quantitative predictor and a categorical predictor, which can represent group-specific intercepts and slopes. After introducing some basic model structures, we present a random effects model including a single quantitative predictor but featuring 'random slopes' for each participant. Finally, this chapter presents a larger model where variation in both the intercepts and slopes of lines is predicted using two categorical predictors and their interaction, in addition to including listener-dependent 'random' effects for all predictors and their interaction.

9.2 Data and research questions

To fit a model with a quantitative dependent variable and a single quantitative independent variable you need a data frame with at least two columns, both of which are quantitative variables (see Section 1.4.4), and which are being treated as numerical by R (rather than as strings or factors). We're going to try to predict apparent height given the speaker's vocal-tract length (VTL). We do this based on the hypothesis that listeners use information about the speaker's VTL to estimate their apparent height (see Section 13.1.6). However, we want to note that what we are calling vocal-tract *length* is

DOI: 10.4324/9781003285878-9

274 *Quantitative predictors and their interactions with factors*

actually an acoustic measurement and might more accurately be referred to as spectral scaling. Please see Section 13.1.4 for more information about this.

We're going to keep working with our experimental data originally described in Section 1.3. Below we load our data and R packages and center our continuous predictor (discussed below).

```
library (brms)
library (bmmb)

data (exp_data)

options (contrasts = c('contr.sum','contr.sum'))

# make a copy of the VTL predictor and center it
exp_data$vtl_original = exp_data$vtl
exp_data$vtl = exp_data$vtl - mean(exp_data$vtl)
```

The relevant variables from our data frame are:

*   `height`: A number representing the *height* (in centimeters) reported for the speaker on each trial.
*   `vtl`: An estimate of the speaker's *vocal-tract length* (VTL) in centimeters.

Initially, we will investigate the linear relationship between these two variables. As we progress through this chapter, we're also going to look for variation in this linear relationship based on the following predictors:

*   `C`: A letter representing the speaker *category* (`b`=boy, `g`=girl, `m`=man, `w`=woman) reported by the listener for each trial.
*   `G`: The *apparent gender* of the speaker indicated by the listener, `f` (female) or `m` (male).
*   `A`: The *apparent age* of the speaker indicated by the listener, `a` (adult) or `c` (child).

We're going to keep our research questions simple for now:

(Q1)   Is there a linear relationship between speaker VTL and apparent height?
(Q2)   Can we predict expected apparent height responses given only knowledge of speaker VTL?

9.3 Modeling variation along lines

We're going to start by focusing on the geometry of different model structures. To do this, we're going to ignore the fact that we have repeated measures data and just fit a big complete pooling model as we did in Chapter 3. This will likely lead to overly precise credible intervals for our parameters because it ignores all the correlations in our data and treats all our observations as independent when they are not. However, this approach will allow us to begin with simple models that are easier to discuss before fitting more realistic (and complex) models later in this chapter.

The equation for a line is presented in (9.1). This equation tells us that x and y enter into what's called a *linear relationship* (see Section 6.3.2). The parameters of a line are called its **slope** (*a*) and **intercept** (*b*). Equation (9.1) indicates that x can be transformed into y by multiplying *x* times the slope and then adding the intercept to the product. The slope parameter indicates how much of a change you expect in your y variable for a *1 unit change* in your x variable. This means that the magnitude of the slope depends on the unit of measurement of x. In general, dividing a predictor x by z will increase the slope of x by a factor of z. For example, imagine measuring the slope of a long hill with a constant rise. The amount of rise measured over one meter (e.g. 10 cm) will necessarily be 1/1,000 as large as the rise measured over one kilometer (e.g. 10,000 cm).

$$y = a + b \cdot x \tag{9.1}$$

We can update equation (9.1) as in (9.2), which changes the name of the parameters and replaces *y* with μ. Equation (9.2) now resembles a regression prediction equation where μ is the expected value of the dependent variable you are predicting using the independent variable *x*.

$$\mu = \text{Intercept} + \text{slope} \cdot x \tag{9.2}$$

In Figure 9.1, we plot the average apparent height for each token against the speaker's VTL. The scatter plot below shows the dependent variable (apparent height, the variable we are interested in understanding) along the y-axis and the independent variable (the thing doing the explaining) along the x-axis. Our models so far have only featured categorical predictors, things like speaker category, gender, and age group. Despite this, and although it might be strange to think of it this way, our regression models have been making lines this whole time. However, these lines had slopes of 0 for any given quantitative variable that we might have shown along the x-axis. This could have been speaker VTL or the number of Star Wars movies seen, it doesn't matter because our model had no way to represent its effect. We see an example of such a relationship in the left plot in Figure 9.1.

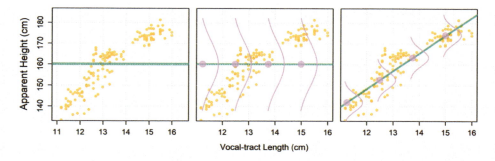

Figure 9.1 (left) Average apparent height plotted against speaker vocal-tract length (VTL) for each token. The horizontal line is at the mean of the observations. (middle) The same points as generated by a normal distribution that slides along a horizontal line with a slope of 0 along the VTL axis. (right) The same points as generated by a normal distribution that slides along a line with a non-zero slope.

276 *Quantitative predictors and their interactions with factors*

The left plot in Figure 9.1 shows the line corresponding to an 'intercept-only model' like the one we fit in Chapter 3. This model features an intercept but no slope, which is equivalent to setting the intercept of our line to the mean of all the data points (160 cm) and setting the slope of the line along VTL to zero, as seen in (9.3).

Intercept = 160, slope = 0

$$\mu = \text{Intercept} + \text{slope} \cdot \text{vtl} \tag{9.3}$$
$$\mu = \text{Intercept} + 0 \cdot \text{vtl}$$
$$\mu = \text{Intercept}$$

When we model apparent height along lines parallel to the VTL dimension, this means our model thinks apparent height is *unrelated to* VTL. This is because VTL can vary from positive to negative infinity and we don't expect the apparent height to change (since the line is flat). So, with intercept-only models you can make horizontal lines, but you only ever change their intercepts. We can see a visual representation of an intercept-only model (for normally distributed data) in the middle plot in Figure 9.1. This model can be thought of as a normal distribution that slides along a horizontal line, generating numbers as it slides. The mean of this data does not vary based on the value of speaker VTL and so it is unrelated to it. The standard deviation of this distribution (σ) does not change as a function of perceived height so the 'width' of the data is stable across values of x.

When you look at the middle plot in Figure 9.1 you might wonder, how could the points all fall below the line for short vocal tracts and above the line for long vocal tracts? Our intercept-only model does not consider variation based on VTL, and so this strange distribution does not 'exist' in the model (i.e. all data points are in 'the same place' along the x-axis as in a boxplot). When we do spread our observations out along the x-axis as in Figure 9.1, we see a clear organization in our observations based on the value of VTL. This suggests that there is a linear relationship between apparent height and speaker VTL, and that our model might benefit from including speaker VTL in its prediction.

To predict apparent height as a function of speaker VTL we include a parameter representing the slope for VTL in our model, i.e. we don't constrain it to be zero as in (9.3). When we tell our model to estimate both an intercept and a slope for VTL, it tries to find the 'best' line that passes through our points. This line might have a slope of zero, but it might not. In general, the 'best' line is one that tends to minimize the square of the *residuals*, the difference between our observed data and our predicted values (see Section 3.5.3). In (9.4) we see that our residual, r, for any given observation (i) is equal to the difference between the observation and the value of our line for the VTL associated with that observation. The reason parameters are generally preferred when they minimize residuals is that smaller residuals lead to larger likelihood values (see Section 2.7.3). Although our Bayesian multilevel models do not solely seek to maximize likelihoods, the likelihood often plays a dominant role in Bayesian model fitting.

$$r_{[i]} = \left(\text{Intercept} + \text{slope} \cdot \text{vtl}_{[i]}\right) - \text{height}_{[i]} \tag{9.4}$$

A model with non-zero slopes for some predictor can be thought of as a normal distribution sliding along a (possibly) *diagonal* line, generating numbers as it slides. In the

Quantitative predictors and their interactions with factors 277

right plot of Figure 9.1 we can see what this might look like. In this model, the y-axis value of the line at a given x-axis location represents the expected value of our dependent variable (μ). The actual values of observations then vary around this expected value in a normally distributed manner with a mean of 0 and a standard deviation equal to σ. This variation around expected values represents the residuals described in (9.4). In other words, $r \sim N(0,\sigma)$. When we model values of apparent height in this way, we're effectively saying that we think apparent height observations vary according to a normal distribution whose mean varies along straight lines *conditional* on the value of VTL.

Notice that the width (standard deviation) of our error distribution is much narrower when we allow expected apparent height to vary as a function of VTL. We've seen this sort of reduction in the error (i.e. σ) before. In the 'intercept-only' model in the middle plot of Figure 9.1, all variation is error, we don't know why any value ever varies from the mean. In contrast, in the right plot, we see that quite a bit of variation in apparent height is (statistically) explainable based on the value of speaker VTL. In this model, it's only variation away from the line that's considered random error.

9.3.1 Description of the model

Just as we did in Chapter 3, we're going to begin with 'incorrect' models that ignore the fact that we have repeated measures data. We can use the `brm` function to find estimates of the slope and intercept of a line through the points in our scatter plot as in Figure 9.1. Our model formula will look like this:

```
height ~ vtl
```

Which tells `brms` to predict `height` based on the values of `vtl` and an intercept which is implicit in the model formula. If the variable on the right-hand side of the ~ is numeric, `brm` will treat it as a quantitative predictor and assume a linear relationship between your dependent and independent variables. You should keep this behavior in mind because it may happen sometimes by accident. For example, if your group names are numeric and treated as such by R, including them in a model will result in them being treated as quantitative by default. To treat numeric predictors as categorical, you can convert them to a factor like this `factor(predictor)`.

The structure of a regression model with a single quantitative predictor (a **bivariate**, two-variable, regression) is shown in (9.5). The first line says that we have a normally distributed variable with an unknown mean that varies from trial to trial $(\mu_{[i]})$. The second line tells us that variation in the mean parameter is along a line with an intercept equal to Intercept and a slope of *VTL* along the VTL axis. We name the slope term (*VTL*) after the quantitative predictor it is associated with (vtl) because this is what R will do. However, we use capital letters to refer to the estimated parameter to help distinguish the two. Note that the predicted value $(\mu_{[i]})$ and the predictor variable $(vtl_{[i]})$ receive subscripts, as these change from trial to trial. However, the slope and intercept *do not* receive subscripts because this model contains a single intercept and a single slope (i.e. it represents a single line) for *every* observation.

278   *Quantitative predictors and their interactions with factors*

$$\text{height}_{[i]} \sim \text{N}\left(\mu_{[i]}, \sigma\right)$$
$$\mu_{[i]} = \text{Intercept} + VTL \cdot \text{vtl}_{[i]}$$

Priors: $\quad\quad\quad\quad\quad\quad\quad\quad\quad\quad$ (9.5)
$$\text{Intercept} \sim \text{t}(3, 160, 12)$$
$$VTL \sim \text{t}(3, 0, 12)$$
$$\sigma \sim \text{t}(3, 0, 12)$$

In plain English, our model says:

> *We are modeling apparent height as coming from a normal distribution with unknown mean (μ), and standard deviation (σ) parameters. The expected value for any given trial (μ) is modeled as the sum of an intercept, and the product of the VTL predictor and the VTL slope. The 'fixed' effects were all given prior distributions appropriate for their expected range of values.*

Here are two other ways to think about this model. First, we can think of it as making a line and then adding noise to it, as in (9.6). From this perspective, each of our observed values is the sum of a line (representing systematic variation) plus a random draw from an error distribution $\left(\text{N}(0, \sigma)\right)$.

$$\text{height}_{[i]} = \text{Intercept} + VTL \cdot \text{vtl}_{[i]} + \text{N}(0, \sigma) \quad\quad\quad\quad (9.6)$$

Alternatively, we could place the formula for the line *inside* the normal distribution function, as in (9.7). There's no particular reason to do this, but it's helpful to see it and realize that it will result in the same output as (9.6).

$$\text{height}_{[i]} = \text{N}\left(\text{Intercept} + VTL \cdot \text{vtl}_{[i]}, \sigma\right) \quad\quad\quad\quad (9.7)$$

In (9.6), we say: The data varies deterministically along a line, and normally distributed error with a mean of 0 and a standard deviation equal to σ is added to this line. In (9.7), we're saying: The data is generated according to a normal distribution whose mean varies along a line, and we expect the variation around this line to have a standard deviation equal to σ.

9.3.2 Centering quantitative predictors

There's one more thing to discuss before fitting our model, and that is the potential utility of *centering* quantitative predictors (first discussed in Section 2.5.4). To center a quantitative predictor you subtract the sample mean from the observations in the sample. When we subtract the sample mean from our observations, each observation will now represent a deviation from 0 and the sum (and mean) of all the observations will equal zero (see Section 2.5.1). For example, if we subtract 4 from the numbers 3, 4, and 5 we get −1, 0, and 1.

When you carry out a regression with a single quantitative predictor, the intercept is the value of your dependent variable (y) when your predictor (x) is equal to 0 (i.e. when the line 'crosses' the y-axis). Often, you won't specifically care about the value of the dependent variable when the value of your predictor is zero. For example, we don't care what the expected apparent height is when VTL equals zero because a VTL of zero centimeters does not exist in human beings. In the left plot of Figure 9.2, we see the intercept of a line going through our observations with an 'uncentered' VTL. This tells us that a speaker with a VTL of 0 cm is expected to sound about 50 cm tall. This is not very useful information, and it is also obviously false (newborn babies are about 50 cm long and have non-zero VTLs).

In the right plot in Figure 9.2 we see the result of centering VTL. Since the intercept of a line is the value of the dependent variable (y) when the predictor (x) is equal to zero, centering our predictor makes the intercept equal to the value of y when x is at its mean value. As a result, centering our quantitative predictors often makes the value of the intercept more interpretable. For example, our mean VTL value is 13.47 meaning that after centering this value is at 0. As a result, we know that the intercept of the line in the right plot in Figure 9.2 corresponds to the expected apparent height for a VTL of 13.4 cm, an actual VTL value that we might be interested in (as opposed to a VTL of 0 cm).

Centering predictor variables affects the intercept of the model, but it does not affect the slope or any other aspect of the model. For example, in the middle and right plots in Figure 9.2, we see that centering has changed the x-axis and moved our intercept to the mean VTL, but has not otherwise affected the plot. Thus, centering is basically like choosing the 'coding' (e.g. sum coding vs. treatment coding) for lines: It affects how the information is represented in the model but not the information itself. As a result, centering can be tremendously useful in yielding more interpretable intercept estimates. It can also greatly facilitate setting priors on the model intercept. For example, when the predictor is centered we just need to think of a reasonable value for our dependent variable when the predictor is at its mean, which is often a meaningful and common value. This is often easier to do than to imagine the expected value of the dependent variable when the predictor is equal to zero.

Based on this, we will be centering our quantitative predictors simply because zero is not a useful or meaningful value for them, and so centering makes the intercepts

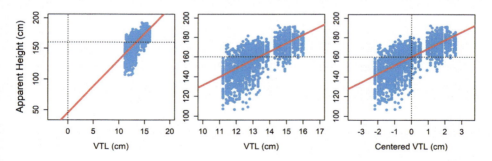

Figure 9.2 (left) Individual apparent height judgments plotted against speaker vocal-tract length (VTL). (middle) The same points as in the left plot, but focused on the region containing the observations. (right) The same points as in the middle, but plotted according to centered VTL. In each plot, the horizontal line represents the mean of the points and the vertical line represents the y-intercept.

280   *Quantitative predictors and their interactions with factors*

more easily interpretable for our data. In your own work, the decision whether to center or not should be based on the information you hope to get out of your model (e.g. is 0 meaningful for your predictors?), just like the decision regarding which coding system to use for nominal variables.

9.3.3 Fitting and interpreting the model

We can use the `brm` function to find the intercept and slope of the 'best' line through the points in our scatter plot in Figure 9.2.

```
# Fit the model yourself
model_single_line =
  brm (height ~ vtl, data = exp_data, chains=1, cores=1,
       warmup=1000, iter = 6000,
       prior = c(set_prior("student_t(3, 160, 12)", class = "Intercept"),
                 set_prior("student_t(3, 0, 12)", class = "b"),
                 set_prior("student_t(3, 0, 12)", class = "sigma")))

# Or download it from the GitHub page:
model_single_line = bmmb::get_model ('9_model_single_line.RDS')
```

The model print statement should be mostly familiar by now. Our model contains only population-level ('fixed') effects: an `Intercept`, indicating the intercept of our line, and `vtl` indicating the slope of the line relating VTL and apparent height. In addition, we get an estimate of the residual error (`sigma`, σ) around our line.

```
bmmb::short_summary (model_single_line)
## Formula:  height ~ vtl
## Population-Level Effects:
##            Estimate Est.Error l-95% CI u-95% CI
## Intercept    160.13      0.23   159.68   160.60
## vtl            8.56      0.18     8.21     8.89
##
## Family Specific Parameters:
##         Estimate Est.Error l-95% CI u-95% CI
## sigma      10.79      0.17    10.47    11.12
```

We can see that the line predicting apparent height as a function of speaker VTL has an intercept of 160 cm and a slope for the `vtl` predictor of 8.6. Let's discuss the intercept first. Recall that for a bivariate regression (like ours) the intercept is the value of the dependent variable when the independent variable is equal to zero. Since we're using a centered predictor, when the mean of our `vtl` predictor is equal to zero, it is *really* (secretly) equal to its *true* mean of 13.4 cm (`mean(exp_data$vtl_original)`). This means that when a speaker's VTL equals 13.4 cm, we expect apparent height to equal 160.1 cm. The model *thinks* the mean of `vtl` is 0, but we *know* it is 13.4 cm, and the centering of the predictor does not affect our ability to interpret it as such.

The slope of the `vtl` predictor is 8.6, meaning that for every 1 cm increase in vocal-tract length we expect an *increase* of 8.6 cm in apparent height. The slope is a *weight* that allows the line to accurately fit the points. In the absence of a slope, regression models would only work if there was a 1-to-1 relationship between the x and y variables. This would mean that for every 1 cm change in VTL we would need to see a 1 cm change in apparent height. What are the odds that the things we measure will be in a 1-to-1 relationship with all of our predictors? Very small. Instead, the slope coefficient in regression models allows a single unit change in the predictor to be associated with different units of change in the variable you're trying to understand.

Figure 9.3 shows our observations compared to the line estimated using our model (height = Intercept + $VTL \cdot$ vtl = 160.1 + 8.6 $\cdot$ vtl). What does this line mean? It means that *if* the mean apparent height is linearly related to speaker VTL *and* the data is normally distributed around this mean with a fixed error (σ), *and* the rest of the details of our model are also true, *then* our best guess for the line relating centered VTL to apparent height has an intercept of 160.1 cm and a slope of 8.6 cm change in apparent height per 1 cm change in VTL. The previous sentence contained a lot of *ifs* and *ands*. Since we know that our assumptions are probably only approximately true, this means that we should treat our model parameters as (at best) an approximation of the underlying relationships we're trying to understand.

We can see that the residuals (as reflected by variation about our line in Figure 9.3) are much larger and more negative for smaller (negative) values of VTL than they are for larger values. Since our model has a single, fixed σ for all values of VTL (10.8), our model should have an error with a constant amount of variation around the predicted values. Since our model can't account for the sort of variation we see in our data, maybe our model could be better. One possible explanation for this lack of fit is that rather than varying around one single line, our data might be thought of as varying

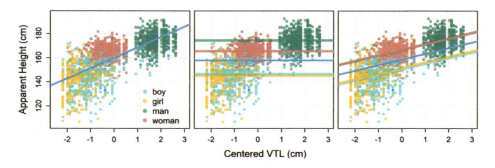

Figure 9.3 (left) Apparent speaker height plotted against speaker VTL for each data point. The line represents the linear relationship between apparent height and VTL for all points. Point colors represent speaker classifications. (middle) The same points as in the left plot. The horizontal lines represent category-dependent lines all constrained to have a slope of zero. The blue line represents the overall intercept. (right) The same points as in the left plot. The lines represent category-dependent lines with shared (but non-zero) slopes. The blue line represents the overall line.

282   *Quantitative predictors and their interactions with factors*

around *four* separate lines, one for each group, as seen in the middle and right plots of Figure 9.3. We will consider this possibility in the following section.

9.4 Models with group-dependent intercepts, but shared slopes

In Chapter 7 we fit a model (`model_four_groups`) that predicted apparent height based on apparent speaker category. This model can be thought of as having one line for each speaker category. These lines differ in their intercepts, however, since this model did not include VTL as a predictor each line effectively had a slope of 0 for VTL (as in the middle plot in Figure 9.3,). In this section, we're going to consider a model that allows for differing intercepts between groups but constrains these to have the same slope, as in the right plot in Figure 9.3.

We allow for category-dependent intercepts for our lines by including a nominal predictor specifying apparent speaker category (`C`) in our model formula, in addition to `vtl`:

```
height ~ C + vtl
```

The formula above says: "model apparent height as a function of VTL, allowing for group-specific variation in the intercept". The `C` and `vtl` terms in our formula represent *main effects*, overall, marginal effects. Our model does *not* include the interaction between `C` and `vtl`. Thus, our model can tell us about the overall slope for VTL but can't tell us if the VTL slope varies conditionally across levels of `C`.

9.4.1 *Description of the model*

The formula above corresponds to the model presented in (9.8). The prediction equation is just like that of our previous model save for the addition of the $C_{\left[\mathsf{c}_{[i]}\right]}$ term. It is also very similar to the fixed effects structure of the four-group model we fit in Chapter 7, save for the addition of the $VTL \cdot \mathrm{vtl}_{[i]}$ term.

$$\mathrm{height}_{[i]} \sim \mathrm{N}\left(\mu_{[i]}, \sigma\right)$$
$$\mu_{[i]} = \mathrm{Intercept} + C_{\left[\mathsf{c}_{[i]}\right]} + VTL \cdot \mathrm{vtl}_{[i]}$$

$$\begin{aligned}
\mathrm{Priors:}& \\
\mathrm{Intercept} &\sim \mathrm{t}(3,160,12) \\
VTL &\sim \mathrm{t}(3,0,12) \\
C_{[\bullet]} &\sim \mathrm{t}(3,0,12) \\
\sigma &\sim \mathrm{t}(3,0,12)
\end{aligned} \tag{9.8}$$

In our model, the C coefficients do not get multiplied by the `vtl`-dependent variable in our prediction equation. As a result, the slope of our line along VTL is *entirely* determined by the VTL coefficient. We can present an alternate, but equivalent, parametrization of this model that better conveys the organization of parameters into those affecting the slope and those affecting the intercepts of our prediction lines.

Quantitative predictors and their interactions with factors 283

The model in (9.9) specifies a line in terms of trial-specific a and b parameters, where a and b are linear combinations of estimated parameters in the model.

$$\text{height}_{[i]} \sim \text{N}\left(\mu_{[i]}, \sigma\right)$$

$$\mu_{[i]} = a_{[i]} + b_{[i]} \cdot \text{vtl}_{[i]}$$

$$a_{[i]} = \text{Intercept} + C_{\left[c_{[i]}\right]}$$

$$b_{[i]} = VTL$$

$$\text{Priors:} \tag{9.9}$$

$$\text{Intercept} \sim \text{t}(3,160,12)$$

$$VTL \sim \text{t}(3,0,12)$$

$$C_{[\bullet]} \sim \text{t}(3,0,12)$$

$$\sigma \sim \text{t}(3,0,12)$$

In plain English, our model says:

> *We are modeling apparent height as coming from a normal distribution with unknown mean (μ), and standard deviation (σ) parameters. The expected value for any given trial (μ) is modeled as the sum of a trial-specific intercept ($a_{[i]}$), and the product of the VTL predictor and a trial-specific VTL slope ($b_{[i]}$). The trial-specific intercept is equal to the sum of the model intercept (Intercept) and an effect for the apparent category of the speaker who produced that trial $\left(C_{\left[c_{[i]}\right]}\right)$. The trial-specific slope is equal to VTL slope (VTL) for all trials. The 'fixed' effects were all given prior distributions appropriate for their expected range of values.*

Although it may be strange to think of it this way, in a sense our model intercept is the 'main effect' for the intercept or the 'intercept intercept'. By this, we mean that this is the reference value we use for the intercept of our line. The C coefficients therefore represent the interaction of our intercept and category, that is, they represent *category-dependent*, variation for our intercept. Unlike our intercept, the slope term does not actually vary from trial to trial in practice, since it simply equals our *VTL* slope parameter for every trial. This single parameter can be thought of as the 'intercept', or the main effect, for our *VTL* slope, a concept that will be expanded on when we include category-dependent slopes in our model a little later in this chapter.

Finally, note that a and b in (9.9) don't get priors, and in fact, were not mentioned at all in our model formula above. This is because these parameters don't actually 'exist', we're just using them as a notational device to organize the way we think of the parameters in our models. As a result, the models in (9.8) and (9.9) are equivalent.

9.4.2 Fitting and interpreting the model

We fit a model that contains the apparent speaker category as a predictor in addition to speaker VTL, but not the interaction between the two. This model corresponds to that presented in the right plot of 9.3.

284 *Quantitative predictors and their interactions with factors*

```
# Fit the model yourself
model_many_intercept_one_slope =
  brm (height ~ C + vtl,
       data=exp_data, chains=1,cores=1,warmup=1000,iter=6000,
       prior = c(set_prior("student_t(3, 160, 12)", class = "Intercept"),
                 set_prior("student_t(3, 0, 12)", class = "b"),
                 set_prior("student_t(3, 0, 12)", class = "sigma")))


# Or download it from the GitHub page:
model_many_intercept_one_slope =
  bmmb::get_model ('9_model_many_intercept_one_slope.RDS')
```

For the sake of comparison, we also fit a model with speaker category as a predictor, but excluding speaker VTL (i.e. no quantitative predictor). As noted above, this is effectively a model with a bunch of horizontal lines, one for each group. This sort of model is seen in the middle plot of 9.3, and an abbreviated model description is presented in (9.10).

$$
\begin{aligned}
\text{height}_{[i]} &\sim \text{N}\left(\mu_{[i]}, \sigma\right) \\
\mu_{[i]} &= a_{[i]} + b_{[i]} \cdot \text{vtl}_{[i]} \\
a_{[i]} &= \text{Intercept} + C_{\left[\text{c}_{[i]}\right]} \\
b_{[i]} &= 0
\end{aligned}
\tag{9.10}
$$

This model is very similar to `model_four_groups` from Chapter 7, except for the omission of 'random effects' related to speaker and listener. We refit this simpler model here to allow for a more direct comparison to the model above.

```
# Fit the model yourself
model_many_intercept_no_slope =
 brm (height ~ C,
       data=exp_data, chains=1,cores=1,warmup=1000,iter=6000,
       prior = c(set_prior("student_t(3, 160, 12)", class = "Intercept"),
                 set_prior("student_t(3, 0, 12)", class = "b"),
                 set_prior("student_t(3, 0, 12)", class = "sigma")))


# Or download it from the GitHub page:
model_many_intercept_no_slope =
  bmmb::get_model ('9_model_many_intercept_no_slope.RDS')
```

It's useful to think about the geometry of our models because pictures are often much easier to interpret than coefficient values. The coefficient values in your model have a one-to-one relationship with a set of lines that make up a plot. Seeing (or imagining) the implied geometry of your model can go a long way toward understanding the meaning of your model parameters. Below, we recover the overall intercept and the intercept for each group from `model_many_intercept_no_slope`. These parameters specify the lines for the middle plot in Figure 9.3. Since this model contains

Quantitative predictors and their interactions with factors   285

no slope terms, these values represent the intercepts of horizontal lines, one for each group (and overall). Since the lines all have the same slope (0), they will necessarily be parallel to the VTL axis.

```
many_intercept_no_slope_hypothesis = bmmb::short_hypothesis (
  model_many_intercept_no_slope,
  hypothesis =
    c("Intercept = 0",                      # overall intercept
      "Intercept + C1 = 0",                 # group 1 intercept
      "Intercept + C2 = 0",                 # group 2 intercept
      "Intercept + C3 = 0",                 # group 3 intercept
      "Intercept - (C1+C2+C3) = 0"))        # group 4 intercept


many_intercept_no_slope_hypothesis
##      Estimate Est.Error   Q2.5 Q97.5                    hypothesis
## H1     158.0    0.2123  157.5 158.4              (Intercept) = 0
## H2     146.5    0.4613  145.6 147.4           (Intercept+C1) = 0
## H3     145.4    0.4531  144.5 146.3            Intercept+C2) = 0
## H4     174.4    0.3738  173.7 175.1           (Intercept+C3) = 0
## H5     165.6    0.3987  164.8 166.4 (Intercept-(C1+C2+C3)) = 0
```

We can also recover the intercepts for each group from `model_many_intercept_one_slope`. These parameters specify the lines for the right plot in Figure 9.3. Like our previous model, this model has a different intercept for each line. However, these lines *can* (and do) have a non-zero slope, albeit one shared by all. As a result, both models are still only capable of representing parallel lines for our four speaker groups.

```
many_intercept_one_slope_hypothesis = bmmb::short_hypothesis (
  model_many_intercept_one_slope,
  hypothesis =
    c("Intercept = 0",                      # overall intercept
      "Intercept + C1 = 0",                 # group 1 intercept
      "Intercept + C2 = 0",                 # group 2 intercept
      "Intercept + C3 = 0",                 # group 3 intercept
      "Intercept + - (C1+C2+C3)=0",         # group 4 intercept
      "vtl = 0"))                           # overall slope


many_intercept_one_slope_hypothesis
##     Estimate Est.Error     Q2.5    Q97.5                       hypothesis
## H1  158.796    0.2138  158.374  159.214               (Intercept) = 0
## H2  150.245    0.5184  149.246  151.258            (Intercept+C1) = 0
## H3  151.503    0.6145  150.317  152.712            (Intercept+C2) = 0
## H4  166.752    0.6352  165.515  167.977            (Intercept+C3) = 0
## H5  166.685    0.3883  165.916  167.450 (Intercept+-(C1+C2+C3)) = 0
## H6    4.604    0.3169    3.974    5.219                     (vtl) = 0
```

286 *Quantitative predictors and their interactions with factors*

9.4.3 Interpreting group effects in the presence of shared (non-zero) slopes

When our only predictor was C, the C coefficients reflected differences between the group means and the intercept (the mean of the group means). In this situation, the C model parameters reflect group-dependent differences in the intercept of the lines for your groups, i.e. the spacing between the lines along the y-axis. When you include a quantitative predictor, the group effects *still* represent differences in the line intercepts *when VTL is equal to zero*. Of course, since the lines will be parallel, the spacing between the lines where VTL is equal to zero will also be the spacing between the lines when VTL is equal to any other value. So, when lines share a slope, group effects change the spacing between parallel lines and this is true whether the shared slope is zero or some non-zero value.

We're going to compare the estimated group effects provided by the two models presented above: `model_many_intercept_no_slope`, and `model_many_intercept_many_slope`. Below, we use the `short_hypothesis` function to get the group effects for our model with no slope:

```
group_no_slope_effects = bmmb::short_hypothesis (
  model_many_intercept_no_slope,
  hypothesis = c("C1 = 0",              # group 1 effect
                 "C2 = 0",              # group 2 effect
                 "C3 = 0",              # group 3 effect
                 "-(C1+C2+C3) = 0"))    # group 4 effect
group_no_slope_effects
##     Estimate Est.Error   Q2.5    Q97.5           hypothesis
## H1   -11.455    0.3893 -12.22  -10.695            (C1) = 0
## H2   -12.574    0.3821 -13.34  -11.817            (C2) = 0
## H3    16.434    0.3411  15.77   17.098            (C3) = 0
## H4     7.595    0.3503   6.90    8.279  (-(C1+C2+C3)) = 0
```

And with a slope:

```
group_single_slope_effects = bmmb::short_hypothesis (
  model_many_intercept_one_slope,
  hypothesis = c("C1 = 0",              # group 1 effect
                 "C2 = 0",              # group 2 effect
                 "C3 = 0",              # group 3 effect
                 "-(C1+C2+C3) = 0"))    # group 4 effect

group_single_slope_effects
##     Estimate Est.Error   Q2.5    Q97.5           hypothesis
## H1    -8.551    0.4272 -9.368  -7.726             (C1) = 0
## H2    -7.293    0.5207 -8.300  -6.285             (C2) = 0
## H3     7.956    0.6702  6.657   9.272             (C3) = 0
## H4     7.889    0.3392  7.218   8.564   (-(C1+C2+C3)) = 0
```

Although the group effects reflect the spacing between parallel lines in both models, the inclusion of a slope clearly results in changes in this spacing. We can use `brmplot` to visually compare the group effects across the models in Figure 9.4. The other two plots in the figure present the parallel lines implied by the group effects (ignoring the slopes) for the model with no slope and the model with a shared slope respectively (seen in the middle and right plots of Figure 9.3). We see that the group effects are smaller in magnitude when the quantitative predictor is included. This is visually apparent in the tighter clustering of the lines in the right plot of Figure 9.4. By the way, since the group effects change the spacing of the lines for each group, in the absence of group effects we would just see four overlapping lines and our model would be just like `model_single_line` we fit above.

Our comparison of the group effects across the two models tells us that the difference in line intercepts according to apparent gender becomes much smaller when we include VTL as a predictor. We can see why this is in Figure 9.3. When VTL is not included as a predictor, the difference in apparent height between women and men, and girls and boys, can only be 'explained' by a difference in line intercepts. In contrast, when we include VTL as a predictor, the difference in apparent height between these groups can potentially be explained based on the average difference in VTL between these categories of speakers.

The fact that the lines representing men and women in `model_many_intercept_one_slope` have the same intercept indicates that, *given a fixed value of VTL*, we expect adult males and females to be about the same apparent height. This does *not* mean that men and women have the same average apparent height in our data, we know that they do not. Instead, it suggests that, if we take into account only the VTL of a given talker, the apparent speaker category does not predict any additional systematic variation in apparent speaker height for adults.

We can again think of this as a reduction in the variation associated with one model component after introducing some more complexity to our model. Previously, our model could only explain the differences in apparent height based on variation according to the apparent speaker category. Now, armed with knowledge of speaker VTL, our model says: "Actually there is no intercept difference between the male and female lines. If you slide the group mean along a line based on VTL, you can get from the adult female mean to the adult male mean using *the same line*".

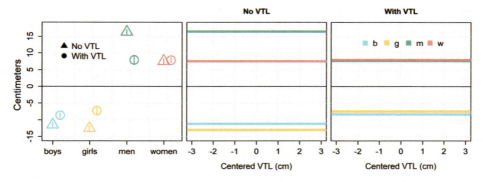

Figure 9.4 (left) Comparison of estimated group effects for the models with and without the VTL predictor. (middle) Lines reflect the triangle coefficients in the left plot. (right) Lines reflect the circle coefficients in the left plot.

288　*Quantitative predictors and their interactions with factors*

9.5　Models with group-dependent slopes and intercepts

Our previous model was ok, but ideally, our model would allow for the possibility of differences in slopes across apparent speaker categories. If we want to include group-dependent slopes, in addition to intercepts, we must consider the value of the VTL slope *conditional* on apparent speaker category. To do this, we need to include the *interaction* (see Section 7.5) between apparent category and VTL in our model using either of the two formulas below:

```
height ~ C * vtl
height ~ C + vtl + vtl:C
```

In either case, the model above says: "model apparent height as a function of VTL (vtl), allowing for category-dependent variation in intercepts (C), and a category-dependent VTL slope (vtl:C)".

9.5.1　Description of the model

In (9.11) we present an 'expanded' version of our prediction equation where each term that relates to the slope (i.e. $VTL, VTL:C$) is independently multiplied by our VTL predictor $\left(\mathrm{vtl}_{[i]}\right)$.

$$\mu_{[i]} = \text{Intercept} + C_{\left[\mathsf{c}_{[i]}\right]} + VTL \cdot \mathrm{vtl}_{[i]} + VTL:C_{\left[\mathsf{c}_{[i]}\right]} \cdot \mathrm{vtl}_{[i]} \tag{9.11}$$

The equation above says that our expected value for a given trial i is equal to the sum of the intercept (Intercept), the category predictor $\left(C_{\left[\mathsf{c}_{[i]}\right]}\right)$, the product of VTL and the VTL slope 'main effect' $\left(VTL \cdot \mathrm{vtl}_{[i]}\right)$, and the product of VTL and the VTL slope by category interaction $\left(VTL:C_{\left[\mathsf{c}_{[i]}\right]} \cdot \mathrm{vtl}_{[i]}\right)$. We can group the terms affecting intercepts, and those affecting slopes, in parenthesis as in (9.12).

$$\mu_{[i]} = \left(\text{Intercept} + C_{\left[\mathsf{c}_{[i]}\right]}\right) + \left(VTL \cdot \mathrm{vtl}_{[i]} + VTL:C_{\left[\mathsf{c}_{[i]}\right]} \cdot \mathrm{vtl}_{[i]}\right) \tag{9.12}$$

We can factor out the VTL predictor from the second parenthesis as in (9.13).

$$\mu_{[i]} = \left(\text{Intercept} + C_{\left[\mathsf{c}_{[i]}\right]}\right) + \left(VTL + VTL:C_{\left[\mathsf{c}_{[i]}\right]}\right) \cdot \mathrm{vtl}_{[i]} \tag{9.13}$$

At this point, despite the complexity, we can see that our model consists of an expanded intercept and an expanded slope. We can break up our prediction equation into three elements as we did in (9.9): One for our expected value, one for the intercept, and one for the slope. We replace the terms on the right-hand side in (9.13) with a and b, and define each on its own line in (9.14).

$$\mu_{[i]} = a_{[i]} + b_{[i]} \cdot \mathrm{vtl}_{[i]}$$
$$a_{[i]} = \text{Intercept} + C_{\left[\mathsf{c}_{[i]}\right]} \tag{9.14}$$
$$b_{[i]} = VTL + VTL:C_{\left[\mathsf{c}_{[i]}\right]})$$

Quantitative predictors and their interactions with factors 289

The three equations in (9.14) say:

- Our expected apparent height (μ) varies according to a trial-dependent intercept (a) and VTL slope (b) parameters.
- The intercept for a given trial is equal to the Intercept (the intercept main effect) and the C predictor (effectively, the Intercept : C interaction).
- The slope expected on a given trial is equal to the VTL predictor (effectively, the slope 'main effect') and the $VTL : C$ interaction.

As our models get more and more complicated, it can help to organize them in this manner. By thinking of all our terms as either 'main effects' or 'interactions' for the different predictors in our data, we can organize our understanding of how different parameters are expected to relate to the dependent variable. For example, (9.14) makes it clear that the $VTL : C$ predictor can affect the *slopes* of our lines, but has no mechanism by which to affect our line *intercepts*. Below, we compare a model specification that puts all our predictors directly in the prediction equation:

$$\text{height}_{[i]} \sim \text{N}\left(\mu_{[i]}, \sigma\right)$$

$$\mu_{[i]} = \left(\text{Intercept} + C_{\left[C_{[i]}\right]}\right) + \left(VTL \cdot \text{vtl}_{[i]} + VTL : C_{\left[C_{[i]}\right]} \cdot \text{vtl}_{[i]}\right)$$

$$
\begin{aligned}
&\text{Priors:} \\
&\text{Intercept} \sim \text{t}\left(3, 160, 12\right) \\
&VTL \sim \text{t}\left(3, 0, 12\right) \\
&C_{[\bullet]} \sim \text{t}\left(3, 0, 12\right) \\
&VTL : C_{[\bullet]} \sim \text{t}\left(3, 0, 12\right) \\
&\sigma \sim \text{t}\left(3, 0, 12\right)
\end{aligned}
\tag{9.15}
$$

To one that organizes parameters into those affecting intercepts and those affecting slopes:

$$\text{height}_{[i]} \sim \text{N}\left(\mu_{[i]}, \sigma\right)$$

$$\mu_{[i]} = a_{[i]} + b_{[i]} \cdot \text{vtl}_{[i]}$$

$$a_{[i]} = \text{Intercept} + C_{\left[C_{[i]}\right]}$$

$$b_{[i]} = VTL + VTL : C_{\left[C_{[i]}\right]}$$

$$
\begin{aligned}
&\text{Priors:} \\
&\text{Intercept} \sim \text{t}\left(3, 160, 12\right) \\
&VTL \sim \text{t}\left(3, 0, 12\right) \\
&C_{[\bullet]} \sim \text{t}\left(3, 0, 12\right) \\
&VTL : C_{[\bullet]} \sim \text{t}\left(3, 0, 12\right) \\
&\sigma \sim \text{t}\left(3, 0, 12\right)
\end{aligned}
\tag{9.16}
$$

290 *Quantitative predictors and their interactions with factors*

We think the latter is clearer and will use it in our model descriptions where appropriate. Our plain English description is now:

We are modeling apparent height as coming from a normal distribution with unknown mean (μ), and standard deviation (σ) parameters. The expected value for any given trial (μ) is modeled as the sum of a trial-specific intercept ($a_{[i]}$), and the product of the VTL predictor and a trial-specific VTL slope ($b_{[i]}$). The trial-specific intercept is equal to the sum of the model intercept (Intercept) and an effect for the apparent category of the speaker who produced that trial ($C_{[c_{[i]}]}$). The trial-specific slope is equal to the sum of the VTL slope (VTL) and the interaction between VTL slope and apparent speaker category ($VTL : C_{[c_{[i]}]}$). The 'fixed' effects were all given prior distributions appropriate for their expected range of values.

9.5.2 *Fitting and interpreting the model*

We fit the model with group-dependent intercepts and slopes below. Remember that the line `set_prior("student_t(3, 0, 12)", class = "b")` sets the prior for all non-intercept 'Population-Level' predictors (i.e. fixed effects). This includes all of our main effects predictors and our interaction terms.

```
# Fit the model yourself
options (contrasts = c('contr.sum','contr.sum'))
model_multi_slope =
  brm (height ~ C + vtl + vtl:C,
       data=exp_data, chains=1,cores=1,warmup=1000,iter=6000,
       prior = c(set_prior("student_t(3, 160, 12)", class = "Intercept"),
                 set_prior("student_t(3, 0, 12)", class = "b"),
                 set_prior("student_t(3, 0, 12)", class = "sigma")))

# Or download it from the GitHub page:
model_multi_slope = bmmb::get_model ('9_model_multi_slope.RDS')
```

We inspect the model 'fixed effects' below and see that our model contains eight parameters. These are necessary because the model we fit looks for a linear relationship between VTL and apparent height and allows for a different line representing this relationship for our four apparent speaker categories. Since each line requires two parameters to be specified, our four lines will necessarily require eight coefficients, four intercepts, and four slopes.

```
# inspect fixed effects
brms::fixef (model_multi_slope)
##               Estimate Est.Error     Q2.5    Q97.5
## Intercept      160.800    0.4525  159.935  161.690
## C1              -9.420    0.6208  -10.632   -8.221
## C2              -4.834    0.8904   -6.580   -3.090
## C3               9.279    1.0062    7.316   11.283
## vtl              4.271    0.3463    3.582    4.937
```

```
## C1:vtl         1.438      0.5067     0.448     2.433
## C2:vtl         3.747      0.6181     2.544     4.937
## C3:vtl        -1.666      0.6069    -2.913    -0.507
```

We can recover the overall (main effects) intercept and slope directly from the model estimates. We can get the group-specific intercept and slopes by adding the 'main effects' and the appropriate parameters. The first five values below are intercepts and the next five are slopes. Note that we are missing one intercept (C4) and one slope (C4:vtl), each corresponding to the last level of the C predictor. To recover the 'missing' intercept (and slope), we find the negative sum of the parameters that *are* estimated (see Section 5.6.2).

```
multi_slope_hypothesis = bmmb::short_hypothesis (
  model_multi_slope,
  hypothesis =
    c("Intercept = 0",                              # overall intercept
      "Intercept + C1 = 0",                         # group 1 mean
      "Intercept + C2 = 0",                         # group 2 mean
      "Intercept + C3 = 0",                         # group 3 mean
      "Intercept + -(C1+C2+C3) = 0",                # group 4 mean
      "vtl = 0",                                    # overall slope
      "vtl + C1:vtl = 0",                           # group 1 slope
      "vtl + C2:vtl = 0",                           # group 2 slope
      "vtl + C3:vtl = 0",                           # group 3 slope
      "vtl + -(C1:vtl+C2:vtl+C3:vtl) = 0"))         # group 4 slope
```

These coefficients are presented in Figure 9.5 and are used to make the lines in the right plot of the figure. We can see that the lines seem to have substantially different slopes and intercepts between the four groups, suggesting that the relative complexity of this model is likely justified.

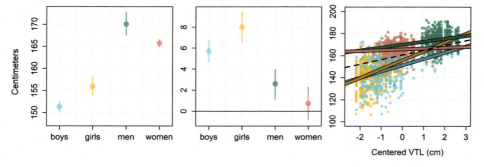

Figure 9.5 (left) Posterior means and 95% credible intervals for group-specific intercepts. (middle) Group-specific VTL slopes. (right) Lines for each speaker group based on the slopes and intercepts in the left and middle plots. Group colors match the other plots.

292 *Quantitative predictors and their interactions with factors*

9.5.3 *Interpreting group effects in the presence of varying slopes*

When the lines representing the groups in our model all share a slope, the intercept is very easy to interpret: It is the spacing between parallel lines representing our groups. Because of this, the group predictors represent the difference between our groups for *all* values of VTL. However, when the lines representing our groups do *not* share a slope, the group intercepts reflect the spacing of the lines *only* when the quantitative predictor (in this case VTL) is *exactly* equal to zero. For example, consider the intercept parameters in the left plot of Figure 9.5 and compare these to the spacing of the lines in the right plot of the same figure. It's clear that the intercepts represent the spacing of the lines when VTL equals zero and *at no other point*. For example, the spacing between the lines is substantially different when VTL is 2 or negative 2.

Recall that we subtracted 13.4 from our VTL predictor so that 0 represents a real VTL value of 13.4. Imagine that we had decided to subtract our minimum VTL value, 11.2 cm, from the predictor instead. This would be perfectly acceptable and would simply move the 0 in the right plot in Figure 9.5 to the point that now says −2. If we did this, our group effects would now reflect the spacing of the lines at the left edge of the plot (at −2) rather than in the middle of the plot (at 0). As a result, the category-dependent intercepts in this model would be substantially different from those we see in Figure 9.5, while at the same time reflecting *the same* lines.

When the lines for different groups in our model do not share a slope, i.e. when there is a non-zero interaction between our slope parameter and the group predictor, intercepts must be interpreted with caution. It is important to avoid seeing that one group has a higher intercept and thinking "this group has higher values of the dependent variable in general, for all values of VTL". This reasoning will only hold if all groups share a slope (as in the right plot in Figure 9.3). Instead, if groups do not share a slope then the spacing between the lines for each group needs to be considered for specific values of the quantitative predictor.

9.6 Answering our research questions: Interim discussion

We're going to provide a simple, interim answer for our research questions, keeping in mind that our models are not 'proper' repeated measures models.

(Q1) Is there a linear relationship between speaker VTL and apparent height?
(Q2) Can we predict expected apparent height responses given only knowledge of speaker VTL?

Yes, there definitely seems to be a linear relationship between apparent speaker height and speaker VTL. And yes, it appears that we can predict speaker height responses given only knowledge of speaker VTL. However, it also appears that the relationship between apparent height and VTL may vary based on apparent speaker category such that using *only* VTL will not result in the best estimates from among the models we've considered so far.

9.7 Data and research questions: Updated

One obvious way to improve our models is to include speaker and listener-related predictors. In particular, we may want to consider how different listeners used VTL in order to make height judgments since this is extremely unlikely to be identical for all listeners. Now that we've covered the inclusion of quantitative predictors and discussed their interactions with categorical predictors, we can start talking about models where these characteristics vary across the levels of our grouping variable (e.g. listener). For example, just like we found that the slope for VTL varies across levels of the apparent speaker category, maybe it also varies across levels of the listener factor.

In addition to adding information about speakers and listeners to our model, we're going to *decompose* our speaker category predictor (C) into the effect of apparent age and gender, in the same way we did in Chapter 7. However, this time we're going to perform this decomposition on both the model intercept and the model slope. Our research questions are:

(Q1) What is the linear relationship between speaker VTL and apparent height?
(Q2) Is the effect of VTL on apparent height affected by the apparent age and gender of the speaker?

We again load our data and packages (just in case), and center our VTL predictor:

```
library (brms)
library (bmmb)

data (exp_data)

options (contrasts = c('contr.sum','contr.sum'))

# make a copy of the VTL predictor and center it
exp_data$vtl_original = exp_data$vtl
exp_data$vtl = exp_data$vtl - mean(exp_data$vtl)
```

We require some additional predictors for this more complicated model. The relevant variables from our data frame are now:

*   L: A number from 1 to 15 indicating which *listener* responded to the trial.
*   height: A number representing the *height* (in centimeters) reported for the speaker on each trial.
*   S: A number from 1 to 139 indicating which *speaker* produced the trial stimulus.
*   vtl: An estimate of the speaker's *vocal-tract length* in centimeters.
*   G: The *apparent gender* of the speaker indicated by the listener, f (female) or m (male).
*   A: The *apparent age* of the speaker indicated by the listener, a (adult) or c (child).

9.8 Models with intercepts and slopes for each level of a grouping factor (i.e. 'random slopes')

To this point, we've been focusing on the geometry implied by different sorts of models. We focused on the fact that categorical predictors that interact with our quantitative predictors affect the *slopes* of our lines, while those that do not interact with them affect line *intercepts*. However, the models we fit so far were not multilevel models and did not properly account for the repeated measures nature of our data. In this section

294 *Quantitative predictors and their interactions with factors*

we will build a multilevel model with a single 'random slope', i.e. a slope term fit using adaptive pooling, before considering a more complex multilevel model in the following section.

9.8.1 Description of the model

The model we fit in the previous section had a formula that looked like this:

```
height ~ C + vtl + vtl:C
```

This means that it included an effect for VTL, category-dependent intercepts, and category-dependent VTL slopes. We noted in Section 4.6 that 'random effects' are simply batches of predictors that are estimated with adaptive pooling. That is, these predictors are assumed to come from a distribution whose variance is estimated from the data. The model above contained only 'fixed' effects simply because we did not use adaptive pooling to estimate any of our effects. We might imagine a model like this:

```
height ~ L + vtl + vtl:L
```

This model would be analogous to the model with category-dependent intercepts and slopes, however, this model would feature *listener*-dependent intercepts and slopes. In actual practice, researchers would not fit a model like this because it treats listener (L) and the listener by `vtl` interaction (`vtl:L`) as 'fixed' effects (i.e. fits the relevant parameters without adaptive pooling). Instead, researchers would tend to estimate the L and `vtl:L` terms using adaptive pooling (i.e. treat these as 'random' effects). The formula corresponding to such a model is given by:

```
height ~ vtl + (vtl|L)
```

The term `(vtl|L)` indicates that we're estimating an intercept (implicit in the formula) and `vtl` parameter for every level of L. Remember that, as discussed in Section 4.6, we treat listener as a 'random' effect not because it is inherently 'random' in a way that apparent speaker category was not. In fact, there is no qualitative difference between C and L in our data: They are both just categorical predictors. The only reason we are treating one as 'fixed' and the other as 'random' is due to the number of levels contained by one vs. the other. We have 15 levels of listener and only four speaker categories. Recall that estimating 'random' effects involved adaptive pooling, which means estimating parameters for each level of the categorical variable of interest as well as a standard deviation that governs the variation among these parameters. Although it is possible to do this with a variable that has a small number of levels, the fewer levels you have, the less information you have to constrain the estimated standard deviation (i.e. the less you are able to benefit from the *adaptive* aspect of adaptive pooling).

In many situations, your data may comprise observations from 50 or more listeners/subjects/participants, resulting in large numbers of parameters for any associated predictors. Treating these as 'random effects', i.e. using adaptive pooling to estimate them, can help out-of-sample prediction and protect us against many of the problems that arise when you estimate large numbers of parameters using no pooling

Quantitative predictors and their interactions with factors 295

(Gelman et al. 2012). For this reason, it's common practice, and recommended, to include all predictors with large (around >10) numbers of levels as 'random' effects. However, we just want to reinforce that there is no qualitative difference between 'fixed' and 'random' effects; the difference is only in the way they are estimated. For example, there are only 50 states in the USA. They are not some infinite population with totally unpredictable characteristics. And yet, if you were modeling something related to the 50 states your model would likely benefit from fitting parameters related to the states using adaptive partial pooling (i.e. treating them as 'random' effects).

The model formula we're actually going to use is seen below. This model says "apparent height is expected to vary along lines as a function of the VTL of the speaker. We expect listener-dependent variation in the intercepts and slopes of these lines and speaker-dependent variation in the intercept of these lines". We include speaker-dependent intercepts but not speaker-dependent VTL slopes. This is because every listener heard every speaker, meaning their responses are associated with a range of VTL values. In contrast, each speaker only had a single fixed VTL value. It's impossible to calculate a slope for a single point as there are an infinite number of lines that pass through it (i.e. the slope is not *identifiable*, see Section 8.8). For this reason, it's impossible to calculate speaker-dependent VTL slopes for our lines, and the inclusion of a term like `(vtl|S)` would cause serious problems for our model.

```
height ~ vtl + (vtl|L) + (1|S)
```

The formal specification of our model is presented in (9.17), excluding the 'construction' of the Σ parameter (as usual). Structurally, this is very similar to the one in (9.16), save for the fact that L replaces C throughout. In addition, our model now recognizes the repeated measures nature of our data and estimates several of our predictors using adaptive pooling.

$$\text{height}_{[i]} \sim t\left(v, \mu_{[i]}, \sigma\right)$$
$$\mu_{[i]} = a + b \cdot \text{vtl}_{[i]}$$
$$a_{[i]} = \text{Intercept} + L_{\left[L_{[i]}\right]} + S_{\left[S_{[i]}\right]}$$
$$b_{[i]} = VTL + VTL : L_{\left[L_{[i]}\right]}$$

$$\text{Priors}:$$
$$S_{[\cdot]} \sim t\left(3, 0, \sigma_S\right) \qquad\qquad (9.17)$$
$$\begin{bmatrix} L_{[\cdot]} \\ VTL : L_{[\cdot]} \end{bmatrix} \sim \text{MVNormal}\left(\begin{bmatrix} 0 \\ 0 \end{bmatrix}, \Sigma\right)$$

$$\text{Intercept} \sim t\left(3, 156, 12\right)$$
$$VTL \sim t\left(3, 0, 12\right)$$
$$\sigma_L, \sigma_{VTL:L}, \sigma_S \sim t\left(3, 0, 12\right)$$
$$\sigma \sim t\left(3, 0, 12\right)$$
$$v \sim \text{gamma}\left(2, 0.1\right)$$
$$R \sim \text{LKJCorr}\left(2\right)$$

296 *Quantitative predictors and their interactions with factors*

The plain English description of our model is below:

We are modeling apparent height as coming from a t distribution with unknown mean (μ), scale (σ), and nu (ν) parameters. The expected value for any given trial (μ) is modeled as the sum of a trial-specific intercept $(a_{[i]})$, and the product of the VTL predictor and a trial-specific VTL slope $(b_{[i]})$. The trial-specific intercept is equal to the sum of the model intercept (Intercept), listener (L), and speaker-dependent (S) deviations from the intercept. The trial-specific slope is equal to the slope 'main effect' (VTL) and a listener-dependent deviation from this (VTL:L). The speaker effects were drawn from a univariate normal distribution with a standard deviation (σ_S) estimated from the data. The two listener effects were drawn from a bivariate normal distribution with standard deviations ($\sigma_L, \sigma_{VTL:L}$) and a correlation matrix (R) that was estimated from the data. The remainder of the 'fixed' effects and correlations were given prior distributions appropriate for their expected range of values.

9.8.2 *Fitting and interpreting the model*

Below we fit the model including listener-dependent slopes and intercepts. We call this our 'simple' model because in the following section we will be fitting one that is substantially more complex.

```
# Fit the model yourself
priors = c(brms::set_prior("student_t(3,160, 12)", class = "Intercept"),
        brms::set_prior("student_t(3,0, 12)", class = "b"),
        brms::set_prior("student_t(3,0, 12)", class = "sd"),
        brms::set_prior("lkj_corr_cholesky(2)", class = "cor"),
        brms::set_prior("gamma(2, 0.1)", class = "nu"),
        brms::set_prior("student_t(3,0, 12)", class = "sigma"))

model_random_slopes_simple =
  brms::brm (height ~ vtl + (vtl|L) + (1|S), data = exp_data, chains = 4,
            cores = 4, warmup = 1000, iter = 5000, thin = 4,
            prior = priors, family = "student")

# Or download it from the GitHub page:
model_random_slopes_simple =
  bmmb::get_model ('9_model_random_slopes_simple.RDS')
```

We can inspect the short print statement below:

```
bmmb::short_summary(model_random_slopes_simple)
## Formula:  height ~ vtl + (vtl | L) + (1 | S)
##
## Group-Level Effects:
## ~L (Number of levels: 15)
##
##                     Estimate Est.Error l-95% CI u-95% CI
## sd(Intercept)          3.67      0.80     2.44     5.56
```

```
## sd(vtl)                          2.84         0.62         1.93         4.31
## cor(Intercept,vtl)              -0.41         0.22        -0.76         0.07
##
## ~S (Number of levels: 139)
##                     Estimate Est.Error 1-95% CI u-95% CI
## sd(Intercept)          4.53         0.34         3.89         5.25
##
## Population-Level Effects:
##                     Estimate Est.Error 1-95% CI u-95% CI
## Intercept           160.60         1.07       158.56       162.76
## vtl                   8.39         0.82         6.73         9.94
##
## Family Specific Parameters:
##           Estimate Est.Error 1-95% CI u-95% CI
## sigma        6.83         0.22         6.41         7.27
## nu           5.24         0.73         4.05         6.82
```

And see that our model contains two 'fixed' effects, the model intercept and the slope. As we know, the model 'random' effects are hidden from us but can be easily accessed in several ways (see Section 5.8.2). Before discussing the random effects let's compare this model to the first model we fit in this chapter, the one that included only a single slope and intercept:

```
bmmb::short_summary(model_single_line)
## Formula:  height ~ vtl
## Population-Level Effects:
##                     Estimate Est.Error 1-95% CI u-95% CI
## Intercept           160.13         0.23       159.68       160.60
## vtl                   8.56         0.18         8.21         8.89
##
## Family Specific Parameters:
##           Estimate Est.Error 1-95% CI u-95% CI
## sigma       10.79         0.17        10.47        11.12
```

We can see that the intercept and VTL slope terms are very similar across the two models. This is to be expected since both represent the average intercept and slope across all listeners and are fit using the same data. What is substantially different is the credible intervals around these parameters, with these being four to five times wider for our model including random effects. As noted in Section 6.3.6 this is a good thing, it means our model recognizes that these estimates are based on only 15 different listeners and that each one of our data points does not represent totally independent information.

We can see from our model output that the standard deviation of listener-dependent intercepts is 3.7 cm and the standard deviation of listener-dependent variation in VTL slopes was 2.8 cm. It's difficult to say whether this is 'big' or 'small' definitively, but here are some things to think about. A difference in height of 3.7 cm (about 1.5 inches) is clearly salient visually and differentiated in many social contexts. This suggests that an average difference of about 3.7 cm in apparent height 'matters'. The VTL slope is 8.4 cm, meaning that the between-listener variation in this is about 1/3 the magnitude

298 *Quantitative predictors and their interactions with factors*

of the slope main effect. Again, something that varies about 1/3 of its magnitude on average between listeners is likely to 'matter' for outcomes. For both of these reasons, it seems that the between-listener variation in slopes and intercepts is worth considering when trying to understand variation in apparent height.

We can use the `hypothesis` function to easily and conveniently recreate our listener-dependent slopes and intercepts. Here, we will use the `short_hypothesis` function simply because the output is easier to deal with for our purposes. Below we set `scope = "ranef"` and `group="L"`. This tells the function to return the listener-dependent intercept $\left(L_{[j]}\right)$ and slope $\left(VTL : L_{[j]}\right)$ 'random' effects for each level of the predictor `L`.

```
# get listener effects
listener_effects = short_hypothesis(
  model_random_slopes_simple, c("Intercept = 0","vtl = 0"),
  scope = "ranef",group="L")
```

If you inspect `listener_effects` you'll see the familiar four-column matrix indicating parameter estimates, standard deviations, and 95% credible intervals. Additional columns present information about the specific level of the grouping factor and the hypothesis for each row. This matrix has 30 rows representing our 15 intercepts and slopes random effects, one for each listener. Since we asked for intercepts and slopes for each level of listener (`L`) in that order, the first 15 parameters represent the intercept effects for listeners one through 15, and rows 16 through 30 represent the slope effects for listeners one through 15. For example, the third row in `listener_effects`, i.e. `listener_effects[3,]` presents information about $L_{[3]}$, and the 18th row (`listener_effects[18,]`) contains information about $VTL : L_{[3]}$. Since these effects represent listener-dependent differences from the 'main effect' for each predictor, we can see below that listener 3 had an intercept −3.5 cm lower than average and a slope that was 3.4 cm greater than average.

```
# get 3rd and 18th row of our listener effects
# these are the intercept and slope effects for listener 3
listener_effects[c(3,18),]
##      Estimate Est.Error    Q2.5   Q97.5       hypothesis group
## H3     -3.482    1.1836  -5.887  -1.186 (Intercept) = 0     3
## H18     3.448    0.8921   1.699   5.226       (vtl) = 0     3
```

Instead of the listener *effects*, we can also reconstruct the listener-dependent intercepts and slopes directly using the `short_hypothesis` function. The listener-dependent intercept is the sum of the listener effect and the model intercept, Intercept + $L_{[j]}$ for listener j. The listener-dependent slope is the sum of the VTL parameter and the listener by VTL interaction, $VTL + VTL : L_{[j]}$ for listener j. We can quickly get these values for all of our listeners by setting `scope = "coef"` in `short_hypothesis`.

```
# get listener coefficients
listener_coefficients = short_hypothesis(
  model_random_slopes_simple, c("Intercept = 0","vtl = 0"),
  scope = "coef",group="L")
```

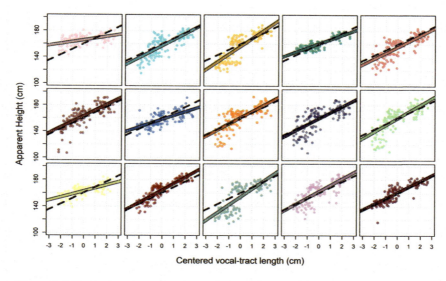

Figure 9.6 Each plot shows responses from a single subject. The line with matched color represents the listener-specific line. The broken black line in each plot is the average 'main effects' line.

We inspect these values for listener three and see that the intercept and slope deviate from the average 'main effect' values of the parameters (160.6, 8.4) in the expected ways.

```
# get 3rd and 18th row of our listener coefficients
# these are the intercept and slope coefficients for listener 3
listener_coefficients[c(3,18),]
##       Estimate Est.Error    Q2.5   Q97.5  hypothesis group
## H3      157.12    0.7981  155.56  158.73 (Intercept) = 0     3
## H18      11.84    0.5667   10.71   12.95       (vtl) = 0     3
```

In Figure 9.6 we see the distribution of apparent height as a function of speaker VTL individually for each listener. Clearly, there is a general tendency shared by all listeners: Each listener-dependent line is reasonably similar to the line drawn using the marginal intercept and slope terms (the broken line in each plot). However, although there are general similarities between listeners there is also noticeable between-listener variation such that the listener-specific lines do a much better job of representing each listener's behavior than the overall line.

9.9 Models with multiple predictors for each level of a grouping factor

We just fit a 'simple' multilevel model in that it contained at most a single slope and intercept term for each level of our grouping factors (i.e. speaker and listener). Now, we're going to fit a more 'complex' model to our data. In Chapter 7 we saw that variation between our groups could be decomposed into an effect for speaker age, an effect for speaker gender, and the interaction between those factors. Here, we're going to apply this same decomposition to the intercepts and slopes of our lines, in addition to including the potential for listener-dependent variation in all these parameters.

300 *Quantitative predictors and their interactions with factors*

9.9.1 Description of the model

If we want our model to investigate the effect of apparent age and gender (and the interaction of these) for our VTL slopes and intercepts, we need to include the interactions between all these predictors. To do this, our model formula needs to look like this:

```
height ~ vtl*A*G + (vtl*A*G|L) + (1|S)
```

This is a very compact way of saying "include the predictors A, G, and vtl, and all possible interactions between them". If this formula were expanded it would look like this:

```
height ~ vtl + A + G + A:G + vtl:A + vtl:G + vtl:A:G +
         (vtl + A + G + A:G + vtl:A + vtl:G + vtl:A:G|L) + (1|S)
```

Recall that any term interacting with a quantitative predictor affects the slope of our lines and any term *not* interacting with a quantitative predictor affects our line intercepts. We can see that there's a symmetry to our model in that we are estimating the effect for A, G, and A:G for both our intercept and VTL slopes. We also see that we're estimating listener-dependent effects for all the fixed effects in our model, but only speaker-dependent intercepts. Our formal model specification is given in (9.18), though we omit many of the priors as they have not changed, are taking up increasingly large amounts of space, and are given when we fit our model below.

$$\text{height}_{[i]} \sim t\left(\nu, \mu_{[i]}, \sigma\right)$$
$$\mu_{[i]} = a + b \cdot \text{vtl}_{[i]}$$

$$a_{[i]} = \text{Intercept} + A + G + A:G +$$
$$A:L_{\left[L_{[i]}\right]} + G:L_{\left[L_{[i]}\right]} + A:G:L_{\left[L_{[i]}\right]} + L_{\left[L_{[i]}\right]} + S_{\left[S_{[i]}\right]}$$

$$b_{[i]} = VTL + VTL:A + VTL:G + VTL:A:G +$$
$$VTL:A:L_{\left[L_{[i]}\right]} + VTL:G:L_{\left[L_{[i]}\right]} + VTL:A:G:L_{\left[L_{[i]}\right]} + VTL:L_{\left[L_{[i]}\right]}$$

$$\text{Priors}:$$
$$S_{[\cdot]} \sim t\left(3, 0, \sigma_S\right)$$

$$\begin{bmatrix} A:L_{[\cdot]} \\ G:L_{[\cdot]} \\ A:G:L_{[\cdot]} \\ L_{[\cdot]} \\ VTL:A:L_{[\cdot]} \\ VTL:G:L_{[\cdot]} \\ VTL:A:G:L_{[\cdot]} \\ VTL:L_{[\cdot]} \end{bmatrix} \sim \text{MVNormal}\left(\begin{bmatrix} 0 \\ 0 \\ 0 \\ 0 \\ 0 \\ 0 \\ 0 \\ 0 \end{bmatrix}, \Sigma\right)$$

$$\cdots$$

(9.18)

Quantitative predictors and their interactions with factors   301

The model specification is getting unwieldy, and we may stop spelling out the full models when they get this big. However, we do think its useful to be aware of how much complexity is involved in what may seem to be a short model formula (`height ~ vtl*A*G + (vtl*A*G|L) + (1|S)`). We can see that with the exception of the speaker predictor, our *a* and *b* equations contain a parallel structure. The parameters represent, for intercepts and VTL slopes, respectively: Main effects (Intercept,*VTL*), the effect for age ($A, A:VTL$), the effect for gender ($G, G:VTL$), the interaction between age and gender ($A:G, A:G:VTL$), listener-dependent intercept and slope effects ($L, VTL:L$), listener-dependent effects for age ($A:L, A:VTL:L$), listener-dependent effects for gender ($G:L, G:VTL:L$), and the listener-dependent interaction between age and gender ($A:G:L, A:G:VTL:L$). We can see above that the eight listener-dependent effects are drawn from an eight-dimensional multivariate normal distribution. Of course, this also entails estimating the correlation between each pair of dimensions resulting in 28 $((8 \cdot 8 - 8)/2)$ unique correlations estimated for the listener random effects.

9.9.2 *Fitting and interpreting the model*

Below we fit our 'complex' model.

```
# Fit the model yourself
priors = c(brms::set_prior("student_t(3,160, 12)", class = "Intercept"),
           brms::set_prior("student_t(3,0, 12)", class = "b"),
           brms::set_prior("student_t(3,0, 12)", class = "sd"),
           brms::set_prior("lkj_corr_cholesky (2)", class = "cor"),
           brms::set_prior("gamma(2, 0.1)", class = "nu"),
           brms::set_prior("student_t(3,0, 12)", class = "sigma"))


model_random_slopes_complex =
  brms::brm (height ~ vtl*A*G + (vtl*A*G|L) + (1|S), data = exp_data,
            chains = 4, cores = 4, warmup = 1000, iter = 5000, thin = 4,
            prior = priors, family = "student")

# Or download it from the GitHub page:
model_random_slopes_complex =
  bmmb::get_model ('9_model_random_slopes_complex.RDS')
```

Our model print statement is very long since it includes eight fixed effects, nine random effect standard deviations, and 28 correlation estimates, among other things.

```
bmmb::short_summary (model_random_slopes_complex)
```

Printing it would use up too much page space at this point, but we can make plots to efficiently summarize the information contained in the model. We can get the fixed effects from our model using the `fixef` function. The book R package (`bmmb`) also contains the functions `get_corrs` to extract model correlations for random effects,

302 *Quantitative predictors and their interactions with factors*

and the function `get_sds` to get the random effects standard deviations from a model. We get this information below:

```
# model fixed effects
fixef_effects = brms::fixef (model_random_slopes_complex)

# model random effect standard deviations
sds = bmmb::get_sds (model_random_slopes_complex)

# model random effect correlations
correlations = bmmb::get_corrs (model_random_slopes_complex, factor="L")
```

And plot it all using the `brmplot` function in 9.7. In the left plot, we see the model fixed effects. In the middle plot, we see the standard deviations of the listener-dependent effects and the model error (`sigma`, σ). For example, the standard deviation of `A1` in the middle plot reflects the variation in the `A1` parameter from the left plot between our different listeners (i.e. $\sigma_{A:L}$). The right plot presents the correlations of different listener random effects. For example, the `G1:Int.` correlation reflects the correlation of listener intercepts and listener `G1` effects across our different listeners.

Figure 9.7 provides a good outline of much of the information contained in our model. We can use combinations of our parameters to predict category-dependent intercepts and slopes just as we did for `multi_slope_hypothesis` in Section 9.5.2 (shown in Figure 9.5) above. This results in parameters specifying four lines, one for each apparent speaker category.

We're going to leave the interpretation of the model for the next section where we attempt to answer our research questions. For now, we're going to think about how to use our model parameters to understand listener and category-dependent variation in responses. In other words, rather than getting a single set of category-dependent lines, as in Figure 9.5, we're going to calculate a set of category-dependent lines for each listener. By using the `scope` and `group` coefficients appropriately, we can use nearly the same code to calculate listener-specific intercepts and slopes for each speaker category.

```
random_slopes_complex_hypothesis_listener = bmmb::short_hypothesis (
  model_random_slopes_complex,
  hypothesis =
    c("Intercept - A1 - G1 + A1:G1 = 0",            # group 1 mean
      "Intercept - A1 + G1 - A1:G1 = 0",            # group 2 mean
      "Intercept + A1 - G1 - A1:G1 = 0",            # group 3 mean
      "Intercept + A1 + G1 + A1:G1 = 0",            # group 4 mean
      "vtl - vtl:A1 - vtl:G1 + vtl:A1:G1 = 0",      # group 1 slope
      "vtl - vtl:A1 + vtl:G1 - vtl:A1:G1 = 0",      # group 2 slope
      "vtl + vtl:A1 - vtl:G1 - vtl:A1:G1 = 0",      # group 3 slope
      "vtl + vtl:A1 + vtl:G1 + vtl:A1:G1 = 0"),     # group 4 slope
  scope = "coef",group="L")
```

The listener-dependent, group-specific lines are presented in Figure 9.8. Two things are clear from this figure. First, there is substantial variation in lines across apparent speaker categories. Second, there is substantial variation in the lines representing each category across different listeners. In both cases, this suggests that this model is preferable to `model_random_slopes_simple` since that model included only a single intercept and VTL slope for each listener.

9.9.3 Model selection

We can approach the question of model selection more formally by using leave-one-out cross-validation (discussed in Chapter 8). First we add the `loo` criterion to each model:

```
model_multi_slope =
  brms::add_criterion(model_multi_slope,"loo")

model_random_slopes_simple =
  brms::add_criterion(model_random_slopes_simple,"loo")

model_random_slopes_complex =
  brms::add_criterion(model_random_slopes_complex,"loo")
```

And compare models:

```
loo_compare (model_multi_slope,
             model_random_slopes_simple,
             model_random_slopes_complex)
##                              elpd_diff  se_diff
## model_random_slopes_complex     0.0       0.0
## model_random_slopes_simple   -494.8      34.7
## model_multi_slope            -578.9      35.9
```

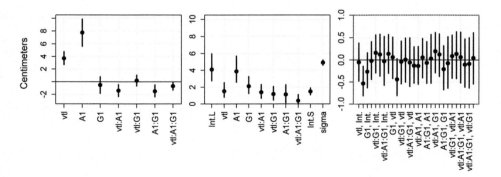

Figure 9.7 (left) Estimates and 95% credible intervals for model fixed effects for `model_random_slopes_complex`. (middle) Standard deviation estimates and 95% credible intervals for listener-dependent random effects parameters, and the error. (right) Estimates and 95% credible intervals for listener random effects correlations.

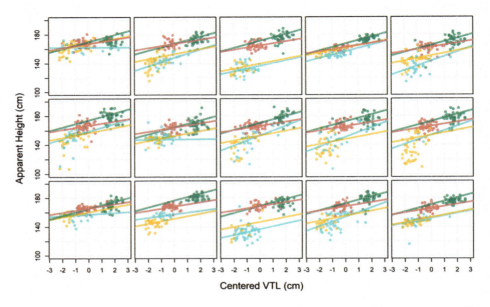

Figure 9.8 Each plot shows responses from a single subject. Lines indicate listener-specific relationships between VTL and apparent height for each speaker category.

Our comparison indicates a *very* large advantage for our newest model with respect to the model with no random effects (model_multi_slope), and the model without age and gender predictors (model_random_slopes_complex). We can get some idea of how much the fit changes across models by using Bayesian R^2. Since R^2 is the proportion of variance in the dependent variable our model explains, we can use differences in R^2 to interpret the differences in elpd presented in our cross-validation above.

```
bmmb::r2_bayes(model_multi_slope)
##         Estimate  Est.Error    Q2.5    Q97.5
## [1,]    0.6715    0.006793    0.658   0.6841

bmmb::r2_bayes(model_random_slopes_simple)
##         Estimate  Est.Error    Q2.5     Q97.5
## [1,]    0.6936    0.006983    0.6795   0.7067

bmmb::r2_bayes(model_random_slopes_complex)
##         Estimate  Est.Error    Q2.5    Q97.5
## [1,]    0.8018    0.004374    0.793   0.8101
```

It's clear that our most complicated model explains the most variance in our dependent variable. By 'explaining the most variance', we mean that this model provides predictions that are closest to our observed data. Based on the results of the cross-validation above, we also think that the most complex model is justified given its expected out-of-sample prediction. In other words, the most complex model offers

Quantitative predictors and their interactions with factors 305

the best prediction *and* justifies its complexity. As a result, we will answer our research questions on the latest, and most complicated, model we fit.

9.10 Answering our research questions: Updated

The research questions we posed above are repeated below:

(Q1) What is the linear relationship between speaker VTL and apparent height?
(Q2) Is the effect of VTL on apparent height affected by the apparent age and gender of the speaker?

Rather than answer our research questions one by one, we're going to attempt to answer these in a narrative like we might include in an academic journal or presentation. We call this a 'narrative' because (in our opinion) reporting your results should not be a long list of numbers like means and credible intervals. Instead, we suggest that it's better to focus on the 'story' of the results as a whole, and to reveal this by presenting individual results (like means and credible intervals). Thinking about the overall story of your results can help the reader make sense of what might otherwise seem like an endless stream of disconnected results. Often things that seem clear and obvious to the researcher, who may have spent months if not years with a data set, are not clear at all to someone reading the analysis for the first time. Using your results to tell 'the story' of your data can help people understand and retain the information you present to them. We will return to these issues in Chapter 13.

Figures 9.7 and 9.8 indicate that our model slopes and intercepts vary based on apparent age and gender, and the interaction of the two. This means that the effect for apparent speaker age varied across levels of gender, and vice versa. As discussed in Section 7.5, in the presence of interactions we need to consider the *simple effects*, the effects of one predictor at a single level of another. The group-specific intercepts and slopes from `model_random_slopes_complex` are presented in the first and third plots in Figure 9.9.

The second plot in the figure presents differences between group-specific intercepts, effectively representing different simple effects. For example, the difference between women and girls (`w-g`) represents the simple effect for age for females and the difference between men and boys (`m-b`) represents the simple effect for age for males. The fourth plot contrasts the differences in group-specific slopes, representing different simple effects for the VTL slope. For example, the difference in slope between women and men (`w-m`) represents the simple effect for gender on the VTL slope for apparent adults, and the difference between girls and boys (`g-b`) represents the simple effect of VTL for gender given apparent children.

As seen in Figure 9.9, the simple effects are the differences between levels of one predictor at a specific level of another predictor. Based on our simple effects we can say that the effect for speaker age is large and somewhat greater for male (`m-b`) than female (`w-g`) speakers. Based on the simple effects for gender within levels of age we can say the perceived femaleness is associated with shorter apparent speakers for adults (`w-m`), but no consistent difference for children (`g-b`). We can use the same approach to discuss the simple effects for VTL slope (fourth plot in Figure 9.9). The only simple effect that has a value that seems reliably different from zero and likely to not be trivially small is the difference between women and girls (`w-g`). This simple effect indicates

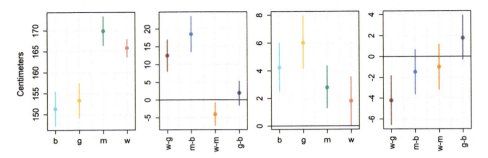

Figure 9.9 (left) Group-specific intercepts from model_random_slopes_complex. (mid-left) Difference between group-specific intercepts (i.e. intercept simple effects). (mid-right) Group-specific slopes from model_random_slopes_complex. (right) Difference between group-specific slopes (i.e. slope simple effects).

that the effect for VTL was substantially smaller for women than for girls. Overall, our results indicate that apparent age had a larger effect on apparent height judgments than apparent gender. In addition, VTL effects were larger for younger speakers, and in particular for girls.

Below, we use the short_hypothesis function to calculate the simple effects for age and gender for intercepts and slopes (seen in Figure 9.9). In each case, we double the value of the effect so that these reflect differences between groups rather than the difference between the group and the main effect.

```
simple_effects = bmmb::short_hypothesis (
  model_random_slopes_complex,
  hypothesis =
    c("2*(A1 + A1:G1) = 0",           # age difference for women
      "2*(A1 - A1:G1) = 0",           # age difference for men
      "2*(G1 + A1:G1) = 0",           # gender difference for adults
      "2*(G1 - A1:G1) = 0",           # gender difference for children
      "2*(vtl:A1 + vtl:A1:G1) = 0",   # VTL difference by age for women
      "2*(vtl:A1 - vtl:A1:G1) = 0",   # VTL difference by age for men
      "2*(vtl:G1 + vtl:A1:G1) = 0",   # VTL difference by gender for adults
      "2*(vtl:G1 - vtl:A1:G1) = 0"))  # VTL difference by gender for children
```

The estimated simple effects are presented in Table 9.1, and you can confirm that the values in the table match up with the information presented in the second and fourth plots in Figure 9.9.

```
knitr::kable (simple_effects, caption="Information regarding
estimated simple effects for `model_random_slopes_complex`
calculated in `simple_effects`.", digits = 2)
```

Quantitative predictors and their interactions with factors 307

Table 9.1 Information regarding estimated simple effects for `model_random_slopes_complex` calculated in `simple_effects`

	Estimate	Est.error	Q2.5	Q97.5	Hypothesis
H1	12.54	2.26	8.16	16.94	$(2*(A1+A1:G1)) = 0$
H2	18.52	2.46	13.56	23.44	$(2*(A1-A1:G1)) = 0$
H3	-4.03	1.56	-7.18	-0.88	$(2*(G1+A1:G1)) = 0$
H4	1.95	1.74	-1.53	5.29	$(2*(G1-A1:G1)) = 0$
H5	-4.21	1.21	-6.54	-1.82	$(2*(vtl:A1+vtl:A1:G1)) = 0$
H6	-1.47	1.05	-3.60	0.66	$(2*(vtl:A1-vtl:A1:G1)) = 0$
H7	-0.97	1.09	-3.13	1.17	$(2*(vtl:G1+vtl:A1:G1)) = 0$
H8	1.77	1.04	-0.27	3.91	$(2*(vtl:G1-vtl:A1:G1)) = 0$

9.10.1 A word on causality

We've specifically tried to avoid causal language so far, saying things like 'is associated with a change' rather than 'causes a change'. In earlier chapters, this was because we were modeling apparent height based on apparent speaker category. In that case, it's totally unclear based on the information we have what is causing what. For example, do listeners determine apparent age and then guess apparent height based on this? Do they estimate apparent height and then use this to estimate apparent age? Are both characteristics estimated simultaneously but in a related manner? So, in our models in previous chapters, we were unsure about the causal direction of the effect and even of the process by which these might be related.

In the case of the models we fit in this chapter, we can be a little more sure about some causal directions, but not much more sure about the process. It's obvious that, if anything, speaker VTL influences apparent height rather than the other way around. We also know based on substantial previous research (see Chapter 13) that speaker VTL does predictably affect apparent height judgments in easily replicable ways in carefully controlled experiments. As a result, we *do* believe that longer VTLs (as measured via speech acoustics) 'cause' the reporting of taller apparent speakers. What we are less sure about is exactly how this occurs.

For example, in this chapter we find that apparent age and gender affect apparent height and also affect the use of VTL. However, we still don't know if apparent age and gender influence apparent height, if the relation is the other way around, or if there is some more complicated way that these variables all affect each other. We also know from previous research (see Chapter 13) and our own models that speaker VTL is also very predictive of apparent gender and apparent age. As a result, we *can* say, somewhat definitively, that independent changes in speaker VTL cause changes in apparent height either directly or indirectly. However, we *cannot* say that the last model we fit (`model_random_slopes_complex`) is a *true* model nor that we know much about how exactly VTL is used to estimate apparent height, gender, and age together, nor about the relationship between the processes underlying the *reporting* (as opposed to perception) of these three apparent speaker characteristics.

The sorts of models that can help you really dig down into causal relationships are beyond the scope of this book. However, these models are usually built out of the model components outlined in this book. The gap between not knowing much about

308 *Quantitative predictors and their interactions with factors*

statistics and understanding this book is much larger than the gap from the end of this book to building models to investigate causal relations. For more information on these sorts of models, we suggest Angrist and Pischke (2009), Glymour et al. (2016), and McElreath (2020).

9.11 Exercises

The analyses in the main body of the text all involve only the unmodified 'actual' resonance level (in `exp_data`). Responses for the stimuli with the simulated 'big' resonance are reserved for exercises throughout. You can get the 'big' resonance in the `exp_ex` data frame, or all data in the `exp_data_all` data frame.

Fit and interpret one or more of the suggested models:

1   Easy: Analyze the (pre-fit) model that's exactly like `model_random_slopes_complex`, except using the data in `exp_ex` (`bmmb::get_model("9_model_random_slopes_complex_ex.RDS")`).
2   Medium: Fit a model like `model_random_slopes_complex` except replace one of the existing categorical predictors with the resonance predictor.
3   Hard: Fit a model like `model_random_slopes_complex` except add the resonance predictor to the model, and possibly some interactions involving the resonance.

In any case, describe the model, present and explain the results, and include some figures.

References

Angrist, J. D., & Pischke, J. S. (2009). *Mostly harmless econometrics: An empiricist's companion.* London: Princeton University Press.

Gelman, A., Hill, J., & Yajima, M. (2012). Why we (usually) don't have to worry about multiple comparisons. *Journal of Research on Educational Effectiveness*, 5(2), 189–211.

Glymour, M., Pearl, J., & Jewell, N. P. (2016). *Causal inference in statistics: A primer.* John Wiley & Sons.

McElreath, R. (2020). *Statistical rethinking: A Bayesian course with examples in R and Stan.* Chapman and Hall/CRC.

10 Logistic regression and signal detection theory models

To this point, we've only discussed the prediction of quantitative variables that can take on a large number of values and are measured on an interval (or ratio) scale. In this chapter, we begin talking about the prediction of categorical variables, variables that take on a (usually small) number of discrete values. For now, we will focus on dichotomous (i.e. binary) outcomes, however, the ideas presented will be extended to the prediction of ordinal (ordered categories such as 1st, 2nd, and 3rd), and multinomial (unordered categories such as English, French, and Spanish) data in Chapter 12. In the second half of this chapter, we will discuss how logistic regression models can be used to investigate the discrimination of categories, and response bias, using signal detection theory.

10.1 Chapter pre-cap

This chapter introduces linear models for the prediction of dichotomous variables, that is, variables that can take on one of two possible discrete values. First, we introduce dichotomous data and the Bernoulli and binomial distributions. After that, link functions and the generalized linear model are discussed. We present logistic regression, discuss logits and their characteristics, and introduce the inverse logit function, the link function for logistic regression. Following this, we fit a multilevel logistic regression model with a single quantitative predictor and use this model to understand the predictions made by our model across the stimulus space, resulting in territorial maps. Finally, we introduce the use of logistic regression to fit a signal detection theory model, estimating response bias and sensitivity using a multilevel logistic regression model.

10.2 Dichotomous variables and data

The models we fit in Chapter 9 featured linear relationships between our predictor and the expected value of the dependent variable (μ). For a model predicting apparent height using speaker vocal-tract length (VTL), like the ones we fit in Chapter 9, this means the μ parameter of a normal distribution slides along straight lines as in (10.1).

$$
\begin{aligned}
\text{height}_{[i]} &\sim \text{N}\left(\mu_{[i]}, \sigma\right) \\
\mu_{[i]} &= \text{Intercept} + VTL \cdot \text{vtl}_{[i]}
\end{aligned}
\tag{10.1}
$$

DOI: 10.4324/9781003285878-10

310 *Logistic regression and signal detection theory models*

We can see an example of a linear relationship in the top left plot of Figure 10.1 where expected apparent height (μ) varies along a line as a function of vocal-tract length (VTL). In this model, the observations we collect are assumed to be normally, and independently, distributed around the expected value (the line). Importantly, our predicted values *directly* model the values we're interested in. What we mean by this is that the values along our line are the actual apparent heights we expect to observe for a given value of VTL.

Unlike quantitative variables, **dichotomous** variables can only take on two different values, and these are not measured on an interval scale. We can easily think of many examples of this kind of data: A response to an item on a test that is wrong or right, a person who is either male or female, or someone who is an adult or a child. None of these examples are meant to suggest that reality is this simple. For example, males and females are not two discrete and internally homogeneous classes that fully explain variation in human sex or gender. Obviously, variation in human age and development is more complicated than being either an adult or a child. And, in fact, it is common that situations or questions can arise that cannot simply be labeled as 'wrong' or 'right'. Despite this, things like gender and age can be *coded* as dichotomous variables so that they have only two possible values within the context of our model.

The decision to represent these groups of speakers using binary variables is just as artificial as assuming that apparent height and VTL relate perfectly along a line, assuming that our errors are normally distributed, and so on. Despite this, we can use

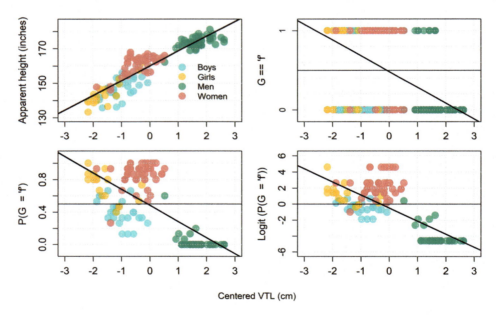

Figure 10.1 (top left) Average apparent height for each speaker against speaker VTL. The point color represents the veridical speaker category. (top right) Individual gender identifications are plotted according to speaker VTL. Female responses were given a value of 1, male responses 0. (bottom left) Probability of a female response as a function of speaker VTL. (bottom right) The logit of the probability of a female response as a function of speaker VTL.

Logistic regression and signal detection theory models   311

our models to look for statistical associations between the dependent variable and our predictors *given the structure of our model*, that is, based on the simplifying assumptions we have made in order to turn an infinitely complicated reality into a regression model with a small number of parameters.

When your variable has only two categorical outcomes (within the context of your model), you need to find a way to represent these numerically. The way this is usually done is by coding one category as 1 (a 'success') and the other as 0 (a 'failure'). The designation of one category as 1 and the other as 0 will not affect your analysis in any meaningful way (it will flip the sign of most coefficients) and can be based on what 'makes sense' given the analysis at hand. In our case we will define a new variable called `Female` and assign 1 to cases where listeners identified a speaker as female, thereby associating female responses with 'successes'. Keep in mind, this variable does not reflect whether the speaker *was* female but that the listener *thought* the speaker was female.

The distribution of dichotomous female (1) and male (0) responses with respect to speaker VTL is presented in the top right plot of Figure 10.1. Plotting ones and zeros against speaker VTL is not very informative, in addition, using a line to directly predict dichotomous data leads to strange outcomes. For example, our line predicts all sorts of values between 0 and 1 that our variable can never actually have. It also suggests a continuous, gradual change in the value of our dependent variable with respect to VTL, which is also impossible.

We can make the situation a bit better by finding the average value of our dichotomous variable for each speaker, where female responses equal 1 and male responses equal 0 (bottom left plot in Figure 10.1). When we do this, we obtain the probability (p) of observing a female response for each speaker. For example, imagine you are playing basketball and keep track of 1,000 free throws over several practices. Imagine you sink 753 of these shots, and let's assume that this represents your actual ability fairly well. You consider these 1,000 shots observations of the variable "successful free throw" which equals 1 when you make it and 0 when you don't. If you add up all your made shots (753) and divide by the total number of observations (1,000), you can conclude that there is a 0.753 (753/1,000) probability of you sinking a free throw (i.e. ($p = 0.753$)).

Since the p parameter is the 'average' made shot, this seems similar to the μ parameter in a normal distribution. However, the p parameter can't be used with a normal distribution to generate dichotomous data. A normal distribution generates continuous variation symmetrically around its mean. Instead, we need a distribution that takes a parameter like p and generates a variable with only two possible values. The two distributions most commonly used to model dichotomous variables are the *Bernoulli* distribution and the *binomial* distribution.

The **Bernoulli distribution** generates individual dichotomous outcomes. This distribution has only one parameter: The probability of a success (p). The p parameter also represents the *expected value* of the Bernoulli distribution. Imagine you have ten observations from a Bernoulli variable and you observe 6 ones and 4 zeros. This suggests a probability of observing a success, p, of 0.6 (6/10). The expected value ($\mathbb{E}$) of a discrete variable is the sum of the values it can take times the probability of each value. For a Bernoulli variable this is relatively simple to calculate as it involves the addition of only two values. In (10.2), we see that to find the expected value of a Bernoulli variable y, we multiply the probability of a success (p) times one, the probability of a failure

312 *Logistic regression and signal detection theory models*

$(1-p)$ times zero, and add the two. Since the probability of failures is multiplied by zero, the expected value of the Bernoulli variable is simply equal to p.

$$\mathbb{E}(y) = \sum_{i=1}^{2} y_{[i]} P\left(y_{[i]}\right)$$

$$\mathbb{E}(y) = (1 \cdot p) + (0 \cdot (1-p))$$

$$\mathbb{E}(y) = p$$

(10.2)

Below, we use the `rbernoulli` function to generate random Bernoulli variables. First, we generate a single Bernoulli variable (a **Bernoulli trial**) and then ten variables with the same probability of success.

```
# a single trial, probability of 0.5
bmmb::rbernoulli (1,.5)
## [1] 0

# ten single trials, probability of 0.5
bmmb::rbernoulli (10,.5)
## [1] 0 0 0 0 0 0 1 0 1 0
```

The **binomial distribution** generates a *set* (batch) of dichotomous outcomes. This distribution has two parameters: The probability of a success (p) and the number of trials (n). The Bernoulli distribution is a special case of the binomial distribution where n is always one. If you were playing basketball and you took 5 free throws and made 3 (3/5=0.6), then the p parameter suggested by your data is 0.6 and the n parameter is 5. If you use this distribution, you are treating all 5 trials as a single observation. This means that your data is 3 (out of five) and not 0, 1, 1, 0, and 1 (or whatever). In this case, another 5 shots would constitute one more 'observation' summarized by the total number of successes. The expected value of the binomial distribution is np since a single observation of a binomial variable is equal to n Bernoulli trials, and the expected value of a single Bernoulli trial is p.

Below we generate random binomial variables using the `rbinom` (random binomial) function, which takes parameters in this order: number of observations, size, probability of success. We can compare the data generated by the Bernoulli and the binomial distributions. In the top row, we get a single number, the total number of successes in the trials. We don't get any information about what happened on any individual trial. In the bottom row, we do get information about what happens on each individual trial.

```
# a single batch of 10 trials, probability of 0.5
rbinom (1,10,.5)
## [1] 6

# ten individual trials, probability of 0.5
bmmb::rbernoulli (10,.5)
## [1] 1 1 0 0 0 0 0 0 0 1
```

Logistic regression and signal detection theory models 313

So, when we have a dichotomous dependent variable and are interested in predicting individual trials, we use a Bernoulli distribution and our data model is $y \sim \text{Bernoulli}(p)$. When our dependent variable consists of groups of Bernoulli trials treated as a single unit we can use a binomial distribution. If this is the case our data model looks like this $y \sim \text{Binomial}(p,n)$, and keep in mind n is *data* (i.e. it is provided by the researcher) and not a parameter that is estimated by the model.

Before moving on we want to note that, unlike the normal distribution, the Bernoulli and binomial distributions do not generate individual data points near their expected value p. Instead, they generate sequences of 1s and 0s whose sample estimate of p is expected to be close to its underlying value *hypothetically* given a large enough sample. For example, below we generate sequences of a dichotomous variable with a true p of 0.5. In each case, the estimate of p gets closer to the true value as the length of the sample gets longer, but it is never exactly equal to the true parameter value of 0.5.

```
mean (rbernoulli (10,.5)) # the mean of 10 observations
## [1] 0.3
mean (rbernoulli (100,.5))  # the mean of 100 observations
## [1] 0.47
mean (rbernoulli (1000,.5))  # the mean of 1000 observations
## [1] 0.488
mean (rbernoulli (100000,.5))  # the mean of 100000 observations
## [1] 0.4999
```

10.3 Generalizing our linear models

The bottom left plot in Figure 10.1 shows the probability of observing a classification of 'female' for each speaker as a function of their vocal-tract length (VTL). We can see that the perception of femaleness is negatively related to speaker VTL: As VTL increases the probability of observing a female response decreases. Despite this, we can't directly model variation in p using lines as shown in the figure. There are many reasons for this but the main one is that using lines to model p causes problems near 0 and 1. For example, imagine a predictor is associated with an increase of 0.2 in probability per unit change in the predictor. If the Intercept is 0.7, a two-unit increase in the predictor is associated with a probability of 1.1, which is not possible. This suggests that a curve with a constant slope (e.g. a line) is fundamentally ill-suited to predict a bounded variable like probability.

The above seems problematic, after all, so far this book has been about linear regression models and we're saying lines are no good for modeling variation in probabilities. The solution to this is to remember that our regression models consist of a bunch of components stuck together. Early on we discussed two general parts: The random component and the systematic component (see Section 3.2). The systematic component predicts variation in expected values using shapes like lines and planes. The random component specifies how our data randomly varies around the expected value. We can add a third component to this called a **link function**, a function that takes some parameter you're interested in (e.g. p) and transforms it so that the *transformed* value can be

314   *Logistic regression and signal detection theory models*

modeled along straight lines. When you rely on link functions, modeling becomes a three-step process like this:

1   Predict variation in expected values (θ) along straight lines (or related shapes), for example $\theta = a + b \cdot x$. This is the systematic component and θ is linearly related to the predictor x.
2   Transform θ using a link function. For example, given the link function f we can transform our expected value θ to p like so: $p = f(\theta)$. The transformed parameter (p) may no longer be linearly related to the dependent variable x or the linear predictor θ.
3   Use the *transformed* parameter (p) in the data generating distribution. For example $y \sim \text{Bernoulli}(p)$. This is the random component.

Our link function literally *links* our systematic and random components: The random component does not *directly* use the information in the systematic component. The models we've been fitting so far featured what's known as the **identity** link function. The identity link function is basically a function that does nothing, the input equals the output like $\mu = f(\mu)$. Using the identity link function is equivalent to modeling μ directly in our prediction equation. This works for the mean parameter of the normal distribution because it can actually vary continuously from positive to negative infinity as lines do. However, it doesn't work for the Bernoulli or binomial distributions since p must fall between 0 and 1. This suggests that we'll need to include a function (f) that maps some continuous predicted value (θ) to a probability (p), as in (10.3).

$$\text{Female}_{[i]} \sim \text{Bernoulli}\left(p_{[i]}\right)$$

$$p_{[i]} = f\left(\theta_{[i]}\right) \tag{10.3}$$

$$\theta_{[i]} = \text{Intercept} + VTL \cdot \text{vtl}_{[i]}$$

The presentation in (10.3) separates our model into a random component, a link function, and a systematic component. Each of these components plays a crucial role in our ability to build regression models that predict dichotomous variables. The random component is the distribution underlying the data-level error in our dependent variable. This component helps us account for the fact that our observations are not perfectly predictable given our independent variables, and that they can only equal 0 or 1. The systematic component allows us to make predictions about variability in the dependent variable using combinations of our predictors. The link function lets us use lines to model variation in parameters even when these may not vary in an unbounded manner.

   This division of regression models into three discrete components is referred to as the **generalized linear model**. The generalized linear model allows the user to change the random component and/or link function as appropriate to model a wide range of data. It's called the 'generalized' linear model because it represents the extrapolation of principles related to the prediction of quantitative variables coming from a normal distribution to the general case. For more information on the generalized linear model see Kruschke (2014) for a Bayesian introduction, or McCullagh and Nelder (2019) for a more advanced, and classic, treatment.

10.4 Logistic regression

Logistic regression is an approach to regression for predicting dichotomous dependent variables. Since it is extremely common, we're going to focus on modeling Bernoulli data (i.e. individual dichotomous variables) in this chapter. However, most of the information presented here directly applies to binomial regression, and binomial regression is simple to carry out using `brms`.

Logistic regression assumes a Bernoulli distribution for the random component and the *inverse logit* function (logit^{-1}, discussed below) as its link function. The systematic component still consists of linear combinations of our independent variables, i.e., adding them up after multiplying by their respective model coefficients, as it has in previous chapters. A general description of logistic regression with a single quantitative predictor is given in (10.4).

$$y_{[i]} \sim \text{Bernoulli}\left(p_{[i]}\right)$$
$$p_{[i]} = \text{logit}^{-1}\left(z_{[i]}\right) \tag{10.4}$$
$$z_{[i]} = \text{Intercept} + \beta \cdot x_{[i]}$$

The information in (10.4) says the following: Our data (y) is a Bernoulli-distributed dichotomous variable with a p parameter that varies on each trial. The p parameter is the output of the inverse logit (logit^{-1}) applied to our linear predictor z. The linear predictor is the sum of an intercept and product of the independent variable (x) and its slope parameter (β). We noted above that p is the expected value of the Bernoulli distribution. Thus, we can see that logistic regression predicts expected values (p) just like our regressions in previous chapters (e.g. μ for a normal model). However, logistic regression doesn't model p directly but instead models the *logit* of the expected value, z.

10.4.1 Logits

Logits are log odds, the logarithm of the odds of success. The odds of success are defined as:

$$\text{odds}_{\text{success}} = \frac{N_{\text{success}}}{N_{\text{failures}}} \tag{10.5}$$

Where N_{success} is the number of observed (or expected) successes and N_{failures} is the observed (or expected) number of failures. For example, odds of 3/1 indicate that success is three times as likely as a failure. We can also define odds by expressing them in terms of the probability of observing a success, p, and the probability of observing a failure, $1-p$, as in (10.6).

$$\text{odds} = p / (1-p) \tag{10.6}$$

We can turn odds into probabilities with the following calculation. For example, odds of 3/1 imply a probability of 0.25 (3 / (3+1)).

$$P(\text{success}) = \frac{N_{\text{success}}}{N_{\text{failures}} + N_{\text{success}}} = \frac{N_{\text{success}}}{N_{\text{total}}} \tag{10.7}$$

316　*Logistic regression and signal detection theory models*

Odds are still bounded by zero on the lower end so they still can't be modeled using lines, however, if we take the *logarithm* of the odds we get a **logit**, the log odds. Unlike odds, logits *can* take on values from positive to negative infinity. This is because, for variable x, logarithms represent the values of x between 0 and 1 with values of log(x) from $-\infty$ to 0. Values of x from 1 to $+\infty$ are represented by values of log(x) from 0 to $+\infty$ (see Section 2.7.2). You can see this relationship by running the code below.

```
# this plot compares x and log (x). Note that log(x)<0 when x<1.
curve (log(x), xlim = c(0,10),n=1000,lwd=2,col=4)
abline (v = 1, lwd=2,col=2)
abline (h=0,v=0, lty=3,col="grey",lwd=3)
```

We can calculate the logit of a probability in either of the two following ways:

$$\text{logit}(p) = \log(p/(1-p))$$
$$\text{logit}(p) = \log(p) - \log(1-p)$$

(10.8)

Equation (10.8) is sometimes called the **logit function** because it turns probabilities into logits. The bmmb package contains a function that carries out this transformation (logit). We can see below that this function takes the second approach to calculate logits.

```
bmmb::logit
## function (p)
## {
##      p[p == 1] = 0.99
##      p[p == 0] = 0.01
##      log(p) - log(1 - p)
## }
## <bytecode: 0x000001de6fef9540>
## <environment: namespace:bmmb>
```

Note that when p is equal to 1 or 0, the function arbitrarily changes those values to 0.99 and 0.01. This is because the logarithm of zero is undefined, and so the logit of probabilities of 0 and 1 cannot be calculated. To accommodate these values, the logit function sets extreme (but manageable) values for probabilities of 0 and 1. The effect of this can be seen in the bottom right plot of Figure 10.1. Several speakers classified as female 100% or 0% of the time appear along horizontal lines at the bottom and top of the y-axis range.

10.4.2 The inverse logit link function

Logistic regression models express expected values in *logits*. The lines represented by these models describe continuous changes in logits as a function of the predictors, and intercepts represent shifts in the values of logits across different situations. However, our data generating distribution (Bernoulli) requires a parameter *p* that is bounded by 0 and 1. This means that the link function for logistic regression needs to convert logits to probabilities. The function that does this is called the **logistic function**, the

Logistic regression and signal detection theory models 317

antilogit function, or the **inverse logit function**. We will refer to it as the inverse logit function to highlight the fact that it is the inverse of the logit, and that it *undoes* the logit transform.

The inverse logit function is presented in (10.9), for logit (i.e. log odds) values, z, ranging continuously from positive to negative infinity. The symbol e represents the mathematical constant (Euler's number, 2.718...) that serves as the base for natural logarithms and for the exponential function so that $\exp(z) = e^z$.

$$P(y = 1) = \text{logit}^{-1}(z) = \frac{e^z}{1 + e^z} \tag{10.9}$$

The inverse logit function may seem inscrutable, but it is in fact very scrutable. First, note its structural similarity to equation (10.7) which describes the conversion of counts of successes and failures to probabilities. Recall that z is the *log odds* of observing a 'success'. This means that e^z is the *odds* of observing a success (since exponentiation 'undoes' log transforms). The odds are the ratio of the number of successes to the number of failures observed (or expected) for some number of trials. As a result, e^z can be *thought of* as the expected number of successes relative to some number of failures. How many failures?

In equation (10.7) we see that the left term in the denominator represents the number of failures. Based on this, it seems as though in (10.9) we're fixing the expected 'count' of failures at 1, and this is effectively what the inverse logit function does. This is necessary because for n trials if you have S successes then you *must* have $n - S$ failures. This means that the odds (or probabilities) of successes *and* failures cannot both be independently estimated. We ran into similar constraints when we discussed contrasts in Chapter 5, and our discussion of why all levels of a factor cannot be independently estimated. To resolve this issue, logistic regression only estimates the odds of successes and not of failures. However, we still need a number of failures in order to turn odds into probabilities. To resolve this issue, the inverse logit function fixes the number of failures to 1 for all cases.

Thinking of e^z as the expected number of successes relative to 1 expected failure may help interpret logits and understand the inverse logit function. For example, since $e^0 = 1$ a logit of 0 means, we expect 1 success compared to 1 failure. This results in $p = 0.5$ for a logit of 0, as shown in (10.10).

$$\frac{e^0}{1 + e^0} = \frac{1}{1 + 1} = 0.5 \tag{10.10}$$

When z is a negative value, e^z is bounded by 0 and 1. This means that a success is less likely than a failure in these cases since we've fixed the number of failures at 1. For example if $z = -3$ then $e^z = e^{-3} = 0.05$. This means that when $z < 0$, we expect probabilities between 0.0 and 0.5, as in (10.11).

$$\frac{e^{-3}}{1 + e^{-3}} = \frac{0.05}{1 + 0.05} = 0.0474 \tag{10.11}$$

On the other hand, when z is positive, e^z will be a number greater than 1, meaning success is more likely than failure. Thus, for positive values of z we expect probabilities between 0.5 and 1 as in:

$$\frac{e^3}{1 + e^3} = \frac{20.1}{1 + 20.1} = 0.953 \tag{10.12}$$

Notice also that the inverse logit function can't actually generate values of 1 or 0. This is because no matter how large the value of z gets, the denominator will always be 1 greater. This sets the upper range of the inverse logit at 1. On the other hand, no matter how negative the value of z gets, exponentiating the value will *always* result in a number greater than 0. This is because the exponential function can only generate positive, non-zero values. As a result, (10.12) will also always provide values greater than 0.

In Figure 10.2 we draw a line with a slope of one and an intercept of 0 (i.e., y=x). We can imagine that this line defines expected values in *logits* as a function of some predictor x. In the middle plot, we've applied the inverse logit function to the line so that $\text{logit}^{-1}(y) = x$. This results in what's known as a **sigmoid curve** relating our x and y variables. If we apply the logit function to this sigmoid curve, the result is a return of our original line again. Thus, we can see that the logit and inverse logit transformations can be applied over and over to go back and forth between a probability or logit representation of the same information.

In Chapter 9 we mentioned that when you do a linear regression you effectively model the data as being generated by distributions that slide along lines, 'producing' data along the way (see Figure 9.1). Logistic regression leads to an analogous but slightly different interpretation. In logistic regression you model the data as a Bernoulli distribution sliding along a sigmoid curve (middle plot, Figure 10.2), generating a ratio of successes to failures based on the value of p specified by the curve.

The second and third lines in (10.4) represent the model link function and systematic component, respectively. We can skip the middleman (z) and just put the prediction equation directly inside the inverse logit function as in (10.13).

$$p = \text{logit}^{-1}\left(\text{Intercept} + \beta \cdot x_{[i]}\right) = \frac{e^{\left(\text{Intercept} + \beta \cdot x_{[i]}\right)}}{1 + e^{\left(\text{Intercept} + \beta \cdot x_{[i]}\right)}} \quad (10.13)$$

We can then take the inverse logit function and put it directly inside the Bernoulli distribution, as in (10.14).

$$F \sim \text{Bernoulli}\left(\frac{e^{\left(\text{Intercept} + \beta \cdot x_{[i]}\right)}}{1 + e^{\left(\text{Intercept} + \beta \cdot x_{[i]}\right)}}\right) \quad (10.14)$$

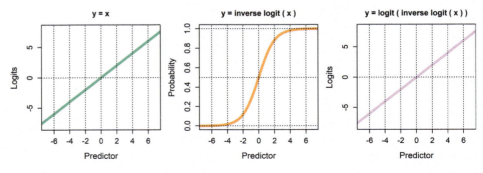

Figure 10.2 (left) A plot of a line with a slope of 1 and intercept of 0. We can treat the y-axis as logits. (middle) The result of applying the inverse logit function to every point of the line in the left plot. (right) Calculating the logit of each value specified on the curve in the middle turns our sigmoid curve back to a line.

Logistic regression and signal detection theory models 319

There's no particular reason to do this, apart from the fact that it illustrates that our link function really does *link* our prediction equation (Intercept + $VTL \cdot$ vtl) and our data distribution (Bernoulli).

10.4.3 Building intuitions about logits and the inverse logit function

The logit and inverse logit functions are **non-linear** functions. In the simplest sense, this means that the relationships they form between x and y variables, when plotted, do not form straight lines. In our case, this means that when we compare logits and their associated probabilities we will not see a straight line. The sigmoid curve in the left plot of Figure 10.3 reveals a changing relationship between logits and probabilities: The slope is very shallow for large negative logit values but increases in value as the curve approaches 0. The slope then begins to decrease in value as the logits become large again. This behavior allows the sigmoid curve in the figure to extend from positive infinity to negative infinity without ever crossing 1 and 0: As logit values become arbitrarily large in magnitude, the slope of the sigmoid curve becomes arbitrarily small in magnitude to the point where it is effectively parallel to the x-axis on both ends of the curve.

In the right plot of Figure 10.3 we see the relationship between the logit of the probability and our predictor. We can see the consequences of the changing relationship between logits and probabilities by looking at the horizontal lines in the plot. These lines represent equal differences in probability (0.1 change per line). The lines are closer together when logits have a small magnitude and further when logits are large. This is a consequence of the non-linearity of the transforms: A one- unit change in probabilities/logits does not always map to the same size of change in the other value. In general, small changes when logits are close to zero (i.e., when p is close to 0.5) map to large changes in probabilities, while larger changes in logits with large magnitudes (i.e., when p is close to 0 or 1) tend to map to small changes in probabilities. As noted above, this is reflected in the changing slope of the sigmoid curve in the left plot.

The top row below contains a sequence of probabilities and the bottom row shows equivalent logits. Notice that the difference between 0.5 and 0.6 is 0.41 logits, but the difference between 0.8 and 0.9 is 0.81 logits. Meanwhile, the difference between 0.9 and 1 is infinity.

```
rbind ( (seq (0.1,.9,.1)),
        round ( logit (seq (0.1,0.9,.1)) , 2) )
##       [,1]  [,2]  [,3]   [,4] [,5] [,6] [,7] [,8] [,9]
## [1,]  0.1  0.20  0.30  0.40  0.5 0.60 0.70 0.80  0.9
## [2,] -2.2 -1.39 -0.85 -0.41  0.0 0.41 0.85 1.39  2.2
```

We can think about the cause of this behavior by thinking about some situation where you're trying to change a probability. Imagine that you keep track of your free throws in basketball practice. You sink 500/1,000 free throws, giving you a 0.5 probability of success. Now imagine you take a further 100 shots and sink them all. Now your probability of success is 600/1,100, meaning your amazing streak has increased your probability to 0.54. However, suppose that you had been a 900/1,000 shooter, a probability of 0.9 of success. If you had the same streak of 100 made baskets you would only increase your probability to 0.901 (1,000/1,100). This change is *forty* times smaller than the change when you begin at 0.5 (0.001/0.040). Thus, we can see that 'the same'

320 *Logistic regression and signal detection theory models*

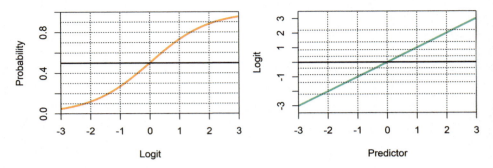

Figure 10.3 (left) A sigmoid curve expressing the probability associated with each logit value along the x-axis. Horizontal lines are placed every 0.1 from 0.1 to 0.9 probability. (right) A line relating some predictor to logits. Horizontal lines are placed every 0.1 from 0.1 to 0.9 probability.

increase in made baskets results in a large increase in one probability (0.5 to 0.54, almost 10%) and a minuscule change in another (0.9 to 0.901, about 0.1%). Basically, as you approach 0 and 1 it gets harder to make large changes in your probabilities, and this is reflected in the logits of those probabilities.

Here are some useful things to keep in mind when interpreting logits, in no particular order:

- A probability of 0.5 is 0 logits. Positive logits mean more likely to be a success, negative logits mean more likely to be a failure.
- −3 and 3 are 4.7% and 95.2%. Basically −3 and 3 logits are useful bounds for "very likely 1" and "very likely 0".
- Since a logit of 3 translates to a P of about 0.95, all of the space between +3 and infinity logits represents the probability space between 0.95 and 1, while logits between 0 and 3 represent the space from 0.5 to 0.95.
- Logits far beyond 3 might not have much practical significance. A logit of 4 is a probability of 0.982 and a logit of 6 is 0.997. For many purposes, probabilities of 0.95, 0.98, and 0.99 are nearly interchangeable. Also, it is very difficult to distinguish 95%, 98%, and 99% in practice since you will be observing very few cases of 0.
- Effects can be considered important or not based on how far they get you along −3 to 3 (or −4 to 4). Basically, anything in the +1 range is very likely to matter, while effects smaller than 0.1 or so are likely to have only a small influence on outcomes.

Here is one final thing to keep in mind about logits: You **must** combine your model parameters as logits **before** transforming them into probabilities. This is due to the fact that the inverse logit function is non-linear, and will be discussed in more detail in Section 10.5.4.

10.5 Logistic regression with one quantitative predictor

In the previous chapter, we tried to predict apparent height using speaker VTL, apparent age, and apparent gender. Here, we're going to predict the perception of femaleness,

Logistic regression and signal detection theory models 321

i.e., the identification of the speaker as female, based on speaker VTL and apparent age, and using a logistic regression.

10.5.1 Data and research questions

Below we load the necessary R packages and the data. We create a new variable called `Female` which will be our dependent variable. This variable equals 1 when listeners indicated hearing a female speaker and 0 when listeners indicated a male speaker. We'll predict this using a single quantitative predictor, speaker VTL, which we also center below.

```
library (brms)
library (bmmb)
options (contrasts = c('contr.sum','contr.sum'))

data (exp_data)

# our dependent variable
exp_data$Female = as.numeric (exp_data$G == 'f')

# make a copy of vtl
exp_data$vtl_original = exp_data$vtl

# center vtl
exp_data$vtl = exp_data$vtl - mean (exp_data$vtl)
```

The variables from our data frame that will be used in this model are:

*   `L`: A number from 1 to 15 indicating which *listener* responded to the trial.
*   `S`: A number from 1 to 139 indicating which *speaker* produced the trial stimulus.
*   `vtl`: An estimate of the speaker's *vocal-tract length* in centimeters.
*   `G`: The *apparent gender* of the speaker indicated by the listener, `f` (female) or `m` (male).
*   `A`: The *apparent age* of the speaker indicated by the listener, `a` (adult) or `c` (child).

We saw in Figure 10.1 that VTL is negatively related to the probability that a speaker will be identified as female. In addition, it seems that the relationship between speaker VTL and the perception of female speakers may differ based on the apparent age of the speaker. We would like to know:

(Q1)   What is the relationship between speaker VTL and the perception of femaleness?
(Q2)   Does the relationship between VTL and apparent speaker gender vary in an age-dependent manner?

10.5.2 Description of the model

In order to answer the questions posed above, our model needs to represent the linear relationship between VTL and the logit of the probability of observing a female

322 *Logistic regression and signal detection theory models*

classification. It also needs to allow this linear relationship to vary between apparent children and adults. The formula for our model needs to look like this:

```
Female ~ vtl*A + (vtl*A|L) + (1|S)
```

The formula above tells our model to predict perceived femaleness using speaker VTL (centered as in the previous chapter), information about whether the speaker was identified as a child or an adult, and age-dependent use of VTL. Since we include the interaction between apparent age and speaker VTL, we are effectively estimating two lines relating speaker VTL and apparent gender: One for apparent adults and another for apparent children. Our formula also includes by-listener effects for all predictors and by-speaker intercepts. This model would be relatively 'simple' at this point if it were dealing with normally distributed data. The prior specification we're going to use looks like this:

```
prior = c(set_prior("student_t(3, 0, 3)", class = "Intercept"),
          set_prior("student_t(3, 0, 3)", class = "b"),
          set_prior("student_t(3, 0, 3)", class = "sd"),
          set_prior("lkj_corr_cholesky(2)", class = "cor"))
```

You'll notice that we're using priors with a standard deviation of 3 across the board. This is because logit values of 3, 6, and 9 correspond to probabilities of 0.9526, 0.9975, and 0.9999 (`inverse_logit(c(3,6,9))`) respectively. So, a prior with a standard deviation of 3 suggests we expect group differences, or a one-unit change in VTL, and have the potential to change probabilities from 50% to 95% (a difference of 3 logits). We think it's plausible that apparent age may, for example, change an expected probability from 50% to 95%. In terms of continuous predictors like VTL, the important thing to keep in mind is that the slope estimated for a predictor depends on the unit of measurement for that predictor. For example, below we see the average VTL in centimeters for each speaker category.

```
tapply (exp_data$vtl_original, exp_data$C_v, mean)
##        b        g        m        w
## -1.0563  -1.5906   1.7052  -0.3748
```

We can see that the average difference between men and women is about 2 cm. If we assume that people at the averages are classified correctly more often than not, this means that the logit of the probability of observing a female response for an adult with a 15 cm VTL may be about −3, and the logit of the same for a 13 cm VTL may be about 3. Thus, we might expect a slope of about 3 logits per 1 cm change in VTL with respect to the perception of female speakers. However, what if we had measured VTL in meters? Then the difference in VTL would be only 0.02, meaning that the model slope would now have to be 300 in order to change from −3 to 3 in only 0.02 units of change (300 = 6 / 0.02). Based on this we can see that it's important to think about the amount of variation there is in your quantitative predictors and how this might relate to the probabilities you are modeling when setting your priors.

Our full model specification, omitting the deterministic construction of the covariance matrix Σ (as usual), is:

$$\text{Female}_{[i]} \sim \text{Bernoulli}\left(p_{[i]}\right)$$

$$p_{[i]} = \text{logit}^{-1}\left(z_{[i]}\right)$$

$$z_{[i]} = a_{[i]} + b_{[i]} \cdot \text{vtl}_{[i]}$$

$$a_{[i]} = \text{Intercept} + A + A : L_{\left[L_{[i]}\right]} + L_{\left[L_{[i]}\right]} + S_{\left[S_{[i]}\right]}$$

$$b_{[i]} = VTL + VTL : A + VTL : L_{\left[L_{[i]}\right]} + VTL : A : L_{\left[L_{[i]}\right]}$$

Priors:

$$S_{[\bullet]} \sim \text{Normal}(0, \sigma_S)$$

$$\begin{bmatrix} L_{[\bullet]} \\ A : L_{[\bullet]} \\ VTL : L_{[\bullet]} \\ VTL : A : L_{[\bullet]} \end{bmatrix} \sim \text{MVNormal}\left(\begin{bmatrix} 0 \\ 0 \\ 0 \\ 0 \end{bmatrix}, \Sigma\right)$$

$$\text{Intercept} \sim t(3, 0, 3)$$

$$A, VTL, VTL : A \sim t(3, 0, 3)$$

$$\sigma_S, \sigma_L, \sigma_{A:L}, \sigma_{VTL:L}, \sigma_{VTL:A:L} \sim t(3, 0, 3)$$

$$R \sim \text{LKJCorr}(2)$$

(10.13)

The main differences compared to our previous models are the lack of terms related to σ, the inclusion of a link function, and the reliance on a Bernoulli rather than the normal or t distributions at the data level. In plain English, this model could be read like:

We're treating our femaleness judgments (1 or 0 for female or male) as coming from a Bernoulli distribution with a probability (p) that varies from trial to trial. The logit of the probability (z) varies along lines. The lines are specified by intercepts (a) and slopes (b) that vary from trial to trial, and there is a single continuous predictor (speaker VTL). The intercept of these lines varies based on an overall intercept, an effect for apparent age (A), listener-specific effects for apparent age (A : L), listener-specific deviations (L), and speaker-specific deviations (S). The slope of these lines varies based on an overall slope (VTL, the main effect), deviations based on apparent age (VTL : A), listener-specific deviations (VTL : L), and listener-specific interactions between apparent age and VTL (A : VTL : L)). The speaker intercept (S) terms were drawn from a normal distribution with a mean of zero and a standard deviation estimated from the data. The listener random effects were drawn from a multivariate normal distribution with means of zero and a covariance matrix estimated from the data. All other effects (e.g., the Intercept, VTL, A, etc.) were treated as 'fixed' and drawn from prior distributions appropriate for their expected range of values.

324 *Logistic regression and signal detection theory models*

10.5.3 *Fitting the model*

We're going to fit the model outlined above. Below is the function call we need to run the model described in (10.13):

```
# Fit the model yourself
priors = c(brms::set_prior("student_t(3, 0, 3)", class = "Intercept"),
           brms::set_prior("student_t(3, 0, 3)", class = "b"),
           brms::set_prior("student_t(3, 0, 3)", class = "sd"),
           brms::set_prior("lkj_corr_cholesky(2)", class = "cor"))

model_gender_vtl =
  brm (Female ~ vtl*A + (vtl*A|L) + (1|S), data=exp_data, chains=4, cores=4,
      family="bernoulli", warmup=1000, iter= 5000, thin = 4,prior=priors)

# Or download it from the GitHub page:
model_gender_vtl = bmmb::get_model ('10_model_gender_vtl.RDS')
```

However, we're going to (retroactively) pause before continuing in order to update our discussion of prior predictive checks. In Section 8.3.1 we discussed these in the context of quantitative variables. In these cases, our predictions take on a range of values and can be summarized effectively using histograms and plots showing the density of the distribution. In contrast, our dichotomous variables only take on values of 1 and 0, and so histograms and densities of these no longer provide as much useful information. Instead of considering the distribution of values of the dependent variable directly, we can consider prior predictions as logits, allowing us to use densities or histograms just as we did for quantitative variables.

We can look at the location of the logit predictions to see how expected outcomes vary across conditions or overall. A concentration around 0 means that predictions are balanced across successes and failures, whereas positive or negative predictions indicate one or the other category is more likely. We can also look at the variation of predictions about their average, and in particular, in the magnitude of the logits being predicted. Predicted logits with very large magnitudes indicate near certainty in the outcome, whereas predictions concentrated near zero indicate that either category is equally likely. We can use the code below to run our prior predictive check and then use the `p_check` function to get and plot our prior predictions (not shown here).

```
priors = c(brms::set_prior("student_t(3, 0, 1)", class = "Intercept"),
           brms::set_prior("student_t(3, 0, 1)", class = "b"),
           brms::set_prior("student_t(3, 0, 1)", class = "sd"),
           brms::set_prior("lkj_corr_cholesky(2)", class = "cor"))

model_gender_vtl_priors =
  brm (Female ~ vtl*A + (vtl*A|L) + (1|S), data=exp_data, chains=4,
      cores=4, family="bernoulli", warmup=1000, iter = 5000, thin = 4,
      prior = priors, sample_prior = "only")

bmmb::p_check (model_gender_vtl_priors)
```

Logistic regression and signal detection theory models 325

Our prior predictions indicate some logits with very high values (>40), with the bulk of variation seemingly between −20 and 20 logits. This indicates that in some cases, speakers would be identified as female with a probability of 0.000000002 (since $logit^{-1}(-20) = 0.000000002$), or about once every 500 million trials. This might seem crazy but it might not be. For example, consider someone with a very deep voice and a deep resonance like James Earl Jones (a.k.a Mufasa in the *Lion King* and Darth Vader in *Star Wars*). You ask: What's the probability that this voice would be identified as an adult female by a random listener, knowing nothing about the speaker other than a single example of their voice? In some cases, you might reasonably think that this might *never* happen, other than perhaps due to accidental responses. But what if you *had* to put a number on never? Well in that case logits as large as 20, or a one in half billion chance, may not seem so crazy.

Although we've spent the last paragraph defending these priors, they probably are too wide, just not excessively so. If our model has problems converging or has any other pathologies (e.g., divergent transitions, see Section 3.6), we may want to reconsider these priors.

10.5.4 Interpreting the model

If we inspect the model summary:

```
short_summary(model_gender_vtl)
## Formula:  Female ~ vtl * A + (vtl * A | L) + (1 | S)
##
## Group-Level Effects:
## ~L (Number of levels: 15)
##                         Estimate Est.Error l-95% CI u-95% CI
## sd(Intercept)               0.55      0.27     0.08     1.14
## sd(vtl)                     1.04      0.31     0.53     1.78
## sd(A1)                      0.95      0.31     0.44     1.61
## sd(vtl:A1)                  0.43      0.24     0.04     0.96
## cor(Intercept,vtl)         -0.06      0.32    -0.66     0.57
## cor(Intercept,A1)          -0.22      0.32    -0.78     0.44
## cor(vtl,A1)                -0.46      0.24    -0.82     0.09
## cor(Intercept,vtl:A1)      -0.26      0.37    -0.83     0.55
## cor(vtl,vtl:A1)             0.24      0.34    -0.48     0.78
## cor(A1,vtl:A1)             -0.26      0.33    -0.81     0.48
##
## ~S (Number of levels: 139)
##              Estimate Est.Error l-95% CI u-95% CI
## sd(Intercept)     1.2      0.16     0.91     1.55
##
## Population-Level Effects:
##           Estimate Est.Error l-95% CI u-95% CI
## Intercept     0.86      0.31     0.27     1.49
## vtl          -3.59      0.39    -4.41    -2.88
## A1            2.65      0.35     2.01     3.39
## vtl:A1       -1.76      0.28    -2.34    -1.24
```

326 *Logistic regression and signal detection theory models*

We see that it looks just like all our previous models except for two main differences:

1 All our parameters, including means, errors, and credible intervals, are now expressed in logits.
2 The absence of the `Family-Specific` parameter section of the model where `sigma` and `nu` (i.e., σ and v) were usually found.

In Chapter 9 we talked about the geometry of models that include a single quantitative predictor, a categorical predictor with several levels, and the interaction of the two. Essentially, these models result in a set of lines, one overall 'main effects' line, and another line for each level of the categorical predictor interacting with the quantitative predictor. Since our model includes effects for apparent age (`A1`), VTL (`vtl`), and their interaction (`vtl:A1`), our model can be thought of as three lines relating VTL to the logit of the probability of observing a female response: The overall (main effects) line, the line for apparent adult speakers, and the line for apparent child speakers. We can recover the parameters for these three lines by adding the appropriate model coefficients together using the hypothesis function. Since `A1` (and related parameters) represent the adult group and we are using sum coding, the effect for children is represented by subtracting, rather than adding, the relevant parameters (i.e. `Intercept - A1` to find the child intercept).

```
gender_vtl_hypothesis = bmmb::short_hypothesis (
   model_gender_vtl,
   hypothesis = c("Intercept = 0",           # overall intercept
                  "Intercept + A1 = 0",       # adult intercept
                  "Intercept - A1 = 0",       # child intercept
                  "vtl = 0",                  # overall slope
                  "vtl + vtl:A1 = 0",         # adult slope
                  "vtl - vtl:A1 = 0") )       # child slope

gender_vtl_hypothesis
##     Estimate Est.Error     Q2.5    Q97.5          hypothesis
## H1    0.8563    0.3084   0.2672   1.4934     (Intercept) = 0
## H2    3.5035    0.5022   2.5716   4.5727  (Intercept+A1) = 0
## H3   -1.7909    0.4337  -2.6816  -0.9702  (Intercept-A1) = 0
## H4   -3.5911    0.3868  -4.4145  -2.8822           (vtl) = 0
## H5   -5.3493    0.5664  -6.5654  -4.3457     (vtl+vtl:A1) = 0
## H6   -1.8328    0.3681  -2.5856  -1.1353     (vtl-vtl:A1) = 0
```

These parameters can be used to plot lines predicting the logit of the probability of a female response given speaker VTL. The left plot of Figure 10.4 presents the overall 'main effects' line and the age-dependent lines, compared to our data. We can see that our age-dependent lines follow the data much better than the single average line does. In the right plot of Figure 10.4 we see what happens when we apply the inverse logit transform on the lines (and points) in the left plot of the figure. The result is a set of sigmoid curves representing expected variation in the p parameter of a Bernoulli distribution as a function of speaker VTL. These curves are a better fit for our probabilities than the lines we originally used in Figure 10.1, and also do not ever result in values below zero or above one.

Let's discuss the values of our fixed effects parameters. The most important thing to remember when interpreting the coefficients of a logistic model is that positive coefficients push us toward a 1 response ('female'), while negative values push us toward a 0 response ('male'). A predicted value of exactly 0 means the outcome is 50/50. The model intercept is the value of the line when VTL=0. Since we centered our VTL predictor, our positive intercept suggests a speaker with an average VTL (13.4 cm) was more likely to be classified as female (with a probability of 0.67 (`inverse_logit(0.71)`). The effect for perceived adultness (`A1`) is positive indicating that a speaker with an average VTL is more likely to be identified as a woman when the speaker is also thought to be an adult. The negative effect for VTL tells us that as VTL increases, we are *less* likely to observe a 'female' response and *more* likely to observe a 'male' response. The interaction between VTL and age is negative, meaning this slope is even more negative when the speaker is thought to be an adult. This is evident in Figure 10.4 where the line for apparent adults has a much steeper slope than the line for apparent children. In addition, the magnitude of the slope increases/decreases by more than 50% since the VTL parameter is −3.6 and the interaction is −1.76.

We can interpret our model entirely in the logit space, focusing on the geometry of our models and interpreting our intercept and slope terms just as we did above and in the previous chapter. However, if we want to think of our model parameters in terms of probabilities (rather than logits), we need to combine parameters as logits first, and then carry out the inverse logit function on these values. It is absolutely essential that the operations be done in this order because the inverse logit function is not an **additive** function. Earlier we noted that the logit (and inverse logit) are non-linear. One of the characteristics of non-linear transformations is that they are generally not additive. A function, $f(x)$, is additive if the following property holds:

$$f(x+y) = f(x)+f(y) \tag{10.14}$$

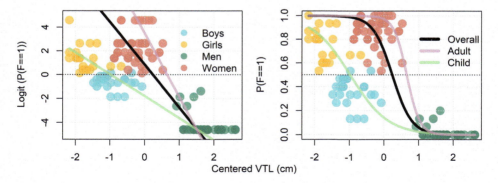

Figure 10.4 (left) Lines indicating the linear relationship between VTL and the logit of the probability of a female response. Point colors indicate modal speaker category classification. (right) Same as the left plot but indicating probabilities on the y-axis.

328 *Logistic regression and signal detection theory models*

A function is additive if it preserves the operation of addition. This means that adding two things and putting them into the function provides the same results as passing them individually through the function and adding them up after. For example, imagine our function is $f(x) = x \cdot 2$. We put in $3 + 2$ (i.e. 5) and get 10 out. We then put in 3 and 2 individually, get 6 and 4 out, add them up and get 10 again. Based on this we say that our function appears to be *additive*. As noted above, the inverse logit function is not. For example, let's consider the meaning of the `Intercept` and `A1` coefficients:

```
# model intercept
inverse_logit (0.86)
## [1] 0.7027

# model A1, adultness, term
inverse_logit (2.65)
## [1] 0.934
```

The intercept reflects the logit of the probability of a female response, overall, when VTL was 0. This intercept is not a difference or a parameter indicating a rate of change. As a result, the probability of 0.7 (`inverse_logit (0.86)`) *can* be interpreted in isolation. But what does 0.934 represent? Nothing useful, actually. The `A1` parameter reflects the difference in logits (2.65) between perceiving a female speaker at 0 VTL overall compared to when listeners indicated hearing an adult. However, since this is a *difference* it needs to be combined with a baseline number in order to be interpreted. For example, if I say "that group was 3 seconds faster", you need to know "faster than what?" in order to know the speed of the group. So, in order to get the log odds (and probability) of observing a female response given some apparent age, we need to combine the `Intercept` and `A1` parameters, and then turn this into a probability using the inverse logit function. Since the inverse logit transform is not additive, we will not get the same output if we combine these parameters and then transform versus transform and then combine. See (10.15) and compare to (10.14).

$$\text{logit}^{-1}(\text{Intercept} + A1) \neq \text{logit}^{-1}(\text{Intercept}) + \text{logit}^{-1}(A1) \tag{10.15}$$

Since they are not equal, only one can be correct. Our model combines parameters as logits, and therefore the appropriate way to consider our parameters is by also combining them as logits. So, in order to turn the `A1` effect into a probability it first needs to be combined with the intercept as a logit, and *then* converted using the inverse logit function. As seen below, converting to a probability and then combining can lead to strange outcomes: 1.64 is not even a valid probability. When we combine first and then convert, we see that the result is a reasonable probability that matches what we see in the right plot of Figure 10.4 (i.e. 0.97 is a plausible value for the adult line at x=0).

```
# intercept + adult (bad)
inverse_logit (0.86) + inverse_logit (2.65)
## [1] 1.637
```

```
# intercept + adult (good)
inverse_logit (0.86 + 2.65)
## [1] 0.971
```

The same reasoning applies to the interpretation of slopes in logistic regression models. Our slope tells us that for every unit change in VTL we expect a 3.6 logit increase/decrease in our expected values. We cannot convert this to probabilities and then multiply this by VTL to predict probabilities. For example, the difference from 0 to 3.6 logits results in a change from 0.5 to 0.97 in probability. We may be inclined to say that our VTL slope suggests an increase of 0.47 in probabilities (0.97−0.5) for every unit change in VTL. Obviously, this will not work since it suggests a difference in probability of 1.41 for a VTL difference of 3 cm. As a result, slopes in logistic models can only be interpreted as reflecting consistent changes in the *logit* of a probability, and not in the probability itself.

Think of it this way. You can move along lines in the logit space (the left plot in Figure 10.4), and you can use the inverse logit to calculate the probability associated with any given value along this line. However, the slope of the curve relating our predictor to probabilities (the right plot in Figure 10.4) does *not have a constant slope*. You can't find the slope of this curve for one fixed position and just move along it in a straight line. Obviously, if you did this you would immediately diverge from the curve in the right plot in Figure 10.4 because that line does not have a constant slope. So, when you want to interpret slopes, just remember that your model only thinks of these as lines in the logit space, not in the probability space.

10.5.5 Using logistic models to understand classification

Our models so far have presented us with the y-intercepts of our lines, the value of the y-axis at x=0. However, when modeling in logits we might also be interested in the **x-intercepts** of our lines. The x-intercept is the value of x where *y is equal to zero*, the point where our line crosses the horizontal x-axis. Why do we care about this? Consider the prediction lines in the left plot in Figure 10.4. When these lines have positive values we know a female response is expected and when these lines have a negative value we know that a male response is expected. Imagine a vertical line placed at the x-axis intercept. This line would represent the **category boundary** between our two possible outcomes along the x-axis (according to our model). Crossing the x-intercept in one direction along the x-axis means one category is more likely, and crossing in the other direction means the other category is now more likely.

We can find the x -intercept by setting y=0 in our prediction equation and solving for (isolating) x, as in (10.16). For complicated prediction equations (and even for simple ones), you can rely on algebra solving websites easily found on the internet. Below, we see that when y is equal to zero, the value of x is equal to the negative intercept (*a*) divided by the slope (*b*).

$$
\begin{aligned}
y &= a + b \cdot x \\
0 &= a + b \cdot x \\
-a &= b \cdot x \\
-a \, / \, b &= x
\end{aligned}
\tag{10.16}
$$

330   *Logistic regression and signal detection theory models*

We can use the equation above to calculate our predicted boundary between male and female classifications along the VTL dimension. For example, based on the numbers in our model summary above, we expect that the overall category boundary is at $-(a/b) = -(0.86/-3.59) = -0.24$. However, remember that to do arithmetic operations on, or otherwise combine, our parameters, we have to use the original samples and not the summaries (see Section 5.8.2 for a discussion on this). We will present three ways to do this, in order of decreasing difficulty/tediousness. The first is by directly combining the fixed effects samples as necessary. First, we get the unsummarized fixed effects samples:

```
samples = fixef (model_gender_vtl, summary = FALSE)
```

Then we divide the column representing the overall intercept by the column representing the overall slope. The result is a vector of individual samples from the posterior distribution of the x-intercept of the line, i.e. the category boundary along the VTL dimension. We refer to specific columns by using the same names seen in the print statement for the fixed effects.

```
# calculate overall boundary = -a/b
boundary = -samples[,"Intercept"] / samples[,"vtl"]
```

To find the x-intercept for the lines for apparent adults and children, we combine parameters in the same way as when we found the age-dependent lines above. However, this time we also relate these parameter estimates as a fraction as seen below.

```
# same but for adults
boundary_adults = -(samples[,"Intercept"] + samples[,"A1"]) /
  (samples[,"vtl"] + samples[,"vtl:A1"])

# now for children
boundary_children = -(samples[,"Intercept"] - samples[,"A1"]) /
  (samples[,"vtl"] - samples[,"vtl:A1"])
```

The result of the above combinations is a set of vectors. Each of these vectors represents the posterior distribution of the category boundary (i.e. the x-intercept) given the structure of our model and our model parameters. We can stick the vectors representing boundaries together and summarize them as seen below. We see that the overall boundary is close to what we predicted using the fixed effect summaries above.

```
boundaries_1 = posterior_summary (
  cbind (boundary, boundary_adults, boundary_children))

boundaries_1
##                      Estimate Est.Error      Q2.5     Q97.5
## boundary               0.2397   0.08613   0.07438    0.4104
## boundary_adults        0.6558   0.07169   0.51829    0.7958
## boundary_children     -0.9925   0.23018  -1.48021   -0.5908
```

Logistic regression and signal detection theory models 331

Our boundaries are expressed relative to a mean VTL of zero. If we want them expressed relative to the true mean we need to add it back in. Below we add the original mean VTL back to our summary (excluding the standard error), and we see the category boundaries relative to values of VTL in the range of our real speakers. This might seem to violate our many (repeated) warnings about summarizing posterior distributions before combining them. Why does this work? Because we are just adding a single number to all our observations, and not a set of values that are possibly correlated with our posterior samples. Adding a number to all samples raises/lowers the sample mean and all the quantiles exactly by that number, but otherwise has no effect on our summaries. Further, adding a single number to all values has no effect on their posterior standard deviation, which means that we don't need to worry about misrepresenting the amount of uncertainty in our estimates.

```
# omit standard error column
boundaries_1[,-2] + 13.4    # i.e. mean (exp_data$vtl_original)
##                     Estimate  Q2.5 Q97.5
## boundary              13.64 13.47 13.81
## boundary_adults       14.06 13.92 14.20
## boundary_children     12.41 11.92 12.81
```

The second way to find boundaries is to use the line parameters we calculated in the previous section. We get the samples from our hypothesis object using the `attr` function as seen below. The individual samples underlying each hypothesis are stored as attributes so that these are not printed out every time the summary is.

```
line_parameters = attr (gender_vtl_hypothesis, "samples")
```

Since we know the first second and third hypotheses represent the overall, adult, and child intercepts, and the fourth, fifth, and sixth hypotheses represent the overall, adult, and child slopes, we can find the boundaries as seen below.

```
# calculate boundary = -a/b
boundary = -line_parameters[,1] / line_parameters[,4]
boundary_adults = -line_parameters[,2] / line_parameters[,5]
boundary_children = -line_parameters[,3] / line_parameters[,6]
```

This process results in identical outcomes to our previous approach.

```
boundaries_2 = posterior_summary (
  cbind (boundary, boundary_adults, boundary_children))

boundaries_2[,-2] + 13.4
##                     Estimate  Q2.5 Q97.5
## boundary              13.64 13.47 13.81
## boundary_adults       14.06 13.92 14.20
## boundary_children     12.41 11.92 12.81
```

332 *Logistic regression and signal detection theory models*

The final way to find the boundaries is to just find the age-dependent parameters, *and* the ratio of these, directly in `hypothesis` (or `short_hypothesis`). We can also add the average VTL value back in at the same time for good measure.

```
boundaries_3 = bmmb::short_hypothesis (
  model_gender_vtl,
  c("-(Intercept) / (vtl) + 13.4= 0",                    # overall boundary
    "-(Intercept + A1) / (vtl + vtl:A1) + 13.4 = 0",     # adult boundary
    "-(Intercept - A1) / (vtl - vtl:A1)  + 13.4 = 0"))   # child boundary

boundaries_3[,-5]
##     Estimate Est.Error  Q2.5 Q97.5
## H1     13.64   0.08613 13.47 13.81
## H2     14.06   0.07169 13.92 14.20
## H3     12.41   0.23018 11.92 12.81
```

If the last way is so quick and easy, why bother learning how to combine and summarize the samples by hand? The problem is if you only know how to use a helper function (like `hypothesis`), you may become reliant on it for your work, and you can be limited by what it can and can't do. If it changes or goes away, your ability to do what you need to do may suffer. If you know what `hypothesis` is doing, and know how to do it yourself, you can use it when it does what you want, but you also have the ability to do things independently when you want or need to.

The boundaries calculated above are presented with our data in Figure 10.5. The right plot below can be thought of as representing a **stimulus space**, a space indicating variation in our experimental stimuli along one or more dimensions. We say *a* stimulus space and not *the* stimulus space because there may be many ways to consider variation in the stimuli, and this is just one of them. In this case, the only dimension we're considering is VTL and all of our speakers can be placed along this dimension. In the right plot of Figure 10.5 the y- axis doesn't matter since this is a unidimensional representation.

We can divide the stimulus space into different regions associated with different expected outcomes of our dependent variable. We do this by finding the boundary and then finding which 'region' of the space corresponds to each response category. In our case, since the VTL slope is negative for all of our groups, we know that larger VTL values correspond to more male responses. As a result, VTL values greater than the boundary must correspond to the male category. Figure 10.5 shows three divisions of our stimulus space based on the three boundaries we calculated above: One for apparent children, one for apparent adults, and an overall boundary. We can see in each case that the category boundary falls at the x-intercept corresponding to each line in the left plot of the same figure. Nearey (1990, 1992, 1997) promoted the use of figures of this kind for perceptual modeling and referred to these as **territorial maps**. Territorial maps divide a stimulus space into regions (or territories) based on the most probable outcome in that region, given the model. These maps have a very simple and useful interpretation: Stimuli falling in a category's 'territory' is expected to be identified as a member of that category.

Logistic regression and signal detection theory models 333

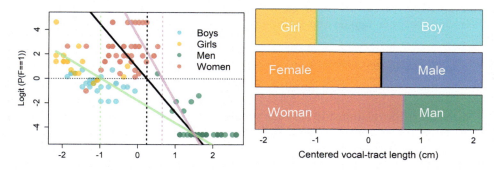

Figure 10.5 (left) Points represent individual speakers in our data based on their VTL and the logit of the probability that they were identified as female. Lines indicate the overall relationship (black), the relationship expected for apparent children (green), and that expected for apparent adults (pink). Vertical lines indicate each line's x-intercept. Point colors indicate veridical speaker categories. (right) Territorial maps implied by each line presented in the left plot. Each map divides the VTL dimension into 'territories' associated with male and female responses.

We can think about the characteristics of our fixed effects parameters, and our age-dependent lines, in terms of what they mean for the classification of speakers as female or male. It can be useful to think about category boundaries when interpreting logits because our model parameters can be interpreted as shifts in these boundaries. For example, our model intercept estimate was 0.86, and the effect for perceived adultness (`A1`) was 2.65. If we consider lines with fixed slopes, the effect of shifts in the y-intercept on classification can be understood in terms of the slope of the line. Since our line has a downward (negative) slope along VTL, raising the *y*-intercept has the effect of moving our x-intercept to the 'right' toward higher values of VTL. In other words, the positive intercept shift associated with perceived adultness increases the category boundary between apparent male and female speakers along the VTL dimension. If the slope of our line had been positive the associations would be reversed: Positive y- intercept shifts would lead to a 'leftward' motion of the category boundary.

Increasing the magnitude of our slopes (positive or negative) does not *necessarily* affect the location of the category boundary. Sometimes there can be a compensatory change in the y-intercept such that the x-intercept remains unchanged. In general, we can say that two lines with unequal slopes but equal x-intercepts differ in terms of how 'categorical' or 'fuzzy' classifications tend to be. This is because a steeper slope gets from high probabilities to low probabilities (or vice versa) faster, and therefore has a smaller ambiguous region relative to a slope with a smaller magnitude. For example, the points representing women and men are further apart along VTL than boys and girls. This means they are more separable along this dimension, and this is represented in the model by the steeper slope for speakers judged to be adults. When lines differ in both slopes and intercepts, the effect on classification boundaries needs to be considered on a case-by-case basis. However, in general, it is quite straightforward: One only

334 *Logistic regression and signal detection theory models*

needs to imagine the effects on our lines and the locations where they will cross zero. In Figure 10.4, we can see that the overall effect of apparent adultness is to increase the boundary between female and male responses along speaker VTL.

10.5.6 Answering our research question

We can answer our research questions based on our model above:

(Q1) What is the relationship between speaker VTL and the perception of femaleness?
(Q2) Does the relationship between VTL and apparent speaker gender vary in an age-dependent manner?

Speaker VTL is negatively related to the perception of femaleness with a slope of −3.59 logits per unit change in cm (s.d. = 0.39, 95% C.I = [−4.41, −2.88])). This effect increased by about 50% when listeners thought the speaker was an adult and decreased by about 50% when listeners thought the speaker was a child (mean = 2.65, s.d. = 0.35, 95% C.I = [2.01, 3.39]). Our results do indicate that the relationship between VTL and apparent femaleness varies as a function of the apparent age of the speaker. These differences can be understood in terms of the information presented in Figure 10.5 and, in particular, the territorial maps presented in the right plot. In the plot, we see that when listeners thought the speaker was a child, the boundary between male and female speakers is at a lower value of VTL (12.4 cm based on our calculations above), which makes sense given that children are smaller overall. When the listener thinks the speaker is an adult, a higher value of VTL (14.0 cm) is required to predict a male response.

We think this model reflects behavior that 'makes sense' for human listeners. Research suggests that listeners more or less 'know' how different sorts of people sound as evidenced by their ability to classify speakers by age, size, and gender. If this is true, listeners need to know that younger speakers have shorter VTLs than older speakers. Necessarily, if there is a category boundary between male and female responses for both adults and children, the one between boys and girls *must* be lower along the VTL dimension than the boundary between men and women. In the absence of this, the model would not result in the accurate classification of stimuli. For example, the overall category boundary in Figure 10.5 would result in the expectation of female classifications for *all* the boys in our sample since they all fall to the left of this line (i.e. in the 'female' territory in the overall territorial map).

10.6 Measuring sensitivity and bias

Previously we considered the probability that a listener would respond female based on speaker vocal-tract length (VTL) and apparent age. What our model didn't really tell us much about was the extent to which listeners were able to correctly identify male and female voices. To do that, we have to carry out an analysis using principles developed in signal detection theory. Whole books can (and have) been written on this topic, and we are only going to deal with it very superficially here. Our intention is to show how *sensitivity* and *bias* (to be discussed momentarily) can be estimated with signal detection theory models implemented using logistic regression. The implementation

Logistic regression and signal detection theory models 335

used here is described in DeCarlo (1998), and a thorough introduction to detection theory can be found in Green and Swets (1966) or Wickens (2002).

Imagine we want to know how well listeners can identify cases when the speaker is actually female. To do this we might just calculate the percentage of trials in which a speaker was female and was also identified as being female. However, imagine a listener identifies 100% of male and female speakers as female. If we only measure accuracy on female speaker trials this speaker would appear to perform perfectly. However, obviously, if they also think 100% of male speakers sound female then they show no ability to distinguish male and female speakers. Clearly, we need a measure that considers whether listeners can detect when female speakers are *not* there, in addition to being able to identify when they are.

First, we need to define some terminology. Consider the general case where the listener is trying to identify some signal or characteristic (e.g., femaleness), and the signal is either present or it is not. We define the **hit rate** (H) as the probability that a listener will say the speaker is female when they are. The **false alarm rate** (FA) is the probability that the listener will identify the speaker as female when they were not. We present this below for our data where Female is our vector indicating whether the listener indicated hearing a male (0) or female speaker (1), and G_v is a vector (G_v) that indicates whether the speaker's veridical gender was male (m) or female (f).

$$H = P\left(\text{Female} = 1 \,|\, G_v = f \right)$$
$$FA = P\left(\text{Female} = 1 \,|\, G_v = m \right)$$

(10.17)

The lines above say: *H* is equal to the probability the Female equals 1 given that the veridical gender is female, and *FA* is equal to the probability the Female equals 1 given that the veridical gender is male. We can calculate the overall hit and false alarm rates for our data with the code below:

```
H = mean(exp_data$Female[exp_data$G_v == "f"])
FA = mean(exp_data$Female[exp_data$G_v == "m"])
```

Or more simply using:

```
tapply(exp_data$Female, exp_data$G_v, mean)
##       f       m
## 0.8219 0.1694
```

Sensitivity is the ability to discriminate categories and is a function of the difference between a listener's hit rate and their false alarm rate. If the hit rate is 1 and the false alarm rate is 0, this listener exhibits perfect discrimination: They can identify all females as females and identify *no* males as females. If a person has a hit rate of 0.5 and a false alarm rate of 0.5 it means they show no sensitivity at all, their hit and false alarm rates are equal. This person would perform as well as someone who was not even listening to the stimuli. However, a person with a hit rate of 0.9 and a false alarm rate of 0.9 *also* shows no sensitivity, even though they are identifying 90% of women as women. The reason for this is that they are identifying 90% of *people*, including men, as women.

336 *Logistic regression and signal detection theory models*

There are potentially many ways to measure sensitivity. For example, we could just subtract the hit rate from the false alarm rate. However, this is not the best idea for many of the same reasons that we do not base our linear models directly on probabilities. One of the most common measures of sensitivity is d' ('d-prime'), which is calculated as in (10.17).

$$d' = z(H) - z(FA) \qquad (10.18)$$

Where $z(\cdot)$ is a function that converts a proportion (or probability) to a z-score (a standard normal variable, see Section 2.5.4). Models estimating d' can be implemented with Probit regression, which is basically analogous to logistic regression save for the fact that they rely on the cumulative Gaussian link function (see Section 12.3.1) rather than the inverse logit link function. The inverse logit function effectively performs the same function as $z(\cdot)$ in (10.17), meaning that logistic regression can be used to estimate d (rather than d'). We define d as the difference between the logit of the hit rate and the logit of the false alarm rate as in (10.19).

$$d = \text{logit}(H) - \text{logit}(FA) \qquad (10.19)$$

When hit rates and false alarm rates are balanced around probabilities of 0.5, this is equivalent to balancing out around values of 0 logits. When hits and false alarms balance out like this, this means that errors were equally likely to occur in response to both male and female speakers. For example, a hit rate of 0.9 means listeners made a mistake on 10% of female trials, and a false alarm rate of 0.1 indicates the same error rate for male trials. But what if they don't balance out?

Imagine a situation where a listener identifies 100% of females as female (hit rate = 1) and 50% of men as females (false alarm rate = 0.5). This seems to suggest that they make no mistakes on female trials but are only performing at chance for male trials. How could this be possible? In order to do well on female trials they need to know the speaker is female (obviously). But if they know when speakers are female, they must also know when the speaker is *not* male. So, why do they perform so poorly on the male trials? Rather than indicating differential performance across the two categories, a lack of balance across hits and false alarms indicates **response bias**, the tendency to select one category more than another. In this case, the listener does not show an increased ability to identify female speakers but rather a bias toward identifying speakers as female. A common way to measure bias is using what is called a **criterion**, defined as the negative of the average of the transformed hit and false alarm rates ((10.20)). Since we are using logits we call this c' to distinguish it from the c criterion measured using a probit model (DeCarlo, 1998).

$$c' = -\frac{1}{2}\left[\text{logit}(H) + \text{logit}(FA)\right] \qquad (10.20)$$

For historical reasons, in signal detection theory a negative criterion (negative bias) is associated with more positive responses, and a positive criterion (positive bias) is associated with more negative responses. Note however that the calculation of c' in (10.17) includes negating the mean of the logit of the hit and false alarm rates. As a result, this definition of bias involves a double negative which unnecessarily complicates things

Logistic regression and signal detection theory models 337

for many purposes: A higher average hit/false alarm rate is *negatively* related to the criterion, which is itself *negatively* related to outcomes. We think it's important to be aware of this convention but do not feel bound to follow it. As a result, we're going to divert from detection theory somewhat and simply define a bias measure b as the negative of the criterion, as seen in (10.21).

$$b = -c' = \frac{1}{2}\left[\text{logit}(H) - \text{logit}(FA)\right]$$
(10.21)

When defined in this way, we see that increasing values of b (positive bias) reflect the tendency for both hits and false alarm rates to increase, while negative values of b (negative bias) reflect the tendency of both hits and false alarm rates to decrease. For our data, a positive bias would indicate an increased tendency to identify speakers as female (since this was the variable coded with a 1) while a negative bias would indicate an increased probability of a male response. As an example, let's consider the detection of femaleness in our speaker's voices. We're going to consider how sensitivity and bias vary according to the veridical (not apparent) age of the speakers. Below we divide our data into trials involving (veridical) children and trials involving (veridical) adult speakers.

```
# adult speaker data
adults = exp_data[exp_data$A_v == "a",]

# child speaker data
children = exp_data[exp_data$A_v == "c",]
```

We can find the hit and false alarm rates by finding the average of our `Female` variable independently for veridical male and female speakers. We see these values below for adults, children, and overall.

```
# hit and false alarm rate, overall
tapply (exp_data$Female, exp_data$G_v, mean)
##       f       m
## 0.8219 0.1694

# hit and false alarm rate, for adult
tapply (adults$Female, adults$G_v, mean)
##       f       m
## 0.86111 0.02667

# hit and false alarm rate, for children
tapply (children$Female, children$G_v, mean)
##       f       m
## 0.7228 0.4074
```

Figure 10.6 presents these probabilities in addition to their logit values. Across all speakers, we see a balanced (zero bias) case, with hits and false alarms equally spaced around 0 logits. For veridical adults, the false alarm rate is lower than the hit rate is

338 *Logistic regression and signal detection theory models*

high. This indicates a negative bias meaning that listeners were more likely to respond male than female for adult speakers. We also see that hits and false alarm rates are more separated for adults, indicating a higher value of d (i.e. sensitivity). For children, we see largely the opposite pattern: Hits were more likely than false alarms indicating a positive bias (and more female responses). In addition, the distance between hits and false alarm rates was much smaller than for adults, indicating a substantially reduced sensitivity and ability to discriminate male and female speakers.

When considered as in the right plot of Figure 10.6, the estimation of hit rates, false alarm rates, and their average, is very similar to the two-group models described in Chapter 5. In Chapter 5 we estimated the effect of apparent adultness on apparent height. In that model, we had two 'groups' in our data: Trials where listeners indicated hearing an adult and trials where listeners indicated hearing a child. So. our model predicted apparent height given the apparent age of the speaker. Since we used sum coding, the intercept in our model was the average of the two group means and the effect for age was equal to 1/2 the distance between the group means.

Here, we are predicting the probability of observing a female response and we have two groups: Trials where the speaker was *actually* a female and trials where they were not. Our model predicts the logit of the probability of a female response given the veridical gender of the speaker. The probability of a female response when the speaker is actually female corresponds to the hit rate, i.e. $P(Female = 1 \mid G_v = \mathrm{f})$, as in (10.17). So, one of the groups in our two-group models is estimating the logit of the hit rate. Conversely, since the probability of a female response when the speaker is actually male corresponds to the false alarm rate, that means that the probability of a female response for actual male speakers represents our false alarm rate (i.e. $P(Female = 1 \mid G_v = \mathrm{m})$. As a result, the other group in our two-group model estimates the false alarm rate. Since we are using sum coding, the intercept in our model is the average of the two group means and so is a measure of *bias* (since it is equal to b and $-c'$, see equations (10.20 and 10.21)). The effect for our group predictor, in this case the group separation based on veridical gender, will equal 1/2 the distance between the hit and false alarm rates. This means that our predictor in this case will equal $d / 2$, meaning that the effect for veridical gender is related to *sensitivity*.

Before continuing, we want to highlight an extremely important property of these models. Any parameter interacting with the predictor indicating *veridical category*, in this case, `G_v`, reflects variation in the separation of hit and false alarm rates. Therefore, any parameters that make the `G_v` effect change in our models reflect variation in sensitivity. In contrast, any predictor that does *not* interact with the veridical category cannot affect the separation between hit and false alarm rates across different conditions. Instead, these effects simply move hit and false alarm rates together in the same direction but do not affect the separation between them. As a result, such effects can only affect response bias, the overall tendency to report one category or the other.

10.6.1 Data and research questions

We're going to keep working with the data we loaded above, which we reload below for convenience. We also center our VTL predictor and create a new predictor representing veridical gender. To represent veridical gender in our model we're going to do something new: we're going to directly specify one of the 'secret' numerical variables our models have been relying on all along (for example, see Sections 5.7.1, 7.2.2).

Logistic regression and signal detection theory models 339

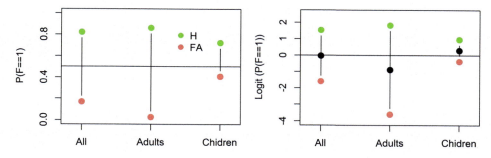

Figure 10.6 (left) Hits and false alarm rates for the detection of speaker 'femaleness', averaged across all listeners. (right) Same as in the left plot, except as logits of the rates. The black point represents the average of hits and false alarms (the bias, *b*) and the distance between the green and red points reflects sensitivity (*d*).

When you have a categorical predictor with only two levels, the coefficient representing one of the levels cannot be estimated because it is the negative of the other coefficient. When using sum coding, this is represented numerically using a predictor that equals 1 for one group (the estimated parameter) and −1 for the other group. Below, we add a variable representing veridical speaker femaleness (F_v) with values of 1 (for female) and −1 (for male).

```
library (brms)
library (bmmb)
options (contrasts = c('contr.sum','contr.sum'))
data (exp_data)

# our dependent variable
exp_data$Female = as.numeric (exp_data$G == 'f')

# make a copy of vtl
exp_data$vtl_original = exp_data$vtl

# center vtl
exp_data$vtl = exp_data$vtl - mean (exp_data$vtl)

# create veridical gender predictor
exp_data$F_v = ifelse (exp_data$G_v=="f", 1,-1)
```

We add the F_v numerical values 'by hand', rather than using a factor as we've usually done, for two reasons. First, as will be discussed below, we need the category coded with a 1 in our predictor (the estimated category) to be the same category coded with a 1 in the dependent variable. Creating a vector that we know equals 1 for a specific category and −1 for the other is a simple way to be sure of this. Second, we do this as a pedagogical device to highlight the fact that, for factors with two levels, a categorical predictor is effectively a 'slope' indicating the difference between groups expected for a 1 unit change in our fake predictor. In our case, our groups have values of −1 and 1

340 *Logistic regression and signal detection theory models*

resulting in a difference of 2 between groups for our fake predictor. This is why, in the two-group case, the difference between groups is equal to twice the value of the estimated parameter (i.e. the real difference is two fake units). In any case, representing a factor with two levels using −1 for one group and 1 for the other has the same effects as sum coding that factor, and we will simply be treating the F_v as a sum-coded factor in the discussion below.

The variables from our data frame involved in this analysis are:

- L: A number from 1 to 15 indicating which *listener* responded to the trial.
- S: A number from 1 to 139 indicating which *speaker* produced the trial stimulus.
- G: The *apparent gender* of the speaker indicated by the listener, f (female) or m (male).
- G_v: The *veridical gender* of the speaker indicated by the listener, f (female) or m (male).
- A_v: The *veridical age* of the speaker indicated by the listener, a (adult) or c (child).

We're going to model the ability of listeners to discriminate the gender of speakers from their voices. We would like to know:

(Q1) How different is listeners' ability to discriminate the gender of children and adults?
(Q2) Is response bias different for children and for adults?

10.6.2 Description of the model

Our model formula should minimally be:

```
Female ~ F_v + (F_v|L) + (1|S)
```

Which predicts the response (female = 1, male = 0) as a function of the actual speaker gender (female = 1, male = −1). Again, note the similarity to the two group models we fit in Chapter 5. For this model, the intercept would reflect response bias and the F_v parameter would reflect sensitivity. The model formula we're actually going to use looks like this:

```
Female ~ F_v * A_v + (F_v * A_v|L) + (1|S)
```

Which we can expand to:

```
Female ~ F_v + A_v + F_v:A_v + (F_v + A_v + F_v:A_v|L) + (1|S)
```

Where A_v represents veridical adultness. As noted above, all predictors in these sorts of models that do not interact with F_v represent bias terms. Thus, the model intercept represents overall bias and the A_v term reflects changes in bias as a function of the veridical adultness of the speaker. All model parameters that *do* interact with F_v reflect sensitivity. So, F_v represents overall sensitivity, and the F_v:A_v

Logistic regression and signal detection theory models 341

interaction represents variation in sensitivity dependent on veridical age. We're going to keep using the same priors we fit for our last logistic model:

```
prior = c(set_prior("student_t(3, 0, 3)", class = "Intercept"),
          set_prior("student_t(3, 0, 3)", class = "b"),
          set_prior("student_t(3, 0, 3)", class = "sd"),
          set_prior("lkj_corr_cholesky(2)", class = "cor"))
```

Our full model specification is:

$$\text{Female}_{[i]} \sim \text{Bernoulli}\left(p_{[i]}\right)$$

$$p_{[i]} = \text{logistic}\left(z_{[i]}\right)$$

$$z_{[i]} = b_{[i]} + d_{[i]}$$

$$b_{[i]} = \text{Intercept} + A_v + A_v : L_{\left[L_{[i]}\right]} + L_{\left[L_{[i]}\right]} + S_{\left[S_{[i]}\right]}$$

$$d_{[i]} = F_v + F_v : A_v + F_v : L_{\left[L_{[i]}\right]} + F_v : A_v : L_{\left[L_{[i]}\right]}$$

Priors:

$$S_{[\bullet]} \sim \text{Normal}\left(0, \sigma_S\right)$$

$$\begin{bmatrix} L_{[\bullet]} \\ A_v : L_{[\bullet]} \\ F_v : L_{[\bullet]} \\ A : F_v : L_{[\bullet]} \end{bmatrix} \sim \text{MVNormal}\left(\begin{bmatrix} 0 \\ 0 \\ 0 \\ 0 \end{bmatrix}, \Sigma\right)$$

$$\text{Intercept} \sim t(3,0,3)$$

$$A, VTL, A : VTL \sim t(3,0,3)$$

$$\sigma_L, \sigma_{A_v:L}, \sigma_{F_v:L}, \sigma_{A_v:F_v:L}, \sigma_S \sim t(3,0,3)$$

$$R \sim \text{LKJCorr}(2)$$

(10.22)

In Chapter 9 we discussed how the model representation above separates our line parameters into those affecting slopes and those affecting intercepts. In (10.22) we can instead see a segregation of parameters into those affecting biases ($b_{[i]} = \ldots$) and those affecting sensitivity ($d_{[i]} = \ldots$). Our plain English model description is now:

We're treating our femaleness judgments (1 or 0 for female or male) as coming from a Bernoulli distribution with a probability that varies trial to trial. The logit of the probability (z) varies based on the sum of parameters related to response bias (b) and discrimination (d). The expected bias for a given situation is equal to the sum of the overall intercept, an effect for veridical age (A_v), listener-specific effects for veridical age ($A_v : L$), listener-specific deviations (L), and speaker-specific deviations (S). The expected discrimination in a given situation varies based on an overall discrimination (F_v, the main effect), deviations based on veridical age ($F_v : A_v$),

342   *Logistic regression and signal detection theory models*

listener-specific deviations ($F_v : L$), and listener-specific interactions between veridical age and veridical femaleness ($F_v : A_v : L$)). The speaker intercept (S) terms were drawn from a normal distribution with a mean of zero and a standard deviation estimated from the data. The listener random effects were drawn from a multivariate normal distribution with means of zero and a covariance matrix estimated from the data. All other effects (e.g., the Intercept, VTL, A, etc.) were treated as 'fixed' and drawn from prior distributions appropriate for their expected range of values.

10.6.3 *Fitting and interpreting the model*

Below is the function call we need to fit the model described in (10.22). Note that it is simply a logistic regression model, just one with a specific structure as discussed above.

```
# Fit the model yourself
model_gender_dt =
  brm (Female ~ F_v*A_v + (F_v*A_v|L) + (1|S), data=exp_data,
       chains=4, cores=4, family="bernoulli",
       warmup=1000, iter = 5000, thin = 4,
       prior = c(set_prior("student_t(3, 0, 3)", class = "Intercept"),
                 set_prior("student_t(3, 0, 3)", class = "b"),
                 set_prior("student_t(3, 0, 3)", class = "sd"),
                 set_prior("lkj_corr_cholesky (2)", class = "cor")))

# Or download it from the GitHub page:
model_gender_dt = bmmb::get_model ('10_model_gender_dt.RDS')
```

We are mainly interested in the fixed effects and combinations of these:

```
fixef (model_gender_dt)
##              Estimate Est.Error    Q2.5    Q97.5
## Intercept    -0.3514    0.2634  -0.8774   0.1545
## F_v           2.2522    0.1851   1.9038   2.6424
## A_v1         -0.7712    0.2255  -1.2340  -0.3309
## F_v:A_v1      1.3446    0.1764   1.0086   1.7019
```

We can find the age-specific intercept terms, representing the bias, and double the age-specific `F_v` effects, representing sensitivity, as seen below.

```
gender_dt_hypothesis = bmmb::short_hypothesis (
  model_gender_dt,
  hypothesis = c("Intercept = 0",               # overall bias
                 "Intercept + A_v1 = 0",         # adult bias
                 "Intercept - A_v1 = 0",         # child bias
                 "2*(F_v) = 0",                  # overall sensitivity
                 "2*(F_v + F_v:A_v1) = 0",       # adult sensitivity
                 "2*(F_v - F_v:A_v1) = 0"))      # child sensitivity
```

We plot these biases and sensitivities in the left plot of Figure 10.7. In the same figure, we also compare listener-dependent biases and sensitivities for veridical adults and children. Since we've covered how to easily recover these 'random effects' previously (e.g. in Section 4.6.1) we only provide a single example below.

```
# listener-dependent biases for veridical adults
biases_adult = bmmb::short_hypothesis (
  model_gender_dt,
  hypothesis = c("Intercept+A_v1 = 0"),group="L", scope="coef")
```

10.6.4 Answering our research questions

The following verbal description of the results in Figure 10.7 is based on the biases and sensitivities reconstructed in gender_dt_hypothesis, presented in Table 10.1. Our model suggests a bias toward male responses for adults, and perhaps a slight bias toward female responses for children. Speaker femaleness appeared to be discriminable for both adults and children, although sensitivity was substantially larger for adults. Based on Figure 10.7 We can also say that all listeners were able to discriminate male and female adult speakers, and most (but not all) were able to do this for children.

We can potentially understand the difference in sensitivity between veridical children and veridical adults if we assume that: (1) Speaker VTL is a useful clue in the discrimination of male and female speakers, and (2) The distribution of VTL between our speaker categories in the whole population is roughly the same as in our data. Consider the distribution of speaker VTL across boys and girls, and women and men in Figure 10.8. Imagine a listener encounters a speaker with a VTL of 15 cm. This value is typical for an adult male but *extremely* unlikely for an adult female. As a result, a speaker with a VTL of 15 cm is very likely to be a male. Because of the lack of overlap along VTL for adult males and females, there are many values of VTL that are plausible for adult males that are implausible for adult females. As a result, adult men and women will be easier to discriminate along the VTL dimension. In contrast, the boy

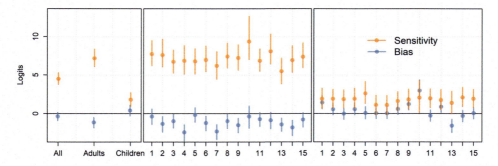

Figure 10.7 (left) Average bias and sensitivity and the 'simple effects' of bias and sensitivity across levels of veridical adultness. (middle) Bias and sensitivity for adult speakers, presented individually for each listener. (right) Bias and sensitivity for child speakers, presented individually for each listener.

Table 10.1 *Posterior means, standard errors, and 2.5% and 97.5% quantiles for bias and sensitivity under different conditions*

	Estimate	Est.error	Q2.5	Q97.5
Overall bias	−0.35	0.26	−0.88	0.15
Adult bias	−1.12	0.34	−1.81	−0.49
Child bias	0.42	0.36	−0.28	1.11
Overall sensitivity	4.50	0.37	3.81	5.28
Adult sensitivity	7.19	0.57	6.13	8.39
Child sensitivity	1.82	0.44	0.94	2.72

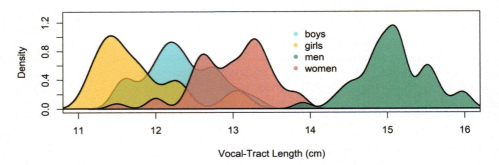

Figure 10.8 Distribution of boys, girls, men, and women in our speaker data according to their vocal-tract length.

and girl distributions largely overlap. This means a VTL of 12 cm could plausibly be either a boy or a girl, and the same could be said for most VTL values for boys and girls. As a result, it will clearly be more difficult to distinguish the gender of children along the VTL dimension and we can reasonably expect sensitivity to be smaller than it is for adults.

We can also potentially explain the changes in response bias that we saw in our results based on Figure 10.8. Below we see a table showing categorizations for adult males and females.

```
xtabs ( ~ adults$C_v + adults$C)
##            adults$C
## adults$C_v   b    g    m    w
##          b   0    0    0    0
##          g   0    0    0    0
##          m  31    0  626   18
##          w  97  109    3  511
```

We see that men are rarely confused with girls or women (18 out of 675 trials, 2.7%). In contrast, women are confused with males in 15% (100/675) of cases, and specifically confused with boys in 14% (97/675) of cases. This is likely because adult males tend to have substantially longer VTLs than women and girls, but the VTLs of adult females

Logistic regression and signal detection theory models **345**

and younger boys overlap somewhat. Recall that a response bias is simply an increase in responses for that category overall. Since men and women are balanced in our sample, if adult males tend to be identified as male almost always, and adult females are sometimes confused with younger males, this will necessarily result in a 'bias' toward male responses.

10.7 Exercises

The analyses in the main body of the text all involve only the unmodified 'actual' resonance level (in `exp_data`). Responses for the stimuli with the simulated 'big' resonance are reserved for exercises throughout. You can get the 'big' resonance in the `exp_ex` data frame, or all data in the `exp_data_all` data frame.

Fit and interpret one of the suggested models:

6   Easy: Analyze the (pre-fit) model that's exactly like `model_gender_vtl`, except using the data in `exp_ex` (`bmmb::get_model("10_model_gender_vtl_ex.RDS")`).
7   Easy: Analyze the (pre-fit) model that's exactly like `model_gender_dt`, except using the data in `exp_ex` (`bmmb::get_model("10_model_gender_dt_ex.RDS")`).
8   Medium: Fit models like the ones in this chapter, but include comparisons across resonance levels. For example, the model formula for a model could be `Female ~ vtl*A+R+A:R + (vtl*A+R+A:R|L) + (1|S)`. This model includes an effect for resonance level, in addition to an interaction between resonance and apparent age.
9   Hard: Fit models like the ones in this chapter, but predict apparent age instead of apparent gender.

In any case, describe the model, present and explain the results, and include some figures.

References

DeCarlo, L. T. (1998). Signal detection theory and generalized linear models. *Psychological Methods*, 3(2), 186.

Green, D. M., & Swets, J. A. (1966). *Signal detection theory and psychophysics* (Vol. 1, pp. 1969–2012). New York: Wiley.

Kruschke, J. (2014). *Doing Bayesian data analysis: A tutorial with R, JAGS, and Stan*. Amsterdam: Elsevier Science.

McCullagh, P., & Nelder, J. A. (2019). *Generalized linear models*. Routledge.

Nearey, T. M. (1990). The segment as a unit of speech perception. *Journal of Phonetics*, 18(3), 347–373.

Nearey, T. M. (1992). Context effects in a double-weak theory of speech perception. *Language and Speech*, 35(1–2), 153–171.

Nearey, T. M. (1997). Speech perception as pattern recognition. *The Journal of the Acoustical Society of America*, 101(6), 3241–3254.

Wickens, T. D. (2002). *Elementary signal detection theory*. Oxford: Oxford University Press.

11 Multiple quantitative predictors, dealing with large models, and Bayesian ANOVA

In this chapter, we introduce models with multiple quantitative predictors and interactions between them. After that, we will have covered the basic modeling concepts necessary to fit most linear models. The models you fit to your own data will include some combination of the elements covered in the previous chapters, and can potentially result in large models with hundreds (or thousands) of estimated parameters. Traditionally, models with many estimated parameters have had three general problems:

1   A model with many predictors may have 'too many' predictors. We will vaguely define 'extra' predictors as those which have no meaningful statistical association with your dependent variable, and which do not appreciably improve your model in any way. Sometimes, the 'extra' predictors have estimated values that are difficult to distinguish from those of the 'real' parameters, leading to incorrect conclusions.
2   A model with many parameters may have more difficulties with fitting/convergence, meaning you can't get good estimates for the model coefficients. Regardless of the approach to parameter estimation, more complicated models make it more difficult to find the optimal parameter values given the data and chosen model structure.
3   It can be difficult to interpret a model with hundreds (or thousands) of parameters. With so many parameters it is important to not miss the forest for the trees, that is, not consider every parameter in isolation to the detriment of understanding what information your fitted model provides in general.

In this chapter, we're going to cover a Bayesian approach to working with large models. First, we're going to discuss how working with multilevel Bayesian models can help us with problems (1) and (2) above. After that, we're going to discuss an easy way to approach problem (3) using our Bayesian models.

Before continuing, we should note that designs with many quantitative predictors, factors, and interactions between these can result in very complicated models which then have to be interpreted. However, the researcher is ultimately the one who determines the complexity of the analysis they are then faced with. Once when Santiago was buying a backpack for traveling, he was looking for the biggest backpack possible. One of the reviews said, "1/5 stars, it was way too heavy when I filled it all the way up with my stuff". However, if we buy a large backpack and fill it with many heavy things, it doesn't seem fair to blame the backpack when it becomes difficult to carry. In the same way, if you are faced with a complex model that you then need to interpret, you shouldn't blame the model, `brms`, or us, for your predicament.

DOI: 10.4324/9781003285878-11

Multiple quantitative predictors, dealing and Bayesian ANOVA   347

In order to avoid a situation where you end up with data you can't analyze or a model you can't interpret, it's worth considering the following questions *before* advancing to the data collection stage of your experiment:

* How will I analyze the data? Will I be able to carry out my planned analysis?
* What will the model structure be?
* What kind of results am I expecting?
* How will the expected results be reflected by the model parameters? How would different results manifest in the model parameters?

11.1 Chapter pre-cap

In this chapter, we discuss why Bayesian multilevel models are well suited for the analysis of complex models with large numbers of parameters, and some strategies for interpreting these models are presented. A model with two quantitative predictors, as well as an interaction between them, is outlined, and the model is fit and interpreted. We introduce Bayesian analysis of variance (BANOVA) and Bayesian ANOVA plots, and use these to investigate the initial model presented in the chapter. Following that, a multivariate logistic regression model is fit and interpreted using a Bayesian ANOVA. After this, we explain how multivariate logistic models can be used to interpret classification and listener behavior. Finally, we discuss model selection and misspecification, and some diagnostics that can help find and diagnose problems in large models.

11.2 Models with multiple quantitative predictors

Our regression models so far have only involved at most a single quantitative predictor. This means that the relationship between the dependent variable and our predictor formed surfaces with a single dimension: Lines. In the left and middle plots in Figure 11.1, we see the linear relationships between speaker vocal-tract length (VTL) and fundamental frequency (f0) with apparent speaker height (see Chapter 1, or 13, for more information on these variables). In each case, the expected value for the *y*-axis variable is the value of the line at each *x*-axis location. The residual, the error in the prediction of each observation, is the vertical distance between the line and the observation.

We can also think about how apparent height, VTL, and f0 vary together. Every point in Figure 11.1 has a specific value of f0, VTL, and apparent height. These three quantitative variables can be thought of as defining a single location in a three-dimensional space. Imagine you had a clear plastic cube containing points arranged as in 11.1 inside it, where each dimension along the cube represented one of the dimensions in the figure. Looking 'through' the cube at different orientations would result in arrangements just like the plots in Figure 11.1. The first plot shows the view through the VTL side, and the second plot shows the view down the f0 side, a 1/4 rotation of the cube. The final plot shows the view down through the top of the cube.

It may be easier to see what we mean in Figure 11.2, which attempts to present our points in three dimensions. The left plot of Figure 11.2 corresponds (more or less) to the left plot in Figure 11.1, while the right plot of Figure 11.2 corresponds (more or less) to the middle plot in Figure 11.1. When we have two quantitative predictors, our models predict values along **planes** rather than lines. If we want to predict apparent height

348 *Multiple quantitative predictors, dealing and Bayesian ANOVA*

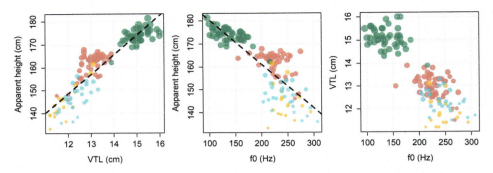

Figure 11.1 (left) Average apparent height reported for each speaker plotted against speaker vocal-tract length (VTL). Point size reflects average apparent height. (middle) Same as the left plot but comparing apparent height to f0. (right) A comparison of VTL and f0 for each speaker.

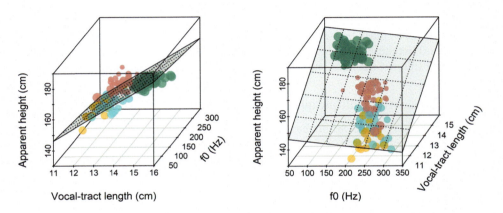

Figure 11.2 (left) A three-dimensional plot of the variables presented in Figure 11.1. (right) The same as the left plot but with a different orientation of the variables.

based on speaker f0 and VTL, we are basically asking: Can we predict the height of a point in our three-dimensional space (i.e. location on the vertical z-axis) based on its x- and y-axis locations?

For example, any given point in the room you are sitting in right now can be specified using three variables that determine its location along the width, depth, and height of the room. Imagine the points in Figure 11.2 were floating in the room with you, arranged just as in the figure. You are given a large flat board (a *plane*) and asked to find the 'best' orientation for the board. When we fit lines, we preferred those that tended to minimize the residuals, the y-axis distance of the points to the line. The same principle holds when we fit models with two (or more) quantitative predictors. In general, planes are 'better' when they minimize the distance from each point to the surface of the plane along the axis representing the dependent variable. Though it's a bit more complicated than this for multilevel models, this general principle (i.e. the minimization of the residuals) still applies. In Figure 11.2, we see the plane that results

Multiple quantitative predictors, dealing and Bayesian ANOVA 349

in the smallest residuals for our points, i.e. the smallest distances between the surface of the plane and the points along the apparent height axis.

In equation (11.1) we see that the height of the plane along the z-axis is determined by an intercept (a) plus the product of the x-axis coordinate and its slope (b), and the product of the y-axis coordinate and its slope (c). When we fit a model that includes two quantitative predictors, the model represents the planes it estimates using their a, b, and c parameters.

$$z = a + b \cdot x + c \cdot y \tag{11.1}$$

Since the plane has two dimensions it has two slopes: A field can be uphill/downhill away from you, but also be up/downhill from left to right. The slope coefficient for each quantitative predictor changes the slope of the plane independently for each dimension. In fact, the slope of each predictor reflects the expected change in the dependent variable when all other predictors are *held constant*. The intercept of the model slides the planes up/down the z-axis without changing their slopes along either the x or y dimensions.

Our discussion above has been entirely about planes, and we will stick to two quantitative predictors for our models. However, your model can include any number of quantitative predictors, it just gets harder to have good intuitions about the geometry involved. If your model has n quantitative predictors, your data specify points in an $n+1$ dimensional space, where dimension $n+1$ represents the dependent variable. Residuals in such models represent the difference between the surface of the n dimensional shape specified by the predictors and the position of each point along the $n+1$ dimension.

11.3 Interactions between quantitative predictors

Models with two quantitative predictors model variation in the dependent variable along planes. The 'interaction' between quantitative variables in regression models is represented by adding a new predictor, the **cross-product** (i.e. $x \cdot y$) of the two variables. We can add a term representing the interaction between our two quantitative predictors to equation (11.2). It's common to refer to this term as the 'interaction' between our quantitative predictors, and we will adopt this convention. Just keep in mind that we are actually referring to the product of the two variables.

$$z = a + (b \cdot x) + (c \cdot y) + (d \cdot x \cdot y) \tag{11.2}$$

In general, interaction terms are parameters that allow for the effect of a predictor to vary according to the value of some other predictor. When it comes to quantitative predictors, an interaction means that the slope of each predictor continuously increases/decreases as a function of the value of the *other* predictor. Consider the equation below which omits the term $(c \cdot y)$ for the sake of simplicity. If we factor out the x from the second and third terms on the right, we can see that the slope for the x dimension, b, will vary as a function of the value of y and the interaction coefficient d.

$$z = a + (b \cdot x) + (d \cdot x \cdot y)$$
$$z = a + (b) \cdot x + (d \cdot y) \cdot x \tag{11.3}$$
$$z = a + (b + d \cdot y) \cdot x$$

350 *Multiple quantitative predictors, dealing and Bayesian ANOVA*

Imagine a case where the slope (b) along the x dimension is fixed at 2 and the interaction term (d) is equal to zero. In this case there is no interaction between x and y. When this happens the slope of x is constant and does not change based on the value of y, as in (11.4).

$$b = 2, d = 0$$
$$z = a + (b + d \cdot y) \cdot x$$
$$z = a + (2 + 0 \cdot y) \cdot x \tag{11.4}$$
$$z = a + 2 \cdot x$$

Now consider a situation where the interaction term has some non-zero value (e.g. 1). In this case, we *will* see the slope along x change as a function of the value of y. In (11.5) we see that as y increases from 1 to 5, the effective slope along the x-axis increases from 3 to 7. This reasoning also holds for the y dimension and also means that negative interactions result in a *decrease* in slopes as the value of variables increases.

$$b = 2, d = 1, y = 1$$
$$z = a + (2 + 1 \cdot 1) \cdot x$$
$$z = a + 3 \cdot x$$

$$b = 2, d = 1, y = 5 \tag{11.5}$$
$$z = a + (2 + 1 \cdot 5) \cdot x$$
$$z = a + 7 \cdot x$$

The inclusion of cross-product terms means that we are not modeling variation along planes anymore, but rather along **hyperbolic paraboloids**. Sometimes these sorts of surfaces are referred to as **saddle surfaces** because they contain what's known as a **saddle point**, a point where the slopes along the x and y dimension are both equal to zero. Informally, a saddle point can be thought of as the flat spot in the middle of a shape that curves along two dimensions in a manner resembling a horse saddle. We're often going to refer to hyperbolic paraboloids as *saddles* because their full name is a bit of a mouthful, and because we are mainly interested in contrasting these with planes. However, it's important to keep in mind that hyperbolic paraboloids are one among many types of saddle surface.

The function for a hyperbolic paraboloid can be seen below, where the height of the surface is equal to the product of some parameter d and its x and y coordinates.

$$z = d \cdot x \cdot y \tag{11.6}$$

Clearly, the interaction of quantitative predictors results in a saddle shape as defined in (11.6). When our models include effects for x, y, *and* their interactions (cross-product), we are effectively modeling a surface that combines a plane and a saddle shape, as in equation (11.2). In Figure 11.3 we can see a comparison of a plane in the top row and a saddle shape in the middle row. In the middle row on the left we can imagine that if we were walking 'into' the plot, the ground would first be sloping down from left to right. However, as we proceeded into the plot the ground would gradually change so that it is sloping up from left to right further into the figure. In other words, the left-to-right slope would gradually increase as we walk further into the plot.

Multiple quantitative predictors, dealing and Bayesian ANOVA 351

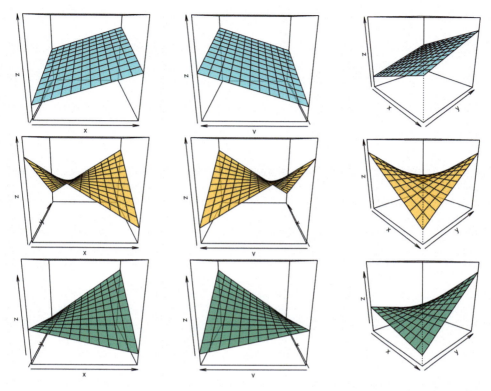

Figure 11.3 (top row) Three perspectives of the same plane. (middle row) Three perspectives of the same saddle shape. (bottom row) Three perspectives of the sum of the plane and the saddle shape in the top two rows.

We can combine a plane and a saddle, as in the bottom row of Figure 11.3. The general formula for such a shape is presented below, and we've placed the terms in parentheses just to make it easier to interpret the equation. Notice that all we really did was add the term for the saddle shape in (11.6) to the plane in (11.1).

$$z = a + (b \cdot x) + (c \cdot y) + (d \cdot x \cdot y) \tag{11.7}$$

11.3.1 Centering quantitative predictors when including interactions

When you include interactions between quantitative predictors in your regression models, it may be useful to center these predictors because this can improve your model convergence statistics, and can also improve the interpretability of the model. Convergence statistics can be improved by centering because this can reduce the correlation between the predictors and their cross-product in many cases. To see why, consider the very simple example shown below:

```
x1 = c(1,2,3)
x2 = c(1,2,3)
```

352 *Multiple quantitative predictors, dealing and Bayesian ANOVA*

```
x1x2 = x1 * x2
x1x2
## [1] 1 4 9

cor (cbind(x1,x2,x1x2))
##            x1       x2     x1x2
## x1     1.0000  1.0000  0.9897
## x2     1.0000  1.0000  0.9897
## x1x2   0.9897  0.9897  1.0000
```

The cross-product of `x1` and `x2`, `x1x2`, increases in value together with both predictors, meaning it enters into a **monotonic** relationship with the predictors (they increase and decrease together). This results in a strong correlation between the cross-product and the predictors seen above. We can help minimize this sort of correlation if we center `x1` and `x2`. When we do this, the centered values will be positive when they are above the sample mean and negative when they are below it. Under these conditions, their cross-product will be positive when both variables are above or below their mean, and negative when one is above and the other is below. This breaks the monotonic relationship between the cross-product and the predictors, i.e. the cross-product does not always increase when one of the predictors increases.

We re-do the example above with 'centered' data, assuming that the mean had been 2. We can see that the correlation between the cross-product and the predictors is now zero, though the correlation between the predictors themselves is still one.

```
x1 = c(-1,0,1)
x2 = c(-1,0,1)
x1x2 = x1 * x2
x1x2
## [1] 1 0 1

cor (cbind(x1,x2,x1x2))
##         x1 x2 x1x2
## x1       1  1    0
## x2       1  1    0
## x1x2     0  0    1
```

We include a less controlled example of this below. We generate two samples of 100 random Gaussian variables (`x1, x2`) with a mean of 500 and a standard deviation of 1. These variables are not strongly correlated (-0.06), and yet their cross-product (`x1x2`) is strongly correlated with both variables (0.67, and 0.70).

```
x1 = rnorm (100,500,1)
x2 = rnorm (100,500,1)
x1x2 = x1*x2

cor (cbind(x1,x2,x1x2))
##            x1        x2      x1x2
## x1     1.00000  -0.05803   0.6747
```

Multiple quantitative predictors, dealing and Bayesian ANOVA   353

```
## x2      -0.05803   1.00000 0.6977
## x1x2    0.67472    0.69768 1.0000
```

We re-do the code above, this time after centering `x1` and `x2`. We can see that centering can dramatically reduce the correlation between the quantitative predictors and the interaction between them.

```
x1_c = x1 - mean (x1)
x2_c = x2 - mean (x2)
x1x2_c = x1_c * x2_c

cor (cbind(x1_c,x2_c,x1x2_c))
##                x1_c     x2_c    x1x2_c
## x1_c      1.00000 -0.05803 -0.05193
## x2_c     -0.05803  1.00000  0.12431
## x1x2_c   -0.05193  0.12431  1.00000
```

In terms of the interpretability of your coefficients, it's very important to keep in mind that in the presence of an interaction, the 'main effect' slope along a dimension is only the actual slope *when all other predictors involved in the interaction are equal to zero*. For example, consider a model including quantitative predictors x_1 and x_2, and the interaction between them. As shown in (11.3), the effective slope for x_1 in the presence of an interaction between x_1 and x_2 varies as a function of the value of x_2. However, when x_2 is equal to zero its influence on the slope of x_1 is erased, and the slope of x_1 reported by your model applies. If you don't center, $x_2 = 0$ may not occur in your data, meaning that the slope reported by your model is not actually expected to occur for your data. In contrast, if you center your predictors the slope for x_1 reported by your model represents the slope along this dimension when x_2 is at its mean.

Because of these advantages, you should consider centering quantitative predictors routinely whenever you plan to include interactions between these in your models, in the absence of a compelling reason not to (e.g. that 0 is a meaningful value for your predictors). Actually, as discussed in Section 9.3.2, you may find it useful to center quantitative predictors even if you are *not* including interactions between them.

11.3.2 Data and research questions

The models we fit in Chapters 9 and 10 were missing an obvious and important predictor: The fundamental frequency (f0) of the speaker's voice. The fundamental frequency of a sound is the main acoustic correlate of the perceived pitch. We know from previous studies that, in general, speakers with lower speaking f0s tend to be identified as taller (see Chapter 13 for a discussion of this). In this section, we're going to fit a model that tries to predict apparent height from VTL, f0, and the interaction of the two.

Below we load our packages and data, and center our quantitative predictors. We also scale f0 so that it has a reasonably similar between-group difference as the VTL predictor. Specifically, the average difference in VTL between adult females and males is about 2 cm, and the difference in f0 between the groups is about 100 Hz. This means that if we divide f0 by 100 the difference between men and women is about 1 unit,

354 *Multiple quantitative predictors, dealing and Bayesian ANOVA*

comparable to the 2-unit difference between these groups in VTL. The reason we don't divide by 50 to make them even more similar is that dividing by 100 results in frequencies being represented in hectohertz (1 hectohertz = 100 Hertz), which is easier to interpret than 50 Hz units.

```
library (brms)
library (bmmb)
options (contrasts = c('contr.sum','contr.sum'))

data (exp_data)

# center VTL
exp_data$vtl_original = exp_data$vtl
exp_data$vtl = exp_data$vtl - mean (exp_data$vtl)

# center and scale f0
exp_data$f0_original = exp_data$f0
exp_data$f0 = exp_data$f0 - mean(exp_data$f0)
exp_data$f0 = exp_data$f0 / 100
```

We're not going to have well-defined research questions this time. Instead, we have a more 'meta' question that we will try to deal with:

(Q1) What do we do with all these parameters? How do we know what to focus on, and where to begin?

11.3.3 Description of the model

We're going to begin with a model that includes all possible interactions between our predictors, and also includes listener-dependent versions of all of our 'fixed' effects parameters. Models of this sort are sometimes referred to as **maximal** models because they include the maximal (i.e. most complicated) random effects structure 'supported' by the data (see Section 8.8). This means that we include corresponding 'random' listener effects for each of our 'fixed' effects predictors. However, notice that we don't include any speaker-dependent predictors in our model (other than intercepts). This is because each speaker had a single f0 and VTL, and many were only identified as either male or female, or only as either adults or children. As a result, estimating interactions between these acoustic predictors and the speaker predictor is not *supported* by our data. Our model formula is:

```
height ~ vtl*f0*A*G + (vtl*f0*A*G|L) + (1|S)
```

We're going to use the same priors we used for our regression models in Chapter 9. We won't present the full model description as this is too long at this point, and all of the required elements have already been presented and discussed at this point. However, we can talk about all our model coefficients and what they mean for our model. Below is an 'expanded' version of our model formula that spells out all of the fixed effect parameters implied by the formula above.

Multiple quantitative predictors, dealing and Bayesian ANOVA 355

```
height ~ Intercept + vtl + f0 + A + G +
         A:G1 + vtl:f0 + vtl:A + vtl:G + f0:A + f0:G +
         vtl:f0:A + vtl:f0:G + vtl:A:G + f0:A:G + vtl:f0:A:G
```

We can group these parameters together based on the way they affect the surfaces they represent: Intercept parameters (a), VTL slope parameters (b), f0 parameters (c), and VTL:f0 interaction parameters (d).

```
a = Intercept + A          + G          + A:G
b = vtl       + vtl:A      + vtl:G      + vtl:A:G
c = f0        + f0:A       + f0:G       + f0:A:G
d = vtl:f0    + vtl:f0:A   + vtl:f0:G   + vtl:f0:A:G
```

Notice that there is a symmetry to the parameters for each 'dimension' in our model. Each one contains a 'main effect' term (`Intercept`, `vtl`, `f0`, `vtl:f0`), an interaction with apparent age (`A`, `vtl:A`, `f0:A`, `vtl:f0:A`), an interaction with apparent gender (`G`, `vtl:G`, `f0:G`, `vtl:f0:G`), and an interaction with apparent age *and* gender (`A:G`, `vtl:A:G`, `f0:A:G`, `vtl:f0:A:G`). This means that our models have intercepts, slopes (along two dimensions), and a saddle component (d), that can each vary as a function of apparent gender, age, and the interaction of the two. This is a complicated model, which is why it has so many parameters. In fact, it actually has many more parameters than this. For example, to calculate the listener-dependent a,b,c and d parameters, which we can call `a_L`, `b_L`, `c_L` and `d_L`, we would need to add the following (hypothetical) parameters (implied by this `(vtl*f0*A*G|L)`) to our calculations.

```
a_L = a + Intercept:L + A:L         + G:L         + A:G:L
b_L = b + vtl:L       + vtl:A:L     + vtl:G:L     + vtl:A:G:L
c_L = c + f0:L        + f0:A:L      + f0:G:L      + f0:A:G:L
d_L = d + vtl:f0:L    + vtl:f0:A:L  + vtl:f0:G:L  + vtl:f0:A:G:L
```

As a result, the calculation of the intercept alone would actually be:

```
a = Intercept + A + G + A:G + Intercept:L + A:L + G:L + A:G:L
```

Which can be rearranged to show that it is simply the sum of each corresponding 'fixed' effect and the corresponding listener-dependent effect.

```
a = (Intercept + Intercept:L) + (A + A:L) + (G + G:L) + (A:G
+ A:G:L)
```

This relatively complex model has been built up out of parts: We discussed the decomposition of intercepts into multiple factors, as in *a* in Chapter 7. We discussed the inclusion of quantitative predictors and the decomposition of variation in these, as in *b* and *c* in Chapter 9. Now, we discuss the addition of more quantitative predictors (*c*) and the interactions between these (*d*). Effectively, we have been incrementally adding complexity to our models and, from here on, increasing complexity mostly consists of sticking together larger numbers of these basic components in different ways.

356 *Multiple quantitative predictors, dealing and Bayesian ANOVA*

We said we weren't going to provide a formal definition of this model, but if we had, the first few lines might have looked something like this:

$$\text{height}_{[i]} \sim t\left(v, \mu_{[i]}, \sigma\right)$$

$$\mu_{[i]} = a_{[i]} + \left(b_{[i]} \cdot \text{vtl}_{[i]}\right) + \left(c_{[i]} \cdot \text{f0}_{[i]}\right) + \left(d_{[i]} \cdot \text{f0}_{[i]} \cdot \text{vtl}_{[i]}\right) \tag{11.8}$$

$$\ldots$$

And the following lines would have described *a*, *b*, *c*, and *d* as the sum of the appropriate model parameters as we did above (for a and a_L). Below, we provide an abbreviated plain English description corresponding to this formula:

```
height ~ vtl*f0*A*G + (vtl*f0*A*G|L) + (1|S).
```

Apparent speaker height is predicted based on two quantitative variables, speaker f0 and VTL, and two categorical variables, apparent gender, and apparent age. Our model includes all possible interactions between these predictors, resulting in 16 'fixed' effects predictors (see above). Our model also included listener-dependent effects for all fixed effects, which were drawn from a 16-dimensional normal distribution whose standard deviations and covariance matrix were estimated from the data. Our model included speaker-dependent intercepts drawn from a normal distribution with a mean of zero and a standard deviation estimated from the data. All remaining parameters were given prior distributions appropriate for their expected range of values.

11.3.4 Fitting the model

We fit our model using the code below:

```
# Fit the model yourself
priors = c(brms::set_prior("student_t(3,0, 12)", class = "Intercept"),
           brms::set_prior("student_t(3,0, 12)", class = "b"),
           brms::set_prior("student_t(3,0, 12)", class = "sd"),
           brms::set_prior("lkj_corr_cholesky (2)", class = "cor"),
           brms::set_prior("gamma(2, 0.1)", class = "nu"),
           brms::set_prior("student_t(3,0, 12)", class = "sigma"))


model_height_vtl_f0 =
  brms::brm (height ~ vtl*f0*A*G + (vtl*f0*A*G|L) + (1|S), data = exp_data,
             chains = 4, cores = 4, warmup = 1000, iter = 5000, thin = 4,
             prior = priors, family = "student")


# Or download it from the GitHub page:
model_height_vtl_f0 = bmmb::get_model ('11_model_height_vtl_f0.RDS')
```

Normally this is where we would discuss and interpret the characteristics of our model. We're going to leave this for Chapter 13, where we present a model very similar to this in a format more similar to what you might see in an academic journal. Instead, we will discuss some advantages of working with Bayesian models over some more 'traditional' (although still modern) approaches.

11.3.5 Advantages of Bayesian multilevel models for large models

At this point, we have learned enough components to build very large and complicated models, like the one we fit above. Traditionally, models with many predictors have presented researchers with some combination of the three general problems outlined at the beginning of this chapter. In this section, we're going to discuss how working with multilevel Bayesian models can help us with problems (1) and (2) above. In the following section, we'll discuss an approach to solving problem (3) as well.

The Bayesian models fit by `brms` have two properties that help minimize the first two problems above. First, the use of prior probabilities and shrinkage, when properly applied, tend to 'pull' weakly-supported parameter values closer to the group mean (or to zero). This can help reduce many of the problems associated with models with large numbers of parameters (Gelman et al. 2012). Second, the fact that credible intervals are provided for all parameters helps distinguish random variation from variation that is unlikely to be small or zero.

To this point, we have not discussed the `lmer` function (from the `lme4` package) very much apart from in 'Traditionalist corner' at the end of some chapters. The `lmer` function (linear mixed-effects regression) is an extremely popular and extremely useful function. In general, `lmer` and an equivalent model specified in `brms` should result in very similar results when fit to the same data. However, there are some important differences between the two approaches. First, rather than provide a distribution of samples for each parameter, `lmer` returns *point estimates* representing the *best* values of parameters, in addition to estimated intervals around some (but not all) parameters. A second difference between `lmer` and our Bayesian multilevel models is that `lmer` doesn't use prior probabilities to estimate most of its parameters. This can cause some problems when estimating large numbers of parameters without large amounts of data.

We're going to compare the output of `lmer` and `brms` for the model we fit above. Just to be clear, our intention in comparing `lmer` and `brms` is not to compare different statistical *philosophies* or epistemological systems. Our aim is much, much more modest than that. We simply wish to compare `brms`, an approach that (1) uses priors, and (2) provides intervals for all parameters, to a broadly similar approach that does not (`lmer`). Below we fit a model equivalent to `model_height_vtl_f0` using `lmer`.

```
# Fit the model yourself
lme_model_height_vtl_f0 =
  lme4::lmer (height ~ vtl*f0*A*G + (vtl*f0*A*G|L) + (1|S),
              data=exp_data,verbose = TRUE,
              control=lme4::lmerControl(optCtrl=list(maxfun= 20000),
              optimizer="bobyqa"))

# Or download it from the GitHub page:
lme_model_height_vtl_f0 = bmmb::get_model ('11_lme_model_height_vtl_f0.RDS')
```

We won't show the model print statements as they are both quite large, but we compare the estimates of our fixed effects in Figure 11.4. Clearly, the two approaches provide very similar estimates for the model's fixed effects. That's reassuring because if results differed dramatically for approximately the same model based on the software used, we would need to think very carefully about the causes and possible meaning of these differences.

Since our model has a large number of parameters we're going to focus on interpreting those that seem likely to result in 'meaningful' differences in apparent height, about 1 cm (as discussed in Section 7.7). We will discuss the Bayesian model fixed effects, which you can see by running `fixef(model_height_vtl_f0)`. Our model suggests non-zero slopes for our plane along the VTL (mean = 3.12, s.d. = 0.64, 95% C.I = [1.85, 4.4]) and f0 dimensions (mean = −3.52, s.d. = 1.45, 95% C.I = [−6.32, −0.63]). However, there is not much evidence that the cross-product term (`vtl:f0`) has a meaningful non-zero value (mean = −1.28, s.d. = 1.05, 95% C.I = [−3.32, 0.81]). This means that our responses can be predicted by a flat plane along f0 and VTL without curving the plane into a saddle shape. The `vtl:A1` interaction suggests a differing use of VTL based on apparent adultness (mean = −2.02, s.d. = 0.51, 95% C.I = [−3.03, −1.02]), but there do not appear to be any other meaningful interactions between VTL, f0 and the other predictors.

In terms of intercept terms (i.e. those not interacting with quantitative predictors), there is a large effect for apparent age (mean = 7.04, s.d. = 1.18, 95% C.I = [4.69, 9.35]) but no main effect for apparent gender (mean = −0.17, s.d. = 0.75, 95% C.I = [−1.63, 1.36]). However, the interaction between apparent age and apparent gender (`A1:G1`) had a 95% credible interval that did not overlap with zero and had a posterior mean value of −1.72 cm (s.d. = 0.61, 95% C.I = [−2.9, −0.5]). This indicates that although apparent gender had an average effect of about 0 cm on apparent height it may have had meaningful, but opposite, effects based on the apparent age of the speaker.

In order to interpret our predictors in the presence of interactions, we need to consider the simple effects. For example, in order to consider the `vtl:A1` interaction we

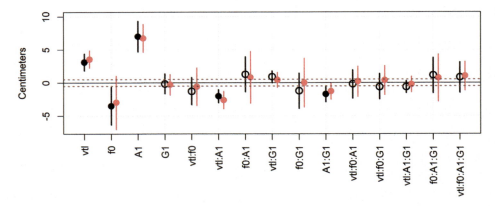

Figure 11.4 A comparison of fixed effect estimates provided by the brms (red) and lmer (black) models. The brms intervals are the 95% credible intervals, those for lmer are twice the standard error of the parameter estimate. Filled points have 95% credible intervals that exceed 0.5 cm.

need to find the simple effect of VTL for apparent children, and then for apparent adults. This is done in the manner outlined in Chapter 9 for quantitative predictors, independently for each dimension (predictor or cross-product). We're not going to go over the interpretation of the coefficients and the reconstruction of the simple effects here, as this will be carried out in Chapter 13.

Whereas Figure 11.4 focused on the similarity of our `lmer` and `brm` models, Figure 11.5 presents some ways that these models differ. In the top row we see a comparison of the 'random effects' standard deviation estimates, and the error terms (i.e. `sigma` or σ), estimated by our two models. For example, the standard deviation of the listener f0 'random effect' (`f0:L`, $\sigma_{F0:L}$) represents the amount of variation between the listener-specific effects for f0 in each model. As we can see, the models provide reasonably similar standard deviation estimates for many, if not most, parameters. However, note that the `brm` model provides intervals for all parameters, while the `lmer` model only provides point estimates for these.

The lack of intervals on parameter estimates makes it difficult to 'rule out' variance parameters since they will *never* equal exactly zero. So, we will always have non-zero estimates for these parameters, and 'secretly' some of these are zero or nearly zero. Notice that it is difficult to predict which standard deviation parameters are distinguishable from zero based on their magnitude alone. For example, consider `G1:L` and `vtl:f0:G1:L` in Figure 11.5. Our `lmer` model provides estimates of about the same magnitude for these two components, but our `brms` model's credible intervals suggest

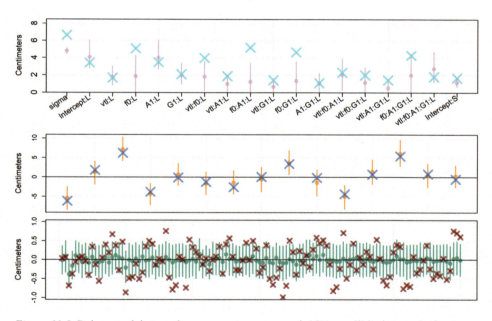

Figure 11.5 Points and intervals represent means and 95% credible intervals for brms parameter estimates for `model_height_vtl_f0`. Crosses indicate point estimates provided in `lme_model_height_vtl_f0`. (top) Estimates of random effect standard deviations. (middle) Estimates for the listener-dependent effects of apparent age. (bottom) Estimates of correlations between listener random effects.

360 *Multiple quantitative predictors, dealing and Bayesian ANOVA*

that one of these is likely to be larger than the other. So, we can use our credible intervals to figure out which variance components are unlikely to matter: Variance components whose credible intervals are concentrated near zero. There are several such components in Figure 11.5. For example, consider the listener-dependent interaction between VTL and apparent gender `vtl:G1:L`. If this variation is non-zero, in the *best case*, this component reflects a tiny amount of systematic variation in our outcomes and so is unlikely to matter much.

Variance components very close to zero can sometimes cause problems when estimating models. For example, fitting our `lmer` model resulted in the following error:

```
boundary (singular) fit: see help('isSingular')
```

This warns us that some of the variance components we are trying to estimate are quite small. However, the estimation of small variance components is not generally problematic for models fit using `brms` (and *Stan*).

In the middle plot of Figure 11.5 we see a comparison of the listener-dependent `A1` 'random effects' (i.e. `A1:L`) estimated using `brms` and `lmer`. Just as with the estimates of the fixed effects in the middle plot of Figure 11.4, we see a close alignment between the two approaches. However, just as for our standard deviation terms, we see that a lack of intervals around our `lmer` estimates makes it difficult to compare our parameter estimates to specific values (such as zero).

Finally, in the bottom plot of Figure 11.5, we compare the correlations for the listener random effects across the two models. Since there were 16 listener-dependent parameters, we needed to estimate 120 unique correlations between these parameters. As with our standard deviation parameters, `brms` gives us intervals while `lmer` returns point estimates. In addition, for the first time, we see a substantial difference between the estimates provided by `lmer` and those provided by `brms`. This is likely a result of the fact that `lmer` does not use adaptive pooling, or shrinkage, to estimate correlations. As a result, we see that the `lmer` estimates vary substantially around 0 while the `brms` estimates are mostly close to zero and have intervals that include zero. We see that in this case, our Bayesian model protects us by: (1) Providing credible intervals for all parameters, letting us accept values of zero as likely, and (2) the LKJ prior we used for our random effect correlation matrices pulls weakly-supported correlations to zero, thereby protecting against spurious results.

The fact that most of our correlation estimates are nearly zero not only lets us rule many out as not interesting, but also focuses our attention on those correlations that deviate from this pattern. For example, the third correlation from the left in the bottom plot of Figure 11.5 represents the correlation between the listener-dependent intercepts and effects for apparent age. Although its 95% credible interval includes some very small values (mean = -0.38, s.d. = 0.17, 95% C.I = $[-0.69, -0.01]$), it seems reasonable that this correlation may be negative and non-zero. In fact, we found this correlation in a previous model and also discussed why we think this correlation 'makes sense' (in Section 6.5).

11.4 Bayesian Analysis of Variance

The information we presented in the previous section can be used to consider which predictors, or groups of predictors, are important for understanding variation in the

Multiple quantitative predictors, dealing and Bayesian ANOVA 361

dependent variable. This approach becomes more and more useful as our models increase in complexity and we end up with dozens or hundreds of parameters that we then need to interpret. The framework to be presented here is outlined by Gelman and colleagues in Gelman (2005), Gelman and Hill (2006, chapter 22), and Gelman et al. (2013, chapter 15).

The **analysis of variance (ANOVA)** is a set of modeling techniques meant to help understand the components of variation in a dependent variable. A 'traditional' ANOVA tries to **decompose** variation in the dependent variable into independent components. It then carries out different statistical tests by relating the different variance components as ratios and comparing values to a reference distribution. If those statements make no sense to you, that's because that approach is fundamentally different from the sorts of things we've been doing with our multilevel Bayesian models. We're not going to talk about a 'traditional' ANOVA in any detail here as that would involve the introduction of a *parallel universe* of statistical concepts and jargon that has not been discussed in this book. In addition, there are many excellent treatments on the subject including Myers et al. (2010), Schmelkin and Pedhazur (2013), and Wickens and Keppel (2004). That being said, we can discuss how ANOVA features concepts that are very useful for Bayesian multilevel models.

At its core, ANOVA consists of thinking of variation in the dependent variable as the sum of a set of **components of variation** related to the predictors in our model. For example, consider the formula for `model_four_groups` we fit in Chapter 7:

```
height ~ C + (C|L) + (1|S)
```

This formula implies a model with a relatively large number of parameters. These parameters can be thought of as 'batches' of thematically related coefficients. For example, we can think of the following batches of parameters:

* 3 parameters representing the fixed effects for apparent speaker category `C`: `C1`, `C2`, `C3`.
* 15 parameters representing the listener-dependent intercepts.
* 45 (15 · 3) parameters representing the listener-dependent effects for parameters `C1`, `C2`, and `C3`.
* 139 parameters representing the speaker-dependent intercepts.

Each of these batches has a thematic or semantic link; these are not just parameters grouped at random. When we break up variation into thematically-grouped parameters, we are doing an **ANOVA-like decomposition** of variation of the dependent variable. We introduced this approach in Chapter 7 without directly referring to ANOVA and have generally been using this approach to understand variation in our predictors throughout the book. Here's what Gelman and Hill (2006) have to say about the analysis of variance in the context of multilevel models:

> *When moving to multilevel modeling, the key idea we want to take from the analysis of variance is the estimation of the importance of different batches of predictors ("components of variation" in ANOVA terminology). As usual, we focus on estimation rather than testing: instead of testing the null hypothesis that a variance component is zero, we estimate the standard deviation of the corresponding batch*

362 *Multiple quantitative predictors, dealing and Bayesian ANOVA*

of coefficients. If this standard deviation is estimated to be small, then the source of variation is minor—we do not worry about whether it is exactly zero. In the social science and public health examples that we focus on, it can be a useful research goal to identify important sources of variation, but it is rare that anything is truly zero.

(p. 490)

Batches of parameters that vary a lot from each other reflect large differences in our dependent variable across the parameters. Batches of parameters that vary a lot from each other will have large standard deviations, i.e. they will be dispersed around the mean for that batch. In contrast, parameters that do not vary much from each other will be represented by small standard deviations, and will generally be close to their mean. These parameters do not have a large effect on our data (since they do not vary much).

For example, in Figure 11.5 we see that the standard deviation of listener-dependent intercepts (`Intercept:L`, σ_L) is much larger than the listener-dependent interaction between VTL and apparent gender (`vtl:G1:L`, $\sigma_{VTL:G:L}$). We can see that this directly relates to the variation of each batch of 'random effects' around zero, as shown in Figure 11.6. Whether or not $\sigma_{VTL:G:L}$ is *exactly* zero, we can look at Figure 11.6 and see that this predictor does not predict much variation in our dependent variable. As a result of this, by inspecting the standard deviations in Figure 11.5 we can see that although there are a large number of predictors, only a couple are having any meaningful effect on apparent height judgments.

Gelman and Hill (2006) distinguish two types of standard deviations for a 'random' effect with J levels (p. 459) (emphasis ours):

> "The **superpopulation** standard deviation, which represents the variation among the modeled probability distribution from which they were drawn, is relevant for determining the uncertainty about the value of a new group not in the original set of J."
>
> "The **finite-population** standard deviation of the particular J values of [some coefficient] describes variation within the existing data."

So, the *finite-population* standard deviation terms reflect the variation we observe in our actual model parameters. This concept can be applied to batches of 'random' effects estimated with adaptive partial pooling and to 'fixed' effects estimated

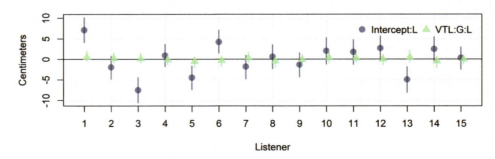

Figure 11.6 Listener-dependent intercepts (Intercept:L) and vtl:G1 interactions (VTL:G1:L).

Multiple quantitative predictors, dealing and Bayesian ANOVA 363

with fixed priors. For example, if your estimated parameters are −1, 0, and 1, your finite-population estimate would be directly based on these values. In contrast, the *superpopulation* standard deviation estimates correspond to the specific σ_β term estimated by our model for some batch β of 'random' effects. No analog exists for our 'fixed' effects, and so we can only get superpopulation standard deviations for batches of parameters fit with adaptive partial pooling (i.e. 'random' effects). Gelman and colleagues suggest the following general process, which can be referred to as a **Bayesian analysis of variance**, or **BANOVA**:

1 Fit the model with the structure you think is required to capture the variation in the data and answer your research questions.
2 Calculate the finite-population (and/or superpopulation) standard deviations for predictors or batches of predictors.
3 Make a plot comparing the magnitudes of different batches of predictors, and the uncertainty in the estimates. The authors refer to this as an **ANOVA plot**.
4 Use the ANOVA plot to make inferences about the relative importance of your predictors, and to guide your analysis.

We could potentially add a fifth step: 5) Refit a reduced model if some components show little to no meaningful variation and if you have some compelling reason to do so. This step is not strictly necessary, and may even be a bad idea sometimes, but we will consider it as a possibility.

11.4.1 Getting the standard deviations from our models 'manually'

The superpopulation standard deviation is our model's estimate of the standard deviation of a batch of parameters. We can extract the superpopulation standard deviations using the `VarCorr` function. This function returns all sorts of information about the variance and correlation parameters estimated by our model. In the second line below we specify that we only want information related to the standard deviation (`"sd"`) of our listener effects (`"L"`). We're not going to go into detail about the information provided by this function, but you can probably figure most of it out by inspecting the output carefully.

```
brms::VarCorr(model_height_vtl_f0)
brms::VarCorr(model_height_vtl_f0)[["L"]][["sd"]]
```

We can also get information regarding our error (σ, `sigma`) using `Varcorr` as seen below:

```
brms::VarCorr(model_height_vtl_f0)$residual$sd
##   Estimate Est.Error   Q2.5 Q97.5
##      4.819    0.1576 4.515 5.137
```

The `bmmb` package contains a function called `get_sds` that collects estimates of all standard deviations estimated by the model, including the error. We show the first five lines of the output of this function below.

```
bmmb::get_sds (model_height_vtl_f0)[1:5,]
```

```
##             Estimate Est.Error    Q2.5 Q97.5 group
## Int.L         4.083    0.8450 2.7530 6.047      L
## vtl           1.767    0.5420 0.8613 3.020      L
## f0            1.868    1.0913 0.1007 4.281      L
## A1            4.009    0.8597 2.6786 6.047      L
## G1            1.970    0.5739 1.0015 3.307      L
```

Getting the finite-sample standard deviations is a bit trickier. First, we should note that although they are called standard deviations, they are actually calculated by finding the root-mean-squared error. The **root-mean-squared** (RMS) error for each batch of coefficients is exactly what it sounds like, it's the (square) root of the mean square. In other words, as seen in equation (11.9), you square a bunch of values, find the average of these, and then find the square root of this value.

$$RMS_x = \sqrt{\sum_{i=1}^{n} x_{[i]}^2 / n} \tag{11.9}$$

Note that this is just like the formula to calculate the sample variance (equation (2.5)) if we assume that the sample mean is equal to zero. In fact, when we use sum coding we *do* assume a mean of 0 for each batch of parameters and our parameters already reflect deviations from the mean. Further, remember that in all our model specifications each batch of random effects is assumed to have a mean of zero (i.e. the prior for L is $N(0, \sigma_L)$). However, the sample mean of any given batch of random effects may not necessarily equal zero. This is because there is no guarantee that the sample mean will equal the population mean (which we know to be zero), and this applies to our 'random effects' as much as it does to variables in general. As a result, we should use the RMS function when calculating the standard deviation for our batches of parameters, since this effectively calculates the standard deviation when the mean is zero.

To calculate the standard deviations of different batches of parameters you need to calculate the root-mean-squared deviation for each batch, *for each sample*. This means you end up with an estimate of the finite-sample standard deviation for each set of posterior samples. For example, equation (11.10) has been updated to show the calculation of the RMS of the listener-dependent intercept terms (L) across J listeners. The little [s] superscript indicates that each calculation is made for an individual posterior sample (s). As a result, the measure below will produce 4,000 estimates of the RMS for L given 4,000 posterior samples.

$$RMS_L^s = \sqrt{\sum_{j=1}^{J} \left(L_{[j]}^s \right)^2 / J} \tag{11.10}$$

The code below shows how to calculate the finite-population standard deviations for the listener based on the random effects parameter estimates.

```
# extract matrix of listener random intercepts from our model
listener_intercepts =
```

```
ranef (model_height_vtl_f0, summary = FALSE) [["L"]] [,,"Intercept"]

# the output is a 2d matrix. dimensions
# are: (rows) samples, (columns) parameters
str (listener_intercepts)
##   num [1:4000, 1:15] 6.1 3.62 7.43 7.5 7.62 ...
##   - attr(*, "dimnames")=List of 2
##     ..$ : NULL
##     ..$ : chr [1:15] "1" "2" "3" "4" ...

# we find the RMS error across each row in the matrix
listener_intercepts_finite = apply (listener_intercepts,1,bmmb::rms)

# we summarize the output
listener_intercepts_finite =
  posterior_summary (listener_intercepts_finite)

listener_intercepts_finite
##      Estimate Est.Error  Q2.5 Q97.5
## [1,]    3.926      0.39 3.243 4.772
```

For the fixed effects, we can use the absolute value of the parameters when these are each a single 'degree of freedom' (i.e. a single parameter). The code below shows how to get the fixed effects standard deviation estimates assuming that all parameters are unrelated.

```
# get individual parameter samples
fixefs_finite = fixef (model_height_vtl_f0, summary = FALSE)

# summarize absolute value
fixefs_finite = posterior_summary (abs (fixefs_finite))
```

Finally, we can estimate the finite-sample error by getting the model residuals, and then calculating the standard deviation of the residuals for each set of samples as shown below.

```
# get residuals
sigma_finite = residuals (model_height_vtl_f0, summary = FALSE)

# find standard deviation for each set of samples
sigma_finite = apply (sigma_finite, 1, sd)
# summarize
sigma_finite = posterior_summary (sigma_finite)

# name row, because it has no name by default
row.names (sigma_finite) = 'sigma'
```

366 *Multiple quantitative predictors, dealing and Bayesian ANOVA*

In the examples above, we treated each fixed effect predictor, and the interaction of each of these with listener, as independent. This is actually appropriate for this model because all our predictors *are* conceptually distinct, so we don't really have batches of fixed effects. However, the process Gelman proposes is potentially more complicated than what we've done above. For example, imagine if we had included `C` as a predictor in our model and calculated the listener-dependent effects of `C`. This would result in the fixed effects `C1`, `C2`, and `C3`, 15 `C1:L` random effects, 15 `C2:L` random effects, and 15 `C3:L` random effects. The process described here would treat each of the 3 fixed effects as independent, and also treat each batch of 15 random effects as independent. In contrast, Gelman and colleagues recommend treating the 3 category-related fixed effects as a single batch, and the 45 category-related random effects as a single batch.

The main reason to do it the way we've shown above is that it can be done easily for all models, and you still get very useful information from the analysis. However, it is undeniable that, for example, treating the 45 `C:L` terms in our example above as related may be desirable in some cases. If you do want to investigate the variation associated with entire clusters of multiple predictors at a time, the code provided above can be modified to do this as necessary, and you should also probably see the readings referred to at the top of Section 11.4.

11.4.2 Using the BANOVA function

The `bmmb` package contains a function called `banova` that can get the finite-sample or superpopulation standard deviations for you. This function will only calculate standard deviations the 'simple' way outlined in the previous section, treating each fixed effect and the random effects for each individual parameter as an independent batch. The output of the `banova` function is a single data frame that contains a summary of the standard deviations for fixed and random effects, and the error term if the model contains one. Below we use the function to get both kinds of standard deviations compared in the previous section.

```
banova_height_vtl_f0_finite =
  banova (model_height_vtl_f0, superpopulation = FALSE)

banova_height_vtl_f0_super =
  banova (model_height_vtl_f0, superpopulation = TRUE)
```

The output of the `banova` function can be used to make a Bayesian ANOVA plot of our model using the `banovaplot` function in the `bmmb` package. An example of a Bayesian ANOVA plot is shown in Figure 11.7. These plots compare the (absolute) values of your fixed effects, the standard deviation of different batches of random effects, and your residual error (σ) if applicable. This is effectively the same information shown in the top row of Figure 11.5 save for the inclusion of the 'fixed' effects in the figure. If we make a BANOVA plot right after fitting our model, we would have a pretty good idea of which of our predictors are associated with meaningful variation in our dependent variable and which don't seem to matter much.

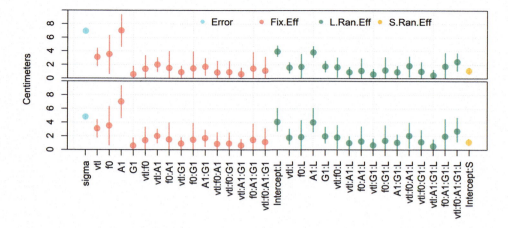

Figure 11.7 (top) Finite-sample BANOVA plot for `model_height_vtl_f0` showing the model error, fixed effects, listener random effects, and speaker random effects. (bottom) The superpopulation BANOVA plot for the same model.

11.4.3 Fitting and comparing the reduced model

Our initial model formula was:

```
height ~ f0*vtl*A*G + (f0*vtl*A*G|L) + (f0*vtl*A*G|S)
```

Because we include all possible interactions between 'fixed' effects and listener 'random effects' for each predictor and interaction, we're basically saying that we think it's possible for every predictor to affect every other predictor, and for all of this to vary in a listener-dependent manner. We might instead consider the following model formula which includes only those effects we (arbitrarily) deemed 'large enough' based on our inspection of the Bayesian ANOVA above.

```
height ~ f0 + vtl + A*G + vtl:A1 + (f0 + vtl + A*G + vtl:A1|L) + (1|S)
```

In some situations, we may be justified in fitting a 'final' model that includes only the important components. We fit the reduced model below:

```
# Fit the model yourself
priors = c(brms::set_prior("student_t(3,160, 12)", class = "Intercept"),
           brms::set_prior("student_t(3,0, 12)", class = "b"),
           brms::set_prior("student_t(3,0, 12)", class = "sd"),
           brms::set_prior("lkj_corr_cholesky (2)", class = "cor"),
           brms::set_prior("gamma(2, 0.1)", class = "nu"),
           brms::set_prior("student_t(3,0, 12)", class = "sigma"))
```

```
model_height_vtl_f0_reduced =
  brms::brm (height ~ f0+vtl+A*G+vtl:A + (f0+vtl+A*G+vtl:A|L) + (1|S),
       data = exp_data, chains = 4, cores = 4, warmup = 1000,
       iter = 5000, thin = 4, prior = priors, family = "student")

# Or download it from the GitHub page:
model_height_vtl_f0_reduced =
  bmmb::get_model ('11_model_height_vtl_f0_reduced.RDS')
```

We can see that the fixed effects shared in common are very similar, as are the estimates of the superpopulation random effects for the listener-dependent parameters (although intervals are wider for the full model).

We can use cross-validation to compare the expected model out-of-sample prediction:

```
model_height_vtl_f0 =
  add_criterion (model_height_vtl_f0, "loo")

model_height_vtl_f0_reduced =
  add_criterion (model_height_vtl_f0_reduced, "loo")
```

And see that the reduced model has a lower elpd, but that the difference is only about 1 standard error, making it not at all reliable.

```
loo_compare (model_height_vtl_f0,model_height_vtl_f0_reduced)
##                               elpd_diff se_diff
## model_height_vtl_f0             0.0       0.0
## model_height_vtl_f0_reduced    -10.8      11.7
```

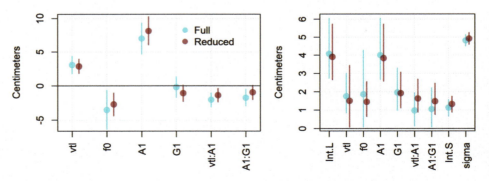

Figure 11.8 (left) A comparison of the means and 95% credible intervals for shared fixed effects parameters in our full and reduced models. (right) A comparison of the means and 95% credible intervals for shared superpopulation standard deviations in our full and reduced models.

We can also consider the variance explained (R^2) by each model:

```
# R2 for full model
bmmb::r2_bayes(model_height_vtl_f0)
##        Estimate Est.Error    Q2.5   Q97.5
## [1,]    0.8064  0.004273  0.7975  0.8142
# R2 for reduced model
bmmb::r2_bayes(model_height_vtl_f0_reduced)
##        Estimate Est.Error    Q2.5   Q97.5
## [1,]    0.7997  0.004404  0.7906  0.8077
```

And see that all of the extra complexity included in our full model gains us less than 1% additional variance explained. All of this suggests that a researcher would be justified in fitting and interpreting the reduced model for their research, especially if there is a compelling reason to do so. However, being able to say "these parameters are near zero/show no meaningful variation" is potentially useful, and we lose that ability when we base our analysis on the reduced model. Of course, we could say something like "we fit a larger model that showed all these effects are zero but we are not presenting it here, please take our word for it". If we *do* want to say something like this it may make sense to present the full model to the reader so that they can reach the same conclusions you did (or not).

11.5 A logistic regression model with multiple quantitative predictors

We're going to fit a logistic regression model with two quantitative predictors and an interaction between them. We're also going to inspect the model using the principles of Bayesian ANOVA (henceforth **BANOVA**) outlined in the previous section. Before continuing we want to talk briefly about the geometry of the models we'll be fitting.

A logistic regression model with two quantitative predictors specifies planes (top row, Figure 11.9) along a third dimension (z) representing the logit of the probability of observing a 'success' (a value of 1 for the dependent variable). We will refer to these surfaces as **response surfaces** because they specify the expected value of the response variable based on the value of our quantitative predictors. When the value on the response surface is negative, the model predicts a response of 0 at this location of the predictor space (i.e. the space defined by the quantitative predictors). When the value of the plane is positive the model predicts a 1. When we want to know the probability expected for any given x and y-axis location, we can transform the value of the response surface using the inverse logit function (equation (10.9)). When the predicted logits are transformed into probabilities, our model defines a curved surface (bottom row of Figure 11.9) rather than a flat plane.

When our models include interactions between quantitative predictors (i.e. the cross-product), our predicted logits will no longer vary along planes. Instead, the surface will resemble a saddle shape based on the sign of the parameter and its magnitude relative to the slopes of the relevant quantitative predictors in the model (top row, Figure 11.10). When we convert these saddle shapes to probabilities using the inverse logit function, the resulting shape can be strange. For example, in the bottom row in Figure 11.10, we see that saddle shapes can result in non-contiguous regions associated with successes, with a canyon in the middle associated with failures.

11.5.1 Data and research questions

In the code below we load our packages, set our contrasts, and load our experimental data. We also add our dependent variable, `Female`, to our data frame. This variable equals 1 when the listener indicated hearing a female speaker and 0 when the listener indicated hearing a male speaker. As with our previous model, we center our

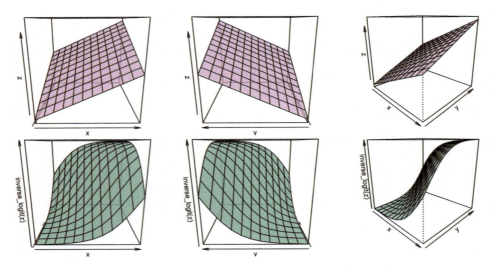

Figure 11.9 (top) Three perspectives on a plane that specifies logits along its z-axis. (bottom) The same plane after undergoing the inverse logit transform, now expressing probabilities along the z-axis.

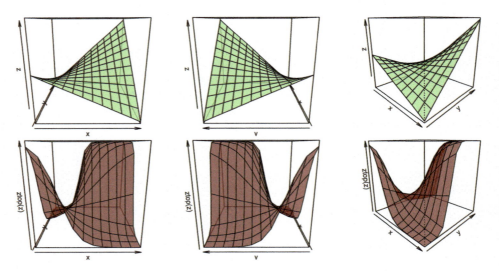

Figure 11.10 (top) Three perspectives on a saddle shape that specifies logits along its z-axis. (bottom) The same saddle shape after undergoing the inverse logit transform, now expressing probabilities along the z-axis.

Multiple quantitative predictors, dealing and Bayesian ANOVA 371

quantitative variables and divide f0 by 100 to make the expected regression coefficients for VTL and f0 more similar in magnitude.

```
library (brms)
library (bmmb)
options (contrasts = c('contr.sum','contr.sum'))

data (exp_data)

# create our dependent variable
exp_data$Female = ifelse(exp_data$G == 'f', 1, 0)

# center vtl
exp_data$vtl_original = exp_data$vtl
exp_data$vtl = exp_data$vtl - mean (exp_data$vtl)

# center and scale f0
exp_data$f0_original = exp_data$f0
exp_data$f0 = exp_data$f0 - mean(exp_data$f0)
exp_data$f0 = exp_data$f0 / 100
```

As with our height model, we'll leave more detailed research questions for Chapter 13. For now, we are only interested in two general questions:

(Q1) Can we use what we've learned so far to fit and evaluate a logistic regression model with two quantitative predictors?
(Q2) Can we extend the concepts from Chapter 10 to classify speakers along two stimulus dimensions (f0 and VTL) using our logistic models?

11.5.2 Description of the model

Our model formula is very much like the one we used to investigate the perception of femaleness in the last chapter, save for the addition of f0 and its interaction with the other predictors. Our formula will be:

```
Female ~ vtl * f0 * A + (vtl * f0 * A|L) + (1|S)
```

We'll use the same priors we used for our logistic models in the last chapter. Since we scaled f0 so that a change of 1 corresponds to 100 Hz, a 1 unit change in f0 represents approximately the average difference in f0 between adult males and females. As a result, we think it's reasonable to use a prior of the same magnitude as we used for our VTL parameter.

We will omit our model specification since it is quite large and very similar to the one presented in Chapter 10 for `model_gender_vtl`. However, we can say what it's doing in general. We are predicting the perception of femaleness using planes, or potentially saddle shapes, that vary as a function of speaker VTL and f0, and the apparent age of the speaker. These shapes can vary arbitrarily, in their slopes along each dimension, degree of curvature, and intercepts, as a function of apparent age. *All* of the aforementioned characteristics can vary in a listener-dependent

372 *Multiple quantitative predictors, dealing and Bayesian ANOVA*

way, and intercepts can vary in a speaker-dependent way. If the preceding sentences make no sense to you, you should review the description of the linear model in Section 11.3.3. All we've done here is briefly say the same thing we said in more detail in that section.

11.5.3 Fitting the model and applying a Bayesian ANOVA

We fit our model with the code below:

```
# Fit the model yourself
model_gender_vtl_f0 =
  brm (Female ~ vtl*f0*A + (vtl*f0*A|L) + (1|S), data=exp_data,
       chains=4, cores=4, family="bernoulli",
       warmup=1000, iter = 5000, thin = 4,
       prior = c(set_prior("student_t(3, 0, 3)", class = "Intercept"),
                 set_prior("student_t(3, 0, 3)", class = "b"),
                 set_prior("student_t(3, 0, 3)", class = "sd"),
                 set_prior("lkj_corr_cholesky (2)", class = "cor")))

# Or download it from the GitHub page:
model_gender_vtl_f0 = bmmb::get_model ('11_model_gender_vtl_f0.RDS')
```

We can inspect the model fixed effects using `brmplot` in Figure 11.11. Besides that we make a BANOVA plot comparing the model fixed effects and the finite-sample standard deviations for 'batches' of our random effects parameters.

In Figure 11.11, we see a relatively complex model, with an important role for f0 and VTL. We also see that unlike our model predicting apparent height above, this model features a prominent f0 by VTL interaction (`vtl:f0`), and an interaction between this and apparent age (`vtl:f0:A1`). Just as with our height model above, we will leave the interpretation of this model for Chapter 13. Instead, we're going to focus on using our models to understand the classification of speakers into apparent females and apparent males based on their VTL and f0, and on whether we actually *like* this model or not.

11.5.4 Categorization in two dimensions

Imagine a horizontal plane such that z=0 for all values of x and y in Figures 11.9 and 11.10. If the *z* (vertical) axis represents logits, this plane would represent an expected probability of 0.5, meaning it is the boundary between successes (1) and failures (0) along the z-axis. Our response surface will intersect with the horizontal $z = 0$ plane, forming a curve at this intersection. These curves represent the division of the response surface into sections with values greater than 0 (expected response 1) and sections with values less than 0 (expected response 0). Thus, the curves formed by the intersection of our response surface and the z=0 plane represent the *category boundary* along the predictor space, as defined by our model.

We will begin by discussing the case where the response surface is a plane, i.e. there is no cross-product term in our model. The intersection of two planes forms a straight line. Although the surfaces in the bottom row of Figure 11.9 are not planes, the intersection

Multiple quantitative predictors, dealing and Bayesian ANOVA 373

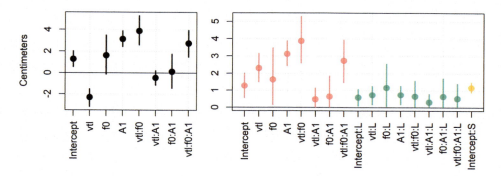

Figure 11.11 (left) A plot showing fixed effects estimates and 95% credible intervals for `model_gender_vtl_f0`. (right) A BANOVA plot of the same model, showing posterior means and 95% credible intervals for the finite-sample standard deviation estimates.

of these surfaces with planes still forms straight lines. Thus, their intersection with the plane at p=0.5 (i.e. the plane where logit(p) = 0) will still form straight lines. To find the intersection of our response surfaces and the plane at z=0, we can use some basic algebra. We take the equation defining the shape of our response and set z to zero:

$$\begin{aligned} z &= a + (b \cdot x) + (c \cdot y) \\ 0 &= a + (b \cdot x) + (c \cdot y) \end{aligned} \tag{11.11}$$

We will arbitrarily decide to draw a line that treats y as the 'dependent' variable. To find the equation for this line we need to solve for y (i.e. isolate it on one side of the equal sign), as shown in (11.12).

$$\begin{aligned} 0 &= a + (b \cdot x) + (c \cdot y) \\ y &= -(b \cdot x - a) / c \end{aligned} \tag{11.12}$$

We can use the above method to calculate the category boundaries implied by a model including a cross-product as seen below. In the interest of full disclosure, we use online algebra solving tools to solve equations like this. There is no shame in doing so, and it minimizes the probability of an error on your part. Of course, you need to make sure the tool you use is reliable, but you can always double (or triple) check proposed solutions across different analysis methods.

$$\begin{aligned} 0 &= a + (b \cdot x) + (c \cdot y) + (d \cdot x \cdot y) \\ y &= (-b \cdot x - a) / (d \cdot x + c) \end{aligned} \tag{11.13}$$

As seen in (11.13), the intersection between a saddle shape and the plane where z=0 will not be a straight line. Instead, it will be a **hyperbola** a shape that resembles a pair of parabolas that approach, but never cross an asymptote (a boundary line). Since saddle shapes can fall and then rise again, a surface of this kind may intersect with the plane at z=0 in more than one location (seen in Figure 11.10). The *a,b,c* and *d* parameters above represent model coefficients for the intercept, VTL slope, f0 slope,

374 *Multiple quantitative predictors, dealing and Bayesian ANOVA*

and cross-product respectively. Below we get the samples for our fixed effects parameters from our model, in addition to the marginal, or 'main effect', estimates of these parameters.

```
# get fixed effect parameters
samples = brms::fixef (model_gender_vtl_f0, summary = FALSE)

# get a,b,c,d coefficients for overall surface
a_all = mean (samples[,"Intercept"])
b_all = mean (samples[,"vtl"])
c_all = mean (samples[,"f0"])
d_all = mean (samples[,"vtl:f0"])
```

We can also add up appropriate combinations of the fixed effects to calculate separate *a,b,c* and *d* parameters for apparent adults and apparent children, as seen below. Note that in each case we combine the necessary parameters first and then find the average across the samples of the parameter. Of course, in both cases, we could have used the hypothesis (or short_hypothesis) function rather than do it 'by hand'.

```
# get a,b,c,d coefficients for adult surface
a_adult = mean (samples[,"Intercept"] + samples[,"A1"])
b_adult = mean (samples[,"vtl"] + samples[,"vtl:A1"])
c_adult = mean (samples[,"f0"] + samples[,"f0:A1"])
d_adult = mean (samples[,"vtl:f0"] + samples[,"vtl:f0:A1"])

# get a,b,c,d coefficients for child surface
a_child = mean (samples[,"Intercept"] - samples[,"A1"])
b_child = mean (samples[,"vtl"] - samples[,"vtl:A1"])
c_child = mean (samples[,"f0"] - samples[,"f0:A1"])
d_child = mean (samples[,"vtl:f0"] - samples[,"vtl:f0:A1"])
```

We can use these parameters to generate curves representing the boundaries between expected female and expected male responses. We do this for our hyperbolic (equation (11.13)) boundaries in Figure 11.12. When we 'zoom out' in the middle plot of the same figure, we see that this model actually predicts male classifications in the top-left corner as well as in the bottom right corner. This is a result of the fact that our hyperbolic boundaries come in pairs, resulting from the bimodal (i.e. two peaked) shape seen in the bottom row of Figure 11.10.

In the right plot of Figure 11.12, we present a *territorial map* of our stimulus space as defined by speaker VTL and f0, for apparent adults. This map tells us the expected classification of speakers into males and females given their voice f0 and VTL, and assuming that they are perceived as being adults (broken green lines in the left and middle plots). Unlike the territorial maps presented in the previous chapter (in Figure 10.5), this map is defined along a two-dimensional stimulus space. In addition, although we only present one map in the plot, we can make three separate maps, one for apparent children, one for apparent adults, and an overall map.

The high-frequency male region in the top-left corner of the plot suggests that speakers with a very high f0 and a very short VTL are likely to be identified as males, even

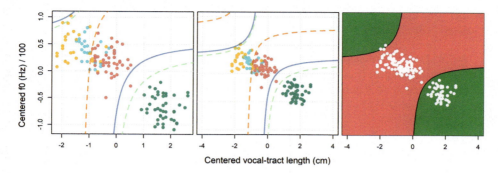

Figure 11.12 (left) Each point represents a single speaker, and labels indicate the most common group classification. Curves indicate male/female boundaries for adults (green), children (orange), and overall (blue). (middle) The same as the left figure but zoomed out more. (right) Territorial maps showing expected classifications for apparent adults in different regions of the f0 by VTL stimulus space.

for adults. Note that we don't have many speakers in these regions and so we can only guess how listeners might have responded to voices there. However, common sense suggests that speakers with a very short VTL and a very high f0 are not very likely to be identified as adult males. Does this matter? Yes and no. Does it matter that the earth isn't flat but our maps mostly act like it is? If it's *flat enough* in the area described by our map, then maybe not. If you're trying to find the shortest flight path between two cities, it probably does.

This suggests we should decide what our model is for. If we only want to understand behavior in the regions where we mostly have a lot of data, then the high-frequency male region may not matter. On the other hand, if we want to understand how listeners might be using acoustic information in general, we might worry that the model predicts behavior that we think is very unlikely to be correct. In other words, we might want our model to 'make sense' even for data we don't have.

11.5.5 *Model selection and misspecification*

In the hopes of finding a model that 'makes more sense', we're going to drop the cross-product and related predictors. Below we fit a reduced model that is otherwise the same as our initial model but without the interaction between f0 and VTL.

```
# Fit the model yourself
model_gender_vtl_f0_reduced =
  brm (Female ~ (vtl+f0)*A + ((vtl+f0)*A|L) + (1|S), data=exp_data,
       chains=4, cores=4, family="bernoulli",
       warmup=1000, iter = 5000, thin = 4,
       prior = c(set_prior("student_t(3, 0, 3)", class = "Intercept"),
                 set_prior("student_t(3, 0, 3)", class = "b"),
                 set_prior("student_t(3, 0, 3)", class = "sd"),
                 set_prior("lkj_corr_cholesky (2)", class = "cor")))
```

376 *Multiple quantitative predictors, dealing and Bayesian ANOVA*

```
# Or download it from the GitHub page:
model_gender_vtl_f0_reduced =
  bmmb::get_model ('11_model_gender_vtl_f0_reduced.RDS')
```

We find the a, b and c parameters for the response plane given our model, calculating the overall (marginal) plane, a plane for apparent children, and another for apparent adults. There is no d parameter this time since there is no cross-product term in this model.

```
# get fixed effect parameters
samples = brms::fixef (model_gender_vtl_f0_reduced, summary = FALSE)

# get a,b,c coefficients for overall plane
a_all_reduced = mean (samples[,"Intercept"])
b_all_reduced = mean (samples[,"vtl"])
c_all_reduced = mean (samples[,"f0"])

# get a,b,c coefficients for adult plane
a_adult_reduced = mean (samples[,"Intercept"] + samples[,"A1"])
b_adult_reduced = mean (samples[,"vtl"] + samples[,"vtl:A1"])
c_adult_reduced = mean (samples[,"f0"] + samples[,"f0:A1"])

# get a,b,c coefficients for child plane
a_child_reduced = mean (samples[,"Intercept"] - samples[,"A1"])
b_child_reduced = mean (samples[,"vtl"] - samples[,"vtl:A1"])
c_child_reduced = mean (samples[,"f0"] - samples[,"f0:A1"])
```

We use these parameters to plot the linear category boundaries in our stimulus space. Figure 11.13 compares the linear boundaries implied by our reduced model (middle) to those implied by our full model (left), ignoring the d coefficients in the case of the full model. We can see that in the absence of the cross-product (middle), the boundaries for children (orange) and adults (green) differ noticeably in their slope. The change in slope indicates that f0 differences matter less for children than they do for adults. This is because since the male-female boundary is almost parallel to the y-axis (f0), it is difficult to cross the boundary by moving along this axis. In general, when a boundary is parallel to an axis this means that the variable that varies along that axis is not strongly associated with category changes. If a boundary is perpendicular to an axis, the predictor may be strongly associated with category changes.

We can use cross-validation to investigate which of our two models is preferable.

```
model_gender_vtl_f0 =
  brms::add_criterion(model_gender_vtl_f0,"loo")

model_gender_vtl_f0_reduced =
  brms::add_criterion(model_gender_vtl_f0_reduced,"loo")
```

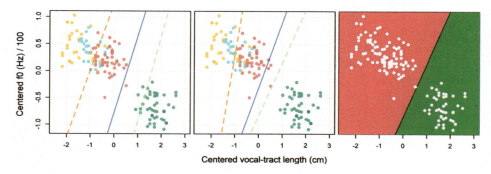

Figure 11.13 (left) Each point represents a single speaker, and labels indicate the most common group classification. Lines indicate male/female boundaries for adults (green), children (orange), and overall (blue) implied by the full model, ignoring the cross-product term. (middle) The same as the left figure but for the reduced model. (right) Territorial maps showing expected classifications for apparent adults in different regions of the f0 by VTL stimulus space, for the reduced model.

The comparison suggests the model that includes the interaction does a better job of explaining our data. The difference between the two models is large-ish, but just under two standard errors in magnitude and so is not terribly reliable.

```
brms::loo_compare (model_gender_vtl_f0, model_gender_vtl_f0_
reduced)
##                                  elpd_diff se_diff
## model_gender_vtl_f0                0.0       0.0
## model_gender_vtl_f0_reduced      -18.2       9.9
```

When adding the `loo` criterion to our models we got error messages like this:

```
## Warning: Found 205 observations with a pareto_k > 0.7 in model
## 'model_gender_vtl_f0'. It is recommended to set 'moment_match = TRUE'
## in order to perform moment matching for problematic observations.
```

When we add the `loo` criterion to our model, `brms` (and *Stan*) don't actually fit a new model for every left-out data point (i.e. a 'real' leave-one-out cross-validation). Instead, there's a way to approximate what the model *would* look like had it actually been refit without each data point. This approximation uses something called **Pareto smoothed importance sampling (PSIS)**. The Pareto-k ($\hat{k}$, `pareto_k`) statistic is a diagnostic for this estimation method that helps you check the assumptions underlying the leave-one-out approximation (Vehtari et al. 2017). Essentially, the $\hat{k}$ statistic is a measure of how unusual a given observation is. A very unusual observation is highly influential in your model and will have a higher value of $\hat{k}$. If an observation is *too* unusual, then the estimate of elpd associated with that observation may not be reliable. The general rule of thumb is that values of $\hat{k}$ that are less than 0.5 are 'good', values

378 *Multiple quantitative predictors, dealing and Bayesian ANOVA*

between 0.5 and 0.7 are 'ok' (not so great but not bad either), values greater than 0.7 are 'bad', and values greater than 1.0 are 'very bad'.

Vehtari (2022) outlines three general situations that cause Pareto-k statistics to be large. To understand these it might help to review the information on model comparison previously discussed in Sections 6.4, and 6.4.3 specifically. The number of estimated parameters in a model is the total actual number of parameters estimated, including all fixed effects, random effects, and 'distributional' parameters such as σ and v. We may distinguish this from the *effective* number of parameters, `p_loo` when calculated using `loo`, which takes the flexibility of the model into account. If a model shows little variability in its random effects, its effective number of parameters may be smaller than its total number of estimated parameters. The three situations that can cause large Pareto-k statistics are:

1   p_loo is *smaller* than the number of estimated parameters: If the estimated number of parameters (p) is relatively large relative to the number of observations (n), e.g. p > n/5, then the model may be too flexible, or your priors may be too weak.
2   p_loo is *much smaller* than the number of estimated parameters: The model is likely to be **misspecified**. A misspecified model is one whose structure contains important differences compared to the processes being modeled.
3   p_loo is *greater than* the number of parameters: The model is likely to be *'badly'* misspecified.

In each case, a posterior predictive check may help understand the issues, as can inspecting the distribution of Pareto-k statistics. Below, we print the actual and effective number of parameters for our full model, as well as our number of observations.

```
# actual number of estimated parameters
ncol (bmmb::get_samples(model_gender_vtl_f0))-2
## [1] 304

# number of observations
nrow (model_gender_vtl_f0$data)
## [1] 2085

# information related to loo creiterion
model_gender_vtl_f0$criteria$loo$estimates
##            Estimate       SE
## elpd_loo    -541.5  23.405
## p_loo        105.8   6.637
## looic       1083.0  46.810
```

Based on the information above, we believe that our model falls into the first case. Our `p_loo` is only about 30% as large as our number of parameters. Although we do have more than 5 times as many observations (2,085) as estimated parameters (304), the ratio of 6.86 is not much greater than 5. In addition, we *do* think there is a possibility that the model is *misspecified* and may be too flexible. We've said repeatedly that no model can really 'prove' itself to be the 'real' model, and even that it's not totally clear what it would mean for a formalism like regression to represent the 'real' process

Multiple quantitative predictors, dealing and Bayesian ANOVA 379

underlying our observations. Given this, it seems that every model is 'misspecified' to some extent, making a focus on the misspecification of this one model seem somewhat arbitrary.

Although the above may be generally true, we can focus on misspecifications that cause noticeable 'misbehaviors' in our models. What might 'misbehaviors' look like? We think an example of this is given by the hyperbolic category boundaries seen in Figure 11.12. We noted above that these boundaries defied logic and were unlikely to represent listener behavior in all areas of the stimulus space. In other words, the model did not seem to correctly reflect the underlying process we are trying to understand: Listener judgments of apparent gender based on speech acoustics and apparent speaker age.

To investigate the issue, we can get the Pareto-k estimates for our initial model using the code below:

```
pareto_k = model_gender_vtl_f0$criteria$loo$diagnostics$
pareto_k
```

We plot these in Figure 11.14, and compare them to the same values for our reduced model. When plotting these, we noted that there was a pattern such that $\hat{k}$ values were highest for adult male speakers, and that the problems largely disappear when the cross-product is removed.

Below we make posterior predictions for the full model, taking the average across all posterior samples:

```
p_preds = predict (model_gender_vtl_f0)
```

Pareto-k values are plotted according to their predicted probability of a female response in the left plot of Figure 11.15. It's clear that the main issue seems to be with adult males who are predicted to be female nearly 0% of the time. In fact, in the data, several men *were* identified as women in 0% of cases. Since a probability of 0 implies, in the limit, a logit of negative infinity, the model appears to have a hard time finding reasonable values for some parameters in these cases. We considered a boxplot of

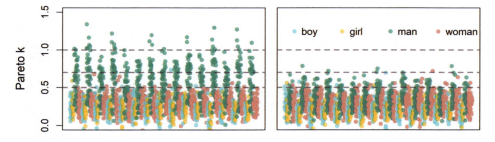

Figure 11.14 (left) Pareto-k estimates for data points in `model_gender_vtl_f0`. (right) Pareto-k estimates for data points in `model_gender_vtl_f0_reduced`. Point colors reflect the veridical speaker category.

Pareto-k values by individual speaker (not presented here), which revealed that a small number of adult males were responsible for most high k values. We found that these men tended to have the lowest f0 values among our speakers. In the middle plot, we present each speaker plotted according to their f0 and VTL, where point size reflects the average Pareto-k value for each speaker.

Based on Figure 11.15, we can see that the problematic male voices are those with extreme values of VTL and, in particular f0. If we think of our saddle shapes (see Figure 11.10), they can have areas where z values (i.e. the dependent variable) can rise or fall extremely rapidly. For example, the right plot of Figure 11.15 presents a sort of topographical map of the response surface for adults in our full model. In this sort of plot, lines indicate differences in 'elevation', and lines that are close together indicate rapid rises/falls in the height of the surface.

We can see that the voices with the highest Pareto-k values were in a region that includes very high values of z that also rise rapidly based on small differences in f0 and VTL. So, it appears that in this case, we have some male speakers whose probability of being identified as female is very low, implying very negative logit values, in a region of our surface that is curved such that extremely negative predicted values are possible. Combining this with our relatively small number of observations (given the complexity/flexibility of our model) results in the very high Pareto-k values seen above.

To resolve this situation we could refit the full model with tighter priors, especially since our priors are actually relatively wide and could be quite a bit narrower without likely having much of an effect on results. However, it may be the case that our full model is simply too flexible given the amount of data we have. Independently of all of this, we are still concerned with the very basic problem that the high-frequency region associated with male responses (presented in Figure 11.12) defies common sense and is probably wrong. As a result of this, we're not going to try to 'fix' the more

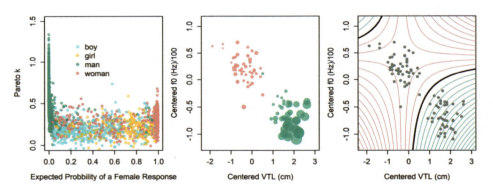

Figure 11.15 (left) Pareto-k estimates for data points in `model_gender_vtl_f0` plotted against the predicted probability of a female response for each data point. Point color represents the veridical speaker category. (middle) Adult male and female speakers are plotted according to voice characteristics. Point size reflects Pareto-k values. (right) A 'topographic map' of our predicted surface for adult speakers. The same points as in the middle figure. Black lines indicate female/male category boundaries (i.e. logit = 0). Red lines indicate 2-logit decreases in expected values, green lines indicate 2-logit increases in expected values.

Multiple quantitative predictors, dealing and Bayesian ANOVA 381

complicated model but simply abandon it, relying instead on the reduced model that does not include the VTL by f0 interaction. We should note that our reduced model *also* had a handful of high Pareto-k values, albeit only a small number (6), and with no values near 1. We don't think this necessarily means that our model is fundamentally misspecified, but rather that sometimes listeners do unpredictable things. It may be the case that a more 'robust' approach to logistic regression is justified in this case, as discussed in Kruschke (2014, chapter 21).

11.6 Exercises

The analyses in the main body of the text all involve only the unmodified 'actual' resonance level (in `exp_data`). Responses for the stimuli with the simulated 'big' resonance are reserved for exercises throughout. You can get the 'big' resonance in the `exp_ex` data frame, or all data in the `exp_data_all` data frame.

Fit and interpret one or more of the suggested models:

1   Easy: Analyze the (pre-fit) model that's exactly like `model_height_vtl_f0`, except using the data in `exp_ex` (`bmmb::get_model("11_model_height_vtl_f0.RDS")`).
2   Easy: Analyze the (pre-fit) model that's exactly like `model_gender_vtl_f0_reduced`, except using the data in `exp_ex` (`bmmb::get_model("11_model_gender_vtl_f0_reduced_ex.RDS")`).
3   Medium: Fit a model like the ones in this chapter but include the resonance predictor, and any interactions you may be interested in.
4   Hard: Fit a model like the ones in this chapter but include the duration predictor, and any interactions you may be interested in. You may also want to predict apparent age using a logistic model.

In any case, describe the model, present and explain the results, and include some figures.

References

Gelman, A. (2005). Analysis of variance—Why it is more important than ever. *The Annals of Statistics*, 33(1), 1–53.
Gelman, A., & Hill, J. (2006). *Data analysis using regression and multilevel/hierarchical models*. Cambridge: Cambridge University Press.
Gelman, A., Hill, J., & Yajima, M. (2012). Why we (usually) don't have to worry about multiple comparisons. *Journal of Research on Educational Effectiveness*, 5(2), 189–211.
Gelman, A., Carlin, J. B., Stern, H. S., Dunson, D. B., Vehtari, A., & Rubin, D. B. (2013). *Bayesian data Aanalysis*, Third Edition. London: Taylor & Francis.
Kruschke, J. (2014). *Doing Bayesian data analysis: A tutorial with R, JAGS, and Stan*. Frankfurt: Elsevier Science.
Myers, J. L., Well, A. D., & Lorch, R. F. (2010). *Research design and statistical analysis*. London: Routledge.
Schmelkin, L. P., & Pedhazur, E. J. (2013). *Measurement, design, and analysis: An integrated approach*. London: Taylor & Francis.

382 *Multiple quantitative predictors, dealing and Bayesian ANOVA*

Vehtari, A., Gelman, A., & Gabry, J. (2017). Practical Bayesian model evaluation using leave-one-out cross-validation and WAIC. *Statistics and computing*, 27(5), 1413–1432.

Vehtari, A. (2022). Cross-validation FAQ.Model Selection. ttps://avehtari.github.io/model selection/CV-FAQ.html

Wickens, T. D., & Keppel, G. (2004). *Design and analysis: A researcher's handbook*. Upper Saddle River, NJ: Pearson Prentice-Hall.

12 Multinomial and ordinal regression

In Chapter 10, we introduced models that can predict dichotomous (two-category) categorical variables using logistic regression. Here, we extend the concepts introduced in that chapter to the modeling of dependent variables with any number of categories. First, we discuss multinomial regression models that can be used to predict categorical variables without an inherent ordering. For example, we could use a multinomial model to predict the perception of vowel sounds from speech acoustics, to predict the lexical category of a word (verb, noun, adjective, ...), or to predict a speaker's native language. After this, we introduce ordinal models appropriate for the prediction of categorical variables with some inherent ordering (e.g. first, second, and third).

12.1 Chapter pre-cap

In this chapter, we introduce models for the prediction of categorical dependent variables with >2 categories. First, we discuss multinomial regression and its relationship to logistic regression. A multinomial logistic regression model with several predictors and random effects is fit and interpreted. We then explain the use of multinomial models to classify data, model participant responses, and make territorial maps. After that, we introduce ordinal logistic regression models, models to predict ordered categorical data. We present ordinal regression as a latent variable model and discuss the use of cumulative distributions and thresholds by ordinal models. An ordinal logistic regression model with several predictors and random effects is fit, interpreted, and discussed. Finally, we present an example of an ordinal regression model with participant-specific latent variable distributions.

12.2 Multinomial logistic regression

Multinomial logistic regression allows you to model data generated by a **multinomial distribution** with unknown parameters. Multinomial data arises when you have a variable that can take on any number of discrete values (often, but not always, a small number). These values do not *need* to have a necessary order (but they can), and the 'differences' between them don't mean anything. For example, in our experiment listeners were asked to identify speakers as either a boy, a girl, a man, or a woman. There was no choice but to report one of these categories, there is nothing 'between' them, and it doesn't make sense to talk about, e.g. boy plus girl or woman minus man. Further, although these categories could potentially be ordered in several ways, no ordering is inherent to the categories.

DOI: 10.4324/9781003285878-12

384　*Multinomial and ordinal regression*

The multinomial distribution is a generalization of the binomial distribution (see Section 10.2) to any number of discrete categories. This distribution will allow us to model the categorization of speakers into boys, girls, men, and women simultaneously rather than modeling this as two binary categorizations (male vs. female and adult vs. child). The multinomial distribution has three parameters:

1　n: The number of trials, a positive integer.
2　J: The number of possible outcome categories, a positive integer.
3　$p_1,...,p_J$: A vector of probabilities of observing each of the J outcomes where
$$\sum p_j = 1.$$

The multinomial distribution (equation (12.1)) takes the above parameters and generates a vector of counts $(y_1,...,y_J)$ representing the number of observations for each category. For every observation of a multinomial variable, the sum of the outcome probabilities $(p_1,...,p_J)$ must equal 1 and the sum of the outcomes $(y_1,...,y_J)$ must equal n, the total number of trials.

$$y_1,...,y_J \sim \text{multinomial}(p_1,...,p_J,n) \tag{12.1}$$

We can begin by thinking about the case where n=1. In this case, our y vector will equal 1 for one category and 0 for all other categories. Actually, data like this could be represented using a **categorical distribution**, which is just like the multinomial distribution except the n is *always* equal to 1. The multinomial distribution is to the categorical distribution as the binomial distribution is to the Bernoulli distribution (see Chapter 10). We will focus on the multinomial distribution here, however, we will provide an example of how to fit our model using a categorical distribution a bit later in the chapter.

Below we draw ten instances of a four-category multinomial variable with probabilities of 0.4, 0.1, 0.2, and 0.3 for the first, second, third, and fourth categories, respectively. In each case, the variable we sample has n=1.

```
rmultinom (10, 1, c(.4,.1,.2,.3))
##        [,1] [,2] [,3] [,4] [,5] [,6] [,7] [,8] [,9] [,10]
## [1,]    1    0    0    1    0    0    0    0    0    0
## [2,]    0    0    1    0    0    1    0    0    0    0
## [3,]    0    1    0    0    1    0    0    0    1    0
## [4,]    0    0    0    0    0    0    1    1    0    1
```

Each individual observation (column) consists of only a single one and three zeros. However, in the code below we can see that if we average across a large number of such observations (across rows), our estimates of $p_1,...,p_J$ closely match the real parameters.

```
rowMeans (rmultinom (10000, 1, c(.4,.1,.2,.3)))
## [1] 0.3985 0.1020 0.1987 0.3008
```

Below we sample ten more multinomial variables, this time each with n=100. We can see that we get a distribution of values across the four outcomes for each variable that resembles the values of p we defined for each outcome. Note that when we average

Multinomial and ordinal regression 385

across these observations, we get a good estimate of the p parameter associated with each outcome.

```
set.seed (1)
multinomial_variable = rmultinom (10, 100, c(.4,.1,.2,.3))
multinomial_variable
##      [,1] [,2] [,3] [,4] [,5] [,6] [,7] [,8] [,9] [,10]
## [1,]   42   37   41   41   41   37   36   47   31    37
## [2,]   10   15    7   14    8   14   13   10   14    12
## [3,]   24   21   18   15   19   18   22   16   22    22
## [4,]   24   27   34   30   32   31   29   27   33    29

# the row means closely approximate p
rowMeans(multinomial_variable)/100
## [1] 0.390 0.117 0.197 0.296
```

Multinomial regression is just what it sounds like: A regression model for the prediction of multinomial outcome variables. There are many ways to think about multinomial regression. We're going to present one that's consistent with the way we presented logistic regression in Chapter 10 and the way we've been presenting regression models in general in this book. For a more complete treatment of the topic please, see Agresti (2013), Agresti (2018), and Kruschke (2014). Before beginning the explanation we can 'spoil' the ending: The number of trials (n) and the number of possible outcomes (J) are aspects of your data and experimental design, and are known to you before you fit any model. Thus, multinomial logistic regression effectively consists of estimating p_j, or values related to it, for each category as a function of your independent variables. In other words, multinomial models let you predict how probable it is that you will see each of the outcome categories, given your independent variables and model structure.

12.2.1 Multinomial logits and the softmax function

Multinomial regression is a surprisingly 'simple' extension of the concepts underlying logistic regression. When we discussed logistic regression in Chapter 10, we introduced the inverse logit function (the link function for logistic regression). In Section 10.4.2, we discussed the fact that this function converts log odds to probabilities by arbitrarily setting the 'count' of failures to 1 and modeling only the expected 'count' of outcomes (i.e. e^z). We see in equation (12.2) that the probability that $y = 1$ (i.e. a 'success') is equal to the ratio of the expected number of successes over the sum of the total number of outcomes.

$$P(y=1) = \frac{\text{success}}{\text{failure} + \text{success}} = \frac{e^z}{1 + e^z} \tag{12.2}$$

The equation above works when we have exactly two categories. However, it can be modified so that it can be applied to three or more categories. First, we assume that rather than exactly two possible outcomes, there are now J outcomes, where J is some integer larger than one. If we stick to our interpretation of the value of e^z as an expected count for that category, then $e^{z \cdot j}$ is the expected count for category j. To find

386 *Multinomial and ordinal regression*

the probability of observing category j we find the ratio of the 'count' of j over the sum of all possible outcomes (i.e. the sum of counts for all categories). This is just an extension of the sum of successes and failures when we had only two categories as in equation (12.2).

$$P(Y = j) = \frac{e^{zj}}{\sum_{j=1}^{J} e^{zj}} \tag{12.3}$$

The function above is called the **softmax** function, and it is basically a generalization of the inverse logit function to more than two categories. When we did dichotomous logistic regression, we modeled only the 'count' of one variable, the one for 'success'. The 'count' for the category set to 'failure' was not modeled and was set to 1 (by setting $z = 0$, and $e^0 = 1$) for all cases. When we model multinomial data we follow the same convention and set one category as the 'reference'. To do this, we modify the equation above to pull the first category out of the summation and set its count to 1 for all situations, as in equation (12.4). Notice that the summation in the denominator of the fraction now begins at two. In Chapter 10, we said that you can think of the inverse logit function as relating expected successes relative to one failure. You can think of the softmax function as relating the expected number of outcomes of one category to the sum of the expected number of outcomes of all categories, where one of the counts (the reference category) has been set to one.

$$P(Y = j) = \frac{e^{zj}}{1 + \sum_{j=2}^{J} e^{zj}} \tag{12.4}$$

The equation above results in a set of probabilities which can serve as the multinomial parameters, $p_1, \ldots, p_j$, for categories $1, \ldots, J$. These probabilities are modeled by estimating z_j as the linear combination of our predictor variables based on some unknown parameters (β_j). Each outcome has a different prediction equation for z_j so that a multinomial regression has J prediction equations, one for each outcome. In addition, each prediction equation combines the same x_k predictors, albeit in a category-specific way (based on the β_j parameters for that category). This can be seen in the equation below representing the prediction of z_j for category j based on the coefficients (but not predictors) specific to that outcome.

$$z_j = \beta_j + \beta_{j1} \cdot x_1 + \beta_{j2} \cdot x_2 + \ldots + \beta_{jk} \cdot x_k \tag{12.5}$$

The prediction equation for the 'reference' category (brm uses the alphabetically-first category) is fixed to have a value of 0 for z_j. One way to accomplish this is to not estimate parameters for the reference category and instead fix these to zero, as seen in (12.6)

$$\begin{aligned} z_1 &= \alpha_1 + \beta_{11} \cdot x_1 + \beta_{12} \cdot x_2 + \ldots + \beta_{1k} \cdot x_k \\ z_1 &= 0 + 0 \cdot x_1 + 0 \cdot x_2 + \ldots + 0 \cdot x_k \\ z_1 &= 0 \end{aligned} \tag{12.6}$$

When we carried out logistic regression, the variable z was referred to as a logit. Sometimes the z_j values involved in multinomial regression are called **multinomial logits** to

Multinomial and ordinal regression 387

highlight their similarity to the dichotomous logit. More often, these values are referred to as the **score** for each category. The 'meaning' of the score is somewhat vaguely defined, in part because there are many ways to think about it. One way to think of the score is that it is a *latent variable* associated with each category that relates to the probability of observing that category given the values of the independent variables.

Latent variables are variables that are inferred mathematically using some statistical models but are not observed directly. For example, in our logistic regression model in Chapter 10 we predicted the perception of femaleness. We did this by predicting variation in the logit of the probability of observing a female response as a function of speaker vocal-tract length. The logit of this probability can be thought of as a latent variable representing something like 'femininity/femaleness' in the mind of the listener. Based on the 'feeling' of voice femininity that the listener has, they produce the surface variable that we do measure: A binary classification of a speaker as female/ male. In this view, the realization of the response variable (a female classification) is the result of a secret, *latent*, variable that is not directly observed (or observable) by us, but which we assume underlies the process.

In our four-category multinomial model we can imagine four latent variables, the score for each category. We can *think* of these as the 'feeling' the listener has regarding the 'boyness', 'girlness', 'manness', and 'womanness' of the voice. What is the 'boyness' of a voice? The difficult-to-quantify internal knowledge a listener has that the speaker is a boy, as opposed to some other sort of speaker. These latent variables are not directly measured in our experiment but we think they underlie the classification of speakers into categories. Thus, by observing the categorization of speakers, we can try to make inferences about these underlying variables, and the way that they relate to our predictors.

12.2.2 Comparison to logistic regression

At this point we've laid out the basics of multinomial regression, however, our presentation has been very quick and fairly abstract. To make our example more concrete we're going to talk about a small toy example using a single predictor and three categories, and show that a multinomial model with a single quantitative predictor is a modest extension of a logistic regression model with a single quantitative predictor.

Let's assume that we're interested in the prediction of a variable Y with two outcome categories, 1 and 2. We arbitrarily set 2 to 'success' and make it equal to 1 in the vector representing the dependent variable. Supposed we are interested in predicting the probability of observing a success, i.e. $Y = 2$, using a single quantitative predictor x. We model the logit of the probability of observing a success using a line with a given intercept and slope for the quantitative predictor. We set the value of failures to 0 logits for all cases, which is equivalent to representing the failure category with a horizontal line whose intercept is zero. So, our logistic model can be thought of as consisting of the two prediction equations in (12.7), presented in the top left plot of Figure 12.1.

$$\begin{aligned} z_1 &= 0 + x \cdot 0 \\ z_2 &= -3 + x \cdot -3 \end{aligned} \tag{12.7}$$

Rather than use the inverse logit function to convert logits to probabilities, we will use the softmax function (introduced above), since we know that these are equivalent when there are two categories. Below, we see that when we set the 'count' for failures

388 *Multinomial and ordinal regression*

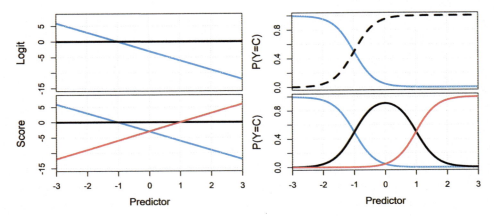

Figure 12.1 (top left) Lines indicate the logit of the probability of observing a success (blue line), or a failure (black line). (top right) Lines indicate the probabilities associated with observing the outcomes in the top left plot. (bottom left) Lines represent scores for the reference category (black line), the second category (blue line), and the third category (red line). (bottom right) Lines indicate the probabilities associated with observing the categories in the bottom left plot.

to 1, i.e. set $z_1 = 0$ so that $e^{z_1} = 1$, the softmax function really does 'become' the inverse logit function when calculating the probability of success $(P(Y = 2))$. We also use this approach to calculate the probability of a failure $(P(Y = 1))$. Of course, this is not usually done because $P(Y = 2) = 1 - P(Y = 2)$; however, we do this explicitly here for illustrative purposes.

$$P(Y = 2) = \frac{e^{z_2}}{e^{z_1} + e^{z_2}} = \frac{e^{z_2}}{1 + e^{z_2}}$$

$$P(Y = 1) = \frac{e^{z_1}}{e^{z_1} + e^{z_2}} = \frac{1}{1 + e^{z_2}}$$

(12.8)

You can use the code below to recreate the lines in the top right row of Figure 12.1, and to find the probabilities in the top right plot. The probability of observing a success (category 2, blue line) looks just like the sigmoid curves we saw when doing a logistic regression in Chapter 10. In Figure 12.1, we also plot the curve associated with failures. Normally this is not plotted for logistic regression since it is just the curve for successes mirrored about the line at $p = 0.5$.

```
# predictor from -3 to 3
x = seq (-3,3,0.1)
# lines for failures
z_1 = 0 + x*0

# line for successes
z_2 = -3 + x*-3
```

```
scores = cbind (z1,z2)
# softmax function, exponentiate and divide by sum
probabilities = exp (scores) / rowSums (exp (scores))

# simple version of the top right plot in Figure 12.1
plot (probabilities[,1], type = 'l')
lines (probabilities[,2], type = 'l')
```

To turn our logistic regression into a multinomial regression, let's imagine we want to model a third outcome category, $Y = 3$. We add a line predicting the 'logit', now a *score*, for this category in (12.9). We now have three lines predicting scores (bottom left, Figure 12.1), one of which is still horizontal (z_1). This is no longer a 'failure' but rather the *reference category*.

$$z_1 = 0 + x \cdot 0$$
$$z_2 = -3 + x \cdot -3 \tag{12.9}$$
$$z_3 = -3 + x \cdot 3$$

To get the predicted probability of observing each outcome we enter these scores into the softmax function, in 'expanded' form in (12.10).

$$P(Y = 3) = \frac{e^{z3}}{1 + e^{z2} + e^{z3}}$$

$$P(Y = 2) = \frac{e^{z2}}{1 + e^{z2} + e^{z3}} \tag{12.10}$$

$$P(Y = 1) = \frac{1}{1 + e^{z2} + e^{z3}}$$

You can use the code below to recreate this process and the lines in the bottom row of Figure 12.1. Note that all we've done is add a third line and a third score. Apart from that, the process is the same as it was for logistic regression.

```
# predictor from -3 to 3
x = seq (-3,3,0.1)

# lines for reference category
z_1 = 0 + x*0
# line for category two
z_2 = -3 + x*-3
# line for category three
z_2 = -3 + x*3
scores = cbind (z1,z2,z3)

# softmax function, exponentiate and divide by sum
probabilities = exp (scores) / rowSums (exp (scores))
```

390 *Multinomial and ordinal regression*

```r
# simple version of the bottom right plot in Figure 12.1
plot (probabilities[,1], type = 'l',ylim=c(0,1))
lines (probabilities[,2], type = 'l')
lines (probabilities[,3], type = 'l')
```

There is one important difference between logistic and multinomial regression related to classification, or expected outcomes, based on probabilities and scores. When there are only two categories, a logit greater than 0 implies a probability greater than 0.5 of success. In previous chapters, we used this characteristic to talk about expected outcomes in specific parts of the stimulus space. Basically, in any part of the stimulus space where a positive logit is predicted, you expect to observe a 'success' (1). In any part of the stimulus space where a negative logit is predicted, you expect to observe a 'failure' (0). Since the logit of failures is always fixed at exactly zero, another way to look at this is that the category with the greatest predicted logit value is expected.

When there are more than two possible outcome categories, there is no guarantee that a positive score for a given outcome means that category is expected. However, it is still the case that the category with the greatest score in a given condition is the predicted outcome for that condition. Another thing to keep in mind is that, unlike in logistic regression, the most probable outcome may not be very probable in a multinomial model. For example, if there are five outcome categories the most probable predicted outcome could have a probability of only 0.24 if the other categories had probabilities of 0.19. Thus, we see that in multinomial regression the most probable outcome doesn't have to be very probable, it just needs to be more probable than the alternatives.

12.2.3 Data and research questions

We load our packages and data below. We also add a new variable, y, representing our multinomial outcome. This variable represents observations of a vector of length four whose first, second, third, and fourth elements represent observed outcomes of 'boy', 'girl', 'man', and 'woman', respectively. After this, we add a variable called `size` that always equals 1 because each row in our data frame represents the observation of a single outcome. Of course, the size information may be higher than 1 for your data if some of your rows represent trials where n>1. Finally, we process our quantitative predictors in the same way as in the previous chapters.

```r
library (brms)
library (bmmb)
data (exp_data)

# new dependent variable
exp_data$y = cbind(b = as.numeric(exp_data$C=='b'),
                   g = as.numeric(exp_data$C=='g'),
                   m = as.numeric(exp_data$C=='m'),
                   w = as.numeric(exp_data$C=='w'))
```

Multinomial and ordinal regression 391

```
# variable representing the size (n) of each observation.
exp_data$size = 1

# preparation of quantitative predictors
# as in previous chapters
exp_data$vtl_original = exp_data$vtl
exp_data$vtl = exp_data$vtl - mean (exp_data$vtl)

exp_data$f0_original = exp_data$f0
exp_data$f0 = exp_data$f0 - mean(exp_data$f0)
exp_data$f0 = exp_data$f0 / 100
```

Below, we print out the first six instances of our dependent variable and compare this to the first six values of the C (apparent category) variable in our data frame. Each row in the matrix below represents a single observation of our multinomial variable. We can see that the dependent variable indicates which category was selected for a given trial using a 1 in the appropriate column and a 0 in the others.

```
# first 6 elements of dependent variable
head (exp_data$y)
##      b g m w
## [1,] 0 1 0 0
## [2,] 0 0 0 1
## [3,] 0 1 0 0
## [4,] 0 1 0 0
## [5,] 1 0 0 0
## [6,] 1 0 0 0

# first 6 elements of apparent speaker category factor
head (exp_data$C)
## [1] "g" "w" "g" "g" "b" "b"
```

We will try to use our data to answer the following research question:

(Q1) Can we use speaker f0 and VTL to predict apparent speaker category?

Keep in mind we're trying to predict *apparent* and not *veridical* speaker category. Our consideration of the accuracy or utility of this model will depend on how well it represents listener classifications of speakers, no matter how wrong or right these may be. Thus, a model with perfect classification of speakers into veridical categories is not the goal: If listeners make predictable mistakes we want the model to make the same 'mistakes'.

12.2.4 *Description of our model*

Our model formula is largely similar to those we have seen before, with two minor changes. Beside the dependent variable, separated by a pipe (|), we need to include a variable that indicates the integer number of trials for each observation. For us, this will always be 1, but in many situations, this can be a wider range of values. We want

392 *Multinomial and ordinal regression*

to predict our counts of categorizations with respect to the value of speaker VTL and f0, and so the model formula we are going to use is seen below.

```
y|trials(size) ~ vtl+f0 + (vtl+f0|x|L) + (1|y|S)
```

Since we're predicting category membership with two quantitative predictors, we know that the surfaces our model defines are planes. In the models we've fit to this point, we had a single dependent variable and a single plane for a single condition. So, our model formulas previously were something like:

```
y ~ vtl+f0 + (vtl+f0|S) + (1|L)
```

However, in a multinomial regression, we have one plane for each response category, so our formula above could really be thought of as:

```
y_1 ~ vtl+f0 + (vtl+f0|x|L) + (1|y|S)
y_2 ~ vtl+f0 + (vtl+f0|x|L) + (1|y|S)
y_3 ~ vtl+f0 + (vtl+f0|x|L) + (1|y|S)
y_4 ~ vtl+f0 + (vtl+f0|x|L) + (1|y|S)
```

As noted in Section 8.6.1, the $|x|$ notation tells our model that the L predictors are related across the prediction equations for each outcome category. In doing this, we estimate the listener effects as coming from a single nine-dimensional normal distribution rather than three separate three-dimensional normal variables. Similarly, by adding $|y|$ before our S predictor we model the speaker effects for each outcome category as coming from a single three-dimensional normal distribution rather than three unidimensional ones and also model the correlations between the dimensions.

Since our multinomial model predicts a response surface for each outcome category, our multinomial model will involve four times as many coefficients as an equivalent Gaussian model. Of course, we noted above that the coefficients of the reference category are set to zero and not estimated. This means that, in general, a multinomial model predicting a variable with J possible outcomes results in $J-1$ times as many parameters as an equivalent model predicting a quantitative variable. Our full model specification is pretty large, so we split it into two parts. First, the part specifying our predictions and combinations of predictors:

$$y_{1[i]}, y_{2[i]}, y_{3[i]}, y_{4[i]} \sim \text{multinomial}\left(p_{1[i]}, p_{2[i]}, p_{3[i]}, p_{4[i]}, size_{[i]}\right)$$

$$\text{for } j = 1, \dots, 4$$

$$p_{j[i]} = \frac{e^{z_{j[i]}}}{\sum_{j=1}^{J} e^{z_{j[i]}}} \qquad (12.11)$$

$$z_{j[i]} = a_j + b_{j[i]} \cdot \text{vtl}_{[i]} + c_{j[i]} \cdot \text{f0}_{[i]}$$
$$a_{j[i]} = \text{Intercept}_j + L_{j\left[\text{L}_{[i]}\right]} + S_{j\left[\text{S}_{[i]}\right]}$$
$$b_{j[i]} = VTL_j + VTL_j : L_{j\left[\text{L}_{[i]}\right]}$$
$$c_{j[i]} = F0_j + F0_j : L_{j\left[\text{L}_{[i]}\right]}$$

Multinomial and ordinal regression   393

And a plain English description of this part:

Our vector of counts $\left(y_{1[i]}, y_{2[i]}, y_{3[i]}, y_{4[i]}\right)$ is assumed to come from a multinomial distribution with unknown parameters $p_{1[i]}, p_{2[i]}, p_{3[i]}, p_{4[i]}$, and an n equal to 1 (size) for all trials. For each of our j response categories, the probability of observing that outcome on a trial i, $p_{j[i]}$, is found by combining the score for each category for that trial $\left(z_{j[i]}\right)$ using the softmax link function. The score for a trial is equal to a trial-dependent combination of an intercept, an effect for VTL, and an effect for f0. The intercept for category j for trial i $\left(a_{j[i]}\right)$ varies according to an overall model intercept for that category $\left(Intercept_j\right)$ and speaker $\left(S_{j\left[s_{[i]}\right]}\right)$ and listener-dependent $\left(L_{j\left[l_{[i]}\right]}\right)$ variations from this. The VTL slope for category j for trial i $\left(b_{j[i]}\right)$ varies according to an overall VTL slope for that category $\left(VTL_j\right)$ and listener-dependent $\left(VTL:L_{j\left[l_{[i]}\right]}\right)$ variations from this. The f0 slope for category j for trial i $\left(c_{j[i]}\right)$ varies according to an overall f0 slope for that category $\left(F0_j\right)$ and listener-dependent $\left(F0:L_{j\left[l_{[i]}\right]}\right)$ variations from this.

In (12.12), we specify the rest of our model (the priors):

$$\begin{aligned}
&\text{for } j = 2,\ldots,4\\
Intercept_j &\sim t(3,0,3)\\
VTL_j, F0_j &\sim t(3,0,3)\\
\sigma_{Lj}, \sigma_{VTLj:Lj}, \sigma_{F0j:Lj}, \sigma_{Sj} &\sim t(3,0,3)
\end{aligned}$$

$$\begin{bmatrix} S_{2[\bullet]} \\ S_{3[\bullet]} \\ S_{4[\bullet]} \end{bmatrix} \sim \text{MVNormal}\left(\begin{bmatrix} 0 \\ 0 \\ 0 \end{bmatrix}, \Sigma_S \right) \tag{12.12}$$

$$\begin{bmatrix} L_{2[\bullet]} \\ VTL_2:L_{2[\bullet]} \\ F0_2:L_{2[\bullet]} \\ L_{3[\bullet]} \\ VTL_3:L_{3[\bullet]} \\ F0_3:L_{3[\bullet]} \\ L_{4[\bullet]} \\ VTL_4:L_{4[\bullet]} \\ F0_4:L_{4[\bullet]} \end{bmatrix} \sim \text{MVNormal}\left(\begin{bmatrix} 0 \\ 0 \\ 0 \\ 0 \\ 0 \\ 0 \\ 0 \\ 0 \\ 0 \end{bmatrix}, \Sigma_L \right)$$

$$\begin{aligned}
R_S &\sim \text{LKJCorr}(2)\\
R_L &\sim \text{LKJCorr}(2)
\end{aligned}$$

394 *Multinomial and ordinal regression*

And provide a plan English description of this second part:

> *We specify priors for response categories 2 to four since all parameters are set to zero for the first (reference) category. The 'fixed' effects and correlations were given prior distributions appropriate for their expected range of values. The three speaker-dependent terms for each listener (one for each modeled outcome category) were drawn from a three-dimensional normal distribution with standard deviations $\left(\sigma_{S2},\sigma_{S2},\sigma_{S3}\right)$ and a correlation matrix $\left(R_S\right)$ that was estimated from the data. The nine listener effects were drawn from a nine-dimensional normal distribution with standard deviations $\left(\sigma_{L2},\sigma_{VTL2:L2},\sigma_{F03:L3},\ldots\right)$ and a correlation matrix $\left(R_L\right)$ that was estimated from the data.*

12.2.5 Fitting the model

There is one major difference in how we need to specify priors for multinomial models: We need to specify priors individually for each response category with modeled parameters. This is done by passing the name of the categorical variable to the `dpar` parameter. Above, we named our response variables according to the letters we have been using throughout this text. We can see this below.

```
colnames (exp_data$y)
## [1] "b" "g" "m" "w"
```

The name passed to `dpar` will be `muCategory` where `Category` corresponds to the category name. This means we need to specify priors for `mug`, `mum`, and `muw`, but not `mub`. We specify our priors below:

```
multinomial_prior =
  c(set_prior("student_t(3, 0, 3)", class = "Intercept",dpar="mug"),
    set_prior("student_t(3, 0, 3)", class = "b",dpar="mug"),
    set_prior("student_t(3, 0, 3)", class = "sd",dpar="mug"),
    set_prior("student_t(3, 0, 3)", class = "Intercept",dpar="mum"),
    set_prior("student_t(3, 0, 3)", class = "b",dpar="mum"),
    set_prior("student_t(3, 0, 3)", class = "sd",dpar="mum"),
    set_prior("student_t(3, 0, 3)", class = "Intercept",dpar="muw"),
    set_prior("student_t(3, 0, 3)", class = "b",dpar="muw"),
    set_prior("student_t(3, 0, 3)", class = "sd",dpar="muw"),
    set_prior("lkj_corr_cholesky (2)", class = "cor"))
```

And here is the code to fit our model, using the `multinomial` family for the first time:

```
# Fit the model yourself
model_multinomial =
  brms::brm (y|trials(size) ~ vtl+f0 + (vtl+f0|x|L) + (1|y|S),
             data=exp_data, family="multinomial", chains=4, cores=4,
             warmup=1000, iter = 5000, thin = 4, prior = multinomial_prior)
```

Multinomial and ordinal regression   395

```
# Or download it from the GitHub page:
model_multinomial = bmmb::get_model ("12_model_multinomial.RDS")
```

By the way, if you wanted to fit the model above using the categorical distribution, you would use the code below. Notice that there are only three changes compared to the code to fit our multinomial model above. First, the `family` parameter is now equal to `categorical`. Second, the `trials` specification is now omitted since the number of observations for each trial is now 1. Finally, we can use our vector representing the outcome category directly as our dependent variable.

```
model_categorical =
  brms::brm (C ~ vtl+f0 + (vtl+f0|L) + (1|S),
             data=exp_data, family="categorical", chains=4, cores=4,
             warmup=1000, iter = 5000, thin = 4, prior = multinomial_prior)
```

Why would we ever use a multinomial analysis when the categorical distribution seems simpler? First, in some cases, individual trials might contain multiple observations such that an individual analysis is not possible. However, a multinomial analysis can also be much faster by substantially reducing the number of individual observations that need to be taken into account when calculating likelihoods. For example, imagine we were only interested in predicting the probability that a listener would report each speaker category. If we run a model like this:

```
brms::brm (C ~ 1+(1|L), family="categorical", data = exp_data)
```

Then our data has 2,085 rows because we have 139 rows for each of 15 listeners. However, if we create a table like this:

```
table (exp_data$C, exp_data$L)
##
##      1  2  3  4  5  6  7  8  9 10 11 12 13 14 15
##   b 29 29 18 42 29 51 40 19 27 30 33  5 26 41 22
##   g 30 34 38 20 21 12 39 31 32 27 20 45 23 23 31
##   m 43 41 39 41 45 42 40 45 42 44 42 43 41 44 43
##   w 37 35 44 36 44 34 20 44 38 38 44 46 49 31 43
```

And use this as our data, then we can treat each column above as a single observation from a multinomial distribution with an n equal to 139. When treated this way, our data has only 15 rows and, as a result, fitting the model below will be much (much) faster.

```
new_data = data.frame (size = 139, L = factor(1:15))
new_data$y = as.matrix(table (exp_data$L, exp_data$C))
brms::brm (y|trials(size) ~ 1+(1|L), family="multinomial", data = new_data)
```

396 *Multinomial and ordinal regression*

This is not an option for us since we want to predict categorizations based on the specific combination of listener and speaker, and we only have one observation for each unique combination in our data. However, it is worth considering if a categorical or multinomial analysis might best suit your specific situation.

12.2.6 Interpreting the model

Below we see the model fixed effects, the intercept, the VTL slope, and the f0 slope for each category with estimated parameters (i.e. no reference category b). The set of parameters for each category defines a category-specific plane whose value along the z dimension can be predicted based on the values of f0 and VTL. We have four planes and four values of z_j for any given location in the two-dimensional space defined by f0 and VTL. For each point, we can select as the most probable category the one whose value of z_j is highest at the point in the space. Another way to look at this is that we select as the most probable outcome the category whose plane is highest at any given location in the space.

```
brms::fixef (model_multinomial)
##                  Estimate Est.Error      Q2.5     Q97.5
## mug_Intercept     -2.4516    0.4508   -3.3802   -1.6018
## mum_Intercept     -2.1677    0.4671   -3.1804   -1.3566
## muw_Intercept     -0.6317    0.4336   -1.5063    0.2166
## mug_vtl           -2.0876    0.3746   -2.8648   -1.3766
## mug_f0             1.4335    0.6987    0.1241    2.8640
## mum_vtl            3.0820    0.5938    2.0761    4.3871
## mum_f0            -2.6146    1.0238   -4.7816   -0.7190
## muw_vtl            0.9464    0.4613    0.0266    1.8643
## muw_f0             2.2001    1.0943    0.1476    4.4024
```

Since the predicted value, the *linear predictor*, is the score for each category, the parameters above are difficult to interpret in isolation. This is because scores need to be interpreted relative to the baseline category value of 0 (for boys), or relative to one another, rather than absolutely. For example, the negative coefficient for VTL for 'girl' (mug_vtl) indicates that a longer VTL made a girl response less likely. We can also see that increasing f0 made a 'woman' response more likely (muw_f0), and a 'man' response less likely (mum_f0). However, it's important to remember that these effects are all relative to the effects for the boy category, and not 'absolute'. For example, the 'boy' slope for VTL is 0, meaning it is 2.09 higher than the 'girl' slope for the same predictor (which is −2.09). We could say this means that longer VTLs suggest a 'boy' response is more likely with respect to a 'girl' response. However, a slope of 0 is smaller than the VTL slope for 'man' of 3.08. So, a longer VTL means that a 'boy' response is *less* likely with respect to a 'man' response. As with all of the parameters in our model, these comparisons can be made more formally with the hypothesis (or short_hypothesis) function as seen below.

```
# difference in VTL slopes between:
short_hypothesis (model_multinomial,
                  c("mug_vtl - mum_vtl = 0",    # girls and men
```

Multinomial and ordinal regression 397

```
                         "mug_vtl -   0 = 0",          # girls and boys
                         "mum_vtl -   0 = 0"))         # men and boys
##        Estimate Est.Error    Q2.5   Q97.5                    hypothesis
## H1      -5.170     0.6927  -6.612  -3.883   (mug_vtl-mum_vtl) = 0
## H2      -2.088     0.3746  -2.865  -1.377        (mug_vtl-0) = 0
## H3       3.082     0.5938   2.076   4.387        (mum_vtl-0) = 0
```

We might wonder how well our model can predict listener judgments. We can do this by finding the predicted probability for each category predicted by our model, as seen below. Note that we use the `fitted` rather than `predict` function. This is because we are interested in the expected values predicted by our model. In contrast, `predict` would give us *posterior predictions* of the actual dependent variable which would incorporate our modeled noise.

```
multi_pred_re = fitted (model_multinomial)
```

The result of this is a three-dimensional matrix. The first two dimensions represent the usual summary matrices generated by `brms`, and the third dimension represents the different response categories. Below we see the two-dimensional summary matrix for the first response category (boy). The first column is the posterior probability of category membership for each observation, the second is the standard error for each prediction, and the third and fourth represent the 2.5% and 97.5% credible intervals.

```
head(multi_pred_re[,,1])
##        Estimate Est.Error    Q2.5   Q97.5
## [1,]    0.2921     0.1244  0.09423  0.5742
## [2,]    0.2104     0.1036  0.05993  0.4504
## [3,]    0.2804     0.1355  0.07635  0.5892
## [4,]    0.4052     0.1483  0.14678  0.7078
## [5,]    0.4385     0.1408  0.18733  0.7212
## [6,]    0.2218     0.1229  0.04973  0.5123
```

Below we see the same information for the second category (girl):

```
head(multi_pred_re[,,2])
##        Estimate Est.Error    Q2.5   Q97.5
## [1,]    0.6190     0.1307  0.3396  0.8427
## [2,]    0.6100     0.1347  0.3243  0.8421
## [3,]    0.6624     0.1380  0.3614  0.8848
## [4,]    0.4507     0.1401  0.1879  0.7200
## [5,]    0.5003     0.1337  0.2454  0.7487
## [6,]    0.6879     0.1367  0.3823  0.9070
```

We can also just select the second dimension from each matrix, resulting in a two-dimensional matrix containing information regarding the posterior probability of being classified into each category across columns, for each observation across rows.

398 *Multinomial and ordinal regression*

```
head(multi_pred_re[,1,])
##        P(Y = b)  P(Y = g)   P(Y = m)  P(Y = w)
## [1,]    0.2921    0.6190   0.0017775  0.08714
## [2,]    0.2104    0.6100   0.0014059  0.17815
## [3,]    0.2804    0.6624   0.0016820  0.05551
## [4,]    0.4052    0.4507   0.0024148  0.14168
## [5,]    0.4385    0.5003   0.0036467  0.05764
## [6,]    0.2218    0.6879   0.0003084  0.09000
```

Since these are probabilities, the sum of each row equals one because only these four outcomes exist. For example, the first row above tells us that, according to our model, the first observation has a 0.29 probability of being identified as a boy, 0.62 probability of being identified as a girl, 0.002 probability of being identified as a man, and a 0.09 probability of being identified as a woman. We can use the code below to find the 'winning' category for each observation, that is, the category with the highest posterior probability in each row. We use the resulting column numbers to get category labels.

```
# find highest posterior probability from each category
predicted = apply (multi_pred_re[,1,],1,which.max)
head (predicted)
## [1] 2 2 2 2 2 2

# use modal category to get a category label
predicted_category = c("b","g","m","w")[predicted]
head (predicted_category)
## [1] "g" "g" "g" "g" "g" "g"
```

Below, we cross-tabulate predicted and observed classifications. Observed speaker classifications vary across rows, and model predictions of these classifications vary across columns. This is a *confusion matrix*, introduced in Chapter 5. Correct classifications fall on the main diagonal and all other values indicate mistakes. For example, we see that there were 269 correct classifications of boys as boys, and 78 incorrect predictions of boys as girls. A majority of observations fall along the main diagonal indicating that the model was relatively good at predicting listener behavior.

```
table (observed_category = exp_data$C, predicted_category)
##                       predicted_category
## observed_category    b    g    m    w
##
##                 b  269   78   27   67
##                 g   74  290    0   62
##                 m    5    1  624    5
##                 w   30   19    9  525
```

Below we find the probability of observing a correct classification overall, and individually for each category. We see that the model was able to predict listener judgments with a high degree of accuracy overall, but that some categories (man) were easier to predict than others (boy).

Multinomial and ordinal regression 399

```
# overall correct
mean (predicted_category == exp_data$C)
## [1] 0.8192

# correct predictions by category
tab = xtabs (~ exp_data$C + predicted_category)
diag(tab) / rowSums(tab)
##       b        g        m        w
## 0.6100  0.6808  0.9827  0.9005
```

12.2.7 *Multinomial models and territorial maps*

We discussed territorial maps for two categories along two dimensions in Chapter 11 where we predicted the perception of femaleness based on speaker f0 and VTL. As we discussed then, when categories are represented by planes, the boundary between categories is defined by the line formed by the intersection of the planes. When we did (dichotomous) logistic regression in Chapter 11, we found the intersection of one plane with a horizontal plane at $z = 0$. In this chapter, we still have a plane such that $z = 0$ for all x and y (the reference category plane), but we also have three other planes with possible non-zero slopes along each dimension. The intersection of the planes representing pairs of categories forms the boundary between those two categories. Since we have 6 unique pairings of our four response categories, we will have six boundary lines.

To find the line formed by the intersection of planes, first we define the values of two planes, z_1 and z_2 based on their respective coefficients as in (12.13). We use a, b, and c for the intercept, x-axis, and y-axis slope for the first plane and d, e, and f for the corresponding coefficients for the second plane.

$$z_1 = a + b \cdot x + c \cdot y$$
$$z_2 = d + e \cdot x + f \cdot y \tag{12.13}$$

We set z_1 equal to z_2 to find the place where the planes equal (i.e. their intersection) as in (12.14).

$$z_1 = z_2$$
$$a + b \cdot x + c \cdot y = d + e \cdot x + f \cdot y \tag{12.14}$$

In order to turn (12.14) into an equation resembling that of a line ($y = a + b \cdot x$), we need to isolate y on the left-hand side as seen in (12.15).

$$y = \frac{-a + d}{c - f} + \frac{-b + e}{c - f} \cdot x \tag{12.15}$$

The equation above is actually much simpler than it looks. Since the parameters (a,b,c,d,e,f) are just constants, the intercept $((-a + d)/(c - f))$ and slope $((-b + e)/(c - f))$ simplify to scalars. As mentioned above, we get 6 such line equations, one for the boundary between all possible pairs of each of the four planes. Figure 12.2 presents each of these six boundaries compared to the modal classification for each speaker.

All six boundary lines are presented in the left plot of Figure 12.3. One problem with considering the figure in this way is that many of the boundaries are not very relevant.

400 *Multinomial and ordinal regression*

For example, the boundary between girl and man will hardly matter for classification because the 'woman' and 'boy' categories fall almost entirely between the 'girl' and 'man' categories. As a result, listeners will rarely be deciding between a 'man' or 'girl' response when 'boy' and 'woman' are available.

The right plot of Figure 12.3 presents only those boundaries that are *relevant*, resulting in a *territorial map* of our categories along f0 and VTL (see Section 10.5.5). This can be stated more formally as: The figure contains only those boundaries that represent scores equal to or greater than the maximal score for that location, from among the response categories. For example, in the left plot, we see that the boy-woman boundary bisects the area where 'man' is a modal response (bottom right in the left plot). This line segment does not feature in the right plot because it has a lower value than the 'man' plane in this area. One way to imagine how territorial maps relate to our planes is to imagine that our planes were opaque but were immaterial such that they

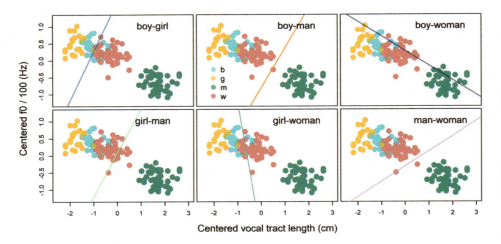

Figure 12.2 Each plot compares a single estimated category boundary between two groups at a time for boys (b), girls (g), men (m), and women (w).

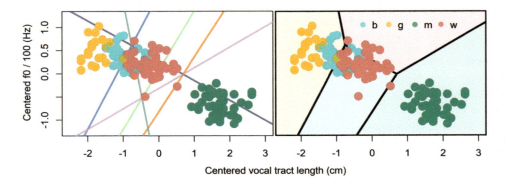

Figure 12.3 (left) Points represent modal classifications for individual speakers. Lines represent the six category boundaries presented in Figure 12.2. (right) Territorial map comparing locations associated with the classification of speakers into boys (b), girls (g), men (m), and women (w).

Multinomial and ordinal regression 401

can intersect and continue past each other. If we were to look 'down' the z-axis onto these planes, we would see something very much like the right plot of Figure 12.3; we would see only those plane sections, and only those intersections, that were 'above' any other plane.

We can find the boundaries of each of the 'territories' in the territorial map *analytically* by finding each boundary, the intersections of all boundaries, and recording only the line segments whose scores were greater than or equal to all of the category planes. Each of these steps is generally straightforward but we know of no algorithm to implement this process easily for any number of response categories. The `make_map` function in the `bmmb` package can be used to generate territorial maps for any number of response categories in a two-dimensional stimulus space. However, rather than find the territorial map analytically, `make_map` estimates its characteristics *numerically*, that is, based on a bunch of guesses and not exact solutions.

The `make_map` function takes in a matrix representing the coefficients for each of the response categories. In the code below we get estimates for our fixed effects and combine these into a matrix, including a column of zeros to represent the 'boy' coefficients. Each column represents the coefficients for a single response category, and intercepts, x-axis coefficients and y-axis coefficients vary across rows. The rows and columns of the matrix below have been named to make this organization clearer, and you should compare the values below to our model fixed effects shown above (e.g. `fixef (model_multinomial)`).

```
parameters = unname (fixef (model_multinomial)[,1])
parameters = cbind(b = c(0, 0, 0),
                   g = parameters[c(1,4,5)],
                   m = parameters[c(2,6,7)],
                   w = parameters[c(3,8,9)])
rownames(parameters)=c("Intercept","vtl_slope","f0_slope")

parameters
##               b       g       m        w
## Intercept    0  -2.452  -2.168  -0.6317
## vtl_slope    0  -2.088   3.082   0.9464
## f0_slope     0   1.434  -2.615   2.2001
```

This matrix can be passed to the `make_map` function, which uses it to calculate the territorial map. It operates in the following manner. First, it generates a 1,000 by 1,000 point grid spanning the desired x and y-axis range. The density of points can be set with the `density` parameter and the x and y-axis range can be set manually or by passing points with the same ranges to the function with the `points` parameter. After this, the function uses the parameters given to calculate the score for each category, for every point in the grid, and collects the winning category for each location. After this, the convex hull encompassing the points for each category is found, and the polygon representing the convex hull for each category is returned in a list by the function. This approach is not *exact*, and so it is not appropriate for making precise claims about your results. However, it can be made arbitrarily accurate by increasing the density of the points, and this approach is sufficient for creating plots to convey the results of your analyses.

402 *Multinomial and ordinal regression*

```
territorial_map =
  bmmb::make_map (parameters, points = cbind(exp_data$vtl,
exp_data$f0))
```

The output of `make_map` can be passed to the `plot_map` function to plot the resulting territorial maps easily. We used this process to create the territorial maps of the figures in this chapter.

```
bmmb::plot_map (territorial_map, colors = bmmb::cols[2:5],
xlab="",ylab="")
```

We noticed something very strange when we made the territorial map in Figure 12.3: The 'boy' territory contains a large number of woman responses. In addition, the boy-woman boundary seems strangely high along f0. If that is really the boundary between boys and women in the VTL by f0 space, then a large number of adult female speakers fall into territory where 'boy' responses are expected. If this is the case then how/why is the model classifying all those women correctly? The answer to this question may lie in Figure 12.4.

In the left plot of Figure 12.4, point colors represent modal listener judgments for each speaker. In the middle plot, we see model predictions including speaker and listener random effects. When these are included the model predictions look very much like the listener judgments and the classifications don't make much sense relative to the territorial map. In the right plot of the same figure, we see model predictions when random effects are *not* included. In this case, we see that model predictions do *not* look like the listener judgments, but the classifications *do* make sense relative to the territorial map. So, it seems that the random effects are causing this strange behavior in our model.

Figure 12.5 presents the speaker random intercepts. Since there are three modeled categories, there are three random intercepts for each speaker. We can see that, in general, the speaker intercepts have small values that vary around zero, and have credible intervals that mostly include zero. However, many female speakers have intercepts that

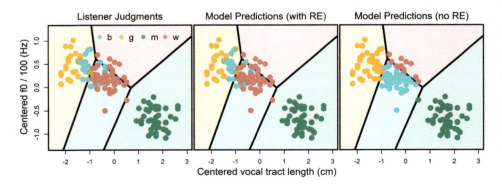

Figure 12.4 Territorial maps compared to modal classifications of speakers as boys (b), girls (g), men (m), and women (w). Point colors reflect classifications made by (left) listeners, (middle) predictions including random effects (RE), and (right) predictions excluding random effects.

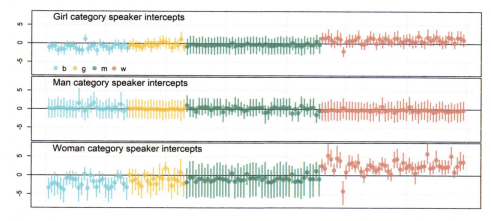

Figure 12.5 Each row presents posterior means and 95% credible intervals for speaker-dependent intercept terms for each category. Colors represent veridical boys (b), girls (g), men (m), and women (w).

have large non-zero values for the female category, and whose credible intervals omit zero and very small values.

Here's what we believe is happening. Think of a female response plane with a specific intercept, VTL slope, and f0 slope. If female speaker categorizations were very predictable based on the value of this plane at a given location, all the female speaker effects would be zero or near zero. This is because if the score based on the plane explains classification, there is nothing left for the speaker intercept to explain. We can see this sort of behavior for adult male speakers: Adult male speakers are mostly easy to identify because of their unusually low f0s.

In contrast, consider a situation where individual female speakers fall way off the plane, in a seemingly random but consistent manner. For example, imagine a female speaker whose score for the female category is way higher than the plane says it should be, but that every listener seems to behave this way for this speaker. This would mean that this is a consistent classification for this voice that cannot be explained by the score according to the plane. In other words, the classification cannot be predicted based on the linear combination of voice VTL and f0. In such a situation, this consistent classification would be 'explained' by the speaker intercept. Effectively, this tells your model "use the general female plane, but move it up/down this much specifically for this speaker". Why are we moving it up/down for this speaker? Our model can't tell us, since we're just modeling this with an intercept (and not an additional predictor). However, it *can* tell us that the up/down adjustment is consistent for the speaker across listeners and improves model performance.

We can think about what these speaker effects might reflect. The information regarding gender and age in voices is complicated, and likely reflects subtle stylistic and rhythmic cues. Basically, sounding 'feminine' and 'masculine' is much more complicated than just f0 or VTL (see Section 13.1.6). This is analogous to the fact that women tend to be shorter than men, but it would be ridiculous to suggest that masculinity/femininity are entirely predictable based on the height of a person. Size is

404 *Multinomial and ordinal regression*

perhaps an aspect of perceived femininity/masculinity but the whole of it is substantially more complicated.

We again consider our model prediction accuracy, but this time make predictions without any random effects.

```
# predictions with no random effects
multi_pred = fitted (model_multinomial, re_formula = NA)

# find winners
predicted_no_re = apply (multi_pred[,1,],1,which.max)
# get winner labels
predicted_category_no_re = c("b","g","m","w")[predicted_no_re]

# overall correct
mean (predicted_category_no_re == exp_data$C)
## [1] 0.5871

# correct predictions by category
tab = xtabs (~ exp_data$C + predicted_category_no_re)
diag(tab) / rowSums(tab)
##       b       g       m       w
## 0.2993 0.7559 0.9827 0.2504
```

The picture without random effects is a bit grim. Overall correct prediction is not too bad (relative to chance at 25%), however, some of the individual categories are predicted very poorly. As expected based on the territorial maps in 12.4, the accurate prediction of 'woman' classifications is particularly bad with only 21% of 'woman' responses being accurately predicted as such.

12.2.8 *Refitting the model without speaker random effects*

The results of our previous model suggest that the inclusion of speaker random effects may lead to some unintended, and undesirable, consequences. The predictions made by our initial model are only good as long as we include the speaker random effects. However, these do not let us understand the prediction of new speakers based solely on speaker f0 and VTL. Further, the territorial map we generate using the model is a bit unreliable because of the influence of the speaker random effects included in the model. We will try fitting the model without speaker effects to see if we get a territorial map that is a better match for our listener judgments. We use the same priors we used before, and fit the same model save for the absence of speaker effects in our formula:

```
# Fit the model yourself
model_multinomial_noS =
  brms::brm (y|trials(size) ~ vtl+f0 + (vtl+f0|x|L), data=exp_data,
             family=multinomial(), chains=4, cores=4, warmup=1000,
             iter = 5000, thin = 4, prior = multinomial_prior)
```

```
# Or download it from the GitHub page:
model_multinomial_noS = 
  bmmb::get_model ("../models/12_model_multinomial_noS.RDS")
```

We jump straight to plotting the territorial map represented by this model, again comparing listener judgments to model predictions with and without random effects (12.6). We can see that the territorial maps in the figure seem to be a better match to the data.

Figure 12.7 compares the territorial maps represented by our models with (left) and without (right) speaker information. In addition to being a better fit to the data, we think the new territorial maps make more 'sense'. This is because the map with speaker

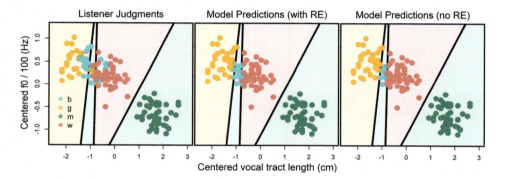

Figure 12.6 Territorial maps compared to modal classifications of speakers as boys (b), girls (g), men (m), and women (w). Point colors reflect classifications made by (left) listeners, (middle) predictions including random effects (RE), and (right) predictions excluding random effects.

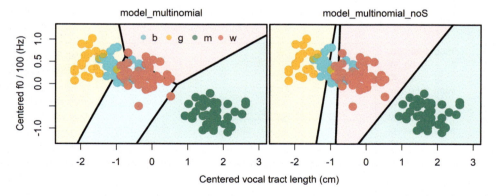

Figure 12.7 Territorial maps compared to modal classifications of speakers as boys (b), girls (g), men (m), and women (w). Point colors reflect classifications made by (left) the model with speaker effects, and (right) the model without speaker effects.

effects suggests that the difference between women and boys was almost entirely due to f0, with women being associated with the higher f0. This is despite the fact that veridical boys, on average, have shorter VTLs *and* higher f0s than adult females. The new map has basically no effect for f0 between these categories and makes it primarily a VTL difference, which seems to be a better fit to the data.

One concern with omitting the speaker effects is that our model doesn't 'know' that we only had 139 speakers in our experiment. This can have the effect of artificially decreasing our credible intervals, as we saw in Figure 6.6. Figure 12.8 compares the fixed effects between our two models, suggesting that the omission of the speaker effects has not had a large impact on most parameters or their credible intervals. The two largest differences are for the woman category: The intercept went from slightly negative to slightly positive, and the effect for f0 went from zero to positive.

We will make new predictions for this model, with and without random effects:

```
multi_pred_re_noS = fitted (model_multinomial_noS)
multi_pred_noS = fitted (model_multinomial_noS, re_formula = NA)
```

We find the maximum a posteriori speaker classification and get a label for each trial for our predictions with random effects.

```
predicted_noS = apply (multi_pred_re_noS[,1,],1,which.max)
predicted_category_noS = c("b","g","m","w")[predicted_noS]
```

We calculate correct classifications overall and by category. Performance is not as good as the model with speaker effects when random effects are included (82%) but not as bad as for the same model when random effects are not included (59%). In addition, we see very good classification of all categories except for 'boy'.

```
# overall correct
mean (predicted_category_noS == exp_data$C)
## [1] 0.742
```

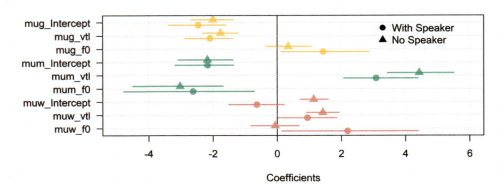

Figure 12.8 A comparison of the fixed effects means and 95% credible intervals provided by the two multinomial models we are considering.

```
# correct predictions by category
tab = xtabs (~ exp_data$C + predicted_category_noS)
diag(tab) / rowSums(tab)
##      b      g      m      w
## 0.3673 0.6737 0.9827 0.8130
```

Importantly, we see that classification barely changes when random effects are not included, except for boy classifications which drop even below chance.

```
predicted_noS_no_re = apply (multi_pred_noS[,1,],1,which.max)
predicted_category_noS_no_re = c("b","g","m","w")[predicted_noS_no_re]

# overall correct
mean (predicted_category_noS_no_re == exp_data$C)
## [1] 0.7223

# correct predictions by category
tab = xtabs (~ exp_data$C + predicted_category_noS_no_re)
diag(tab) / rowSums(tab)
##       b       g       m       w
## 0.09977 0.72770 0.98268 0.90566
```

12.2.9 Answering our research questions

We can use our models to answer the question we posed above:

(Q1) Can we use speaker f0 and VTL to predict their apparent speaker category?

Yes, we can use speaker f0 and VTL to predict apparent speaker with relatively high accuracy. If we consider baseline correctness by chance of 25%, then our classification of 72% from two predictors (with no random effects) isn't bad at all. However, the importance of the speaker random effects for female speakers strongly suggests that there is 'something else' being used to identify women as women and boys as boys, apart from VTL and f0. So, the results of our first model tell us that we should probably try to understand what that 'something else' is.

The speaker random effects are not particularly useful for understanding the categorization of new speakers. However, understanding what causes the variation in these random effects is. Our model tells us that even though we know there is something else to it, we can still predict categorization fairly well using just speaker VTL and f0. So, the first model may be better to really try to understand what listeners are doing when they classify individual voices, while the second model may be better to understand classification from just f0 and VTL.

12.3 Ordinal (logistic) regression

Ordinal logistic regression involves the prediction of ordered categories. Although in some senses ordinal regression is 'simpler' than multinomial regression, we decided

408 *Multinomial and ordinal regression*

to present it after multinomial regression. This is because, as discussed above, multinomial regression is mostly just a multivariate generalization of logistic regression (discussed in detail in Chapter 10). In contrast, ordinal regression, although related to logistic regression, is in many ways conceptually its own thing. We will present one way of thinking about ordinal logistic regression however, as usual, there are other ways to think of it. For more information about ordinal regression, please see Agresti (2013), Agresti (2018), and Kruschke (2014) (the same citations we provided for multinomial models, actually).

A simple example of an ordinal variable is first, second, and third place in a race. These values are categorical and not on an interval or ratio scale. For example, fourth place is not 'double' anything with respect to second place, and the distance between first and second doesn't necessarily represent the same difference as the difference between second and third. However, there is clearly an inherent ordering in the categories such that first < second < third < fourth < and so on. A common experimental example of ordered categorical data arises from survey data that asks listeners to respond to questions using a small number of discrete, categorical choices. For example, respondents might be asked to evaluate whether they (1) strongly agree, (2) somewhat agree, (3) are neutral, (4) somewhat disagree, or (5) strongly disagree with some proposition. This is often referred to as a **Likert scale** and the data resulting from this is often referred to as **Likert scale data**.

Likert scale data was originally meant to have response scales ranging from agreement to disagreement (as above). However, the concept of Likert scale data can be generalized to a very broad range of possible questions. For example, rather than height in centimeters, we might have asked listeners "use this 10 point scale to indicate how tall this person sounds". This could be made into a more 'traditional' Likert scale by asking it in the form "this person sounds very tall" and asking people to agree or disagree on a 10-point scale. Rather than ask for binary gender judgments, we might have asked "Use this 7 point scale to judge the perceived femininity/masculinity of the speaker" (or the more traditional "this person sounds very feminine" and asking people to agree or disagree on a 7-point scale).

Although Likert scale data is sometimes treated as quantitative, there are some characteristics of this data that make an ordinal analysis a better fit. First, it is not necessarily the case that the 'distance' between adjacent responses is equal across all categories. We can say with absolute certainty that the difference between 150 and 151 cm is equal to the difference between 151 and 152 cm. However, is the difference between strongly agree and somewhat agree the same as the difference between somewhat agree and neutral? This is difficult if not impossible to determine. Further, the small number of outcome categories may result in subjects reserving extreme categories for extraordinary cases. What if a subject somewhat strongly agrees? There is no such option, and this subject may instead indicate they somewhat agree lest something they *really* strongly agree with comes along later.

Here's what we said in Chapter 1 about when to treat a variable as quantitative:

- Is the variable on a ratio or interval scale? This is a prerequisite for a quantitative value to be used as a dependent variable. An interval scale means that distances are meaningful, and a ratio scale means that 0 is meaningful.
- Is the underlying value continuous? Many variables are discrete in practice due to limitations in measurement. However, if the underlying value is continuous (e.g.

height, time) then this can motivate treating the measurement as a quantitative dependent variable since fractional values 'make sense'. For example, even if you measure time only down to the nearest millisecond, a value of 0.5 milliseconds is possible and interpretable. In contrast, a value of 0.5 people is not.
- Are there a large number (>50) of possible values the measured variable can take? For example, a die can only take on 6 quantitative values, which is not enough.
- Are most/all of the observed values far from their bounds? Human height does not really get much smaller than about 50 cm and longer than about 220 cm, so it is technically bounded. However, in most cases, our observations are expected to not be clustered at the boundaries.

If survey participants were given a survey with 5 discrete numerical categories and were told that this represented some continuous value 'agreement', then we could perhaps argue that that 5-point Likert scale data abides by the first two considerations above. However, our data runs afoul of the bottom two considerations: There are only a small number of discrete outcomes, with nothing 'in between', and many of the observed values are likely to be near the boundaries and are likely to be constrained by these.

We don't actually have any ordinal variables in our experiment, but we still wanted to provide an example of an ordinal analysis. To do this, we're going to make a fake ordinal variable that we think is actually relatively plausible. In Figure 12.9, we see a boxplot of apparent height judgments organized by apparent speaker category, with boys and girls collapsed into one category, 'child'. Note that apparent children are judged to be shortest, apparent women are judged to be a little taller than that, and apparent men are judged to be a little taller than women. In addition, there is not very much overlap in apparent heights between categories. Based on the above, we could potentially think of our apparent speaker categories as reflecting classifications of speakers into small (boys, girls), medium (women), and large (men). We might imagine that if we *had* asked listeners to identify speakers as small, medium, or large, listeners would have labeled most apparent children as small, most apparent women as medium, and most apparent men as large.

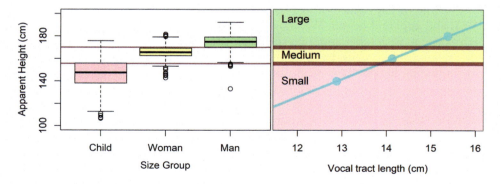

Figure 12.9 (left) Distribution of apparent height judgments for apparent children, women, and men. (right) A hypothetical linear relationship between apparent height and speaker vocal-tract length. The apparent height axis is divided into three size groups: Small, medium, and large. Points indicate three possible apparent height judgments, leading to three different size-group classifications.

410　*Multinomial and ordinal regression*

The right plot in Figure 12.9 presents the *y*-axis divided into three sections. The boundaries (or **thresholds**) between sections are halfway between the means of apparent children and adult females (155.7 cm), and apparent adult females and adult males (170 cm). We can think of these sections as reflecting the expected categorization of speakers into small, medium, or large based on their apparent height. We can see how this might work using the code below. First, we convert our observed speaker classifications into a new variable that we will treat as ordinal. This variable is *size group* (SG), and it has the values 1 (small), 2 (medium), and 3 (large).

```
SG = 0
SG[exp_data$C=='b' | exp_data$C=='g'] = 1
SG[exp_data$C=='w'] = 2
SG[exp_data$C=='m'] = 3
```

Then, we create a new variable that will hold our size group predictions, SG_hat. After this, we set this variable to 1 if the apparent height is less than the threshold between small and medium (155.7 cm), to 2 if the apparent height is greater than the threshold between small and medium (155.7), but less than the threshold between medium and large (170 cm), and to 3 if it is greater than the threshold between medium and large (170 cm).

```
SG_hat = exp_data$height * 0
SG_hat[exp_data$height <= 155.7] = 1
SG_hat[exp_data$height > 155.7 & exp_data$height <= 170] = 2
SG_hat[exp_data$height >= 170] = 3
```

This relatively primitive 'model' is able to correctly predict size group responses in 75% of cases.

```
mean (SG == SG_hat)
## [1] 0.7549
```

The line in the right plot in Figure 12.9 reflects the relationship between speaker VTL and apparent height. We know from earlier chapters that a longer speaker VTL is associated with taller apparent speakers. Let's assume for the sake of simplicity that this relationship is causal and that there is a direct connection between speaker VTL and apparent height. This means that when we hear a voice, we can be thought of as sliding along the line in the plot based on the VTL of the speaker. Then, based on the apparent height value at a given *x*-axis location, we can arrive at a size group classification based on the method above. Note that in this scenario we were not collecting or observing apparent speaker height but rather predicting size group using VTL. However, we assume that apparent height underlies this process and connects the two variables we do observe. By assuming that apparent height was driving this process but not trying to measure it directly we are treating it as a *latent variable*.

The latent variable was presented as apparent height, however, the latent variable could have had any name and used any other units. For example, in our situation, we can think of this variable as 'size' or 'bigness', but its name is not important, and neither is us having a rock-solid conceptual grasp of what it is exactly. Instead, all we need to understand is that we think there is some latent variable, something like 'bigness', that

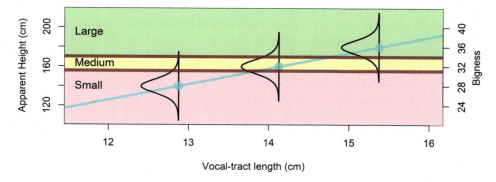

Figure 12.10 Our three possible size group classifications from Figure 12.9 are presented again, this time with error distributions around predicted values. The right side of the plot shows an alternate *y*-axis, the made-up latent variable 'bigness'.

allows listeners to classify speakers into small, medium, and large groups based on their voices.

The right side of Figure 12.10 is labeled "bigness" to correspond to our hypothetical latent variable. This variable is just apparent height divided by 50, but the point is that the values of this axis are entirely arbitrary. Notice that the change in axis units has absolutely no effect on the way our conceptual model works. If the latent variable units are 50 times smaller than some other variable, that just means the slope of the line relating x to y is 50 times smaller and the boundaries between categories are 50 times closer. The same logic applies to the relationship between our latent dependent variable and our predictors.

Our 'model' so far would do a reasonable job of predicting classification but contains no random component. As a result, given a certain speaker VTL, it would always predict the same size group response. In Figure 9.1, we show that bivariate linear regression with normally distributed errors can be thought of as a normal distribution sliding along a line based on the value of the dependent variable. The *y*-axis value of the line at an *x*-axis location tells you the expected value of *y* for that value of *x*. However, we will hardly (if ever) observe the expected value exactly. Instead, we assume that we have normal errors centered around our expected values.

We show a similar situation in Figure 12.10, with a probability distribution sliding along a line. However, in the case of ordinal regression the values that this distribution generates are not the observed values of the ordinal dependent variable, but rather random values of the *latent* variable (e.g. 'bigness'). The observed ordinal variable is then based on the value of the latent variable with respect to the boundaries, called *thresholds*, in the space (the horizontal lines in the figure). In this chapter, we will use a *logistic* distribution as the error distribution (more detail on this in the next section), hence the name, ordinal *logistic* regression. We will do this because it is commonly used and has some useful characteristics, but a basically equivalent model can be constructed using a normal distribution to represent randomness in the latent variable.

Ordinal regression estimates the location of thresholds between categories along the latent variable. It also tries to predict the expected value of the latent variable for each observation, based on the combination of the dependent variables. For example, in Figure 12.10 the boundaries are at 31 and 34 bigness, and you have an expected bigness of around 32 for a vocal-tract length of 14.1. We can think of it this way: Given a VTL of 14.1 we know how big people will sound in general (32), but these things are fuzzy and necessarily noisy. So actually, there is a distribution of expected perceived/apparent 'bigness' given our predictors. Given the actual value of the latent variable for a trial (including the random component), the ordinal response is based on the value of the latent variable with respect to the estimated thresholds. So, for a fixed expected value of 32, sometimes the distribution might 'generate' a bigness value of 28, resulting in a response of small. For another observation with the same expected value, the value of the latent variable may be 36, meaning the speaker will be identified as large.

12.3.1 Cumulative distribution functions

In order to understand ordinal regression, we need to talk about cumulative distribution functions first. We haven't explicitly talked about cumulative distribution functions yet, though we did see one in Chapter 10 when it was referred to as the *inverse logit* function (more on this in a moment). To this point, we've been focused on what are called *probability density functions* (PDF), functions that assign a density to different values of a variable. Examples of PDFs are given in the top row of Figure 12.11. **Cumulative distribution functions** (CDF) tell you the probability that a variable will be *less than or equal to* some value. Since a PDF has an area under the curve equal to 1 (representing the total probability of the variable), a CDF tells you how much of that area (out of 1) is to the left of the value, and has a range from 0 to 1.

For example, in the left column of Figure 12.11, we see a standard normal distribution with a mean of 0 and a standard deviation of one. We know that the normal distribution is symmetrical about its mean so that half the area under the curve of this density must be below 0. If we look at the bottom row of the first column, we can see the CDF corresponding to the PDF in the top row. If we look at the value of this

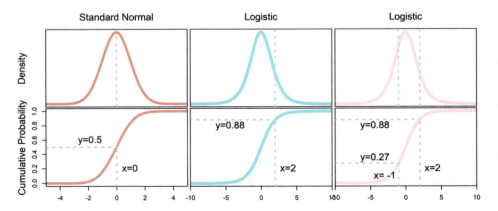

Figure 12.11 (top row) Probability density functions for standard normal and standard logistic distributions. (bottom row) Cumulative distribution functions for densities immediately above. Numbers indicate x and y values at different points along each curve.

Multinomial and ordinal regression **413**

function at x=0, we see that it is exactly equal to 0.5. In other words, the cumulative function tells us that the standard normal has exactly half its mass at values less than x=0, i.e. the probability of observing a value of x that is less than or equal to 0, the mean, is exactly 0.5.

We can use the `pnorm` function (discussed in Chapter 2) to get the value of the normal CDF for any value of x. Below we calculate this for x=0, x= −2, and $x = 2$. See that in each case, the output of the function corresponds to the y-axis value of the CDF at that x-axis location (bottom left, Figure 12.11).

```
# cumulative distribution at x = -2, 0, 2
pnorm (c(-2,0,2),0,1)
## [1] 0.02275 0.50000 0.97725
```

The CDF is the **integral** of the PDF, and the PDF is the **derivative** of the CDF. We've already explained the *integral* part of this: As you move left to right, the value of the CDF equals the cumulative (i.e. added up total) area under the curve (i.e. probability) in the PDF to that point. To say that the PDF is the derivative of the CDF means that the value of the PDF reflects the *rate of change* (i.e. the slope) in the CDF for different values of x. Imagine you were in a tiny car driving along the standard normal CDF in Figure 12.11, left to right. As you drive along around −4 the 'terrain' is flat and the value of the density is near 0. As you near −2 the slope of the CDF begins to increase, as does the value of the PDF. The value of the PDF is largest at x=0, telling us that the slope of the CDF is greatest at that point. As we drive past x=0 in the CDF, we see a gradual decrease in the slope until we more or less reach 'flat ground' again at just past x=2. This is reflected by the gradual decrease in the value of the PDF between x=0 and x=2.

In the middle column of Figure 12.11 we see a logistic distribution. The **logistic distribution** is a two-parameter distribution similar in shape to the normal distribution but with 'fatter/heavier' tails (like the t distribution). The logistic distribution has a location parameter (μ, equal to the mean) that determines its location along the number line, and a scale parameter (s, equal to the standard deviation times $\sqrt{3} / \pi$) that is positively related to the 'width' of the density function. In the bottom row of the middle column, we see the CDF of the logistic density. It turns out that the inverse logit function we use as the link function for logistic regression is simply the CDF of a logistic distribution with a mean of 0 and a scale of 1 (i.e. a *standard* logistic distribution). This is also why you might commonly see the inverse logit function referred to as the logistic function. We avoided using this name for the function to avoid confusion.

In the middle column of Figure 12.11, we see that we can use the same approach we used for our normal distribution to calculate values of the CDF of our logistic distribution. Below, we use the `plogis` function to calculate the probability of observing a value greater than or equal to 2 form that distribution.

```
plogis (2,0,1)
## [1] 0.8808
```

In the right column of Figure 12.11, we've placed two vertical lines at x= −1 and x=2. We use the code below to calculate the area under the curve to the left of each line.

```
# area left of first line
plogis (-1,0,1)
## [1] 0.2689
# area left of second line
plogis (2,0,1)
## [1] 0.8808
```

At this point, the connection between CDFs and ordinal regression may be clear: We can use a set of thresholds and the CDF of a probability distribution to calculate the probability of observing different values of the latent variable, within certain intervals. For example, in the bottom-right plot of Figure 12.11, if 0.27 falls to the left of the first line and 0.88 falls to the left of the second line, then 0.61 must fall between the first and second lines. Thus, we have effectively divided the distribution into three parts and can discuss the probability that the observation of the variable will fall within each part.

```
# area between first and second line
plogis (2,0,1)-plogis (-1,0,1)
## [1] 0.6119
```

In Figure 12.12, the thresholds and distributions from Figure 12.10 have been rotated clockwise 90 degrees so that our latent variable (the arbitrarily named 'bigness') varies along the *x*-axis. The distributions presented in the figure have means of 28, 32, 36, and scales of 1. The probabilities in each subsection of each plot represent the predicted probability of observing size group responses of 1, 2, and 3 for each distribution. These probabilities were calculated based on the area under the curve of the distributions falling between different intervals of the latent variable space.

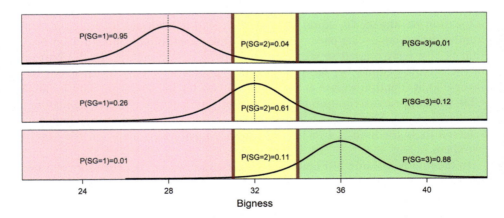

Figure 12.12 Error distributions from Figure 12.10, presented in more detail. Vertical lines indicate the expected value for each distribution. Numbers indicate the area under the curve of the density function inside each category's section of the 'bigness' dimension. These values correspond to the expected probability of observing each of the size group responses for each expected value of the latent variable.

Multinomial and ordinal regression 415

For example, below we calculate the probability of observing each size group based on the distribution in the middle plot of Figure 12.12, a latent variable distribution with a mean of 32 and a scale of 1. First, we find the probability of observing a bigness value less than 31 (the first threshold). This tells us the probability of observing a response of size group 1 for this expected value of bigness (P(SG=1)=0.26). Then, we again find the probability of a bigness value less than 31 (the first thresholds) and subtract this from the probability of a bigness value less than 34 (the second threshold). This operation gives us the probability of observing a bigness value between the first and second thresholds, i.e. the probability of observing a medium-size group response (P(SG=2) = 0.88 − 0.26). Finally, to find the probability of a large-size group response we find the probability of a bigness value less than 34 and subtract this from 1. Since there are no more boundaries above the largest response category, the entire probability above the highest threshold must correspond to the final category.

```
# probability of observing category 1
plogis (31,32,1)
## [1] 0.2689

# probability of observing category 2
plogis (34,32,1) - plogis (31,32,1)
## [1] 0.6119

# probability of observing category 3
1 - plogis (34,32,1)
## [1] 0.1192
```

This conceptualization of our model leads to both **hard classification** and **soft classification**. An ordinal regression model will predict, for every observation, an expected value of the dependent variable based on the values of the predictors. This value can then be used to find response probabilities for each category. A *hard* classification classifies each observation into a predicted category, 1, 2, or 3, based on the value of the highest predicted probability across the categories. A *soft* classification provides the probability that an observation is classified into one or more categories. For example, in the middle plot of Figure 12.12, it may be useful to say that the most probable classification is of a 'medium' speaker. However, it may be just as, or more, useful to indicate that the probability of this response was only 0.61, making the observation of a small response (P=0.26) not unlikely.

12.3.2 Data and research questions

We load our packages and data below. We also add a new variable, SG (size group), which will act as our dependent variable. This variable represents children with a 1, adult women with a 2, and adult males with a 3. We don't need to do anything special to make this variable 'ordinal', but we are using three consecutive integers to represent the categories to make things simpler. After this, we process our quantitative predictors in the same way as in the previous chapters.

416   *Multinomial and ordinal regression*

```
library (brms)
library (bmmb)
data (exp_data)
# new dependent variable: Size Group
SG = 0
SG[exp_data$C=='g'] = 1
SG[exp_data$C=='b'] = 1
SG[exp_data$C=='w'] = 2
SG[exp_data$C=='m'] = 3
exp_data$SG = SG

# preparation of quantitative predictors
# as in previous chapters
exp_data$vtl_original = exp_data$vtl
exp_data$vtl = exp_data$vtl - mean (exp_data$vtl)

exp_data$f0_original = exp_data$f0
exp_data$f0 = exp_data$f0 - mean(exp_data$f0)
exp_data$f0 = exp_data$f0 / 100
```

We're going to keep our research questions relatively simple this time, as this is mostly a demonstration of an ordinal regression analysis and not a 'real' ordinal variable:

(Q1)   Can we predict size group responses for a speaker given their f0 and VTL?

12.3.3   *Description of the model*

To fit a model predicting apparent size group from speaker f0 and VTL, we can use the formula below:

```
SG ~ vtl+f0 + (vtl+f0|L) + (1|S)
```

This model formula is very much like ones we've used several times in earlier chapters. The formula says "predict size group using a plane based on voice f0 and VTL, allow for listener-specific planes, and speaker-specific adjustments to the height of the plane". However, the relationship it represents between our predictors and our dependent variables is substantially different from what we've seen before. Let's begin with the relationship between the independent variables and the expected value of the latent variable (i.e. the mean of our logistic distribution), presented in equation (12.16):

$$\mu_{[i]} = a_{[i]} + b_{[i]} \cdot \text{vtl}_{[i]} + c_{[i]} \cdot \text{f0}_{[i]} \tag{12.16}$$

We model this latent variable as being distributed according to a logistic distribution with a mean of μ and a scale parameter equal to 1, as in equation (12.17). Actually, for reasons that we won't get into, for ordinal regression brm uses a parameter called

Multinomial and ordinal regression 417

the **discrimination** parameter, which is the inverse of the scale. However, since we are using a scale of 1 we can ignore this for now (since 1/1=1).

$$z_{[i]} \sim \text{Logistic}\left(\mu_{[i]}, 1\right) \tag{12.17}$$

Our observed (dependent) ordinal category is then predicted based on the value of the latent variable $\left(z_{[i]}\right)$ for that trial, relative to the model boundaries, called **thresholds**, or **cutoffs** $\left(\theta_{[1]}, \theta_{[2]}\right)$. We see this in (12.18) below.

$$SG_{[i]} = \begin{cases} 1 \text{ if } z_{[i]} \leq \theta_1 \\ 2 \text{ if } \theta_{[1]} < z_{[i]} \leq \theta_{[2]} \\ 3 \text{ if } \theta_{[2]} \leq z_{[i]} \end{cases} \tag{12.18}$$

The above says: "SG is equal to 1 if the latent variable is below the first threshold, 2 if it's between the first and second thresholds, and 3 if it is above the second threshold". Here is a full description of our model:

$$SG_{[i]} = \begin{cases} 1 \text{ if } z_{[i]} \leq \theta_{[1]} \\ 2 \text{ if } \theta_{[1]} < z_{[i]} \leq \theta_{[2]} \\ 3 \text{ if } \theta_{[2]} \leq z_{[i]} \end{cases}$$

$$z_{[i]} \sim \text{Logistic}\left(\mu_{[i]}, 1\right)$$

$$\mu_{[i]} = a_{[i]} + b_{[i]} \cdot \text{vtl}_{[i]} + c_{[i]} \cdot \text{f0}_{[i]} \tag{12.19}$$
$$a_{[i]} = L_{\left[4_{[i]}\right]}$$
$$b_{[i]} = VTL + VTL : L_{\left[4_{[i]}\right]}$$
$$c_{[i]} = F0 + F0 : L_{\left[4_{[i]}\right]}$$

Priors:
$$S_{[\bullet]} \sim \text{Normal}\left(0, \sigma_S\right)$$

$$\begin{bmatrix} L_{[\bullet]} \\ VTL : L_{[\bullet]} \\ F0 : L_{[\bullet]} \end{bmatrix} \sim \text{MVNormal}\left(\begin{bmatrix} 0 \\ 0 \\ 0 \end{bmatrix}, \Sigma\right)$$

$$\theta_{[1]}, \theta_{[2]} \sim t(3,0,3)$$
$$VTL, F0 \sim t(3,0,3)$$
$$\sigma_L, \sigma_{VTL:L}, \sigma_{F0:L}, \sigma_S \sim t(3,0,3)$$
$$R \sim \text{LKJCorr}(2)$$

418   *Multinomial and ordinal regression*

And here is a plain English, verbal description of our model:

We are modeling an ordinal variable, size group (SG), with possible outcomes of small (1), medium (2), and large (3). The value expected for any given trial is based on the value of a latent variable (z) in relation to two thresholds $(\theta_{[1]}, \theta_{[2]})$, which were estimated from the data. Our latent variable is modeled as coming from a logistic distribution with a scale of 1 and a mean that varies from trial to trial. The mean of these distributions varies based on the combination of 'main' (e.g. VTL) and listener-dependent (e.g. VTL : L) effects for vocal-tract length and f0, and a listener-dependent intercept. The speaker intercept (S) terms were drawn from a normal distribution with a mean of zero and a standard deviation estimated from the data. The listener random effects were drawn from a multivariate normal distribution with means of zero and a correlation matrix (R) estimated from the data. All other effects were treated as 'fixed' and drawn from prior distributions appropriate for their expected range of values.

Notice that the model in (12.19) does not contain a term representing the overall model intercept. This is because the important thing for our model is the distance between the expected value of the latent variable and the thresholds, and not the value of the latent variable itself. For example, imagine an 'intercept-only' model (Chapter 4) that had intercept = 3 and thresholds of 1 and 5. The behavior of this model would be exactly analogous to a model with an intercept of 13 and thresholds of 11 and 15. In fact, there are an infinite number of models that maintain this structure, one for each possible value of the intercept. Under these conditions finding the 'best' model is an impossible task (i.e. the model is not *identifiable*, see Section 8.8). To resolve this issue, the overall intercept in these models is usually set to zero and not modeled, and instead, only the $J-1$ thresholds are modeled (for J categories).

Although ordinal models do not usually estimate the overall intercept, they *can* estimate listener-dependent (and speaker-dependent) intercepts, and our model in equation does contain these. Since the boundaries are shared by all groups, using group-dependent intercepts can be thought of as sliding the thresholds up and down the number line by different amounts for each level of a grouping factor (e.g. listener), or as moving the predicted values by the same amount. This sort of adjustment *can* have a meaningful effect on predictions, unlike changes in the overall model intercept outlined above.

12.3.4 *Fitting and interpreting the model*

To fit an ordinal logistic model, you set `family=cumulative` when fitting your model. The logistic distribution is the default error distribution for these sorts of models, but other distributions such as the normal distribution can be used.

```
# Fit the model yourself
model_ordinal =
  brms::brm (SG ~ vtl+f0 + (vtl+f0|L) + (1|S), data=exp_data,
          family="cumulative", chains=4, cores=4, warmup=1000,
          iter = 5000, thin = 4,
          prior = c(set_prior("student_t(3, 0, 3)", class = "Intercept"),
                    set_prior("student_t(3, 0, 3)", class = "b"),
```

Multinomial and ordinal regression   419

```
                    set_prior("student_t(3, 0, 3)", class = "sd"),
                    set_prior("lkj_corr_cholesky(2)", class = "cor")))

# Or download it from the GitHub page:
model_ordinal = bmmb::get_model ("12_model_ordinal.RDS")
```

We can inspect the short summary to see the information it contains:

```
bmmb::short_summary(model_ordinal)
## Formula:  SG ~ vtl + f0 + (vtl + f0 | L) + (1 | S)
##
## Group-Level Effects:
## ~L (Number of levels: 15)
##                      Estimate Est.Error l-95% CI u-95% CI
## sd(Intercept)            0.54      0.15     0.30     0.89
## sd(vtl)                  0.45      0.20     0.07     0.89
## sd(f0)                   0.67      0.40     0.04     1.55
## cor(Intercept,vtl)       0.07      0.33    -0.58     0.67
## cor(Intercept,f0)        0.14      0.36    -0.58     0.79
## cor(vtl,f0)             -0.11      0.37    -0.78     0.62
##
## ~S (Number of levels: 139)
##                      Estimate Est.Error l-95% CI u-95% CI
## sd(Intercept)            1.27      0.14     1.02     1.57
##
## Population-Level Effects:
##                 Estimate Est.Error l-95% CI u-95% CI
## Intercept[1]       -1.86      0.22    -2.32    -1.44
## Intercept[2]        2.58      0.24     2.13     3.07
## vtl                 3.16      0.29     2.63     3.76
## f0                 -1.78      0.60    -2.98    -0.58
##
## Family Specific Parameters:
##      Estimate Est.Error l-95% CI u-95% CI
## disc        1         0        1        1
```

In the population-level effects, we see the two estimated thresholds `Intercept[1]` and `Intercept[2]` representing $\theta_{[1]}$ and $\theta_{[2]}$ above. We also see our 'main' effects for VTL and f0 in this section. Our results indicate that VTL is positively related to a larger size group response, while f0 is negatively related to this (no surprises there). In the group-level effects section, note that we get listener-dependent intercepts, VTL, and f0 effects. The intercepts correspond to the *L* terms in the model described in (12.19), and do not refer to listener-dependent thresholds/cutoffs. Below we make 'fixed effect' predictions using our model. These predictions omit the random effects structure to let us see how well our fixed effects can predict our data. In addition, we set `scale="linear"` so that we get predictions of the latent variable rather than the probability of category membership.

420 *Multinomial and ordinal regression*

```
# make latent variable predictions
predictions_latent = fitted (model_ordinal,scale="linear",
re_formula = NA)

# inspect first 6 predictions
head (predictions_latent)
##        Estimate Est.Error    Q2.5   Q97.5
## [1,]    -5.000     0.3558  -5.742  -4.330
## [2,]    -4.545     0.3958  -5.330  -3.783
## [3,]    -5.864     0.4669  -6.817  -4.994
## [4,]    -5.645     0.3486  -6.376  -4.978
## [5,]    -4.728     0.2945  -5.340  -4.171
## [6,]    -7.115     0.5044  -8.168  -6.163
```

Below, we predict our latent variable using our posterior mean fixed effects. We do this just to show that it does, in fact, result in the expected predictions. Below, we get the posterior mean model fixed effects and use these to come up with an expected value for our latent variable for each observation (mu).

```
# get fixed effects
fixed_effects = brms::fixef(model_ordinal)

threshold_1 = fixed_effects[1,1]
threshold_2 = fixed_effects[2,1]
vtl_slope = fixed_effects[3,1]
f0_slope = fixed_effects[4,1]

# get expected values
mu = exp_data$vtl * vtl_slope + exp_data$f0  * f0_slope
```

We can see that the prediction above results in basically the same expected values for our latent variable as obtained using the `fitted` function. Of course, the `fitted` function finds these estimates the right way, computing a prediction for each posterior sample rather than only using the posterior mean.

```
cor (predictions_latent[,1], mu)
## [1] 1
sd (predictions_latent[,1] - mu)
## [1] 3.571143e-16
```

We can also ask for predictions as probabilities, rather than latent variable values, by not specifying the scale:

```
# predict probability of category membership
predictions_latent = fitted (model_ordinal, re_formula = NA)
```

In this case, our prediction results in a three-dimensional matrix where the response category varies along the third dimension (very much like our multinomial predictions).

Multinomial and ordinal regression 421

For example, below we see the probability of observing the first response category (small), for the first six observations.

```
# see first six for the first category
head (predictions_latent[,,1])
##          Estimate  Est.Error    Q2.5    Q97.5
## [1,]     0.9557    0.016006   0.9184   0.9803
## [2,]     0.9314    0.026561   0.8714   0.9714
## [3,]     0.9799    0.009882   0.9566   0.9933
## [4,]     0.9763    0.008675   0.9561   0.9896
## [5,]     0.9435    0.017720   0.9035   0.9723
## [6,]     0.9941    0.003051   0.9866   0.9981
```

If we consider only the first element of the second dimension (columns), we can get the expected value for each category, for the first six observations.

```
# see first six for each category
head (predictions_latent[,1,])
##         P(Y = 1)   P(Y = 2)    P(Y = 3)
## [1,]    0.9557    0.043713    5.615e-04
## [2,]    0.9314    0.067657    8.960e-04
## [3,]    0.9799    0.019885    2.480e-04
## [4,]    0.9763    0.023454    2.943e-04
## [5,]    0.9435    0.055775    7.227e-04
## [6,]    0.9941    0.005824    7.232e-05
```

We can use the expected value for the latent variable calculated manually above (mu), combined with the model thresholds, to calculate the expected probability that the observation will belong to each category (rounded to 5 decimal places).

```
predictions_manual =
  cbind (round (plogis (threshold_1, mu),5),
         round ((plogis (threshold_2, mu)-plogis
(threshold_1, mu)),5),
         round (1-plogis (threshold_2, mu), 5))

head (predictions_manual)
##             [,1]      [,2]       [,3]
## [1,]  0.95834   0.04115   0.00051
## [2,]  0.93592   0.06328   0.00080
## [3,]  0.98201   0.01778   0.00021
## [4,]  0.97772   0.02202   0.00027
## [5,]  0.94604   0.05329   0.00067
## [6,]  0.99478   0.00515   0.00006
```

Again, we can see that this approach results in basically the same values as those calculated with the `fitted` function.

422 *Multinomial and ordinal regression*

```
cor (predictions_latent[,1,1],predictions_manual[,1])
## [1] 1

cor (predictions_latent[,1,2],predictions_manual[,2])
## [1] 1

cor (predictions_latent[,1,3],predictions_manual[,3])
## [1] 1
```

Below we find the maximum value across each row of our predictions in `predictions_manual`, representing the *hard*, categorical prediction for each observation.

```
SG_hat = apply (predictions_latent[,1,],1,which.max)
SG_hat_manual = apply (predictions_manual,1,which.max)
```

We can see that these two approaches lead to the same outcomes and that in either case, we can correctly predict about 83% of our observations using only our fixed effects.

```
# manual and automatically-calculated predictions
mean (SG_hat == SG_hat_manual)
## [1] 1

# predictive accuracy for actual size group responses
mean (SG_hat == exp_data$SG)
## [1] 0.8264

mean (SG_hat_manual == exp_data$SG)
## [1] 0.8264
```

Our focus has been on manually replicating some of the helper functions included in `brms` in order to highlight the relationship between our model parameters and expected outcomes. For more complex models, the specific effects of parameters or combinations of parameters can still be investigated using the techniques discussed in earlier chapters. For example, imagine an ordinal model involving a single quantitative predictor and a single categorical predictor with four levels. The geometry of the lines formed to predict expected values in such a model would be the same as that of the models discussed in Chapter 9, and many of the strategies discussed in that chapter could be directly applied to such an analysis.

12.3.5 *Listener-specific discrimination terms*

Before wrapping up our discussion of ordinal models, we want to talk briefly about the `disc` (discrimination) parameter. As mentioned above, this parameter is equal to the inverse of the scale parameter of the logistic distribution. In our previous ordinal model, the `disc` parameter was fixed at a value of 1 for all observations, However, this parameter can be predicted just as the error term (`sigma`,

Multinomial and ordinal regression 423

σ) of our normal or t-distributed errors was predicted in Chapter 8. Since this value cannot be negative, our model will predict the logarithm of `disc` just as it did for `sigma`.

Below we fit a model with listener-specific discrimination parameters. We're not going to discuss this in detail, however, the additional model structure is extremely similar to that presented in Chapter 8 (in particular, Section 8.6.1), and should be clear based on the information provided in that chapter.

```
model_formula = bf(SG ~ vtl+f0 + (vtl+f0|L) + (1|S),
                    disc ~ 1 + (1|L))
priors =
  c(set_prior("student_t(3, 0, 3)", class = "Intercept"),
    set_prior("student_t(3, 0, 3)", class = "b"),
    set_prior("student_t(3, 0, 3)", class = "sd"),
    set_prior("student_t(3, 0, 1)", class = "Intercept",dpar="disc"),
    set_prior("student_t(3, 0, 1)", class = "sd", dpar="disc"),
    set_prior("lkj_corr_cholesky (2)", class = "cor"))


model_ordinal_disc =
  brms::brm (model_formula, data=exp_data, family="cumulative", chains=4,
             cores=4, warmup=1000, iter = 5000, thin = 4, prior = priors,
             control = list(adapt_delta = 0.99))


# Or download it from the GitHub page:
model_ordinal_disc = bmmb::get_model ("12_model_ordinal_disc.RDS")
```

We can see that our model summary now includes a fixed effect for the `disc_Intercept` and the standard deviation of the listener-dependent discrimination terms (`sd(disc_Intercept)`) in the listener random effects section.

```
bmmb::short_summary (model_ordinal_disc)
## Formula:  SG ~ vtl + f0 + (vtl + f0 | L) + (1 | S)
##
## Group-Level Effects:
## ~L (Number of levels: 15)
##
##                      Estimate Est.Error l-95% CI u-95% CI
## sd(Intercept)            0.95      0.42     0.36     1.99
## sd(vtl)                  0.62      0.43     0.03     1.68
## sd(f0)                   1.07      0.77     0.05     2.99
## sd(disc_Intercept)       0.42      0.11     0.25     0.67
## cor(Intercept,vtl)      -0.19      0.36    -0.81     0.56
## cor(Intercept,f0)        0.21      0.37    -0.58     0.82
## cor(vtl,f0)             -0.03      0.39    -0.76     0.72
##
## ~S (Number of levels: 139)
##                      Estimate Est.Error l-95% CI u-95% CI
## sd(Intercept)            2.43      0.85     1.11     4.33
##
```

424 *Multinomial and ordinal regression*

```
## Population-Level Effects:
##                  Estimate Est.Error 1-95% CI u-95% CI
## Intercept[1]       -3.57      1.24     -6.36     -1.61
## Intercept[2]        4.97      1.72      2.30      8.83
## disc_Intercept     -0.52      0.35     -1.17      0.21
## vtl                 6.11      2.13      2.78     10.93
## f0                 -3.31      1.51     -6.95     -0.95
```

We can get the listener-dependent disc terms using the `short_hypothesis` function. Since these values are the logarithm of the discrimination, we need to exponentiate and then invert the parameter estimate to get the scale. We can do this inside the
hypothesis function so that we summarize after manipulating (rather than exponentiating and inverting our summary).

```
listener_scale = short_hypothesis (
  model_ordinal_disc,
  "1/exp(disc_Intercept)=0", group="L", scope="coef")

# omit hypothesis column so this fits in the book
head(listener_scale)[,-5]
##     Estimate Est.Error   Q2.5 Q97.5 group
## H1     2.947    1.0599 1.3115 5.406     1
## H2     2.157    0.7857 0.9580 4.006     2
## H3     1.423    0.5277 0.6223 2.619     3
## H4     2.730    1.0239 1.1936 5.062     4
## H5     2.180    0.7832 0.9581 4.014     5
## H6     2.229    0.7954 0.9919 4.038     6
```

In Figure 12.13 we compare the distributions implied by these `disc` parameters for
a value of 0 for the latent variable. We can see that these distributions imply substantially different behaviors across listeners, given the same predicted value for the latent
variable.

12.3.6 Answering our research questions

Our research question was very simple:

(Q1) Can we predict size group responses for a speaker given their f0 and VTL?

Yes we can, and with reasonable accuracy (83%) based only on two acoustic predictors. Below we find the predicted category for each trial based on our first model,
including the random effects, and for the second ordinal model, we fit that included
listener-specific `disc` parameters.

```
# predictions with random effects
predictions_latent_full = fitted (model_ordinal)
# predictions with listener dependent disc
predictions_latent_disc = fitted (model_ordinal_disc)
```

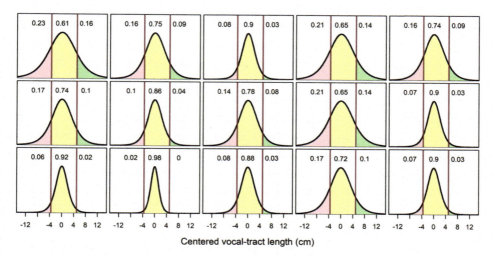

Figure 12.13 Listener-specific distributions of the latent variable given an expected value of zero. Numbers indicate the expected probability of observing each size group for this expected value, for each listener. Plot *y*-axis ranges are determined relative to the height of each density and are not all equal.

```
# find highest predicted probability
SG_hat_full = apply (predictions_latent_full[,1,],1,which.max)
SG_hat_disc = apply (predictions_latent_disc[,1,],1,which.max)
```

Below, we calculate the probability of a correct size group prediction for the fixed effects predictions, the predictions made by the full model with a single `disc` parameter, and the model with a listener-dependent `disc` parameter. We can see that the random effects noticeably improve prediction whereas the inclusion of listener-specific `disc` has a much smaller effect.

```
# fixed effects
mean (SG_hat == exp_data$SG)
## [1] 0.8264

# full model, single disc
mean (SG_hat_full == exp_data$SG)
## [1] 0.8887

# full model, listener-dependent disc
mean (SG_hat_disc == exp_data$SG)
## [1] 0.8911
```

In any case, it seems clear that ordinal variables related to apparent talker size/height are likely to be very predictable based on speaker VTL and f0. However, we're not going to dig into these results very much since this dependent variable

426 *Multinomial and ordinal regression*

was sort of 'made up', and our intention was mostly to provide practical examples of ordinal regression analyses that take advantage of the information in repeated measures data.

12.4 Exercises

The analyses in the main body of the text all involve only the unmodified 'actual' resonance level (in `exp_data`). Responses for the stimuli with the simulated 'big' resonance are reserved for exercises throughout. You can get the 'big' resonance in the `exp_ex` data frame, or all data in the `exp_data_all` data frame.

Fit and interpret one or more of the suggested models:

1   Easy: Analyze the (pre-fit) model that's exactly like `model_multinomial`, except using the data in `exp_ex` (`bmmb::get_model("12_model_multinomial_ex.RDS")`).
2   Easy: Analyze the (pre-fit) model that's exactly like `model _ ordinal`, except using the data in `exp_ex` (`bmmb::get_model("12_model_ordinal_ex.RDS")`).
3   Medium: Model `SG` using a multinomial model and compare results, predictions, coefficient estimates, etc. with `model_multinomial`.
4   Hard: Expand on either of the models fit in this chapter, either by adding duration as a quantitative predictor or by including resonance and its interaction with the other predictors.

In any case, describe the model, present and explain the results, and include some figures.

References

Agresti, A. (2013). *Categorical data analysis.* Chichester: Wiley.
Agresti, A. (2018). *An introduction to categorical data analysis.* Chichester: Wiley.
Kruschke, J. (2014). *Doing Bayesian data analysis: A tutorial with R, JAGS, and Stan.* Frankfurt: Elsevier Science.

13 Writing up experiments

An investigation of the perception of apparent speaker characteristics from speech acoustics

In this chapter, we will present an analysis of our experimental data based on models similar to the ones we considered in Chapter 11. This chapter will be written in the general structure of an academic paper, but less formally, and will include a meta-discussion of what we are doing and why we are doing it. Writing a paper is like directing a short (maybe slightly dull) movie. A movie is made up of hundreds or thousands of discrete 'shots', stuck together to give the impression of a single, continuous, coherent story. Do you ever watch a movie and wonder, why is this scene here? What is this character's motivation? Where are the characters right now and how did they get here? If so, either the director or the editor (or both) may have been careless with the way they have stuck their shots together, or the shots they've chosen to include, resulting in problems with your understanding of the story.

In the same way, the papers you write based on data analysis need to present the reader with dozens or hundreds of individual pieces of information, information regarding your research questions, data collection, analysis, results, interpretation, and so on. You are in charge of stitching these pieces of information into paragraphs, sections, and ultimately, into a paper. When the reader reads the paper, they should feel like they are reading a coherent story regarding your research questions and what your experiment says about them. If someone reads your paper and thinks: Why are they telling me this? Why/how did they do this? What does this parameter mean? How did they reach that conclusion? Then there may be problems in terms of the information you've presented to the reader, or in the way that the information has been presented.

We're going to present two independent models: One predicts apparent height based on acoustics, apparent age, and apparent gender, and the other predicts apparent gender based on speech acoustics and apparent age. Our intention in this chapter is simply to provide examples of analyses of a quantitative variable and a dichotomous variable. Imagine a pair of researchers who ran the same experiment in two parallel dimensions where everything is the same, except for these researchers deciding on slightly different research questions. One of these researchers, the one predicting apparent height, treats apparent age and gender as given in order to understand height. The other researcher, the one predicting apparent gender, treats apparent age as given in order to understand apparent gender. We might consider a third researcher (in another dimension) who decides to consider both apparent age and apparent height simultaneously in a model with multiple dependent variables in some configuration. This sort of thing is possible with *Stan* and `brms`; however, it's not something we'll be getting to

DOI: 10.4324/9781003285878-13

428 *Apparent speaker characteristics from speech acoustics*

in this book. Luckily, building these models is mostly a modest extension of the things we *have* covered.

Because of the similarity in the subject areas, much of the background information in the introduction of the two 'experiments' would be repetitive. In addition, since only one experiment was carried out there was only one set of methods. As a result, a single introduction and methods section will be presented for both 'analyses.'experiments'. After that, the experimental analyses diverge substantially, and so are presented separately for each 'experiment'. However, in order to avoid jumping back and forth between topics, we present contiguous results, discussion, and conclusion sections for each of the two experiments.

13.1 Introduction

The acoustic characteristics of the human voice vary in a systematic way between speakers with different indexical characteristics such as age and gender. Listeners are familiar with these patterns of co-variation and use this information to guess speaker indexical characteristics from their speech. Although listeners are often incorrect in their assessments, they tend to be fairly consistent. Thus, listener judgments of speaker indexical characteristics are often incorrect but generally precise: People often make errors but their errors are fairly predictable. In this experiment, we will investigate how listeners assess speaker characteristics from speech acoustics.

Our discussion of the perception of apparent speaker characteristics will focus on three of these: Apparent height, apparent age, and apparent gender. We will begin by talking about the perception of speaker size and height more generally. The main acoustic predictors of apparent speaker age, size, and gender are the *fundamental frequency* and the *resonance* properties of speech. Both of these acoustic characteristics will be introduced in the following sections, and the veridical relationships between these and apparent speaker characteristics will be discussed. After that, we will briefly review the current state of knowledge regarding listener perception of these characteristics.

13.1.1 Fundamental frequency and voice pitch

Your vocal folds, housed inside your larynx (in your neck) vibrate when you speak. For example, you will feel the front of your neck vibrate when you produce a 'zzzzzz' or a vowel sound. The rate of vibration of the vocal folds varies as a function of the mass and length of the vocal folds, and the size of the laryngeal structures in general. Think of guitar strings and the fact that the lower frequency strings tend to be thicker while higher frequency strings tend to be thinner. In addition, the rate of vibration of the vocal folds is easily modifiable within a large range by speakers in the same way that a guitar player can adjust the tightness of a string to modify the note it plays. Rate of vibration is measured in units of cycles per second, referred to as Hertz (Hz).

The repetitive vibration of the vocal folds results in a repetitive speech sound. Repetitive sounds can feel 'musical' or 'harmonic' to humans; these are terms that are difficult to define but that most people intuitively understand. A whistle or flute is harmonic, a waterfall or the noise a fan makes is not. The repetition rate of sounds is referred to as the fundamental frequency (f0) of the sound. The f0 of a sound is the strongest determinant of the perceived pitch. We say strongest because perceived pitch can also be (weakly) affected by the loudness of a sound, among other things (e.g. spectral shape), however, it is still primarily dependent on f0.

Pitch is the internal *sensation* associated with sounds such that they can be ranked from 'low' to 'high'. Think of pitch like spiciness, it's the way something *feels*. In general, spiciness may relate to the amount of capsaicin in food, but other factors such as the amount of sugar in the food may also affect how the food *feels* (i.e. tastes) when we eat it. You can rank foods from more to less spicy, you can rank sounds from lower to higher pitch. When you do this, in general, the ranking will result in an ordering of the sounds according to f0: Sounds with higher f0s generally have higher pitches. So, when you hear someone with a 'high pitched voice', that is your auditory system (and brain) telling you, in its own way, that that person's vocal folds are vibrating at a high rate (i.e. they have a high speaking f0).

13.1.2 Variation in fundamental frequency between speakers

There are two main sources of average f0 differences between speakers. First, there is age-related growth, meaning that f0 tends to decrease as humans age into their full adult size, as seen in Figure 13.1. Second, there is a substantial growth of laryngeal structures, including the vocal folds, during the typical course of male puberty. For this reason, most adult males produce speaking f0s that are lower than those of adult females of the same body size and age. This tendency is also clearly evident in Figure 13.1. In summary, we can say that taller speakers tend to have lower f0s than shorter speakers, adults tend to have lower f0s than children, and adult males tend to have lower f0s than the rest of the population.

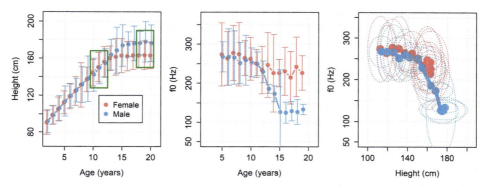

Figure 13.1 (left) Average height of males and females in the United States of America, organized by age (Fryar et al. 2012). Error bars indicate two standard deviations and boxes highlight the age ranges featured in this experiment. (middle) Average f0 produced by male and female speakers from five years of age until adulthood (Lee et al. 1999). Error bars indicate two standard deviations. (right) The heights from the first plot are plotted against the f0s from the second plot. These data were collected from different sets of people, so this comparison is simply illustrative. Ellipses enclose two standard deviations and assume no correlation between the dimensions.

430 *Apparent speaker characteristics from speech acoustics*

13.1.3 Voice resonance and vocal-tract length

Another way that speakers vary systematically in their speech acoustics is in their voice resonance. **Resonance** occurs when a sound wave bounces back and forth in an enclosed cavity so the energy can't leave the system easily, and builds up inside. Resonance forms the basis of the sounds produced by most musical instruments and (loud) animals. So, dogs, cats, and humans, but also guitars and pianos, all make sounds by comprising structures that can produce resonances. A common way of generating a resonance is by putting acoustic energy into a tube or enclosed space. For example, an acoustic guitar uses its strings to introduce energy into the cavity in its body, which serves to substantially amplify the sound. Without this amplification, the guitar strings alone would only make a quiet and unappealing buzzing sound. In the same way, resonance is what allows us to produce very loud speech, with relatively little effort. Think of the fact that babies that aren't strong enough to hold up their own heads can scream surprisingly loud, for a very long time.

For human speech communication, the enclosed structure used to create acoustic resonances is the **vocal tract**, the space between the vocal folds and the lips. The vocal tract is an empty space comprising the oral cavity (your mouth) and the pharyngeal cavity (your throat). As you speak you push air out of your lungs toward your mouth. The vocal folds are like the reed of a saxophone: They periodically open and close letting through (periodic) puffs of air. The puffs of air go from your larynx (in your neck) to your mouth and, even if your mouth is open, their energy 'bounces' back and forth between the mouth and the vocal folds. The small amounts of energy reflected between the mouth and vocal folds add up and result in what are known as acoustic resonances, which are build-ups of acoustic energy inside an enclosed space.

Resonators, that is, structures like the vocal tract that can resonate, usually have one or more preferred **resonant frequencies**, frequencies that they amplify the most. A complete explanation of this is beyond the scope of this chapter, but see Johnson (2004) for more information on the topic. Here we will provide a not-entirely-right but conceptually simple explanation of the topic. The speed of sound is fixed for a given environment (temperature, pressure, gas composition, etc.). This means that the bouncing back and forth between your mouth and your larynx occurs at a fixed speed (i.e. the speed of sound). As a result, the number of times per second a sound wave can travel back and forth along the vocal tract, measured in Hertz, is determined by the length of that vocal tract. This is obvious: A longer travel time at a fixed velocity entails fewer repetitions ('laps') per unit of time.

As a consequence of the above relationships, longer resonators have lower **resonant frequencies**. All other things being equal, if resonator x is 20% shorter than resonator y, waves will take 20% less time to complete one travel back and forth. This means that resonator x will have resonant frequencies 20% higher than those of y. In general, sounds with lower resonances *sound* and *feel* bigger to listeners. The difference between a violin and a cello playing the same note, or a small child and a large adult singing the same note, is resonance. In each case, listeners can detect the sound with lower resonances and identify it as the larger object.

The resonance frequencies of most sounds can be estimated using analysis software such as Praat or the `phonTools` package in R (Barreda, 2015). This means that, for speech, we could potentially estimate the length of the vocal tract (vocal-tract length, VTL) that produced some speech based on the frequencies of its resonances.

Apparent speaker characteristics from speech acoustics   431

13.1.4 Estimating vocal-tract length from speech

We may define a 'true' **anatomical VTL** measuring the distance between the vocal folds and lips of a speaker in units of distance, perhaps measured using magnetic resonance imaging or x-ray images. It's not clear how one might establish a 'true' anatomical VTL for a speaker or what the direct relevance of this for speech communication would be. For example, anatomical VTL varies across the different gestures employed by the mouth in the process of producing speech. Which of these is the 'true' anatomical VTL, or, how should the different VTL estimates be combined across speech samples?

In fact, the estimation of anatomical VTL from speech acoustics is an underdetermined problem: There are an infinite number of combinations of vocal tract anatomy and gesture that can result in a given resonance pattern (Wakita, 1977). How can any acoustic estimate of VTL know that a speaker isn't adopting some gesture that causes their acoustic VTL to diverge from their 'resting' anatomical VTL in meaningful ways? As a result, it is difficult, if not impossible, to reliably associate the acoustic speech signal to certain knowledge of the speaker's anatomical VTL (however that's defined). For example, imagine trying to estimate the height of a person using only their shadow. If everyone is standing up straight this might work, but given random differences in body posture, this becomes a much more difficult problem.

Instead of worrying about speakers' *anatomical* VTL, we're going to focus on their **acoustic VTL** or **effective VTL**, which we define as the VTL implied by the resonant frequencies produced during speech. When two speakers say 'the same thing', the differences in their vocal tract resonances will primarily reflect differences in their effective/acoustic VTL. Thus, if two speakers saying 'the same thing' differ by 10% in their resonant frequencies, they differ by about 10% in their (acoustic) VTL, and by some indeterminate amount in their anatomical VTL. Unless otherwise specified, when we refer to VTL we will be discussing acoustic VTL, an estimate of VTL based on estimated resonant frequencies.

13.1.5 Variation in vocal-tract length between speakers

In Figure 13.2, we see a comparison of age, height, and (acoustic) VTL for males and females. We can see that VTL increases as a function of age (and height) for both men and women. In addition, we see that male and female speakers are approximately the same in height until around 13 or 14 years of age, at which point female and male averages begin to diverge in height (and VTL). However, note that male and female averages are always within two standard deviations of each other, meaning that a degree of overlap is expected.

We would like to highlight two aspects of the variation seen in Figure 13.2. First, there appears to be a sex-based difference in VTL. However, there is evidence that this is a difference in height masquerading as a difference in VTL. That is, speaker height is strongly correlated ($r = 0.93$) to anatomical VTL (measured using magnetic resonance imaging) across the human population (Turner et al. 2009). As a result of this relationship, the average adult female is expected to have a shorter VTL than the average adult male if they also have a shorter overall body length. Given the same height, men and women are expected to have approximately the same anatomical VTL. Thus, the average difference in VTL seen between adult males and females seems to be more about height than sex specifically.

432 *Apparent speaker characteristics from speech acoustics*

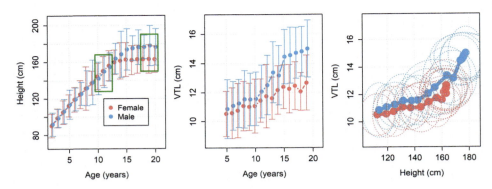

Figure 13.2 (left) Average height of males and females in the United States of America, organized by age (Fryar et al. 2012). Error bars indicate two standard deviations and boxes highlight the age ranges featured in this experiment. (middle) Average acoustic vocal-tract length (VTL) of male and female speakers from five years of age until adulthood (Lee et al. 1999). The average adult male VTL was set to 15 cm. Error bars indicate two standard deviations. (right) The heights from the first plot are plotted against the f0s from the second plot. These data were collected from different sets of people, so this comparison is simply illustrative. Ellipses enclose two standard deviations and assume no correlation between the dimensions.

Second, since speech output is a combination of anatomy and gesture, very similar anatomies can produce quite different sounds when used in different ways. As a result, the relationship between veridical speaker height and any VTL estimate based on acoustic measures may be an unreliable estimate of anatomical VTL. This may be seen as a weakness of acoustic VTL, however, we see it as a strength. For example, we see in the middle plot of Figure 13.2 that there is a consistent difference in VTL estimates for boys and girls. However, there is no corresponding difference in body size between speakers of these ages, nor is there compelling evidence of corresponding anatomical differences between these speakers (Vorperian et al. 2008). Instead, it's been suggested that the apparent difference in (acoustic) VTL between boys and girls may be behavioral (see Barreda and Assmann, 2021). In other words, little girls and little boys may be trying to sound 'masculine' or 'feminine' and adopt gestures that lead their similar anatomies to produce diverging acoustic outputs.

Which are we more concerned about in speech communication? The speaker's anatomy, or the acoustic output of that anatomy? Our acoustic VTL estimates capture the fact that when the girls represented in the middle plot of Figure 13.2 speak, on average they produce resonant frequencies that tend to be higher than those of boys of the same age. This acoustic information is the only information available to the listener when considering the speaker's indexical characteristics, and a focus on anatomical VTL would obscure this difference.

13.1.6 *Perception of age, gender, and size*

In this section, we will review the perception of speaker age, height, and gender from speech. This is the process by which a listener hears a speaker's voice and guesses what sort of person they are speaking to. We will focus on the use of two gross acoustic cues, f0 and VTL. We call these 'gross' acoustic cues because they are very general and overall cues, and there are many more subtle acoustic characteristics that we will not be discussing. This is a bit like talking about basketball players in terms of height and weight. There is much more to being a good basketball player than a person's height and weight, however, these two variables can still tell you a lot about the player.

13.1.6.1 Height

There is substantial previous research on the perception of speaker size/height from speech. Experiments have repeatedly found that f0 and VTL cues individually affect the perception of size. The following general statement can be made: All other things being equal, listeners will identify a speaker with a lower f0 or longer apparent VTL as being larger. As seen in Figure 13.2, there is a strong association between anatomical/acoustic VTL and human height across the entire population. For this reason, listeners can generally guess the veridical height of speakers with good accuracy if the entire range of possible human height is considered. For example, given that most human speakers plausibly range from about 100–200 cm in height, a guess of 170 cm for a speaker who is 160 cm might be considered fairly close even though 10 cm is a noticeable difference in height.

However, evidence suggests that height can no longer be reliably estimated when speakers are restricted to adults (see González, 2004). Because height varies substantially less for adults than it does for humans overall, the systematic relationship between height and VTL becomes smaller relative to the amount of between-speaker variation. As a result, errors must be much smaller to be equally impressive. For example, if about 95% of adult females are between 150 and 177 cm in height then the same error of 10 cm (a guess of 170 for a speaker who is 160 cm) seems less impressive.

13.1.6.2 Age

The perception of age can be divided into two general situations: Before and after adulthood. As seen in Figure 13.2, from the ages of 2 to 15, age and height are almost perfectly correlated, 0.995 in Fryar et al. (2012). After this age, the average female height stops increasing much and the average male heights increase at a smaller rate until around 18. Based on this, we see that for many children (<18 years), identification of speaker age is effectively identification of speaker height, and vice versa. Barreda and Assmann (2018) report that age can be estimated with reasonable accuracy from speech acoustics, and Assmann et al. (2018) have found that height can be estimated with good accuracy from speech. In both cases, speakers with longer VTLs and lower f0s were more likely to be identified as older and taller.

We will not discuss the perception of age past adulthood in any detail, as variation in speech in adulthood does not have simple growth-related explanations, and is not expected to vary as systematically with respect to average speaker f0 and VTL. As a result, any ability to distinguish speakers who are, for example, 30 from those who are 40, is necessarily a more subtle and complicated process than distinguishing a speaker who is 3 from one who is 13.

13.1.6.3 Gender

Finally, we will discuss the identification of speaker gender from speech. First, we must make a distinction between sex and gender. Sex refers to the classification of humans into categories like *male* and *female* based wholly on anatomical/physiological considerations. Gender categories like *male* or *female* refer to social categories and the set of customs and behaviors that individuals engage into signal belonging in one or another category. For example, the most common 'scientific' definitions of biological sex center around reproductive capabilities. Such definitions are scientific objects, neither true nor false, and subject to change. Even if we accept a reproductively centered definition of 'biological women', there is little to no connection between many of the behavioral and social characteristics of 'biological women', on the one hand, and reproductive capabilities, on the other. For example, there is no logical connection between the physical characteristics of the female sex and the stereotypical expectation that women have longer hair than males.

Despite the arbitrary association of many (if not most) gendered *behaviors* and biological sex, there is a connection between biological sex and the expectations listeners have regarding variation in VTL and f0 between men and women. The most common way by which speakers are assigned to gender categories is via superficial inspection of the reproductive organs at birth. As a result of associations between reproductive organs, the endocrine system, and human development, most speakers assigned male gender at birth are also likely to be relatively taller and have lower speaking f0s than speakers assigned to female at birth, within the same 'population'. This constraint is important because although men tend to be larger than women within a given population, there are large differences across global populations. As a result, it is not the case that men everywhere are taller than women everywhere.

Speaker f0 and VTL can be used to predict the gender of adult speakers with a high degree of accuracy. Likely because adult men and women are well separated along these dimensions, listeners can usually identify the gender of adult speakers from their voice in a large majority of cases (e.g. 99.6% in Hillenbrand and Clark, 2009). However, the perception of gender in voice is more complicated than what can be explained by f0 and VTL alone. Gender information in speech also involves performative aspects that cannot be explained solely due to average differences in body types. For example, Hillenbrand and Clark (2009) played listeners' adult male and female voices and asked them to guess if they were men or women. They also manipulated stimuli to flip f0 and VTL characteristics between men and women: Adult male voices were matched with female VTL and f0, and adult female voices got male VTL and f0. Even in this flipped condition, around 20% of speakers were still identified as their original gender. In addition, the tendency to identify speakers as their original (unflipped) gender was greater for sentences than for syllables.

The results above tell us that although f0 and VTL are important for the perception of gender, they do not entirely determine it, and some 'other' information is involved. Listeners heard originally female voices with speech acoustics that are *extremely* rare for a female speaker, and listeners *still* identified the speaker as female in a large proportion of cases. This suggests that not only does this 'other' information matter, but it matters enough to overwhelm extremely strong evidence in the form of f0 and VTL that the speaker is an adult male. In addition, this information is better conveyed by

Apparent speaker characteristics from speech acoustics 435

entire sentences, rather than just syllables, suggesting that it may be 'stylistic' information regarding speech rhythm or intonation.

The identification of gender in children's voices is more complicated, mostly due to the lack of many reliable anatomical differences in the vocal tracts and larynxes of boys and girls before puberty. This similarity can be seen by the almost complete overlap of speaker height, VTL and f0 seen for children under 13 in the figures above. Despite this, however, previous studies have found that the gender of pre-pubescent children can be identified at a greater than chance level. For example, Barreda and Assmann (2021) presented listeners with the voices of boys and girls between the ages of four and 18 and asked them to guess their gender. They found that listeners can identify the gender of speakers as young as five, and that this ability increased for sentences over syllables.

The findings reported by Barreda and Assmann (2021) support those of Hillenbrand and Clark (2009) in two important ways. First, they support the idea that although they are the most important determiners of apparent gender and can predict a large majority of variation, there is more to apparent gender than just f0 and VTL. The boys and girls presented to listeners did not differ much if at all in their gross acoustics, and yet listeners were able to distinguish them. Second, they both show that given longer stretches of speech, gender identification is better. This suggests that the 'other' information allowing gender identification in ambiguous cases is *performative*, that is *gestural* rather than anatomic. What we mean is that two humans may have an anatomical basis for having a different f0, but it is difficult to suggest that anatomy would constrain the 'style' with which we say an entire phrase. These performative aspects of gender may come across better for longer stretches of speech and may come across in the way that listeners stitch words together to produce sentences (i.e. **prosody** the rhythm and melody of phrases and sentences).

13.1.7 Category-dependent behavior

First, we will discuss the age-dependent relationship between speaker VTL in apparent height, and a possible cause for this. In Figure 13.2, we can see that the average female height stops increasing substantially at about 14 years of age, and the average male height stops increasing at about 18 years of age. We can also see that relatively modest changes in VTL, in the order of 2 cm, are associated with large changes in height (around 40 cm) between the ages of 5 to 15. Let's imagine that listeners associate each 1 cm difference in VTL with a 20 cm difference in height between speakers. However, in Figure 13.2 we see that adult VTL has a standard deviation of about 1 cm (about 1 cm in Pisanski et al. 2016). If listeners applied the 20/1 height to VTL ratio for adults, they would expect adults who differ by 3 cm in VTL, a fairly typical amount of VTL variation, to also differ by 60 cm in their height, an *extreme* amount of variation for heights in adults.

In response to this, Barreda (2017) has suggested that listeners likely use acoustics in a category-dependent manner if they are to correctly guess the height of both adult and child speakers. Specifically, listeners must have a 'steep' relationship between VTL and apparent height when they think they are listening to children. This would allow them to relate 'small' VTL differences with 'large' differences in apparent height. They must also have a 'shallow' slope between VTL and apparent height for apparent adults, allowing them to relate 'large' VTL differences with 'small' apparent height changes. Of course, this presupposes that listeners *know* whether they are listening to an adult or a child, which is obviously itself related to the size of the speaker. As a result, this suggests that the relationship between speech acoustics and apparent speaker characteristics is not 'simple' (i.e. a single regression line between VTL and apparent height), but rather 'complex', featuring a complicated relationship between the determination of multiple apparent speaker characteristics and speech acoustics.

For example, consider the expected dependence of estimates of speaker age, height, and gender for a wide range of speakers. Figure 13.3 presents average VTL and f0 for the speakers in the Lee et al. (1999) data, for different ages. We can see in the left plot that males and females largely overlap in gross acoustics save for post-pubescent males, and in the right plot, we see the age groups involved in this experiment in more detail. Since adult female acoustics overlap substantially with those of younger males and females, if a speaker makes a gender error for these voices, they may also make an age error. For example, if an adult female is identified as a male, it is also very likely that they will identify this speaker as younger than they are (i.e. a 'boy'), making certain sorts of identification errors likely to be correlated.

In fact, previous research has found that the perception of age for children between the ages of 5 and 18 is affected by the apparent gender of the child (Barreda and Assmann, 2018). Similarly, the perception of the gender of children between the ages of 5 and 18 is dependent on the perceived age of the child (Barreda and Assmann, 2021). This behavior can largely be understood in terms of changing expectations for female and male speakers of different age groups. For example, the category boundary between male and female speakers in the f0 by VTL stimulus space clearly needs to be in a substantially different place for 18-year-old speakers vs. 5-year-old speakers if its to be of any use. Overall, this also strongly suggests that a simple deterministic mapping between speech acoustics and apparent speaker characteristics is not reflective of the process underlying the perception of these characteristics.

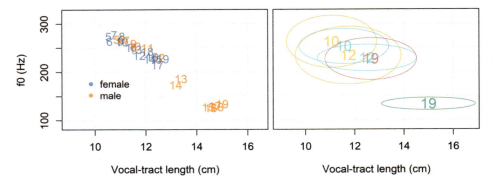

Figure 13.3 (left) Average f0 and vocal-tract length for each age group in the Lee et al. (1999) data. (right) The same data as in the left plot, but only age groups similar to those included in our experiment are included. These are 10–12-year-old children, and adults over 19 years of age.

13.1.8 The current experiment

The experiment presented here is meant to investigate the relationship between speaker VTL, f0, and apparent height and gender. In each case, we are also interested in the role of apparent age in the use of speech acoustics and in the determination of height and gender. Listeners were presented with a set of voices and were asked to classify the speakers as female or male and as children and adults. Two separate analyses will be carried out. The first predicts apparent height based on speech acoustics and apparent age and gender, the second predicts apparent gender based on speech acoustics and apparent age. In general, we are interested in a few basic questions:

(Q1) What is the relationship between speech acoustics, specifically speaker f0 and VTL, and apparent height/gender?
(Q2) Do the effects for speaker f0 and VTL on apparent height/gender vary based on apparent speaker characteristics?

We may consider two general views on the processes that underlie the perception of apparent speaker perception: Simple and complex. The 'simple' view suggests relatively stable mappings from speech acoustics to apparent speaker characteristics. Such mappings could be thought of as logistic regression models with a small number of parameters with fixed values, as seen below.

```
characteristic ~ f0 + vtl
```

In contrast, the 'complex' view suggests that the mappings between acoustics an apparent speaker characteristics are complex and flexible. For example, this might be thought of as a logistic regression model with a larger number of parameters and interactions between them as seen below:

```
characteristic ~ (f0 + vtl + X) * (Y * Z)
```

Where X represents some other acoustic characteristic(s), possibly strongly affected by behavior, and Y and Z represent non-acoustic information, such as apparent speaker information or perhaps listening conditions or instructions. Generally speaking, a strong role in perception for non-acoustic information such as apparent age or gender is incompatible with the 'simple' view, and suggests that a more 'complex' process underlies the determination of apparent speaker characteristics.

13.2 Methods

In this section, we will discuss the methods we used to collect and analyze the data. The goal of a methods section is to provide enough information so that a person reading it could potentially replicate your experiment and analysis. You should keep in mind that the person reading your paper may have no idea what you did or why you did it, and things that seem obvious to you may not be obvious at all to your reader. For example, in an experiment like this, it is nearly *always* the case that you present stimuli to listeners in a random order. Readers may strongly assume that you presented your stimuli to listeners in a random order. However, this still needs to be explicitly stated

438 *Apparent speaker characteristics from speech acoustics*

if it is true because your readers shouldn't have to *guess* what you did in the experiment. Basically, if you presented stimuli to listeners in a random order, then be sure to mention that in your methods section. Finally, when describing your methods you should try to keep in mind that readers may not be in your specialized area or even in your field. As a result, it's useful to either provide background information in highly-specialized subjects or methods, or at least provide adequate references for readers to figure things out for themselves.

13.2.1 Participants

Listeners were 15 speakers of California English. Listeners were not all native speakers of English but all spoke English well enough to attend a university in the United States. All listeners participated in the experiment for partial course credit. Listeners were told that this was not a 'real' experiment, but rather that the resulting data would be analyzed in a book and released publicly. Participating in the experiment and contributing their data to the book were both opt-in on the part of the student. For example, students could participate in the experiment for credit even if they did not wish to have their data included in the book. Several other ways to get equivalent course credit were also offered.

13.2.2 Stimuli

Stimuli were isolated productions of the word 'heed' produced by the 139 speakers in the Hillenbrand et al. (1995) data set. Productions represent speech produced by 27 boys, 19 girls, 45 men, and 48 women. Speakers were all from Michigan and had the northeast cities dialect (i.e., they 'sounded' like they were from Michigan). In addition, speech samples were collected in 1995 meaning the local dialect may have changed substantially in the meantime. However, dialects of English do not usually exhibit much variation in the vowel sound in "heed" meaning that the speech should have sounded relatively 'normal' to speakers of California English. In any case, any possible dialectal difference is not expected to have much effect on the important research questions we hope to address.

As noted above, the fundamental frequency (f0) of sounds is the repetition rate of the acoustic wave measured in Hertz, units of cycles per second. This means that the f0 of vowel sounds can estimated by measuring the rate at which the 'shape' of the acoustic wave repeats as a function of time. For f0, we use the Hillenbrand et al. (1995) measurements for the stimuli, provided with the original data.

Speaker vocal-tract length (VTL) was estimated based on the vocal-tract resonances provided in the Hillenbrand data. To estimate speaker VTL based on resonant frequencies, we found the geometric mean resonant frequency for the vowel in each production of the word 'heed'. We then found the speaker with the lowest overall resonances and arbitrarily set this speaker VTL to 16cm, basically appropriate for an adult male with a long VTL. This speaker served as the reference VTL. We then set each speaker's VTL to reflect the proportional difference between their resonances and those associated with the reference VTL. For example, imagine a second speaker who produced resonances that were 1.04% higher than those of the reference speaker. This speaker would then have a VTL of 15.4 cm (16/1.04), meaning it is 96% (1/1.04) as long as that of the first speaker.

Apparent speaker characteristics from speech acoustics 439

What we did above is a reasonable estimate of the differences in *effective*, or *acoustic*, VTL between speakers. However, it should be clear that this does not reflect an estimate of the absolute anatomical VTL for our speakers. We could have left the VTL predictor as a unit of frequency scaling, simply representing proportional differences in resonant frequencies between different speakers. However, we've found that readers find estimates of VTL in units of distance such as centimeters much more interpretable. Since this is not a 'real' experiment and exists in service of learning about statistics, we went with the more interpretable predictor.

All syllables were also manipulated using the 'change gender' function in Praat. This function allows you to scale the spectral envelope of speech sounds up/down according to uniform scaling, thereby changing resonant frequencies in a way that mimics the effects of differences in VTL. The spectral envelope of each syllable was scaled down by 8%, replicating a VTL increase of 8%. The fundamental frequency, duration, and other characteristics of the sound were not affected by this processing. Manipulated syllables were marked with a value of `b`, for 'big', in the `R` (resonance) column. These responses are not discussed or analyzed in the text as they are reserved for exercises, however, they are available in the `exp_ex` and `exp_data_all` data frames included in the `bmmb` package.

13.2.3 Procedure

Listeners were instructed that they would hear the word 'heed' produced by adult males (>18), adult females (>18), girls (10–12 years old), and boys (10–12 years old). They were asked to indicate how tall the speaker 'sounded' in feet and inches, and the category of the speaker. Responses could be provided in any order. Height responses were entered on a slider ranging form 4'0" to 6'6". The slider displayed the selected height to the listener to the nearest tenth of an inch. Category responses were entered by selecting one of four category buttons labeled 'women (18+ years old)', 'man (18+ years old)', 'girl (10–12 year old)', and 'boy (10–12 years old)'.

The experiment was conducted over Qualtrics, an online survey tool, with very little control over listening conditions. For example, listeners may have had headphones or speakers of very different qualities when carrying out the experiment. We have a pretty good excuse: Data collection was carried out in 2021 during the covid-19 pandemic and both of the authors, in addition to the research participants, were mostly confined to their homes. However, if this were a 'real' experiment, we would have exerted more control over the listening conditions. Listeners were presented with syllables one at a time, randomized across stimulus dimensions. This means that all 278 unique stimuli were presented in a completely unpredictable, random manner. This randomization was carried out independently for each listener.

13.2.4 Data screening

Data were collected from approximately 30 people, however, we only wanted 15 for the book in order to keep plots and model outputs manageable. As a result, we needed to eliminate about half the original listeners. In part, because the experiment was done online via Qualtrics and not in a controlled environment like a lab, the data were of varying quality between listeners. In light of this, when removing participants we tried to remove the 'bad' data and tried to keep the "good" data. In general, this meant

440 *Apparent speaker characteristics from speech acoustics*

removing listeners that exhibited 'unusual' behavior, or behavior suggesting that they were not conducting the experiment in good faith. For example, some listeners identified adult males correctly at a low rate despite the fact that they can be identified correctly nearly 100% of the time based on f0 alone (see Chapter 10). Based on what we know about the perception of gender from adult male speech, this behavior is likely to reflect inattentiveness on the part of the listener.

The above screening might be more difficult to justify in a 'real' experiment, and that's why we would like to stress that this is not a 'real' experiment. The data presented and analyzed here is 100% real, provided by actual listeners participating in the experiment described above. They did not know each other and did not co-ordinate their behavior in any way, nor where they 'prepped' in any way regarding what sort of responses were expected for the experiment. However, the data has been 'curated' to make it suitable for use as a pedagogical tool, and so any inferences made using this data should be taken with a grain of salt. That being said, we expect most findings would hold up to replication and, in fact, many of the conclusions we reach (later on) are confirmations of earlier findings.

Normally, this section wouldn't be in a 'real' paper since we wouldn't have chosen our data in this way in a real experiment. However, if you *have* omitted listeners, individual observations, or modified your data in any way prior to analysis, you should be completely transparent about this and make this clear to the reader early on. You should also be prepared to explain your decisions and to discuss the possible consequences for your analysis.

13.2.5 *Loading the data and packages*

This section *definitely* wouldn't be in a real paper, but we want to load our data and packages in an easy-to-find place so that the code, later on, works for anyone following along.

```
library (brms)
library (bmmb)
options (contrasts = c('contr.sum','contr.sum'))

# load data
data (exp_data)

# create gender analysis dependent variable
exp_data$Female = ifelse(exp_data$G == 'f', 1, 0)

# center vtl
exp_data$vtl_original = exp_data$vtl
exp_data$vtl = exp_data$vtl - mean (exp_data$vtl)

# scale and center f0
exp_data$f0_original = exp_data$f0
exp_data$f0 = exp_data$f0 - mean(exp_data$f0)
exp_data$f0 = exp_data$f0 / 100
```

Apparent speaker characteristics from speech acoustics 441

13.2.6 Statistical Analysis: Apparent height

We're going to re-fit the apparent height model we fit in Chapter 11, without the f0 by VTL cross-product. What follows is something like what we would write in a paper or journal article describing the analyses we carried out. Sometimes these descriptions happen in the methods section, and sometimes the analysis is described in the results section when the results are presented. Each approach has its positives and negatives. Presenting the modeling information in its own section early on makes it easy to find and makes the paper more organized. However, as a reader, it can sometimes be difficult to remember the details of the model by the time you get to the results, so that you have to flip back and forth to remember what the different parameters mean, and so on.

Apparent height was treated as a quantitative variable coming from a t distribution with a trial-specific mean and fixed (but unknown) scale and nu parameters. Apparent height responses were converted to centimeters prior to analysis. Expected apparent height was predicted based on the following 'fixed' effects: 1) Speaker vocal-tract length (VTL) (`vtl`) measured in centimeters, 2) speaker fundamental frequency (`f0`) measured in hectohertz (1 hectohertz = 100 Hertz), 3) apparent speaker age, a factor `A` with levels adult (`a`) and child (`c`), and 4) apparent speaker gender, a factor `G` with levels female (`f`) and male (`m`). All categorical predictors were included in the model using sum coding.

All possible interactions between fixed effects were included in the model, save for the interaction between f0 and VTL (and all related predictors). In addition, listener 'random effects' intercepts were calculated, as were listener-dependent effects for all fixed effects and their interactions. Speaker-dependent random intercepts were also included in the model. The model formula used is presented below.

```
height ~ (vtl+f0) * A * G + ((vtl+f0) * A * G | L) + (1 | S)
```

Data were analyzed using a multilevel Bayesian model fit with *Stan* (Stan Development Team, 2022), using the `brms` (Bürkner, 2017) package in R (R Core Team, 2022). Model 'fixed' effects were all estimated as coming from t distributions with a mean of zero, a scale of 5, and a nu of 3. The model intercept was given a t prior with a mean of 160, a scale of 5, and a nu parameter of 3. Speaker random intercepts were estimated as coming from a normal distribution with a mean of zero and a distribution-specific standard deviation estimated from the data. Listener random effects were estimated as coming from a 16-dimensional normal distribution. Each dimension was assumed to have a mean of zero and a standard deviation estimated from the data. An LKJ (Lewandowski-Kurowicka-Joe distribution) prior was used with a *concentration* parameter of 2, meaning our model would be somewhat skeptical of large correlations. Finally, the error term (`sigma`, σ) was given a half-t prior with a mean of 0, a scale of 5 and a nu of 3, and the nu parameter for our error distribution was given a gamma prior with scale and rate parameters of 2 and 0.1, respectively.

Here's the code we used to fit this model. Note that the code below has the same information as the verbal description of our model above.

```
priors = c(brms::set_prior("student_t(3,160, 5)", class = "Intercept"),
           brms::set_prior("student_t(3,0, 5)", class = "b"),
```

442 *Apparent speaker characteristics from speech acoustics*

```
        brms::set_prior("student_t(3,0, 5)", class = "sd"),
        brms::set_prior("lkj_corr_cholesky(2)", class = "cor"),
        brms::set_prior("gamma(2, 0.1)", class = "nu"),
        brms::set_prior("student_t(3,0, 5)", class = "sigma"))

height_model =
  brms::brm (height ~ (vtl+f0)*A*G + ((vtl+f0)*A*G|L) + (1|S),
            data = exp_data, chains = 4, cores = 4, warmup = 1000,
            iter = 5000, thin = 4, prior = priors, family = "student")

# Download the height from the GitHub page:
height_model = bmmb::get_model ('13_model_height_vtl_f0.RDS')
```

We would also like to note that it is good practice to do a prior predictive check *before* fitting your model in order to see that your prior generates reasonably plausible values of your dependent variables. Below is the code to carry out a prior predictive check for our model, and to plot the resulting predictions. You may have noted that above we use tighter priors than we have used so far in this book for our models with quantitative dependent variables (i.e. 5 cm as opposed to 12 cm). We decided to use the more constrained priors in our final analysis as this leads to prior predictions that are more concentrated in the 100–200 cm range we are mostly interested.

```
height_model_priors =
  brms::brm (height ~ (vtl+f0)*A*G + ((vtl+f0)*A*G|L) + (1|S),
            data = exp_data, chains = 4, cores = 4, warmup = 1000,
            iter = 5000, thin = 4, prior = priors, family = "student",
              sample_prior = "only")
p_check (height_model_priors)
```

13.2.7 *Statistical Analysis: Apparent gender*

Apparent speaker femaleness (`Female`) was treated as a binomial (dichotomous) variable coming from a Bernoulli distribution with a trial-specific p parameter. For the purposes of analysis, responses of female were coded as 1, and responses of male were coded as 0. Expected apparent gender for a given trial was predicted based on the following 'fixed' effects: 1) Speaker VTL (`vtl`) measured in centimeters, 2) speaker fundamental frequency (`f0`) measured in hectohertz (1 hectohertz = 100 Hertz), and 3) apparent speaker age, a factor `A` with levels adult (`a`) and child (`c`). All possible interactions between fixed effects were included in the model, save for the exclusion of the cross-product of f0 and VTL (and all related predictors). In addition, listener 'random effects' intercepts were calculated, as were listener-dependent effects for all fixed effects and their interactions. Speaker-dependent random intercepts were also included in the model. The model formula used is presented below.

```
Female ~ (vtl + f0) * A + ((vtl + f0) * A | L) + (1 | S)
```

Model 'fixed' effects, including the intercept, were all estimated as coming from t distributions with a mean of zero, a scale of 3, and a nu of 3. Speaker random intercepts were estimated as coming from a normal distribution with a mean of zero and a distribution-specific standard deviation estimated from the data. Listener random effects were estimated as coming from a 6-dimensional normal distribution. Each dimension was assumed to have a mean of zero and a standard deviation estimated from the data. An LKJ prior for the correlation of these dimensions was used, with a concentration parameter of 2. Since we are using exactly the same model we fit (and described) in Chapter 11, we load it below.

```
# Download the gender model from the GitHub page:
gender_model = bmmb::get_model ('11_model_gender_vtl_f0_reduced.RDS')
```

However, we include the code to carry out a prior predictive check on this model to remind the reader that it is a good idea to do this *before* you fit your final model. We present these after our model description here because these are not something that necessarily needs to be discussed in the paper (though reviewers may ask about this if relevant).

```
gender_model_prior =
  brm (Female ~ (vtl+f0)*A + ((vtl+f0)*A|L) + (1|S), data=exp_data,
       family="bernoulli", sample_prior = "only",
       chains = 4, cores = 4, warmup = 1000, iter = 5000, thin = 4,
       prior = c(set_prior("student_t(3, 0, 3)", class = "Intercept"),
                 set_prior("student_t(3, 0, 3)", class = "b"),
                 set_prior("student_t(3, 0, 3)", class = "sd"),
                 set_prior("lkj_corr_cholesky (2)", class = "cor")))

preds = p_check (gender_model_prior)
```

13.3 Results: Apparent height judgments

In this section, we'll outline a structured way to present large models to the reader. In general, we suggest figuring out what 'story' you are trying to tell with your data, and making sure that everything you tell the reader is in service of helping them understand the story. This approach helps people understand your data better than loading up a cannon with numbers and blasting it at the reader. In general, it may be a good idea to present the 'big picture' before moving on to more specific details of the results. The 'big picture' can also help motivate more detailed investigations of specific questions.

Before discussing any statistical model, it's useful to talk about the results a bit, and to present some visual representation of the data without much processing. Although we've discussed our experimental data ad nauseam at this point, we will present this as we would at the beginning of a results section, assuming that the reader has never seen these results before. Figure 13.4 presents a boxplot showing all size responses across all listeners, grouped by apparent speaker category. There are clear systematic differences in apparent height across the different apparent speaker categories. As seen in the middle and right plots of the same figure, it appears that apparent speaker height is relatively predictable based on speaker VTL and f0.

Since our model has a large number of parameters we're going to focus on interpreting those that seem likely to result in 'meaningful' differences in apparent height (see

Section 7.7). For human height, apparent and veridical, we define meaningful differences as those that 1) are likely to be different from zero, *and* 2) have magnitudes of at least around 0.5 cm. We see in Figure 13.5 that only a small number of the fixed effects exceed even this modest threshold. In addition, roughly the same subset of predictors exhibit the largest systematic between-listener variation in parameters. These predictors are the main effect for VTL (`vtl`), the main effect for f0 (`f0`), the main effect for apparent age (`A1`), and the interaction between apparent age and VTL (`vtl:A1`). Our discussion below will focus on these effects.

Table 13.1 presents information regarding our model fixed effects. We can see in the table (and figure) that f0 and VTL variation between speakers is associated with meaningful differences in apparent height. For example, a difference of 100 Hz between speakers is associated with a change of 3 cm in apparent height, and a 1 cm difference in VTL is associated with a change of 3 cm in apparent height. However, the largest effect is that of apparent age, indicating a difference of 14 cm in apparent height between speakers based on their apparent age.

Results also indicate a varying effect for speaker VTL across levels of apparent age. To investigate this, we considered the simple effects of VTL across levels of apparent age (calculated below).

```
# vtl main effect + adult, vtl main effect - adult (i.e. + child)
age_vtl_slopes = bmmb::short_hypothesis(
  height_model, c("vtl + vtl:A1 = 0","vtl - vtl:A1 = 0"))

age_vtl_slopes
##      Estimate Est.Error    Q2.5   Q97.5       hypothesis
## H1      1.345    0.6705 0.06048   2.722  (vtl+vtl:A1) = 0
## H2      4.740    0.7800 3.24153   6.286  (vtl-vtl:A1) = 0
```

We can report the simple effects as follows. The simple effect for VTL when listeners thought the speaker was a child was 4.74 (s.d. = 0.78, 95% C.I = [3.24, 6.29]), meaning

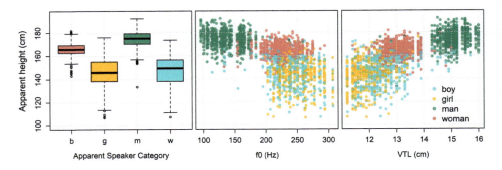

Figure 13.4 (left) Distribution of apparent height judgments across all listeners, grouped by apparent speaker category. (middle) Distribution of individual apparent height judgments based on the fundamental frequency (f0) of the stimulus. (right) Distribution of individual apparent height judgments based on the vocal-tract length (VTL). Point colors represent the modal category judgment made by listeners, for each token.

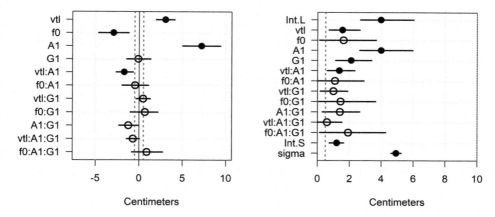

Figure 13.5 (left) Posterior distribution of model fixed effects. (right) Posterior distribution of random effect standard deviation estimates. Points indicate means, lines indicate 95% credible intervals. Dashed vertical lines indicate 0.5 cm away from 0. Points whose 95% credible intervals are at least 0.5 cm away from zero are filled.

Table 13.1 Posterior means, standard deviations, and 2.5% and 97.5% quantiles for our regression model 'fixed' effect parameter estimates

	Estimate	*Est.error*	*Q2.5*	*Q97.5*
Intercept	160.17	1.14	157.90	162.41
vtl	3.04	0.54	1.97	4.10
f0	−2.92	0.88	−4.67	−1.17
A1	7.20	1.12	5.01	9.39
G1	−0.09	0.70	−1.43	1.34
vtl:A1	−1.70	0.49	−2.64	−0.67
f0:A1	−0.46	0.78	−1.97	1.10
vtl:G1	0.47	0.42	−0.35	1.30
f0:G1	0.67	0.81	−1.00	2.20
A1:G1	−1.23	0.57	−2.32	−0.11
vtl:A1:G1	−0.70	0.37	−1.43	0.05
f0:A1:G1	0.90	0.90	−0.83	2.75

we expect an increase of 4.7 cm in apparent height for every 1 cm increase in speaker VTL, on average. However, this value dropped all the way to 1.34 cm (s.d. = 0.67, 95% C.I = [0.06, 2.72]) for apparent adults. So, differences in speaker VTL appear to be associated with much larger differences in apparent height when listeners think the speaker is a child.

13.4 Discussion: Apparent height

In the discussion section, we can delve into any questions that arose but remained unresolved in the results section, and tell the 'story' of our data using more prose and more of a narrative. Here is where you can explain your results to your reader and how they relate to your research questions. You can also develop interesting or unexpected findings in more detail, especially as they relate to previous literature in the field, and possible future studies. We're going to divide our discussion into thematic subsections, which can be a good idea since it allows the consideration of one topic/question at a time, and helps the reader find the information they may be looking for.

13.4.1 Age-dependent use of VTL cues on apparent height

In the results above, we found that the slope relating speaker VTL and apparent height was substantially different in apparent children and apparent adults. Below, we calculate the age-dependent intercepts.

```
age_intercepts = bmmb::short_hypothesis(
  height_model, c("Intercept + A1 = 0","Intercept - A1 = 0"))

age_intercepts
##      Estimate Est.Error   Q2.5  Q97.5            hypothesis
## H1      167.4     1.273  164.9  169.9   (Intercept+A1) = 0
## H2      153.0     1.860  149.3  156.6   (Intercept-A1) = 0
```

Figure 13.6 presents age-dependent intercepts (left plot), VTL slopes (middle plot), and a comparison of the lines implied by these parameters to our data (right plot). Age-dependent intercepts were 167.4 cm (s.d. = 1.27, 95% C.I = [164.88, 169.93]) for adults and 153.0 (s.d. = 1.86, 95% C.I = [149.28, 156.62]) for children. Combined with the slope differences described above, the result is a higher but flatter line for adults and a lower but more steep line for children.

Results suggest that the perception of size from speech is not the simple relation of VTL and f0 with a predicted height, as is suggested by some simpler models of size perception (e.g. Smith and Patterson, 2005). We can relate this back to patterns in our data to show that this is not just an 'abstract' association made by our model. For example,

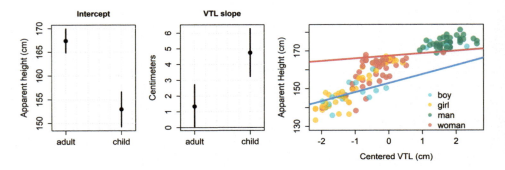

Figure 13.6 Posterior means and 95% credible intervals for model intercepts (left), and slopes (middle), of the lines relating speaker vocal-tract length (VTL) and apparent height, for apparent children and adults. (right) Average apparent height for each stimulus plotted against stimulus VTL. Point colors represent modal classifications for each speaker.

Apparent speaker characteristics from speech acoustics 447

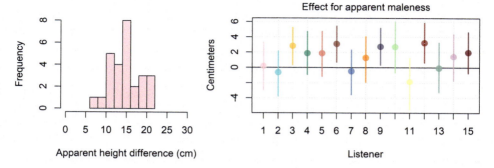

Figure 13.7 (left) Distribution of apparent height difference for 27 speakers identified as both adults and children at least five times each. The difference reflects apparent adult height minus apparent child height. (right) Posterior distribution and 95% credible intervals for listener-dependent effects for apparent maleness.

we found the 27 speakers who were identified as adults and children at least 5 times each out of 15 total classifications. These speakers included 5 boys, 2 girls, 1 man, and 19 women. We then found the average reported height for each speaker when identified as an adult, and the average height for the same speaker when identified as a child. The distribution of these differences is presented in the left plot of Figure 13.7. We see a range of differences in apparent height, however, in each case, individual speakers were identified as taller on average when they were also identified as adults.

13.4.2 The effect of apparent gender on apparent height

In Figure 13.5, we saw that the marginal (fixed) effect for apparent gender was effectively zero, however, the standard deviation of the listener-dependent gender effect ($\sigma_{A:L}$) was not. In the right plot of Figure 13.7, we see the listener-dependent effects of apparent maleness on apparent height. We can see that although many of these are not reliably different from zero, they differ *from each other* and are large enough to meaningfully affect apparent height judgments. As a result, we can say that although apparent gender may not have a consistent average effect, it can still be associated with meaningful differences in apparent height across listeners.

13.5 Conclusion: Apparent height judgments

The conclusion summarizes what you consider the main findings of your paper and points in the direction of future study. Writing conclusions is hard but important, it is the last part of your paper so its important to keep in mind that the reader may walk away with the things you mention in your conclusion in mind. Do you ever leave a bit of food until the end thinking it will be good, then it turns out to be a stringy piece of meat and it leaves you feeling disappointed? Don't let your conclusion be that stringy piece of meat.

Since the conclusion needs to be focused on the 'point' of the paper and this is not a 'real' experiment, we won't spend much time on this. However, we can summarize what we consider to be the main take-aways in relation to the general research questions posed above. We can say that we have strong evidence of the fact that the determination of apparent speaker height is not independent of apparent age such that even

448 *Apparent speaker characteristics from speech acoustics*

a single speech stimulus can be judged in different ways based on the apparent age of the speaker. This suggests that the determination of apparent speaker age, height, and gender are very likely related processes and not a simple mapping directly from speech acoustics to apparent speaker characteristics.

13.6 Results: Apparent gender judgments

Figure 13.8 presents the probability with which individual speakers were identified as female, plotted against their gross acoustic characteristics. It's clear that there is a positive association between f0 and the probability of a female response, and a negative association between speaker VTL and the same probability. In addition, our figure suggests that the locations of category boundaries between male and female responses must differ for adults (women vs. men) compared to children (girls vs. boys). For example, we might place the boundary between boys and girls at around 12 cm VTL, while the boundary between women and men along the same dimension might be at around 14 cm.

Although this analysis is focused on the relationships between predictors and responses, we may also want to consider how accurate listeners tended to be and the mistakes they tended to make. For example, below we see that listeners were more accurate at identifying the gender of adults than of children. In particular, the gender of adult males seems quite easy to identify.

```
# find cases where reported and veridical gender matches, across levels
# of veridical category
tapply (exp_data$G==exp_data$G_v, exp_data$C_v,mean)
##      b      g      m      w
## 0.5926 0.7228 0.9733 0.8611
```

Below we inspect a confusion matrix comparing veridical and judged apparent speaker class. Based on this we can see that boys were confused with girls and women in 40% of cases, and girls were identified incorrectly in 57% of cases.

```
# table comparing reported (C) to actual (C_v) category.
xtabs (~ exp_data$C_v + exp_data$C)
##             exp_data$C
## exp_data$C_v   b   g   m   w
##            b 234 133   6  32
##            g  79 184   0  22
##            m  31   0 626  18
##            w  97 109   3 511
```

Figure 13.9 presents the model fixed effects and the standard deviation estimates of the random effects. Results indicate large effects for f0, VTL, and apparent age, and meaningful interactions between both acoustic predictors and apparent age. The effects for the acoustic predictors are as expected: A lower f0 and a longer VTL are associated with male responses. The magnitude of these effects is enough to make a meaningful difference in expected outcomes. For example, our results suggest that a 2 cm difference in VTL is associated with a logit difference of about 5.4, enough to

Apparent speaker characteristics from speech acoustics 449

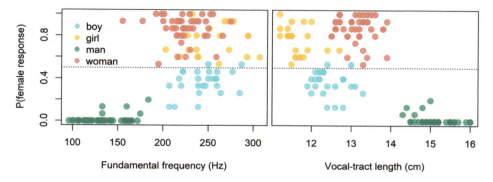

Figure 13.8 Probability of observing a female response for each speaker, across all listeners. Point color reflects modal speaker classification. Points are organized according to speaker fundamental frequency (left) and speaker (acoustic) vocal-tract length (right).

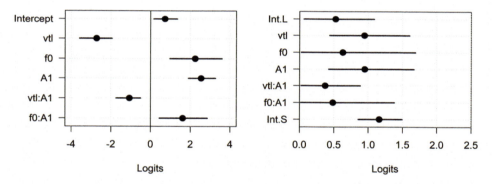

Figure 13.9 (left) Posterior distribution of model fixed effects. (right) Posterior distribution of random effect superpopulation standard deviation estimates. Points indicate means, lines indicate 95% credible intervals.

change the probability of a female response from 0.06 (logit^{-1}(−2.7) = 0.06) to 0.93 (logit^{-1}(2.7)). In addition, apparent adultness also seems to have an important effect on apparent gender: Apparent adults were more likely to be perceived as female given and average VTL and f0, and the effects of f0 and VTL changes on apparent gender were *stronger* for adults compared to children.

The random effects standard deviations indicate substantial variation in only three effects: Listener-dependent variation in the use of VTL ($\sigma_{VTL:L}$), the effect of apparent age ($\sigma_{A1:L}$), and speaker-dependent variation in intercepts (σ_S). Below we print a table of the standard deviation estimates presented in Figure 13.9. We don't present both tables in order to save space, but it is generally a good idea to provide actual numbers (even in an appendix or supplemental files) in addition to graphical representations of your results.

450   *Apparent speaker characteristics from speech acoustics*

Table 13.2 Posterior means, standard deviations, and 2.5% and 97.5% quantiles for the standard deviation estimates for our model random effects parameters

	Estimate	*Est.error*	*Q2.5*	*Q97.5*
Intercept	0.72	0.31	0.15	1.34
vtl	−2.73	0.41	−3.59	−1.96
f0	2.24	0.67	0.97	3.59
A1	2.54	0.35	1.90	3.27
vtl:A1	−1.08	0.32	−1.75	−0.50
f0:A1	1.62	0.61	0.44	2.85

13.7 Discussion: Apparent gender judgments

We're going to focus on three aspects of our results: 1) The age-dependent classification of speakers, 2) Between-listener variation in gender classifications, and 3) The speaker effects and more 'subtle' cues in gender perception.

13.7.1 Effect of apparent age on the perception of femaleness

Apparent adultness increased the probability of observing a female response and also increased the effects of VTL and f0, leading to steeper slopes along each dimension. For example, the interaction between f0 and apparent age (`f0:A1`) has the effect of reducing the effect of f0 to nearly zero for children (`f0 + (-A1:f0)`, mean = 0.62, s.d. = 0.71, 95% C.I = [−0.77, 2.08]), and nearly doubling it for adults (`f0 + A1:f0`, mean = 3.85, s.d. = 1.07, 95% C.I = [1.86, 5.97]). The joint effects of f0 and VTL, and the way that these vary in relation to apparent age can be considered using territorial maps, as in Figure 13.10. Territorial maps present category boundaries in a stimulus space and indicate which categorical outcome is most probable in each region of the space.

We discussed territorial maps and how to make these for models with two quantitative predictors in Section 11.5.4, so we won't go into much detail regarding them here. However, when using 'esoteric' approaches like this, it's important to give the reader enough information so that they understand what they are looking at. For example, we can explain that our model specifies planes that vary along f0 and VTL. The intersection of these planes forms a line, and this line represents the category boundary between predicted male and female responses. The territorial maps in Figure 13.10 indicate the expected gender response in different regions of the stimulus space defined by speaker VTL and f0.

In Figure 13.10 we can see that the category boundary becomes more parallel to the f0 axis for apparent children. This reflects the decreasing importance of this cue in the prediction of responses for apparent children. We can also see the larger slopes along f0 and VTL for apparent adults reflected in the density of the white dotted lines on the territorial map. These lines reflect the increasing/decreasing value of the planes predicting female responses in our model. For example, we know the category boundary has a value of zero logits, so the closest set of dotted lines must reflect ±2 logits, the second line reflects ±4 logits, and so on. As a result, the spacing of the lines in the child territorial map reflects a slowly changing slope and less

Apparent speaker characteristics from speech acoustics 451

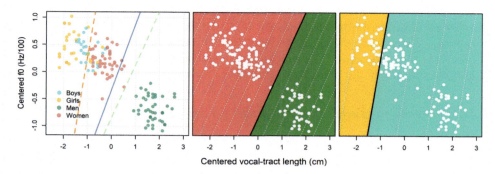

Figure 13.10 (left) Each point represents a single speaker, and labels indicate the most common group classification. Lines indicate male/female boundaries for adults (green), children (orange), and overall (blue) implied by our model. (middle) Territorial map showing expected classifications for apparent adults in different regions of the f0 by VTL stimulus space. (right) Same as the middle, but for apparent children. In each territorial map, dotted lines indicate an increase/decrease of 2 logits in the expected value of observing a female response, starting at a value of zero for the solid black line.

certain predictions, while the tightly packed lines in the middle plot indicate rapid changes in predicted logit values and more certain predictions. Basically, you can get to ±4 logits (i.e. a probability of 0.98 or 0.02) by moving very little with respect to the category boundary for adults, but you need to move quite a bit to reach this level of certainty for children.

13.7.2 Between-listener variation in gender perception

Our random effects standard deviations (Figure 13.9) indicated substantial variation in listener-dependent effects for VTL and apparent age. To investigate this, we calculated listener-specific intercepts, f0 slopes, and VTL slopes. We did this separately for apparent children and apparent adults using the code below. This process was discussed in detail in Section 11.5.4), and so will not be described here. The only novelty here is that we are repeating this process individually for each listener rather than only calculating the marginal (overall) boundaries, similar to what was done in Section 9.9.2.

```
listener_coefficients_adult =
  bmmb::short_hypothesis (gender_model, scope="coef",group="L",
                    c("Intercept+A1=0","vtl+vtl:A1=0","f0+f0:A1=0"))
listener_coefficients_child =
  bmmb::short_hypothesis (gender_model, scope="coef",group="L",
                    c("Intercept-A1=0","vtl-vtl:A1=0","f0-f0:A1=0"))
```

Using these parameters, we found category boundaries for apparent adults and apparent children, independently for each listener. These are presented in Figure 13.11. We see that there is a general consensus between listeners in terms of an approximate acoustic boundary between adult males and adult females. However, there is much more variation in the boundary between boys and girls. This likely reflects the fact

452 *Apparent speaker characteristics from speech acoustics*

that the acoustic characteristics of adult men and women are generally more predictable and stable relative to children 10–12 years old. In addition, the listeners in our experiment (undergraduate university students) likely have substantially more recent experience interacting with adults than with children in that age group. Finally, the greater separation between women and men relative to boys and girls might also result in more stability in the boundary between the former categories.

13.7.3 Beyond gross acoustic cues in gender perception

Our model attempts to predict female responses given a small number of acoustic predictors and their interaction with apparent age. It also allows for these relationships to vary in a listener-dependent manner. When there is systematic variation in the way that individual speakers are classified that *cannot* be explained by the acoustic predictors, including by listener-dependent variation in these, this is captured by the speaker-dependent intercepts (for a discussion of this, see Section 12.2.7). As a result, the speaker-dependent intercept effects reflect systematic tendencies in the identification of individual speakers as male or female above and beyond what can be explained given the other parameters in the model.

The speaker-dependent intercept effects for our model are presented in Figure 13.12. We can see that the effects for boys are mostly negative, indicating that boys were less likely to be identified as female than expected. Conversely, adult females were more likely to be identified as adult females than expected. As we can see in Figure 13.3, boys and women overlap substantially in their gross acoustics. As a result, to the extent that

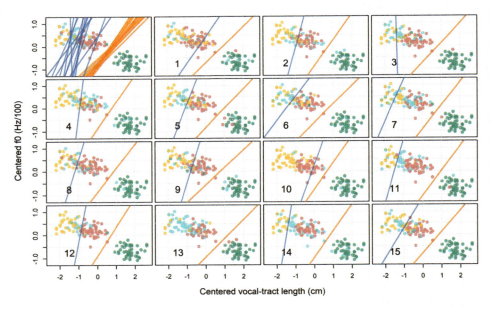

Figure 13.11 The first plot compares all listener-dependent category boundaries between men/women (orange) and boys/girls (blue). Subsequent plots present each listener's individual boundaries. Point colors indicate the listener's individual speaker classifications. The number on each plot indicates the listener number.

Figure 13.12 Speaker random effects. Point colors indicate the veridical speaker category for boys (b), girls (g), men (m), and women (w).

their gender is identified correctly, we might expect that this would be on the basis of 'something else'. We can contrast the effects for boys and women with those of adult males, which are nearly all centered around zero with fairly wide intervals. The intercept terms for veridical adult male speakers suggest there is no 'something else' necessary in the prediction of adult males. In other words, the classification of adult males is easy to explain in terms of f0 and VTL and there is no 'left over' systematic variation to explain for the speaker effects.

What could the 'something else' aiding in the classification of boys and adult women be? One candidate is what is known as *prosodic* information, that is, information about timing, rhythm, pitch movement, and so on. It's also possible that other more subtle acoustic information is involved, for example, information about the breathiness or creakiness of the voice. In any case, results highlight the fact that the communication and identification of gender from speech is more complicated than what can be explained by speaker f0 and VTL.

13.8 Conclusion: Apparent gender

In conclusion, we can say that the determination of apparent gender from speech acoustics seems to also involve the estimation of apparent speaker age in the process. In addition, there seems to be 'other' acoustic information that is very important for the perception of speaker age/gender that is not captured by the gross acoustic cues (f0 and VTL) included in our model. Further research is needed to investigate these topics.

13.9 Next steps

This book is over, now what? We tried to provide thorough examples of working with different types of common model structures and data types. However, it is impossible to cover everything in one book, and in fact, there are many important topics and methods that we didn't cover. We leave you with a very brief discussion on some of the topics we didn't get to or chose to not discuss.

13.9.1 Research design, variable selection, etc.

In this book, we focused on introducing important concepts and putting them into practice. However, we *began* with a completed experiment and began at a point where

454　*Apparent speaker characteristics from speech acoustics*

we know what predictors we wanted in our model, how we wanted to use them in our model, and how we wanted to represent our dependent variable. In a typical case, the researcher must make all these decisions.

For example, in the example regarding coffee and reading times mentioned sporadically throughout the book, the researcher has to decide which, if any, other manipulations (and associated predictors) to include in their experiment. They also need to decide which *observed* variables they want to include, these are things that were not manipulated such as reader age or gender. The famous statistician Ronald Fisher said: "To consult the statistician after an experiment is finished is often merely to ask him to conduct a post-mortem examination. He can perhaps say what the experiment died of". Your experiment is like a cake you put in the oven. Once it comes out, it's too late to add the eggs. All of this is to say that a successful statistical analysis hinges on a properly designed experiment and having a model that reasonably reflects the relations between the variables in your model. Mostly any decent introductory statistics book will feature a discussion of these topics, and so we chose to rehash these issues.

13.9.2 *Non-linear models*

The models we have fit in this book are all *linear models*, meaning we have made predictions by adding together predictors after multiplying them by coefficients. A **non-linear regression model** is one in which predictions are *not* linearly combined. Since non-linear regression is simply characterized by not being a very specific combination of parameters, there are a very large number of possible non-linear models. For example, consider the following prediction equations:

$$\mu_{[i]} = x_1 \cdot a_1 \cdot x_2 \cdot a_2$$

$$\mu_{[i]} = \frac{x_1 \cdot a_1}{x_2 \cdot a_2}$$

(13.1)

Although very 'simple', these equations do not represent linear combinations of the terms and will not generate lines or planes for most values of x and a. As noted above, there are a wide variety of non-linear models, often highly-specific to different subfields. The good news is that both `brms` and *Stan* can be used to fit non-linear models, as well, and a majority of the content in this book will directly translate to working with these sorts of models.

13.9.3 *Other data distributions*

In this book, we discussed some of the more 'basic' and common data distributions in use: Normal, t, Bernoulli, multinomial, etc. However, there are a large number of other distributions that can be used in `brms` (and *Stan*) simply by changing the `family` parameter in the function call. You can think of this parameter as below, where the distribution specified by the family parameter generates your data y given some parameter (or parameters) θ.

$$y \sim \text{family}(\theta)$$

(13.2)

Apparent speaker characteristics from speech acoustics 455

For example, setting `family=poisson` uses the Poisson distribution to model your data, i.e., it assumes that $y \sim \text{Poisson}(\theta)$. The Poisson distribution is used to model discrete count data that is bounded by zero at the lower end but unbounded at the higher end. You can get more information about the link functions and data distributions included in `brms` using the command `?brms::brmsfamily`, and you should refer to the current *Stan* manual for information about the link functions and distributions supported by *Stan*. You can get more information about the different distributions in a large number of textbooks and web pages online. In this book, we modeled quantitative data (that we treated as unbounded and continuous), binomial, multinomial, and ordinal data. If you are modeling any other kind of data, it's worth thinking about what kind of probability distribution (and link function) would be best suited for that data.

13.9.4 Multivariate analyses

The models in this book have all had univariate dependent variables. In other words, at all times we were predicting variables with a single dimension. However, we might imagine wanting to predict multivariate dependent variables, for example, from a multivariate normal distribution. Below, we see an example where we predict bivariate normal data (y_1, y_2) by predicting expected values for each dimension (μ_1, μ_2) and estimating the covariance matrix of the distribution (Σ). Notice that in the prediction equations below, the predictors (x) are shared by both dimensions but the coefficients (a) are not.

$$\begin{bmatrix} y_1 \\ y_2 \end{bmatrix} \sim \text{MVNormal}\left(\begin{bmatrix} \mu_1 \\ \mu_2 \end{bmatrix}, \Sigma \right)$$

$$\mu_1 = a_{11} \cdot x_1 + a_{12} \cdot x_2 + a_{13} \cdot x_3$$
$$\mu_2 = a_{21} \cdot x_1 + a_{22} \cdot x_2 + a_{23} \cdot x_3$$

(13.3)

These sorts of models are actually very similar to the models we have fit in this book in that each dimension is represented by its own independent prediction equation. However, there are three main differences between fitting, for example, a single multivariate model predicting both variables at the same time, and fitting two independent models predicting each dimension at a time. First, by fitting the model above as a multivariate model, we can test for differences between, for example, μ_1 and μ_2 or $a_{1[1]}$ and $a_{2[1]}$, that could only be made indirectly if the two models are fit independently. Second, treating our data as multivariate allows us to estimate the correlations of coefficients across dimensions, which is particularly useful when estimating 'random effects'. For example, suppose we had collected both height and age judgments in the experiment used throughout the book. We could use a multivariate model of both judgments to see if there is a relationship between how listeners used one predictor (e.g., f0) for height relative to how they used it for age. Finally, when we treat data as univariate, under certain conditions we can also estimate the correlation of the residuals across dimensions. This will tell us, for example, whether our model overestimates one dimension when it underestimates the other, or if errors are unrelated.

456 *Apparent speaker characteristics from speech acoustics*

There are also other reasons you might want to build multivariate models, such as to carry out structural equation modeling or path analysis. Those topics are beyond the scope of this book, but these (and many other) multivariate models can be fit with relative ease using `brms` and/or *Stan*.

References

Assmann, P. F., Kapolowicz, M. R., & Barreda, S. (2018). Perception of talker height and sex from children's voices. *The Journal of the Acoustical Society of America*, 144(3), 1964–1964.

Barreda (2015). *phonTools: Functions for phonetics in R. R package version 0.2-2.1.*

Barreda, S., & Assmann, P. F. (2018). Modeling the perception of children's age from speech acoustics. *The Journal of the Acoustical Society of America*, 143(5), EL361. https://doi.org/10.1121/1.5037614.

Barreda, S., & Assmann, P. F. (2021). Perception of gender in children's voices. *The Journal of the Acoustical Society of America*, 150(5), 3949–3963.

Bürkner, P. (2017). "brms: An R Package for Bayesian Multilevel Models Using Stan." *Journal of Statistical Software*, 80(1), 1–28. doi: 10.18637/jss.v080.i01.

Fryar, C. D., Gu, Q., & Ogden, C. L. (2012). *Anthropometric reference data for children and adults*; United States, 2007–2010.

González, J. (2004). Formant frequencies and body size of speaker: A weak relationship in adult humans. *Journal of Phonetics*, 32(2), 277–287. doi: 10.1016/S0095-4470(03)00049-4.

Hillenbrand, J., Getty, L. A., Clark, M. J., & Wheeler, K. (1995). Acoustic characteristics of American english vowels. *The Journal of the Acoustical Society of America*, 97(5), 3099–3111.

Hillenbrand, J. M., & Clark, M. J. (2009). The role of f0 and formant frequencies in distinguishing the voices of men and women. *Attention, Perception, & Psychophysics*, 71(5), 1150–1166. doi: 10.3758/APP.71.5.1150.

Johnson, K. (2004). Acoustic and auditory phonetics. *Phonetica*, 61(1), 56-58.

Pisanski, K., Jones, B. C., Fink, B., O'Connor, J. J., DeBruine, L. M., Röder, S., & Feinberg, D. R. (2016). Voice parameters predict sex-specific body morphology in men and women. *Animal Behaviour*, 112, 13–22.

R Core Team (2022). R: A language and environment for statistical computing. R Foundation for Statistical Computing, Vienna, Austria. https://www.R-project.org/.

Turner, R. E., Walters, T. C., Monaghan, J. J. M., & Patterson, R. D. (2009). A statistical, formant-pattern model for segregating vowel type and vocal-tract length in developmental formant data. *The Journal of the Acoustical Society of America*, 125(4), 2374. https://doi.org/10.1121/1.3079772.

Smith, D. R. R., & Patterson, R. D. (2005). The interaction of glottal-pulse rate and vocal-tract length in judgements of speaker size, sex, and age. The *Journal of the Acoustical Society of America*, 118(5), 3177–3186. https://doi.org/10.1121/1.2047107.

Stan Development Team. (2022). Stan Modeling Language Users Guide and Reference Manual, Version. https://mc-stan.org.

Vorperian, H. K., Wang, S., Chung, M. K., Schimek, E. M., Durtschi, R. B., Kent, R. D., Ziegert, A. J., & Gentry, L. R. (2008). Anatomic development of the oral and pharyngeal portions of the vocal tract: An imaging study. The *Journal of the Acoustical Society of America*, 125(3), 1666. https://doi.org/10.1121/1.3075589

Wakita, H. (1977). Normalization of vowels by vocal-tract length and its application to vowel identification. *IEEE Transactions on Acoustics, Speech, and Signal Processing*, 25(2), 183–192.

Index

0 130
1 67, 129
- 224
: 169, 224
* 169
^ 224
| 100, 224–225, 391–392
~ 67
$ 11

a posteriori 60
a priori 13, 27
adaptive partial pooling 96
additive function 327
analysis of variance 361
analytically 63
ANOVA *see* analysis of variance
ANOVA plot 363, 367
antilogit function *see* inverse logit function
apparent speaker characteristics 8
auditory sensation 5
autocorrelation 74

banova 366–369
BANOVA *see* Bayesian analysis of variance
banovaplot 366–367
Bayes theorem 59
Bayesian analysis of variance 360–363
Bayesian models 58–63
behavioral measures 7
Bernoulli trial 312
between-subjects 124–126, 201–202, 210
bias 337–338
bias-variance tradeoff 181
bivariate regression 277
bmmb 9
boxplot 22
brm 68

category boundary 372; along one dimension 329–334; along two dimensions 373–375
causality 307–308
CDF *see* cumulative distribution functions 412
cell 210

centering 41; multiple predictors 351–353; predictors 278–280
chains 64, 74
coefficients 57
collinearity 266–268
complete pooling 94
components of variation 361
conditional effect 166
conditional expectation function 216
conditional probability 30
confusion matrix 126
contingency table 19
contrasts 132–135
convergence 73
cor 173
correlation 141, 171–174
covariance 172; matrix 176
credible interval 69
criterion 336
cross tabulation 19
cross validation 190–194
crossed 167–168
cross-product 349
cumulative distribution functions 412–415
curve 154
cutoffs 417

data frame 9
decomposition of variance 212; ANOVA-like 361; between groups 135–137
degrees of freedom parameter 150
derivative 413
dgamma 154–155
dimension 174, 209
distributional models 250
distributions *see* probability distributions
divergent transitions 76
dnorm 43
domain knowledge 244
d-prime 336

effect 2
effective number of parameters 189, 194
effective sample size 73, 267

458 *Index*

error 57, 67
ESS *see* effective sample size
elpd *see* expected log pointwise predictive density
exchangeable 15
`exp_data` 28
`exp_data_all` 9
expected log pointwise predictive density 182–185, 194
expected value 36, 182, 311–312
experiments 1–5
exponentiation 41

f0 *see* fundamental frequency
factorial design 210
factors 14, 92, 131; with more than two levels 239–241
false alarm rate 335
finite-population standard deviation 362
`fitted` 217, 397, 420
fitting 58
fixed effects 105, 169
`fixef` 139
`forpaper` 235
fundamental frequency 5, 428

generalized linear model 313–314
`get_corrs` 179
`get_prior` 77
`get_samples` 70
`get_sds` 179
grand mean 133
`group` 147
`Group-Level Effects` 103

hard classification 415
`head` 9
`height_data` 6
Hertz 5, 428
heteroscedasticity 250–251
hierarchical models 97
histogram 22
hit rate 335
holdout data 191
homoscedasticity 250–251
hyperbola 373
hyperbolic paraboloid 350
hyperprior 97
`hypothesis` *see* `short_hypothesis` 144

identifiability 265, 295
indexical characteristics 5; perception of 432–435
induction 3
inference 3, 27
in-sample data 181
integral 413

interaction 166, 220–222; effects 166; modeling of 222–225; plots 221, 228–229
intercept 275
intercept-only model 66, 276
interquartile range 22
inverse logit function 317–318

joint density 61
joint probabilities 32–34

$\hat{k}$ *see* Pareto-k 377–378
`kable` 306
k-fold 191

latent variable 387, 410–411
leave-one-out cross-validation 191
levels 14
likelihood 45–52; function 45
likert scale 408; data 408
linear: combination 58; correlation 172; dependence 132, 266; predictor 216; regression models 58; relationship 172, 275
lines 274–277
link function 313–314
`lm` 85, 184
`lmer` 105, 119, 161, 198, 241, 357–360
log density 49
log likelihood 51
log odds *see* logit
log pointwise predictive density 182–185
log posterior density 80–83
log prior density 80–83
logarithms 49
logistic function *see* inverse logit function
logistic regression 315–318
logit function 316
logits 315–316; combination of 327–329
long format 9
`loo` 191
lpd *see* log pointwise predictive density

main effect 166; plot 220
`make_map` 401
marginal: distributions 30; effects 166; probabilities 60
maximal models 354
maximum-likelihood estimate 47, 53
mean 36; of a sample 37–39
median 21
misspecification of models 378
mixed designs 210
mixed-effects models 104
model formulas 67, 100, 129–130, 168–169, 204–206, 223–225
model selection 181, 194–197, 303–305, 375–381
models and inference 42–44

Index 459

monotonic 352
multilevel model 89–91
multinomial logistic regression 383–385; comparison to logistic 387–390
multinomial logits 386–387
multivariate analyses 455–456

nearly-saturated model *see* saturated models
nested 167–168
no pooling 95
noise 57
non-linear 319
non-linear, models 454
normal distribution density 41
numerically 64

odds 315
one-sample t-test 84
ordinal logistic regression 407–415
ordinary least-squares 84–85
orthogonal designs 210
outliers 22
out-of-sample data 181
overfitting 181

parameters 35
parametric distributions 36
Pareto smoothed importance sampling 377–378
Pareto-k 377–378
partial pooling 96
p_check 217, 246–247
PDF *see* probability density functions 412
Pearson's correlation coefficient 172
penalizing predictive accuracy 185–187
perception of age, gender, and size *see* indexical characteristics
perceptual experiment 7
pitch 5, 428
planes 347–349
plot_map 402
pnorm 44, 413
population 13
population-level effect 69
post hoc 180
posterior, distributions 61
posterior, prediction 216–220
posterior, predictive checks 217
posterior, predictive distribution 216
posterior, probabilities 59, 61–63
posterior samples 70
posterior samples, Inspecting and manipulating the 140–144
posterior_summary 143
pp_check 217
predict 217, 246

prediction 216
prior predictive check 245–248, 254–255, 324–325
prior probabilities 59–61, 244–245, 248–250; informative, weakly-informative, and vague 62; multivariate normal 175–177
prior_summary 248
probability 29; empirical 29; theoretical 43
probability density function 35, 37, 412
probability distributions 34–35; Bernoulli 311; binomial 312; categorical 384; Gaussian (*see* normal); LKJ 177; logistic 413; multinomial 383–384; multivariate normal 174–177; non-standardized t 151; normal 36–42; other 454–455; standard normal 41; t 150–151
problem of induction 4
proportional constant 82
prosody 435
PSIS *see* Pareto smoothed importance sampling

quantiles 21
quantitative predictors 274–277; interactions between 349–353; multiple 347–349
quartiles 21

R^2 232–235, 304
r2_bayes 234
random component 57
random effects 104–109, 169, 174–175; correlations 179; inspecting and manipulating 106–109, 145–149; recovering heteroscedastic variances 261; standard deviations 180
random slopes 293–295; inspecting and manipulating 298–299; with multiple predictors 299–301
ranef 106
rank 15
rbernoulli 312
rbinom 312
region of practical equivalence 238
regression 56–58
regularization 95
repeated-measures data 87–91
researcher degrees of freedom 263
residuals 67, 72, 276
residuals 72
resonance 6; frequencies 430
resonators 430
response bias *see* bias
response surfaces 369
Rhat 73
RMS error *see* root-mean-squared error
robust 149–150; distributional robustness 150
root-mean-squared error 364

460 *Index*

saddle surface 350
sample 13
sample, space 28
saturated model 271–272
scaling 41
scatter plots 22
scientific 1
scope 147
score 387
sensitivity 335–336
short_hypothesis 144–148; group-specific
  error parameters 261; multiple factors
  215; multiple factors and interactions
  230–232; ordinal models 424; recovering
  error parameters 256; recovering individual
  random slopes 298; recovering individual
  random slopes with interactions 302, 451;
  recovering missing levels 208; recovering
  missing levels and slopes 291; recovering
  missing levels with a quantitative predictor
  285–286; signal detection theory 342–343
short_summary 80
shrinkage 63, 95, 115–117
shrunk *see* shrinkage
sigmoid curve 318
signal detection theory 334–338
simple effects 221, 305; calculating 230–232
simple main effects *see* simple effects
simulating data: predictive accuracy 183–185;
  for a single group 109–112; for two groups
  157–159
slope 275
soft classification 415
softmax function 386
Stan 64
standard deviation 37; of a sample 39–40
standardization 41
statistical: dependence 32; independence 31;
  inference 37
stimulus 7
stimulus space 332
str 9
sum coding 133–135

superpopulation standard deviation 362
supported models 265
systematic component 57

territorial maps 332, 374–375, 399–402,
  450–451
testing data 190
thinning 75
thresholds 410, 417
training data 190
treatment coding 133
t.test 84
type M errors 236–237
type S errors 236–237

uncertainty 27
underdetermination 263

variables 12–18; Boolean 16; categorical 14;
  continuous 15; dependent 13; dichotomous
  310–311; discrete 15; independent 13; logical
  16; nominal 14; ordinal 15, 408; ordinal *vs.*
  quantitative 408–409; random 12; selection
  of 453–454
variance 37; of a sample 39–40
vector 9
vocal tract 6, 430
vocal-tract length 430; acoustic 431;
  anatomical 431; effective 431
voice resonance *see* resonance 430
VTL *see* vocal-tract length

WAIC *see* widely available information
  criterion
warmup 68
whiskers 22
widely available information criterion
  187–190
within-subjects 124–126, 201–202, 210

x intercept 329

z score 41